S0-BDN-974

True Reflections

TRUE REFLECTIONS

The International Library of Poetry

Laura Michele Diener, Editor

True Reflections

Library of Congress
Cataloging in Publication Data

ISBN 1-58235-964-4

Proudly manufactured in the United States of America by
Watermark Press
One Poetry Plaza
Owings Mills, MD 21117

The International Library of Poetry
poetry.COM

FOREWORD

Throughout life, we store information collected from experiences and try in some way to make sense of it. When we are not able to fully understand the things that occur in our lives, we often externalize the information. By doing this, we are afforded a different perspective, thus allowing us to think more clearly about difficult or perplexing events and emotions. Art is one of the ways in which people choose to externalize their thoughts.

Within the arts, modes of expression differ, but poetry is a very powerful tool by which people can share sometimes confusing, sometimes perfectly clear concepts and feelings with others. Intentions can run the gamut as well: The artists may simply want to share something that has touched their lives in some way, or they may want to get help to allay anxiety or uncertainty. The poetry within *True Reflections* is from every point on the spectrum: every topic, every intention, every event or emotion imaginable. Some poems will speak to certain readers more than others, but it is always important to keep in mind that each verse is the voice of a poet, of a mind that needs to make sense of this world, of a heart that feels the effects of every moment in this life, and perhaps of a memory that is striving to surface. Nonetheless, recalling our yesterdays gives birth to our many forms of expression.

Melisa S. Mitchell
Senior Editor

Editor's Note

"The Rubicons which women must cross, the sex barriers which they must breach, are ultimately those that exist in their own minds."—Freda Adler

Women have often been defined by their roles—wife, mother, caretaker, etc. All of these roles not only limit women, but stereotype them as well. Throughout history, women have struggled with the confines society has placed upon them. It is only in the last century that women have broken barriers and transcended many confines, changing the idea of women's roles. However, sometimes more harmful than the confines society has placed on women are the limits women place on themselves.

Two poems in this anthology explore clearly female personas and their unique barriers: "In Her Favorite Room" and "Belly." "In Her Favorite Room" (1), by Pamela Hill, describes a woman who seems to have no use for the outside world. The room itself has its duality in that the kitchen is the persona's favorite room, because it provides her with mental stimulation, and, at the same time, serves as a barrier to the outside world. She seems content, if not pleased, with having limited contact with the world at large. Everything that she wants to know comes from her recipes and cookbooks, and the things that she wants to experience she does through her recipes.

The snow falling outside makes the world appear as a white void. It seems that all of the persona's travels and flights of fancy take place in the kitchen—the proverbial "woman's place" in the home. Newspapers, cookbooks, and exotic spices from around the world surround her. Her knowledge of the world comes through cookbooks, not the newspaper that "lies useless in its box, bringing only halves of tales."

The language of the poem gives more clues about the persona. The foods and spices used are intriguing. Cardamom, a Greek word, is an expensive, exotic spice from India, enjoyed and used extensively by Russians and Japanese. It is sometimes called "the queen of spices" because of its long history and distinctive taste. Saffron, commonly know as the world's most expensive spice, is also mentioned in the poem. Used in ancient Persia before being exported to India, it has many uses, including medicinal. The presence of these two spices alone lead the reader to believe that the persona in the poem treats herself well and appreciates the finer things in life.

The seventh line of the poem states, "She wants to see Asia." Immediately following that, she peels chestnuts and soaks rice. It appears that she does not actually want to visit the regions mentioned in the poem, but would rather create her own ideal Asia, Greece, and Spain, an ideal that manifests itself in her cookbooks and recipes. Perhaps she is unable to travel to the places she reads about and is content to "visit" them through the cuisine she creates. Regardless of the reason, she is happy in the world of the culinary delights she creates in her kitchen.

The persona mentions twice in the poem that it is Sunday. The first time, it is stated outright. The chosen day gives the feeling that she considers her cooking as a religious ritual, as she "creates" her universe with recipes and diverse spices. Except for the day of the week itself, specific time has no meaning in the poem, but the reader can deduce that it is winter by the presence of the snow. This lends a timeless quality to the poem, as the action could have taken place on any winter Sunday. The only other time references are historical: the Spartans and "leaders of ancient nations." Already having expressed a fondness for history, it is quite possible that the persona prefers days gone by to the present.

"In Her Favorite Room" concludes with "four truths: one of spice, one of lodestar, another of tongues, and a fourth of fantasies that never leave the chair." Once again, we are offered more clues about the persona. Lodestar is a guiding star, such as the North Star, but it can also refer to something that serves as an inspiration, a guiding principle, or an ambition or goal. The "spice" mentioned as one of the four truths alludes to the aforementioned spices, but also to the cliche "the spice of life," which does not apply to the persona. She seemingly has little or no variety in her life. The "tongues" represent the foreign languages that lie in the regions in which the spices originated, and in the spices themselves. The fourth truth, "fantasies that never leave the chair" is a direct statement about how the persona has chosen to lead her life. Although the persona seems to have lived a life unfulfilled, it seems to be by choice, fashioning her own world, one in which she "caresses the walls and rattles three spoons for their sound."

"Belly" (1), by Beth Dugan, features confines of a different type—those of the body itself. In our society, women have struggled with the unrealistic ideal of beauty portrayed by the media. While it may be a familiar theme, the woman in the poem is struggling with the drastic changes her body has gone through. She describes how her muscles "tear like cloth," a description that conjures up two very different images: one of someone who has simply outgrown her clothes, and one of a woman delivering a baby. It bothers the woman that she cares about what others think of her body, but she, too, is affected by the societal ideal:

> The loss of an interest I should have never wanted
> Gives tooth to the smooth wood of my ego,
> Roughens its veneer, hard fought, dearly won.

She thinks back to before her body changed, reminiscing about a past love: ". . . I try and remember caresses felt / a rough palm over this stretched, ridged skin marked with scars of expansion." By the end of the poem, the persona is victorious, vividly describing the physical act of comforting a child:

> arms thrown around my hips as I soothe his worry
> brushing the tangled hair away from his ear with a cool, sure hand.

While "Belly" may seem like another poem bemoaning extra pounds, it does indeed become almost a celebration of them, a celebration of self-acceptance, regardless of what others may think. Unlike "In Her Favorite Room," "Belly" explores the one constant in life—change. The persona not only undergoes physical changes, but mental changes as well. While the persona begins with her belly as a source of "shame," she gradually becomes more secure with her body. Now, instead of finding comfort with a lover, she will find her consolation in not only being an emotionally strong figure for her child, but a physical comfort as well. She knows a child has no concept of the social ideal; he will instead seek the comfort of soft flesh in times of distress.

Like "In Her Favorite Room," "Belly" does not have a specific time frame. The persona's reminiscing about a past lover also includes the memory of comforting her child. When presented in this way, her memory, as well as the child's birth, could have taken place years earlier, possibly meaning that the persona has been struggling with her emotions for quite some time.

Both "In Her Favorite Room" and "Belly" discuss physical confines, but the prevailing confine is ultimately the mind. While the mind of the woman in "Belly" is affected by the ideals of society, the woman of "In Her Favorite Room" has created her own ideal society in her mind. She has different circumstances to overcome from the woman in "Belly." While both personas have very different lives and struggles to overcome, both of their stories fit into the broad spectrum of the life stories of women finding a place where they are accepted by others, as well as themselves. It is the level of self-acceptance that seemingly gives both women a sense of purpose, perhaps not present to the rest of the world, but ever-present in their own lives. Regardless of the genders of the personas, both "In Her Favorite Room" and "Belly" are original, well-written, and thought-provoking pieces. Although these poems reflect the lives of two individuals, the poems themselves are for everyone.

A poem written on any topic and done with vivid clarity can be accessible to anyone, much like the other poems in this anthology. Please have a look at some of my personal favorites: Lyska S. Mondor's "Don't Go to Florida and Leave Me Here" (4), Rachel Louise Weber's "Notable Absence" (6), Carly Michele Southworth's "Pink Elephants" (5), William Hampton's "Green Monsters" (9), John Wallace's "Chinese" (10), Holly Nix's "Unwilling Goddess" (16), and Kaitlin Conway's "Phoenix" (17).

I would like to thank all the poets who contributed their work to this anthology. I wish all of them success in their future writings. The publishing of this anthology was made possible by numerous judges, editors, assistant editors, customer service representatives, data entry staff, office administrators, graphic and layout artists, and mailroom personnel. I truly appreciate all of their assistance and support.

Patty Davis
Editor

Cover Art: "Reflecting Light" by Cynthia Becce

Belly

My belly, edged and fleshy carries my shame, is my shame.
I force it in when I pass by, pulling so hard
I can almost feel the muscles tear like cloth,
imagining that sound when it nearly rends apart with the effort.
I despise that I care what they think of my pouchy belly
but I hate their contempt and dismissal more,
eyes sliding over me,
assessing me slickly
disregarding me swiftly.
The loss of an interest I never should have wanted
gives tooth to the smooth wood of my ego,
roughens its veneer, hard fought, dearly won.
Combatively, I try and remember
caresses felt, a rough palm over this stretched,
ridged skin marked with scars of expansion
my breath fluttering,
or a child's head burrowed deeply there,
arms thrown around my hips as I soothe his worry
brushing the tangled hair away from his ear with a cool, sure hand.

Beth Dugan

In Her Favorite Room

On Sunday, the snow is white as sun. She drinks tea
and learns history from cookbooks.
Greece: she crushes cardamom with the back of a spoon.
Spain: she threads saffron into a soup.
It must be Sunday. The newspaper lies
useless in its box, bringing only halves of tales.
She wants to see Asia. Peel chestnuts from their hulls,
soak rice in big bowls, and squat over the New York Times.
By ten, she has read a wine list, and discovered
what the Spartans ate. Leaders of old nations
stand around her and break bread into small triangles.
They smear them with avocado and feed in silence
while it snows. Their chins turn green. Oil drips
onto a spread of old dailies, she caresses the walls,
and rattles three spoons for their sound. A woman
in her favorite room rocks slowly through the morning,
moving her skin to the scent of breath,
suckling four truths:
one of spice, one of lodestar, another of tongues,
and a fourth of fantasies that never leave the chair.

Pamela Hill

Where the Whirlpools Sleep

Our silken water whispers on
cutting through the cluttered forest.
Flowing memories here and gone
telling of lives lived before us.

With rapids placed to keep our interest
twists and falls, we so enjoy.
Whirlpools swirling in time held dearest
while the current meanders; heavens' ploy.

Growing always as we fade
our strength only drifts us home.
Down these highways we have paved
towards the ever-growing storm.

There we'll finally meet ourselves
there we'll view the truth
there we'll tell collected tales
there we'll find our youth.

Scott William Soltys

Mercury

Mercury
although
it is
a metal
it
flows
flows here
flows there
Mercury
I
sometimes
wish
I
could
be.

Caroline Landers

Asleep

My hands, they said, fell asleep from fear,
the trigger fingers first, one each in Chu Lai and Ben Hoa.

My arms went silent after Bart Embry disappeared
in the Mekong Delta.
My feet and legs stopped when they found
his bearded jawbone floating in the river.

At night my limbs die completely,
a muted protest to the fragmented memories of fragmented lives.

William Matthews

Lines to a Friend

I dance to
the way your hair sweeps
on freckled skin and it is the

Dancing of things, the movement
that becomes like the trees
floating on the moon, a swollen
melon, that is, the tongue
swinging in utter wetness

I dance to
your seaweed hands
the way they fall around shoulders

I am sure
it is slowing inside this room

Where you are
the sheets, the rain,
the Earth rotating.

Kiley Amber Cogis

The Big, Blonde Bomb

That big, blonde bomb shell of a car still cruises
one grassless expanse of the lawn as I crack
peas on the front porch. The air liquefies,
runs down my neck and into my faded print dress. Husks
dry between the spread of thin cloth my open legs create.
This was my favorite time of day:
Maggie at school, Frank on deliveries, or the line, and it's
just us blonde bombshells—neither painted recently and both
beginning to corrode.
Neither of us moved without difficulty,
and we're both prone to overheat.
Eleven years. Then last winter
you decided, with a choke-sputter, you couldn't take anymore
and quit.

Moiz Mansoor Kasimali

The Cry Of

The cry of an infant is the end of a thought
That began with the sight of a beer can rusting
At the far end of the fallow garden. I think
Of infants often in the evening when the sun
Has set and the night wraps 'round my feet, climbs over
My shoulders until I almost choke. My neighbor
Calls for her lover to come join her in the grass.
Car horns, bird calls, cicadas, and the excited
Taunts of loitering teenagers converge beyond
My grasp that witnesses the end of metal, hears
The insatiable gnawing. Yellow jackets swarm.

Pat J. McCormick

The Farmer

As long as he contends with dirt
Crumbles, and breezes found in dust,
History is the row of grapes
Lying straight down the dimpled hill, becoming.
The future fuses to the sunshine
Sweating down his back,
Arched with satisfied muscle, tanning.
Alone the day, night must be
Peopled with reflection,
Or do views from porches finally develop into views?
Longing must turn around the trellis, the captured chase of buds
A slowed tear,
Or do eyes wander to the roadway, now and then,
Anticipating the long black car of letters,
Jumping behind themselves to: come for me?
Sip of Coke, and back inside
I bustle, rendering the wrinkled Mexican
A farmer once again.

Rider Strong

Weather Alert

In his pocket sleeps a postcard
from somewhere he has never been.
Hours from now, he will board a plane
to a place where winter is a slight
dip in temperature overnight.
In a living room a wife waits
for her husband, impatiently
looking out the windows,
holding back the yellow
curtains she does not realize
she is holding. She listens
for his truck in the driveway.
Snow falls. It does not know
there is danger in its fall.
One flake can balance on a fingertip
and easily melt. Burgeoning,
they obscure, they bury, they blind.
The snow thinks nothing of this world.

Eric Hoffman

Don't Go to Florida and Leave Me Here

Don't go to Florida and leave me here,
as the weatherman shadows your whole state
into darkness with one hand;
he says that the climate will be lukewarm
like a puddle.
I am drinking in a country bar,
listening to cowboys sing old Merle Haggard
songs as the TV blares an ad for Disney World.
I have been left for a lukewarm mouse,
not even singing "The Rose" pressed
against "Big Abe's" belly seems comforting.
I am a pink haired, tattooed lesbian in a room
full of Texas loving sons of Uncle Sam.
I am waiting to be killed,
then I can prove you were wrong for leaving.
My head hangs over my scotch;
they only tip ten gallons of pride at me.
I am more pathetic than any of the drunkards
in this room.

Lyska S. Mondor

The Enemy

My old enemy came to visit
today: a man hermetically sealed
in this truth, like a castle
or strongbox
With this own style of breathing
and a singular swordplay
sedulously stropped to draw blood.
I saw the years in his face:
the eyes of tired water,
the lines of his loneliness
that had lifted his temples
little by little to consummate self-love
the sun on all sides an struck at the sky.
I think he was silent,
the flint of his soul
stayed impenetrable.

Clodualdo Orozco

Halcyon

Big black crow too old to caw,
sitting on barbed wire, watching the rising dawn.
You've been there so long
the ugly sound of your voice, rasping
cuts through the air.
Horrid. Distracting. Noise.
You are old, worn; Go, bother me no more.

Red tailed hawk and falcon brown
puffed against the cold;
strength in your body, speed in your wings
power in your talons, keen eyes cast down.

If choices are ours,
and who we will be,
and what we take with us,
then I choose the crow dies today
and the hawk
and the falcon
fly below the dove.

Ria Sanacore

Van Gogh's Quiet Lines on the 716

I've been watching you since Stockton,
on through Denair, Merced, and Madera.
I've studied some of the quiet lines
that make up you. Sitting on your suitcase
waiting for the 716, reading
with your face in a scowl.
A strand of your hair falls,
and you make no effort to remove it.
Immersed in your reading you await
a revelation. "25 minutes to Fresno!"
I see the conductor remove the ticket
from your seat. As I approach you
this is what I finally say: "Pardon me,
but I would hate myself if I did not meet you."
You tell me that you have a boyfriend.
I say, "I'm not looking for a girlfriend,
but an intelligent conversation with an intelligent girl."
Epilogue: Still, fear kept me from that
possible encounter. I watched her walk off
that train to Fresno, leaving me with questions
of fate and divine appointment.

Michael James Eddy

Dance to the Dead Pantoum

Night where light from dead stars still glow
above the flat corn fields acres on through Iowa's isolation
where two old friends in a blue Toyota sail past silver silos.
A dried rose petal past swirls above and beyond their conversation.

Above the flat corn fields acres on through Iowa's isolation
Old friends smoke fine cigars and drink dark German beer.
A dried rose petal past swirls above and beyond their conversation.
Van Gogh's abyss-black crows hover near.

Old friends smoke fine cigars and drink dark German beer.
One turns up The Grateful Dead's improvisations.
Van Gogh's abyss-black crows hover near
while they remember decades ago dream desolations.

One turns up The Grateful Dead's improvisations.
They dance to Cassidy in a recently harvested corn field.
While they remember decades ago dream desolations,
the goblins of should've, would've and could've stay concealed.

They fall then crawl towards a lonely black road
where two old friends in a blue Toyota sail past silver silos
and marijuana memories and into the eternal ebony cold
night where light from dead stars still glow.

Robert Kendell Akin

Cede Forfeit, Mother

Crumpled in your favorite armchair,
Gazing out across a rain-soaked street,
Watching listless through your window painted silver
A small girl playing baseball,
Shoeless.

This leviathan of flame
Has exploded from your brain,
And you have watched
As it battled for your life.

Crushed beneath the weight of marriage,
It choked to death on jackfruit brine.
You lost it like a copper circlet
Around the span of years you gave
Love; when lightning strikes the pavement
And when your window clears,
You will see me running, running
Through the rain,
To be free.

Daniel Pelletier

Fate of Clay Hands

I know what you're made of without even
looking—water droppings trapped
in silicate structures, crystalline
repetitions, kisses from an unabashed
heat source, frozen in the fissures,
multiplying on the needs of the obsolete.
habit can't even unhook itself from your claws.

gripped aimlessly (almost)
in a muddy clay glaze, burning to be
conceived, swollen from mineral embraces,
running my fingers through you, smelling
traces of everything that made me smile,
molding, kneading you with my bare
thoughts, watching you grow a hand, a heart.
how many times I could slip and fall
to your fate.

see me as that last look a maker gives to a
giant sunflower, just enough to open its
world toward the warmth.

Nellie Evelyn Freydin

Motel Scene

Sun shines through the window
Hard to find my shoes
Packing up what they didn't steal
In the motel room
Woman's sleeping off boredom
TV's nothing but news
They ain't found a body yet
But it's safe to assume
Cigarettes are soaked, found 'em in on the tub
Woman tends to forget things
Says it's 'cause she's in love
She's gonna hit the ceiling
When she wakes up at noon
Can't say I blame her, then again
Can't say I left too soon
Thought of leavin' her money or maybe a note
Words are more like poison than an anecdote
So I just blow a kiss as I slide out the door
After all, it's expected from
A motel troubadour

Darin K. Henderson

The Night Sacrifice

July stole in like a black bear
And I admired the night stars as if I knew them
Felt the breeze and moon on my face
Floated above the earth in the old porch swing
Its creaking my oxygen.
Measuring of night by the mind's eye and not moving
Barely, the consumption of a summer fragrance of
Sweet unnamed flowers, these were the things
I thought I should do then. I could not
Just then conjure up all the things I would have
To conquer or had already.
I started to stir once making tea, painting words.
I should have written, found what was lost, but the oak
Branches made a noise like rubbing paper. The sky
Began to laugh. Moon bloated with its own glistening
As I watched to see it burst, the old blanket
At my chin my amulet.
I fended off the hungry need of seeking
Blinked the bear god in the face and sacrificed the
Night into nothing.

Diane Smalley

Pink Elephants

I lie belly up on your secondhand couch
like an elephant waiting for the sun to ferment the berries
in its belly (something you are watching on the Discovery Channel).

Her black bra is under the end table.
It somehow managed to escape the rest of her
laundry, piling up in one corner of your room.

My hand lifts the strawberry wine cooler to my dry lips.
You are still talking about elephants.

Maybe it's the berries in my belly,
but I want to tell you something
I have discovered, or uncovered.

I want to tell you I would turn
down that bracelet she asked for
(or even the layaway ring that matches)
for a late night on this musty couch.

I want to say I love you.
But instead, I say, "What kind of elephants?"
And wait for your voice, the one thing I can have.

Carly Michele Southworth

Love Poem

I do not dream of you;
you do not lend yourself to rhetoric
but move in calligraphic paths
untraceable with words.

I dream of small gray birds
with dark-streaked wings cupped in my hands;
I fling them out to fly,
soft cries and feather-thin,
beating arcs into the air,
leaving barbs and thorns caught in my fingers.
I move between the pain of touch and joy of sight:
the etching of those bodies on the sky.

I do not dream of you
but of the mysteries you hold me in,
in feathers, winds, and wizardry,
yet if I spoke
my voice would gleam in hard, bright fragments
you could not hope to catch or comprehend.

Benita Adoree Budd

Turning Soil

My heart divulges its scars as it is turned
Inside out by the garden spade
Insects inside me from long ago
Scurry in circles or poke up their silvery, pointy, heads
And dive back down only to emerge again and again

My earth is ready for conception, but I haven't the seeds
And I can see I'll have to trade something in for them
Something old and familiar, for something foreign and new
What can I plant that will flourish in this untested soil
This unpredictable weather?
I don't know if I want raspberry bushes or apricot trees
Parsnips or peas, tulips or weeds

The hoe leans on the side of the shed awaiting its instructions
The workers lie in their cots: boots and gloves at the ready
Everything is in place, still and silently humming
While I hold my breath with calm uncertainty
The universe awaits my nod

Danielle Ellis

Art of Gaucherie

Stumbling upon an art form,
the lead and ink
flow onto the pulp of creation.
A plethora of nigrescence
furthers its absence as
the clearest of ideas tames
the most feral of entities:
the mind.
Control no longer a trepidation,
the images painted with such ineptness
now contrive blueprints for appreciation.
It is on this very plane that the
wooden wand conjures up its most
basic and purest of splendors.
The artist merely a puppet
reacting to the stringy antics
of the quill.
Stumbling as he may . . . however,
discovering a gift of gracefulness.

Joseph Donald Teague

The Bee Box

In this small box, my love,
you'll not find a ring,
but instead, a brave, little bee.
He'll be dead by morn, having given his life
defending his flowers against me.
I felt his sting
while picking the small, purple pansies
growing wild along the roadside,
in hopes of an afternoon bouquet for you.
And I grieved the sting,
more for him than me,
knowing full well the price he paid
for my small pain.
And I allowed him his victory,
leaving his flowers as a memory,
and brought you instead
this brave, little bee,
who proves there is love
even in the smallest
of things.

Lowell Parker

Fortune

As she files my nails she talks about herself,
Her six year-old daughter,
Her escape from Vietnam,
Her family
Rich enough to send her here
To escape the chaos.

She was ten.
Old enough
To take her younger brother.
A child raising a child.

By eighteen
Raising another.

She wants to get married
"Husband bring me happiness."
But she doesn't expect anyone to ask.
She says she is too skinny,
And looks like a boy.

I interrupt to tell her I would kill for her figure.
She stares at me, and then smiles.
She says a fortune teller once told her she would be rich by thirty.

Nancy Castaneda

Typical Teen

I wash my hair with Capitalist Shampoo
Clean my body with The Newest Fad
Dress in Conformity's latest fashions

A base of self-esteem cakes my face
A bit of hypocrisy powder follows
Rumor proof mascara smothers my eyelashes

I grab my cloak of popularity
And head off to teenage hell.

Jessica Rae Hatlestad

The Broken Shell

Like a shell that has been left by the bird,
we will never be looked back upon—
for we are no longer of any use.
It served its purpose and it is now cast
aside.
Cracked. Shattered.
Like the bird, we started out as nothing.
Our love was a pinpoint in the void of
emptiness.
But we too, like the bird, protected, grew.
Into something so special that could never
be matched.
Comfortable, though we were, we soon
realized that love was our captive, and we
must break free.
Because refusing to grow is ceasing to live.
So we, like the bird, broke out of our shell
and flew.
Alone.

Erica Lynn Thalmann

The Last Night

White skin on white sheets . . .
(There is a point where nothing can remain)
Red hair on red blood . . .
(And each visit only leaves a stain)
Flowing out, mingling with tears . . .
(A scar that never heals)
Arms at odd angles . . .
(Hidden away, but constantly revealed)
Like broken wings . . .
(In gestures, in slips of words)
Tiny cuts innumerable . . .
(Fragments of a story that should not be heard)
Bruises blue and brown . . .
(Cannot be told, Should not have been)
Smelling of smoke and sex . . .
(Things that can only be whispered sin)
And all the things that shall remain secret . . .

Matthew Alvin Smith

Notable Absence

In the winter, when you're away,
I imagine the world mourns with me.
The candy floss clouds turn dark in suspension,
The bus on Canal street runs late, and the milk sours seconds faster.
When ice grows on the oak, I do the things I can't when you're here.
I let the hair on my legs entwine, the soy sauce on my chin congeal.
I watch Oprah and sob, sing Abba with my mouth full.
On Christmas day, the only stockings I see
are wrapped in gaudy paper,
A present from Aunty Ena to wear
as I eat my radioactive meal for one.
And then suddenly it's spring, the world rises groggily from slumber,
And finds me shaved and scrubbed and scented.
The house dusted, the cushions laid on the couch in order of shade.
Everything ready so I can tell you I didn't even notice you were gone.

Rachel Louise Weber

Arranged Marriage

Sickly-sweet jasmine coils in her
serpentine braid,
bathed in rose water and mystic oils,
swathed in scarlet silk and burnished in gold.

Mirrored orbs of eyes lined with kohl
to ward off the evil eye,
startled bindi marks her forehead,
center of her being, as one with the universe.
Rich stains seep through ivory skin,
of crushed henna, as an unending maze.

Sunburst marigolds squat on dewed grass
hearing hushed whispers upon mumbled mantras.
Stiff old aunts in starched saris,
crusty vermilion in their hair as
flaking proof of marriages that last.
Watching young girls dance to flute melodies,
plotting upon future brides for sons.

Downcast timid bridal eyes harboring
resentment within
an ebbing heart—the seat of her soul.

Hina Qidwai

Julie, You Can Smell Cyanide

Like the grace of God,
a weapon against weapons,
an aversion to death—
the scent of survival
brings bitter almonds to mulled wine.
Like every chair becomes electrified in your presence,
and every gun becomes a gun,
the trash rot is underlaid by the exotic, the tang of poison.
Like the spice that tints the dregs of morning coffee
and evening milk—
the taste of a warning,
the sky turning gray,
the smell of it everywhere,
the bodies shot three times
fading to snow on your lawn.
Still, you sliver almonds for Christmas cake,
crying a little when the knife slips, and when it doesn't.
For your secret, you would cross the street without looking,
because there are other means of murder
not sensed, unknown.

Jocelyn Gillece

Ending's Chill

Depression settles in
Like an old dog on its favorite rug
And the dark
That crept in would not untie me.

I feel lions within me
But I only show demons.

A dizziness comes over me
As though life has spun me 'round
And the clawed hand
Of the morning's frost touches my shoulder.

I build mountains inside me
But I only show cowardly eyes.

And wind can be so cold.
And snow can fall in the summer's heat to me.
And seconds can grow so old
While I'm waiting,
Growing old for you.

Ken W. Griffin

BROKEN PUPPETS (About Dependencies)

The audience is full capacity—
The velvet curtain begins to part.
But the broken puppet lies there,
Immobile from the fear in his heart.
And soon the intro music starts to play
But how can he dance without his strings?
Without outside help to guide his moves,
Why, he's just a heap of wooden things.
But as the solemn prelude slowly ends
With all eyes upon this broken heap,
His fingers quiver and arms weakly rise
As he struggles on to shaky feet.
First one slips back, and then one ahead,
As his wide eyes meet those looking on.
Then the music seems to carry his limbs
In a marriage of pathos with song.
And this tale is ours—no mystical chance
'Cause if we but try,
All broken puppets can dance,
Yes, all broken puppets can dance.

David (Dave) Cummings

No Title 3

She sighed and walked outside.
He was asleep, the entire house was asleep.
She ducked under the trees,
tugging the long sleeves of his shirt over her hands.
Her bare feet chased each other across the grass,
sinking into the mud of the field.
She stood for a second.
A hot wind pushed her hair upwards,
and for a moment she seemed to be pulled by her hair up
into the night sky.
The house watched from behind her;
the stars blinked for a moment, confused.
She began to cry, but no tears fell from her cheeks.
The night seemed to hold its breath for just a moment,
waiting for her.
Then the night blew a gust of wind, swirling it around her naked legs.
His shirt billowed up and around her and she crouched down,
pulling it down and around her knees.
The tears fell.

Elisabeth Blair

Insomnia

By the breathing pond
While consumed by its misty breath
I met Insomnia.
"Why are your eyes wide and soul tired?"
"My wife," he replied, "has disappeared into
the moon light."
"Can I help you find her?" I asked.
"Yes. She's pale with dark features and an
air of peace."
"What is her name?" I asked.
"Rest."
We looked high upon grassy peaks
And low into snowy valleys.
At last we found her
Under a tree down by that pond
Having an affair with Slumber
Insomnia lay down beside her
Embraced her
And then Insomnia was no more.

Brad Alan McClain

The Sphinx Is Crumbling

i wander the biggest city
embraced by neon cobwebs
clouded by cheap wine
an afterthought of love
kissed by spit-stained pavement
and she's a sculpture of venus
there in front of the sex shoppe
a heart of cold marble
still the streets are hissing with morbid desire
and the lust for salvation
cursing chinatown; crawling on hands and knees
the rank smell of digestion
a cornucopia gone rancid and musty
wretchedly grievous are we
hardened in feelings we proliferate
budding like fungal blossoms
clinging to the skyscraper jungle
we crumble together
and fall though the cracks like human gravel

P. John Donnie

The Bee Box

In this small box, my love,
you'll not find a ring,
but instead, a brave, little bee.
He'll be dead by morn, having given his life
defending his flowers against me.
I felt his sting
while picking the small, purple pansies
growing wild along the roadside,
in hopes of an afternoon bouquet for you.
And I grieved the sting,
more for him than me,
knowing full well the price he paid
for my small pain.
And I allowed him his victory,
leaving his flowers as a memory,
and brought you instead
this brave, little bee,
who proves there is love
even in the smallest
of things.

Lowell Parker

About the Woman

as if she just dripped off the page
ink still sweetly warm and wet
she's sprawled in my naked mind

a series of elaborate images
rolled on pure white parchment
outlined with a faint black trace

inches from untouchable
she's a gracious host
to a humbled artist

my fearful hands shake
as if I were playing god
creating this vision

from the grace of her cheek
to the waves of her swelled chest
my hardened pen a willing captive

possessed in a furious, fervent reverie
the electric words are transformed alive
burned into the pulp with abandon

Justin Michael Doyle

Motel Scene

Sun shines through the window
Hard to find my shoes
Packing up what they didn't steal
In the motel room
Woman's sleeping off boredom
TV's nothing but news
They ain't found a body yet
But it's safe to assume
Cigarettes are soaked, found 'em in on the tub
Woman tends to forget things
Says it's 'cause she's in love
She's gonna hit the ceiling
When she wakes up at noon
Can't say I blame her, then again
Can't say I left too soon
Thought of leavin' her money or maybe a note
Words are more like poison than an anecdote
So I just blow a kiss as I slide out the door
After all, it's expected from
A motel troubadour

Darin K. Henderson

For the Boxer

He was the grenade,
and she, the pin.
After she left, well, I think
you can guess the rest.
And the same story's etched
in stone on side-by-side graves
across our land,
the single-digit differences
separating "Mr." and "Mrs.,"
the simple arithmetic of grief.

My grandfather was a fighter.
Orphaned, he fought
for everything he cared for.
And when his wife died, her mind
hollowed by disease, he kept
his arms to his side,
the meager years beating him
mercilessly, into a ground
he'd paid for with cash.

Bruce Cain

Untitled

You chip at the blue gray porch floor
while I squirm sitting on the stoop.
The brick is shedding its white paint,
unmasking the burnt red underneath.
The chines have attached to the bottom
of my hands and thighs.
I trace against the cast of
the brick on my hand
and stare at the color of pressure.

You hold my hand and enquire
of the impressions left behind.
Your finger moves softly and slowly
along my skin like a kiss from an angel.
Then I watch as you magically massage
the reddened skin to my normal porcelain beige.

Danielle Lynn Mencl

the birth of picasso

standing outside your mother's Malaga home. clinging,
the moon above me and almost full, blue clouds
sanding it smooth. I, your uncle Salvador, am waiting
for you to stroke the blue in clouds and be born.
my sister, the reclining nude, a portrait of the artist's mother,
is lying, legs spread wide enough to deliver the head of a fawn,
bloated and red, bleeding the chance
of some teary screams that reach me in the cold,
the moon still waxing and blue.

I enter into La Vie, only you have fallen to the floor, forgotten,
the midwife turning to your mother, sleeping by shutters,
near death, a few aching streaks around the base of her seat
and numb. my cigar aches between thick stubs of quiet fingers,
blue smoke making clouds and a solid stream blown into your face.
you are born, eyes cracking to the haze of smoke,
screams that split the light between you and I. you see the light
refracting through me. you see me as hundred year old
liquid window panes, grown fat at base and thin at top,
like the bellies of old men and the thinning of their hair.

Patrick Davidson

Lost in Guadalajara

when I'm lost
when the universal
fluorescent convenience store
is across the street
and a taxi driver stops
to buy chopped sugar cane
decisions that'll affect my whole life
can't bring me down
neither can my familiar room
or 10 p.m.

I know someone else lives inside me
and has nothing to do with me
and listens to a seashell
in the light of their childhood

it doesn't bother me
the way snakes have sex
or that seven generations ago
I had 128 grandparents

I'm happy to be lost
among neon crosses and bus routes

Jim Rushton

West Virginia

i know of love and of beer cans
i have felt breasts and tears
just taking the midnight train throughout the years
lonesome guitars, slammed doors on cars
i put a premium on the quality of scars
mountain side rushes hit the deep underbrush
the strokes of the heart, the bones in my fist
hit the breakfast tables just in time
sleeping-bag reveries are what we find
rolling, wavy fields and hermetic jack rabbits
hollowed-out silos and starlit skies like
colored festival lights at this late-night barbecue
the lips touch, the hot blood rushes and throbs

Frank James Berlanga

The Mouth

Drives cockroaches from a rooming house
with a banshee's gale against her husband,

as his, like the gentle quiver of a two-lip
through the hell-wind December noon.

In time, the gale resides
and the two lips open once again
only to yield the shotgun shells
that tear the curtains from the walls.

Some, nimble as Gershwin's right hand,
while others are jagged pavement
after a juggernaut's parade.

Most have and will assume them all:
From motorbike to Magic Flute,
From keyholes to sliding doors,
From arsenic to honey.

Rob John Kelly

When I Come to Ireland

When I come to Ireland, Mayo will whisper
from her piled stone fences
through her blowin' willows
that I have too long tarried,
and which farm's for buyin'.

I will find St. Martin's dream
down dirt road tracks
a mile outside Westport.
I will hear uplands airy
carry fiddle tunes to taverns,
heart-tearing tributes
to the dead of '16.

When I come to Ireland,
I will learn to dive—deep
as gray geese from green-moss cliffs
into the blue-eyed water
of a woman,
whose hair burns my fingers
and soft Gaelic tongue
calls me "Gallagher" again.

Michael L. Dellger

Green Monsters

The picture hangs on my wall, filled with intent
Ty Cobb sliding into Jimmy Austin's shins at third
The dirt spewing up in agony, as the Georgia Peach's spikes
Slice through more than the basepath
It was a time of madmen and green monsters, when Cobb knew Navin
When the summer sun cut through the savage symmetry of the infield
Like quicksand, ready to swallow you up just for standing still
When the stench of stubborn glory was carried up by the urgent dust
And the roar of the crowd was a roar for blood
In the shadow of Navin field that became Briggs and then Tiger Stadium
Now as empty as Cobb's grave, crying out for its madmen
That picture carries the hate spit through Ty Cobb's gritted teeth
Hate spit not at Austin but to the world in general, to life, to me
At the end of his career, when asked if he had any regrets
Cobb only said that he wished he had made more friends
That what he really missed was the warm memories
Of friends sacrificed to green monsters and the glory of the next base

William E. Hampton

Today

When you served me breakfast in bed this morning,
You suddenly said you loved me.
Without thinking, I unknowingly returned the gesture,
Even though I didn't know if I felt it.
By lunchtime, you were saying it again
And this time I honestly said it back.
As a matter of fact, we said it a lot,
Almost after every bite.
Then at dinner, I said, "I love you," first.
This time, you mumbled when you said it.
Maybe you still had chicken in your mouth,
But I hardly heard it clearly.
I wonder what dessert will be.
Maybe you'll skip saying anything,
And be more concerned with your cake.

Crystal Rhodes

Morning Sun

we are ugly laying in the morning light,
the magic of last night's darkness
now just dried alcohol and sex sweat.
i can see the dark circles beneath your eyes
sitting naked before me, knees bent, legs spread,
your tangled hair falling to your lips.

we were beautiful last night, dressed and primed,
dancing and elegant, smart and witty, stealing
flesh beneath the table and in the crowds.
we closed the club, drove to my place, lit candles
and incense, undressed before the flames,
made love on top of the sheets.

we wake beneath each other, tangled, tired, hung over.
in the morning light we are just naked and ugly.
we are ourselves and we are unsure.
such an honest beauty grows from the morning sun.
i may just love you.

Kip Silverman

Naive Me

Today I spied a Grape
that never got to BE—
It Clung to the mother-vine
on the thickness of a thread.
Its pinhead Green-being
Suspended, almost nonexistent,
next to its purple-plump partners.

That minuscule Grape
that never got to Be
Reminds myself of Me—
This lack of sustainment
means Stagnation,
yet Agonizing Longevity.

Because I was so Naive
You never chose to Consume me.
And I'm Cast Away to
Rot . . . Yet Always Remember thee.

Lisa Mikula

Chinese

The first time I ate Chinese
She made me use chopsticks
The sticks hung like broken fingers
But she insisted I try

She had traveled to China
Slept in a tent on the steppe
Where little villagers
Marveled at red hair

All that I understand of China
A custom here, a forbidden temple
Spilled from her pink mouth
And crept inside of me

Now, I cook my own Chinese
In a tarnished wok on the stove
The smell lingers in the carpet
Of this dim apartment

And some nights, I hear through walls
Two making love
Their whispers and cries sound foreign to me
And could be Chinese

John E. Wallace

Burger King

He sits in his own booth.
Arguing with the ghosts of people he has never met.
He eats french fries, stares into space
Remembering the man he must have been.
The man looks right at me, or through me perhaps
Seeing someone he used to know in me.
Away I glance, shivering from his memories
Almost, I can see his phantoms.
I suddenly feel guilty looking into his secrets
Like trying to gaze upon wavering spider webs.
He begins to argue again, pausing to chew his fries
Telling jokes to his delusions.
He hides all the lies from himself.
Silence envelops the place,
And I look over.
He sits there, intently analyzing his Coke.
I try to understand him.
Then I realize, I was trying to touch
Someone else's moment.
Then I look away.

Jenna Bowen

The Boys of Labadi Beach

On the shores of Labadi Beach, live harbingers of treasure:
Star fish, cowry shells, snails sweet as coconut,
Coke bottles, broken, cut and polished into ocean emeralds,
Magic stones—sacrificial offerings.
Oblation for the sons of Teshie, the children of Nungua,
Barefoot village boys, no shirts, no knickers, no fees for school.
Yet they are abosom—gods of the beach.

Up and down Labadi, they alone, can find the treasure
Power-drilled by sand and water, spiral tunnels, filled with magic.
"Good luck . . . in here," the beach boys promise,
Raising them to the African sun: transubstantiation.
Ancient magic, under the species of stone.

"Five thousand cedis," they say, "six on down the way."
Two dollars can feed a family for a day; I buy the useless rock.
The boys of Teshie and Nungua, heads bowed,
Counting money and good luck,
Disappear, leaving behind only land-turtle trails
To be eaten by the next hungry wave.

Ellie Widmer

A Grown-Up Way

Sitting in a green plastic chair,
She is crying,
And it is not the winter that makes her cold.
I stand in awkward silence.
One foot pointing toward her,
The other poised to step away.

Take back the hurt, dry up the tears.
Reassure me that everything is as carefree
As it used to be.
I long for childhood,
When it was understood that I did not mean
The things I said, and all I ever did was
Step on toes.

I have amended and spring has again descended
On this house.
There is a grown-up way of saying I'm sorry.
But I understand now what she means when
She says, "They'll step on your heart."

Kirsten Rebstock

Here, Present Baggage (18 Days)

It's not a me-centered universe
somewhere, somehow it could be though
in your eyes I lie along those lines
nail-biting's lost its edge
like my nerve, like my will
here I am, stuck again in the mud
created by tears and an overactive mind,
pictures whirling through my head—
didn't I tell you I'd never find a moment
in which I could keep you
time is always fleeting
and this bar of soap won't float—
heads up, grab hold, I'll pull you to shore
soul's a little heavier, though body's lithe
and the ceiling's spinning with my mind
you're gone again, tapestry's fraying
to something I can use
hearing your voice, filling like chocolate
and good enough for the moment
(pray it will pass)

Stephanie A. Kessler

Nick for Real aka Caralina's Lament

What was she to say to his list of Isabellas, Francescas and Marias?
What should she have sung
When he tangoed in the cobblestone streets of Granada?
Green eyes, green roots
Polished shoes reflect the tattered woman selling peaches
Her porcelain mouth irritated by the velvet skin
The juice staining her white charade with a deep red
How many minutes does it take to fall in love?
With moonlight? With reflection? With love?
Serenading fortune with questions, fingers callused by the strings
Where does laughter find its nurture
when the eyes are too tired to smile?
Maybe she blinked away the tears
At sight of a coarse linen dress
At sight of a full-skirted candle flame
At sight of her frigid ways and how the sea shrunk away from her
What was she to say to his list of Isabellas, Francescas and Marias?
What should she have sung as he danced away from her, shivering
Comforted by the arms of the Spanish night

Margarita Rayzberg

Silence

Four lilac walls surround me,
I sit alone.
The lilac makes think of flowers,
Flowers that gently get swayed by the wind.
But not a sound is present,
Because there is nothing but silence.
Beneath me there is a beige carpet,
My feet lay barefoot, tickled.
The beige carpet makes me think of the sun on snow.
It gently shines
On the snow and pines.
Then wind comes by, drifting snow,
But not a sound is present,
For there is nothing but silence.
My canopy bed beside me.
The canopy bed makes me think of a large ship.
Water beneath me gently pushes me along,
The wind pushes the sails gently.
But still I hear nothing,
For silence is golden.

Lauren Elizabeth Agyekum

My Better Half

As the rain falls on my thatched roof,
I panic, for there'll be some leakage on the floor;
Helter skelter I run about,
Placing the calabashes on the usual spots.
Wrapped in the thread bone wrapper on the bamboo bed
you left behind,
I reminisce on the times we spent in the twilight,
Playing and dancing to the tunes of the drum beaters,
Coupled with the noise of the crickets.
At dawn, the cock will crow;
Then I recall your warm embrace,
Your confident and reassuring smile,
Revealing your gaped tooth,
And on your powerful shoulders,
You would want me,
Telling me, "No one else can replace your better half."

Nkeruwem Udofia

Flowers of Remembrance

The lovely daisy signifies secrets told or kept
Roses, regardless of their color, always betoken love
Purple violets bring to mind lavender place and grandmother football
Chrysanthemums, blooming golden during harvest and season
Zinnias and marigolds beside the sidewalks, speak of stability
Dawn breaks to the glisten of dew upon reliable morning glories
Day lilies' blooms last only one day, but such glory!
Colorful snapdragons with their unique ability to snap
Bluebonnets make me think of Texas and the Alamo
A gift from your lover tied with lace and blue forget-me-nots
White magnolias, memories of deep South, plantations, slavery
From the hidden depths of the jungle to the ballroom, the orchid
Tall hollyhocks outside the window of a long ago farmhouse
Running as a child among fields of wild black-eyed Susans
Lacking would be the prom without the fragrances of gardenia
New England homes with sidewalk borders of primrose
Childhood memories of Chinese bellflowers worthy of the home
In shapes and sizes and many shades of color, the faithful petunia
Among the night-blooming moonflowers
when I stargaze to the Heavens,
I see Jesus Christ, the rose of Sharon, most precious flower of all

Lucille Simmons

Sacred Places

I met a Tamil hajji
in Buddha's backyard

the pool carved by
Kandyan kings who
imprisoned a Portuguese
cleric and watched women
dance like buffalo

an elephant chained
to a tooth devours danT
and waits to be painted
for a parade

legless beggars sell
betel nut and king
coconut to policemen
waiting for a bomb
to send the temple to
Heaven

the hajji says in perfect
English: I am from Toronto
and shakes my hand

James Steven Kessler

The First Day of the Rest of My Life

For Paolo

In a downtown mall are smiles on bars of soap
Psychotic memorabilia, Marilyn Monroe merlot
In a hidden corner booth in a downtown diner
I saw and felt rainbows, sunshine in clouds
If only on a coffee mug

Your onion-smacked lips
Sweeter than the brandy we shared that night
A night unto nightmares

Now I imagine you will say, "Hello, Joseph"
With forgiving uncolored eyes
Once unanswerable by me, now no more
I imagine you will say it so that I can say
"I hate you," but mean "My love, it cannot be"

Oh, heavy heart, I am drowning
Every day since the one we kissed is cold
Neither to be warmed by spirits or smiles

Joseph G. Pino

11 a.m., Alone—A Tribute to Edward Hopper

A lonely nude woman
sits in a stuffed chair
a plastered simple smile
enamored, blissfully silent
hands clasped together
looking outside a closed window
afterglow of spent desire
all that remains of the magic
when bodies touched and gracefully
slid along the contours of flesh
drawing contentment, sighs of joy
in dreamy memories of figure eights
drawn by her finger over and over
the outstretched body of her lover
lingering hours after he walked out
and never returned

George Edward Kimball

ROOM G159

Caught off balance on the patio

by a direct question of fingers and toes,
a lover's abacus that calculates the
distance between my lips and yours,
or the reach of my hand to your hair,
which releases a jasmine dream so vivid
and fragrant that we lose each other
in the rhythm of a midnight chat

about digits and the sum of tomorrow.

David Jones

Father

I was 11 when I tried to kill you.
I snuck into your bedroom with the knife
you gave me, ghosts of Vietnam rusting the blade.
You had showed me how to slide it into the neck, a silent kill.
The way you killed.
I imagined mother horrified, not understanding how my act
had set her free.
I imagined no more drunken nights,
no more screaming into my tear-streaked face,
no more beatings,
no more.
No.
I went back to my room with the Holly Hobbie
sheets and pink stuffed elephants
and dreamed of Athena rising out
of her father's split skull.

Shannon A. Akui

Valley of the Bees

imagine me in this garden,
arms outstretched to be tasted by bees,
and the numbness in my toes
from the cold grass.

dew trickles down my face
as I gaze at the newly risen sun,
your companion,
so near that I can feel your warmth.

trace the fingers down, down,
following all that isn't ours,
to the roots of spring
and the birth of your spirit.

imagine me in this valley,
hiding among the sunflowers,
waiting for you to rise
and dry the dew from my skin.

Christopher Griffiths

Through the Wires

The trees outside look lonely.
A bruised sky pouts in a blue-black
corner of clouds.
Even the sun dims in
mimicry of a pale moon.
Inside the house
a conduit of sad tidings
slivers through the wires
and we take the words like
razors to our throats.
The last great ghost before death
dances us against slabs of giant
dominoes where we fall bloodless
again and again in quick succession.
Only unrequited love endures.

Salvatore Buttaci

Franny

After four years I'm still sweat and faith
And sometimes weakness
Thinking that bed in the hot summer quiet with you
Is love
And I'd pull on my jeans at four a.m.
To get you a pack of smokes
Or a cherry Slurpee
Or even another box of condoms
To make the night last without
Our universal fear of conception
But now you're no more sweat
And faith in something I can't understand
Or stand and all I hear is your glassy-eyed affirmation
That "I'm better now with medicine and therapy"
And all I see is a shattered favorite Christmas
Ornament, fragile but still shiny and
Unable to from the broken shards of itself

James Barber

nameless

Take comfort; you have dreams ahead
And worlds to explore within and about
And even here
The Earth spins webs of nothingness
Which we are left to fill with somethingness
Our minds are filling in the sky
Our fantasies sleeping in the clouds
Listen to the morning tell her story
Learn the sound of evening's gentle lullaby
Loves and joys are sparkling in the air
We breathe and exhale them everywhere
Take comfort; you have wealth
Of all the world
And every time you feel, you fill the space
Laugh as springtime leaves of time unfurl
You are an atom of the living race;
You are a soul, whom time cannot erase

T. Cavanaugh

Oswald and Hess Meat Packing Plant, Papa Bud, 1956

So small, the girl looked up and straight ahead
Into the rafters of that bleak, steel cell.
Cows hung head down, tail up tied by the swell
Of their thighs and chains.
Men bound and wrapped the threads
Of metal up and through the beams.
The dead maze wrapped around her, made her feel the smell
Seeping into her throat, burning like hell in her lungs.
She grabbed her father's hand and wept.
He slices steaks up on the Hill.
He wraps them up in paper and he ties
The white string tight around the top.
He looks up, slaps them down on the counter.
Calculates, writes the price on top.
Wipes his hands on his lap,
Thinks about his kids, waits hard for the night.

Katie Rose Horowitz

Then and Now

You were a young horse, nostrils flaring,
and I rode your heaving breath until like kittens we squinted,
hearts purring, heated numb and slower than backwards,
fish mouths gulping water, air, sound, any wave—
finally light, pure sheen and vibratory—
the shimmering promise of forever.

While we knelt, crumbling to our altar one last time.

Now free but empty, I crave brilliance outside me,
searching the glossy hard eyes of dogs, sullen and forgotten,
who no longer need men.

Or love.

Susan Gardner

Supermarket Baby

In the checkout line looking around
For the baby whose cry sounds familiar;
Months ago my womb ceased weeping:
Tears resigned without a two weeks' notice.

Yet I still find myself scanning tiny
Faces whenever I'm in the supermarket—
Looking for eyes that mirror mine.

It's been 8 months since I saw the one
I thought had given me life—
When it was I who had given birth to her;
Nevertheless I worshipped at pint-sized feet.

The invisible umbilical cord;
I feel her without hands,
Scanning while I shop:
What I want to take home is not on the shelves.

Maria A. Page

Conversations with Charles Hendricks

The piano plays itself a fantasy
Old brown half-emptied, eyes glazed, you look over to me.
They put you away you say, 160 days
I get these answers for questions I haven't asked.
I don't know what to do with them
Your paunchy laugh against my white skin
animation dies into awkwardness
as you get more drunk and I, less and less
I seemed to have nowhere to hide my contradictions
I am a young lady. I am white, I am American.
You've seventy-six, dispossessed of any compunction
with vehemence covered by slurs
you rattle off a history of whatever occurs.

Geoff Hammond

The Sphinx Is Crumbling

i wander the biggest city
embraced by neon cobwebs
clouded by cheap wine
an afterthought of love
kissed by spit-stained pavement
and she's a sculpture of venus
there in front of the sex shoppe
a heart of cold marble
still the streets are hissing with morbid desire
and the lust for salvation
cursing chinatown; crawling on hands and knees
the rank smell of digestion
a cornucopia gone rancid and musty
wretchedly grievous are we
hardened in feelings we proliferate
budding like fungal blossoms
clinging to the skyscraper jungle
we crumble together
and fall though the cracks like human gravel

P. John Donnie

Ave de Champ E'lysees, Late Summer, 1999

Hemingway has gone away
and taken Paris with him.

I'd walked the streets for days and found nothing
—save the absolute perfect croissant
with chocolate studs like jewels—
that could convince me I was in
an old world den of culture.

I went to McDonald's to see if they really
called them
Royales with cheese.
They did,
but that joke wore thin on Mickey D's #43
as I sat out front drinking coffee
in the lengthening shadow of glory
and triumph.

Charles Reed

Meadow at Midday

Elysian fields of grassland tapestries,
embroidered bright with little flowers sweet
by ancient fairies stitching eulogies
with threads of time where past and future meet.
Perennial matron bending as you weave
each precious moment spinning from your loom.
Delightful blossoms that your love conceives,
this turfy heath without you surely doomed.
Green earthy carpet soft beneath bare skin
in motley iridescence of soft hues,
whose quilted edges quiet woodlands trim,
and overall, the sun, its rays diffuse.
This terrace frocked in spring's fresh dressing gown.
Breathtaking marvel spread upon the ground!

CoCo Mimms

Sunday Morning

My mother came, in righteous green, ribbons
trailing roots I feared would take hold
among the corpses of canned dinners
unpaid bills, letters from their lawyers and mine,
curtains locked in misery, ashes of old dreams.
These roots, good Christian roots, will drag me
back to the Cross and down the hill to Marie,
plain but Pentecostal, warming her Bible and Campbell's soup.
These roots, family roots, lead to Smiths, Browns,
meaning well, though useless as a broken mirror.
They watch me with yellowed eye, dentures
in murky water, like plastic sharks.

Trevor Valerie Yearwood

Prayer to the Rain God

Oh, hard rain that drums on the tin eaves,
Smacks the blacktop with nonstop splattering,
Raps the window glass with each wind gust,
And spouts out the drain pipe an artesian spring;
Oh, anti-liturgical benediction;
Oh, rampant and wanton redemption;
Oh, most holy gully-washer and moisture-laden westerly offshore flow:

Make frothing brooks in the dry ditches
And roiling creek beds out of rock-strewn arroyos;
Swell the stream to a leaping, swirling, dusky rush,
And let it billow out a silt cloud into the big river.
Drench all desire and longing,
All pleasure and depression,
All scheming and regret,
Be they solitary leaf or uprooted tree,
And, in the wild ebullient overflow,
Sweep them out to sea.

John Williams

tragedy of an unspoken word

he missed the morning rain sitting in the dark
in a womb of blankets that curled around a spine
that dared fingers to trace down its boulevard
eyes peeked out like a wish split in two
mouth strangled remarks like a guilty man
with nooses embracing his fish-bone collar

but behind the chapped lips and worried tongues
sat hanging like ribbons on a wall that coughs at night
burrowing between taste buds and hiding

when blankets were tossed aside like
the birthing fluids of ten thousand babies born
and windows hesitated open
with all the distress due any toad in water
regret colored sighs escaped
fugitive thoughts tossed aside handcuffs

the sky was blue
and it was bluer than
leaves that held its breath at twilight

Malinda C. Auk

Yin and Yang

You are Yin, waving purple corpulence
tighting your feline horizons
like the sunset to the sea
like the sea to the drowned.

I am Yang, complete coarseness of blue muscles
and abyssed flanges
that roll down the no-summer trail
shaking off the mass of fire.

However, it is the call of your sex
the unexpected hyphen.
The Yin feeling and the Yin tenderness
watch under that intruder.

And this, my deaf borrowed sex
is by happy coincidence
the gear that fits in the nonconformist yours,
setting the antithesis
of the perfect piece.

Marcela Valdivia

My Girl

I still remember that long, lonely road,
Ten months and ten days long.
At the end you arrived,
Piercing through my womb,
Clenched fists drenched in blood.
Grandmothers wept, Grandfathers spat.
Well-wishers hung sad charcoals on the front door.
"It's a girl!"
Only I smiled, because I knew.
The sweat of my sweat covered your body
When the sun drilled through my pores
In the brick kiln, the rice fields,
Endless realms of my burden.
Your blood sprang with every dirty touch
I endured.
Now, when you start walking this earth
On your wobbly feet,
You will know exactly which door to walk in to.

Arna Seal

Piano

Flanks smooth as silk even their color, flowing like clear tea.
A poised hand floated in air
As the fingers danced over keys like willow branches in the wind.
Everything seemed so effortless,
Only a slight swaying visible
As two hearts and twin souls poured out through taut strings
And when she saw him, she brought up one graceful arm,
Smooth and slim (though slightly more pale on that side),
And smiled as she called his name
He smiled too

Her hair loosely pulled back,
The locks lounging down her back,
There was a slight sheen of sweat on her flawless forehead,
Not obscuring the perfection, but emphasizing the beauty
And with that sheen,
Scarcely visible now that she turned back to play
It was clear she was human.
She was woman
He was man
He smiled . . . and sat down to listen

Daniel Jacob Rubinstein

Untitled

She said her name was Marsha
her hands dangling from her wrists like wet clay
as she sat on the steel horse in the playground backward

They said her name was Carol
and she laughed from the bottom of her stomach

Roger with the body of a man pushes Carol to the sky
and her laugh bounces off the trees in the park

Roger's face fits like the pieces of a puzzle
sewn together with care
locking in a mind that will always see itself as only four
and then will always be as now and as before

They leave the playground like a small tornado
whisking leaves, rocks and twigs from the earth
they disappear inside the yellow school bus
waving ever wildly as they chug down the road

Ducks still float on a leaf-covered pond
brown bark remains on the trees
and the blue-gray river flows perfectly

But there's no sound
only a stillness an emptiness left in the park.

Jennifer DeSalvo Cortner

Orbit

Moving through space, endlessly.
Two celestial bodies find their way
through an ocean of dead, cold nothingness—
Emerging as coexistent entities,
no longer revolving around the sun.
To me, that girl was the sun.
I was Pluto,
too far away to bask in her radiant beauty,
yet close enough to admire her from afar.
How could such phenomena occur?
Could she have been reaching for me—
as I was reaching for her?
Or were we both sister planets?
Earth and Venus,
Identical in shape and size—
but with little differences that scream their uniquity.
Closer we move to one another,
waiting for collision.
To shatter our Earth bodies.
and become something eternal.

John Ryan Hoskins

Rocks to Give

She searches for hours, toddling
daughter of mine, through rocks
for that special one made by the sun
for glowing conversation.
Once found, it's presented to me
with generous smiles and unknown words,
her eyes flashing colors
the jealous rock can only whisper.

She owns the universe.
Fences are for climbing. Coins are
shiny collectibles, and music is everywhere.
Soon she will know how poor she is.
Learn fences are boundaries, money is
power and music is copyrighted.
Knowledge squanders a wealth of innocence.

But for now she is Queen of the World—
My world. My all and everything,
even though she has only worthless rocks to give.

Pamela Haddorff

When Last I Was Rummaging

When last I was rummaging
Through those tucked-away memories
I usually keep for cold, rainy days, such as this,
I found that old copy of Jack Kerouac
You had shoplifted from the bookstore on the corner.
And I remember how you couldn't stop giggling,
As you snuck past the shriveled, gray man at the counter.
We ran, how we ran,
But, when we stopped,
You took out your pen,
And scribbled something on the inside cover.
"I want you to have this," you said,
As you thrust the book at me.
Now, years later, as once again I open the book,
Those words you scribbled on the inside cover,
So yellow with age,
Will forever remain a mystery to me.
I never could read your writing.

James J. Jenkins

Every Morning

Every morning we drive to the same coffee shop,
On the same road, up that same hill—
Castaneda would be disappointed.
There's a girl that walks up that hill,
Presumably to class.
Every morning we see the girl with plum red hair,
And every morning I try not to look at her.

The sound of the milk being steamed,
While the coffee grinder grinds the espresso beans
(Just right, like the texture of sugar),
I am violently reminded of what I have not become,
And what has become of us because.
It was not shooting-magic; it is not a curse.
There will be no witch doctor stalking me, I think;
Yet the sounds of every morning are like echoing incantations.

Every morning amounts to this,
Since she told me her awful secret.

Barker Fariss

Elvis in Hell

On days when he is not condemned to shake
off death and rise again
before the startled rearview gaze
of white-line-wired big riggers highballing
through Peoria or reflected in
the window-shopping reverie
of a Tulsa football widow, he's
imprisoned in a velvet painting in El Paso,
a plaster statuette in Nashville,
a T-shirt on the rack or
cursed with impersonators, harpies in white,
spangled bells drawling
old songs that scald like bacon grease.
But evening brings real agony
when night lights up the strip:
no headliner, just a warm-up, he
opens every night for the big marquee,
the boss of Mephistopheles,
who sets 'em howling with lines like:
"Take my dignity . . . Please."

Michael Stuart Waterson

Wait for You

you said it will only be a few days . . .

I counted the fingers on my left
then my right hand
then once again, and once again

Spring bloomed all around me
like the flowers on the caressing sheets
that comforted me each night

Summer burned with the moist air of sleepless
visions long and countless, hot and restless

Fall ripened our bed with blankets
like the growing red peas beneath the Ormosia
round, solid, and delicious.
the Chinese called them "love peas"
for thousands of years.

Winter whispered purity
beneath the blankets of snow and promises

Tonight, as I climbed into bed
alone
I left the light on for you
again.

Guili Zhang

An Addict's Colors in the Lines

tracing textures of his
dusty Chicago smiles
I contemplate the idea of broken metaphor.
more specifically, a
thousand Mondays
spent drawing black liner across our wrists
pondering Exacto knives instead
his now fading into pools of confession
his now fought by newborn freckle
his now swallowed with a glass . . . of . . . water . . . me
I don't want a coloring book
64 Crayolas all lined up.
still no shade as comfortable silent
as the blue of our veins
his absence leaving only
the frost of my clinging last to glassy addiction.
and beauty drawn
up in lines.

Danielle Li

The Night Sacrifice

July stole in like a black bear
And I admired the night stars as if I knew them
Felt the breeze and moon on my face
Floated above the Earth in the old porch swing
Its creaking my oxygen.
Measuring of night by the mind's eye and not moving
Barely, the consumption of a summer fragrance of
Sweet unnamed flowers, these were the things
I thought I should do then. I could not
Just then conjure up all the things I would have
To conquer or had already.
I started to stir once making tea, painting words.
I should have written, found what was lost, but the oak
Branches made a noise like rubbing paper. The sky
Began to laugh. Moon bloated with its own glistening
As I watched to see it burst, the old blanket
At my chin my amulet.
I fended off the hungry need of seeking
Blinked the bear god in the face and sacrificed the
Night into nothing.

Diane Smalley

Airbrushed In

Sleep well tonight
beneath this Starry Night
or at least if you wake tossing
imagine me a good thing
even the light of those dangerous things I said.

Entertain thoughts and dreams of us;
pictures of forever and fairy tales,
that reach beyond the stratosphere.

Remember my voice like I remember yours
echoing in my head phone against my ear
all that is missing in sound quality and visuals
gets airbrushed in like Hubble pics
of far off planets and gaseous clouds.

Howard Garwood

Unwilling Goddess

He has made me the unwilling goddess of his pagan heart.
He has claimed me with his savage soul.
A common deity, I am ignored when all is well in his world.
He neglects me when the sun is warm and the hunt is good.
But . . . When the icy wind bites, he comes to me
and pleads for Sanctuary.
He seeks my protection when he is afraid.
He prays to me with plaintive cries when he is ravaged by hunger.
And when I have blessed him with comfort and with safety,
He worships me with adoration and with sacrifice.
Blood spilled upon an altar that bears my name.
The dead mouse upon my pillow
That he has slain with his . . .
Cruel Cat Claws . . . In my honor.

Holly Nix

Timeless

We were cruising through the wind, timeless
Time couldn't touch us, even if it tried
Her blacker than black hair must have been warm
'Cause that sun was hot, but it didn't stop us
Jump the canal, I screamed, didn't matter if she did
'Cause in my mind we had jumped it a thousand times
Just like General Lee, except we were in the War Chief
No feathers to mark us, no moccasins on our feet
The real thing, cruising through the wind
Listening to the Eagles and leaving everyone behind us
Like dust in the wind, but this was no Kansas
We were cruising through the wind, with the sun ahead
Like a lighthouse in the desert, guiding us somewhere up ahead
So we kept cruising through the wind, to forever
I think she kept cruising and I don't remember getting off
But what a ride, what a ride
Cruising through the wind side by side

Michael Valenzuela

Elevenses with Ghosts

Soldiers walk in whispers in Flanders fields
Unseen by the air that breathes on slim trees.
But I have a sense of having been
In this place once, when the Earth was rent
Open and spilled out and whistles summoned us
To immortality
Like obedient dogs.

But the land is green now, smoothed inscrutable and
The unknowing wind sighs between white stones.
The gray voices of the boys now wonder how we used
The gift they gave to us.
At the going down of the sun, I kneel and wonder too
Why I wear my poppy
Like sackcloth and ashes.

John Beevers

Unlike Lazarus

Brittle-boned and bruised in this black nest.
Barely breathing, like a bird just born.
And I believe in the resurrection.
I see you through the cracked earth rising
Like the full, white moon.
Unlike Lazarus, your flesh clean and sweet.
Alabaster roses.

J. M. Yates

Untitled

in silent waves
in hushes and whispers
the sand dunes roll over
the ages
of nothingness
from under
the camel hair tent
rushed out the sounds
of familiar voices
sitting
cross-legged
in front of the blank screen
my fingers typed out her name
Gaia
Pierre would probably think
my search is vain . . .
we go through life the way
a kiss would fade
away
in slow motion

Abdelfetah Chenni

Pool-Watching after Fencing Drills and Too Much T. E. Lawrence

The sabre gripped in dirty sweat, all grit
And ache; the grinning velvet scabbard hung
In gold and lazuli, inlaid with pearl
And silver.

I have seen you swim, and dreamt of noble sheikhs
And T. E. Lawrence in oases: palm
Trees, date trees, khaki uniforms, but off—
White turbans, robes, and camels slipping sandwise
Beneath the sickle moon that harvests heat.

My rhymes all left me then and I was burnt,
Embarrassed, blushing by the pool with you;
A fencer in his denim whites all soaked
To skin with saline sweat, the sabre gripped
In rotten, leather gloves inside the gym
Where noble sheikhs are far away, and I
Know there was only one Sheherezade,
My dear.

Weldon Michael Goree

Roadside

On the way to Fresno, we pass almond orchards,
a weave of trees, like stitches across the land,
as precise as fine lace or crossword puzzles.
We talk past empty fields, abandoned acres
of bleached earth that reflect only heat,
not the light piercing our noon hour.

Between Merced and Chowchilla, somewhere
along 99 South, I spot a man on the shoulder,
loosely sprawled atop the sun-softened asphalt,
limbs flung out as though disjointed—one arm across
his face, the other pointing south. Like a shadow,
he has fallen away from the sun, and by the stillness
of his body, by the fine coat of dust that covers
his clothes like sifted flour, I know that he has
been there for a while, that he fell long before
our journey started. Caught in the speed
of highway driving, we do not stop, and in the small
rectangle of the rear view, I see how the hot gusts from
each passing car rock his body ever so gently.

Jennifer Mie Margareta Hayashida

Phoenix

His voice, scratchy like sandpaper
or an unshaven chin
scrapes against my skin,
sending strips of flesh falling,
forming a neat pile, the pieces
in the shape of curled pencil shavings.
The shavings are dry,
crispy like a brown pile of leaves.
The kind that catch instantly
from a carelessly dropped cigarette.
Licks of flame reach up,
grasps of smoke
trying to tear even more flesh,
layer by layer like husks from corn.
But my eyes stare upwards,
past the pyre's grip.
I rocket to the sky;
the hands couldn't reach me,
and they sank back to become ashes,
as my wings reached for an even hotter fire.

Kaitlin Marie Conway

Direction

Driving southwest
(like misguided geese),
we peer out into the
gray December dusk.
The electronic highway sign
shouts, "6:34 p.m."
like a 21st century night watchman,
forgetting to comment
that all is well.
A sleek jet rushes overhead,
and I wish I were on it
(no matter where it's going).
I can't help thinking my life
has become a slide show of some
Leave-It-to-Beaver world—
full of repetitive small talk
about the price of gas
while picking lint off an old, gray sweater.

Christina R. Spurlock

Dogma

I have a god,
an obsession, a way of life.
His constant and ruthless energy
merely reminds me of the past,
as the moment evaporates like a morning dew,
thrusting me into the unforgiving sunlight.

My god has control, I don't;
I pretend and feign,
but this pompous charade
is destroyed by the sight of my bible
which burdens me with guilt
and an unfading regret for the unalterable.

An escape is absolutely impossible,
at least while my heart still beats,
mirroring the patterned hand,
with which my god reigns.
But this too shall pass,
for I, unlike my god, won't last forever.

Vince Robert Grzegorek

Gardens in the Sand

On the dunes of this Kuwaiti desert
Parched by years of greed and conflict
The north-easterlies weave patterns learnt
Perhaps an incarnation or two ago
Over the exquisite rock gardens of Kyoto.

Amidst the debris of invasion and occupation
The chiaroscuro of browns and burnt oil sludge
Weave a carpet of Rohrsach blots on the sand
Inviting us to project onto the undulations
The anthers and petals of pain and maybe hope
Hidden in the dark recesses of our minds.

Like the parched winds shifting the sand
Looking for a tinge of moisture
We sift through the debris of our lives
And find nothing but flotsam and jetsam
In the garden of sand in our minds

Ravi Nayar

el diario

el diario and the book man
walked hand in hand to the corner.
he spoke of his wife, the whale with lash tongues,
and his measly wage,
dried out by hard drinks and a soft son.
el diario and the show man
sat at a table in the back,
and clicked spoons over the morning's deal.
i'll admit this, he said,
i never shook hands with a man i liked.
i've never been right about the weather.
el diario and the god's man
met behind the gym on game day.
he answered every question with,
it's hard to say,
and left before finishing his cigarette.
then behind his back, to himself perhaps,
no matter that the lord can't fix,
he sighed. no matter that the lord can't fix.

S. M. Ahmed

Nude

His nude body becomes
a clean, new canvas as I
slather paint all over
his primitive stature of old
white, hot, meaty flesh
I hold in my hands as
I attempt to understand
the meaning of this epiphany,
"Grace falls from us, not us from it,"
he whispers, shattering my mind
All of this time, wasted. Trying,
grasping, hoping to ascend.
the crisp sound of the bell
tolls in my mind as I realize
the truth of a life of piety
I don't need it anymore
I have my primordial soldier
to keep me occupied in any fashion
as we travel through life's revelry

Ann Catherine Clemens

The Kissing Tree

A nostalgia for cloaking leaves—

Thin-lipped passions of a child
Asserting in spite of familial damage
And other normal molestations
Herself with me
High above up
In the kissing tree

We quaintly called ourselves
By nicknames or grown-up
Endearments, disarming faulty
Embraces, touching all places
On a branch beyond
The big kids and fathers

No one could find us
But our selves became
A verdant rising sacrifice
Of childhood

Patrick Henry Diener

Innocence

My heart calls out on the darkest of nights,
Life without joy? Incomplete.
I pray that my soul will one day be light,
But sadness plagues me still, a fire without heat.
My mind cries out!
But there's no one to hear.
I wallow in doubt,
And shed bitter tears.
Innocence lost.
But love never found.
Too great is the cost,
And too quiet is the sound.

Thomas Dowling

Destiny

For Sandy . . . who was and always will be . . . my destiny!

It is there, I know . . . somewhere it is there

It rings in my head, day upon night
Night upon day an elusive voice
Beckoning from a dream somewhere
In the distance . . .

"Come to me, come to me"

It is there, I know . . . I can hear it knocking
Quietly knocking . . . begging to be let in
Its siren call lures me to the door.

It is there, I know . . .

I can see it through the keyhole . . .
A vaporous shadow flitting like a tiny bird
From treetop to treetop summoning me . . .
From every branch.

It is there, I know . . . somewhere it is there

A tiny Island on a darkened sea,
It whispers in the wind
Day upon night, night upon Day
From somewhere in the distance . . .

"Come to me, come to me."

Susanne Lee Math

A Second Chance

We awake every day not knowing the extent of our lives.
We are what we eat, we are what we preach.
We can only predict the future,
and act on what we have to do to make it work.
We see people on drugs, alcohol and what it does to their bodies.
We can try it all and there's always a first time for everything.
The first time for something can mean an addiction for life.
For nine months we are created, yet at the snap of a finger,
we can be gone.
I feel that you have been through a lot.
You've overcome a lot of trials and tribulations.
You have a wife who cares and two beautiful children who will
always love you for what you are, not because your their dad.
Before you can be a dad, a husband, a lover,
you have to be a friend first.
That conquers all and life goes on.
I sat back and thought you could have been history,
if it weren't for your knowledge of what to do.
I believe that being the person that you are
and knowing what you knew to survive,
you were given "a second chance."
When situations like this happen,
it's a shame we have to stop then and think of how lucky we are.
What we have to be thankful for?
What can we do to make life better?
Why can't we think about these things when the going is good?

Priscilla M. Hagins

Aladdin's Cave (21st Century)

To a housewife the department store is a vast toy shop
With such a wealth of choice it's difficult to know when to stop.
To a newly housed it's an adventure in lining the nest
And her first impulse is to look for the best.
Economic caution is not always the prime consideration
When her mind is poised on the point of deliberation.
It's a house of dreams even when she's not money to spend
Where she can search the floors for the current trend.
She can admire the clothes she'll never wear
Because there never will be that much money to spare.
The cosmetic section is a delight to her nose and eye
Where she can muse over expensive items with a sigh.
Finally of course she can break off for tea
With a sandwich and a cold dose of reality.

Allen Jessop

A Grandmother's Love

My lovely granddaughter, Jasmine Lee Jenkins,
was born October 3, 1994.

Weighing in at six lbs. 12 oz.,
19 1/2 inches long,
on a crystal clear and pleasant morn.

She was such a heavenly baby with her vivacious beautiful eyes,
and a smile that immediately was to her gain.

Now she's the terrible two's,
forming her own individual, charismatic personality,
with a slight temper to maintain.

She's indeed smart, intensely observant,
alert, and oh! what a challenging test!

We, as parents and grandparents, even a potential positive
stranger on the streets, are prepared
by the creator, generationally, to do the rest.

My granddaughter's parents are independently sown,
spiritually grown, with lifelong endeavors
that are unquestionably known.

Jasmine Lee is the love of the land,
that's why her daddy calls her his, "Little Girlie Man."

Janice L. Jenkins

Nature

There was a time, long ago
When the world was alive, and everything would grow.

Every spring, the flowers would bloom
Unaware of their certain doom.

Year after year the same old thing
Till everyone knew what spring would bring.

But then one spring the sun wouldn't show
The smog blocked its rays to the world below

The flowers stopped blooming, the trees didn't grow
All because of ignorance from men who didn't know.

Slowly it died, the world, you see
Until it came down to the last and final tree

And there it stood, that powerful oak
It was then the men realized this wasn't a joke.

They began to wheeze, for they could not breathe,
They were dying, now they believed
The trees provided oxygen, which they had all but relieved

So they all rushed around the powerful oak
In hopes that it's oxygen would not make them choke

But no oxygen they got, and they soon all died
For the tree gave no oxygen, it was petrified!

Justin Geer

My Love to Linda Marie

Linda Marie, you are the sea which floats my boat. You fill up
the hole in my heart with warmth and cuddles. I have never
had such a wonderful lover in my life. Cause your smiles
and wonderful eyes holds me captive in the spell of your love.

Bill Nichols

The Web

The sunset reveals a glimmering,
silk silhouette,
casting a shadow of doom over the ground,
sealing the fate
of whatever may pass through it.

Steven Haney

Poem of the Ocean

I went to the beach.
I found a little peach.
I threw it in the ocean.
I made a new potion.
That gave me the notion to swim in the ocean.

Jori Baldwin

Fireflies by Moonlight

Take leave of me, and find your wings.
Join the others for all to see.
Our lives will pass like a moonlit night.
All I ask . . . is to remember me . . .
Remember me.

D. Wayne Austin

Because I Care

You told me you have Cancer and I go numb
in disbelief. I want you to know that I'm
here to support you when a hug is needed or
a shoulder to hold on to is best. Just call and I'll do the rest.
I'm here for you because I care

Althea B. Washington

Just to Let You Know

Just to let you know I'm here
Just to let you know I'm not scared
Just so you can see who's behind closed doors

I'm not just a man who walks on all fours
I see the light when I see you
I feel darkness when I can't hear you

And when you shut me out
I wonder what's it all about

Is it a women thing, or is it a me thing
What you bring is smiles, but when you leave it's frowns
That's when my body lays on top of the ocean and drowns

I guess there's no life guard
To stop my heart from going down

They say time heals all wounds
But to me life is like a balloon

What you see is what you choose
But what you choose you can also lose

Just to let you know don't be cruel
Just to let you know we're still cool
And just to let you know I'm not a fool

Craig T. Allen

Where My Journey Begins

Pelting rain drives through the sky
and slaps the car windows.

It trickles down in kaleidoscopic patterns
and is quickly forced away by the velocity of
the wind.

Each brush of air even more chilling than the
one before.

My breath is whiter than the snow outside:
Outside where the highway becomes a conveyor
belt of needless rushing and where the only
difference between day and night is the
ticking Timex on my left wrist.

This is where my journey begins.

Andrea Lawless

The Feelings I Feel

As the morning arrives,
My heart for you it thrives .

I want to call you
I place my hand on my heart, 'cause you know it's true.

I am lost without your laugh or smile,
Like the saying goes, you have to walk a mile.

I have walked the walk,
I so long for your voice, touch, and that joyful talk.

You had a way of making me smile,
Until I had to hold my side and then rest a while.

With your gentle voice,
You never judged or gave me a choice.

You loved me with all your heart,
From day one until we had to part.

With every effort of your being,
You made me laugh, and I'm still gleaming.

Your love will live within me for as long as I live,
I am so blessed for you gave me all you could give.

I miss you so very much,
But I just have to remember, my heart to touch.

Terry L. Buser

untitled

whispers in the night of lonely lost lovers
calling my name a familiar memory
lost to the spring breeze
escaping their exhausted lips
out of habit—purely habit
sitting by my bedroom window
i hear their calls beckoning me to travel with them
to explore a world
now possible only in their dreams
a lone tear falls
down the cheek of my fragmented reflection
the stars stare down at me as they scream
this isn't how it's supposed to be
my insides tell me to turn, run, leave this place
a message received constantly
my heart absorbs it once again
. . . breathe and move on
air embraces me, a warming ember
in the chilled night
scents of sandalwood, mint, and rose petals
rock me to a calmed state as I lay awake and listen
to lonely lost lovers sewing dispirited stories
of everything they loved, everything now gone
another night expires in celestial hands
drifting away into memory bliss

Jackie Cote

What Is Love?

Is it love we fall in love with when we're burning with desire?
Or something that the Lord had planned when he set our hearts afire.
What commitment do we make when we finally come together?
To Honor, love and cherish in fair or foul the weather.
Were we old enough to realize we must commit to love?
And just not take it blindly this blessing from above.
Are we here to just raise children, and send them on their way?
Or is love an everlasting theme that grows from day to day.
When passion wanes, and hair turns gray in the final years of life;
Our god must look with favor on a loving man and wife.
Dear Lord, I thank you for my love that's lasted through the years;
That's given joy and laughter through the good times and the tears.
To cuddle up together when the day comes to an end,
I know I have a one true love and a very faithful friend.

Valerie Ann Tudor

Waiting for My Love

I look at the window, what do I see?
I see the sky crying out to me.

The sky is black, and I cannot see,
Where, oh, where can he be?

If only I can see him on this night so weary,
To ease my mind, so that I may see so clearly.

As I pause to hear the rain break through the glass,
My heart skips and trembles just like being in mass.

My eyes are closed in fear
The men in Black are coming near.

I hear their footsteps coming close.
Oh, how I wish it was all a joke.

Louder and clearer I hear the steps
I even hear it in the depths.

I feel hands covering my eyes.
My heart just wants to die.

As I turn to see who it is.
It is my love, who gives me a kiss.

His kiss is warm, his kiss is pure.
My love has found my cure.

Lyli De Jesus

My Life with M.S.

This poem is dedicated to my family, Roque, Rosha, and Dustin.

The world is a beautiful place,
But when my sight is taken, it leaves me alone, giving me my space.

With steroids I blow up like a balloon,
Making my face look like the moon.

I am not angry with my disease.
Being not terminal puts me at ease.

Each day is different from another
Putting my present day from the others.

God made us feet to feel the sand,
While I have lost use of my hands.

When my brain is scrambled and cannot think,
My memories and thoughts are gone and that stinks.

Wheelchairs, walkers and all other aids
Keeps me living many happy days.

Fatigue, migraines and stress are part of my life,
But my family is always by my side.

Each day I pray Heaven will be my cure
Because I know God will not make me handle
more than I can endure.

Shelba J. Williams

Flower

Flowers, flowers grow so high
You look so pretty, almost up to the sky
I water you twice a week so you can grow
The sun is shining over you that makes you glow.

Kerri Jo Foster

Paper Weight

The written word from the profound to the absurd.
Scribe it down so that it can be heard.
The voice in your head resounding what is said.
To give life to the paper it is the ink that is fed.

Richard Soule

The School Year

Throughout the year there have been some mad times.
There have been some bad times.
But we all are here that's what counts.
The school year—it's been tough, have a great
summer through and through.

Philip Christopher Hansen

Angel's Wings

For some of us, today is a day to rejoice,
for others who have lost a loved one . . .
remember to always listen for their voice,
they are with you in your time of need . . .
they will be sent to you on Angel's Wings.

Angela Rich

My Computer Friend

Never heard your voice, but you were my choice.
Never saw your face, don't even know your race.
Big, tall, short, or small; doesn't matter much at all.
But chatting with you a lot makes me think of what I've got.
"GOOD FRIEND" feeling goes to the bone.
I wrote this for you on my own.
"FOR YOU, MY FRIEND."

David Dale Renfrow

Broken Heart

I can no longer fall in love again.
Because once I fell in love with a friend.

I often thought of us together.
But when she said no, it ruined my dreams forever.

And I never thought it to be true.
That my heart would be split in two.

When she said no I thought I would die.
But instead of killing myself I went home and cried.

Never had I felt so much pain.
Another rejection can drive me insane.

So much pain and frustration caused by this friend.
Will this feeling I have ever end?

So never again will I fall in love with a woman I adore.
'Cause I don't think my heart can break much more.

But why do I feel pain, when I knew it could never be.
Because a woman as pretty as she would never have chosen me.

I really loved her with all of my heart.
But in the end I had to let fate do it's part.

And until the day we meet again.
The girl I love will remain a friend.

Osberry William Diles

Birth

Birth is a mess. . .fashionable undress,
A spiritual miracle for the main.
But how can a hugging become such a mugging
The moment my domicile is drained?
I was squeezed, flushed, wrenched and thrust,
I was pinched and rolled about.
When the tongs clamped on, was I so wrong
To consider another way out?
They sprang me to hang me upside down,
And paddled my rear till I scream.
The cries and the cheers challenged my fears
To go right back in was my dream.
I felt the warm reach of mom's arms beneath
I was Life. . .a born-to-be Winner.
But wait just a minute, the doc will begin it
"Say hello to a little 'ol Sinner."

H. H. Rutledge

A Song of Memory

To Robert G. Chester, my true but unhappy love in the U.S.A.

On the day,
It was a flowering month of May,
The greatest singer and poet
Has passed away.

[refrain:] Goodbye, Frank Sinatra, good-bye!
You were a famous guy!
The singer of the century
And who left us the wonderful legacy.

You're now resting in the land,
But your songs are marked with a brand
Of a beautiful poetry, and a National Band
Plays your songs accomplished with a backhand. [refrain:]

I learned your songs,
They came in my life along,
I grew up under the overlong,
Influence on me by your songs so strong, so strong.

[refrain:] Goodbye, Frank Sinatra, good-bye!
You were a famous guy!
In my heart your name is written with the light,
In my memory you'll never die!

Victoria Clinton

Vicksburg, Arizona

We awake to gaze at the rising sun
Knowing another day has begun
When wondering through the desert so free
Realizing God's goodness, for you and for me
The beautiful cactus that depends on the rain
So cactus flowers can bloom again
The white winged doves flap their wings
The prettiest tune they love to sing
The picturesque mountains with shapely peaks
And the coyotes howling for something to eat
The lizards running through the sand
With creosote bushes on every hand
Crowder wiser ranch handling cattle with care
Rising each morning with work prepared
This tiny town of Vicksburg stays busy each day
With a slow pace of life style, we like it that way
The old windmills turning shows progress from before
If only I could have strolled into that old country store
with ten gallon hats and dresses sewn by hand
If this still existed, wouldn't life be grand
Some say there's gold in them hills
And some tell it so free
Just talk to some little miner
And Vicksburg will rejuvenate you and me.

Ruth Nelson

Alone

I live in a big house, alone
Since my mate has gone to Heaven
He was my Honey, Soul Mate, and Protector
Oh, how I miss him deeply, thoroughly
I miss him more and more each day
It hurts
Alas, nobody knows, nobody cares
I hate to see the sun rise
It is an another day begun without him
I hate to see the moon shine
It is a dark, lonely night without him
Beyond, it will be an another day
Time floating by, the world never stops moving
Why, I am still here on this planet
Why, my Honey is not here anymore
Oh, those precious memories with him
It gets harder and harder to live with memories
I need my Honey, I want him back with me

Emmy Muyu Hartwick

At Risk—AIDS

It started that spring, went right through the fall,
I was living it up, having a ball,

Roaming around out looking for pleasure,
Convivial in hours of leisure,

In bars, discos, clubs, with pick-ups many,
Yet failed to take precautions with any.

The urge so strong, the need to have it off
Caused most to forget, or simply to scoff—

Exchanges of pleasure when in good health
Lulled suspicions of contagion by stealth—

Diseases, S.T.D.'s, not on the mind
When encountering others of your kind.

Much the same no precautions did I take,
Afraid to lose out with those on the make,

I was diagnosed to be HIV—
My devil—may—care had caused it to be.
What had been passed on was the virus AIDS,
I knew once stricken by it all hope fades,
It simply becomes a matter of time
Before one sinks into final decline.

Laura Edwards

Sadness

Sitting in solitude
Quiet reflection on a lifetime past; moments forever gone

Love, lives, friends; lost in time
Disappointments and joys, only memories now

Reflections of things
That never were, and will never be in this lifetime

A sadness descending
For what the future appears to be bringing once again to life

And a weariness settles within
Robbing the strength that once beat proud

No bitterness, no anger
Just disappointment, and a resignation to fate

The tears once feared
In the open light and feared no more, only acceptance of destiny
The tears to be shed are the final tears
And then a hope for the end of sadness

A new journey awaiting
Towards an unknown place where no pain exists, only an eternal peace

The undiscovered country; the land of forever
Land of dreams, forever serene

Christopher Banks

An Ode to My Loving Husband

You have held the key to my heart for
fifty-one years. I appreciate the
care and caring, the love and loving
we share and continue to share.

You are my love, my best friend,
a loving husband, a loving father and also a
loving grandfather to our grandchildren.

I have wonderful memories of all the fun
and happiness over these fifty-one years
and nobody can ever take away the love I feel for you.

Our life together is a living testament
for a perfect marriage and I hope the
future years will continue to hold the
magic we have known as sweethearts,
husband and wife and lovers.

In honor of your seventy-ninth birthday
with my love forever. Your loving wife!

Sylvia A. Vayda

Aspire

Aspire;
Dream about yourself and your future.

Try to move beyond what you already are;
Strive for a higher plane.

Elevate, motivate, and uplift yourself;
Don't let anything or anyone sway you.

Choose the positive path and walk it;
Keep God inside.

Tell yourself that you will not fail;
You don't stop! Keep on.

Let the people closest to you guide your steps;
Knock down all barriers to success.

Attain your goals, then set new ones for yourself.
Keep your head up.

Take some friendly advice,
But don't let anybody turn you around.

People might say that you'll never amount to anything.
In that case, aspire to be something—something good.

Leniah Antwoine Johnson

Reliable

Flowers are gorgeous to enjoy today—
Tomorrow the petals are falling off
And soon you have to throw them away . . .
Our cars are great while they work properly—
But what happens once they break down and fall apart . . .
Computers are truly marvels of the "New World"—
However let one malfunction and our world is totally in despair
And at a loss to do anything . . .
There are so many things which are reliable
For a period of time, so many things we count on—
Until that dreadful day happens when something breaks,
Falls apart, doesn't work, or malfunctions—
So many things . . .
But look above your head for "True Reliability"—
Look up as far as you can see, look up what's beyond,
Imagine what is out there . . . the Big Dipper, Little Dipper,
The North Star, our "Glorious Moon" . . .
Every 365 days a year, all you have to do is look up
For things that are "Truly Reliable"—
They are always there, they never break or fall apart,
When everything is going wrong in your life
And all hell is breaking loose, just look up into the night sky,
Everything good is still there.

Steven Jacobs

Money

All your money can't buy a sunny day.
It can't make love come your way;
Nor buy a summer rain,
Nor ease the pain
Of a broken heart.
It surely may impart
A measure of temporary pleasure.
It can also drive you mad
If you keep up with every fad.
It can spoil your child
Who will then drive you wild,
Trying to keep him out of trouble;
Turn your dreams to rubble.
Yet to have no money is a sorrowful state.
A life of poverty is not great.
It's a problem; too much, too little.
How can you manage to be in the middle?
Work, get paid for all you merit,
Be nice to relatives; with luck, you may inherit!

Mary Lois Lind

Mystery of Our Love

To Tiffany. I love you.

When I look into your eyes
I know that it's true
The love that I have looked for, for so long
I found it in you

Will a kiss
Prove our love
You're an angel baby
From the heavens above

I gaze into your eyes
And from this point on
I lead you into my soul
And forever, we'll always be one

I hold your hand
And whisper into your ear
"You'll never forget
What you're about to hear"

All this time, we soon find out
Forever, our love is true
I softly whisper,
"Baby, I love you"

Chad McGee

Your Other Lover

You walk alone
beside me.
Here where the surf rages against the sand.

This is your silence.
Here where the tide breaks against the land.

Your short, annoyed glance, as the shrill cry of my world
interrupting yours, makes me more the stranger.
Here, where blood washes over bone.

I stand still,
speaking, watching;
you walk your invisible ledge,
between Earth and man.

It is Her
pulse, you feel beneath your feet.
Her breath
that tussles your hair.

There is no bridge long enough to reach you
in Her embrace.

Phone in hand,
I turn back to the car. To wait.

Jamie Moffatt

Dreams

So often we see them, so little we understand them,
Like little bubbles of reality that only exist in our minds,
Shaped and changed by our very thoughts.
They give and yell messages like aggravated dogs,
But we are too blind to see and too deaf to hear.
He who can hear them is truly great,
And he who can understand them is truly wise.
When shall we ever learn?

Like fleeting bubbles of reality,
They are nowhere but everywhere, never but always.
Contradictions, they're full of them, dreams are.
But one thing is certain, they are not real.
Some people dream of this, some of that.
Most dreams never come to reality,
But the ones that do come out in all their glory and splendor,
Such is the nature of dreams.
Dreams are a dying man's only consolation,
Dreams . . .

Glenn Myers

A Solution

It rained a solution from the skies
and that solution was known as peace,
found in its ability to dissolve the skin,
man's skin.

Alas, one skin.

One could no longer discern
a difference and point,
He's black, she's white, he's yellow, she's
red, they're green.

So now there is one less thing
with which man has to judge his fellow man.

And now we need a "solution" for religion.

But instead it rained a solution of love . . .
and that solution embraced all,
Protestant, Catholic, Muslim and Jew.

That solution of love
caused chaos,
for it was still one less thing
with which man has
to judge his fellow man.

Veronica Owens

I Hope

I hope that when he wakes up,
You are the first thought that enters his mind,
and I hope that when he goes to sleep,
You are the last person to leave his conscious thought.

I hope that when he sees you, his life lightens up.
His mind becomes flustered with a thousand
thoughts and dreams to share with you.

I hope that when he touches your soft gentle skin
His heart explodes into the color of a thousand autumn leaves.

I hope that when he holds you close,
all his foolish dreams of fame and fortune fade away.
And he realizes the only thing he needs in this life is you.

I hope that when his lips touch yours,
the world and all its pains disappear.
Even making him cry, because he realizes
that when he dies, Heaven could never be this good.

I hope.

I hope all of this is true,
because then maybe, just maybe,
He can begin to love you the way that I do.

Nilanga Gihan Fernando

Daddy

Daddy, this is your baby girl,
I wasn't here when you left us,
I would of been, but didn't know.
You've always chased rainbows in the wrong places.

If you had turned around, you would of seen beautiful rainbows,
standing behind you with open arms.

Daddy, why weren't you there to hold my hand when I'd fall,
you could of hugged me, and said it's all better,
tomorrow the pain will all be gone.
A little pat on the head and an I love you would have been okay.

Daddy, today I chased rainbows so far away,
but I turned around, and saw my rainbows with open arms.
I gave love, understanding, and affection.
When I open my arms, I get big hugs and love in return.

Daddy, you're so far away, did you find your rainbow?
Just turn around, and let me give you a big hug and I love you.
This is where your rainbows was that all along.

Janice Anderson Wills

Simply You

We are so blessed!
For at our backs does rest, a wise and patient eye.
For in our family God did not deny, simply love!

"Christ is all" our hero sings,
for she's the wind beneath our wings!

"Blessed assurance" is another song that followed our path
to keep us strong!

We are so blessed!
For at our backs does rest, a wise and patient eye.
For in our family, God did not deny, simply love!

This day cannot tell the stories I'm sure she could write.
Of worried hours and long burning lights.
Of lies and pain only the sun could shame.
Of held back fears and smiling faced fears
through her sickness down through the years.

But through it all, we are blessed!
From chicken feet to black-eyed peas,
Lord, we would like to say, we're so very pleased!

From chitterlings and so rare steaks, we are certain
there's been no mistakes. We've been blessed, by simply love!

April Sims

He Was a Dancing Smile at Light

To my husband, Jerry, the first and last love of my life

The facets of light were a lifeline that appeared through the cracks
of your smile that night. A stranger's shadow lit in the
darkness with feeling once remembered from just such a sight.

You were a gift sent merely to set me free and in your eyes,
a loud light just for TC to see.

No longer just a burnt memory, this smile will remain.
I'll etch in stone somewhere for all will see the painted stain.

This light you take with you for all others to see,
But this smile you planted deep within, and it stays with me

I can touch and be touched, I can sing a happy song.
Tell me in your arms is where you want me and where I belong

I feel a warmth from you, and I love giving.
It was you sent to make one more try at living.

When you need to see what you gave shine through,
It may be vague, but remember that girl in Havasu.

She shines from your light that crossed her way.
Smiles from her shine beside you,
hoping you'll feel the same as I someday.

Tricia Taylor Speer

She Sees Him; He Hears Her Voice

And she sees him; she hears his voice.
He needs love and devotion;
He needs to be needed.
He needs appreciation, dedication.
He needs someone to care
When he doesn't care anymore.
Is there hope? Is there a chance?
Will he find the one he needs?
Does she dare ask herself, or anyone else,
If who he needs is she?
And he sees her; he hears her voice.
She needs love and devotion;
She needs to be needed.
She needs appreciation, dedication.
She needs someone to care,
When she doesn't care anymore.
Is there hope? Is there a chance?
Will she find the one she needs?
Does he dare ask himself, or anyone else,
If who she needs is he?

Adrianne L. Colson

Kind Gentleman, My Song

Such tenderness your voice doth hold
A gentleman you are and cherished one indeed,
Ne'er harsh, ne'er cruel, nor cold
My mentor, my true great need.
God planted goodness with this gentleman's seed
With whom I am richly blessed, yes, as a songbird
I stretch my neck to chant high o'er the glebe
All just from hearing your softest words . . .

That by any other would not seem to unfold
With quite the same puissance, so pure without greed.
Nay, thou art ne'er selfishly bold
Nor one to ne'er make me plead
For this kindness about which most men only e'er read
Let alone come to know in a lifetime of great rewards.
This lady with naught to say in such splendid esprit
All just from hearing your softest words.

Now filled with ecstasy this warmth I behold
Nay my heart will ne'er bleed,
For tears of happiness gleam like gold;
(To have this timeless feeling is Godspeed)

Darlene Fremgen

Walking Rock Run

I walked a stream that is Rock Run,
Shallow water, cooled ankles, and feet.
Walking over or around moss-covered rocks,
The thick canopy prohibited day's heat.

Many photographs were taken of the run,
As rays of sun fought to penetrate.
A sunbeam reached a moss-covered rock,
To become a photographic focal trait.

Lush hemlock branches overhead intertwined,
Wild rhododendron branches touched moist ground.
Rocks were strewn side to side, unaligned,
Large ones, small ones, both flat and round.

Many hues of green, born of shade and moisture,
Added color to the natural bounty.
The voice of Rock Run, just a murmur,
All senses partook of natural beauty.

I walked Rock Run on this day,
Mind centered in center stream.
My psyche was soothed a natural way,
My persona acquired a wondrous gleam.

Joseph M. Grusky

Dare to Dream

Dream of tomorrow.
Imagine the world a better place.
Don't hesitate!
To see a world without limits, cruelty, and hate
Before it's too late.
Just because you make believe
What you see and know in your dreams and heart
Is real and true,
And people may laugh at you,
Don't get discouraged or blue.
The dreamers of yesterday, today, and tomorrow are few
And may fade away
Except for you!
So, no matter what you do,
Keep the faith, dreams alive,
And . . . believe!
Dare to dream.
It happens.
It's up to you, making
Dreams come true.

Marie Wadsworth

The Wall

There it stands bold and black the wall that
brings sad memories back.

Memories of bombs and mangled men torn piece
by piece and limb by limb.

Memories of those who finally came home leaving
parts of their bodies in places unknown.

Those who still have restless sleep as they dream
of their buddies blown up at their feet.

There he stands in front of the wall, one lone
soldier who survived it all.

I believe I see a tear in his eye as he looks
for a buddy's name who died.

He stands there on crutches straight and proud
with one leg gone, he pays tribute with the crowd.

Special care should be taken of the bold black
wall so it can always be there to remind us all.
So that it should never crumble and fall.

Linda J. Buie

For God I Am Challenged

The morning arrives with the dew
and sunrise of yet another day.

I lie and listen, the birds singing
with the beckoning of my rise,
for yet another day of uncertainty.

My body says, don't move,
while my mind humming, be brave you'll endure.

I up my body, at first feeling
hindered, the sustenance of the day begins.

What I can do gets done.
I walk, dream and wonder what God
in my future will entail.

A child of God, a day at a time I take.
Thanking him for yet one more chance
with family and friends,
the dew and one more sunrise.

My being determined,
I pray and give thanks with my love
and my destiny, I leave with God.

Judith E. Weiss

Companion for Life

I am just a lonely cigarette!
I come in a package of twenty and twenty-five.
I wait patiently in a carton of two hundred cigarettes
for someone to buy me and strike up a companionship with me.
I have no life without a light. Once you light me up and give life,
I'll become your companion for life.
If you don't want me to be part of your life,
then don't buy the first package of me.
It's a pleasure to smoke me, but it will be a greater pleasure
in getting rid of me, once you're hooked on me!
I bring revenue to the government coffers and at the same
time deteriorate your lungs with nicotine.
The warning signal you read on the package protects the
cigarette companies if sued and not you.
If you're underage, don't sneak that cigarette!
When you become of age, think of your health before buying
that package of cigarettes.
And if you're already hooked and addicted and want to get rid
of me, don't hide me away, just destroy me so someone doesn't find
me the next day—of course you know that someone will.

Boniface Idziak

True to Myself

I have to be true to myself, and so
I have to be someone I'd like to know.
Here in the struggle for fame and wealth,
I want to be able to like myself.
I don't want to go through life as a sham
So I must be careful of what I am.
I want to walk with my head held high
And be able to smile, when I'd rather cry.
I want to respond to a friend in need,
And not clutter my life with envy and greed.
I don't want to stand at close of day
Wishing I'd done things a different way.
I want a clear conscience so I can sleep.
I don't want to make promises I can't keep.
I can't fool myself or hide my deeds,
For I know and respect my inner needs.
And so I must be all the things I admire,
And not a bore, of which people tire.
I can never hide myself from me,
For I know what others can never see.

Lorraine Bennett

A Plea to the God of Bards

The Stratford Bard lurked ghostly in my brain,
As I roved the verdant hills and wild terrain.
In solitude, I strolled in sombre mood
Endeavouring to describe the scenes I viewed.

What rhyme or flowing phrase would he invent
Were he here with me in this environment.
What would his sight and hearing hear and see
If he were wandering down these paths with me.

To what depths of description would he go,
Immortalizing moments we would read and know.
Just how long and desperate would he try
To portray with his words an azure sky.

If we both described the landscape and skies
That would regale our four discerning eyes.
I'm certain that his turn of phrase and rhyme
Would evermore, be loftier than mine.

Oh, God of poets, may you grant to me two boons—
That my words and rhyme be greater that a loons.
And if you should feel more generous still . . .
As fetching as a mating blackbirds trill.

Frank McGowan

All My Life

All my life, I been searching
Searching for the meaning of it all
Why I existed in this world
And why I wanted to fall

I wanted to fall
To fall in love with you
My heart is waiting for the call
So I can talk to you

Deep in my heart
Is an empty surrounding
Half of it is okay but the other is apart
Why am I frowning

Searching the sky
Falling on my knees
Asking God, "Why?"
Is this is only decree

To be alone forever
Make my life miserable
My heart weight like a feather
Being alone is not so fallible

Sopheap Pal

My Blue-Eyed Boy

My precious Jason with sparkling blue eyes.
So handsome he lights up the skies.
Running and frolicking, jumping up and down
Even his teachers say he is the class clown.

My sweet little dumpling all cuddly and cute
Why you're so adorable you're a real hoot!
You twist your hips and act so silly
You're really a dilly, dilly.

So all through your life you will always be mine.
Mama will always know that you're just so fine.
God will lead you each step of the way
'Cause Mama has prayed for you every day.
You see the Lord and Mother's have a direct line
Because our hearts are totally entwined.
Yes you will fall and stumble,
But that's life and it can be a bumble.
Straighten your face, square your shoulders
For you will climb over big boulders.
You are blessed my son, so go in His grace.
Be proud of you heritage and put a smile on your face.

Paula Wright Niehelson

It

On a cold and lifeless day,
Wherever the trees have
been stripped of their beauty,
and the sun has gone away,
We sat looking out our windows.
Wondering why it has passed us by
Did it not hear our hearts fall to its feet?

Can it not see the love on our faces
or hear our hearts beating at a faster pace?
Does it not see the longing in our eyes,
that someday we might meet.

They say it makes the world go around.
Everyone wants it, we all say we deserve it.
We act as if it has grown wild underground.

Such fools, we all are to think,
Because we say we need it.
It would come to us in a blink.

Well, I'm here to tell you all that it
Doesn't work that way, love must be earned.

Nancy J. Wood

Rocking Chair Song

Would you like a piece of me
To look at when you're feeling stronger?
Will you keep the peace with me
When I'm not here any longer?
Put me in the flower bed
The one next to your rocking chair
Remember all I said and was
The empty space where I'm not there
Please will you say hello to me?
I still want to hear your music
Then say one last goodbye to me
I need to hear your "sorry song" once more
Staying was too much for me
I'd cry each time I saw your face
I couldn't bear to see the one
Whose smile you chose to take my place
Have you yet forgotten me?
Have my flowers died of sadness?
I long to hear your rocking chair
Creak its rhythmic, rock-a-bye madness

Tanya Hart

Growing Up

Life is ever changing
Every day is different
New challenges, dreams, and priorities

Loves have left
Friends have gone
Time has passed and yet goes on
Every aspect changes body, mind, and soul

Self-discovery
Mistakes made
Searching for the meaning of life
Trying to make sense of it all growing
Learning, winning, losing, trying, and quitting

Outlook shifting constantly
A little wiser than before maturing
Working, playing, living life to extremes
Slowing down
Creating
Taking risks
Being cautious
Growing up!

C'atie Bateman

Little Tommy Comes to Visit

My boys are eight & ten . . . I forgot how much fun a two-year-old could be!

There he goes at lightning speed
with a devilish grin.
I knew that he was wondering,
"Now where do I begin?"
"What happens if I push this button?
Boy, those stairs look fun!
I think I'll play with those golf clubs.
Watch Aunt Sandy run!"
"I guess I'll have to climb this stool
to get to those french fries.
It seems Aunt Sandy can't keep up,
but boy, she sure does try!"
Then he thinks he'll take a break
and sit down for a minute. (HA!)
It's not that long when trouble calls
and Tommy's right there in it!
There he goes at lightning speed!
But what's a boy to do?
The world is full of mystery
when you're only two!

Sandra Early

Christ Has Died, Christ Has Risen, Christ Will Come Again

Christ has died, Christ has risen, Christ will come again
We need Him today like we needed Him then.
He is still the same as he was then.
Christ has died, Christ has risen, Christ will come again.
We all drink from the cup of his blood.
We all shelter ourselves from the flood.
We need to make it through this mud.
We all drink from the cup of his blood.
We pray for all of those who may have died.
We all pray and show respect and pride.
We give thanks for those who gave us a ride.
We pray for all of those who may have died.
We all make a living will and a sacrifice.
Our treasures we wish for are very nice.
We would rise up into paradise.
We all make a living will and a sacrifice.
We show praise, we show mercy, we show our glory,
We show love and commitment and the story,
We have the power to offer an oratory.
We show praise, we show mercy, we show our glory.

T. J. Woods

The Tale of Plots & Targets . . .

For Jackie, Laurie, & Dean—We've all been here! Love you!

Bored in his position of self-proclaimed power.
Drunk in his ambition! Erratic in his tower!
Picking at random, in twisted perception!
A new game begins! A new Target's reception!
A sneering facade with a glaring reflection!
"I'll file the ledger!" Zero detection!
Numbers once clear, the game rearranges!
Now Plotters' visit to the shooting ranges!
Arrow in place with bow string pulled taut!
Shooting Target in surprise with guilt deflected!
"Come, let's talk! Problems in our ledger!"
Target suspicious! Retrospective detections! !
Plotter had assisted! Reprimands rebuked and resisted!
No word explains! No proof to disclaim!
"Embezzlers are fired and prosecuted! The ledger shows . . . !"
Targets' trial a ruse and rhyme! Plotter glows in his jail time!
Shackled Target weeps, as his dreams sweep quickly by!
Sentenced! Seven years for a pseudo-crime!
"So many targets, so little time!"
"For now, for a while—Plotter will keep a low profile."

Paul Arthur Nicholson

The Flavor of Your Voice

The flavor of your voice still loiters in my brain.
As I strain to remember the depth of its pitch,
I am wrapped in its smoothness and can hardly refrain
from its blanket as osmosis takes over with each painstaking stitch.

Its boldness and directness awaken my senses;
Like a peacock in full bloom,
I am lured by its colorful expenses
As its musk fills the room.

Entrapping aromas of this fresh brewed container
flavors my morning and refreshes my sight.
Until the next reunion, I'll gladly invite a retainer,
As this everlasting memory blankets my night.

This full-bodied sonnet tantalizes and chocolates my appetite.
Its lusty texture brings a glow to my face
While this stupor envelopes me as I fall from its grace.
Should I abandon this hearty feeling and be contrite?

As this escrow consumes me, I look for my escape.
Short lived in this entity, I am gladly entwined in this drape,
And delighted with rapture, when given a choice,
That the memory preludes me to the flavor of your voice.

Linda D. Boutin

Through My Eyes

There is a special bond between two friends that only they know and that only their hearts share.

Our two hearts have shared in some special memories. Memories that will play over and over again through my eyes.

Through my eyes I see a friend that means a great number of things to me. You are the friend who lights up my life, and the one I will always need in my presence.

Everyone needs something or someone to keep them going, and your friendship carries me forward. You are a haven to me. I feel safe from all the wrong in my life when I am near you.

Wherever I go or whatever I do. I see a friend who is my shadow. One who never leaves or turns away, and one who will always be with me.

Dolores A. Fox

My Dear Friend

To Luisa Lipar, Shannon Jose, Leizl Ochavillo, and Glaiza De Veas

You were always there to brighten my day
And you never left, you were here to stay.
At the moment my heart was seriously broken,
You took away my sorrowful burden.
Thank you for stopping the flow of my tears
And for vanishing my greatest fears.
When I was faced with major denial,
You enlightened me with your uplifting smile.
You are the friend I have always dreamt of,
I guess you're my angel, sent from above.
I thank you for lifting and guiding my soul
And for taking the place of my angel's role.
Our friendship, I swear, I will never regret,
You are my friend that I'll never forget.
You've given me a friendship that is rare,
Now I know that you truly do care.
You are the sister I've never had,
Life without you will be very sad.
If someone asks me to rate you as my friend,
I'll say, "She's, no doubt, a perfect 10!"

Jennifer David Oledan

My Refuge

In the deepest, darkest storm,
Lies my refuge, safe and warm.
In the corner hangs a light;
I will stay there all the night.

Wrapped in a quilt of ancient days,
As my refuge rocks and sways;
Reading books from dusk till dawn,
Books by authors whose days have gone.

Alcott, Steinbeck, Twain, and more,
All sit stacked upon the floor.
I never cease, I never stop,
And one by one the books do drop.

And as the morning dawn does break,
I feel a book slip from my embrace.
While in my refuge, safe and warm,
The world turns from stormy night to calming morn.

In my refuge I sleep till noon,
Knowing night will come again soon.
Instead of a refuge, an old hammock you might see,
But it is my refuge, and I its refugee.

Haley Leigh Phillips

The Soldier's Letter

It's the graveyard shift on Christmas Eve;
there's rustling—the leaves.
Walking guard duty far across the sea,
along a dark perimeter lined with trees,
with only the stars to see. Putting my hand
on my rifle comforts me, relaxing anxiety.
"Be alert; don't fall asleep. Keep walking."
Like a deer hunter listening for any noise,
movement, it seems. But this night my mind
keeps wandering. Thoughts of home, lighted
trees, snow, caroling, things dear to me.
I hear music, marching music. Eyes right,
footsteps in unison. Marching to the stars
and stripes that keep our country free.
Been a long time, but tomorrow morning
mail call. Maybe, like the old saying goes,
"If God is willing and the creek don't rise,"
there will be a package, letter, something for me.
I love my job; it's my duty, you see.
But sometimes we wish it weren't so, oh, you know what I mean.

William Grotz

Happy 25th Anniversary

Love is what makes the world go round.
It can make your feet come off the ground.

There are laughs and tears
All through the years.

Happy and sad times,
They help you to grow.

The things you can go through,
Only you two will know.

There are times to remember,
Things you'd like to forget—
All the people you've dealt with,
Those you haven't met yet.

This year your anniversary is silver.
On good days it can make your heart quiver
But on off days it can make you feel like chopped liver.

Lots of memories we give you as a gift
For you to remember when your minds start to drift.

Remember memories are small packages of love,
Always blessed from above.

Betty Paul

What Can I Do?

You told me today, we're growing apart.
I want you to know that's breaking my heart.
I really don't know just what I can do.
You know, my dear, I don't want to lose you.

So, what have I done to cause this to be?
I beg you, darling, please, to tell me.
What have I done to cause you to say
That our love has gotten this way?

I'm so ashamed that I had not a clue
That I may have been neglectful of you.
I'm sorry, my love, that I have not seen
That I have not been what I should have been.

Please believe me when I say this to you,
I really want to know what I must do.
Please tell me, my sweet, so that I can start
Pulling us back together, not farther apart.

My heart is so sad because I now see
I have not been everything I should be.
So tell me, my love, just what I can do
Because I know I don't want to lose you.

William Farnam Durfee

The Darkest Depths

For Dave, who always believed . . .

The darkest depths of life do tell
Of golden years and years of Hell;
Of sacrifice, of homage paid,
Of richness, of wealth, of foundations laid;
Of poverty, of hardship, of plagues where death does play,
Of fearing life and fearing death, of fearing fear each day.
The darkest depths of life do scream
Of plotting, of deception, of failing dreams;
Of conspiring against and conspiring within,
Of accepting loss when expecting win;
Of courage, of faith, of heavenly bliss,
Of wanting to aim, but yearning to miss.
The darkest depths of life do chant
Of those that rave, of those that rant;
Of those whose minds have lost themselves,
Of those whose memories are boxed on shelves;
Of those who are saved, of those not worth saving,
Of those who will live and those death are craving.
The darkest depths of life do stake,
It molds, it casts, it sets, and it breaks.

Natalie Rene Sheffield

Mercy of Reality

It's a feeling of dissatisfaction, transforming into frustration.
The distaste of direction becomes apparent with every turn.
It was not meant to be, yet explain to me why is it?

I am what I am not. Semi-functioning each day.
Going through the motions. Displeased with every step.
Day by day life drifts by, to be observed, yet unchanged.
I am merely a puppet of reality.

The play has begun. A never-ending plot or changing
with every act? Ups and downs are inevitable.
The closing act is in question. The lines are controlled by
the mercy of the puppeteer, by the mercy of reality.

"Oh, give me strength to cut the binding strings."
As fast as the spirit prevails me to grasp the courage,
yanking at my heels are the doubts and fears.
"Overcome such foolishness!" a voice within screams out;
yet another reasons with thoughts of frustration.

The backdrop is a complex maze of struggles between
heart and mind, yet the question is always the same.
Control the ending or be controlled by the end. Follow another's
path or make my own. Control reality or fall to its mercy.

Victoria W. Mattox

Friends

This world, without friends, would be a barren place,
Cold and lonely, an endless race.
A merry-go-round with no music inside,
Purposeless people, along for a ride.
But God didn't intend that we go it alone,
For He created others to share in his home.
Two souls that meet, a personality endears,
A deepening feeling that spans the years,
Sharing of joys, occasional tears.
It doesn't take much, if it comes from a friend,
To give us such peace and a warmness within.
A telephone call, a touch from a hand,
Just knowing, and caring, not fearing to tell.
"We love you, we are with you" makes all our hearts swell.
Neither diamonds, nor dollars, nor riches and such
Can ever, not ever, mean half as much
As having good friends that come to our side,
Who lighten our burden and soften our ride.
I pray that I have learned to show that I care,
To offer my friendship, to give and to share.
I am thankful for God and His marvelous grace.
With my God and my friends, it's a wonderful place.

Len Gibbens

Unknown Rage

There is a rage inside of me,
for which I can find no peace.
Even in my sleep I toss and turn.
There's a demon after me.
Wondering why I dreamed that dream?
With tears streaming down my face.
Drop on my knees and pray.
Then back to sleep I go.
This rage is still inside of me.
I cannot find the reasons why.
Go through the day they pick my brain.
They say, humble yourself.
This quiet rage we don't understand.
So for us to find the reason, for this rage.
Let us pick your brain! There is a rage in my soul.
I don't know the reasons, why.
The mystery has not been solved.
I guess I'll replay my mind.
There is a rage inside of me, for which
I can find no peace.

Sharron Rossum

Follow Your Heart

The time had come to bid farewell,
What lay ahead we could not tell—
A bag full of memories we carried along
While our dreams soared on the wings of a song.

Relatives came to lend a helping hand
And show us the way of this great land.
With Spring in the air and the scent of the pines
From the rule-book we were made to study our lines.

"Leave the children alone," so we were told,
"Let them fend for themselves and grow more bold."
Emotions and sensitivity with indifference were treated
Homesickness made us feel so defeated.

Luckily friends and colleagues were understanding enough,
And showed that the going need not be tough.
Adjusting seemed easier when they were around,
Making us realize that happiness can be found.

So remember, fellow immigrants follow your heart
And don't let anyone influence you from the start.
Confidence in your abilities is what you need,
Your life style may change, but to your instincts pay heed.

Marian Cecilia Valadares

Comrades of the Mountain Snows

Of lofty crag and timeless heights,
Clouds forming ever after
Through storms of ice, snow, and hail,
The mountain soldier's laughter.
Come, our comrades of the mountain snows,
Swiftly, silently, descending . . .
To ski blue timber, forest glade and meadow,
A narrow trail remaining,
Etched on the canvas of alpine lore
Whom no one knows,
Except the wind that blows
Across the dense drifts forming.

The slopes will end, the wind cries out
Our fallen comrades' memories true,
Crosses of white on fields of green
Eternity softly beckons,
Yet Death's dark grasp not strong enough
To hold a mountain soldier's spirit.
Hark! From on high his shackles break,
Here skiers come once more,
God's glory shows,
Our comrades of the mountain snows.

Ernst F. Baumann

World

The World, my World
The World consists of America,
Europe, Australia, Africa, and Asia.
My World is a round ball rotating 'round the sun,
With the other balls rotating in their orbits.
The World has a friend called the Moon,
Which we can see every day. Ah! The Moon.
So big like this? Ah! The World.
The only ball with life.
Full of humans, plants, and resources and animals.
A World of many people and many places;
The home of Negroid, Australasian, Caucasian, and Mongoloid.
A place with different cultures.
Different ways, different colors.
Seeing the wonderful stars at night
And the wonderful rivers and oceans;
The fantastic cool breeze,
The fantastic seasons.
How can I stop thinking about it, dreaming about it?
The home of all, the World, my World!

Ifedayo J. Olaleye

Mommy, I Miss You

When God looked down from above
He saw your glowing face
He picked you with all his love
And said, "She'd be perfect for this place"

You looked back one last time
With all the love you had
And left me all alone
In a world so dangerous and bad

But still I forgive you
Because I know you were needed up there
And I know you are watching down on me
With all your love and care

And someday I'll be with you
Through those golden gates
But for now I'll stay down here
And pray for your embrace

Every day I think of you
And wish that you were here
Because I miss you, Mommy
And want you very near

Stephanie Heisdorffer

A Hint from Above

Gaze up at the morning sky,
His glorious canvas painted high,
His wondrous hand from up above:
A message of his undying love.

I have a plan though not foretold,
Have faith, my son, your story is gold.
Of lessons learned, heartache and pain,
You've only got to call my name.

A colored canvas as sunset falls,
His way of reminding one and all.
You are never alone, you are part of a plan:
See all of my promises in the stroke of my hand.

A star a sign saying, "I'm still here,"
I never left you; to me you are dear.
Believe in me as I do in you,
I know just what you are going through.

Every day there are signs, just a hint from above,
to remind us of his gift of love.
Stop and take notice of the promise it brings,
for these are truly life's finer things.

Angela Kay Phillips

Word

In motion
With intention
To stimulate a nation

Be still, and listen to the list of the breeze
Bare witness to the rhythm of the trees
Feel the spirit moving upon the seas
Locomotion
In union
Having holy communion

Flowing tides of inspiration
Like the open waters of the ocean
Neither clinging or possessing
Merely expressing
Consciousness
Moving with finesse
Taking evolution
To it's highest elevation
Creation
Unveiling as revelation

Shearer Williamson

Lullaby, Good-bye!

Hope, once held so close
Yellowed from time gone by
Illusions of what wasn't
Evaporate on the shore of eternity

He didn't want to know her
He didn't want to care

Still, a sliver of engraved hope remained
On a childlike hand she brings to her heart
And silently blowing all that remains to the wind
Never again to return

Can't show the pain, hide the tears
No one would understand, as man she never knew
He was a ghost that was real, never to be seen
But alive is her dream of one day

Tell her he's not worth it
Bring faith to forget another's existence
A dream of a wish
That died in the wind

He didn't want to know her
He didn't want to care . . . good-bye, Dad

Lorna Donnelly

Tolerance

A young girl stood and questioned her mother
"How do you tolerate the world?"
Her mother quietly said. . .I don't

I can't give in for I will trip and fall
My mind will roam and I will stall
I'm destined the most suitable life for you
One without. . .and she pauses her daughter sadly knew

. . .One without crime, wars, and hate
The struggles began but this time it's too late

I've built my barrier to protect you
It's deteriorated over time
I can only give you the ways to live
By words, knowledge, and insightful lines

Soon I will no longer be here to guide you
The world will help you there
And that's what I'm most afraid of

If you keep the thought of me in the back
Of your mind when you're grown and far away
You won't have to tolerate the world
You'll be able to stand up and face the day

AnnaLee Wagoner

Should I . . .

Confusion in the heart brings doubt to the mind.

Should I for you my whole soul bare
for only glimpses I have yet to share
Too much or too little this is yet known
only the parts I dare have I let to be shown
Should I lie to you and say words untrue
if only to spare this confusion for you
Being so careful with these words I write
putting to paper and bringing to light
Should I cross the line in the words I say
expose myself with nowhere to stay
For once they are said there is no going back
no recoil no retreat no way to retract
Should I reveal that for you I have cried
holding this back I have truly tried
Giving more of myself with each passing day
in the feelings I have and the words I say
Should I leave my thoughts for another time
and live in this place where reason has rhyme
Hold on to this dream of a tomorrow with you
please tell me my love, what I should do

Billy

Before You Die

We went out on a couple of dates,
and soon enough we were mates.
We weren't careful, you lied to me.
You said good-bye, that's how it's got to be.
I called you later to tell you why
when you dumped me, I started to cry.
You're a daddy now, what can I say?
You have a son; he was born today,
Please come and see him, he's very sad.
He wants to know, where's his dad.
He's growing up without a father.
It's very depressing, you won't even bother.
Pretty soon he will grad,
but I have to say, he isn't that glad.
Today he will fly off to college.
Of his father, he has no knowledge.
I cry myself to sleep at night,
and wonder why you're nowhere in sight.
I love my child, together or apart.
You need to know, it was you who broke his heart.
I hope one day, I will not lie,
you'll see your son, before you die.

Brandi Barefoot

Left Behind

Life for us has stopped
as a friend and loved one has departed,
having chosen a different path
and leaving us sadly behind.

The loss is overwhelming
and we are shaken without understanding,
what would cause them to decide
that living was not worth the pain?

Could we have seen it coming
as we retrace in our minds
to somehow change the course of events
that left us all behind?

How could this final decision be made
without a word or good-bye
the final chapter written without the chance to say I love you
for the first or last time?

So we send our prayers to the heavens
that God would be so kind
to open his arms in our absence,
and give them our final good-byes.

Sally Jo Grubaugh

Final Glimpse

She waits upon a mountain.
Bitter, swift strides of wind permeate the aura.
She glances across the barren field and
spots a single, blue bulb.
She advances through the knoll, focused on
the only dash of life around. She smiles.
She notices the brightly colored painting of
a sunset above, and dances with her shadow
while there is still time.
She sings a duet with her soul, and though
she seems slightly off key, creates the
most placid vibration. She came to escape.
She listens with her heart and lives through her mind.
As the Conductor singles for the last
measure, she holds on to the final note as
long as she can . . .
And so her soul flies to the rhythm of the
sweet song of eternity.

Otilia Ghetes

The Day I Cried

I sat and I watched the pain in your soul
The timing was all wrong, I needed you so
You fought your hardest, I fought with you
I prayed and I prayed, not knowing what to do

Inside I was dying, my heart had a hole
I watched, as your sparkle started to lose its glow
Each day grew longer and turned into night
Time was a circle, with no end in sight

Your breathing became shallow
Your eyes lost their smile, they soon turned hallow
Almost as if peace were on your side
I cried and I cried that day that you died

The tears, they won't stop flowing
A smile, I put on just for showing
Five years have past since that morning
Life is so full, then ends with no warming

I sit and I stare at the stars at night
Just hoping to see a glimpse or a sight
Not knowing, if peace is really around you
I'm sad and lonely and feel so blue

Linda Dionizio

Multiple

I want to run a race for the cure
I would love to see people live more
To be whole and healthy, mentally awake
This is the least I can do, for mankind's sake

I'll stretch, I'll dress, I'll even warm up
Watch my cholesterol, drink juice from my cup
My muscles ready, I'm in place
The gun goes off, sweat on my face

I can do this, I know I can
Competition between all women and man
I won't go fast, I won't go slow
My tennis shoes help me flow

There are hundreds of people today
What a great cause; it's worthy, I say
To help the afflicted, ease their pain
Common goal, erase all blame

I look up at Heaven, thank the Lord
I'm rounding the bend to collect a reward
Muscles ache and I am last; I still get roses
I finished even though I have multiple sclerosis

Linda Cegan

Love Comes Once in a Lifetime

To have love for another,
makes everything possible.
To feel love through the beholder's eyes,
gives much satisfaction.
To hold love brings much happiness.
To you, I send my love.

We make our life what it is,
with the help of a few Dear friends.
It seems when we need a lift, our friend is never far.
Through thought and sound,
our Dear friend gives us nourishment
that we need to get through the day.
To you, I send my love.

May you always know
what a difference you have made in my life.
May you always feel
the warmth that you have given to others.
May your life always
be filled with much happiness.
To you, I send my love.

Cindy L. Nabors

Paramedics

First you call 911, you know something's wrong,
You are told they are coming, and it won't take long.
They say not to worry, they're almost here,
They'll be able to help, have no fear.

You know you are terrified, nothing's scared you more,
But you feel great comfort when they walk through the door.
They go right to work, they know what to do,
But in just moments, their work will be through.

They'll arrive at the hospital, flashing lights of blue and red,
They jump out of the ambulance and pull out the bed.
The patient's given to the doctors for further care,
For this is someone's life; it cannot be spared.

They try their hardest to save those in need,
Sometimes it doesn't work, people need to be freed.
Their lives are taken, and yes, it is sad,
But you've got to move on and get past the bad.

Paramedics are vital, it's obviously true,
Don't put them down, the one in need could be you.
Always remember, they help us a great deal,
Never forget, life's all very real.

Lindsie Read

On Our Anniversary

Twenty-five years ago today
I promised to love, honor, and obey,

To stand by your side in good times and bad,
In sickness or health, whatever we had.

I knew that no matter what fell in our path,
We'd move it with love, a tear, or a laugh.

We stayed on our path so straight and so true,
My darling, I'll always believe in you.

Our life is not over; it's still going strong.
We're still going forward with love and a song.

If times should get easy or harder to bear,
My darling, you know that I'll always be there.

And now today, as I did back then,
I'd make that same vow
All over again.

To stay by your side
'Til my life is through,
My darling, I'll always,
Always love you.

Linda Steele

Dreams and Wishes

To my love, Jeffrey Jonathan Salyers

Dreams will come
And dreams will go
So hold on to them
And never let go
Keep your heart open
And your hopes up high
Then all your dreams
Will come alive
Because dreams are forever
So let them be your guide
Wish on the first star
You see tonight
And never let it slip from your life
So keep your spirit
Like a shooting star
And never lose hope of your wishes
Because wishes are forever
So let them be your light
So put your dreams and wishes together
To be your guiding light to happiness forever

Melissa Margaret Vucci

My Special Place

Above the sky of gray and blue,
There is a place of dreams come true.
A place of love and tenderness,
To keep us safe from all sadness.

Where skies are never black or gray,
And the sun's caress is here to stay.
Where birds will fly sure and free,
To announce the freedom that is sure to be.

A place where people will never sin,
A place where life will again begin.
Without the hunger and life's disease,
We'll find our peace and live with ease.

Where the grass will shine with the touch of dew,
And fields of flowers spread through and through.
Where the breeze will brush kisses upon our face,
And honor us with its loving grace.

This place of love and tenderness,
Which keeps us safe from all sadness.
Is given to us with undying love,
From the Holy Heavens up above.

Carol Proulx

Broken Soul

Stop clinging to me!
I can't breathe
I'm trapped among your sneers
And your harshly critical words

I can't get out
You're pulling me in
Is it your purpose
To kill my innocence?

You're so far away
And so untouchable
Yet I feel your breath
Hot on the back of my neck

Must you rip out my insides
And make my life an endless downward spiral?
Your snide remarks
Becoming a deadly part of me

It will never stop
For this is my destiny
To never die
But to live as a broken soul

Cari Smith Pierre

Relentlessly Dreaming?!?

This is a symbolic poem kept close to my heart.

Relentlessly dreaming of all that could be
Hiding behind my analytical monotony
Look at that boy
Look at that girl
Two beautiful beings
That never fail to amaze me
Now tell me
Are you dreaming?
I want your words to have meaning
So intimate and personal
We can be
Two existing bumblebees
Floating on Mother Earth's lilacs
Drifting petals
Weeping willow trees
Come with me
To places encapsulating mystery
Fantasy
My warm flesh serenading your body
Dreaming and dreaming . . . still dreaming . . .

Nicole Cimorelli

Heart of a Rock Star

How can you say you love me
If you don't even know me?
How can you say you know me
If you've never even met me?

You don't try and hide your stares
If only you knew what's there
Inside this heart of mine
Would you still love me?

And maybe you don't want to know
What lies behind these shields
But if you did, what would you do?
Turn me away, or would you stay?

I'm drowned in a pain like a thousand knives
Ripping at my heart
Sometimes I can't sleep
Sometimes I can't breathe
I guess I am just falling apart

They ask me to smile
But what for?
I have no reason to anymore

Jocelyn Ember Baird

Just Me

I am the same person
deep within Me

With dreams and ambitions
things you can't see

I am the same person
who breaths the same air

My emotions and feelings
are forever there

My strength has diminished
that's surely true

I can't do the things
I wish I could do

We all have our moments where we dwell in the past

to have what we had
it just didn't last

But I am the same person
God created to be
and nothing can take that away from me.

Michelle Mary Hirt

Season Change

Cold ashes in the fireplace,
downtrodden grass,
silence everywhere.
Marshmallow sticks abandoned by a child.
Empty beaches, undisturbed ponds.
Beach house closings, gateways locked!
Moorings without boats, docks on dry land;
Summer ending.
New sneakers,
pretty dresses,
stiff jeans;
Shirts telling stories
of summer past.
Happy smiles,
anxious mothers,
eager teachers;
excitement in the air,
sports, drama, homework;
yellow buses,
flashing lights;
school beginning.

William H. Moses

A Dream Once Dreamt

I believe we were meant for be,
An angel from Heaven that was sent for me.
I see you and know what dreams can be,
A dream once dreamt, now reality.

Your eyes, they shine so brightly
Of hope and all you want for me.
Your touch, so warm and comforting,
To ease all pain and worry.

A love so strong with clarity,
With souls so close they cannot breathe,
A long-lasting love, what I believe,
A life with you is what I see.

A life with so much ecstasy,
And all the things I cannot see,
and everything we hope to be;
Two lives once lost, now loving.

Now, life with you may be a dream,
But has the makings of reality.
If I could, it would be
a dream once dreamt, now eternity.

Josh Beauregard

Till the End

I'm not a soldier
Just a soldier's son
Always so proud of
three wars that he won

When my turn came
Sarge took me aside
We've suffered enough
not you, family pride

Still never be a hero
Always first feed the men
You'll do the job that needs doing
When you stay till the end

Let them forget war
but remember, gold and blue
Never let them forget
Our warriors loyal and true

The war is over for some
we must stay till the end
They can't make us leave them;
sons, brothers, fathers, husbands and friends

King Cavalier, II

My Inmate's Prayer

It's hard to keep my chin up
When I am accused of a crime.
It's hard to keep my chin up
At the thought of doing time.

It's hard to keep my chin up
When I already know,
My prison record will follow me
Wherever I go.

It's hard to keep my chin up
When I'm surrounded by gloom,
Locked in at night, in my nine by fifteen room.
It's hard to keep my chin up
Being treated like a child,
Walking two by two, instead of single file.
It's hard to keep my chin up
When the food that we eat
Is the same stuff I would
throw away out on the street.

It's hard to keep my chin up
and keep believing in God.

Elisia Green

Invisible to Birds

I am invisible to birds.
I can walk among them
becoming part of the flock.

Because I am Serenity
moving a step at a time
I am barely discernible.

Also, I am Stealth,
avoiding the twigs and leaves,
a mist to be flown through.

I am invisible to birds.

I lie motionless on the ground
while they circle overhead or walk through me
as if my limbs were branches.

I avert my eyes from theirs,
look down at my bare feet, or
cast a glimpse up and to the right.

This way they are not threatened,
so they allow me to exist among them,

as one of them.

Al Chiodi

I Am the World

Aggression pumps through
My veins like blood, my only life line.
I feel the pain of a thousand sharp knifes
Stabbing me in my heart
As it transforms from Flesh
To cold steel.

Not human or anything living,
But frost bitten emotions
Joyless, decaying vision.
No sunrises, only sunsets can I see.

The world is infiltrating my soul
Leaving a cold shell of emptiness and death
Inside is a foundation of rage,
Aggression, fear, and failure.

I am the world
Heartless, monstrous, unable to feel,
Feeding on selfishness and Deception.

To many shackles dragging me down
Forbidding any hope to sneak into my heart
Leaving me only as this world.

Erin Hogshead

Grandmother—after Karen Volkman

Dear Lord, she said,
leave a memento for me,
a kiss, a hug, a warm
bed sheet beside me at night
to remember him by.

Because, she said, I miss him so dearly.
You know how dearly I loved him, from
the time we met in that Penn. restaurant,
back when life was good.
Please spare a kiss, a hug, a warm
bed sheet beside me at night
to remember him by.

And because, she said,
we loved each other for so many years.
Now he is gone, not a day goes by, I don't
long to see his handsome face and feel the
sensitivity and kindness of his heart.
So please, leave a kiss, a hug, a warm
bed sheet beside me at night
to remember him by.

James William Endress

War Helicopters on the Floor

Missiles go flying away
Beyond the mirrors that we pray
Targeting places we don't know
And all the people with no control

Now sing along with me
Let's call out for peace
Throw weapons away
And watch how nice it stays

On the rocks and villes
Seas, oceans and fishes
The eyes and hands of
Everyone who

Lives the world of no war with peace coming up to
You and me and those
Who love each other to live in peace and say it
For helicopters on the floor

Sing a song and see how easy it is
To pick a flower and not a gun,
And more to live in peace and say:
I need you darling every day

Fabio Penna

The Apology

I apologize on behalf of all mankind
For the ingenuity to destroy instilled in their minds
I apologize to all the children of the world
For the way we introduce them to the violence and gore

I apologize to all the women far and near
Who are beaten and battered and live in constant fear
I apologize for all the men whose one goal in life
Is to bring pain and suffering to the one they call wife

I apologize to all God's creatures great and small
For living their lives in labs to make life better for us all

I apologize to all animals killed for sport
For this is not God's will I am glad to report

I apologize for all your loved ones killed in battle
For the war to end all wars is just a fable
I apologize for the invention of the bomb of mass destruction
For now we do not know if tomorrow is fact or fiction

I apologize for all the pushers, murderers and rapists
For they bring so much pain and make life without bliss
I apologize for everything that brings us so much demise
For life is not meant to be like this; for this, I apologize

Lucien Lozier

Special One

There have always been some special ones.
They were there to hold my hand.
I could lean on them when I was down.
Right beside me is where they'd stand.

But there are times in life you must let them go,
For they won't always be with you.
Someday you will be that special one,
The one that someone looks up to.

Just remember that these special ones
Need to hear what's in your head.
And don't make the mistakes that I have made
With the things you should've said.
That's when you think back and realize
All the things you could have done.
And feels like everything has died,
Along with that special one.

There are feelings bottled up inside,
But don't keep them in your head,
'Cause there's nothing you can do about
The things you should've said.

Jeffrey Langston

Remember the Brave

Born of British Souls,
But with very different goals,
Settlers descended upon this land,
With their families in hand.

They came to escape repression,
They came to escape their depression,
No matter what their reason,
They now had a country to believe in.

Even though we're built of many different races,
Have so many different faces,
We all have one unique trait,
Freedom, isn't that great?

We often don't take time to recall,
Those who gave us their all,
Who died for this country,
To free people like you and me.

So please remember those who gave,
Those who fought to save,
This great country we know today,
And the freedom we enjoy every day.

Ryan Bushland

As I Look at This World

As I look at this world, all that I see and hear
Of countless murders, child abusers, wars,
Divorces, and many, many tears.

As I look at this world, how much more can we stand?
It's not just happening in one country, but all over the land.

As I look at this world, there is so much pain,
Does the sun shine anymore? Are there only storms and rain?

Some say that it will get worse instead of better,
Others mumble about it and another just chatters.

As I look at this world, families are homeless and hungry.
Abundant babies, depressed old people,
And many are sad and lonely.

As I look at this world, can we find a positive observation?
Can all be neutral? There is no speculation.

There may be still a bright side to all the madness,
Because there has to be more than negativeness and sadness.

A man once recited this passage, when he was a little boy;
"Weeping may endure for a night,
But in the morning, there is joy."

Reese Audrey

I Wish He Knew

I dedicate this to Dustin, my best guy friend. I just wish he knew.

I wish he knew how much I like him.
I wish he knew all of my dreams about him.
I wish he knew what goes through my head,
every time he smiles, looks in my eyes, says
my name, or even just walks by.
I wish he knew how much I just want to hug
him, kiss him, just have him near.
But one big thing's stopping me; it must be fear.

I'm guessing he will never ever know.
He says I shouldn't let it show.
He says, be patient it will all work out.
Somehow I know there's reason for doubt.
He'll never really know what he means to me.
Or even how he makes me weak in the knees.
Sometime he'll know, if it's even too late.
I believe this is somehow all fate.
I just wish he knew!
Please just let him know!

Suzanne Marie Sutton

The Lost Heart

I had a love that made my heart sing
and dance to the rhythm of a child's swing.
But no more does it laugh with delight,
but cry to the loneliness of the night.

To lose that love is such a crime,
and to never again share that time.
With such sweetness replaced with sorrow,
I can only hope the best for tomorrow.

Oh, how I long to sing
the music that love always brings.
The sparkle that's in one's eye,
and the smiles that just won't hide.

I ask myself, where is thy love my heart aches for?
Or is it possible, that I may have just . . . closed the door.
Is it amidst me all the while,
Or do I have to search across the miles?

I pray for guidance through this storm
of confusion, anxiety and forlorn.
And I hope only that time will tell
how long I must be under this spell.

Paul R. Palazzo

Thoughts on the Physical Paradox of an Egg's Interior Gravity

There is also the theory of binary bodies.
These things: A holding of something at bay.
Inside, a salty smallness, protected, thin,
overlaid, two-yolked, this single layer
of membranous faille restored by time and laced
in shapes like stars and maps.

There is the theory of courage. All violence
meets at the event horizon. We, inside.
It feels like wind, or tide. This part
isn't fragile at all. Walk to the rim. Look.

A curvature. Inside, no thoroughness of
caution. Or chance. Doom is nothing.
A reminder, one single stable element.
To the naked eye: change. You have broken through.

We are all whole, everything; dimensional,
particulate, prayer; wave, frail, weir.
That book, this touch, you. Graceful. If I wait, I
am galaxy forming. If I don't, this world
breaks apart.

Margaret Howard

Why?

Why does he yell and scream?
Just because something doesn't go his way
Why are his eyes filled with hate?
Just because someone proves him wrong
Why does he cuss under his breath?
Just because someone makes a mistake
Why does he claim to be saved?
When he's not doing God's will

Why did he call me fat?
Just because my pants were tight
Why does he like me to be hurt?
Just to see the pain in my eyes
Why is he so demanding?
Just because everything isn't his way
Why doesn't he care how I feel?
Is it because he's scared that I'm hurting so bad?

Why do I love to hate him?
Why do I hate to love him?
Why doesn't he understand?
Why doesn't he care . . . Why?

Tahnea M. Black

A Rehearsal Dinner Toast

To the bride and groom, I toast to you tonight
On this eve of your wedding day.
The day your two hearts will join as one
In the most splendid and glorious way.

May this new life together be good to you both,
May good times and good fortune be plentiful,
May troubles and worries stay far away
And may each day you encounter be beautiful.

If understanding and patience should ever run low,
Take a moment with each other to share
The memory of the day you committed for life,
And the love it took to get there.

And any disagreement, whether it big or it little,
In your lives, it will play a small part,
Because no disagreement will ever out power
The feelings you both feel in your heart.

May your lives be filled with lots of love,
With hope and joy and with laughter,
And from this day forward, may the two of you
Live happily ever after.

Karen Cook Mayfield

No Time to Say Goodbye

She left him for dead by the shore that night
To go and find help nearby.
No time to take a moment and stay,
To stop and say goodbye.

"Forgive me," she whispered as she ran away
With tears running down her face.
"If I lose you now, how will I go on?
For your love I could never replace."

She reached the road as it began to rain
And waved at every car.
A black station wagon finally stopped.
The man asked, "Where to, how far?"

As she got in the car she related to him
What had happened down by the sea.
Then they reached the place where her true love lay,
Both afraid of how he would be.

The man looked at her and said, "It's too late."
So again she began to cry.
She knelt by her lifeless love and said,
"There was no time to say goodbye."

Elizabeth Wood

Memories

When the sun has gone down,
and the shades are all drawn,
it's time to reflect on another day gone.

Of hours that were spent
that I'll cherish forever,
like the beauty of flowers
that are happily gathered.

All time is precious,
and each day a blessing
to keep in my heart
like a rose in a book
put there for pressing.

To remember again
through the years yet to come,
a memory that remains of another day gone.

Just one day in my life,
nothing special to do,
but a day worth remembering,
because I spent it with you.

Lucille Lutz

Dad

I am young, only three
I think he is as tall as a tree

He's the one who cuts on my night light
And tucks me in at night

Now I am a teen
With him I'm not seen

I am embarrassed of him
In these years I hurt him

I am now a parent
I now know the joy he feels being my parent

I wonder how he did it
He tells me that he too wanted an instruction kit

Now I am very, very old
He is not here to tell me what I need to be told

He is gone, he left me behind
I miss him so, why did he leave me behind

He is my father
I am his daughter

Robin Yocum

The House by the Sea

There is an old house that sits by the sea
Watching over waves, rolling wild and free
Made of brick and wood and glass
Quietly watching the century pass

Through many, wild hurricanes
With howling winds and beating rains
Stout and sturdy she would remain
Atop her sand dune, proud and vain

If only these old walls could talk
What a story they could tell
From ghosts who roam her widows walk
To electricity and a telephone with a cell

She saw the pirates come and go
And, on occasion, even saw snow
She watched as carriages drawn by a horse
Changed to cars racing around an oval course

Until the wind no longer makes a sound
And the rain and surf no longer pound
Until the tide no longer kisses the sand
In silent vigil, she will forever stand

Sandra Carol Polson

A Prayer for Peace

Before I rest,
I pray to God
That when I awake,
My life won't be lost.

There is much violence in the world,
As everyone knows;
To the people who suffer,
My heart goes out to those.

I pray for peace,
I pray for love,
I pray for belief,
I pray for trust.

I pray for my life,
My sisters and brothers.
I pray for my Lord, my dad and my mother.

I lay my head down to rest,
To sleep for the night.
I pray that when I awake,
The world won't be in a fight.

Kenda Charolette Swanson

Life As I Know It

I can always see the things of need,
but to succeed, I need to do these things.
In my mind and in my soul, I fly so high in the sky,
but in my heart it's not a fact,
so just sit back and watch the act.
And now I have fallen to my knees
because I have chosen to ignore our needs,
and now we must pay the price,
and it is indeed only a partial fact.
My whole family shouldn't have to pay for things I did,
But in the end, it's a reality act.
So as this act shouldn't become a fact for the people I love,
I must stand up and take the responsibility on myself
for the good of her and myself and three siblings,
who are on the enrollment act
to the facts and crimes in my life.
I'd better start standing with both shoes on my feet,
being an all-time survivor at life's defeats.
No matter how many times I've fallen down
just to pick up the pieces,
just to perform the act again and again . . .
Life as I see it.

Joseph Wagner

My Lonely Heart

Everywhere I turn,
There is something that I don't have,
People all cozy with each other,
And me by myself.

I thought once that no one loved me,
Maybe I'm right,
I could be wrong,
But it hasn't happened yet,

Love is a complicated game,
Some win some lose,
I seem to be on the losing end,
Because I love someone who doesn't know.

Thoughts of her fill my head,
My heart beats a little bit faster at the mention of her name,
I could tell her,
But the fear of losing her leaves me mute.

So I'll stay quiet,
Until I have the guts to tell her,
So all the secrets and lies that are kept and said,
Will be stored in my lonely heart.

Shannon Standiford

Vision of Contentment

To Willard

As I gaze out the window that faces the North
I quietly survey what God has brought forth.
A five o'clock shadow is cast through the trees,
And dry foliage waves in the cold evening breeze.
Beyond stands our cow herd, heads bent to the ground,
Grazing on stubble and new grass they have found.
A newborn stands near its mother on wobbly legs
And step by step follows as though walking on eggs.
Two playful calves stop for a moment and stare
Then take off like the wind with their tails in the air.
The scene suddenly changes, there is noise and commotion
As the cows change direction and follow the motion.
A pickup appears stacked with bales of hay,
And the sound of the horn moves them out of the way.
The bales split open as they reach the ground,
And peace settles in as the herd gathers 'round.
I reach for my pen to put this vision to verse
Then pause for a moment to watch the calves nurse.
Something inside me is moved by the sight,
And I am filled with contentment as they bed down for the night.

Audrey Kay Wells

Favorite Son of America

A jet plane flying in the sky,
Brave and strong over the sea.
Heaven and ocean look as one,
Fly, fly so high!

Young boy, you capture the world's attention.
Your actions have lessons to find a way.
Peaceful home in our father's land—there you go.
Joy and freedom have all come true.

Junior Kennedy, you are a simple man,
With a touch of class in an Irish blend.
No matter what you wear, you're still fashion's best
Your gentle choice is an endless style.

You're like a shining star to every man,
We'll miss you, John—we'll miss you.
You will always be remembered for who you are.
Favorite son of America.

Life in water, forever you will be
Love has no pain, forever it will be
Fly . . . fly . . . so high!
Fly . . . fly . . . so high!

Victor A. Miller

The Lord and I

God holds us in the Palms of His hands,
Gives us the world with the beautiful lands.
Rainbow, the sun, the stars, and the moon,
If we walk with the Lord we are never alone.

He will listen to everything we have to say
But would rather we would always do things his way.
Your prayers and your songs would come from your heart,
That way Jesus and you would never be apart.

There is many a day we are deeply depressed,
We rant and we rave, we rarely confess.
As long as it's mine, who cares about the rest?
So many ways we think we are always the best.

The Lord will forgive if we only ask,
But to many of us that's too great a task.
My prayers today and always will be—
Lord hold my hand and always lead me.

In these very hard and trying days,
They always seem dark, no sunshine rays.
So many times I let go and fall down,
Once more he holds on and again, I am found.

Arlene Marie Dohn

Skippy

I hear you bark outside the door.
You know I'm coming before my feet hit the floor.
I open the door and there you stand.
A greater presence known to man.

I fell asleep with you at my feet.
When I woke up, I knew I had a great treat.
Something was wrong that one clear night.
You were quiet as a mite.

I closed my eyes and fell back into dreamland.
My feet were walking me through the great sand.
That night you woke me with a start.
I didn't know what was wrong, but I didn't have to look far.

I saw you lying there, with old age in your hair.
You looked up, I looked down, afraid of what I had just found.

I ran to get my mom and dad.
I said, "Please hurry my dog looks bad."
I saw the look on their faces, as they took me into their embraces.

We took you to the vet, I was very upset.
You were my very best friend!

Catherine Lorraine Stanley

Jesus Loves Me

I used to be so lost, there was no hope in sight
Everything looked dark until you showed me the light
You came to me, you loved me, you stole my very heart
And on that day you gave me life and a brand new start.

I thought no one could ever love me or that I could ever love,
You taught me not to look down, but to look above,
As I lifted my eyes to you, you spoke with that small voice,
Saying I love you, follow me, but it has to be your choice.

I gave my heart to you, and you dried away my tears,
You gave me peace, joy, and hope after all my wasted years,
You said, "I forgive you, child, so please don't look back again."
"Take my hand and follow me, as I forgave your sin."

Jesus, you truly are the best thing that ever happened to me,
I want others to know you, if they could only see.
I pray they will come to know you and give their hearts to you.
That they will know you want them, and that you love them too.

Teach me, Jesus, to be the person you want me to be,
Teach me all that I should know, until I clearly see.
Fill me with the Holy Spirit and guide and lead my way,
Cleanse me and use me for your glory every single day.

Barbara Knock

Love Never Dies

Walking in the darkness I heard you call my name.
I couldn't help but be drawn to you like a moth to a flame.
The heat was so intense, the light was so bright.
It was just like a noontime sun in the middle of the night.
Standing in the wilderness that's full of hate and spite.
You took me up so high like an eagle in flight.
Once in a lifetime you meet someone that makes you feel this way.
Now that I've found you, I pray you'll always stay.
You're like a needle in a haystack, like a white dove in the snow.
You were so hard to find I'll never let you go.
The most valuable treasure a man could ever hold.
You're a true one of a kind; when they made you they broke the mold.
This world may try to separate us but they'll never tear us apart.
They only see what's on the outside,
they can't see deep into our hearts.
If they could see the whole picture, they'd put it in a frame.
Then they would take it and hang it in the lovers Hall of Fame.
One day soon, from our oppression we'll be set free.
The world could crumble around us as long as your with me.
We will withstand the test of time, it will be to their surprise.
Because we know something they don't know—
Love never dies.

Jeff A. Groves

Tell Me How You've Bruised My Heart

Tell me how you've bruised my heart
with your cheats and lies
You took my heart and threw it back in my face
Show me how you've bruised my heart
with your strong fist
You hit me once and I let it go
You hit me again and I ignored it
'cause it happened before
Teach me how you've bruised my heart
With your strong voice
You yelled and yelled I cried and cried inside
wishing it would all stop
Listen to how you've bruised my heart
While I walk away from you laughing
as you scream at me to stay
I can't stay with someone I don't love
Why do you love to bruise my heart
to make me fell small and unneeded
and try to heal it with a simple sorry
Oh, how you love to bruise my heart
let me count the ways

Heather Diane Clark

Halloween

Dusk is falling; porch lights on
Goofy jack-o'-lanterns leer and yawn
Ghosts and goblins rattle and moan
All Hallow's Eve is back again.

Brush strokes of orange across a blackened sky
Excitement sparkles in a child's eyes
Hot dogs and french fries to fortify
Then out into the frosty night.

Wizards with crystals and tiger eyes
Hippies in beads and tie-dye
Ballerinas in tights with wings held high
All with the same modus operandi.

Wrestlers full of testosterone
Gypsies in scarves with big gemstones
Cheerleaders shouting into megaphones
And a bride in white wearing eau de cologne.

All under the watchful eyes
of Moms and Dads and an autumn sky.
A dusting of frost and a sleepy eye.
Home for a treat before shut-eye.

Molly Titus

The Storms of Life

When trials and tribulations come our way
And we wonder if we can make it through another day,
Put faith and trust in God; he'll make things right,
Leading us through the storms of life.

Circumstances and situations may test our endurance
As we lose our patience searching for some reassurance.
Look to the Heavens and you'll see the light
To see you through the storms of life.

One day we may find ourselves locked in a prison cell,
The one place on Earth that truly can be called hell.
Separated from loved ones, our children and our wife,
Caught up again, in the storms of life.

But there is an answer, and God is the key,
Holding the solution for you and for me.
He can open the door any time, day or night,
Saving us again from the storms of life.

Remember this, my friends, we are not alone,
Even though we may be far away from our homes.
We can see with our eyes and never lose sight,
God has made us survivors from the storms of life.

Mark Haure

A Daughter's Grief

In Daddy's memory

Daddy, Daddy, I miss you so
I know with God you had to go
In God's hands you'll be in peace
And though our hearts are filled with grief
We'll try to think of times we smiled
Times we laughed and hugged a while
They say with time the heart will heal
But that doesn't help the way I feel
I miss your face, your smile, your walk
The times we'd sit and fish and talk
You loved us all as we did you
Not often said, but we all knew
I love you, Daddy, and miss you so
I know with God you had to go
Left in our hearts an empty space
Filled with memories of your warm embrace
In God's hands we'll be in peace
And look to him in times of grief
And when we need you for so many things
You'll come to us on angels' wings

Charlene Arriaga

It's Over Now

It's over now, I understand
I'll never be the one to hold your hand
Never again will we embrace
I'll never, the same way, look upon your face

I appreciate the times of fun
It was awesome, when we were with everyone
But by ourselves we couldn't speak
Our choice of words was always weak

Through it all, we tried to get along
And times without you were too long
Our relationship could never be strong
Together we just didn't belong

I'm afraid that tomorrow is another day
Another time, another way

You're special to me, I want you to know
In my heart I'll never let go
You've always meant the world to me
You've always made me smile for free

It's over now, I understand
But I don't think it ever began

Daryl Austin

Martin Luther King

Martin Luther King was one heck of a man,
For justice and freedom, he made his great stand.
He lead his Black Brothers against social wrong,
A man such as he simply had to be strong.

He was inspired one day by Rosa Park's ride,
A tired Black Lady who would not step aside.
She was determined to ride in the front of the bus,
Which opened a new chapter in history for us.

A man so unselfish, so dedicated his life,
Taking the criticism, the abuse and the strife.
A natural born leader, his people so needed,
Following his leadership the movement succeeded.

He forced the government to fight for the cause,
Changing old legislation and making new laws.
To protect the rights of the second-class man,
Who didn't have the power to make his own stand.

But the King was a strong man, courageous and brave,
For the love of a people his whole life he gave.
For Martin Luther King did not live by the sword,
'Cause Martin Luther King was a man of the Lord.

Mary A. Payne

Sublime

Smoke everywhere,
Endless noise permeating
from the coal-black speakers.
A chaotic scene
representing archaic times.

People everywhere,
Constantly pushing and shoving
in the middle of the steel tensed barriers.
A complete pandemonium,
the unwelcoming gates of hell opened.

It is everywhere,
Always ready to make your dreams come
true or nudge you to darkness forever.
The scene is freedom—
did the '60s never leave?

He is everywhere.
The scene is forever carved in my mind,
endlessly haunting the silence of my dreams.
A funeral scene
black roses placed on his grave.

Jeremy Andrew Dizon

Forever Mom

I knew a woman a long time ago,
Who held my hand with love to show.
Who would wipe the tears off my face,
Her heart held love in a special place.

To listen to that soothing voice,
Loving me no matter what the choice.
Looking high to see that face,
Cradling me with loving grace.

A gentle touch to feel secure,
Staying with me what ever I endure.
Waking with a beautiful smile,
If only it wasn't just for a while.

He had his plan I shouldn't judge,
So hard to keep from holding a grudge.
Many times I yearn for the past,
Very grateful for the love that has last.

I know I will see again,
That smile from way back when.
I know she's there I just can't see,
My mom is with me eternally.

Kristen F. Lippa

A Chance Worth Taking

I got a chance, and so did you.
But you took your chance
And your dream came true.

I kept my chance
Close to my heart
I thought I'd save it.
That wasn't smart.

I figured I would save it, until a rainy day.
But it was like a snowball that had melted,
It was a dream to pay.

What have I learned from this?
What won't I do?
I won't save chances
until I have a hundred and two!

I'll live each day as the sun rises high,
And I'll snatch every chance before it passes me by.

And my parting words to you,
the ones my lips make,
are the only thing in your life that you'll regret
are the risks you don't take.

Katherine Melonakos

Why?

The wars of man will not subside,
Unless we can be unified.
We're taught that "love can conquer all,"
But man is weak—to sin we fall.
There's jealousy, hate and lust—
Every man is afraid to trust.
As competition rises high,
can no one hear that heart-torn cry
of frightened children asking, "Why?"
Why does Daddy fight with Mom?
Why does that policeman carry a gun?
Why do we have to lock all our doors?
Why must big brothers go to fight wars?
Why are so many people rich—
while others are struggling or starving and sick?
When we grow up, will we be the same,
fighting and hating and passing the blame?
And if we see someone who is in need,
will we toss them a penny and brag of the deed?
"We don't want to grow up that way.
'Cause grown-ups don't listen to things that they say."

Janet Ippolito LaFata

Love Someone

In a world filled with sadness and hate,
Where crime is growing at a very fast rate,
Where we criticize the difference in everyone,
Why can't we all just love someone?

Where poverty-stricken countries are in despair,
But does anyone who matters really care?
And in our world, when push comes to shove,
All everybody needs is a little love.

Without love and devotion we wouldn't survive—
Caring for others keeps us alive.
We need to trade guns in for a hug,
And give someone else a little love.

Some people just don't understand
That love is lending a helping hand.
Love is turning up your frown—
We need to spread love all around.

Spread this message around the world
To every boy and every girl.
One word that everybody shares,
Love is the answer to all of our prayers.

Meg Snyder

Heroes

I wonder what or who heroes really are,
They might be unknown or a movie star;
Are they the people who fight a fire?
Or the ones who McDonald's often hire.

Maybe it's the nurses who care for the sick,
Or the magician with a brand new trick;
Is it the judges and attorneys who keep law and order,
Or the immigration officers stopping drugs at the border?

Maybe it's the guys who drive the 18-wheelers,
Or Sunday School kids and the devout believers;
Could be it's just a man, a plain ordinary Joe,
Maybe a farmer who ploughs and buys seed to sow.

I think it's the ones who are very ill,
With something that can't be cured with a pill;
They struggle up each morning, put on clothes and a smile,
Though they feel like they've just run a bloody mile.

They try to keep going because that's the only way . . .
To live with loved ones day after day;
They are the heroes, the ones to look up to,
And ask, "Is there anything I can do for you?"

Shirley J. Stone

You're a Part of Me

Although you said goodbye, I still hear your cry.
How could this be? You never really knew me.
Now you're gone, my love remains unknown.
Being away from you, it's been the hardest thing to do.
Since we've been apart, the memories are breaking my heart.
Every day I ask myself why you went away.
My heart tells me you would've stayed, if only you knew who I am.

Look into the mirror, it will show,
Look into the mirror and you will know

You're a part of me!
Tonight I wish for you upon a falling star, no matter where you are,
hear me when I say, my love will never fade away,
I'll wait for you 'cause dreams do come true,
and deep down inside my soul,
I know that one day you will be told who I am.
Every day I ask myself, why you went away.
My heart tells me you would've stayed, if only you knew who I am.

Look into the mirror, it will show,
Look into the mirror and you will know
You're a part of me!

Curtis Andre Baucham

God's Angel

With God's angel on your shoulder,
And the Lord to light your path,
You can accomplish anything,
Just forget about the past.

With God's angel on your shoulder
There isn't anything you can't do.
Think honestly and positively,
And good things will come to you.

With God's angel all around you,
And kept close by you all your life,
Through good times, hard times, and pain,
There is no doubt you will survive.

With God's angel on your shoulder,
And you must always remember He's there
To lead you down the right path,
God will show all He has for you to share.

So God bless you with His love,
And His angel keep you safe.
Then one day we'll meet in Heaven
Where He's saving us a place.

Karen Moore

Courage

What is courage,
Do we have to ask?
Finding out is a huge task.

Seven years old, a boy got sick,
Doctors were puzzled, but acted quick.

A rare germ was what was found,
From hospital, to hospital
Family traveled all around.

They were strong, the boy
Full of life,
Never willing to accept strife.

Thirty-five years he lived in pain,
Never complaining, or giving blame.

Life went on, happy days followed,
He brought sunshine, no time did he wallow.

One night the stars came out,
This one with courage had a terrible bout.

He slipped away from those he loved,
Time long ago had been granted from above!

Sylvia Bott

The Passing of My Children, Ages Nine and Eleven

My heart was torn out of my body,
the day I received a call my kids went away.
No one can tell the pain I feel, it's anger,
sadness, and pretend it's not real.
It's like a nightmare that never goes away,
because I'm left to wake up each day.
Your hopes and dreams have fallen so low,
each day you wake you want to go.
Instead of feeling happy about the day to come,
you hope and pray God will take you to his kingdom.
This is my feeling when my head lifts off my pillow,
I guess it's another day of pain and sorrow.
You try to go on if the kingdom doesn't come,
you laugh and joke but your body is numb.
The hurt is there, nobody else can see, the outside's okay,
but the inside's torn beyond belief.
You get the feeling that you just don't care,
you've got people around you, but my heart's still bare.
They always say, "Life must go on,"
but everyone can't say their kids are gone.

Dan Moyer

For You

You ask me for a cure
and I can give you none . . .
But I can hold your hand in mine
and tell you what others have done . . .

They put forth your name
when they sent their prayers above . . .
They prayed for you to know
internal peace and ever lasting love . . .

A cure for all cancers
is a search to all mankind . . .
To answers some God has given us
the rest is ours yet to find . . .

I pray I could "cure" you
but alas this is not meant to be . . .
a special prayer will go to Heaven
It will be for you from me . . .

Please for give me if when I pray
that my prayer is mixed with tears . . .
for I pray you find inner peace
and happiness for many years. . . .

Mary Wright

The Life of a Butterfly

Beginning as a caterpillar, rolled in a cocoon
Becoming a beautiful butterfly very soon
Wings of many different bright colors
Flying in the wind, the butterfly flutters.

Perched upon a single pedal of a rose;
Does he grasp the greatness of his beauty? Nobody knows.
Soaring away into the skies
He disappears the further he flies.

You never hear the slightness of a sound,
If there were it'd surely be astound.
Imagine his song to match his grace;
Slow and high pitched but keeping its pace.

If the butterfly has any sadness to bare
We wouldn't even notice and to notice is to care.
If he could speak to us, what would he say?
Would he say to come close or to just stay away?

Such a short and simple life,
With little or no strife.
When their life ends they'll collapse and then fall.
The life of a butterfly, yes and that's all.

Julianne Marie Zahm

Charity Shows We Care

As I walk around and wonder, why life is so unfair
Why the good ones are never spared
And the bad ones are always there
Why the sick ones are always happy
But the healthy ones are always sad
Why the new ones come in crying
And the older ones go out smiling

As I walk around and wonder
Why no one is ever there; it comes to me;
No one has the time to spare

As I walk around and wonder
God has always had the time to spare
So let's all take the time
To be there and share

For love is what we need to share
And charity shows that we care
So let's all be there with our love
And charity, to show we care
And that God is always there,
To help us find a way to share his love

Donna Stephens

Hope, No More

Can't believe it's back to the old way,
Still hurtful, still mean,
Fighting to survive, but still green,
It has its price to pay.

Can't afford it so now must stop,
Just can't keep up the pace
Takes too much work and no breathing space,
Can't run, nor jump, nor hop.

Why keep on trying when all is lost,
Stuff loses its charm fast,
Now the present becomes the past,
Couldn't get it at any cost.

Some were too many to have to deal,
Nothing makes sense anymore,
Everything starts to hurt, feel sore,
Not enough strength and everything's too real.

As all begins to accumulate,
No way is the way out,
Searing pain creates more doubt,
Please say this is not an act of fate.

Isanne C. Zoller

Amethyst

She soars with wings as an angel
With the light of the stars in her eyes,
And as the midnight air fills her lungs,
She throws her head back and cries deep into the night.

Begging mercy from the moon
and pleading the forgiveness of the stars.
The man in the moon then looks at her and smiles.
Come here, sweet child, and wipe the tears from your eyes,
Tell me again where your passion lies.

Suddenly she felt comfort cover the pain
She spoke and told the man all she wished to gain.
She wanted the strength of the sun
A heart of gold
She wanted a price for what could never be sold.
She asked for the power of the one whom she prayed
To touch the beauty in all that he made.

Ambition and courage that pulled like the tide
Simply she said she was dying inside
She wanted to fall, a change to be made
Even if it was from angel to slave.
Finally he agreed and granted her wish

Holly Curcio

Angels Are with You

Don't worry angels are with you.
They are watching over you.
A mother's loving fight is true.
This will keep the angels by you.

In time all your joyous light will show.
All who cross you an angel's wrath will know.
The angels will help your heart to heal and grow.
This will cause your face to show a happy glow.

Tabatha Kay Hall

The Barefoot Girl

A dirt country road was the scene
Where the barefoot girl could often be seen
Riding her bike in a childlike dream,
Free from worry, so it would seem.

The simple life became an oyster without a pearl.
She left one day to give the unknown a whirl.
Gone forever is the barefoot girl
Who didn't have a care in the world.

Jane F. Bass

Beach Peace

As I repose on nature's silicious beaches
And peer over her reservoirs of blue
And breathe the iodine-misty spray
As I see the distance that seeing teaches.

As I experience the kisses of her waves
And play the games of her styles
And to realize the language of water and ray
As I repose in things of natural naves.

Warren Calvin McCain

Mist of Morning

The cool rise of dawn softens the morning
As the sun begins to shine,
The mist and the dew forgotten
As a new day opens and yesterday's falls behind.
As nature's creatures awaken
And some begin to sleep
God and his angels will weep,
For some of nature's wonders never seem to die.

Norah Elise Johnson

A Myst of Time

Glancing from a distance,
My eyes calculate the distance between her and you.
I spy your hands softly caressing hers.
My heart aches, and in a split second, breaks.
Jealousy empowers my being,
And a sense of confusion invades me.
Suddenly the confusion vanishes,
And jealousy no longer has control of me.
I open my eyes to the sight of your beautiful brown eyes,
staring deep into my soul.
The chemistry and passion so intense, it weakens my body.
Your fingers stroke my hair.
Then, with such fragileness, your hands caress my face.
As they softly smooth over my lips,
I kiss them, as if engraving your fingerprints on my lips.
Your body draws closer to me.
I can feel your heart beating against my chest.
My heart begins pounding as I feel the warmth of your breath
mystifying over my lips.
Tension increases as our lips invite themselves towards each other.
Unexpectedly, a sudden instant in time forces me to look away.
When I direct my eyes toward you,
your lips are kissing hers. . . .

Angelica Martinez

For I Am

I'm here to find if you want me,
  but I'm just so very hard to keep.
I bring pleasure to those who do have me,
  but when I'm lost, thus the sky does weep.
I'm in the joyful smile of children,
  in the thoughts of lovers embraced,
and in the peace you find within yourself,
  when you put aside your life's mistakes.

I've been sought after through all the ages,
  in every culture the world around,
and died many deaths in the darkness of life,
  but in this light again I can be found.

Oh, I'm wanted for so many reasons,
  some good, some bad, you would deem.
For I am what is called, "Happiness,"
  desired by all, yes, by all indeed.

Sharon Bennett-Williams

The Man from Nowhere

There was a poor man from nowhere.
He lived nowhere.
And when winter came, he tried to look for a warm place to lie down,
But a warm place could not be found.
So he walked around with a frown.
As the poor man was walking around, trying to find
A place to lie down,
He saw some birds flying around.
So he put his hands in his pocket to see if some
Crumbs could be found.
He found some crumbs, and spread them around.
The birds flew around, found the crumbs,
And went to eat them. Not one crumb was left to be found.
The poor man saw the birds eat the crumbs.
Then walked away, still searching for a place to lay.
He found a place—it's an unhappy place where
No man will ever be found, way down in the ground.
This poor man will not be around,
To put crumbs on the ground.

As he lies deep in the ground, the birds fly
Around, looking for the crumbs the man used
To put on the ground.

Loretta Berman

In Darkness

The moon stood high above the sky
And looked down at the world below.

The wind seemed like a lost child,
Running all around on its own.

The sky was a canopy of velvet,
Tossed far up above my head.

The stream slowly flowed along the rocks,
The water looked black, like the blood of the dead.

The woods were empty, yet filled my mind,
With curiosity and fear.

I wondered if something was standing in there,
Just waiting for me to come near.

A sleepy yet restless cloud wandered by
And settled in front of the moon.

In a second the moonlight had run away,
And the darkness seemed to stand still.

I moved from my window,
And fell into bed, then laid my head on the pillow.

I said my prayers, then closed my eyes,
And called to the day to come hither.

Louise Martin

Eyes on Me

he thinks all is well
because I smiled at him across the room—
all I wanted was to ease the tension
of his glare.

it stuck me to the wall
like an animal frightened by the light.
nothing to do but
look up and be caught.

Rachel Elisabeth Wilson

Deep, Sorrowful Sobs

Have you ever seen sobs that stem from the soul?
Deep sorrowful sobs . . . let the pain flow.
Have you ever felt tears boil over from inside?
Let the hurt show . . . the pain can't always hide.
Have you ever empowered emotions to rule over intellect?
Let the feelings fly free . . . release what you can't forget.
Has the hate and hurt inside taken too much of a toll?
Deep sorrowful sobs . . . let the pain flow.

Joseph Aaron Barnes

Try and Understand Me

Don't look at me and misjudge me.
I may be shaking or moving more than you—
Don't say I am on drugs.
My voice sounded like yours once.
I was healthy like you, but my genes just went out of control.
Try and help me all you can; you see, I have MS.
I am still the same person—
Changing, so please still love me.

Loretta Anderson

Welcoming of Spring

I walk, in the cool morning of spring rain.
Down paths of few evergreens,
new grass and wildflowers comforts the plains,
Brilliant sun glows, my umbrella turns to a parasol!
I gain a warm welcoming of an array of colorful magic sand,
birds appear and sing, spring is ready,
tree blossoms soft wind, pink and white confetti.

Baby cottontails quickly leap, and hide for shelter.
A pair of shiny snakes coiled around each other.
It's a new beginning, new life, spring rings.

Carolyn C. Spily

Little Children

Little children roam the streets hungry and so cold
Little children roam the streets where has your family gone
Little children roam the streets so far away from home
Little children roam the streets they have no place to go

Little children don't you know there is food for you to eat
Little children don't you know your family has been found
Little children don't you know that this is your home
Little children don't you know you have a place to go

My God is the father of His little children here
He feeds and clothes and loves and scolds His children oh, so dear
Just take a moment of your time to gaze upon his face
And you will know the love He has, the power and His grace
My God, you've opened up your arms you've asked them to come in
I pray your little children ask forgiveness of their sins
My God is so loving, little children do not wait
I pray you find my father so you can enter through His gates

Enter in little children, enter in one and all
Enter in little children, at my father's call
Do not wait, do no hesitate, trust your heart and you will see
When you enter, little children, there's a glorious place you will be

Jackie Phillips

A Wake

I lay in summer's golden rye
You frolic in your gentle lie
Your silver flows, a touch of ice
Kiss no more my weary eyes.

A bed of oak, my cloak of pine
You snuffed my heart out a thousand times
My bones no more wear flesh and sighs
Kiss no more my weary eyes.

Lev Anenberg

Without the Lord

One thousand dollars, a luscious reward.
Tell me friend, what is money without the Lord?
You could do many things with that kind of money,
Like buy some school books, pay tuition,
or see a movie that's funny.
Without the Lord, where would we be in life?
Probably lost in the realm of our own minds,
sick, poor and with no pride.
I know what I'd do with that luscious reward,
but I can only not win it without the Lord!

Alicia Gravely

Baby Santanna

Baby Santanna
Born on the eve of the third world war
Her future
Death by radiation
Her family
Living in a nightmare
No one celebrated her birth

Baby Santanna
Lay in her crib crying
Little did she know
Her family would spend
The next few days
Slowly
Dying

Baby Santanna
Dried tears on her cheeks
Everyone dead
She in a deep sleep

Baby Santanna only a few hours old
The baby to whom stories could never be told

Alicia Renee Ogletree

They Are Yours Too

Little children enter our world with innocence, and grace.
How their beauty glows throughout a tiny face.

Children can give. You too can give as well.
Open your minds, open your hearts,
Speak with love, and never yell.

You must make time and give your all.
If you're at their sides, share your love.
If you cannot be, then write or call.

You must share both sad and happy days.
Your promises must never shatter and break.
You must turn inward and hear the voice within yourself.
Do this for your children's sake.

Do not walk into, and then walk out
of the life that you helped to create.
It does not matter if you live with them or in another state.

A lifetime commitment is what you owe
to the child that is born unto you.
You need not have wealth, or fine fancy gifts,
But only the gift of yourself.

Michelle Testa

Poem

To write a poem is fun.
To write a lot of poetry is real neat,
To write a poem of origin and where you're from can't be beat.

To write a love sonnet,
Or to pretend in words to love someone;
And more love sonnets on it,
Is a never ceasing run.

To not run away from the sonnet,
Is to love the words,
Is love, the words or the paper; from it?
The affairs of the sonnet is heard.

Sazs S. Sexigs

The Vow

I always try and make the vow
to take the time to tell you how.
It's thought of often throughout the day,
but lost in thought, no time to say.
I know it hurts, the words unsaid,
I just assume, you know instead.
My promise to you, to make the time,
and declare the words, to me divine.
My devotion for you, the want to pronounce,
"I Love You" dear, each day I'll announce.
I will not just try, I have made the vow,
I will make the time, and tell you how.

Mary Trocke

Lost, Not Knowing What to Do

Oh, I've looked at the sky for days,
Oh, I've stared at the clouds in many ways.
Oh, I can wait until the end of my days,
But will you do the same for me?

Maybe I went wrong some way,
Maybe it was something I didn't mean to say.
Maybe I can forgive anything,
But will you do the same for me?

How can I sit here and not think
About you, when you're dressed in pretty pink?
This is where I tell you that I love you and wink,
But will you do the same for me?

Matt McEuen

Boot Camp

At time it seems hopeless,
And hard to handle the loneliness;
So confused, and far away from home,
Not willing to refuse, but oh, so all alone
No matter how much you pray,
The sky still gets gray;
Seems it's not worth it
The puzzle will not fit
The rules are so severe,
How can I endure
Seems the gain,
Oh, it's not worth the pain;
Then remember you are not out to gain fame,
Just your future you want to frame
Then you'll look back and realize, oh, how time flew,
Oh, how your knowledge and wisdom grew
That's the time you'll understand what God was saying,
The whole time you were praying;
"Just don't question or ask who"
"Instead, trust me; I'll get you through"

Jay/2000

Jessie Soileau

Long Faraway Cat

Long faraway cat, you are gone away,
We all hope you'll be back some day,
When you are here you will see us shine
For all of my life you'll always be mine
In the long, dark, cold night,
I will see you in the light,
At first it will seem like a great scheme
Then I'll know it was all just a dream
Long far away cat you are gone away,
We all hope you'll be back someday,
When you are here you will see us shine
For all of my life you'll always be mine

Amanda McRae

A Beauty of a View

To Angelee, with all of my heart . . .

Seeing the sun set behind the clouds, makes
me wonder; what this is all about . . . A
wonderful golden haze surrounds the trees;
what a beautiful sight she is to me. She has
such beautiful blonde hair; I catch myself
with a wondrous stare! I sit and ponder
the thought at times, as I put these
words into rhymes. She is so beautiful to
see; I wonder in my heart, for her to be;
choices are made every day, at times I
wonder; which way? The answer is quite
clear; I want to call her dear. . . .

Wade Matthew Gardner

Daddy

Since the first time you held me, I captured your heart.
From my first step till the day I became your graduate,
you've been there to see me grow and change,
and you have taught me many a thing.
You taught me how to ride my bike, to hunt, fish, and work on cars.
Even how to enjoy life.
But more importantly, you've taught me how to live and love.
You've been a hug when I needed it, a friend I could always turn to.
Someone I look up to and respect,
a model of the kind of person I want to be.
I'm proud to be your daughter, and to have you as my father.
Even until the day you give me away and beyond . . .
Always your little girl I'll be, and you, my Daddy.

Anita A. Nielsen

Only You

Why do I want you?
Is it because of the desire I feel . . .
When I look into your eyes,
Your gentle caress and warm embrace,
Or maybe the touch of your lips as they meet mine.

Why do I care for you?
It is because you always seem to . . .
Be there when I need a friend,
You love me just the way I am,
Or maybe because you make me feel special.

Why do I need you?
Is it because when I am with you . . .
I feel like I can do anything,
You always want the best for me,
Or maybe because you believe in me.

Why do I love you?
Is it because my heart soars . . .
Every time you walk into a room,
And I would give anything to be at your side,
Or maybe because you are not only my partner . . . but my best friend.

Nancy E. Runstedler

Untitled

Quietly sitting, patiently waiting for another game.
Dropped alone in the playpen with yesterday's favorites.
Grown old and tired.
Dust fills my wide, open mouth.
Left so from your innocent remarks.
Why so forgotten?
Why so alone?
Embarked on your own vacation.
You bought a new toy.
Paid with a smile.
And left me here in the corner.
Wondering why you sailed so swiftly.
And why you didn't take me along.

Jeff Benarick

A Fisher's Tale

I'm sure the fishing was the best in the world,
And the ride on the boat was just grand.
For the fisherman's story is a long tall tale
And the fish that he hooked are on land.

Oh, yes, says he, as the fish are unloaded
and the boat continues to sway
You know how it goes when you put in your line,
the biggest fish just gets away.

This fishers tale from the far Northland
was written with love to you brother.
I hope that the fishing was the very best
And that you soon get to go on another.

Elaine Gustafson

Life

What is life?
I can't explain life.
Life begins and ends each day.
It seems we live to die.
But why does it have to be this way?
At birth we're young and innocent.
With age we're ripe with sin.
Who draws the fine line between life?
Who decides when it begins and ends?
Is it a higher power?
Or the Grim Reaper on his harvest at night.
I don't understand life.
I just want to live mine right.

Brandon Beasley

Leaves of Conscience

It's weird how a day,
Can turn from bright blue to gray.
An early mornings sunshine,
To an evening shade.

But thus is something to accept.
Another unpleasantry of life,
Better forgotten,
Than remembered.

But the mind does not forget.
No.

The Leaves of Conscience don't shake from a limb,
Don't float around, in winds gentle descend.

Not an easy task,
Shedding ones guilt.
Correcting a problem,
That one has dealt.

Nature itself does not compare,
To the human mind,
That grew from its vine.

Brandon Gene Lucas

Night

As all turns dark a light approaches from the west.
All turns silent except the tall grass.
It turns a bright yellow.
All turns silent except the tall grass.
The creatures watch it from dusk to dawn.
All turns silent except the tall grass.
Then the noise begins and it is dawn.
Now all is loud except the tall grass.

Casey Michelle Ansell

A Plant's Cry

Yesterday as I sat in this very same spot
I saw something outside that gave a great shock
The workmen there were doing their job . . .
They didn't realize, that trees also sob

Where those trees once spread their branches
Are now only holes, what are their chances
If you put yourself out there in the dry
You can also hear the plants cry.

Sarah Catherine Dodt

The Scarecrow

I am a scarecrow
A sad and mischievous scarecrow
I stand with a bird on my hat
I stand in a field where love grows

My head did no thinking
My arms didn't move
My heart . . . I have no heart
I'm just standing in a field where love grows

Vahd Nabyl Mulachela

Illness

I is for isolation you sometimes feel
L is for life, so use it wisely
L is for love we all need to feel
N is for not now, but maybe there may one day be a cure
E is for energy you will need
S is for how special each day is
S is for Savior, and hope one day He accepts you for who you are
and not what you did

Sally Lewis

Body and Soul

Montel needs rest from the MS.
He cries in pain and tries not to complain
from the fight that takes his life
and brings his spirit to a great test.
One day there will be a cure.
Then shall come the rest,
for he has done his best
for everyone's body and soul with M.S.

Darlene J. Martin

Fall Harvest

When it turns fall, the hunters get their licenses,
and the geese are on the way South. The deer are on
the run. The combines are running, the augers are set
up, and the corn is being hauled to the nearby co-ops.
When I come home from a hard day's work, I walk
through the leaves hearing the crunch of the dryness.
I sit down and listen to the roosters calling their
mates to the cornfield where they will feast their
eyes on golden corn.

Tonya Rose Arensdorf

End of a Beginning

Dedicated to Joshua Brockman

Heart and soul and mind control,
a dream too wanted to come true,
a love to hold forever somewhere lies in you
Empty thoughts and broken dreams,
reality sets in
a love is lost at a simple cost;
it was over before it even had a chance to begin

Tiffany Wilhelm

Down Deep

Far below the ocean depths lies my depression.
So a smile from you could lift my oppression.
Without your love I find myself beside the river.
Please tell me why you won't be the giver.
All the love I have for you is a waste.
I still have a taste of you on my lips.
Stillness holds me when all hope is lost.
Buried at the bottom of the ocean is my soul.

Donald Sidman

Heart Strings

The curtains open wide, the universe displayed,
God directs time, His plans in Christ are made.
The moods of God balance to celestial sound,
Man hears it's voice, and in Christ he does abound.
Angels play their harps upon His golden street.
As God plays our heart strings all the while, we meet.
Listen to His music, oh, how beautiful it is,
Playing upon our heart strings, singing that we're His!

Judith Myers

My Child

You are my past. Every memory of innocents.
You are my present. Every heartbeat belongs
to you. You are my future. Every dream and
hope lies within you. You are my sun. The
light that burns without end. You are my
moon. The mystery of all that amazes. You
are the stars. The universe that holds life.
You have been, you are, you will be a miracle.

Linda Volpe

Love Waits for No One

Wanting to trust you, but not knowing how.
Wanting answers from you, not willing to hear the truth.
Wanting to love you, but not willing to fall.
Wanting the understanding, but not willing to let you in.
Wanting you near me, but scared to be close.
Wanting the relationship, but scared to trust completely.
Wanting to give you my heart, not willing to have it broken.
Love waits for no one and the time has come to move on.

Katie Bounds

The Best Life

my grandfather has a very optimistic view of life
it's always the best hot dog
the best plane ride
the nicest day
the best barbecue
I wonder if it was the best aneurysm surgery
the best time as a general in world war two
the best loss of hearing
the best macular degeneration
if you think like him, you will certainly have the best life

Alyssa Helen Mackenzie

Angel's Advice

Can you hear the voices of angels?
Do you hear what they are whispering?
If I could I know what they'd be saying,
she's the one for whom you should be praying.
But do they know what you do to me?
What I go through no man can see.
For the pain I suffer is deep within,
because your love I can never win.

Eliseos Thomas Anenoglou

Dream of Color

Mine are eyes that have seen only gray
and dream of vibrant colors of a future day.
With the sky and the earth meshed together as one
only inner visions cradled by hope can I pray overcome.
My eagerness to envision to visit and to stay
with the colors outside myself grow stronger each day.
For that which I desire such as depth definition and hue
will become a reality as the rainbow is in you.

Tonda Dohse

Autumn Leaves

Blowing in the wind,
Fall is just a passing thing,
Winter soon will be with us.
The days grow shorter, time seems to rush,
Ice and snow is what it will bring,
Then suddenly it is spring,
grass, flowers and budding trees.
The cycle begins again

Josephine Duncan

My Life

The more I learn, the more I still have to learn.
The more I know, the more I still do not know.
Is it really more knowledge I yearn,
Or is it a satisfaction I take in what I already know?

The more I see, the more that still remains to be seen.
Is it really more of life's experiences that I yearn,
Or is it a satisfaction I take in where I have already been?
One thing for sure, there is still much to learn.

Chris Jardin

The First Kiss

It seems as if the world has faded away
Subsided to facilitate our foray
Of curiosity of each other's being
As our soft touches become our seeing.

In wonder, hesitation, we should meet,
Our uncertain caresses, purely sweet.
What a moment it shall be, such perfect bliss,
The very first instant of our first kiss.

Constance Jeanne McCormack

He Went out for a Skateboard Ride and a Cigarette

He went out for a skateboard ride to calm his nerves.
He went out for a cigarette to ease his stress.
The tar cools his boiling blood
that's been building up and boiling up his pressure.
The carbon monoxide he breathes in and out
takes him to his fantasy in his own mind and world.
He loves it there, he not only loves it, he enjoys it,
So he continues smoking till the tar is inhaled
and the pain has been exhaled.

Jeffrey Franklin Sommers

Quietness

His chest it did ache for no reason he knew
Except he was in love this time all new.

She wasn't denying him or playing hard to get
He just hadn't asserted his presence quite yet.
She wasn't being heartless or just didn't care
He just hadn't said he was devoted to her.
He just wouldn't say all his heart meant.
So his love just lay there and could find no vent,
Yet he needs only tell her the love that he felt.

Deeper and deeper the yearning and ache
For this sweet young damsel he needs aught take
Had grown greater and greater each passing day
While over the years they'd been away.
Oh, for a few precious moments to let words utter forth
To end the great silence of that terrible swath.

Till the end, pent up feeling he still held within.
But he never did say it, and in love it's a sin,
To hold great affection silent and afar
And never to speak how you feel things are.

Anthony Wyant

Despised

Drunk he ignored my plea and plight
A wicked child conceived that night.
Gaze not upon her face, do not define
I wish that she, wasn't one of mine.
Despise; this girl child of disquiet.
Don't help, discourage, lest she riot.
Waste not affection, pathos, nor your love.
She's not fit for man, or God above.
Loathsome creepy crawly's, make her scream.
Let her languish, not indulge with dream.
Fate steps in, throws open wide the door.
A child's life, no choice, it must explore.
Tattered remnants, a soul now underfed
Wishes—longs—only to be dead.

Yet life, full of goodness promised there.
This child kneels down to God in prayer.
Please make me; someone else today.
Take this pain and anguish all away.
A gift of Love—kindness—make me be.
Trapped—unloved souls—to set free.

Jacqueline Yvonne Young

Just Because

Just because I do not always say it
Does not mean that I don't care.

Just because I can't always be around
Does not mean that I don't wish I was there.

Just because I don't always ask for it
Doesn't mean that I don't need your helping hand.

Just because we sometimes disagree
Does not mean that we are not friends.

Just because I do not always seem to be listening
Does not mean that I don't here what you say.

Just because I do not always understand your troubles
Does not mean that I don't feel your pain.

Just because we may not always be near
Does not mean that you are not close to my heart.

Just because I am always busy
Doesn't mean that I am not thinking about you.

Just because I may not always say it
Does not mean that I don't love you.

Just because I am all grown up
Does not mean that I can't still be . . . your little girl.

Heather Woods

The Tearing Down of Timber

He painted a corner inside his mind
With thick strokes of pain and thoughts unkind
Ever pensive, defensive and hard to forgive
Unable to try, and unwilling to give

She gave him the brush, and taught him the stroke
Burning the kindle to fire and stoked
The logs, the flames till the last dying ember
Then chopped another tree, and sighed, "Timber. . . ."

Hollie Rebekkah Wyatt

The Carbon Copy

Two witnesses in nature, alerts life.
The beauty of God, or, devil's strife.
Should I think of living, or to death?
Of a beast, holding one's breath?
Life is breath to all, living abound.
In breath, most refrain, graved underground.
Should we burn after a death jargon?
And so creating more element, "carbon."
In the image of God we are a "copy."
Whether a beast 666 is carbon sloppy.
Chemistry evolves that, deep insight.
Removing the beast, entails a plight.
Does scripture remain of God unseen?
Or carbon beast 666, and life to dream!?!

William G. Robinson

I Did Try

I tried harder and harder every day
to do things your way
But you know what they say
love can't go one way
I tried so hard to make you mine
if only you would have given me more time
I know that time
has taken its toll
And it's long past time
for me to go
That's why I am going
getting out of your way
Because I love you
more than words can say
So I guess it's time
to say good-bye
One day you will realize
I did try

Christina Warnock

My Tree

My tree, so beautiful, like pure gold,
For years withstood the winter cold.
Then came to life each spring, so green,
To stand majestic as a queen.

For four years now I've watched my tree,
But now it's through my tears I see
You lying crumpled and so broken.
I saw that you trembled just after you fell,
And this is a secret I'll never tell,
My heart trembled with you.
Another dream gone, that is my token.

I'll not miss you so much
While your limbs would be bare,
But next fall when your leaves
Would have turned to pure gold,
I'll listen, and maybe upon a sweet breeze
I'll hear my tree whispering a prayer to God, please.

Roberta Marie Coppenbarger

Forever Burned

Forever burned in my mind are memories
forever imbedded in my body are memories forgotten
in you I find consolation and hope
in my dreams . . . freedom
reliving trauma unintentionally
forging the constitution of my disease
simple words invoke my body's bank of the past
in my body the past is relived
in my nightmares I can't remember
the horrid visions of yesterday's bliss

Mark Jacob Freeby

Life and Love

Life is always a challenge, you have to be strong
It may not be right, it may be so wrong
When your body and mind are racked with pain
And when you feel you have nothing to gain
When you're feeling lonely and scared
And when you think that no one cares
You have your faith, you have your pride
Even when your illness is a thorn in your side
Just remember God's love and let it fill your heart
Let it fill your spirit and be a new start
His strength will help ease the pain of body and mind
His love will surround you like no other kind
Spread that love to family and friends
Feel it returned and never feel lonely again

Nancy R. Weaver

Winter Splinter

Withered Away Without A Cause To Promote.
Bliss In The Hay.
Without A Trend To Follow.
Shallow As The Shadow Under My Heal.
You Cannot Appeal.
You Play The Cards Unfettered, So Surreal.

Child Of The Tidbits, Infringing On Privacy.
Appalled By Caustic Winds Of Jealousy.
A Feather In Your Hat For Being Out Of Whack.
If That Is Where You Are At, Take A Breather.

Winter Claims Its Victims Throughout.
These Grueling Times Duel Like Aaron Burr.
It Lingers On Like Dandruff.
In Tune To An Icy Vice-like Grip.
It Clamors A Frothy Clam-tight Bite.

Winter, Whether You Like It Or Not.
Arthritic, Arsenic Seasonal Du Jour.

Alan Brian Kraus

The Mind

Though our eyes have never met, our arms have never embraced,
My mind is filled with thoughts of you, with images of your face.
As flowers in the springtime reach their fullness with the rain,
Your love inspires my heart to joyful vibrancy again.

Though our lips have never touched with passion in our eyes,
I taste your kisses hungrily as for you my soul cries.
As a river stops for nothing on its journey to the sea,
So my desire to feed the fire grows with intensity.

Though my hands have never felt the softness of your face,
If I could be the hand that did, I'd gladly take its place.
I'd feel like the climber when he clears the mountain's peak
If I could just caress the subtle curving of your cheek.

Though distance has prevented me from melting with your touch,
It hasn't kept my heart and mind from loving you just as much.
It's true, I cannot hold you close as willingly I fall;
But isn't loving with mind the most intimate of all?

K. L. Kingsbury

Love

Love is so important to give.
We have to Forgive, to live.
Then we have all good memories out there,
To spend our lives to love.

Barb J. Chase

Get Out and Try

Those days you sit alone and cry,
And think, what's the use to try!

You wish for all your dreams to come true
But you still sit there thinking of how you are blue.

But if you don't try
And really apply . . .

Life won't be fun,
In fact life wouldn't even have begun!

If it wasn't for the man who went out and tried,
And really applied . . .

The world would be gone,
And our lives would be done!

So Get out and TRY
And really Apply!

Michelle Sofakos

Failure Is . . .

Failure, it's only a word
But it carries so much pain
And so little concern, so
Much frustration and so little
Respect, so much stress and so
Little understanding that people
Spend their lives running
Through their days in hope of
Avoiding the long arm of this little word.

To test your vision, you must risk failure.
To temper your ego, you must attempt the impossible.

To tell your story,
You must take a chance
To see beyond the horizon,
You must spread your wings.

Failure is not negative;
It's life's lesson on how to live.

Josh Glover

Symphony of the Night

The breeze starts a song, carries it along,
The old moon looks down, and he grins.
Each creature's been placed, as a tenor or bass,
And the melody is given to the winds.
The owls hoot-e-hoo; nightingales say, "I do,"
For love is the theme that takes flight.
While the oak and the pine sway there in time,
To the symphony of the night.

The whippoorwill's cry adds a sweet lullaby
To the voices all joined in the song.
To the sound that's so sweet, bulrushes beat,
A drum solo that makes the work strong.
And the wind's blust'ry roar calls an "encore,"
So, the music goes on till daylight.
There under the moon, the world's all in tune,
To the symphony of the night.

The things in the forest make up the chorus,
For the symphony of the night.

Tom Russell McNeil

Love in Hindsight

Did I love him
then?
For what I knew of love, I loved him
then.
Do I love him
still?
I love my memory of what my love was for him
then.

Marina Salazar

How to Love

You said I taught you how to Love. We met along time ago. We were young and still getting to know who we were, and each other. You said I taught you how to love. Through the years, the joy we shared, and the tears, we grew and grew. You said I taught you how to Love. Through the years, the fights we had, the affairs you had, the break ups and the make ups. You once said I taught you how to Love, but through the years you have taught me why not to Love.

Brenda Davidson

My Angel

Her hair slung down around her neck;
She drives me into the upper deck.
She is the one, the one that's right
I dream of her each and every night.

I'd give my life and limb,
To be with her in the end.
She's an angel when she sings;
My angel from Heaven with hidden wings.

She's a Goddess of beauty, of love.
Her eyes, handpicked from the stars above.
I've loved her from the very start
My angel, my Goddess, the sunrise of my heart.

Charles W. Johnson

One Step at a Time

This is me. . . .

I am a woman, I can withstand any
task I am given.
I am beautiful, graceful, and righteous.
I am strong in my fight to be acknowledged.
If I fail I will try again; I do
not give up after my first try.
I am not always right, but don't criticize me when I am wrong.
Respect me and I will be
generous to you, but don't ask for the world.
I am a woman and must take my
climb to the top
one step at a time.

Kerry Ann Nichol

Untitled

The sun fades against a sea of blue,
As stars awake from their sleep.
The night is filled with dreams from times
Long ago or fantasies of things to come.

Wondering minds and restless hearts
Fill the bodies of unsuspecting beings
How has my day been and what will
the darkness bring?

Minds twist with unease.
Sleep, I must, until day once again appears,
And my fears diminish with the night.
Light is sanctuary for my soul.

April Arnett

Myself/My God

I am sitting here quietly within myself
Just as a toy on a very tall shelf
With my thoughts of mine that are all alone
I share with God often, with my low tone
Between the two of us, there is a great love
And the strength that I receive from him above
He gives me the will power to deal with life's pain
That special feeling, just like a falling rain.

Karen Hatch

Disappeared

The night was cold and stormy when I heard a knock upon my door.
I rose to answer quickly to find no one there.
I closed the door behind me and felt a cold chill in the air,
I looked and then I saw him the man I never knew,
He said I've come to see you, and tell you who I am,
but first you need to tell me am I really who I am.
I said I couldn't answer his question, for the answer wasn't clear,
and in a flash before my eyes he swiftly disappeared.

Norman George

A Soulless Statue

I see him sitting there, just staring
with this look of confusion on his face.
He looks as if he were a statue
and that his soul has gone from his body.
He sits and stares, unaware of his surroundings,
unaware of me watching him.
He look so peaceful,
but at the same time like he is in pain.
I wonder what he is thinking
and how he feels.
But then the bell rings,
and his soul returns from its journey
And he passes to his next class.

Catherine Margaret Lenois

Lost

Once I lost you forever,
I felt I lost a big piece of me
Not knowing how to go on, thinking
I should do the same as you
That's the only way we could be together,
and the painfullest way at that
Debating day to day if it's worth it,
but to see your face again it might be
I miss you, missing you in the worst possible way
I guess you could say losing you made
me love you, but not realizing it until you were gone
I hate myself for treating you the way
I did, and now it's too late for I'm sorry.

Krystal Nicole Shell

Forbidden Midnight

Every year in the dark autumn's haze;
Lies the moon full and bright, in the midnight sky, gold and white.
You can hear the owls' anxious cry,
When their prey comes tiptoeing by;
For which the wolves howl and yap;
At the vibrant rays of the moon,
The darken hearth that crumbles beneath your feet as you move.
The swaying motion and shadows of the trees that surround you;
Swish, swish, as a gust of wind pulls you down,
Where unseen creatures lurk around,
Where the town's horsemen forbid to go and ride;
Closer and closer, the ghost comes by,
Leaving you with a frozen chill that leads to your spine.

Candace Rae-Rockwood Fields

Butterfly

Could you be my butterfly?
Could you open your wings and fly in my direction?
Could you stop on by for a while?
Would you fly away if my heart flutters too quickly?
Would my touch suffocate you and make you circle me nervously?
Could my shoulder satisfy you as a tender perch?
Could you be my butterfly?
If so, land on me

Taunya D. Hatchett

Behind Closed Eyes

The single candle glows,
the bed, covered by the pedals of a rose.
The love of my life is here next to me,
I'm holding her, tight, against my body.
She looks into my eyes, and grins,
I know what she means with her, subtle hints.
We start to touch, and then kiss,
I feel the emotion, extreme bliss.
My eyes open and I then realize,
everything that happened, happened behind closed eyes.

Daniel Lee Gathman

I Hid You in My Heart

I hid you in my heart, beneath its very beat
I knew you'd be safe in there till God's work is complete
I hid you in my dreams, among dazzling stars above
I knew God would watch over you, He gave me you to love
I hid you in my hopes in whispering winds you blew
When those winds brushed my face, I knew that it was you
I hid you in my mind, memories so tender and fair
Tucked away deep down inside till our hearts one day we share
I hid you for a long, long time; then God said it was okay
To unlock the doors and tightly embrace you that I hid away

Anna M. Easley

Twist of Fate

The road of life twists.
The road of life winds.
Sometimes you'll stop to rest by the side.
Pictures and voices that race through your mind,
The things that occur, when you've crossed that thin line
Are often defined by the person inside.
The waves of the ocean roll and collide.
I stare at the setting sun with wondrous pride.
I look to the heavens with a tear in my eye
And know how I'm thankful that I'm along for the ride.

Carla Dawn Morris

A Lost Love

I feel as if I am trapped. Mind, Body and Soul.
My Emotions are in complete turmoil.
If ever I loved another as much as I loved you,
I would surrender myself to his arms,
in hopes to escape this silly obsession.
Pushing myself to wake in the morning, you're gone.
Physically near, you taunt me with your words.
I hear you love another, and my heart crashes to the floor.
My dreams are shattered.
The power of love stands higher than any other.
Yet I am weak, and have succumb to a life of self-pity
and complete depression.
While you continue to find happiness, I am left alone.
Hurt, Broken, and Hidden forever.
I am now experiencing a pain far greater than any pain
that I've ever felt before.

Tara Sansoni

Happy Does It

Multiple Sclerosis is no fun
It stops you from being on the run
It keeps you from singing like a lark
It keeps you from walking in the dark

It keeps you medicated every day
It keeps you from your friend at play

Keep a sincere and happy thought each day
And all diseases refuse to come your way
You'll live a long and happy life
Completely rid of "Multiple's" strife

Maxine Payne

Soft, Gentle Breeze

She's like a soft, gentle breeze
On a hot summer night—
Refreshing, uplifting, welcomed.

Her fragrance is the sweet scent of honeysuckle—fresh, clean, pure.

She wraps him in her tenderness and calms him with her love.

She is his treasure, his purpose, his reason for living,
The soft, gentle breeze that drifts through his life.

Mary Beth Boggs

Naked Lies the Earth

Bright and beautiful are the trees in fall,
as the leaves begin to sprinkle upon
the frosty ground.

Colors of orange, red and violet
lighten up the bare tree so that
you and I may enjoy our sky.

But soon the leaves are all
gone, only to leave a
picture of a
bare tree.

Stuart Edward Dobro

Friends

Friends are always there for you
Friends always care for you
I don't know how lucky I can be
To have many friends that are sweet to me
My friends have never let me down
But sometimes they have made me frown
We always laugh and share our smiles
Even if we are apart for miles and miles
Friendship is a special gift
It will give your heart a lift.

Katelyn Somers

A Child's Prayer

May the Lord's light shine wherever you roam,
And its brilliance guide you safely home.
May it steer you on seas forever calm,
Always keep you safe from harm.

May it radiate the brightest beams
To always keep and fulfill your dreams.
May it never flicker when trouble brews
And lead to safe harbors for you to use.

May it shine eternal from high above
And always fill your life with love.

Melody Cain

Someday

Someday I'll fly without a plane,
Someday I'll travel with out a train.
Someday I'll see all the world's land,
Someday I'll have the upper hand.
Someday I'll swim the deepest sea,
Someday I'll be famous and drink rich tea.
Someday I'll be the best athlete ever,
Although these somedays may be never,
That's okay.
Because the achievements of tomorrow
all begin with somedays.

Stacy Olson

Silence

Lost in Silence is where I shall be
Both wild, and pure voices shall be found here
Voices of water on stones
The movement of light on the ocean
Foam, stone both storming travellers
Come here and look perhaps it's nothing
Come here and look, for man and woman shall not say where or when
Some will look here and some will not
Back again I am between the mouth of time
As for me I shall afterwards be found here
Here, here my heart shall stay alive

Sherif Khaled Abdel-Khabir

Everything Is a Blessing

Dedicated to my Lord, Jesus Christ

As I look to the sky
As I ask questions that end in why
You finally answer me
With everything is a blessing
The grass that grows on the ground
The little blue jay with the wonderful sound
The sky that is above me
Everything is a blessing
I want you to have everything
Starting with love and ending with gain. :)

Celia Deanna Eddy

Special Twinkle

There's a little twinkle in you eyes Grandpa
One that I will never forget
It tells me that you love me
And sings to me a beautiful tune
It smiles an enormous "grandpa" smile
And say that you are proud of me too
It tells me you wish that you could say
At least a few words
But please don't worry Grandpa
The little unforgettable twinkle in your eyes told me
So I have already heard

Darla Roberts

I Love Jesus

I is for the Incredible miracles He does.

L is for how much He Loves us.
O is for how much He cares for Others.
V is for how He takes Very, Very good care of us.
E is for His Everlasting love for us.

J is for God gave us Jesus
E is for you getting Executed for us.
S is for helping us in hard Situations.
U is for making us, Us.
S is for Sacrificing yourself for us.

Joshua Canevari

Untitled 1

telephone wire sings with new babies, old
friends, relative-ish gossip, dirty
jokes,
and
Aunt Betty Jean's New, Improved, and
Absolutely Fab-O
Tang pie recipe.
telephone pole
just stands there
concentrates on withering away
a splinter at a time.

Beverly Shannon Norman

Unconditional Love

There is a cloud hanging over my head, it is
there when I wake, there when I sleep. It is a
symbol of my pain, which I carry so deep.
It's a pain that I cannot bear to let go of
for it is a pain caused by love. Love for a
soul that I long to be near, love for a soul
that I hold so dear. A love that can pass
any given test. Love that I will carry with
me till my last breath. Love that is truer
than any one thing you can conceive. Love
that brought forth a seed.

Gemetra Wicks

The Way I Wished He Looked at Me

Those eyes, those eyes that call to me . . .
Those beautiful brown eyes which sing to me . . .
I wish that every time I looked into those eyes,
I would feel like dancing.

In my dreams those eyes give me hope, love,
confidence, and courage, but most of all,
they would give me faith.
That one look of love, I wish I could see . . .
for the one he adores, for the one he would give his heart to,
for the one he knows is for him, I just wish I could see it . . .
The way I wish he looked at me is magical.

Ronnetta Denae' Rideout

Band Leader

Beating like a runaway drum
Your rhythm sings of love
And from this rhythm we taste our shape
Our lives blister from the searing heat you generate
So I scan the horizon and search for the day
When I may finally shake your hand
When I can finally look at you and see my own, true reflection
And we can cry in harmony, sing in symphony, laugh in infamy
A long, arduous journey culminating in our pulse
Has nothing more exquisite ever been felt
Than the meeting of one's own heart?

Patrick S. Oliver

True Love

Without you, why am I here?
I am just a swing in the wind
with only one rope to hold me up.
I need the other piece of my life to go on.
You are the one and only thing that holds me together.
Though in your heart we stand apart,
in mine we will always stand with one another,
I will love you forever, no matter what the cost.
In my dreams, we have a love to last all time,
but in life I have yet to feel the soft touch of your lips to mine.
I will do anything for you . . . and you must know this.

Kevin Robinson

Lost Dreams

Who's dreams are these lost in the shadows?
Flittering here and there on the winds of change?
Who is to find and ground these wayward dreams?
Dreams once held in high hopes . . .
Longing expectations of what a better life may hold
Some just a fleeting glimpse
Others held many years before being lost to the winds
Many sad and disheartened at the loss of a friend once held dear
Others content with those flittered away upon realization of reality
We must remember that happiness lies upon the dreams we keep
For what is hope without dreams?

Joel Adrian Sanderlin

Reborn at Fifty-Two

Like a freak from a side show,
Cast into your path,
No direction, no love, no hope, no future,
doors tightly shut, suddenly flung open,
crossed arms unfolded into outstretched acceptance.

Love, pain, fate, hate,
sarcastic comedy, spiritual conversation,
All painted in the most fantastic pastels,
Wayward journeys taken in abundance,
Yet the love you've shown always shone
brightly in the distance to light the way home

Kevin C. McGuigan

Friends

How do we count them?
These friends of ours.
One by one.
A smile, a kind word, a hug now and then.
Listen, share, care.
Knowing that this friend will always be there.
Laugh, cry, that's what we've done.
This friend and I.
Pray for others, pray together, pray alone, pray for each other.
Friend,
I thank God for you.

Joyce Dupont

Lady Blues and Windowpanes

Paint up your face
To cover battle scars and waif
To be black and blue and sore all through
To be glazed
She pulls up her hose
To hide scars that chose
With this fist full fight and humming my blues
So, for all the pain and all the fear
I can look out my window
I can wipe a tear
But damn it God, I am still standing here

Joey Adami

One Night

I didn't know you long
But it took only a night for me to fall in love with you
I think about each moment we had together
I miss everything about you
When I think of you it makes me happy
Then happiness turns to into sadness
I am scared that I might never see you again
I believe that we could have had a true love
But what do I know of true love?
I am young and have not felt true love
Until I was with you

Ashley Marie Grone

I'll Meet You at the Moon

In loving memory of Kyle Birch

I miss you so much—why did you leave?
When I think of you, all I do is grieve.
I miss all the humor—you were so sweet.
I can't wait to come to Heaven, so again we will meet.
You were really quiet; you always listened and sat.
But inside you were mischievous, just like a cat.
I hope you like Heaven; you have my blessing and love.
And if I ever need to talk to you, I'll mail it by dove.
I will be coming to Heaven, hopefully not too soon.
I'll meet you halfway; I'll meet you at the moon.

Jillian Audrey Kelly

Sickness

Sickness shows no discrimination
It can devour Anyone at anytime regardless of how noble we are
So be conscious of the way you live
Because your health can erupt when you least expect it
We are never too rich to fall downwards
And never too large to be conquer
You did not bring yourself into the world
Therefore you are not your own
Learn to be humble and when you reach the upward heights
Of progressiveness and is stricken by an illness
You will not be alone

Dawn Hamilton

Remember Your Spirit

Remembering God gives you a reasonable service
to acknowledge your spirit.
It's vital to good self-esteem no matter what the situation
or sickness is cancer, AIDS, drug addiction, families separated,
poverty, positions, authority, leadership,]
power of authority bills—remembering God. There's an answer.
Remembering your spirit you'll get your answer
everyone answer want be the same
it is our reasonable service to learn your spirit to think positive.
I will not accept defeat or can't—remembering God
is remembering your spirit.

C. Mitchell Wilson

I See Angels

Forgive me, if I seem to stare,
but much to my surprise,
I thought I saw an angel in your eyes.
I suppose it might have been,
the sunset's amber glare.
For just one fleeting moment,
I saw wings and flowing hair.
And also it may have been
my imagination running wild.
For I see angels every time, that is,
every time I look into the eyes of a child.

Debra Tate

Spring

A tapered shaft of sunlight glanced through the valley green,
Climbing through the shadows a beautiful golden dream.
Drops of silver imagery, within petals of muted dust,
Caroling waves of tranquility, allow the wind to adjust.
Scarlet pansies pecking through layers of demur tall grass,
With opal wings above the sky, the angels calmly pass.
Hypnotizing waves of violet sky float above ivy walls.
Ivory doves challenge the silence with their virtuous calls.
A breath of early dusk, melted away by rays of noon.
The monarch patiently settles upon a valley of midnight's birth,
Where the only hand to touch the soil is the gracious Mother Earth's.

Heather Cadarette

What Do I Think about Fourth Grade So Far?

I think it is very fun all my teachers are very nice.
My favorite class is math.
We always have lots of homework.
Fourth grade is a lot different than downstairs.
I like it and I hope you do too.

Meghan Clarke

The Granddaughter Clock

Into the charming Antique clock store,
My soul is filled with amazing
Beauty and sounds of many ornate clocks.
The Grandfather clock with deep tones,
Struck twelve, the sun, moon, and stars
Moved at once, the grandmother clock
Chimed in time, a melody of love.
The granddaughter clock stood out,
With her delicate charm, pink-baby roses,
Graced her face, so sweetly, her darling
Melody would repeat every hour,
A reminder of the past and present,
A timeless, paradox of sounds and beauty,
Which shine the better times.
Chimes, the sounds of sweet notes,
So precious . . .
Create a endless sound,
And smile upon her face.

Sharon L. Sullivan

Daddy-O

I've had the privilege of growing up with "live" music
Because of your "Stan Getz" sounding sax
Every day was filled with "rock," "pop," "top 40 . . ."
"big band," "r & b," and all that jazz!
"Savitt, Como, Spivak, Crosby, or Sinatra . . ."
You've played with them all, to name a few
Your "looks" are always compared to "celebrity"
You even sing like "ol' blue eyes" too!
And on top of all this, you were a landscaper by day
To which I owe you my passion for gardening, to say the least
This is how I will always remember my father
Since he adopted me as a "little baby girl" of just six weeks!
We've certainly had our times of misunderstanding . . .
In between the "loss" of your loving wife, son,
And now, your close companion of many years
Always remember, Dad, "the 12 steps" and this poem . . .
Both written out of love, respect, and admiration,
Whenever you feel the need to hold back those deep, heartfelt tears

Paula Massey Murphy

This Fear

This fear has become a big part of my life,
A part of who I am.

It doesn't make me happy, this fear,
The fear that trembles through my body,
That guides my hand, controls my speech.

How many chances have I missed,
Relationships have I lost,
Victories have I forgone to cling to fear?

In place of fear, I'd like to trust . . .
Hold on, close my eyes, and just be led.
In place of fear, I'd like to act,
Just do, just live, just say, just believe.

But fear clings to me as well,
For it and I cannot live without one another.
And so we two live together, alone together,
Without hope . . . without trust . . . without life.

DeBorah Graham

The Stay Awake at Nighter's Prayer

Now I lay me down to sleep
That's a prayer I'd like to keep
As I lay in my bed with my eyes open wide
To keep them closed, I certainly tried
And if that works in the time I spent
Then I know that I'll be content!

Bernice Follett

More Than Just a Wife

Do you ever look at your life and
want to be more than just a wife?
Do you ever see yourself free,
with no ties or responsibility?
Do you ever see yourself in the company of another man,
being loved by a stranger's hand?
Do you ever look at your life and
want to be more than just a wife?
Do you ever see yourself going where you want to go?
Having no one there to tell you no?
Do you ever look at yourself and think,
"What have I done?"
And questioned if he was really the one?
Do you ever see yourself taking a long look in the mirror,
and wished things were more clearer?
Do you ever look at your life and
want to be more than just a wife?

Amanda Thomas

The First Kiss

The Headlights of Heaven's highway shimmer.
The moon lights the sky.
The feeling, all but melancholy

A breeze softly blows. The waves wash up shore
The humming of crickets is clear,
in this night of perfection.
However, the seconds that lay ahead,
make perfection seem futile.

Laying softly on my shoulder, as they look on
I feel the love inside, the heads slowly turn
I am overcome by the beating of my heart.

Two lives meet as one, the world goes silent.
The great emotion takes over all surrounding.
As we part the world is alive once more,
but the two bodies ponder on what's to come,
Again she lays on my shoulder,
We sit silent, and listen to Cupid sing.

Sean James Giovanni

Angels Watch over You

Angels were watching when you were born,
We didn't see them, they didn't blow a horn.
Angels were there when you contracted polio,
You weren't in the iron lung, you know.
Angels have always been around,
To watch and protect you, but no sound.
Through all phases of life, they're there,
Surrounding you with love, showing they care.
When you feel down, want someone to hear,
Remember your angels, they're always near.
Tell them, they'll listen, they're there.
Disappointments, anger, spurts of despair.
Mother's angels, children's angels too,
Sometimes chat, I believe, don't you?
I hope when ours get together, you'll know,
I remember that day many years ago.
I wanted a girl, smart, but pretty too,
I got just what I wanted—I got you.

Betty Jo Anderson

I

I
And I am.
and I could be more, but I am
And I care that I could be, but I am,
And, you never know me, 'cause I might be You.
You never know. . . .

Igor Mirkovich

Euphoria

Just one kiss, and I knew
My knees turned to unsteady rubber
As I tasted the salt on his lips
A knot of fear and excitement tied into my stomach
And I longed to open my eyes
Knowing at any time it could be over
But an eternity flew before we parted
Fate pressed our lips together
Reality drew them apart
His blue and my green gazing together
Into each other, drawing emotions from within
But the kiss was not repeated
The tingle that danced my spine subsided
And the sensation passes away as a flower
Budding, in bloom then wilting to the cold earth.
To decay, leaving only its scent to the dew
Like the memory of his lips
And the electricity sparked in the moment

Katie Patricia van de Kamp

Happy Mother's Day!

Happy Mother's day,
to the mother who showed me the way.
Happy Mother's day,
to the mother of the day.
Happy Mother's day,
to the mother who showed me right,
by the night.
Happy Mother's day,
to the mother who brought me up the right way.
Happy Mother's day,
to the mother who has a brother.
Happy Mother's day,
to the mother who is special,
in such a special way.
Happy Mother's day,
to the mother who sat by the bay.
Happy Mother's day,
to the mother who is on the payroll.

Stacy Ford

Light in Darkness' Place

I live in the black,
I am lost to this world,
Scared and all alone.
There are those who come to me;
They drain emotions right out of me
And laugh at me when I moan.
I once thought that I was fine,
But that was then and this is now.
I knew I could never be loved again.
Then when my last hope draws near,
You appear,
Bringing no critical eye or words of pain.
I thought I was done for,
Old clothes tossed away,
But that is not the case.
For you are here;
You draw me near,
Light in darkness' place.

Alana Rachele Paul

My Love

I can't live without you, the way you
move, your sweet skin flows in the wind, the
sweet smell your body gives off, that smell
that attracts my nose, the way your lips move
as words flow out of your mouth, like water
down a stream, I just can't live without My Love

Wayne C. Baehr

I Still Believe in Thee

If a photo contains all our memories,
then why can'st I seest thee?

If I only had one more day,
and one more hour . . .

I'd asketh to let thine eyes
be cast upon thee.

We could share my fondest memories
with my friend from long ago.

And be not ashamed anymore
from fear, persecution, and pain;
that I held no grievances against thee.

As I cast thine eyes upon thee
one last time, with a clear consciousness . . .

I'd tell the world,
I still believe in Thee!

Jacqueline Sue Bird

Bobby

He was my first, so proud was I
He was what I wanted, 'til the day I die.
He got into boy stuff, busy as a beaver
He was a pistol, so happy, so eager.
Now he's grown, turned into a man.
I'd change him now, if I can.
I worry quite often, I wait to see
If he makes it home, that satisfies me.
He drinks a little much and dabbles in drugs.
He doesn't run to me with my baby boy hugs.
I worry, I fret. I fuss, I plead
I give my love, of which he needs.
Mama's hard, he may think
But, Lord, I know ,
His life could go in a blink.
Give me patience, Give me strength.
I love him so, Lord:
Let me go first.

Marcia R. Hodges

Remembering You

As I sit in the house on a cold December,
Trying very hard not to remember
The times we spent together
In this beautiful, white weather.
The time you said you loved my beautiful hair
When we were teenagers and we just didn't care.
As we sat there side by side,
You sat there and lied.
You lied about what you had said;
You told me you were fine instead.
You died on New Year's Day,
While in the waiting room I stay.
Only then I knew you were going;
You should have told me,
I had the right of knowing,
But the doctor told me the whole story.
The only good thing is that you are not hurting,
But I want to tell you, I Love You, Michael.

Kimberly Nicole Brindley

Sunny Nights

Rely on stormy nights becoming sunny days,
'cause everybody sees things in so many different ways,
don't think that you're the awkward one,
because of looks and style,
'cause your life is everlasting,
and your purpose is worthwhile . . .

Rebecca Weber

The Grendels' Money

Speak I say?
Or hold your frivolous tongue.
You cry to me for pay so undeserved,
and say it's for a job well done.
But I see no beauty in my garden,
for winter has willed out its last churn.
Oh, how can I pay you for a job not done?
There are still two seasons to come.
You rent for free and have unlimited food and fun.
The time you have kept in the presence of my home,
has been lived in a life style even I don't condone.
I watched day by day and not even a rake
touched that infertile ground!
Now winter has come, the ground so dead,
thanks to little work been done.
Yet you ask for pay?
Explain to me why I say!
Oh, do tell why you deserve that money today!

Christopher T. Collins

Day 09: Total Awareness

The politeness flickers out,
But he knows in her eyes
That she could show him the world.
And behind the shades of decency,
She shows him how to hurt
And how to hang on.

His insecurities rise in his throat,
But she drinks them
And weaves him into her web,
Knowing he is helpless.
Music floats in the background
As he tries to break loose,
And she cries for fear of losing him.
Of course, she's vowed before
Never to be so vulnerable,
Never to hurt someone like she's been hurt.
All vows broken
As she steps over herself.

Rachel Middleton

Red Is the Color of a Mother's Love

Red is the color of a mother's love
That burns a tearful hole through her heart.
Who knows what could trigger it?

The sight of a child, forlorn and sad,
Alone, deprived of a loving heart.
The mother's tears fall freely and sad

Compassionate hands, so gentle yet firm,
Brush falling tears from the face,
And loving arms encircle those with burdens on their hearts.

The first to realize, first to understand,
Caring for the weakened of body or mind,
Is the mother, soul mate, and tear-sharer.

An unconscious presence in our lives,
Her diligent eyes are gently guiding,
Always there, yet strong and silent.

Red is the color of a mother's love.

Devon Marie Gan

Today I Smelled the Rain

Today I smelled the rain.
As the billowing, slate blue clouds drifted aimlessly
across the sullen summer sky,
even before the first silent, silver slivers
fell upon the soft, brown earth,

I smelled the rain.

Barbara B. J. Nelson

Eagle

Freedom high up in the sky,
that's how I feel when I fly.
With the eyes of an eagle, I view the world.
It's so beautiful, but now I'm getting old.
You wanted to feel my feathers.
I let you touch me, now I regret it.
You clipped my wings so I can't fly,
I keep falling, now all I do is cry.
How did I become an object of your possession?
All I know is to fly is my obsession.
Against the wind I used to fly.
It was a great challenge, all I can do is try.
Those wings once took me to places
where there was no pain, just smiling faces.
Those wings one day will grow,
a little reminder to let you know.
That freedom high up in the sky,
is how I'm going to feel when I say GOOD-BYE.

Maria M. Cade

Essence of Love

Gazing into your eyes I see your innocence
Yet I feel the fire of desire as we embrace
Sharing a magic Kiss whispering words of love
Take your hand in mine as we walk down the lane
Stopping 'neath a majestic oak we lie down
Looking up to the peaceful Heavens above
A moment of silence our eyes closed
We share a common vision of two people in love
We embrace eyes locked we merge into one being
Our minds linking hearts touching we smile
Moments seem like years our souls mesh as one
We are alive with blissful fulfillment
An inner peace sweeps over us
We separate returning to our natural state
Without a spoken word we rise
Taking each other's hand
We begin to walk once more
Now two spirits of eternal love

David Annichiarico

Alone

It's dark outside, and I'm all alone.
I don't know where I am
Tonight it is as cold as death. Sometimes the clouds tease me.
They give me a glimpse of light to show
Me where I am, but as soon as I look
To find my way, the light is engulfed
By the devouring clouds.
A harsh wind has picked up,
It feels like sandpaper
Against my fragile skin.
It throws dirt and tiny stones at me,
So that I am blinded and cannot see
My path. I am all alone and I am lost.
The dark night is trying to break me. Tonight I will not bend,
I will not give up.
All I can do is continue along
My way and hope that soon the foul night
Will surrender to the gentle sun.

Lori Ann Kuziek

Coming Home

We waited patiently with our two small children, for the
Plane to land. We heard the sound approaching, and then
Suddenly the honor guard appeared. And as the plane
Released Jim's remains, we remembered that our country
Was not at war. Only that he had died protecting what
All of us held so dear. The day that Jim came home. . . .

Denise Phelps

Reading Lies

Sleeves wet from the tears you've shed.
All night you've been sitting up on your bed.
The room dark, tranquil, dull filled with quite noises of your sobs
And the sounds of your headache throbs.
Letters from him neatly stacked tied up in two blue rubber bands.
Sound of paper unfolding as you open one with your trembling hands.
In an instant more tears appear on your face.
You feel cold; you need his warm embrace.
You were in love and now it's all broken.
It's been so long since the last time you've spoken.
Agony taking over your body.
Diseased is your soul with despair and heartbreak.
Another sentence—another promise.
Asking yourself if this is what love is.
Every word written means much more now than before.
"Lord, help me, please!" on your knees you implore,
And until someone from above hears your cries,
You will sit here sobbing reading these lies.

Armine Grigoryan

Brother of Balance

Envisioned,
Cold fury, Ice hatred, no desire.
Who turned off the furnace?

A heart placed in my upturned palms.

Delusions,
Steaming discussion, a set confusion . . .
Spinning downward,
Is the furnace turned on?

Oh, . . . Where is my brother of balance?
Innocence was our protector.
Shyness was the secrets kept hidden.

Casting off your innocence and shy-like
Ways, as dirty rags thrown at my feet.

Did you turn the furnace on?
Walking into the filth of the world.
Or did you turn the furnace off?

Roscoe A. Warren

Best Friends

Best friends are forever,
Because they are always together.
It may be in mind and body,
But it will always be in spirit.
They will always share memories,
Even when they are old and grey.
Our friendship is very special,
Because you are a special part of me.
We have our arguments,
But we always work through them.
Never forget the way we are now,
For some people change over the years.
I never want our friendship to change,
Because you are an important part of my life.
I will always be there for you,
And I know you will always be there for me.
Take care and enjoy life,
For you never know when it will end.

Mary Short

Comforting Thoughts

Oh, God, I know You alone hear my prayers,
that my loved ones are in Your care
in a heavenly place where they never grow old.
You have placed them in mansions of silver and gold.
All their pain and tears faded away,
with You, oh, Lord, for eternity to stay.

Julie Lapach

How I Miss You

Oh, Grandpa, Oh, Grandpa,
You were the best!
But not just better,
Then all the rest!
You cared about everyone,
Not just yourself.
And no one who knew you,
Could say anything else.
I love you Grandpa,
And I want you to know,
That I did not ever,
Want you to go!
We shared happy times,
And sad ones too.
I hope that you know,
I still care about you.
I think of the times that we spent together
And why you could not stay forever!

Jessica Phillips

Fatherless Child

I stand on the outside of your little glass world
wondering if you even care that
I am your little girl
I know I have one parent
But, I should have two
I wish that second one could really be you
I see you in your glass world and your happier then due
Yet, I am the off spring that came from you
I don't think that happiness should be given to you
Because you have yet to recognize the pain that you've
put me through
Remember, I am the off spring from the love of two and
I want some of that happiness and
I want it from you.
I know I have one parent
But, I wish I had two
You see this fatherless child
was created through you.

Linda L. Nunnally

Love Endures Forever

There is no way out, He cried to Me, within this pit of black.
I try and try to upward climb, to nevermore go back,
I look inside my own dark self, to see what hides inside.
I don't like what I see, the pain just won't subside.

My child, I said, just look at Me. I know what's hurting you.
And if you trust, I tell you, just what you need to do.
I've been with you all through this hell. I won't let you down.
Just look to Me, not what you see, to know just what you've found.

I'll give you love so precious, no one can take it away.
I'll give you clothes so beautiful, as Heaven in all its array.
I'll give you food so tasty, you'll always be satisfied.
You'll find my clothes, food, and love will make you sanctified.

Lord, if you can to all that, my life to you I give.
If You can help me from this pit, and show how to live,
Humbly Lord, I thank you. I believe you'll help me cope
Because I know within my heart, with You, there's always hope.
His love endures forever.

Brian J. Polley

Headtrippin'

My devotion is as deep as the ocean
In love I'm a giver as sweet as the river
When other gals dole out the ice
I serve up portions of paradise
I am woman
I am love

Eileen Worthy

Wedding Day Gifts

The road you have chosen will not be easy by far,
But you'll shine through like the brightest star.

The Precious relationship, the two of you share,
Is something so beautiful, something so rare.

The talks that you'll have, the laughter, the tears,
Are all part of life, and your future years.

With each day that passes your love will grow,
Just as the soft breeze will sing, and the
harsh winds blow.

The pledge to each other spoken today from the heart,
Now binds you together——You shall never part.

God has brought you together and blessed you today,
With family and friends from so far away.

And a wedding gift——I bring to give.
The Like, Love and Friendship one needs to live.

Mary Maglish

A Sea of Music

I sit down to the piano, ready to play,
Play just for me, no force, no other way.
I play for the music, the emotions, the feeling,
Much better than any chatting, talking, or squealing.
Music, I play, reaches deep inside the soul,
Mixing the emotions like a giant salad bowl.
I play of anger, frustration, and sorrow,
I play of love and the hope for a happier tomorrow.
My favorite thing to do, as you can see,
Is to create a sea of music so touching, so free.
To me, music tells a story, a wonderful tale,
More exciting than any handsome, young male.
The music reaches to people, whose spirit cries,
Seeks out the unhappiness and little white lies.
It soothes, it comforts, those of all age,
It tells you amazing things like a wise, old sage.
Thus, you can understand why I love it so,
Why I'd rather play music than read, talk, or sew.

Grace Lin

New Millennium

From horse and camel travel—to cars and planes
From paper information—to network games
From black and white boarder—to the equality lane
From total annihilation—to six billion names

We have made it, we have made it—through the millennium
We have made it, we have made it—to the new millennium

Two world wars—atomic nuclear bombs
Religion, communism—now the capital thrown
Deep sea wonders—exploring outer zones
DNA decoding—growing human bones

We have made it, we have made it—through the millennium
We have made it, we have made it—to the new millennium

We'll take the best of history
Get rid of things that cause misery
Make peace a part of our chemistry
In this new millennium, we'll solve most mysteries

Jacob Joseph Muntazar

clusters

all these roses together, made from nature's hand,
have a powerful bond between a woman and a man.
for it is a perfect love, a perfect dream come true,
that these roses formed this cluster to show my love for you.
and as these pretty flowers wilt and fall away,
our love will always flourish to bloom another day.

harold medford

'Til Death Do Us Part

Dedicated to my husband on our wedding day

Sometimes it's hard to believe, today we'll be man and wife.
I promise to you my love and commitment all of the days of my life.
I'll try my best to be patient and kind in all I do and say
May God grant me the gift of an unselfish
heart, to successfully guide my way
As we travel down life's road together, no
doubt they'll be mountains to climb
May we keep in mind to look to Our Father,
for in Him the strength we will find
The strength we will need to overcome all
obstacles unfortunately placed in our path
May we learn and grow in our faith and our love,
for that's what gives us the strength to last
Our life has been "perfectly planned" and
this day Our Father knew . . .
We were going to be joined as one, for He's
temporarily given me to you!

Michelle Lynne Middaugh

To Higher Ground

Days in the valley are numbered now.
Children playing in green grass,
Laughing from their bellies, soft, unguarded.
The smell of spring-wet earth,
The faint memory of a dog barking.
I am preparing for the rocky trail upward,
Leaving behind the morning mists
For crystal air cracking against rock surface
To see you on your life journeys.
Sometimes I will smile, sometimes rejoice.
And I know that sometimes I will weep,
Carrying the memory of who you were, once.
You, from the seed of my valley,
Your stories, yet to unfold, not by my design.
I head for high country above the timberline.
And now I make myself light,
Climbing higher than the alpine flowers
To higher ground that meets the night—

Linda Friehling

The Shadows Dance

He comes to her cloaked in his velvet armor
of darkness. He asks of her to show him the
light that he seeks. She smiles, a sad sweet
smile, at his request for she knows the Dance
of Shadows will soon commence. Slowly does
Light open her arms and beckons Darkness to
come. As Darkness moves across the abyss,
the Shadows begin to dance. He stops
hovering over the abyss; for now the Shadows
Dance within. He screams and rages within
himself; for the light is changing his
darkness. He tears at Light, trying to
destroy and run from the Shadows. Light
stands silent with Shadows tears running upon
her skin. For all Light can do, is watch as
the Shadows Dance unfolds. She waits with
arms open for light and dark to embrace and
to become the Rainbow Colors of Emergence.

Kathryn A. Menard

Morning Dove

A mourning dove sang in the morning,
Strongly, softly, with sounds full of joy!
It was just as the day finished dawning.

In the morning, the morning dove saw me.
We were friends! He gave his song blessing!
Then his feathers flew over a tree.

Annie Lloyd Condit

Early Morning Rainstorm

Lightning stabs through the fabric
of early morning darkness,
probing around curtain edges,
casting fleeting scenes of surreal shadows
on the south bedroom wall,
followed quickly by the deafening crash of thunder.

Then rain, at first a gentle patter,
then rushing, gushing to a torrent
that seems it's right outside my door.

Awakened, reluctantly, from the depths of
peaceful sleep, I throw back the blankets.
I must check to see if all the
windows are closed against the deluge.

The cool, damp air against my sleep-warm body
causes goose bumps as I hurry, checking,
closing, to keep us safe from nature's
early morning onslaught.

Janie M. Hubbell

To Our Sweet, Lovable Damian

We are all in such horrid despair!
Mommy, Grandma, and Grandpa think life is so unfair.
The state took away our baby boy.
He will be one year old on December 31st, 2000.
Mommy and I made a mistake!
We now have been condemned by the state.
We are all missing you.
The world doesn't know how much we love you,
Right down to our souls.
Our home is so empty without you.
These days there isn't much to smile about.
Our hearts have been bound with a very thick chain.
I wish the world could feel our pain.
Help us, dear Lord. Ease our pain!
We need to love once again.
With all our love, sweet Damian.
Hugs and kisses,
Mommy, Grandma Tina, and Grandpa Mike.

Tina Marie Tessier

Soul Road

Bring me an ounce of your finest emotions,
And I'll show you,
Show you something,
Maybe nothing.

Just assure me of your life.
Its offerings—
(Contributions from the soul that you
alone have created among the billions.)

And to say that you have satisfied me,
I hope not.

My quest should not end with you,
Only alone.
To derive what drives me,
Madness may soon follow.

To what end?
To the end of what?

Jeff Martin

Grandmas

Grandmas are someone special indeed.
They always help us when we are in need.
When we are sad, or when we are blue,
they always know just what to do.
Whether they bake us some cookies or give us a hug,
they always find a way to show us their love.

Maranda Mareen Bond

Grandma

Dedicated to my Grandma Joyce

I dream upon this star I see, and
all I see is a picture of you and me.
Holding each other so close and sweet,
wishing how true this fantasy could be.
Oh, how I see your face in the sky,
and all I see is you tonight.
Grandma, I want to be with you today in peace,
but all I can do is wait for my time
and meet all my needs.
Seeing you in pictures of mine can only
repeat memories in time.
How I wish these memories would come true,
but all I remember is sitting on your lap.
At times, I see your face in my dreams,
and saying, "Man, I shouldn't have pulled that mistake."
One day, Grandma, you'll see me by your side,
and sharing with you days that go by.

Amanda O'Dell

Bitterness

Teachers—
Who are they
Are they human
Can they feel
Or are they merely machines
Programmed to do one task
I am bitter
Teachers have no feelings
They have no time to spend with one student
Some give no hope, but plenty of despair
If you flunk,
It's your fault, they have no shame
I am bitter
I try my hardest to succeed
In may cases I am victorious
But there are those classes I do hate
I do my best and hope to pass
I am bitter

David John Schwarz

Birth—Life—Death

The light pours in from all around,
For a great new sense of reality has been found.
The sphere of thought is new and fresh,
And is covered with a new flesh.
It takes in all it sees and hears,
Spawning fetishes hates and fears.
Love and agony fill a tremendous space,
Leaving the sphere of thought open to deface.
Goods and bads are frequent along the way,
That which is unpleasant, that which is play.
Sins tear at the fabric of tranquility,
Leaving the sphere of thought all but free.
Followed by decay and remorse,
As the long road becomes quite coarse.
The realization of sorrow and emptiness start to come,
And a curiosity about what it has all become.
The dark creeps in from all around,
For eternal silence and dormancy have been found.

Ben Lee Heintz

Christmas

It is here it is here, Christmas it's right
Under the tree.
Ho, ho, ho, he is on his way
So you better watch out because he will shout
So go, go, go, to sleep my little dear
And you will hear the cry of Old St. Nick.

Alexia Bailey

Someone Else's

She touched me in Times New Roman font
heartfelt letter to someone else
no poem, no schemes, straight-up raw feelings
in size ten letters from margin to margin
the lump of mixed emotions started to outgrow
my throat, tears held back, clouding my mind,
flooded my being and made me flushed—words
hitting hard and sticking, knowing my feelings
will never see daylight, only time to heal this pain.
As she approached the end of one very long page,
I swallowed my rock, breathed, forced a
yawn to hide my tears and somehow willed away
my excess red just in time to see her look up
for my approval. AND I LIED . . .
"That's pretty good; I think he'll
appreciate that you're being straightforward with him. . . . "

Matt C. Levine

Autumn's Angel

In a lifetime, in this world
Where there is crime, pain and hurt,
People have to have something to believe in.
I believe in beautiful angels.
In a lifetime in this world,
I've met an angel on a warm autumn day.
He had a broken wing.
I ached for his fate.
In a lifetime, in this world,
I took care of his broken wing;
He took care of my broken heart.
In a lifetime, in this world,
Winter was coming, it was getting cold,
the trees were losing their leaves.
I had to let him go, he must leave
In a lifetime, in this world.
I believe I've met my beautiful angel
On one blissful autumn day.

Jenny Jeannot

Where I Live

I live in the city of Uncertainty,
In the land of Not-Knowing,
On the continent of Indeterminate Time.
I have breast cancer!

The leaves lie brown and yellow at my feet.
Slowly I trudge through them, keeping the beat:

I live in the city of Uncertainty,
In the land of Not-Knowing,
On the continent of Indeterminate Time.
Will I see another fall?

Gold leaves shimmer overhead in the sun.
Oh, is this autumn my very last one?

I live in the city of Uncertainty,
In the land of Not-Knowing,
On the continent of Indeterminate Time.
I have breast cancer!

Laura June Kenny

God's Gifts to Me

P: is for the precious gift that God has given us
E: is for the everlasting love
O: is for others and what they give to us
P: is for prayers that God has answered
L: is for the love he sends us with the people who are friends
E: is for eternity with God and his gifts to me

Doreen Linder

Castle by the Sea

Old castle by the sea,
Wicked kings and queens were not meant to be.
Stay they way you are,
And I will be amazed by far.
I will put aside my fear,
I keep on standing here.
I hold the golden sand
In the palm of my hand.
As I remember long ago,
The windows inside would glow.
But then one night,
You gave me a fright.
And as the glowing died out,
I gave a loud shout.
I walked away,
For I felt astray.
Old castle by the sea,
I guess this was meant to be.

Rachel Bosworth

The Puppet

The puppet sitting in his chair, just as his master
Put him there, says not a word, makes not a face; he only
Sits there in his place. His lips are red, his
Cheeks are pink, but there's more to him than most would
Think. He lifts the heavy weight of age as he laughs and
Plays upon the stage. Silencing the cares of life, he'll
Free you of your pain and strife . . . replacing each with
Happiness—a simple love, as one might guess—the love
That's found in children's eyes as they're taken by
Surprise. And in this puppet soon you'll see he's much
The same as you and me; this love that's placed within
Each heart, that I'm expressing in my art, is the string
Attached to live each day as we learn our role in this
Big play. Our character's carved one piece at a time
While we merely try to keep in line, and acting out our
Hopes and fears, through the glare of smiling tears, we
Wait patiently for our puppeteer, just as our Master put
Us here.

Jillian Anderson

Where I Am

I used to know who I was and what I loved
to do. Then I met someone who I thought I
Loved and thought he Loved me too.

We had a child then got divorced. After
that the child was my life as I thought
it was supposed to be. Now I'm lost within
his life and there is no longer a me.
I'm told to do things I used to Love to do.

I no longer know who I am or how to find
out what happened to me.

I Love my son with all my heart! Yet along
the way I forgot to still be me. Now I don't
know who I was or where I am supposed to be.

I have my son and all his Love just as he has mine.
Maybe I don't need to know where I am,
For I am where I am supposed to be!

Kathleen Diamond

An Ode to the Old

Every day when I awake
My torso has another ache
Even though I have some pain
I never ever do complain
I am grateful for this life I live
It's better than the alternative
So you see no need complaining
Just be glad you are still remaining
Life's greatest gift is in reaching old age
And having the wisdom to keep turning the page
These days that remain need not be of sorrow
If you only remember to have a pleasant tomorrow
So live to the fullest, and cease your worries
You will never see your name in the obituaries

Frank Branca

Immortality of Transcending Beauty

A bright morning out of nowhere
quickly touches upon the shadows,
bending my will as a weed in the wind.
Let my heart escape out of emptiness.
Let forgotten yesterday sink into a crevice,
while today enraptures my tormented soul.
The seeds of tomorrow fall upon an empty womb
of earth forever struggling to become. . . .
Let love come out of a loveless world,
into an innocent heart of a new born child,
And beauty erupt out of passive nothing
into a bursting force of sparkling sun,
Then let intense ugliness become a desperate part
of the wonderment of art and surpass all else.

Dorothy Blasius

The Light of Angels

Why do we speak so, of angels, more openly in these days
Is there a sense of knowing, or just an "Angel craze"
Are there some thoughts that seize us, tight in a grip of fear
Can it be love that relieves us, (bringing our angels near?)

Now, in dark days of peril, when everything seems to fail
Angels appear, to protect us—bearing the "Holy Grail"
Let not hate be our burden (hearts can be lightened with love)
Loosen the chains that bind you—look to the promise, above

There is a hope for redemption, new paths are shown, every day
Humans have guidance, to aid them, always, whenever they pray
Earth lies so closely, to Heaven, death's but an open door
Beckoning to light and to glory, with angels, angels, galore!

A. C. Hart

Forever and a Day

The day has come for us to say our vows,
You look so beautiful; I think I'll forget how.
Our parents are crying, you finally say, "I do,"
No one must realize how much I love you.
Our families are joined; I can't find the words to say,
But I promise our love will last forever and a day.
Our parents are filled with an abundance of joy,
They know we are expecting a girl or a boy.
Time has passed quickly labor is near,
You look into my eyes and have nothing to fear.
The baby is born healthy and okay,
Just like our love that lasts forever and a day.
The kids are all grown and moved on with their life,
And our love grows stronger each day you're my wife.
I know we have been one from the very start,
One mind, one soul, one body, one heart.
I think of the day when one of us cannot stay,
And I comfort in knowing our love still lasts forever and a day.

Christopher Michael Sneed

What a Father Is to Me

A Father to me is the answer!
To everything I need to know.
For I am the seed of my Father,
and on this earth I'll grow.
Until I go home from which I came,
for it's my Father and I that send the rain.
The water of life will always be!
Bringing life to you and me,
for in my Father's house, I am free.
To look upon the earth,
to watch the growing of my seed!
From your heart you should understand,
this is the Father of Glory and His divine plan.

John Henry Wright

I Was but Now

I was a prisoner, a captive, a slave,
But now I am free, unhurt and unscathed.

I was wandering, hopelessly lost,
But now I am found for He paid the cost.

I was in bondage to the sin that I bore,
But now I am unchained, in shackles no more.

I was in darkness, unable to see,
But now I have sight, to see other's needs.

I was alone, with no friend to call mine,
But now I have Jesus and a friendship divine.

I was a sinner, with no conscience, no care,
But now, by believing, I have faith to share.

Kim Fields

(Add on to "Thank You") Only You

You've showed me time after time that you'd
stick by me to the end. You've promised the
world to me and gone out of your way to get
a silver platter to put it on. Thank you for
keeping your promises and sticking with me.
You stood next to me and took my hand to
lead me through the dark and I thank God
that you still do that today. We have
laughed in the past and we're still laughing
today. You listen to my problems and offer
your advice. I wish I had more to offer then
my love and thanks. You say my smile is
enough, so I guess I better stop shedding
tears of memories and start smiling my thanks!

Caitlyn M. Jones

Promises

Too many tomorrows have come and gone,
Too many promises broken.
Too many harsh words uttered, words that
should have remained unspoken.
How much time is left to right all the
wrongs we have done?
If we would just think before we speak and
smile instead of frown,
The world would seem more cheerful and
pleasant for all of the people around.
One kind word is all it takes to cheer
someone that is blue.
That isn't too much to ask from someone like
me or you!
Next time you encounter someone with a
nasty look on their face,
Just smile or grin and say, "Hi" and watch
a miracle take place.

Mae Noreen Rosensteel

Does Darkness Consume All?

We are lost in a world of despair,
a kingdom of darkness
but does any one care?

Darkness consumes our every thought
it dwells deep within us,
but are we caught?

There's a light at the end of the tunnel,
but very few choose to follow.
Are we caught up in the devil's funnel?

Can we get out?
With God . . .
there is no doubt.

Stephanie O'Quinn

To the One I Love

The look in yours eyes is like fire
You smile like the sun lighting up the room
I love you for your beauty and mind
Your personality is loving and caring
You never look down; You always smile
You seem as if sadness does not exist
You care for all who are sad and down
You light up there day with happiness
You are the angel of grace
The one people will remember for your smile
I love you for your qualities of love
I love you for who you are
You are perfect in every one way
Not one thing could change my love for you

Dustin Lee Gwin

Love

Love, can it really be explained
in words like a teacher to a student
explaining a lesson?
No, I think not.
Love, can it really be shown,
like a movie in a theater?
Yes, through all its acts and actions
it will be put together,
not to explain
but to show and allow an individual
to interpret the feeling,
and after the interpretation is complete,
the heart would either turn cold or weak.

Heriberto Torres

The Voice

My mission, to make this place better
My mission won't help to write a letter
One voice won't make a difference
One voice speaks, no one listens
Where is the freedom in our land
It was never here no one can understand
Teens are harassed, when they're outside
The police's job, is to take their pride
Nobody sees a problem of this sort
By the age of 18 you've already been in court
Criminals are what they're labeled as
So who pointed their finger, society has
Who can make a difference, society itself
It takes more than a handful to get some help
Most towns are dull, so they have no choice
But get into trouble, no one hears their voice
My mission, to create this voice
My mission, make them see the right choice

Davin P. Norgoal

The Beautiness of Life

As the water flows gently down the stream,
the sun brightly beams down on the grass
that is, oh, so green!
No one can resist this wonderful feeling.
There's always blue skies, birds chirping too,
there's nothing better then life coming down to you.

Brent William Gallaugher

Fear Not

In God's strength we can survive
Keeping our bodies healthy and alive.
Nutritious foods, good exercise
What it does for you is no surprise.

Cancer, blood pressure and diabetes
Will keep you in prayer on your knees
We fear them less, we know them best
But we consider multiple sclerosis a new contest

What is to be is going to be;
To be happy and healthy is precious to me.
So eat right, exercise much
Keep in touch with reality as such.

Your life can be long, it can be sure.
Think healthy and keep your mind pure
God granted us three score and ten.
Fight the odds so you can win.

Margaret E. Snorten

Channeling Nature

The nature of things.
It starts from an urge, an animal calling.
It becomes.
It evolves.
It moves inside into a man-made world. It becomes a dance.
Curtsy and smile. Take a hold and spinning raw.
It becomes.
It evolves outside back to earth. Calling
somewhere from the ground, the eternal want.
Animal instinct.
Prowling.
Lusting for love.
Romance is of man. Love is of mother. Mother Nature.
The dance ends. Breathing hard. You're enthralled.
The chase is on. You must have.
You must hunt and have.
It evolves. It becomes.
It's the nature of things.

Skarlett Lee Davolt

Dreams of Home

Misery, despair, and hopelessness
 are my friends now.
Happiness I know no more.
Distant visions of the South and
 my home in the mountains constantly on my mind.
No good-byes to the loved that
 has now passed on.

Weeping—I am ever weeping
 for my home so far away.

May I see my beloved
 Arkansas before I go to
 my grave?
If not, I will accept my loss
 of family and home.
But
 I then will know I'm finally home
 in my Beloved Arkansas.

Tamara J. Hansen

"33"

Teacher Goose tells Piglet: "Please
Write on the board your 33's."

Piglet went, but stood stock still.
"Ready then? Write what you will."

Poor Piglet stood there feeling his worst,
"I just don't know which 3 goes first."

Ferit Lamaj

Listen with Your Heart

When you listen to a friend,
What do you hear or feel deep within?

The mouth may speak words of
joy, but deep inside, the soul employs
the feelings of pain, desperation, of fear.
Listen real close—What do you really hear?

Listen with your heart, you'll feel
every word—Emotions or sadness, even if
they never speak a word!

It's amazing the power we have
within—Just listen with your heart—
This is where it begins.

Sharing and caring, results in
healing of pain—Be there for one
another, and always teach others the same.

Linda D. Calhoun

A Thousand Monks

He was walking at vespers.
Surely it was vespers, he could hear the intonation of the tenors.
He had been pruning the pyrocanthus . . .
branches lay snarled about his feet like horns
snatched just now from heads of devils.
It seemed all calumnies were piled there . . .
forked thoughts howling, tongues lapping at his habit.
Lord, who had devised this lattice?
Oh, yes, he was now pacing vespers,
hoping against vain hope the distraction of dusk,
with its vague sedona hues obscuring day,
might dispel the brambles setting snares.
Oh, what density of sin?
Look! Not one moth stirs, and ivy trembles yet on stone.
Sadly, nightfall harbors no Gilead's balm.
Alas, psalms hang in tender niches on sullen air.
Hurry. Rush toward the sound. To safety hasten. . . .
Hie thee to the brethren.

Rev. Dorothy-Yorke Alloway, Ph. D.

Life or Death

Life is Death in its fullest form.
Live it to death, until you're reborn.

Life is but once
And we should rejoice;
But everyone goes with choice after choice.

Just do what you feel,
As Life may be Death.
It can be taken away with only one breath.
Is that Life or is that Death?

Who knows and who cares?
We only know One.
We think it is Life,
And that's what we've done.

But what if our Life was not full of fun?
We've messed up our Life
And Death has won.

P. R. Smith-Taylor

Born Again

Born again, he endeavored me to live for him,
so he could set me free from within.

Through him, I manifest his works and place a
set of concrete morals with my words.

I've unfolded before his very eyes and live, a
new born babe, thrust out of sight,
he's forgotten my rotten past and clothed me anew
with rays of light within my path.

Christina Y. Acevedo

In Your Eyes

With you,
my life could go on for eternity. For your
luster and beauty would have me caress the
wings of time, and dare to defy all the rules
that have been placed before me.
In your eyes,
I will stare and be held captive for all to
see.
In your hair,
I will play and fondle for the years to come.
For my heart,
who has never been tempted to love as easily,
before the glorious sight of you.
For my mind,
who never thought that I would ever have a
chance with someone as beautiful as you.

David Gautier

Tell Me You Love Me

Tell me you love me, show me just how much you care,
A loving hug, a soft caress, fingers lightly stroking my hair.
Your nearness to my being will always be in my dreams,
Our love will last forever, an eternity it seems.
Tell me you love me, we'll seal it with a kiss.
I never knew your love could make me feel like this.
And when I hold you close to me, my heart beats very fast,
Making a loving rhythm that unites us both at last.
Tell me you love me, with your very heart and soul,
A lifetime together will be our one and only goal.
If love becomes eternal, then ours will never end,
A gift from the Lord in Heaven, a wonderful Godsend!
We share the gift of love, it's ours to freely give
We pledge our life together, as long as we both live.
Our hearts are overflowing, our love will always be
As endless as an ocean, as lasting as a sea.

Charles R. Swain

Loveliness in Bloom

A rose is but another name for loveliness in bloom
Its fragrance fills the air as it swirls around the room
No other flower that I know of is given so much grace
For no matter where you see a rose it's never out of place

I've seen it grace the fancy rooms in palaces of Kings
Often it shares the pillow that carries wedding rings
It has caressed the headboard of a little baby's bed
Could be that it's placed there to frame a tiny head.

But no matter where you view a rose it sets the mind in motion
Its petals have been used to make a soft and silky lotion
Some people throw its petals along a winding lane
Others grow some roses 'round a cottage window pane

I like to see the roses in a lovely flower bed
In yellow, pink, and orange, and also, the deep red
Its fragrance can be carried by a gentle blowing breeze
It circles 'round and fills the air, its fragrance sure to please.

Katie Lazette

O. C. D.

i met this guy once
he suffered from obsessive compulsive disorder
he described it to me
as being similar to the times
when you find yourself
reading the same sentence over and over again
the same sentence over and ov
reading the same sentence over and over
ag again

Gina L. Sweet

Love Spit Lust

Shut me up and bury me under,
The life I had known has all gone asunder.
Pierce my heart so I may bleed,
To purge all but the e'erlasting seed.
I want to show you all that I am,
So easier it may be to take hold of your hand.
However, the mazed fortress which I have built,
Leads to nothing but our guilt.

I wish you wanted to come inside;
You'll see I've nothing left to hide.
My sin and shame: All's bore on the cross;
This will not be my final loss. . . .
If what you want is nothing more,
Please say goodbye and shut the door.

Here I am—alone again,
Adoring you . . . my only sin.

William Michael Moring

A Simple Plea

Soft tears fall silently through the night,
Fading quietly into the past,
Emotions rendered to the dark,
Deep scars that ever last.

As rest descends on tired eyes,
My heavy heart too sleeps,
But restless dreams no peace allow
And into my soul they seep.

Awake with sadness in my heart,
I turn to see your face,
A smile, a wink, and "I love you,"
The doubts and fears to erase.

But still the sorrow hides within,
Suppressed for one more day,
Rescue me, I ask of you, please
Make it go away.

Valerie Kay Grisham

Each Morning and Evening

Each morning when I awake, I strive to see
what I can give to this world
rather than to see what I can take.
Giving is a bit harder to do,
but you always feel better after
you've tried after you're through.
I take each day as it comes, then
I try always to make it better
right down to the letter.
After I've finished my day, I reflect.
What could I have done differently to gain
someone's respect?
With this I think when this chapter
of my life is over,
will I have done all that I can do
to have left this world a better place
for the whole human race.

Thomas Allen Warner

After Life

Death is like a crash.
You don't think, you just react.
The world, with all the people in it is
Like a fantasy, a daze.
After a while, it just seems natural to be sad.
You yearn to remember
the past conversations and feelings
Regrets don't even faze me;
All you have left is memories.

Laura Stiverson

Hold You

Your love was my comfort
It was my sun that rose when I saw you
My heart and soul was lifted by your voice
Now every moment I spend
Is spent watching your eyes
Hoping one day you'll lay them on me again
But I fear
A breath will be smothered by your kiss
And I will crumble in your palms.
In time I know those wings will molt
And you will no longer appear an angel to me
But now is not that time
For your kisses have burned imprints on my heart
That will only heal if I could hold you
For one minute
And then
I could let go

Stephanie Kearley

If I Could . . . Just To . . .

If I could die a thousand painful deaths,
and somehow come back
as a person who could love only one,
I'd do it just for you.
If I could live a life that's not cursed
by self indulgence,
then by all means,
I would, just for you.
If I could make you happy, by loving you,
I'd give my life to see that day happen
and totally submit myself at your feet.
Just to see that beautiful smile on your face,
Just to see your eyes light up at my presence.
Just to feel your "I love you's"
when my lips touch yours.
Just to make you content with me.
With life. With us. With . . . Everything.

Jonquille Marie Rice

aspects of self

a loud youngster who loves to be wild
a softly crying wounded child
the shy one who's always meek and mild
she only shows once in a while

a loyal friend who will not smother
a nurturing caring emotional mother
the wildly vibrant passionate lover
she is stronger than the others

a philosopher who thinks every hour
a small voice who'd love to have power
the firmly built tall strong tower
she always causes others to cower

a humorous joker who loves the attention
a keen observer of things you don't mention
the artistic lover of life with moral intention
she alone is God's invention

Rebecca Cribb

Ice Maiden's Call

She looks at me with her distraught eyes,
in pain, and tears of shards of ice,
to wander and breach the memories
of hurt and loss and enemies,
I hear her call, I watch her sleep,
her smiley gaze, her saddened weep,
alone again, a whisper cold
of ice and tears that pave glass floors,
and slip under my feet as I fall. . . .

Philippa J Adamson

My Love and Hope Are Fading

Oh, sweet music set me free,
I pray that thou shall not banish me.
For if thou shall banish me
how can I live in silence without thee?

Oh, sweet music dance for me,
do not banish me
do not leave me
stay with me,
until thou sets me free.

For I am lost in despair,
how dare thou forget my soul
to leave me all alone in sorrow.

Now no soul can compare to my sorrow,
Because of thee my soul is lost without hope,
Oh, sweet music listen to me,
and set me free from all despair and sorrow.

Melissa Lee Smith

Searching No More

Deep in my heart there was a hole.
I tried everything but it still would not close.
I 'd pray every night to fulfill this dream.
But something went wrong; that's what it seems.
I searched and searched 'til I could no more.
I threw up my hands and gave it to the Lord.
I learned a lesson that I'd like to teach,
but I'm not the kind to lecture or preach.
Life is like an ocean of time with every
droplet of water representing the precious
seconds that go by.
So I treasure each drink or sip that is given to me
'cause I know not when my ocean will run dry.
Surely enough my hole is filled,
but only because of God's great will.
Deep in my heart I'll always believe,
if you ask God you will receive!

Ashley Cole

Said a Prayer for You

I said a little prayer today
Hoping for you, no "gray" day
Wishing you the best in all
Everything big and small

Wishing God will be by you, all the time
And letting your goodness shine
To be there to protect you
In whatever you may do

Didn't ask for wealth or fame
Just to make you win life's game
. . . I knew you wouldn't mind
As I asked for something of a more lasting kind

To be by you, with you, beside you
Is what I asked God to do
To make sure you don't endure a single day that's blue
All this I asked for you. . . .

Bandhna Kaur Bajaj

Alone

Embracing a loved one while only embracing the soul.
No shell is there to hold.
Embracing his scent to only inhale the air;
I turn and no one is there.
The sky is spinning without reason;
loneliness hovers me.
I embrace myself only to wish for him to be near.
Darkness embraces me in silence.
Daddy's little girl.

Tammy Sanchez

What the Stars See

Staring at the stars as they stare at me
If they could what would they see
Death, Destruction and kids having kids
Women being beaten by the men they so love
Kids turned into junkies by the drugs given
To them by a friend they trust
Abortion taken lives before they are given
Divorce splitting families
As the torn pictures start to pile
Dreams shattered by the
Pull of a trigger
You can hear all the dreams
Shatter all at once
If this is what the stars see
They see it right
But only the strong survive
That's because they fight.

Jonathan David Flores

Angels Live among Us

Angels live among us, and walk, with us on earth.
Sometimes we do not notice, or realize their worth

Is it the one who shares your life; who lives with you each day?
The one who holds you close, and loves you in every way.

Was it the dad who fed you, and kissed you every night?
The one who held you in his arms, when nothing seemed to go right.

Was it the Mom who cared for you, and made that house a home?
The one who always loved you; no matter where you roamed.

Was it the child you rocked to sleep; that grew to be your friend?
The one you know will love you right up to the very end.

Yes angels walk among us, in our loved ones and our friends.
Or maybe it was that stranger, who so willing her hand did lend.

Who is that person beside you? Look close, if you will dare.
It may be you are looking at an angel unaware.

Mary E. Rogers

What Beginning?

In the beginning there was Adam and Eve
and as we went on there was a lot greed.
In the beginning there should be a star,
a moon a river and even a bar.
But in this beginning it's hard to say,
It's hard to see a world this way.
Imagine this no grass, trees or life,
we live on a ship out in the night.
Our Earth is gone we killed her so fast,
then we blast off into the vast.
Maybe to live in a bubble or some far off place.
We'd live in the space only some have seen.
Our homes would be small and maybe bright green.
Just imagine the new found life we might live . . .
But personally I'd just rather eat beautiful figs.
The figs and the fruit like Adam and Eve
May be us or we have just been deceived.

Allison Jensen

Have You Seen the Wind?

I ask you have you seen the wind?
Have you cast your eyes on the gentle breeze
That caresses the leaves of autumn trees
And bends the boughs that hold them firm?
In a windy waltz their trunks do sway.

I haven't seen the wind today;
The sun shone rays and seemed to stay,
How rich the scene in every way.
Have you seen the wind today?

Mykal Spencer McNee

A Special Thanks

Dedicated to the people of Desert Storm

A special thanks, to those who go
to bring the food, to those who know
of how it feels, to cry in pain
to see their mentors, being slain
A special thanks, to those who fight
the pain and sorrow, to make things right
for those who starve, and those who feed
to make them better, and cure the need
A special thanks, to those who feel
I give you courage, to help them heal
the pain they have, that lingers inside
I give you wisdom, for every stride
You are the reason, for them to live
the things you do, the way you give
I hope you strive, throughout the ranks
for I give you now . . . A Special Thanks

Daren Duane Gaut

Delight

Forbidden fruit,
raped and bruised
eaten upon the desires of he who ponders.
Small and docile,
kept and unkempt in the same breath.
Do not tarry, yet—go far away.
What do you mean by these words you say?
Better yet, what should I do?
Maybe I'll understand a diagram drew. . .
Kept on a shelf, taken out to play.
Oh, please do not handle me this way.
Bewildered and confused,
so maybe I could find better than you.
Call on me whenever you like,
try to remember I'm not a doll, all right?
Just another creature of delight
who cannot be held to what is wrong or right.

Shelley W. Wallace

From Day to Night and into a Dream

Your eyes shine like the summer's sun
beaming down to meet me.
So kiss me
under the shadows of the full moon glowing
brightly.

Tonight the breeze is flowing swiftly,
brushing against the bluebell trees.
As their sweet scent wafts around me,
their leaves start to rustle,
singing sweetly in the wind.

The night rolls on,
just you and I together in sweet harmony.
So let it be,
let us not spoil the peace.
So hush the words you urge to speak,
just let it be.

Fritha McKenzie

Only the Sacrifice

Secret symphonies not ready to be heard.
Eclectic static, so desolate and desperate.
Only with the emptiest of feelings . . .
Loneliest of notions, dispersed through aerosol.
Beautiful golden whispers.
Tangible thoughts longing for introduction.
Enchanted delight, so pleasing and sacred.
Harvesting anguish and maintaining only sorrow.
Only the sacrifice is saved.

James Andrew Barta

Lost

All the pleasure and all the pain
Was endured with no gain
As if all that kept us sane
Will be washed away with the coming rain
Love, life, and liberty will be faded
When will they see that we are jaded?
Those incompetent fools!
Can't they see that it is our own blood that pools?
Why has compassion on this Earth ceased to be
It's all because of that Biblical tree!
Because apples and snakes
Are all it takes
To damn this world to those fiery lakes
Now my life line is taut
As I realize that all for which we have fought
And all the destruction that we have wrought . . .
It was all for naught

Foster Nyles Smedley

Gift of Life

God gave me life
To give me a chance to understand
To fulfill His plan for me not the
Plans of man

Many days come that cause frustration
And despair; but I can always take it
To God in prayer

He will never fail me or leave me to
Endure more than I can bear: God hears
My tears when one by one they fall and
Wipes them away with His gentle hands
And catches me when I fall

I remember God through all times of strife

I remember God because He gave me the
Gift of life.

Patricia D. Johnson

God's Little Angels

Our smiles show the love we bring,
For this time of year,
To celebrate a baby
With a festive season's cheer.

His son's bright eyes sparkle with warmth
just like our eyes do,
We follow in his footsteps
We are God's children too!

From our head down to our wiggly toes,
with grins, and giggles full of bliss,
with tender cheeks for you to kiss;
We are God's present of youth and innocence!

We are God's little Angels,
Bringing you Christmas cheer,
Wishing you "Merry Christmas,"
And a "Happy New Year!"

Jennifer Ivy Peters

Painful Path

My eyes bleed from this pain I received,
Sacrifices are made to allow innocence to be freed.
Believe in a higher hope, faith is all you need,
Believe in me and not what you read.
Forget everyone you ever envied.
Within a world of so much greed, so much to be pitied,
Believe there's a better life, this is my creed.
So take heed, in which this wisdom I plead for.
I am lost, but on your path, good luck and Godspeed.

Darren J. Taylor

My Favorite Time of Year

The wind is blowing though my hair.
The leaves are flying everywhere.
The days grow short but I don't care.
It is my favorite time of year.

The air is crisp with the scent of fall.
The smoke is wafting from the chimney tall.
It is October after all.
And it's my favorite time of year.

The pumpkins with their candles bright.
The windows glowing with soft light.
The clouds are thick, oh, what a sight!
This, my favorite time of year.

I love the blustering, windy days.
I love the smoky, foggy haze
Of twilight with its frosty glaze
During my favorite time of year.

Pearl Nitsch

Humiliation

He has a name but no face.
Toward the feelings of others he give no space.
Everything is uncensored on His behalf
because He always get the last laugh.
Irritating the souls of the weak
to reach the goal for power at its peak.
Inside of Him lies a beast,
forever causing confusion that brings no peace.
To change or make peace is His right to choose,
although inside the weak He leaves an eternal bruise.
He makes the weak feel foolish and dumb,
making our hearts feel beatless and numb.
After the laughs are over, the weak is scorned
with feelings of wishing they weren't born.

His name is humiliation.
He doesn't know the meaning of love.
But He can only find out that it comes from above.

Felita McElroy

I Wonder Why?

As I lie in the grass at night and stare
at the bright beautiful moon I wonder, why?
Why did the Lord make something look so
beautiful and look so close, yet make it
so barren and put it so far away from me?
I stare at the stars and I wonder, why?
Why does the light look so bright
and so close, yet so far away?
I close my eyes and I wonder, why?
Why does the Lord make us feel so close to Him,
yet in our times of desperation He feels so far away?
Then I think to myself that if all of these
things I wonder about were different then
I would not get the chance to wonder.
I wonder why the Lord did that?
I wonder why I ask?
I wonder why?

William Robert Stoecker

My Husband

I married you with a conscience
of never-ending love.
Your spirit surrounds me with a peacefulness.
Our hearts are now intertwined as one.
Our thoughts hold us as individuals.
You have helped me become the person I am,
the woman I intend to be.
With your grace and wisdom, you help me
understand the world around me.

Melissa Passer

TIME

i wait in the shadows of my mind
i grow older waiting
i'm left behind
words can't express the way i feel
my heart still warm, his, cold as steel
what has happened with life as a whole
why, dear god, must i grow old
grace has nothing to do with years
i was robbed of that through all my tears
i'm lonely, it's hard, i've climbed so high
to have fallen so low, i was touching the sky
time doesn't heal like they say it will,
it pushes back memories that you can still feel
i will always love this man of this earth,
and i learned to love me, i've been here since birth
time will come soon and i'll touch the sky
am i alone? please, are you near by?

sonja williams

Losing You

Sitting here shivering, I don't know what to do. The air around me is Oh, so cold. I think about you and wish that you were still here to warm me up. Ever since that dreadful day when you left me, cold days have gotten colder, and lonely days have gotten lonelier. Oh, I'd give anything to have you back again. To hug you, to kiss you, to curl up in your arms and let the bad memories slip away. But no, there are no more kisses, no more hugs, no more arms to curl up in when things are going bad. There will be other loves in my life, but none as great as you. You meant something to me. Something real and you still do, but you don't see it. Have fun my love, have fun while I sit and cry.

Danielle Sarah Wyman

Death

Death it came, woe to the living
It robbed us of a precious life
It can come in the day, or the still of the night
Like a thief, it hits with all its might

Death is something we all must share
At times it seems it's all we can bear
Death can remove that precious body we see
However, it cannot take the memory

Morn for your loved one
shed a tear or two
Be glad that their suffering is through
Know that death isn't all that bad

As we remember our loved ones lost
We'll pick up the pieces and go on at all cost
One day we also shall go that way
Until then be thankful for every living day

Geneva Francis Austin

The Thought of You

I silently recalled a cherished moment,
My face drew a smile. . .
With a contented heart,
I sat motionless;
Remembering;
Emotions expressed without words;
Just responsive glances. . .
Our moments together to remain in our hearts,
For Always.

Terri L. Cook

My Lake

When silver wings spread across my lake
And air's so fresh each breath I take,
My head grows numb and heart takes flight,
As twilight gives away to night.

And as I shake in nature's clasp
My heart leaps up, my breath a gasp.
The glowing moon then spins its spell
'Tis much like Heaven and all is well.
Then comes the morn of sometimes mist.
Alas! My heart cannot resist.
I sit and watch and often stare.
A duck swims off to who knows where.

The wake a V on a mirror, a shine.
I know what I see is only mine.
The shining sun now casts its spell
'Tis much like Heaven and all is well.

Donna Wooden

Five

I can hear you whisper my name.
I can hear your breath caress my body.
I can hear your heart pound as I listen to you touch me.
I can sense the sound.
I can see your warm smile, watching me.
I can see your eyes,
seeping into mine like golden stars.
I can see myself with you.
I can smell your body.
I can smell the reason I fell in love with you.
I can smell your passion back.
I can taste your sweet lips.
I can taste the sweet thoughts melting in your mind.
I can feel you.
I can feel your soul,
I can feel you breath,
I can feel the pain you give.

Vanessa Kathleen Hagan

Unfulfilled

Reach out to me, Oh, enchanted evening.
Wrap me within your silken embrace.
Tantalize me with scents that entice.
Whisper, so softly, my name.

If only my heart were free of this bedazzlement,
unenamoured, entranced no more.
Able to cast off the fervid longing,
that has transformed my very soul.

I stand in silence, arms outstretched and ever beckoning.
Lay hold of me, envelop me within your twinkling veil.
A compassionate mingling, is all I require,
a fleeting endearment, or charitable caress.

Will you not relent your affection?
Or release me from the never ending infatuation that consumes?
Please, I beseech that you no longer deny me.
For can you not see how I languish for you?

Donna Cagle

Escape

To fly, Oh, how I wish that I could spread my
wings out to the sky;
to soar, to float, drifting weightless on the air;
soft and downy like a feather, sailing here, gliding there.
Though heavy foot be bound, tethered firmly to the ground;
My heart, light and free,
takes flight like gulls upon the sea.
And in dream-flight I shall go
to heights of freedom I have yet to know.

Reva Colclasure

New Love

The introduction of this day
brings leaps of heart
Fearing the feelings of baggage beckoning
Holding them back
hoping to become free of old pains
Setting the dial for the future
The words yet to be spoken
Joy begins to win
We have begun again

Fear is present in each move taken,
caressed by the hand of joy
Settle the fear with warm touches of emotion
Comfort sets in with all things unknown
The heart expresses, follow the stillness spirit has known
Love sets in
Love begins to win
We begin again

James Henry Beaton, III

Alone

You were loved, revered, wanted, breathed,
When you were whole.
Broken,
You are lonely, denied, less than full.
Goodbye is not new,
It's the single constant left.
Loving I don't know,
No one stayed to profess.
Alone,
Familiar and able to
Happen without resistance.
I sunk,
(At least one constant)
and you
Jumped, swimming
Shorebound and
Saved yourself.

Lindsey Foster

Life

Falling, falling leaves upon a ground so cold,
Falling, falling hearts upon a world so old,
Falling, falling memories of life's soiled clothes,
Falling, falling thoughts of life—of loss.

I think of Fall as cleansing time,
The old and dried up fall away, as leaves do,
But something clings to hearts easily broken,
Just like leaves—their thoughts unspoken.

There is a season for each of us,
A time of cleansing, a time of shedding,
A time of pruning, and then, of rest,
To sleep awhile, and then. . . .

As spring slowly rises from the cold,
The once pruned and rested heart
Brings forth a new, and sweeter song—
Then life again begins. . . .

Donna Mae Merrifield

Thirst

a tumbleweed rolls past
and because of my thirst, i pray

i happen upon dry, dusty bones
and because of my thirst, i pray

the sun beats down upon parched earth
and because of my thirst, i pray

because of my thirst of eternal life with you—
because of this thirst, i pray

Gary Salazar Gregorio

Fallen

Once I thought I was strong
A legate form of great magnitude
A standard from which I oft exhumed
Unbeknownst to the faltering stature within

Once I thought I was right
Of having a universal white grip on life
An entrenched theory of self-evolution
But soon gave way to a moist silhouette

Once I thought I was saved
Yet encompassed truth swayed tirelessly within
The changing winds would smite reason
If the bellows hadn't already been scathed

Once I thought I was heard
Gasping forth on prodded knees
For all benign whispers lest sight unsheathed
Have now but fallen into the river of dreams

Eric Eskelson

Love Sorrows

It's the feeling that you get inside
It's the person you place on the throne above
It's the one thing you sometimes want to hide
What I speak of is a thing called love

Oh, how is it that love can be
Something so sweet and yet something so tasteless
My trials with love have only left me
Feeling alone and very useless

It seems my heart cannot dare take
Another chance on love willingly
For fear of another harsh heart break
Do I dare risk my heart repeatedly

As the sun sets and night appears
My one bright star shines in the sky
And to that star I weep silent tears
Wondering why my love had to die

Jamiru Foday Bangura

Love

Love, love, when do you know if it's true?
Is it when you like me and I like you?
Love, love, is it worth all the pain?
Is its joy worth going insane?

People say friends are forever,
But lovers come and go,
But if that's so,
Then what's the point though.

In life, there are few things that last forever,
Is true love so? I wouldn't know.
I guess it's something we'll all have to find out over time,
When we're about 89 and running out of time.
Then we look at life's ups and downs,
And see who was there to help us get the rebounds.

Is true love out there and we just have to find it?
Or do we have to create it and bind it?

Ronique Wright

Seasons

Fall: When stately oaks bow low their heads
to shed their summer tresses.

Winter: When babbling brooks are bedded down
by icy blankets of snow.

Spring: When the sun beckons sleepy crocus
from their winter hibernation.

Summer: Lonely sand castles silhouetted
against the setting sun.

Camilla Ruth Priddy

Big Sister

Donna,
You were my Big Sister
I always looked up to you
You were the eldest and the most wise
You were my Big Sister
You led the way
You followed your heart and listened to your soul
I wanted to be just like you
You were my Big Sister
You shared with me and I with you
We fought and made up
We knew that's what sisters do
You were my Big Sister
Now you have taken the final path
To peace and love you have gone
But you remain always in my heart
You are my Big Sister

Mary Wilkins

Healing Smiles

M uscles are not working well,
U nable to use my hand, I tell.
L egs are weak and wobbly, too.
T ime to make them believe it's true.
I feel like it's happening to someone, not me,
P raying each day just to be free.
L ying awake at night wondering what to do,
E ach day waking to something new.

S ometimes I wonder how I found such good friends,
C aring and concerned, truly Godsends!
L ove around each corner I turn,
E veryone is there for me, I begin to learn.
R eflecting on my friends and family, too,
O nly if they knew the healing all their love will do.
S miles and hugs making me feel better, and so
I t's time to tell everyone so they will know
S omeone out there could use a smile, to help them go that extra mile!

Anne Bridget Enright

For Jesus I Would

Some say the risk is not worth taking,
I cannot explain why I would.
They say that I'm a martyr in the making,
but if they knew Him, they surely could.

Jesus has done so much for me.
He gave me peace I could not find.
He saved my soul and set me free.
A sinful past is all I left behind.

If persecution should affect me,
I would not turn away for anything.
I'd stay close to Jesus who loves me,
even though they strip me of everything.

My whole life I would sacrifice.
They can take all that I own.
Riches and gold may entice,
In Jesus all my faith I've sown.

Chesley Lynn Hogue

The Look of Joy

Don't look so sad, there are wonderful things all around.
The sound of the calming ocean,
the smile of a child.
The beauty of the trees,
the sound of your favorite song.
Don't look at the bad; there is so much beauty to see.
Think of your happy day, where joy is to see.
Take a deep breath, look deep within, you will see
Your smile and a kind word will make many glad.

Loraine Pratt

A Rose for You

Times like these, I wish could last forever
Just the two of us, alone and together
A moment from dreams, or just a passing glance
My feelings contented to be given that chance

An ear to listen, a shoulder to cry
A sharing of passion, a friend to rely
A touch, a smile, a time between two
My heart, my love and a rose for you

Feelings that show my love and admiration
Only to grow through your inspiration
Time spent together, forever a memory
Missing your smile, eternally within me

So give me a sign, show how you care
I will give you my heart, between us to share
So if we must part, my heart will be two
One beating for me and one, a rose for you

William Mickel

Motherhood

What do you come into knowing?
How are you trained or prepared?
You work months and years to perfect them,
The lives you begin, then share.

We knew you from our inception,
We loved and learned from the start.
The time we spent together growing
Was time you gave from your heart.

Looking now at our changing lives,
A miracle has shaped and grown.
The miracle of four people showing
And a love mother and daughters have known.

This birthday is a special occasion
We find as a reason to say:
Where would we be without you Mother, and
Thank you on your seventieth birthday.

Evelyn W. Still

Endless Cry

Within your body, a spirit lies through eternity
Love never dies
The constant throbbing of desire
The chronic waves take you higher
Collective feelings of one another end in travail
As life starts to smother
Your eyes are filled with certitude
your heart is full of pain
It is clearly assuring now,
your emotions are driving you insane
Painful screams fill the midnight air
People surround you,
but they just don't care
Sometimes it gets so hard
you wish you would die
but just remember this,
people are deaf to the endless cry

amber jorgensen

Soak

Madness is barreling through the rain
as rain barrels through tunnels underneath streets,
bending with curves and slapping the cold metal like it hurts;
water never changes, it borrows the shape
of anything it meets
and bleaches the pain from this troubled temple
when droplets fall to the thirsty ground,
bleeding forever into the sunken earth
until a reason why is found.

Michael Raymond Sarnacki

Acceptance

I know not what you desire
I fear that it's not me
Should I pursue in this attire
Or should I just leave it be

These emotions that I am having
You clearly don't share the same
I hope that I am not annoying
Because it's these feelings that are to blame

I wish to be accepted
Rather than turned away
I know that I have been rejected
But the feeling I have I can't betray

I strive for this acceptance
As an outcast I can't remain
I struggle to close the distance
In this endless journey I will sustain

Edwin Scott

The Brave Ones

I wish I could be faithful just like Nephi,
Alma, Ammon, Jacob and Moroni.
To live a most exemplary true life
And share the truth with all my faith and might.

What a peaceful mind I could obtain
If I could be more like them day by day
And learn with all my humble heart to say
Come unto Christ, then follow and obey.

The world could come against me with its pain,
But I would surely not withdraw nor faint.
Trials could be worse than I thought,
But I'd resist and I'd come out on top.

As I'm not yet like all of those Great Ones
I beg the Father in the Son's own name
To fight by my side each and every day
So, I may gain the strength to make me brave.

Rubia Fagundes

Election Time

Do you have a TV?
Then you know it's time,
Time for the election,
To choose the one in the light of lime.

The mud slinging will be over,
The name bashing ended.
If the winner keeps their promises,
Our country will be splendid.

Our nation will quickly move on and forget,
The drama and hype of this biggest elect.
If we all do our part and try each day,
We can improve ourselves in a positive way!

So live each day to fullest,
And try to positively touch another's life.
I hope whoever you wanted to win,
Is now the President and the First Wife!

Matt P. Neff

One Day

Girl, whoever you might be, or should I just let all women
Know on this Earth! Before I leave this
World I'll make one of you my one and only,
my bride, the one that will have it all!
My love, my world all of me!
Someone who will complete me!
Someday, someone who will bring a state of entirety to make
my life wholesome, perfect to fulfill, to accomplish
And conquer the biggest monogamy of all—marriage.

Dereck Rutherford

A Painted Poem

Father, a poem is like a painting, you start line by line.
All of a sudden it blossoms, and the sun begins to shine.

It's colorful, it's bright, it makes you feel alive.
You feel so good inside you, Dad, you feel you need to strive.

Further and further you go, you think you cannot stop.
Then finally you're toward the end, you are almost at the top.

Then, oh, no! Now what, I think I need a change.
This poem, this painting, is looking, sounding strange.

Dad, I know how you work that stress, how you wipe out that strain.
You feel that you have made it, when you are back on track again.

This art, this work, this labor, you feel you're tied in chains.
It's our life, our love and favor, not judged by monetary gains.

The work is done, it's finished, it's finally at rest.
You sit back and look at it. Father, you have done your very best.

Phillip C. Tremelling

Only Love Is Real

Speak to me of love, and I will say, only
love is real. Speak to me of patience, and
I will say, patience is the guardian of
love. Speak to me of humility, and I will
say, humility is the mother of love. Speak to
me of trust, and I will say, trust is the
path that leads to love. Speak to me of
integrity, and I will say integrity surrounds
love and keeps it whole. Speak to me of
kindness, and I will say kindness solicits
love. Speak to me of passion, and I will say
passion ignites love. Speak to me of the
soul, and I will say the soul drinks from
the chalice of love. Speak to me of Fear,
and I will say Fear builds walls and keeps
love from you. Speak to me of love, and I
and I will say Only Love Is Real.

Harley S. Duff

A Valentine's Day Poem

Today I celebrate our love
these roses, twelve, symbolic of

the bond between us, true and strong
together is where we belong

We've laughed and cried through joy and pain
danced in the sun, hid from the rain

We've shared our lives, our hearts and souls
and talked of dreams and reaching goals

So precious are the memories made
for nothing would I ever trade

those tender moments that we've shared
Leave me convinced our souls have paired

A touch, a kiss, a warm embrace
this world of ours, a loving place

Gardner Quinn Broadbent

Shadowland

Diamond mountains, tranquil streams,
Phantom images evoked in dreams.
Diaphanous waterfalls cascading,
Imagery that is hazy, yet haunting.
A kaleidoscope of scene and sound
No longer finite, no longer bound.
Ascending in dreams to ethereal heights
Softly, then thunderous, a fantasia played
by the shadowland nights.

Eva Bullock

Through the Eyes

The eyes are the window to the soul
or so I was always told
Through our eyes we see many things
a rose, a sunset, a blue bird sing
We see beauty when we open our eyes
but if we close them it passes us by
When we look through a child's eyes we see
the world is a wondrous place to be
In the eyes of a stranger you may seem
old, young, or most anything
But when they look into your eyes
what will they see
Your soul, your thoughts, your dreams
or maybe all three
So as you look out through your eyes
remember one thing
Life is too short to let it keep passing.

Donna Marie O'Neill

A Time to Accept

Two little arms, a smiling face,
A dream that once belonged,
Has gone away and left an empty place,
A part of you, a part of me, is gone.

A hurt so deep, the root unseen,
Leaves pain no words can tell.
A feeling strong, so much it means,
Each letter of emotion, the word of love it spells.

The unborn child we'll never see,
A future alone, once again.
Sorrow has come, to you, to me,
Only time will cure this pain.

Time to continue and accept this past,
But never will it be forgotten.
The love and memory of this child will last,
It's now time for the future to begin.

Lori Kutz West

Written in My Soul

The Earth, the moon, the sky sang your name, your eternal name
I searched myself for wisdom there in your arms
I felt lost surrender we searched ships of souls
Your poetry of life and death
Written in my soul
We enter the divine, we enter the light
Of our newborn child
We enter beyond place and time
Blessed by the gods, blessed by the grace ones
Engaged to eternity we enter death and life
We are ageless, sexless, we are one
Sailing into nowhere we chant with the higher skies
Floating the clouds we break the ties
We see the truth we see our spiritual bond
We are soul mates forever
I love you forever
Written in my soul

Abir Lillman

One Thousand Dollar Poem

I'm writing this poem, which I'm hoping to win,
So that I can go to New York, just to meet Mr. Williams.
I thank Mr. Williams for the response and autographed pictured,
And if by chance, I happen to win,
I will be one thousand dollars richer.
I'm trying my best to get this poem won,
Because, I truly believe it will be one great day of fun.
If, in any case I shall fail,
I will be sure not to tell.

Diane L. Smith

Somewhere in Time

Somewhere in Time
I knew I would find
The love of my life;
Who's heart I'd hold in mine.
Somewhere in Time; I believed you would come
I dreamed of you often, if only in my mind.
Somewhere in Time
Seemed so out of reach
But, I always had faith
For my Heavenly Father did teach.
Somewhere in Time
Grew closer each day,
When a Mother and friend
led us the way.
Somewhere in Time
came and went like a dream,
And with the lords blessing holds our love in its beam.

Julie E. Smith

For the Love of a Caring Mom

She was so sweet, my dear mom,
Who struggled tirelessly to bring up her child
In a world fill with wrongs.
I felt her love, as she sang her songs,
Teaching me daily to forgive all wrongs.
She left me early; now I struggle along
With the memory of my loving, special, caring mom.
Forget her? I never will!
For she's helped me to forgive all ills.
None like her can ever be.
She was the most special mom in this world to me.
Still feeling the pains as the day she past away.
Now I go through life living it in her humble way.
Though death is a cheater, this is a truth I know.
He will lose this battle, for this is my vow.
Glad the day I'll be, when my loving mom I'll see.
Resting in the arms of sweet Jesus, my mom and me.

Roderick C. Clarke

Fall

Candy is like a tickle to the tongue!
A hay ride is like leaves that have sprung.
The scarecrow smiled as we went by.
The squirrels were eating pumpkin pie.

The fall fairs are a cyclone of yellow and brown.
The turkeys are singing and dancing around!
Fall is like the rain of leaves.
Now naked stands the trees.

Fireplaces are dancing with orange and yellow.
as the deer play football—what lucky fellows!
Fall is now upon us, I am told.
No wonder it's getting so doggone cold!

Thanksgiving day is here once more.
The turkeys are hiding behind the door.
Which one will it be?
Tom the turkey says, "I hope it's not me!"

Whitney Ann Walton

Untitled

I know a man who does all he can.
He makes me happy and loves me when I'm sad.
He gives me hugs, and kisses too.
He talks to me when I'm blue.
I love this man that can.
He loves to hold me when it rains.
He listens when I complain.
He gives me all his love and all of his self.
He doesn't put me on the shelf.

Toni Gere

I Always Wanted You

I always wanted you, I always believed
That the best gift of all I could only conceive

I thought about you and what you would be
Little did I know that God would only see

You grew in my stomach with heart beating wild
I only wished that I could've seen you smile

You were my second; another one passed
Why were you taken? So quickly, so fast

Now you're in Heaven to make everyone smile
I wish I could've held you for only a while

When I lie down in bed with tears in my eyes
I dry them right up and stop wondering why

God blessed me with life and a great family too
So now I am glad I can bless him with you

Brandy Fischbach

My Life

My body is turning to stone
He is leaving
I am grieving
How do I raise two babies alone?

Our vows have been broken
For eighteen years, I've been their mother
Yet the illness continues
I've not been just a token.

I'm almost blind and I walk like a drunk
yet we three have laughter
I will not let MS take my spunk.

Each day the sun comes up
I feel its kindness on my skin
No arms hold me
but the earth is my lover
as the smells of life drift in.

Linda L. Strohfus

A Wondrous Love

In thine eyes only beauty can appear

For thou holds in the palm of your hand,
My world,
For in my heart, if it were a mirror, would
Show a reflection of thee

Could it be my dream fulfilled?
Which each day in splendor to me,
Thou love is revealed

With each breath of love I take
Is upon my soul a blessing that is
So insurmountable that if caution be not
Advised,

I could lose myself in this,
For it to me is a wondrous love
That plunges my every being into true bliss. . . .

Lillian Louise Biagas

Tears

Blue raindrops fall down the sleek but frail porcelain,
The salinity represents the presence of something more than rain,
The tears that fall,
They eat away at the substance below.
The bitterness of the heart inside
envelopes the surrounding body.
Falling down I turn my worthless body to Christ.
I've let Him down,
So soon to fail Him once again.

Melissa Danielle Matticola

Drunk Driver

The night I got the phone call
I knew something was wrong
How can it be
You're not here with me?

I flew down the stairs
With my uncombed hair
Losing you was one of my biggest fears
No longer able to see through blinding tears.

They told me you were gone
Good grief this night has been long
I feel so alone
Beside you is where I belong.

Responsibility is the only cure
For this I am sure
Have a designated driver
If you want to be a survivor.

Torie Leigh Inman

My Gift to You

My gift to you, my friend of old,
would be kind words about your soul.

Lots of contentment to warm your heart,
and the dizzy feel when love first starts.

I would give to you the morning light
and the way the moon looks on a starry night.

The smell of Christmas to bring you home,
and the magic of winter to set the tone.

My gift to you would also bring
the blossoms of each early spring.

I would gather all the angels' wings
and fill your heart with peaceful things.

So my gift to you, my old friend,
Is the love for you that I always send.

Lisa Haley

Angels without Wings

When God created Earth and all surrounding things,
he created some angels . . . angels without wings.
The people that have been blessed with this magnificent chore
have made such a difference and so much more.
They walk the Earth each and every day,
touching so many people in so many ways.
It's easy to tell when you've met an angel on Earth;
almost everyone does, and it's usually at birth.
I know the facts of this poem to be true,
I've known since the beginning, the day I met you.
I've truly been lucky and I thank God above
for all your friendship and all your love.
If I should go before I'm old and gray,
I hope I've had a chance to say
a million times over, I LOVE YOU and I THANK YOU.
You are always there, my angel without wings.
With you by my side, I can conquer anything.

Jeff Eugene Cooper

Untitled . . .

Leaving what you think you hate,
Leaving what causes you pain . . .
When you are gone, does it leave too?
Does your pain leave you?
Or does it follow you each time you run?
In case you haven't noticed
You've left more than once,
So if you are running away from your pain,
It is chasing after you.

Carissa Ann Engel

Interlock

Glance into the painting, a story unfolds,
that of which is seldom told.
Look quick, think fast.
A story of the future preoccupied in the past.
They bloom into roses that will never wilt,
for it is kept in the sun.
It cannot see the twilight, for it does not yet grasp the horizon.
The mind sees the inside, but is blind; for it cannot see the out.
When all these work together, no one can defy.
This is a puzzle, it is not easy,
trust me, no lie.
One last piece I'll give to you.
The tomorrow meets the yesterday,
they feed each other connected as one.
Bound in such a way that they part.
Until you merge the two, stumped you'll be.
Wonder why, figure out, my friend, try.

Alexandra Ileana Demet

Why Is the World Going Crazy?

Why are mothers killing their babies
School shootings like Columbine
Why are there Oklahoma City Bombings?
Why so many evil minds?

Evil minds are ruling times
Tell me what your thinking?
Murder rage, front page, juvenile delinquents

Murders, burglaries, robberies, home invasions
Kidnapping, raping and child molestations

Television and Movies are clocking trillions
Feeding our Children Billions
of deadly doses of negativity
Viewers starting ages two and three

Violence in cartoons, doesn't have to be
For the love of money they care less about society

Tanya E. Whitfield

Pogo Love

Pogo love, it's just a game,
where people flirt to find a flame.
Relax, enjoy this could be fun,
who knows,
you might be the lucky one.
it happened to me, a few times see.
they all were worthwhile p's
I think they would say the same for me.
In pogo land there is lots of fun,
mostly for me I've found the one,
it's now more than a game to me,
'cause this nice guy has found his luvey
so let me say to all of you
no matter what it is you do,
there is that special someone who,
can fulfill your wishes and make your dreams come true
with pogo love there are quite a few.

Brent Jenkinson

The Door Was Shut

You told me once my friend you'd always be,
Your door always open and never shut to me
But once I knocked, the door was shut.
My cry you did not heed.
Angry or bitter? No longer.
Surprised? Oh, yes I was!
Hurt? Wouldn't you be?
But, worry not, my ex-friend.
This fool will never knock again.

Dottee Anderson

I Give You This Heart

I give you this heart on St. Valentine
I give you this heart this heart of mine
Look inside
It seems almost bottomless it is so very deep,
A place with no secrets from you to keep,
It captures the light brought its way,
Throwing it back in colorful display.
This is a heart of great beauty crafted with care,
It is a heart so very rare,
A heart so strong in character
But fragile, delicate, easy to break.
So please be careful and tender
With this heart of mine you take,
For another just like it you can never make,
Give all you have of what it needs, oh, love of mine
And it will withstand all the tests of time.
And now you see—it's no longer mine

Michael Orrick

White Lady

White Lady, you treat my love unkind.
He has no peace of mind.
You make him do things he normally wouldn't do.
Then throw him away and leave him feeling blue.

There seems to be no end to you, White Lady,
for there is destruction in your path.
You take him away from family and friends
thinking you are showing him a good time,
but you're not there for the aftermath.

Go away, White Lady, leave my love alone!
Don't tempt him no longer
with your loveless heart of white sandstone.
You make him give promises and he says things
he later regrets,
While the ones that love him
have sat at home and wept.

Sieglinde Dozier

Life's Equations

I wake up in a cold sweat
I still see it just beyond reach
Not some faraway mountain or glorious beach
Just a minuscule piece of something so transparent
And yet so vivid

With my eyes I cannot see
Clear enough to set this phantasmal force free
I must embrace this darkness and so fear the light
It's messing with my mind, I seem to be artificially blind

Upon whose name do I cry
Your exploits of me bring me to my knees
My blood flows freely upon the ground
My tears entrance the eyes of the passerby
Is it inhuman to cry

Is it wrong to wander about in a morose trance
I embrace my death with open arms but not with open eyes

Douglas Paul Smith

To You

I think I could climb to Mount Everest and stand,
If I could hold your hand.

I think I could go on a roller-coaster,
If you were a big jokester.

And run by a tiger who was hungry.
If you were there to comfort me.

I think I can do anything at all,
If you were there to catch me if I fall.

Kelsey Baxter

Nighttime

Mystical smoking dew,
Mornings whisper through,
I only thought about you
in the nighttime

Fog lifted from smoking tall grasses,
sunrises also in the hidden passes
our life is like a series of train crashes
in the nighttime

In the nighttime we just might,
renew our turbulent flight,
we always seem to end up in the wreckage
. . . in the night time

glimmering tear tracks shriek
my spirit grows steadily weak
my soul? You can have it to keep
in the nighttime. . . .

Nadim Ahmad

Father

Your wings have spread far too soon
I wasn't ready for you to soar higher than moons

A spirit as strong as body weak
And through it all, on your lips, all the answers I seek

Explaining away the bumps in the night
Through every pain and joy, you held us tight

Teaching two boys how to be men
Nurturing daddy's little girl the best one can

Kindness, patience, pride—all your legacy for sure
The lights of your life left behind will endure

A life cut short by ironies of chance
In mom's heart the two of you will always dance

We shared borrowed time, for which I am glad
So much to say, most of all, I'll miss you Dad

Robert G. Ebbole

Dad and Me

Tall and proud he always stood,
With the strength of a big oak tree,
And piggy back rides on shoulders so wide
was how he carried me.

Whistling tunes as we walked along
With no words to be sung or rhymed,
Just Dad and me, with our old dog made three—
This was my favorite time.

Strong hands that worked hard all day
But gentle when we would play,
Getting chores done yet making them fun,
This was my father's way.

But time passes on, and a child now has grown,
It has taken its toll on Dad too.
He is slower these days, so I walk at his pace
As we whistle our little tunes.

Elizabeth J. Potts

Times Like These

Times like these are where a man is tested,
Facing the day tired and unrested.
The courage to continue must come from within,
Faith in success is the power not to give in.
Looking ahead I hope where I'll be,
Is feeling all joy and tranquillity.
For now it's a test of what I am made of,
I pray for the power from the Lord up above.

James Frederick Biteman

A Tragic Loss

When you think about her,
And the tears come to your eyes,
Try not to think about the tragedy in which
She was taken from our lives.
When it feels like the pain will never be at ease,
Just think, one day we'll be with her again.
Remember the life you'll always see in her eyes.
Remember her energy, her spirit for life,
Her ambition, her personality.
Can you see her?
She's part of you as long as you remember.
Think about conversations you had with her,
Or advice she once gave you.
She left us with a lot of good memories—
Memories you'll want to remember forever.
She'll forever be alive in those of us who loved her.
Forever loved and missed, in our hearts and minds.

Lisa Marie Ransom

Art

He was a very hard working man
There was nothing he couldn't do,
If you ever needed a favor
He was always there for you.
He so loved his children and wife
Sometimes more than his own life.
No one ever imagined what would be his fate,
But it turned out to be—a young thirty-eight.
There was no cure for the dreaded cancer
That invaded his brain,
And even though, we knew—he never
Showed his pain,
He was tough and courageous and waited
For what God would send,
Never giving up and fighting to the end.
The day that God called and came
He left with a smile and no shame.

Norma Linda Ramos

People

Some people are nice
While others are mean
Other people are dirty
Yet others are clean

Some people can make you laugh
While others can make you cry
Other people may live a long time
Yet others might be very young when they die

Some people can cheat
While others can be true
Other people can be so happy
Yet some people are so blue

For almost twenty-three years
Of being around
Now I know for sure
All kind of people make this world go round

Allan M. Minnowsky

You and Me

When times are tough with you and me,
I feel like this world is no place to be.
When we're not together, I fall apart,
Where are you? Can we please talk?
You light up my life, you make me breathe,
You open my eyes to things I don't see.
Please take my hand, I'll give you my heart,
Come with me and you will see that
times aren't so tough with you and me.

Marcey Asselin

My Dear Tooky

I think of you as days go by.
I think of you no wonder why.
You were the best of brothers you see . . .
You were the best "My Dear Tooky."

At thirty nine you left us here.
No more to teach the children dear.
It's been twenty years since you've been gone
and still I wonder what went wrong . . .
I've been told that time will heal.
So now I've said just how I feel.

I'll miss you "Tooky," all my life.
But I will always remember your good advice.
To be yourself, be the best you can be.
That's what you told me "My Dear Tooky."

The memories I will hold dear to me.
As a beautiful part of your legacy. . . .

Peggy A. Soward

Passing Time

Why does time go so fast?
Can't it take a break?
Seems like yesterday I was skipping to pre-K,
Not aware of what lay ahead.
Why did I grow so fast?
I want to go back
But it keeps pulling me into the tornado—
The tornado of infancy, adolescence, and old age.
Life, death, in-between
All a blur.
It's not like ice cream.
You can't choose between
mint chocolate chip and strawberry,
nor between stopping time or traveling back.
You must keep moving, moving, moving.
Why does time go so fast?
No choice—not fair.

Danielle Delashaw

The Essence of Dew

Does dew fall from the sky
or float about in the air?
Or rise up slowly from the ground,
extracted by the cool, night air?

Does dew evaporate during day?
And when day transcends to night,
the condensation of it precipitates,
and spreads just as light?

As roofs cast about shadows,
and deprive dew of the ground,
It is proof that dew cannot spread
'round about and all around.

It is true that dew will wet your shoes
if you walk in the morning grass.
It is true that dew has wet my shoes
many mornings on my way to class.

Jeromy Lane Young

Tenderness

One can only guess the sadness of others this time of year. We hold our head high and put on airs to keep the truth of our hurt inside while all along we try to hide our cry, for love, compassion, happiness, where will we be tomorrow? Who will share a little warmth and tenderness?

With hidden feelings no one can express, we try to cry but nevertheless we still hide deep inside the one deep secret we don't want anyone else to see, for all the sadness in the world began with me. . . .

Laura Burke

The Other Side

There's a beautiful place where most people go;
what this place is like, well, someday we'll know.

When people go there, they rarely come back;
I guess there is only a one-way track.

This place is so sacred, it's beautiful, too;
when you're finished in this life, you start out brand-new.

No one comes back to tell how it is;
it's a personal thing, it's none of your biz.

I know many people who have gone to this place;
it's pretty sad, though, 'cause I miss their face.

Are people really happier without all their friends,
with unfinished business and loose bitter ends?

Some people are happy when they enter this gate;
for some it's an accident, for others it's fate.

Belinda Robertson

I Thought about This Often, and Still Do

I'm royalty, in my own way.
I'm a king to myself every day!
I do know people are hard to convince,
I came to this world like a wanted prince . . .

I'm used to not being a real royal
But born of parents, to whom I was loyal,
And was loved from day one, like a real King!
I know, both have done for me everything.

There are still days when tears run down my face
When thinking far back into childhood days,
The time I was brought up like a real King,
But one finger, without a royal ring . . .

I often return to that nice birthplace
And kneel there at the grave, saying a grace
For my dear parents, both lie there now still,
Beneath nice wreaths, when I visit that hill.

John Balogh

Bottled Tears

Tears may fall like pouring down rain.
But I shelter myself under his wing
I look in the mirror, but the past isn't visible.
I find myself in wholeness, putting away all that's miserable.

God has shown me to look past the pain,
Warm sunshine covers all that is rain.
I hold myself from letting go my bottled tears,
Captured like a dream; no more do they flow like a running stream.

Shine on me my father of grace,
You guide my steps into a better place.
I leave my trapped tears behind my steps that do not fall,
God has healed my hurt once for all.

Jesus died on the cross to wash away my tears.
That have been falling down for many years.
Now bottled up and never to be free,
Because the tears that fell was me.

Garzelous M. Curd

Time Gone By

I looked across the grey sky wondering where the time has gone. No matter how long it is, time is still so short.
I remembered days when skies were blue.
White clouds drifting by. And, suddenly I knew, and began to cry. Those were days long ago. When I thought things were slow. Had I known then what I know now, I wouldn't have been in such a rush to go.

Andria Lumpkin

The Storms of Life

When love ones began to let you fall,
All of a sudden, you feel like a bouncing ball.

So much confusion fill the air,
It makes your head feel like a drum snare.

Everywhere you go, there's so much strife,
I want to let you know, it's the storms of life.

Life is a highway with many roads,
Keep your eyes open, they just might unfold.

You might hit one or two bumps,
But someone far away, only had a few crumbs.

Some days there are rain and many thunder,
And other days just makes you wonder.

Remember to prepare for the storms of life,
You will never make it, without the light.

Violet T. Cannon

Goodbye, My Love

I have cried many tears,
laughed many laughs,
fought many fights,
and overcome many fears.
As God has chosen me now, the thoughts of my life overwhelm me.
My soul will be free to watch over you,
my body and mind finally put to rest,
for my life has been full of joy.
God has chosen me to fill an opening,
to become an angel in his Heaven.
There is a need for me there,
as the need here has passed, for you are now strong.
Do not cry for me, but let the sadness pass,
for all you must know is that I am at peace;
there is no greater peace than the peace I feel now.
Do not cry for me, as I am happy the Heavens have accepted me.
Goodbye, my love.

Sherri Landry

Colors of a Sunset

Part orange, part peach
Descending slowly
From a half-dark sky

A speck of yellow
Can be seen
Though that is what I saw
One early evening
Out of the corners
Of my eyes

I stood in awe
Such a sight
Stood inside a warm comfortable home
And watched the orange-like peach-like sunset
Drift
Down slowly with coffee in hand
One early night

R. Collins

Why It's Me

A glimpse of her stole my heart.
I kept strolling to see her—every moment
A feeling rose my desire,
She the moon, my only moon.

Words can never please her,
Neither my dreams nor my love.
She flies far away, shining down the sky
Yet she stole my heart,
Suffering another suffering.

S. S.

Together

In the arms of our love we've faced storm clouds
We have danced on life's rainbows serene
We have cradled our share of life's burdens
Together my love, you and me

We have basked in our share of God's blessings
with impossible dreams coming true
You've been my partner, my friend and my lover
Yes, God gave me an angel in you.

Through our faith we have gained inspiration
and forever your hand I will hold
You're that rock that my heart seems to lean on
and your love is my true pot of gold

And when our God in His infinite wisdom
calls one of us to His mansion on high
I will have no regrets for God gave me the best
for I've had you my love by my side.

Evelyn Daugherty

Word Song

Words can comfort, words can sting,
Some can make our spirits sing.
Some are sacred, from above.
And tell us we should live in love.
Words take flight from stationery,
Some require the dictionary.

Words delight us,
Some ignite us.
Words befriend us,
Some transcend us.

But there's one word which we hold dear,
A word that many long to hear.
One we chant throughout the night
To help us make it till daylight.
A word so wondrous, bright, and pure;
A magic word, the word is cure

Mell Morris

A Time for Spring

When the snow geese honk overhead
And crocus and snowdrops awake in their bed;
When remnants of winter's blackened snow
'Cause the creeks to overflow;

When on the lake swans drop in
And the peepers begin their din
And pussywillow's fuzzy catkins grow;
When, spying fresh fields, the gulls fly low

And you feel the soft sweet rain of spring
And all the hope that rain can bring,
Then winter hearts begin to sigh
As spring bursts in on a windy high!

Stream beds dispense old winter's gloom
When marsh marigolds begin to bloom.
Give yourself a happy breather
That warm glow you feel must be spring fever!

Lyn Hirst

Seasons

Winter, quivering cold, blast of magic.
Spring, creeps in like an unmuffed kitten.
Summer, explodes with heat so amazing,
it tickle your toes and is so exciting.
Fall around, I'm ready—are you?
Everyone is looking with eagerness for the seasons.
Winter, spring, summer, and fall.
You've come a long way; it is always
nice to see and feel your masterpiece.

Carol M. Pollard

The North Wind Is a Hungry Hunter

I hear you, you're early, yet wait angry.
To be fed, you start by devouring the golden, red leaves.
It is hard to believe summer was just here,
We now begin another winter year.

A time to hibernate, your big brother winter's strong
Whispering voice, waits
At times a silent hunter, with a spray of brilliant snow,
Yet others he makes us lose our way home.

It is ten a.m. and I am on the third floor, and my apartment
Is cozy and dim; I smell the fresh coffee I just brewed.
Today is laundry day, I have my walker cart all ready.
To go, it costs $1.00 to wash my clothes.
From my office window, I see and hear your mighty north wind voice.
I rejoice, I rejoice, for my God, has allowed me to see
And hear you, my friend, once again.
Before, brother winter, begins.

Sue Sheehan

The Journey

Life is like a road that never ends
For many a journey unknown
That can lead us around the world and back again.
In hopes through it all you'll have faith and keep growing.

Our paths not always pleasant and pure
Perhaps a dream that was left untrue
Leaving is cynical and unsure
Wondering if God has given up on you.

We often question how to make it through
Each faced with trials and put to the test
You pray to find what's inside of you
When it appears it's not enough after giving it your best.

If your soul is lost and hope seems far away
Live each moment remembering what it is that's special in you
For tomorrow may be a brighter day and
Life will reward you if to yourself you remain true.

Kelli Byrd

Thinking of You

Silence is broken by the sound of the wind;
Things being heard will never again.
Whispers were once as loud as a gun;
Now they are absent, as struck by one.

Who would've thought change happened so fast?
Things that were here are gone in a flash.
A friend was once here, but suddenly gone;
Peace, Rest, and Happiness are what he won.

Now he is living in a place in the sky,
Not scared of living, not afraid to die,
Safe and secure in the clouds up above,
While remaining down here is the feeling of love.

But I guess there is a time for everyone to go;
Why his was so soon, I'll just never know.
There are no regrets, just memories of you,
One of my friends, my brother Drew!

Shaylon Wade Haberman

Mother's Home

As I walked from my garage to the red brick

house where my Mother always lived,
I remember all the good times and some bad
times that flowed from within.

There is a hollow emptiness from her
presence gone, like a fleeting dove.
This house is now my cherished home with

Mother watching from above.

William J. Siegrist

Our Heavenly Father

Get on your knees if you want to please
Our Heavenly Father, who knows and sees
All we do and all we say
and every thought throughout the day

He loves us all, each and every one
that's why he gave his only son
To save us from these lives of sin
and change these blackened hearts within

That we may turn away from disgrace
and only look upon his face
Let go of the flesh and grasp his hand
so that one day we too might stand . . .

Before the throne and see his face
In all of his glory and all of his grace
He loves us all, we know it's true,
so follow his commands and He will see you through.

Cathy L. Peoples

Choice

I have the pain and confusion of a child
needing direction of an angel.
Perseverance can be a strength, but is often
misread as a threat.
Success is gained when all tears replenish
the surface and soul.
When will all desired accomplishments be recognized?
Those who feel threatened by other's strengths
will be the failure of their own destiny.
Strength, honesty and belief are the three
keys from a higher power—
needed to guide the determined spirit willing to follow.
An angel is any form you choose to see and believe;
choose to see it, choose to believe it,
because it is you.
You have been given a higher power—
conquer it and never lose it in life's delusion's.

Collette Corbett

my journey

my soul is bonded with shackles and chains
beneath the metal are visions to see
but no one will ever get a chance to
the only one will be me

my eyes have witnessed grief and sorrow
where I wander from here is unknown
I have no idea where the road leads
nothing is shown

my face has been fronted with many people
anger and insanity infest our existence
soon the only thought of "nice"
will be a reminiscence

my feet have traveled over treacherous ground
I have not seen all of what I have been told
the only thing for me to continue
is to live till I am old

Jeri White

Angels with Unseen Wings

Little angels with unseen wings,
are sent from Heaven to fill our dreams.
Sometimes, too soon, we must let them go,
for God just lent them to us we know.
Although they were here for just a short while,
they taught us to love, feel pain, and to smile.
The memories we cherish and hold so dear,
we wouldn't have if they hadn't been here.
Thank you, Lord, in Heaven above,
for lending your angels for us to love,
and giving us the memories of wonderful things,
brought by "Sweet Little Angels with Unseen Wings."

Katherine Evon Donoho

Hour of Leisure

An apple, a book and a bench 'neath a large spreading oak,
Contented, I browsed, as I munched, then removing my cloak,
I gazed at two chattering birds in the old flowering gum,
Among all the red, fluffy flowers, where the bees go and come,
All buzzing while filling their bags with the nectar so sweet,
And happily gathering pollen on small, sticky feet,
Then placing my book with my cloak on the bench by my side,
I watched a hawk gracefully circle, and silently glide,
To rest, on the well covered branch of a tall, stalwart pine;
It stealthily peered from its shelter, an ominous sign;
The two bright rosellas, their chattering done, flapped right by;
The hawk was so quick as he rose from the tree, flying high,
Above the two victims, who fluttering, passed from my view;
I saw the hawk swoop and I felt rather sad, it is true;
I picked up my cloak and my book, turning back to the house,
But swiftly the hawk passed me by, 'ere I left, with a mouse.

Phyllis Horner

Guidance

To not be able to see where one is going,
not to be able to see anything but the
deepest of deep darkness,
the blackest of black nights,
one could, and quite easily would
feel so entirely lost,
and be needing something, someone
to be holding onto,
to be their light,
to guide them through a pathway
of uncertainty and despair
A light being held in the hand of my saviour,
in the hand of my creator.
The light being my creator.
The light being God.

Natalie Pope

Evening Glow

The sun is fading into an evening glow
As I trace my footsteps through my quiet abode
Looking for the love and laughter from the ever after.

I feel the absence, but then I know
Time without you, passes sometime slow
Through the time is short and is not flouted
The moments of parting are those that were counted.

Hurry my love to my arms again
The essence of where it all began
Knowing that once again you will be near
Makes my heart leap with joy and quiets my fears.

So as the sun does fade into the glow
I can feel your presence in my soul
You are a feeling, a presence from above
For you will always be, my special love.

Marilyn Borsik

Once upon a Time

What is the purpose
Of this thing called time . . .
Has anyone ever been able to truly define . . .
Maybe it is confined
Within the simplest of a rhyme . . .
To be detected by a scientist of the mind . . .
Are we blind to our fathers of time . . .
Hear the ringing of the clock's chime . . .
Can we change its design . . .
Or is that only for the divine . . .
Seek and ye shall find . . .

Michelle Burton

The Lord Brought Me You

I searched and I searched for a love that is true,
For someone who would be mine.
When all hope was gone, the Lord brought me you,
And now, my darling, I find
That I love you so, something I thought
That I could never, ever do,
But you gave me love, dear, a love that is true,
And oh, my dear, I love you.

I thought in this world that a love such as yours
Must surely exist just for me.
The Lord brought me you, and such joy I've known,
And now, my darling, I see
That true love exists; my life is complete.
I love you, and you, dear, love me,
And all through the years, dear, my love will just grow,
As I know your love will for me.

Jonathan Palmiter

Maze

My soul has been caught! In this maze called life.
Wondering which way shall I go?
Also wondering, how can I ever be free?

I have been drawn into this maze of life,
like so many others before me.
However, I continue to go forward!
While knowing it would be easier
for me to return from where I came.

Something keeps drawing me forward!
My soul tells me, "just maybe
there's something better
at the end of this maze for me."

Not knowing what's ahead,
knowing what's behind. So I continue!
The journey forward.

Helen L. Rush

On Your Wedding Day

For Amy, from Dad

To my precious first-born child, the twinkle of my eye.
Today is your wedding day, look forward and fly.
If you get nervous or scared,
Look up above I'm all prepared.
Give me your hand, I will wrap it around mine.
Take a deep breath, everything will be fine.
You made wonderful preparations.
Let me be the first to give you my congratulations.
Your gown is so beautiful, with satin and lace.
You look like your mother, so full of grace.
Don't shed a tear because you can't see me there.
I know baby girl, things in life don't always seem fair.
Everyone is waiting, let's go and do this.
Let me walk you down the aisle,
so I can witness your first married kiss.

Kimberly Vandevelde

Forever Friendship

We think our friendship is the best friendship
anyone could ever have!
Since the first day we met and exchanged smiles,
we have shared a special connection that keeps us close
even when we are far apart.
We will be connected all of our lives,
even until death and beyond, for our souls,
our sprits will visit even after our bodies expire.
We are so happy because a forever friendship
is hard to come by, and we are very blessed
that we have found each other!

Phoebe Spiers

From Darkness to Light

Our frustrations are just windows that
drift open along our ways . . .
but God in all his powerfulness
can blow them close for us every day. . . .

The looming of disasters that we
face in our day . . . aren't meant to stay. . . .
The promises of God will drive them away. . . .

When there is darkness: Pray for the light.
In sadness pray for joy, because
God is a light, and with him things

Will always be right . . .
For he brings the joy that has made life complete. . . .

. . . God is the light, and in him is no darkness at all.
1 John 1:5

Angela Michele Moore

Did I Tell You?

Did I tell you that I loved you?
Did I say how dear you've been?
Did I ever stop to thank you . . .
for being my best friend?
Did I tell you how the thought of you helped ease a lonely night,
and the memories of our yesterday
make all the wrong seem right?
Did I tell you that your strength to me
when doubt starts to take control?
And how your smile has touched
the very being of my soul?
Did I ever offer one kind word
for little things you say and do?
Just in case you didn't hear me,
Did I tell you I loved you?

Jody Arndt

Six Feet Underground

In both hands I carry my life
Digging, digging, and dug until reaching end
Upon the sky are gray vultures awaiting me
And a hooded man of bones carries a sickle
I look into my after-war affected hands
My chest poisoned from lead and drug powder
My legs weakened from the endless poverty
My feet and toes scoured from glass and nails
I still feel the eager to die with damage
No magic to change time or to turn back
Absented of the possibilities of fixture
But the only choice to fall deep
Very hollow into the depths of my endzone
My voice calls its final, but weak plea
And now I must fall in the narrow grief
Goodbye

Vernon Alexander Fairley

Goodbye, My Friend

This is in memory of my best friend, Josh.

I received a call from your grandmother this morning,
and she told me the most shocking news I have ever heard,
that you went to be with our lord last night.
It wasn't your fault,
just your time to be with your son once again,
to see his face,
hear his laughter,
hold him in your arms,
and hear the words you had been longing to hear, "DADDY! ! !"
No more thinking of why him and not you,
but I wish I could have said, so long, to my best friend.

Brandi Hobbs

My Mom, the "Dad," and My Best Friend

Mom, it is funny why I call you, "dad."
But really you are the best one I ever had.
Even when he was gone, you never put him
down. You told us he loves us
And he would someday come around.
You would work long hours to provide for us,
Still, mom, you always made time to be there for us.
I can't thank you enough for all that you
have done. I know God has blessed me
to have you as my mom.
I can always laugh and talk to you about
anything. You never judge me or put me down.
If I could begin to thank you for all you
have ever done, my list would never end.

I would start by thanking you for being,
"My mom, 'the dad,' and my best friend."

Ranye Godbolt

Midnight Moon

There once was a man who could hold a tune.
He held in his hand the midnight moon,
making it shine bright with his loving glow.
Everyone told him to never let go,
looking at his only love, her skin so soft and white
as a dove, not knowing how to hold on tight.
He did everything wrong, instead of everything right.
Now, people warned and people told,
If you don't hold on tight, your love will unfold.
The man who held the midnight moon had no fears
as his true love continued to shed tears.
The fire in the sky turned to ash with every lie.
In his love's heart, she slowly will die.
Now in her heart and in her soul,
there is no man who can hold a tune,
nor a man who will ever hold the midnight moon.

Leatha A. Ferguson

Lonely Nights

Million nights in grief I cried
'cause our memories were still on my mind.
I had wished to end it all and
losing you was a great big fall.
You didn't even care,
but I held what we shared.
So many tears for such a long time,
wishing that you were still mine.
And how I missed you it's hard to explain,
but all those nights you drove me insane.
I couldn't leave our love behind,
all the feelings I had inside.
I just wanted to erase it all,
make my heart go blind.
I feel so bad, and it seems as if all
you made me feel was sad.

Aline Franco

The Fight

How do you deal with the thought of someone so close being so gone?
How do you handle the reality of knowing the dead or dying?
How do you find the strength to accept that he's not living?
There is no way it's right,
He's too young to have to fight this,
To fight for his life that he's not even living.
Every night I think of the old times,
The happy times of before.
As tears fall from my eyes, I try to convince myself that
He'll pull through.
Hoping and praying that he will.

Stephanie Rice

Paint Me a Picture

paint me a picture of your love,
anything you've been dreaming of.
paint it with anything or in any way,
but forget not to put in the grey
paint it with blood or paint with wine,
work with your heart or with your mind.
erase the blemishes for love is divine.
i beg to differ, but love is not of that kind.
love is flawed only so, for man is too,
and hoping that a love is true to you,
is like praying that you'll live forever,
or saying that he'll stay—he'll never.
care where care is needed best,
color where the canvas is loveless,
paint a picture of limitless love and beauty,
but paint one of love that is not for your eyes only.

Rahul Keerthi

Never Ending

My pain is immense, unbearable.
Like the mountains around
it seems as if there is no end.
Uphill, Uphill,
the down just a tease.
A moment to catch my breath,
to make me feel I have conquered my pain.
Then up again, steeper than before.
I am out of breath at trying to cope.
I have no confidence to go on.
You took that when you left.
You took my confidence, my judgement,
even my belief in my worthiness.
I have no strength left to climb
the mountains of my pain.
So here I lie, awash in my own sorrow.

M. J. Cadle

The Door

For my loving husband, John Autry

This feeling I feel, I've felt before.
The feeling of the shutting door.
It's very hard, but God keeps commanding
It's time to move on, please don't be left standing.
I need you here now!
To spread your gift further on.
To open hearts, and sing my song.
Your gift is needed, it must be used.
You didn't choose it, it chose you,
Because of your heart, your soul, and compassion.
To love anyone, in any form or fashion.
To see in their hearts, and touch their soul.
Is the greatest gift that I know.
When time shall come, that I shall depart.
My love for them, shall remain in my heart.

Louisa Autry

showers of eternal rain

awakened in the night as my spirit is filled with the sound
of a thousand rain drops marching to Heaven's orders,
showering a parched and hungry soul,
that longs for the living waters of life,
dancing drops of spiritual rain,
beading on the window of my soul,
pools of water giving visions of GOD'S plan,
as the thunder of his voice strikes destiny
and lights up the chambers of my heart,
giving way to the promise of his rainbow,
coloring the hopes of all,
brought in by showers of eternal rain

Michael Malloy

My Poems

My poems are a mirror of my thoughts.
My poems, a reminder of my feelings.
Only there I really live.
Only there I really sing.
I sing about love, I sing about pain
I sing only for you.
Only for you I sing, my only one.
Only for you, who are waiting for me
Somewhere in the months and years to come.
Only you I need,
You, who will know my poems,
You, who will recognize my eyes,
And gently take my hand
And take me away
Towards the Sun,
Towards the Moon.

Sonja Mustra

Deathwatch

The space in life that you occupy
Is a place called suicide,
And all the drugs that you buy
Will be the reason why you die.
We look at you when you're high
But we no longer sympathize,
For as the lies multiply,
We look at you and wonder, why?
You let drugs rob you of your pride.
Someday your life with death will collide.
So now to you I will confide,
We will always be at your side
And our tears we will always hide
Until the day that you die,
And all the tears we shall cry
Will be tears that say good-bye.

Joyce Gilbert

The Second Time Around

When first you meet "him" and fall in love,
The world is seen through rose-colored glasses.
You marry, have children, build a future, a home.
He gets ill, suffers, dies; you're alone.

Time passes, life goes right by,
The 14 years seem to fly.
Then suddenly life is turned upside down;
A new "he" has appeared for
A second time around.

It's your golden years now,
And love continues to excel.
Life is wonderful—complete;
You're so happy you fell.
To complete happiness you're bound,
Because of the second time around.

Rose Louise Pothier

Masquerade

Self-inflected, post-traumatic stress,
the cards, all on the table now.
The obscurity you'll be subjected to,
creating a new plan, when disaster strikes.

Contradictions, just mentally existing,
in your cellular mobility.

Carve a sister out of pine wood,
is she more alive than you?
Crawling cowardly into your hiding place,
shameful existence is haunting.

Mikael Jedhamre

A Mother's Prayer

Take me, oh, Lord, to another level
High above the realm of the Devil.
Help me to shed this robe of sin.
Make me ready to enter in,
Into the arms of my precious Savior,
Out of the midst of all evil behavior.

When God says it's time to close my door
And to dwell in His house forevermore,
I will ask one favor in the name of His son:
That He will show the right road to my loved ones.

Give them wisdom to judge which is fake,
So they will know the right road to take.
I will then rest assured without any fear,
For my Lord is their Lord and
He will always be near.

Louedythe Kilpatrick

Drowning in a Sea of Emotions

My heart is heavy, soaked by the vexatious emotions of life,
and yet I walk on, keeping it all bottled up inside.

When will it become easy to breathe again?
When will the tears cease to flow?
I grasp at useless life rafts of the world,
all the while, knowing that only He can keep me afloat.

Why, when lost in my feelings,
do I ignore the only love I need?
Why torture myself with whys and hows
and not just let Him lead?

Only the Lord can carry us through;
it is only He that frees us.
So, before drowning in a sea of emotions,
we must ring out our heavy hearts
into the comforting hands of Jesus.

Christy Larance

Wrinkled Faces

Old ladies with wrinkled faces,
he moved from one to another.
He'd grown to love them all
in this home where he visited his mother.
He touched their pale, translucent skin,
smoothed back their hair so gray,
or silently sat and held a hand
when there wasn't a thing to say.
Sometimes he sang them show tunes
and would act out every part.
He'd found a showcase for his talent,
they'd found a place in his heart.
He would bid them a fond farewell
and step through one last doorway.
He crossed himself in the darkened room
where his mother used to lay.

Shelby M. Metz

It's True

I am your angel, this much is true,
'cause baby, I really do love you.
I feel all of your pain,
and I promise never to do it again.
I can't stand to see the hurt in your eyes,
knowing it is all from me and my lies.
I want to love you with all my heart,
so let's try to make a brand new start.
If we start over I'm sure you will see,
this time will be much better for you and me.
Yes it's true,
I LOVE YOU!

Nancy Mote

Ping Pong

Once when the basement seemed less musty we went down stairs
and played ping pong for a while:

"The light's in my eyes, damn it! I'm on the wrong side!"
"Are you sure? There is no light on my side."
"The ball blends in with your stupid white shirt! You're cheating!"
"No light on my side."
"The table's obviously shorter on your side!"
"Old ginger is spicier."
"Ginger? What the hell are you talking about?"

The musty air crept in again and he and I put
the worn paddles down and went up stairs.
He went right to his office to read his ________
(I was never good at reading Chinese).
I went left and up to my bedroom and turned on Emeril:
"Your good wines will be gettin' better with age. . . ."

Jack Qian

A Slave's Day

The sun slowly rises in the sky
Another day of hatred and lies
Enraged voices and a striking fist
Must finish all the chores on the list
Failing could lead to harsh beatings
Emptiness and loneliness are my feelings
Working until my hands are sore with pain
Wishing for my fear to be washed away by the rain
Tears run down my cheek
While the other children play hide and seek
Freedom is my only thought
If only I hadn't been bought
Going to bed at night with no dinner
Another day of becoming thinner
Before falling asleep, I begin to pray
That God will save me from another slave day

Nicole Irene Ybanez

FEWW

As fire can easily end strife
So can disdainfulness cause love to fall into a hole
But just as fire can rekindle life
So can trust make love again whole

As the Earth itself can destroy creation
So can hatred destroy a friendship
But as the Earth itself can cause jubilation
So can openness create a relationship

As the fierce wind blows over the deserted land
So does anger blow through a broken heart
But as the gentle wind flows through a welcoming hand
So does love flow through a mended heart

And just as water can nourish all
So can trust, openness, and true love be a
nutriment for all

David P. Suarez

Written in the Stars

When the day's at an end, and the stars are bright,
I look up to the heavens and smile at the sight.
For we are both stars, formed of the same dust.
And though created apart, towards each other were thrust.
Each day, in its close, brings us one step nearer.
Each night, in its silence, shows our destiny clearer.
Our paths are aligned; the timing is right.
And soon our two lights will shine as one in the night.
And then, time will tell, as momentum draws us together,
If the attraction is right, and we orbit each other.
When next you look up and gaze at the sky,
Look for your star—I'm the one nearest by.

Shadow Bosman-Golata

A Moment of Peace

Nobody knows . . . the pain inside.
I search for an escape. . . .
wanting to be surrounded by velvety darkness,
to a place where there is no pain.
I reach for a release,
where it hurts no longer. . . .
I struggle to hold on,
to the serenity of the darkness,
the end of the unwanted.
But it will not welcome me into its arms,
it pushes me into coming back to reality
to feel the pain once again,
devouring me, taking control of my every being.
I reach for the darkness once again,
only to be pushed back to the place
where nobody knows . . . the pain.

Barbara L. Walter

September 19th

My best friend died today.
It was hard to say goodbye,
But I couldn't ask him to stay.
I miss him every moment of every day,
But I wouldn't wish him back sick.
We had M.S., you see.
We, you say?
The last time he went dancing,
Was my last dance.
He was my world.
Father, husband, lover,
My best friend.
When life left his twisted body, M.S. did as well.
There are no wheelchairs in Heaven.
He is at peace.
His suffering has ended; mine has just begun

Carol Hamilton

The Will to Go On

We come in this world a sweet and innocent newborn.
Our first breath of life and no knowledge of where it is going.
Like a roaring storm out of nowhere.
In our body we find problems there
We struggle and try to understand
So we leave it all in God's hands.
Knowing that we're not all alone.
As we search for the will to go on.
We look toward Heaven with a prayer.
We look for support, love, and care.
We pray for a miracle to find a cure.
Trying to be brave and hide our fear!
Knowing that God has all power and can change anything.
So with joy and hope in our heart we sing.
As we travel down the road of life until he calls us home.
We keep the faith and pray for strength and the will to go on.

Kelvin Brewster

The Leader in You

You aim so high you can't see the top,
You persist when your heart says no,
You reach for heaven to give it away,
You extend your hand when no one else will,
Your destiny is to become a dream for others,
Your wisdom encourages a chance of hope,
Your courage assures another to try,
Your smile brings joy to all who cry,
When you stand between an ocean and a mountain,
Will yours be the footsteps followed?
When the grains of sand have fallen through,
Will yours be the name remembered?

Swati Patel

Life

You asked a questions. What was life all about?
I was surprised to hear your answer.
You did not know, and knew no one who could give you an answer.
You do know my dear friend, you just did not realize that . . .

Life is being born and growing old.
Life is problems and solutions
Life is joy, happiness and laughter,
Also, grief, sorrow and tears.
Life is dark clouds and rain, blue skies and sunshine.
Life is surprises and disappointments.
Life is friendship, understanding, kindness;
Also, sharing and giving
Life is a handshake, a hug and a kiss.
Life has a beginning and an end.
Life is generous and can be explained simply in one word
Loving.

Agnes C. Hagan

A Crush Is Only a Small Piece

It all began with a simple smile
I had known him since kindergarten
I would talk to him occasionally once in a while,
And the bond between us began to harden
Then began the innocent glances,
Like signals sent from above
I held him close at one of the dances,
That's when I think I fell in love
My heart raced whenever I saw him
And slowly I began to obsess
His muttered no tore my heart in half like a tree limb,
That's what turned my life into a painful mess
It doesn't hurt anymore right now,
Because pain does fade away,
For you see, a crush is only a small piece
In the game of life we all must play

Tawnya Renee Molina

Safety

You can see the sorrow's worth in my face,
To tell you how to live your life that's not my place,
I want to lie down and cry until life passes by,
I want to be in my dreams, but most of all I want to fly,
I want to stand in the midst of you fears,
But I want to be to salt released inside your tears,
I want to explore the jungle of feelings inside you,
I want to treasure the time and you, just like new,
Lift up your feet and put your trust in me,
Close your eyes and just imagine what you see,
Listen closely to the little voices inside your head,
Rest your pain on me, for I want you to be content when you're dead,
The holes in your heart are what I hope to fill,
You want me to open my world to you, don't worry, in time I will,
So believe in me and have faith,
Until then, hold me in your arms where I know I'm safe.

Jen Pfeiffer

Paint Me a Picture

Paint me a picture black and blue
paint me a picture of me and you
paint an apology on the wall
telling me you won't hurt me no more
paint me a reason to stick around
even after the bruises I've found
paint a smile across my face
to make you happy I'll dress in lace
paint a crack across my heart
on that been growing from the very start
paint me a picture then you can picture me
gone. . . .

Chel Campbell

Hostage

The pain fills my mind
Sometimes it feels like a knife
Sharp, digging, tearing at my sanity
Held hostage, invisible bonds
Too many thoughts, too much time . . . too much time

I miss the peaceful times
So long since I felt at ease
So long it seems, it will never end
And then it does . . . if for but a brief time

But it's always there
Lurking in the back of my mind
Hiding in the core of my being
Waiting to be seen, to take control again
And then it does . . .

I miss what life was. . . .

Isham Collier

Truth

People are deceiving no doubt. Always
wondering what lies beneath the words
they are saying. Sorting through the lines
they spill out as if they truly mean
anything at all. Why does each word have to
have a double meaning.

Keep the faith that is yours I keep telling
myself. Am I much different from them I
wonder. I want to be a better person than
the one I just encountered.

I have discovered that truth is everything
and lies have no meaning. I know in my
heart and in my soul that I love the people
I love and have no feelings for those who
deceive me.

Brenda L. Davidson

Lonely Thoughts

I sit here bein' blue
And it don't help havin' a chew.
I think 'bout it all the time
Just sittin' here, fiddlin' with a dime.
I can't stand this feelin' of bein' alone.
It's twice as worse than breakin' a bone.
I try to get my mind off of this thought,
But it all brings back what God has not yet brought.
I rub some rosin into my glove,
Or stare out the window into the Wyoming sky above.
I clean off the dirt from my rope.
And put in another dip of that satisfyin' Cope.
But with all that I do, I can't hold back
What I still want and what I lack.
I want love to last within my dreary life,
And maybe someday, even a wife

J. T. Mesite

To a Gone Friend

To V. R. A.

Suddenly she'll leap from our thoughts,
wearing a crazy hat, long Indian dresses,
caressing a cat,
doing her hair in tresses,
getting into a mess,
having a fit of rage.

Of course, she never left;
of course, she's always there,
and of course,
as we go on getting from life ages and ages,
she'll be twenty-three forever.

Betty Vidigal Hastings

Tortured Soul

A stranger walks in the night
Silent as the innocent
Sinful as those he seeks to stop
A tortured soul unable to know
How he really feels
In his hands lies the power to heal
In his hand lies the strength to kill
So young in years with a soul so old
Longing to feel real love
Needing to be held
But not knowing how to let go
To let go of the darkness
To let go of the fear that he holds inside
To come into the light
To trust is to surrender
Something he could never do

Karen A. Sullivan

My Love

At first, I saw you as a friend
Now, I see you as more
I see you as my light, when it's dark
I see you like my world
Out of my whole life
I loved a lot of people
But I never thought that
I would love you the way I did to them
I just loved them because I wanted to love someone, You're different
I Love you and I am in love with you
I hope you understand that
And don't play me for a fool
To tell you the truth
you are my first love
Your the first person who I'm really into
and Hopefully the last!

Vanessa Ortiz

Graduation Farewell

Dedicated to my friends—FHS, Class of 1992

Together we shared a lifetime
Of laughter and tears
Forever we must stand
With pride and cheers
Look into the future
Where it's bright and clear
Look beyond the past
And what we might've feared
We can do what we can
To be the best we've always been
And "to strive for better than for worst" is our theme
A day will come again
When together as one we will be
For our bond is as strong
As friends will always be!

Marie Amian

Untitled

On wings of angels do we fly, but for the
fallen gaze high in the sky for their loss
innocence of a time long past,
and weep a sad cry my wings my wings.
Can you tell me, where are my wings
of a childhood long past?
A voice cries out with a simple truth,
you broke them with your pride filled eyes
all so long ago when you thought your selves
gods flying so high in the sky.
So when you fell, no hand was given,
so cry your sad cry.

Chase Miller

The Black Granite Wall

The names are many, and emotions run high.
Tear stained eyes peering from within,
To reach out and touch this mighty Black Wall.
A feeling of helplessness overcomes us all.
Mothers and Fathers, Sisters and Brothers,
Wives and Lovers, Children and others.
We stand in silence and feel the pain,
For those who did not die in vain.
We gather our thoughts, and see our
reflections, combined with the names
of those we loved.
This Wall is awesome, it brings us together,
to ease the heartache that overwhelms us all.
Never to be forgotten by those left behind.
We will surely remember them
Till the end of time. . . .

Lil Abrams

Ragamuffin Worship

Who am I, to say what God accepts
As worship that is pleasing to His ears
Who am I, but a frail piece of mud
Trying to explain what I cannot comprehend
Who am I, who am I

Useless pots are we
Chosen by an omnipotent being
To stand in His presence and sing
Songs of little words, with soft voices
Worshipping, worshipping

But loved is the voice of His children
And cherished are the weak, and puny offerings
We lift them up hoping to find acceptance
And He smiles down, full of pride for His kids
Abba, and child

David Holland

My Brother's Keeper

Am I my brother's keeper?
Yes! I am
I shall know at all times where my brother be
For my strength remains strong with "Thee"
Never to be cursed because I do not know
That my brother cried; yet I still had to go
I am my brother's keeper from day one to day none
Keeping my promise never to look back on what I've done
Together we will shout gracious songs
In being his keeper I see no wrong
Jesus is whom I want to see,
For He always knows where my brother may be
My soul will get stronger and never weaker
For we all will sow what we reap
Today as always my brother I will forever keep
Yes! I am my brother's keeper

Lisa K. Yarbough

God's Children

Across the meadow, a cool wind blows,
High in the mountain top, it softly snows.
A rippling brook flowing along,
A bird sweetly singing a beautiful song.
Deep in the woods the animals play,
Paying no mind to the time of day.
Children laughing and having fun,
Enjoying the gift of God's precious sun.
How lucky we are to have such a place
And to be blessed with such wonderful grace!
Children of God is what we all are,
Sharing His love near and far.

Beth Ann Roberts

If You Disappear

If you started to hate me
I'd live life in fear
If you went out of my life
I'd burst out in tears
If you went away
I'd have bad luck like broken mirrors
If you disappeared
I'd search for you for so many years

You cheer me up when I'm so down
Without you I'd be in sorrow
Your voice is an angelic sound
Without you I'd be standing hollow
You bring me in when I'm so out
Without you I'd jump straight into a black hole
Your presence makes the world go around
Without you there'd be no tomorrow

Yusuke Hasegawa

I Understand

I understand.
You don't have to say a word.
I understand.
Maybe I was told by a little bird.
I understand.
You see, I have been there before and, yes, others know.
I understand.
Don't explain. I can see.
The answer is plain.
I understand.
Don't cry. Dry your eyes.
No more lies,
I understand.
Just close your eyes, relax, and look deep
Into your soul and tell yourself
I understand, I understand.

Mamie Kerr

What Is God's Word

Do not simply read about God
Understand God
Do not simply read God's word
Understand God's word
God sent Jesus for the forgiveness of our sins
All sins, all men
God sent his commandments to show us how we will sin
And how much we will need a savior
God sent us a Savior for the forgiveness of our sins
God's words show us how much we need Jesus
not to set up a judgement system for Jesus to love us
God's love is unconditional
He wants us to be happy and to fulfill our potential and his will
Judgement is not a word God invented
It is a word Man invented
God's word is forgiveness

Anne Elizabeth Leedom

Life's Long Road

We travelled far,
We travelled wide,
We even travelled side by side.

Throughout it all,
I always knew that it
Was God seeing us through

The tunnels of darkness of cold and fear,
Yet always knowing that He was near

To show the light of another day,
And helping us to find our way
Down life's long road.

Mary Roberts

Woman-Child

Who is this unfamiliar girl
with caramel-colored skin speckled by
hormonal eruptions of adolescence masked under
the odor of Clearasil;
hair that smells of beauty parlor chemicals
curled, combed, and lacquered
into obedience;
face twisted with anger;
eyes the shade of cinnamon glazed over with a
"What do you know" look;
blossoming body hidden under
two-sizes-too-big clothing that
denies gender;
and a mouth that has mortally wounded
with words of judgment
flung from its lips?

Paula J. Lewis

A Sense of Perspective

Seize a moment—for it may never return
Pass on a lesson—for another to learn
Thoughts that capture—memories intertwined
Dreams that dance—in the mind
From every struggle—a strength soon grows
Through tainted soil—blossoms a rose
A life of happiness—is what our soul seeks
Bonds of friendships—at their peeks
Sensing the warmth of the sun—through a cloud
Noticing a playful child—amongst a crowd
No moments to do over—no statements recanted
Tell your parents you love them—and never take it for granted
Hold onto God's faith—with vigorous conviction
Let love hold no bounds—or mounts of restriction
From this moment on—hold a smile a minute longer
Keep passion in your vision—and perspective will grow stronger

Cassandra Marie McCann

Nine Minutes

Just as I am ready to leave,
A loud snap, then music, weather, or traffic.
You are rudely brought to morning, and moan.
I press the long button and we are alone again.
Our bodies lay puzzled together, and it begins:
My fingers rake through your hair, my hand
Slowly mapping your shape, and I watch
As you fall back into the dark, breathing deeply.

Again you are awoken from sleep,
And I from somewhere else—
The most perfect place
Where we cannot hear the sounds
Or feel the pull
Of morning,
And the length of nine minutes
Is indefinite.

Manuel I. Gonzalez

The Debt of Love

I owe for the love you've given me
For every time I smile, or every kind word I say
I owe you for the happiness I feel inside.
You've made me blind to the hurt and pain
That's in this world today.

I owe you for the warmth I feel as I start
Another day.
And when I tell you what I owe for all the love you gave
You turn to me and smile, and say it's just another day.
You owe me nothing the debt is fully paid
Just because you're mine for another day
I love you.

Peggy S. Zajac

Too Bad

Too bad it just ain't gonna happen
I really want it to
Too bad it just won't take the right
direction 'cause I really think it should
too bad
I am just so sorry that my life
over, gone, vanished incompletely, discretely
in and out and in again
gone
I wish I knew
too bad for me, too bad for you
How I often wonder which chance I've lost
could be the time to take
Pas mal, muy mala, tres bon, muy bueno
Naw, no just, no, and I can't finish this, I am
tongue tied but I really want to

Rolanda Alexis Wright

The Poem (10/10/00)

I wonder if in Heaven
there'll be those special bells . . .
those over there on my bookcase,
which replaced my special shells.

And what about my plants
adorning the patio door?
Will Heaven be just that . . .
an array of collections galore?

My dolls and spoons, plates and thimbles,
Mary statues and angel pillows . . .
snowmen, bears and reminders of cats—
Could this be Heaven or more than that?

I think so . . . because of love—
because of God's open arms above,
welcoming me to His collections!

Karen Marie Andersen

The Struggle of an Unknown Disease

I feel invisible, vulnerable, and alone . . .
Doctor's compassion seems to have flown.
I struggle each day hope and pray for relief
But specialists give me no hope, I need belief.
I was promised a support team to cover my needs
They don't return my calls, they ignore my pleas.
I want to live and be happy and gay.
I got two dogs to lift my spirits and play.
My counselor gets frustrated and mad.
She tries to get me to speak out, but I'm sad.
I feel that I've paid the price of life's lessons
But the diploma you receive isn't worth the depression.
The days go by and I look for the bright light.
They say that its there but it's not in my sight.
Someday, when this struggle is over
I look forward to a life filled with four-leaf clovers.

Susan Grill

Best Friend

I'll be there for you when your skies turn gray.
I'll be there for you and keep the fiends at bay.
I'll be there to help when the good times are gone.
I'll be there to help when your world seems done,
And I'll be standing by to keep your spirits high,
And I'll be standing by to share the tears you cry.
I will understand you when no one else will try.
I will understand you when you say you want to fly.
Just remember me and that I'm always here.
Just remember me and that I'll always care.
My door is always open, my shoulder always clear.
Whether it's advice I can lend, or just a friendly ear.

Mary J. Woosley

Red to Black

A slice of watermelon on a hot summer's day
Pink flesh glows radiantly
Champagne bubbles ascend like angels to Heaven
A shiver of pleasure runs up my spine
Contrast; red for danger—a warning
Black, the depths of despair
Rain clouds fill the sky, black and molesting
Summer turns to fall
Once again the red appears—only deeper
Much deeper
Flowing, running—escape
All is dismal until that glimpse
The flash of red, crimson, fresh
Just for a moment, taste the champagne,
Feel the bubbles,
Then black.

Maria Joy Kingsbury

Who Are You, Teenager?

Who are you, Teenager? What have you done to me?
To that girl filled with laughter; So careless and so free?
Who are you, Teenager? To make me feel this way?
Moody, sad, frustrated; And more confused each day.
Who are you, Teenager? Tell me, why did you hide
The confidence and self-assurance; That I used to feel inside?
Who are you, Teenager? Please, I need to know.
Will you help me find my dreams as I learn and grow?
Is that you, Teenager? Showing me how to care
For hidden pieces of me; I never knew were there.
Is that you, Teenager? Helping me find and explore
My long-lost confidence; stronger now than ever before!
Is that you, Teenager? Playing a young woman's part
Maturing body, changing feelings; Yet always a child at heart.
Is that you, Teenager? You're helping me to see
That I am uniquely special; I'm so glad you are me!

Dallas Nicole Woodburn

Icy Insecurities

What you said was icy cold
The same goes for your heart
A place inside you that you sometimes wish was warm
Where you keep tally on a chart
Do you write exactly what you said?
Or who you made break down and cry?
Do you put down how hard you laughed?
Or who you made wish they would die?
You laugh in the day and cry at night
And though you hate to admit it
Inside you know it's you who's insecure
A fuse waiting to be lit
And where your conscience used to be
You can think of childish things to do and say
So that tomorrow it will be them crying and not you
And maybe, for a fleeting moment, your pain will go away

Louis A. Peitzman

The Peace within

We used to wish upon a star, then say our bedtime prayer,
A "trust" we learned as children, always knowing He was there!
Tho' we may not recognize it, looking back, it still is true,
Whatever life has dealt us, it was faith that saw us through!
So when turmoil and anxiety are heavy in your heart—
If tomorrow seems unknown, and you don't know where to start.
When you tire of the struggle, just reach out and take His hand,
For even if the words won't come, He still can understand. . . .
If that trust is hard to find, and troubles never cease
Just reach away down deep inside and find that inner peace—
The place that says, "I've done my best—I put it in your care—"
You will find a load is lifted if you only leave it there!

Audrey K. Thompson

A Dream

Never had much of a life,
mostly heartache and strife.
Everything changed when he came along,
gave her the faith she needed to be strong.
He'd given her everything she'd ever dreamed of,
including his Powerful love.
Swept her right off of her feet,
this love couldn't be more sweet.
They both had big plans together,
this love they had was going to last forever.
She was sure these dreams came true,
when he whispered, "I Love You."
Then with a sudden wind from the open window,
she felt a cold breeze come across her toes.
She realized she'd waken up from a dream,
she felt torn, she wanted to cry and scream.

Crystal DiRosario

Recipe for a Mother's Love

A child or more:
Three or four,
Or more if desired.
Add: lots of love, devotion, understanding.
Many laughs here and there.
Few tears and bumps.
Many talks and long walks.
Few broken hearts.
Also add joy, happiness,
Patience, hard work,
Sacrifice.
Mix together
And you have a mother's love.
Preparation one second.
Lifetime to develop.
Serving: rewards endless.

Kay Jeffries

The Day the World Cried

We are at war, I heard them say,
The bombing started late this day.

I couldn't stop the tears that flowed
And I didn't care to whom they showed.
I love the lives I know we'll lose,
All for the war we didn't choose.

My heart bears such pain and tears,
My heart cries out with all my fears . . .

The targets, the bombs, the lives all lost . . .
Did anyone stop to think, what cost?
The war if won . . . the war if lost?

This war . . . they're calling "Desert Storm" . . .
What does that mean? It doesn't really matter . . .
I mourn, I mourn, for all lives lost in this "Desert Storm."

Joan G. Hazelwood

Deep Water

The rivers of my love run deep and true,
Pooling in lake I know as you.
Where the water stays calm and the birds always sing,
I sit there waiting on the love you bring.
When we come together, no one can part,
Nor fence in or make boundaries, chaining our hearts.
This world sounds so perfect, so very untrue,
Till I wake in the mornings gazing at you.
With your eyes so sleepily staring back at me,
I know what it's like to finally be free.
You make me feel loved, so very complete,
I'll stay forever in the water that's deep.

Rodney Tiffee

The Long Fight

Multiple Sclerosis, such frightening words to hear.
Can strike at any time, to someone we hold dear.
It comes without warning, no time to prepare.
Like a bolt of lighting, from out of nowhere.
The tests have been run; the results are in.
The battle is hard one, one I hope we can win.
It takes over your body and your mind.
Making you forget stored memories of a whole lifetime.
Pain, pain, and more pain, but no relief in sight.
Makes life a constant unbearable fight.
The struggle of each hour every day.
What a high price one must pay.
But fight and fight hard, we must.
Putting our faith in God whom we trust.
God works miracles every day.
Let's hope and pray he sends one your way.

Gladys Ehrhardt

Are You Listening?

Do you see the signs that time is showing
Do you see the changes whenever the wind is blowing
Do you know that nature is showing us these signs
Or are we just merely blind
The hurricanes, the tornadoes, the floods, and the storms
Are the anger from the Earth, from which we've torn
Do you see the losses, accidents, sickness and the pain
Do you see the tears that come within the rain
Do you know that nature is playing its role
When the thunder roars and the lightning unfolds
Do you know that a rainbow is a sign of hope and peace
Do you know that wonders never cease
Do you know you have a role to play
By trying to live better day by day
Just like nature you have a task
Open your Bible and just ask.

Brenda J. Hollingsworth

Thank You!

Thank you Lord for another day.
Thank you for the clouds that you can roll away.
Thank you for the sunshine on a cloudy day.
Thank you for being God and you can work that way.
Thank you for doing it without any pay.
That, we can't do,
But we can say thank you!
Early this morning I saw the sun peeking through the clouds,
And to be your child I felt appreciative and proud.
I was able to say thank you real loud.
Thank you for bringing me through sunshine, clouds, and rain,
And for easing my pains, by just calling your name.
Thank you for being so dear,
You aren't far off, you are always near.
Even if we whisper you can hear.
Thank you Lord for the cheer.

Everline H. McGhee

I Release You

I release you,
May hills and valleys pass beneath your feet.
May many people smile as you come and go.
May you taste fully of all of life's beauty.
I hold you
That as you roam I will remain in your heart and mind,
And that someday you may return from your roaming
Knowing that I will be here.
Always,
You will be free to follow your own path and do as you choose,
Knowing that you are loved unconditionally.
You will always be welcome at my side.

Teresa Lynn Creath

Life

People sit and wonder about their life
And what kind of goals they should have for their life.
Wondering what is good for them
And what is going to happen.

I know what my goals are and what I want,
but who knows what will happen
To me and what kind of traumatic things
Will happen to me during my time here.
But I do know this, I want a family that
Will love and care for me, a wife and children I can love

But most of all I want people to care
More about what is going on in the world
And do things to change what is wrong
With it, instead of always talking about it
Until then, I will keep going on with my life.

Joshua Ralko

A River of Many Oceans

I can feel you surround me
as your vibrations jolt through my body like a thunderous roar.
My veins from within combust from the overwhelming feeling
of love and acceptance that you have.
I can hear you knocking; I can hear you calling my name,
your voice is the silence from all around.
My ears may not hear you, but my heart will always cry for you.
When I close my eyes, I can see you; not with my eyes,
but with my spirit, for only our spirit is true and pure.
You are with such beauty, so elegant and pure.
You have no shadow of darkness; you are of a brilliant light.
I trust and believe in you because I know we'll never fight.
I know you have felt my pain.
I know you have a river of many oceans
because you have always been there to pick up our tears
that have fallen from beneath us all.

Michelle Patton

Time to Fly

There must be a change a comin' as tension reaches the sky.
Oh, yes, a change is comin'.
It's time for someone to fly.

Her wings have grown too strong.
There's no comfort in the nest.
She looks out from the doorway.
It's time to take the test.

Her senses have reached their peak.
She's doing what feels right.
She's spreading brand new wings.
And now she takes to flight.

Everything will look different now.
She's left the nest, her home.
The freedom, the fear,
the awe—they are hers, she's on her own.

Connie L. Novotny

The Harsh Words

Shoulders turned away in anguish
A misunderstanding so painful
The lover's hurt shown with tears
Why, I pray, did we not understand
The winter's frozen scorn on our souls
The words torn from me
Oh! for the chance to take those words back
Who was right and who was wrong?
Did we really need to strike the blow?
My body screams out for the mistakes made
Please come back to me, my love
I did not mean the harsh words I said

Dominic Edward Elliot Rouse

Twilight Time

Reluctant to depart, the day slowly dies,
With crimson fingers grasping the darkening skies.
The sun disappears, o'er the rim of the world,
Its brilliant banners gleaming, in magnificent unfurled.
And as its pennants fade, I hear the vespers chime,
Soft and sweet, yet clear, they herald twilight time.
It is a magic moment, betwixt the night and day,
When everything is hushed, and the world is lost in fey.
For thought the darkness lurks, in the shadows everywhere,
Still, for a while, time stands still, as though it was not there.
Not light, nor dark, but somehow a part of each,
Like paradise lost, and paradise found, it seems our souls to reach.
With the promise of tomorrow yet clinging to the past,
Until toward the evening star, our souls fly, free at last,
And upward soar in ecstasy, above this worldly clime,
For each will know, within himself, when he reaches twilight time!

John Munck Probasco

We Are Meant for Each Other

I remember the first time I heard your voice.
I knew I enjoy the conversation.
You are the type of guy, I could get along with,
without hesitation.
Then when I finally saw you, the feeling I had grew,
and seen to be endless
Your nice smile and gorgeous blue eyes to me
you're worth my love and true happiness
I know it is impossible and yes, it's true
The only thing that is worth more is my love
I offer to you.
I can see myself 50 years from now,
and my love would still be burning.
I want you to know I want to be your lover,
your best friend, and your soul mate.
But right now I know we are meant for each other.

Ashley Mendoza

God's Kiss

As life goes on, painful memories mount,
For some they are far too numerous to count.
These are the memories that linger the longest,
They are never forgotten by even the strongest.
Only God can save us from the pains we will feel,
Only through him will our hearts ever heal.
He takes from among us the very best,
To have for Himself in his own little nest.
To have the best people, He first gives them birth,
Then allows them to prove themselves here on Earth.
Their carefree childhood he gives them here,
Then he takes them to shelter from pain and fear.
He makes sure while on Earth they feel sorrow never,
Before taking them home to be carefree forever.
So grieve not for what life young loved ones may miss
For they are the chosen few touched by God's kiss.

Theresa Poffenberger

Who's Better

Beauty Queen
Pageant winner
Biggest prep
Biggest phony
You may be a beauty queen
but you'll never be as beautiful as me
because I'm really smiling, I'm doing what I love
while your face is plastered with fake happiness
buying votes from people you hate
like me
Inside you envy me and you don't even know it
but you will

Miranda Earnest

Don't Tell Mama

Shh! Don't tell Mama or she'll be sad.
If she knows our little secret, her heart will surely break.
She can't know right now. I don't want to hurt her.
Mama may be strong, but not strong enough for our secret.
Shh! Daddy. Don't tell Mama.

We will have to tell her before it's too late.
But now's not the time. She is too weak right now.
When will we be able to tell her? That I don't know.
I don't want her to know while she's sick.
Shh! Ricky. Don't tell Mama.

Why does this have to happen to our family?
Mama is sick and so am I.
But Mama will get better. I won't. I am dying.
Please don't tell her, for my heart will shatter with hers.
Shh! Jem. Don't tell Mama.

Marina Wise

Experience Someone Else

Look into the eyes of a stranger,
take the path they chose to walk,
experience the life they have lived,
relate to the loves they have lost,
feel the pain they have endured,
shake from the fear they have faced,
dance in the joy they have seen,
fight the battles they have won,
touch the tears they have cried,
understand the consequences of the lies they've told,
run from the whisper of their truths unknown,
crawl through the cracks in their heart,
watch in amazement visions uncontrolled,
break through a surface that has never been
scratched and find the soul that no one else has seen.

Stephanie Victoria Brandon Clark

Mom

She makes sure I am always loved,
and keeps a roof over my head.
She makes sure I am safe at night,
and tucks me into bed.
She's always there to hold me tight,
even if I'm wrong or right.

Mom will always be there for me,
No matter what happens in our life.
She loves me deeply,
That I will always know.

Mom teaches me many things,
Like how to love and think,
But the best thing that my mom has given me,
Is the power to be myself.
I love my mom.

Carleen Richele Driesen-Allyn

Tidings

Hasty violence strikes the heart
With an unconscious dart.
Lips sealed with ice in the souls tidings
Whom can see of what can be
Or the sound of thee endless flee . . .
A seldom fight with the taste of light
In a hale are there the precious tales
For few can be the doors of the sea
In thy souls of our dueling poles
But again the war takes the beings to a shore
Of where the mighty shall be
Hope, love and honesty . . .

Filiz Ayse Aksoy

Even Me

Is it true that You extend Your grace
To all who pause to seek Your face
For any who will run the race
For even me?
Do You really guide the Christian life
Through times of trial, mortal strife
And bond the love of man and wife
For even me?
In other lives, I see Your touch
In ways for which I yearn so much
Would you do the same in the life of such
As me?
And yet, You know, as I look back
I see You're faithful—on the track
You were the fullness for what I lack
Yes, even me.

Kimberly Arnold

Mariel

A ginger haired little
niece
I treasure like a precious
piece
She is only four years
old
But she acts so very
bold
Nine months since I saw her
last
This is a long way in the
past
I wish her life and hope she keeps
well
Then I will be gone
but I will not tell

Graham Wrench

A Tribute to Montel

A few weeks ago, my friend and I saw your
show, and it was a blast,
The discussions were so interesting;
we wanted it to last.
Montel, your personality is such a charm.
With Montel you feel no harm.
Along with Jerry, Ricki, Jenny, they will put
one through a test,
But Montel, you're still the best.
It's really sad that, Montel, you have M. S.
and sometimes are sick.
Hopefully with new medicines and other
Advances—that will do the trick.
Montel, I only wish you the best each day,
We are Happy watching your show in
Every Way! ! ! !

Nancy Jane Kirsch

The Hue of You

It is you, the cause of my smile,
you who fills my thoughts
It is you, who has tamed my mind,
you who has caressed my soul
It is you, who has occupied my dreams,
you who makes my body tingle
It is you, the image behind my eyes,
you who has broadened my view
It is you, the scent that intoxicates me,
you who brings light to my life
It is you, the only lover for me,
you who has captured my heart

Ashley Wong

The Origin of My Sin . . .

The origin of my sin is that which eats away
at my bones . . .
coursing through my veins,
pounding inside of me.
It will remain there, if I let it,
sustaining that which must be broken.

Its infidel life feeding off of mine
Praising my conformity of passion
Yearning for my affection it turns,
burning inside of me . . .

"Go On! Do you have it in you to let me go?"
We had a common goal but now,
I have reached my wholeness
That which was missing now remains
And my heart will now sustain what once was yours.

Alejandra DeLuna

The Thought that Flickered through My Mind

We danced all night, danced into the soft morning light,
so soft I could not see what was lurking right in front of me.
I smelled the night air; her scent was crisp and fair.

My eyes were heavy as the night began to spin.
Suddenly I was faint and weak when he leaned over to softly speak.

Though his voice 'twas not above a whisper,
every sound I'd remember as he laid me down ethereally on the bed.
I'd known him only a second, yet I'd know him all my life.
The moments ticked by.

As the world lay blanketed in darkness,
while sweet cherubs softly slumbered,
I walked along the dimly lit road
and the thought flickered through my mind
that I hadn't said goodbye
to this man I had slowly danced by.

R. J. Isabelle

Father of Lies

Whisper, then scream,
Which is more frightening—
To be alone or to know you are near?
Better to cry, better to die alone in peace
Than to tremble, dry eyed, in your presence.

If it's my blood you wish to see
My destruction you desire . . .
How could I call to you, to you in my despair?

Lust, hate, a ravening lion
I know you now for what you are,
The father of lies.
Dead, yes, I'm dead to sin.
Your nemesis freed me.
I live in His love,
And your power is gone.

Angela Joyce

My Fallen Hero

My hero fell during September of '96.
He had no fears, and had a heart of gold.
He was murdered after a Mike Tyson fight,
on that cold fateful night.
He fought for seven days after,
but five bullets were just too much.
He shouldn't have died, he was just 25.
Some say he was the best rapper ever,
others say he was just weak,
but no matter who you are,
you must say "Rest in Peace."
Rest in peace Pac, you will be missed.

Jonathan Chittum

Soft Memories

Into the heart of darkness comes a light,
Shining bright and illuminating.
"Are you my light?" asks the darkness?
"Yes." replies the light, dusting off forsaken memories. . . .

I remember times when the breeze,
Soft and sweet,
Warm and wonderful,
Love and loving,
Accompanied my own heart's song.

Sighs escape my dry lips
And I Cherish then, my memories
That slowly filter through time immemorial,
Substance never to be understood,
Seen through a haze of overwhelming
Emotion.

Akua Gyanewah Asare

Winter Dream

As I sit here staring at the snow
Feeling the cold at ten below
Too cold to go out
Bored with the house
I gaze off and dream of Spring and Summer
Warm days with bright shining sun
Our day that is coming this very June
I dream of a beautiful day as we stand
in front of the river
Those solemn vows from my heart to yours
Our family and friends gathered round
You in your white tux and me in my pearl gown
The laughs the tears the beautiful sky
This is where I belong no need to ask why
Now the wind whistles and brings me back
Time to stop dreaming and get back to my task

Lynette L. Baudino

Lovers

The black sea, and endless night,
Move as boundless lovers.
They are not two separate bodies,
But one essence, one being, one element.
The stars cradle the moon in loving caress.
With the stars as a soft spider's webbing,
The soft tinge of color is that of a soft sound.
The Universe . . . the delicate solar systems' guardian.
The folds of deep space . . .
Are dark folds of a blanket for the stars to hide in.
To be protected from black
gaping, hungry, grasping, greedy,
monsters of death,
and bringers of an unknown, cold, distant fate.
The folds are ocean waves at night . . .
Caressing a sleeping lover. . . .

Jake Marie Bennett

An Evening Prayer

Dear God, I send you my humble prayer
For sending me a bit of your kingdom up there.
Then you bequeathed from your treasures rare,
Three little angels with golden hair.

Three little cherubs, now fast asleep.
May your Holy Spirit His vigil keep.
Watch over them, Lord, and let me be
Worthy of the trust that You placed in me.

Deloise Tilton

Those Golden Years

The young kids' great desire
They can't wait till they retire,
Their first real job, they plan retirement
They want to know what's the requirement.

They can't know it's all a dream,
They've worked so hard to reach that scheme
They spend their money oh, so free!
As if it grew upon a tree.

There's nothing left but their small pension
The amount is hardly worth the mention
Travel, sightseeing, sounds so great
But suddenly they find, it's all too late.

By the time you reach those golden years,
To their surprise, they shed some tears
Arthritis hits and you can't walk
About their ailments we talk.

Jewel Robinson

Sensation of Spring

I watched the sunrise of the morning sun shining up high
And saw the multitude of colors that aligned the sky.

I could feel the warmth of the green spring grass
I ran my fingers across blades in mass.

Flowers are now blooming with radiance so fine
And their fragrance of sweetness, textured divine.

I captured a cool breeze that gently combed back my hair,
Stuck out my tongue and tasted the honeysuckle air.

Birds are singing and leaving their nests
Happy to flee from the long winter rest.

I pulled off my shoes and placed my feet in cold water,
In a large pond full of ducks that scampered and squandered.

Then I heard children laughing and playing, so now it must be true,
The sensation of spring has been long overdue!

Paulette Hill Tarot

Running Home Again

You'll surely have trials; you'll have plenty of woes,
And hard are the choices you'll make.
Of course, blinded by love, frustrated by fate,
You're unheeding of roads that you'll take.

Your mind's in a whirl! They're all pushing you, girl;
Where's the balance that you thought you had?
Your whole life's before you, but you can't find the door you
Must pass through to find peace and be glad.

Oh, it's okay to cry when dark clouds fill your sky;
Even flowers need water to start.
But, just back up a while and shine up your smile . . .
Get in touch with yourself and your heart.

Then when storm clouds have flown
and you're out on your own,
Choose wisely your hearth and your home.
No fears, no deceit, vowing vows you can keep,
Then, wherever you are, you'll be home.

Loraine Stephenson

A Lifestyle

water water, slowly flowing
giving no care to which way it is going
around the rock and under the log
the path of the water is like that of the fog
flowing and flowing, flowing some more
not waiting or watching, for what is in store
moving and flowing any which way it would like
to flow like the water, that's what i'd like

Jason William Warner

Portrait of a Homeless Man

Never judge a man till you walk in his shoes,
Especially a man with nothing else to lose.
He used to hold his head up high, he used to walk with pride.
Now nobody knows the hurt he feels inside.

He's done a lot of wrong and he's done a lot of right;
His day to day survival is a struggle and a fight.
People say he's worthless but oh, are they so blind,
'cause nobody can see what's inside his mind.

Some have served this country so we could all be free,
Some have fought the wars all across the sea.
Some have been a doctor, a lawyer, and a cop,
Even though he's on the bottom, he used to be on top.

Now you should never judge him, still you walk down his road,
For you don't know his burden, it's a mighty heavy load.
Be careful how you treat him, what you say and do,
'Cause you never know what lies in store; one day it could be you!

Mark A. Hilligas

Higher

As I flew up in the sky
On wings of steel in an F-16
I rolled and swooped among the team
Following the commanders every cry

Soaring, roaring through the majestic blue
Floating, swift as an airborne falcon
Commanding my vessel like a sea captain
With only myself as the crew

I fly higher, higher towards the stars
Where the air is quite thin
I can almost touch our planets rim
For someday I hope to fly to Mars

Now, the sun's hours end is near
And night once more sets in
You land you craft as skies dim
And thoughts once strewn are clear.

David B. Ingraham

One in the Same

Kindness and gentleness flow from within
Whenever I think of my wonderful friend . . .
There's no sweeter song that the nightingale
sings . . . than the sound of your voice,
when you speak to me . . .
For where would I be without you, Each time
My heart beats it calls out your name . . .
For you and my heart are one in the same
Together we grow even though we're apart
Distance shall never separate our heart
Though I walk alone I am not afraid
For I feel you beside me every step of the
way . . . Comforting me, Loving me, Guiding me
Through . . . To the time and place I can
Be with you . . . When I lay my head down to rest
I can hear your heart beat through your chest
I swear that I can hear my name . . .
For your heart and I are one in the same

Susan Lyn Raccine

A Feeling

It's kind of funny, this feeling inside.
It's like the breeze that blows the tide.
It can be gentle and yet so strong,
And blow you down like nothing's wrong.

It just a feeling you cannot hide.
It takes you on a tumbling ride.
Through the fields of love and hate,
Right straight up to Heaven's gate.

Though now it's gone, completely dead,
It's still remembered inside my head.
It'll be there till time is done
'Cause no other feeling can match this one.

Colleen Francis

Endless Romance

I'm in love with a girl,
If I had it, I'd give her the world.
Would I give her the universe?
If I had it, of course.
If I were a king, I'd give her my throne
and let her reign on her own,
unless she wanted to share it with me.
I'd be as happy as can be but I'm just a normal man
wondering where he stands,
getting knocked down and never getting the chance
to ask her to dance, while wishing for an endless romance.
If I could have just a kiss, I would live in a bliss.
If only wishes came true, I'd be forever loving and pleasing you.

William Harold

11:2

I'm burning vegetables, wary of fire-building
Match lighting the corners, feeling for sand deposits
Mistaking the ruined bellies of spiders
For a flattened tapestry or a map of storm
Endings on the porch, we didn't worry
About winter, certain our region would be skimmed
Over later, with both of us swinging, I tried
Preventing our shoes the wear of hesitation, the barely
Holes obvious and splintered blue.

Since then, I've built caves with ground water faucets
Leaking, they choir for desert or a dinner
Of burnt vegetables I hear others talk about winter,
Sure to skim these regions or the trees that have
Orphaned themselves to longing after birds gone
To highway telephone poles, the peat half-empty
Rising to weather patterns, embossed
with the imprint of your worn-out shoes.

Nicolette Mcfaddin

Be Here Now

Be here now, all the time
It's the best friend for anyone.
If you are being nice to it,
It will be nicer to you.

You can use this tool forever.
It will never perish if we use it.
One when it's out of mind,
It's out of service within no second.

Be here now to save to your time.
Be here now to digest your task.
Be here now to avoid procrastination.
Be here now to acquire success.

Often minds drift from here to there now.
Bring it back at once, as time never waits.
Be here now, as now or never;
Now counts each and every second.

Lobsang Lhamo

Tired Eyes

Black in blue, blue in white
sometimes surrounded by darkness bright,
if possible, but even so
always black at the heart
these are my tired eyes waiting to die
my innocent blue trapped and corrupted
by black

Ryan Tonkin

At Night

Like a black and white phantom,
she crept silently into my bedroom.
A smaller, multicolored shadow follows.
Carefully they move from floor to bed where I lay sleeping.
The small one cuddles by my leg.
Her partner pauses, then creeps up onto my chest
and rubs her face against my cheek, purring softly.
I waken and reach out to caress both silky heads,
speaking my feelings for them quietly,
careful not to disturb the moment.
Silently, softly, they crept into my heart.

Norma F. Carroll

Rat Race

Today's my destiny. It will shape into what's in store for me.
This moment on will determine my purpose.
My karma. So confusing to others.
So busy working, running, hating, and thinking.
"I did, so you should too," is what's banging on my walls.
So much to protect while everyone's destroying.
Hate putting up walls; but they love breaking
them down, what's good for you isn't.
How do you preach then? Back up against those walls
stand tall, and protect your choices, follow your heart
Run your own life. Everything else will follow.

Natalie Fitzgerald

Multiple Sclerosis

Multiple Sclerosis is serious disease
Many people are suffering from
We want a cure and need it now
Too many lives has been lost
This disease of the nervous system
Can eventually paralyze
Our scientists are working hard on a cure
Let's pray one day it will be found
Special funding is needed for MS
Give what you can afford
Every dime will be appreciated
One day they'll find a cure
You'll be glad you were a part of it

Mary Ann Branch

This Woman

This woman, this powerful woman
Mother of all living things
Life, air, breath, she brings
Someone that relieves, something to receive
She is introvert, she is in your face
Something never to replace
This woman so full and tall
Representing the beauty of it all
Like circles in her pattern created
Like the light from her emanated
My mother, my blood, my unconditional love
Let her hands cool my skin
The one she bore me in.

Mandy Zuniga

Little Snow Bird

Why fly? We fly for the journey not the trip!

Why do we fly south?
We fly south because it's warm!

When we get there we just fly back, why?
Because we need to come home!

So why fly? Because we can!

Kelly Decker

Last Dance of the Fireflies

A crimson canvas blankets the sky
Auburn leaves float to the ground
The gentle day's rain takes a pause
Wind chimes jingle as the breeze blows
And the shops close for another day
Darkness falls and the dance of the fireflies begin.

Intertwining paths, figure eights, and loops
I shall puck away a few melodies at your last dance
Whether be at wedding or funeral
We grieve and celebrate the same as you
Daybreak draws near, soon the dance will end
I bid you farewell till the next year

Carlton Hwa

The Time of Our Lives

The sand in an hourglass ticks the time away,
time affects life much the same way.
Days, months and years can be measured in life by tears.
Some tears of gladness from things that brought us happiness,
Other tears of sadness, of sorrowful things that have happened.
As life passes by, the question of how to live begins to arise.
We can let the sand in the hourglass drop with a sigh,
and give in to our fears and die.
Or feel the energy to be alive,
and embrace the sand of our lives.
The time is ours to lose;
how we live it, is ours to choose.

Thomas H. Gunderman, Jr.

Why?

"Why is the grass green?"
"Why is the sky blue?"
Asked the child to whom these things were new.
"Why does the computer work?"
"Why does the car work, and how?"
Asked the child, a little older now
Why and how, so often asked,
Are questions of today are questions of the past.
"How does the brain work? Why do we live? Wow!"
Said the child, a philosopher now.
Still asking why,
Still wondering how.

Kyle Bellinger

Arms of Love

To my twin sons, Matthew and Marc

Because my mom loved me so,
She gave me away and let me go.
But in her heart she was never free
Of the loving feeling she had for me.

So she prayed to God from up above,
To wrap me in His arms of love
And keep me in His loving care
Until one day she could be there.

Thirty years have come and gone,
But her love for me has still stayed strong.

Cecile Marshall

The Miracle

He brought me blood-red cherries from Siberia
and kissed my tear-stained cheeks in an April
dream while the world looked on and wondered
if it could be done; if rainbows could come
right in your window, if flowers could bloom
in the winter, if water could really be turned into
wine, if lily-white love could grow . . . in the snow.

Helen Ann Dimitriev

Father, Can You Hear Me?

As twilight sets, darkness floods the sky
While gusts of wind whispers greetings to the treetops
Natures music fills the air, its voice so
beautiful and soothing to the demon of pain in my heart
Trapped between mourning your lost life and
praying for the rebirth that will release
you from your undeserving Hell
Hiding under the armor that blankets me,
I look to the Heavens to fill you with
strength and to guide your soul back home

Shrell Dawn Krawczyk

My Winter Poem

Winter is frozen children making mischief
Winter is old ladies muttering in grief

Winter is blizzards, not very nice
Winter is snowstorms, and a whole lot of ice

Winter is snowdrifts, horrible to the bone
Winter is ploughmen with hearts of stone

Winter is frosty sleet, making me cold
Winter is chamomile tea, faithful as gold

Winter is snowmen melting down
Winter is people slipping in town

Erik Runeson

A Rose

When I met my sweetheart, she seemed to be a rose,
so perfect in form.
On our first date, she blossomed as though
reaching out to me with all the love
that life has to give.
Now the years have passed by,
and now there is another rose
that has blossomed in full
as each day goes by,
and that rose is my heart.
Now my sweetheart, so beautiful as a rose,
is now also my wife.

Granville (Bud) Bullard

One Magical Day

I love her dearly and she is missed.
Even though I know she's with God in His
Heavenly bliss.

I told her my secrets and she told me hers too.
I knew not what the Lord had planned
and what he was about to do.

I will remember her forever.
She will always be in my heart.
I just don't understand why we have to be so far apart.

Now I lay my head down and silently I pray,
and hope we will be together again, on one magical day.

Erica V. Blake

I Saw a Dead Woman Smiling Today

I saw a dead woman smiling today, I looked into
her eyes and smiled back, I have never seen
anything quite so serene as her physiognomy

Her arms by her side, legs slightly crossed, she
sees the Jekyll I Hyde within, the dead see the
truth I cannot escape, I hold her hand as the
day slowly comes to a close, she gets up and goes

Jamil K. Tajik

Time

Brisk autumn air through trees of red,
Feels almost like spring, but you know what looms ahead.

The inevitable happens when all turns to white:
It's beautiful at first but then turns to spite.

A blossom appears when the cold starts to fade;
brilliant colors appear in a wonderful cascade.

New life is reborn in all you can see,
the songbirds chirping with glee.

So as the autumn air approaches to breathe once more,
time begins the cycle and opens a door.

Michael J. Luksch

Vision of Me

I am like a tulip . . .
Beautiful to gaze upon, but easily damaged if
touched too harshly
I look vibrant and strong, but am fragile and hollow
I bloom briefly in the coolness of spring
and wither under the brutality of summer's heat

How I wish for eyes to gaze upon me,
hands to touch gently the depths of my soul,
leaving me whole and not broken,
to be vibrant, full of substance
and for the coolness of spring to last a lifetime,
that I may forever bloom.

Amber Smith

Luminous Beverage

I see the light around you and I must be closer still,
As a moth is drawn to flame I'm called beyond my will,
A glow transcends all appearance and intentions paved,
I see the light around you as each to now be saved,
I give the light inside me to shine from deep within,
As one cannot become this whole hiding fearfully from sin,
The spirit born within us calls for each to look inside,
I give the light inside me as this love can't be denied,
I hold the light within us a gift from higher up,
To give us drink and quench the thirst from overflowing cup,
Nourishment that soothes quiets painful hearts to still,
I hold the light within us drinking deeply to my fill.

Kathleen K. Harris

The Girl under Glass

Through the glass I watch the girl in the box;
She cannot see me from where she now stands.
I speak to her, she hears nothing at all;
The sound's absorbed in the walls of her cell.
I reach for her hand to take her away;
Despite my advance, she pays me no mind.
Her box is her world, it's all she has known;
It is her wish to remain in her room.
Mesmerized by her eyes, I cannot leave;
Hypnotized by her beauty, I must stay.
Transfixed by the girl, I am her captive,
She in the prison, I the prisoner.

Brian Kennedy

Good-bye

Good-bye, I will miss you so. Good-bye, my dear Grandma Hogle.
I know you are the only one. And good-bye. Your journey
here has just begun. Don't cry. I try to say. As I say
good-bye I can't let you slip away.
Grandma, I hope you have a good day, I can never say but
there I say,
Good-bye.

Aloura Lynne Morgan

Your Eyes

Are your eyes the windows to your soul?
And I imagine what lies beyond your eyes.
But should I dare to be forward and bold?
When I look deeply will I find my desires?
Will my own soul be captured by what I see?
Being pulled into you will I become infused,
Unable to turn back, run away, and flee?
Or a prisoner of passion for you to use.
If I dare to feel all of these things I feel,
In your eyes will I see love or feel fear?
My soul will know that all I see is so real.
Your eyes will see my heart crying crimson tears.

Nancy Lou Summers

Just a Child

Just a child, small and weak.
Looked toward the sun, but could not speak.
A silent world was all around.
And could not hear a single sound.
Then one day an angel came.
Just a child, spoke His name.
The silence broken, the sun aglow.
The angels singing, just a child could know.
The voice was heard and believed,
just a child would received.
The promise made so long ago,
lived in a child we all know.

LaVonne Murdock

Life

There comes a time in everyone's life where
there is a miasma.
A gleam of enlightenment amongst the
darkness of ignorance.
The question is, When do you sense it? When
do you feel it? When do you know it?
The answer is not a mystery. It is your time
when you feel wise at a young age, mature
towards your actions, and enjoy doing things
for others

You are within such miasma.
You are officially an adult

Florian Boyce

The Journey

The Earth in rotation as it spins the wind round
Blowing through the trees of golden brown
Halfway between where the leaves start and stop
Is my same experience as I am lost in thought
A learning experience with each different current
From a branch to a limb, to being stung by a hornet
And as I think of the little leaves' journey,
I keep in mind next year's blooming
See, time is for healing, each spring and fall
It's a time to pollinate and that's not all
To bring out the blossoms of my life's tree
And let go when it's time and just be me.

Kim Nichols

It Wasn't Meant to Be . . .

Standing over your Grave
I see what happened.
Was it rave? . . .
Or was it Passion? . . .

You yell,
You scream,
Your lungs so piercing.
There's something wrong,
something missing.

Those hands of cold,
Upon your body . . .

And that's where it all ends!
And now I stand here cowardly.
If I only had been there
In your time of need.
I would have saved you,
But I let you bleed.

Remember, it wasn't meant to be . . .

But then . . . maybe it was. . . .

Katherine Rollins

Unlove

The sun is setting and
I am letting you leave
Your eyes are telling
Secrets of how you feel
If you hate as much as you stare
In your mind, I am burning in Hell
Your tears remind me that I don't know
Quite as much as I thought I knew
The lies I've told
The love I sold
Just for one night without you

Anthony Karl Rose

Josapp

You never were a real great guy,
In fact, you often were a pr*ck.
You were a real big thief,
And your mind was really quite sick.
But you could always make us laugh
Or gag in disgust,
'Cause you really were
A good friend to all of us.
But then you left us all,
And we wish it were some other way.
Oh, why did you have to pull the trigger
On that sad, sad Easter day?
Yet time will move on,
And I know we'll meet once again.
Oh, and when we do,
Remind me to kick you in the shin.
Josapp, you meant a lot to me,
I wish this hadn't happened at all.
'Cause about a week beforehand,
You fink, you stole my golf ball!

Paul Miller

Horses

Horses
run, fast
loving, training, kissing
eating, soft, stupid, useless
hating, jumping, frightening
old, warm, dead

Britnee Felton

A Sacrifice

Impaled, I lay before you
Before your alter of eternity
I offer myself
A sacrifice of my soul
. . . for pleasure . . . ecstasy . . .
Never ending euphoria
My flesh is consumed
My blood spills forth
—to nourish your hunger
—to feed your desires
—to stain your blackened heart
My soul consumed
Salvation in return
The depths of Hell
Devour and burn

Bradi Hooker

Pure Conscience

Silent and alone he stands
bloodied blade loose in hands
Heavy conscience on his mind
pure redemption he must find.

Walks away fast as he can,
runs away, no more a man
tries to run, tries to hide
can't escape feeling inside

Eyes wide like frightened child
blank stare, young and wild
leaves the town, all he knows
silent watches river flows

Turns his back on innocence
inside brain hums resonance
tries to run, tries to hide,
can't escape his guilt inside

Andrew Symes

B*tchin' II: The Sequel

Everything gets worse
Never any better
I cry my tears of sadness
My face only gets wetter

First there's the screaming
Then comes the tears
I hurt so bad
I think only of my fears

So many things hurt me
My smile's almost always a fake
I'm never truly happy
For my heart always aches

I feel as though everything's my fault
And that no one wants me around
I know the time has come
I'll be careful not to make a sound

I don't do anything right
Everything is always wrong
What else is there to do
I haven't felt truly happy in so long.

Lenore Elizabeth Gerun

In Darkest Room of Darkest Night

In darkest room of darkest night
By the moon and candle light
Look at your eyes and your soft skin
My open lips to let you in
My heart it races, beats and pounds
Your sweet voice the only sound
You push me one way; then I pull
A cover drops; the air is cool
My bare skin pressed against your touch
I catch my breath; it's all too much
I cool down, then fires again
Within my soul do flare, and then
I grab you, tumble, kiss, and roll
Happiness our only goal
Passion stays till sleep sets in
Rest until we start again

Jeffrey Michael Oyler

silence

silence is September,
taking a leak in the dark
beside a parked car,
the pitter-patter,
like raindrops on the dead
leaves between my feet,
no music playing,
no sound at all now,
just steam rising from the ground.

David Rubin

Cocaine

Once we have met,
You will never be the same.
Then you'll ask yourself
"Who is to blame?"
I've turned the rich
Into the poorest of the poor.
I've changed good women
Into helpless whores.
I'll turn a brand-new Mercedes
Into a beat-up Chevy,
Because my pull on you
Is irresistibly heavy.
Once you use me,
I'll be your best friend.
And I may run out,
But it's never the end.
You'll try really hard
To someday finally quit.
But sooner or later,
You'll take another hit.

Susan Stack

Death

Death is coming for you
So you had better hide
He will eat up your soul
And spit out your pride

The moment he comes
To swallow your soul
The life which you had lived
Has entered the eternal hole

Death is eternal
And will never die
He will follow all souls
Until Apocalypse arrives.

Kellie Lubin

Drugs Can Screw with You

You think smoking is cool
You think weed is great
But what's this . . .
Your best friend is in the obituaries
Now it's not cool
Now it's not great
You had to wait
Find out if it could really kill you
Well God let the Devil do his job
He killed your best friend
Just so you know how it feels . . .
To lose a friend over drugs
I hope you're happy because I'm sure not
But one person is happy
Guess who that is?
The DEVIL!

Chelsea Francine Chevrette

Hungry?

How hungry are you?
Enough to . . . kill somebody?
Sell yourself for sex?
Pick it out of garbage bins?
Steal for it?
Stand in line at a soup kitchen?
Sell a pint of blood?
Deliver or sell drugs?
Rob, or be on food stamps?
Line up at an elderly meal site?
Take free lunches at school?
Beg on national television?
Eat, sleep and breath mom's dope for it?
Be ashamed to be living in America
Where hunger still exists!

Veneta F. Winkelman

Your Voice

As sweet as a cello serenading,
it captures my attention,
stimulates my senses etched
in my mind and heart,
lingering.

I've fallen to a surety,
but a gentleness I hear
awakening a stillness within,
inspiring.

As the voice of an angel,
it calms, softens my heart
strengthening my soul, so soothing.

Sensually caressing my ears,
seductively undressing me
gently disarming, embedded passions
surrendering.

Keep talking, never is it
enough. Bring me to you whispering.

Denise M. Dacunha

(Untiedled)

werds thrown togetherr in hayst.
mie [lie]f is,
was
neverr. and foreverr shall bee
cumming and going with the tydes. . .
neverr and foreverr shall bee,
was
mie [lie]f. is
werds thrown togetherr in hayst.

Catharine Stokes Emlen

Greenbriar Satori

ice cubes melt into metal grating
which burns my bare feet
steam rises
into faded blue
the soul escaping the body
consciousness will fall away
and we will melt into the sky
together
to be born again
in beautiful storms—
phallic lightning, quaking thunder
anticipates consummation
the earth buckles to meet their thrust
grass cools my blistered feet
the throbbing hum
of the highway
i feel no distance between myself
and the people in those cars
metal and glass shells
fall away

Matthew Guerrero

The Fight

He threw a left,
I threw a right,
That is how we started to fight.
He threw a hook,
So I hit him with a book,
When the teacher ran to stop us
I slammed him into the bus.
That's it till next time.

Jonathan Ray Chavez

Rest in Peace, the Final Farewell

The day grows longer each step we take.
The Lord is my shepherd. Do something for Heaven's sake!
The path of destruction is written for his fate. Candles burn
in honor of his life, it's too late! Hear my words,
remember what they said. Hear my words; remember what
they read. Reality filled the air, nothing scared him awake.
Now we lay him down for his soul to take.
What could I have done? He threw out his sword?
Now I'm on my knees, forgive me, Lord!
What was on my mind? I can't understand!
He needed my help! I extended my hand!
My mind had to learn what happened that night. I lost my son! I
let him out of my sight! Through my eyes,
the lessons they'll learn. And for this reason,
his candle still burns. His life is over now at a drop of a dime.
I need one last chance, to tell him one last time.
And on my face does it really show? That I loved you
once a long time ago? Now put down your guns.
And let the fighting cease! So that my oldest son may finally rest
in peace! I hope he can still hear me, I promised I shall—while I'm
on my knees, for the final farewell.

Arilita Moore

Open Your Eyes and See

Open your eyes and see . . .
A woman who lost her baby to the gun.
A man who lost his legs to another man's war.
A baby abandoned on the steps by a mother long gone.
Help too late for a woman on a cold steel table.
A man unleashing his anger on the innocent he loves.
A baby eternally asleep from the neglect of a father.
Open your eyes and see what is wrong with the world today.
All I have to give is the glory of God
And the power of hope for all who are left to live.

Elizabeth Peterson

Audra

last night i watched over you as you slept, my angel
caressed your cheek
brushed the hair from your face
my touch, deep and tender
still feeling that look in your eye
the look, the exhale of a heart's surrender

i called with a fervor to the skies to send an angel
to fill me with this piercing, throbbing warmth that is your love

it's a 111.111.111 vibe that feels like soul-coitus
a triple seven ecstasy that was meant to be

our hearts once beat in harmony
now in perfect synchronizing
two chambers of the same heart
two chambers of the same heart

wiped the tear from your face
that fell from my eye

last night i looked upon you and wept, my angel
there's no shame in tears of joy

Adrian Barret Johnson

Different

You label me as different,
Because I don't look like you.
I don't wear the same shoes as you.
I don't wear the same clothes like you.
I don't comb my hair the way you do.

You label me as different,
Because I don't act like you.
I don't cough like you,
I don't play football like you.
I don't eat the way you do.

You label me as different,
Because I don't like the same girls as you.
I don't flirt as badly like you.
I don't rub all over girls as much as you.
I don't grab girls . . . um . . . "butts" as much as you.

Wesley Ray Driggers

So, So Tired

I died alone in my bed last night,
So, so tired
Tired of all that is,
Leaving out all that can some day very well be,
So youthful, so alone.
If I handed you my feelings in a box,
You'd probably wrap them up,
Bury them six feet deep.
I'm am so tired of the hopelessness I feel within.
Sometimes I wish people could see, maybe could even understand,
Lend out a helping hand.
I tried to make every single one of them understand,
But they refused my offer,
so I decided to let it all go,
Let it remain buried deep within my soul.
I laid down, closing my eyes to my past,
I let go of that which identified me.
Last night you see,
I died all alone in my bed,
Just me. . . .

Helena Rios

My Brotha's

Brotha's, my brotha's, please tell my why
Why do you kiss on us sista's, then constantly lie?
Why do you mislead, mistreat, and call us out our name?
B*tches, tricks, and 'ho's. Baby we're all not the same.

Brotha's, my Brotha's, there's something else on my mind.
Why do you call her your girl, yet treat her so unkind?
You beat her and abuse her both mentally and physically.
But sista's we need to wake up. We're to blame equally.

Sista's, my sista's, we need to speak up loud and clear.
Sex isn't the only reason we are here.
We are here to be loved, admired, and respected.
Nowhere in the book says we are to be neglected

Brotha's, my brotha's, let me tell you one more thing.
You need to stop fronting when your around your friends.
So straighten up your act or find the door.
'Cause us beautiful, black sista's isn't taking it no more.

Akeliah Adia Stewart

Anonymity

He casually asked if he could pet my hair,
So I let him.
She told me: I hope you like the books;
I know I will, but she'll want them back soon.
He called out from behind me:
So what are you doing tonight?
I exhaled and continued on.
The psychological twin I passed said hi, turned;
rolled her eyes.
She thought I wouldn't notice.
I arrive, and inside my green cage,
I write on a piece of worn material: Buy more bread.
I do this only to appear stranger than I really am.
He stole my mirror and proclaimed, D*MN I'm fine!
I shrug and laugh, although he speaks honest truth.
But I still like my chemistry partner
with the sultry smile and sensitive eyes.
I turn suddenly and laugh.
She'll be terrified when the sh*t hits the fan
and she realizes she has no REAL friends.

. . . I walk in and admire my artwork.

Stephanie Crocker

Composer

until she finds me beautiful, I'm laughter
without a face. Eyes, I see; when echoes sleep.
Ears here, hear nothing under calm seas,
water morphing into every cup, that's how
I want her drip to feel: that's when drops splash
and symbols crash! Time to feed my pet Fantasy.
". . .Libido hungry too!" "G., keep your dog
on a leash." But woman, no man-animal-male-
beast, should be caged . . . lights on, ominous;
Death rattles the chain, "Awake Love,
this appears to be your lucky day." [yawn]
Love's rabid, and her fingers glitter
I bit her arrow, butter bean hearts
succulent and juicy, like liquid squid
writing "ball point pen," in eight indigo inks
"tentacle tongue want to taste."
mammal belly and mammary glands
to sniff notes off lady symphony
and to make music with my bare hands

Ra Graves

Lingering Passion

i met you in the fall of a year
you seemed to be so genuinely dear
one day you were here
and the next you were gone
i wondered for months what had went wrong
then you left my mind like an old
forgotten song
life went on
but then that day you returned . . .
our eyes met with unsaid desire
our bodies longing to share
each others fire
entangled together we became
the unsaid desire became one in the same
that day we began the game
sharing the sensual with no shame
remembering . . .
the rich passion will not so easily
be forgotten. . . .

Teresa Heyden

You Are

The day ends and I close my eyes
As the light begins to fade
I see your face . . . I can't sleep

A hot steamy shower warm water soothes me
lulls me into bliss. I'm reminded of your
touch . . . I can't sleep

A book to fulfill the need
Strength and comfort in every word
Your arms
around me . . . I can't sleep

A late walk; Gentle breezes, swaying
branches. The quiet seduction of the night
The soft sounds and sensual movements
of our lovemaking . . . I can't sleep

You are everything and everywhere
Exhausted, drifting and content
Wrapped tight and cozy in my covers
Secure and warm in your Love

As the light begins to fade I close my eyes
and Dream of You . . . As I Sleep

Kelly R. Roberson-Haney

The Game

She plays with mesmerized delighted eyes.
She knows of tenderness, but self-denied.
Lives and loves a way you don't expect too much.
Her touch is amplified by mine.
We play the game.

She wears a tattered, torn, faded smile.
It shows while stripping to her naked pose.
Clutching endlessly to hold me tight,
Pressing her breasts softly to my thigh,
And whispers, "Love is not a friend of mine."
We play the game.

David Buzzelli

Endeavor

Ride the snake, said the beast, out of his cave
For he will do you no harm, only if you are brave
He will show you the things that you yearn to know
Leaving you with no other place to go
He will show you the way through the desert sands
Ripping away your goodness to the escaping lands
Where fear and darkness finally cave in
Is when all the pain subconsciously begins
Under the sheets lies nothing but dirt
Losing your love and numbing your hurt
Leaving confusion trapped in your mind
Pushing for death all in due time.

Misty Marie Rzepniewski

Beer for Me

As I drive to Octoberfest,
I hope that there is beer for me.
I know that I will get no rest,
Especially if the beer is free.

Beer still flows as the night goes on,
Then someone yells "the keg is gone."
We are all feeling good and feeling fine,
But that's okay, We got wine!

Leighton Schoenberger

Spoken Words

Your words pierce me like a dagger to my heart.
Your ever-threatening moves only dig the dagger deeper.
My dark, red blood seeps slowly to the uncaring, cold earth.
Drip, drip, drip, drip.
I scream out in unholy terror at the pain it conceives,
My every breath getting shorter, shorter, until . . .
Nothing, my body is a pale, lifeless form lying on the hard gravel.
Night comes and swallows all light.
It is over, I will never be the same.
This is because of you.
This is how it feels to be teased, taunted, stereotyped.
It is an ugly, cruel thing to do.

JewLea Dahleen Hatton

I Can't Handle It Anymore

Gun in mouth. Finger on trigger.
It's the moment, the moment of TRUTH.
Slowly pulling the trigger, I see everything
I want to live for. BANG! Now it's too late.
No chance to rethink my thoughts and change my mind.
I regret having ever pulled that G**damned trigger.
I had a lot, but now there is nothing.

Insane Devil

That Dreadful Night

It's happened a couple of times, maybe seven or eight;
it's never a bone or a ligament, it's my heart that breaks.
I know that he loves me and sometimes he gets sad;
I don't know if it's stress, alcohol, or how easily he gets mad.
I try to be smart and say the right things;
if he only knew the heartache in the impact his fist brings.
My mind tells me to leave but my heart says get him help;
if he's not hurting me then he's hurting someone else.
I know I shouldn't take it, I should fight back;
he is stronger than me and he has a lot of impact.
Last night he came home and knocked me out by the bed;
when I came to, he was sleeping, and I shot him in the head.
There he lay in his own pool of blood right there on my satin sheets;
this way he wasn't hurting anyone else and he wasn't hurting me.

Stephanie Alexander

Lost

I hate where I wound up
Yet I am immobile.
To move forward I'm scared,
To go back is a dream.
Do I wallow in my despair,
Take a knife and end my life,
Or try to find solace in days gone by,
Resurrect the past when long ago I would dance
Around the thoughts of my unforeseen future?
Oh, how I ache for the times
When I still had the integrity to imagine
That I could one day be happy.

Jackie Hermes

The Crazy Ones

Crazy in the head
Wishing we were dead
We run far away from civilization
Fearing differentiation
Gashing with a blade
Hoping the pain we feel will fade
Hours of lecture from psychiatrists
Trying to prevent us from slitting our wrists
We scream into the echoing abyss
Trying to find a way out of this
We are swallowed up by the great escape
The spitting product of a cruel rape
Society refuses to see our tears
And doesn't seem to understand our fears
We are the crazy ones
We come in bundles by the tons
But we run and hide
Hoping to find a softer side
To this lovely, ugly, brutal world!

Kara Marie Hansen

Black Dream

Last night I had a dream of despair. There
smoke filled the streets. Fog kissed the
air. Buildings of crumbling stone stood like
fragile old men. I walked slowly down a
street of darkness. I found a gate. Its
skeleton arms guarded memories. It invited
me into its world of emptiness. Rows and
rows of cemetery stones lay deserted and
forgotten. I looked into a freshly dug hole
and saw a glimmering candlelight. A
frightened girl sat like a hiding shadow. It
was me. Tears fell from my pale face. A
nervous blade caressed my wrist. Slowly my
body disappeared. I looked up to see tearful
people passing over me. My father stood
there lifeless. He began to laugh. His wild
laughter tore the silence. I clapped my ears
until silence broke. I awoke in my bed,
sweat dripping down my brow. I looked up and
found my father standing over me.

Jenifer Andrews

House in the Familiar Crack

Crack in the screaming hot beams up there in the basement
beautiful hands remember, she doesn't
they are where to be through here,
dead bodies right side up there behind light
close to actually miss it
only to be reached by old, wrinkled hands
I go there usually—hallway with no walls,
frantic cleaning and cleaning glass everywhere
remember dreams right side up
only to be reached before she notices
every wall not being right behind the door houses
very familiar crack in beautiful, old, wrinkled hands
however moved not to miss it crack in the no walls hallway
the little door screaming hands rinsing me off
hanging from thin, plastic circles
rough, textured, old hands beautiful, wrinkled clothes thrown
everywhere please, please remember . . . she can't
how long can you stand it, light where no one has ever been—
beautiful by ladder, old from whatever is up there,
wrinkled by screaming feelings—remember the familiar crack.

DeAnna Pelleccia

Sandman

Another night all alone
My bed is cold, my pillow stone
As I slowly drift asleep
This lonely prison does not keep
In this place never-never land
We walk together in the sand
The moon is full the stars are bright
My love is strong the feeling right
The waves crash into the shore
Our flesh sweats, our bodies soar
The night is crisp, desires come
Together we become as one
Your breath brushing softly against my skin
Your hair blowing wildly in the wind
I kiss your lips and hold you tight
We make love throughout the night
But like always dawn will break
And in the morning I awake
No sea, no beach, no stars, no sand
Just this empty room and a lonely man

James Stockard

Sweet Seduction

SEXY, SULTRY, SUAVE, SENSUAL, SEXUAL,
STERN, SWEET, AND SAVORY . . .
This is the seduction of him.
TEMPTING, TANTALIZING, TEASING, THRUSTING,
THROBBING, TOXIC, AND TASTY . . .
This is the turmoil caused by him.
MOUTH-WATERING, MESMERIZING, MYSTERIOUS,
MISCHIEVOUS, AND MIND-BOGGLING . . .

This is the moment of madness experienced from him.
So WHY do I love him so much?
He seduces me with his gentle kisses.
He infiltrates my privacy with his tempting thoughts.
He masks me with his sexy strength.
And he intoxicates my willing mind with his subtle deeds . . .

This is the SWEET seduction of him.

Monica Marie Smith

daydreaming

awaiting his arrival
i shower, daydreaming, romanticizing me!
standing dripping wet
while the water beads against my flesh
yearning to give off a sultry effect
i let the water run down my breast
seductively inviting him in
with a bowl of cherries that lies beneath my frame
i grin
a lavish scent inundates the air
the fragrance draws him near
i shower, daydreaming, romanticizing
kiss me, baby, kiss me all over
whisper in my ear
ahh, don't stop there
embrace me, tantalize me, arouse my every need
daydreaming, romanticizing , enthralled me!

sandra jervay

Seek Ye the Caduceus

Oh, loathe the starting timer, turns the pages in your eyes
and dares you bring your nogginball and race to your demise

and grabs you with his learnedness to twist and turn and rent
your nogginball and steal away compassion you have lent

aye run and hide your gray ones from the red-eyed beastyteach
who takes and laughs and prods you all the more as you beseech

then gather beastyteaches to confound and devastate
and drink the life from nogginballs and feed on noggin hate

the brave and daring seekers of the snake and staff alone
will cower as their nogginballs lie gnarled to the bone

and when the beastyteach can taste sweet victory on his tongue
arising from the sweat and blood the seeker's bell is rung

and gathered up their nogginballs and find their hidden gray
Oh, rise, ye seekers find your snake and pave your golden way

then comes the beastyteach for help when beastyteach is ill
and gray in hand the seeker helps . . . as seekers always will .

Edward Scott Umlauf

Better Parenting through Ignorance

Free-floating thoughts I may now discuss
Night visions are all affright
Sensuousness abound, fiery sounds
Tasty touch, licking the sights

Not always so, I say in foresight
Not knowing what Mr. Death will bring
But for now, bi***y Tippy's gone
In praise for a new dawn, I sing

Self-regulating record pimps all p*ssed off
No self-effacing hack to be ripped off
Sponsors of slavery shall have no pie
No third world members today will die

Not losing sleep over ousted pseudos
With their hypocritical pathos
Hippie flowers wilting for all to see
Psyochonaut delusion of reality

Ian Keith Kennedy

Finished Life

In the light of dark . . .
They lay there, sweating drops of hate and pain
Madness due to hunger,
consumed by the hopelessness and the darkness
They sustain on a deep-rooted psychosis
The hard rain washes nothing but the love and propinquity
Drip . . . drip . . . drip, incessantly falling in the same place
Minds blank—hearts filled with emptiness and hatred
Overflowing with the paucity
The abyssal loneliness! Who's there? !
Given up on life . . .
People seem to be procreated to destroy
Raze everything in sight
Where's the kinship and care? Who's there? !
Times lost, it seems to be running away
The closer you want to get, the farther it goes
Unbalanced and incognizant, so they seem
Nothing new or different is accepted!
How can it be?
Vomiting malevolence . . . Tired and pathetic, why carry on the misery?
End it right here . . .

Shahid H. Karachiwala

Club Love

I don't know you but I'll spend this time with you.
You're probably not my type, but I'll still bump and grind with you.
We'll exchange phone numbers and maybe talk once or twice.
You're probably a freak but you seem nice.

Gentry Luanne Kestner

Sophistication

When you come home
You come to me, knowing you're not alone.
What you see?
Hazel bedroom eyes, my beautiful face with a lovely smile,
long black wavy hair and a coca-cola shaped body
in a black and lace see-through negligee, showing you all of me.
Passion, love, and pleasure bringing us both sure satisfaction in reality.

Sherritha L. LaFleur

A Moment

My whole life's been crooked, nobody can overlook it.
Self worth's at an all time low, nobody can move it.
I thought I had a baby boy, but DNA couldn't prove it.
These suicidal tendencies, thinking about going through it.
See suicidal thoughts come and go like the wind.
And even though the bible be stating that it's a sin,
To be doing yourself in, I'm at war from within.
So which side's going to lose, and which side's going to win.
Slap myself in my own face, try to get back to a normal place.
Surround myself with love and homies, some of those things
Keep my mind off those things that make my life so harsh.
And the people that don't understand, wonder why I start.
With a twelve pack in the middle of the day, also the middle of night
That seems to be the only way to stop the constant fight.
Between the devil and the angel that sit upon my shoulders.
Get them both drunk and now they act like home boys for
A moment.

Gonzalo Belmonte

No Distance Is Far Enough

No distance could ever come between our never-ending love
No distance could ever take away
the lasting memories of your soft and tender touch
No distance could ever silence the sweet charm of your voice
No distance could ever erase the enchanting fragrance of your essence
No distance could ever keep me from getting back to you

James A. Marrow, Jr.

The Desert

The morning dew is like a magic powder to my land,
It is fresh water on top of the dry, arid sand.
When I wake up and see my day is magical,
I know that I will see the sky for another three weeks, which is to me, special.
I don't know when the mist will come down from God,
But I do know that it will always come as a magical flood.

Risto Stevcev

This Guy

This guy I know cares, trusts.
This guy I know believes, tries; he is not the best.
This guy I know has strength, integrity, the power to do anything.
This guy I know loves me.
This guy I know is my father.
He is my strength, my life, my trust, and most of all, he has my love.
This guy I know is my father.

Erika Lindberg

The Integral Part

As the four winds blow, you appeared into my life.
not knowing which direction you came releasing me from love's strife.
Walking softly into my heart, and now you are the most important part.
You know—the tick that goes with the tock—the time from the clock.
And without that—time would stand still.
You are the integral part of my life.
You are my wife.

James Porch

Their Baby

The news is here—she is having a baby,
She looks forward to all the joy—their baby will arrive.

She tells the father their baby is due,
He seems amazed, but wishes it wasn't true. Their baby will arrive.

Then she loses the father, her man, her love—can she ever be one again?
Their baby will arrive.

Now the pain and anger have begun. She is hurt, upset, and full of tears.
Her life is changing—there are so many fears.

She feels the anger deep inside, hoping, praying—she will survive.
Their baby will arrive.

One day she is awakened. Her baby is gone.
She feels scared and shaken
She is lost, confused and torn apart, wishing she had a new start.
Their baby will not arrive.

She tells the father, and what does he do? Questions her and acts like a fool.

He yells and screams, her shattered dreams, knowing they will never have a family.
Their baby will not arrive.

Tears of pain and sorrow fill her nights,
She prays that everything will turn out right.
Their baby will not arrive.

Her baby is close, always on her mind.
We love you forever, until the end of time.
Only in heart has their baby arrived. Good night.

Naomi Sotero

Thanksgiving

Thanksgiving is a time for caring,
Having fun and people sharing,
Outside the sun is shining bright,
Unhappy souls will see a sight,
Giant turkeys smelling great,
Harvest times will forever create,
Tasty foods so good to eat,
Favorite pies that are a treat,
United together for one special day,
Lasting memories that never go away.

Sara Frankovic

Ghosts of the Titanic

All my love, Garry

As we raised up the old titanic
From the deep dark coasts
What of its mysteries
Did we too dig up the ghosts

Are they haunting the old "murderess"
Would this be their thirst quencher
All wishing to speak
Of their fatal adventure

We wonder on, what they would tell us
Those deeply unfortunates
Would it all be
Happenings of their last minutes

The day the mighty iceberg was struck
By "unsinkable" Titanic
Most were hysterical
Some, bravely kept up the music.

Those ghosts must surely be so lost
Moaning for their sad losses
Does the sea care at all
In her splashings and tosses

Oh, rock-hard iceberg
What have you done
But sorted the survivor
From the sea-claimed one.

Barbara Sherlow

Part of Me

Alone
Trapped without myself
Scared
Do I really know myself
Afraid
Where did my world go
Betrayed
Deprived of all hope
Should I try to make amends
Should I accept this bitter end
Should I believe you're just a friend
No, I can't
I cannot believe you would feel this way
Cannot decide if it's love or hate
Cannot determine who's wrong or right
Cannot endure another fight
Will not accept this bitter end
Will not believe you're just a friend
But I will try to make amends
For love
For need
For hope
Not greed
I take what life has dealt to me
But will not accept so easily
And I will be here readily
Waiting for the other part of me

Jeremy Dawley

Stone to the Bone

To my brothers, black, white, red, yellow or brown,
please listen to my sound, you say, you want to get stone to the bone.
Get stone to the bone with a heavy education.
There is no time for any hesitation.
Get stone to the bone with a specific skill.
There is no reason to kill.
Get stone to the bone with a heavy trade.
Sooner or later, you will have it made.
Then no one can call you a simple spade.
Get stone to the bone and earn some money.
You will be like all the bees with all that good honey.
Get stone to the bone with a healthy mind.
Darn that unemployment line.
Use your brains, enjoy your gains.
Get stone to the bone.
Baby, be on your own!

Bettie Ann Siler Henderson

The Wolf's Round

He had his way! He won today! My will just up and went away.
I am so weak with despair. How much longer can I hang in there?
This time and tried to will him away.
But he was more driven, you might say.
He only had one thing on his mind, and that was to win this time!
It's harder and harder with each passing day
to find the strength to will him away.

My thoughts turn to my children and what they will become.
A doctor or a nun, it's hard to say; but they still need me
to help them guide their way.
I want so much to see that day when would give them away.
Hand and hand with that special someone
as two people unite as one.

God has a plan for us all it seems.
I am not certain what He has in mind for me.
As for now, we will wait and see in hopes that they find
a cure for this disease!
There is one thing I know is that this wolf has got to go.
So I am going to reach deep inside me to find a way
to get through another day.
I don't know what time will bring; but I am in for a battle it seems.
He may have won this round,
but rest assured, I won't take it lying down!

Susan Trancynger

Reflections

Looking back what do I see? Many, many reflections of me.
Images and faces who can they be? Can they really, really be me?

A tiny baby innocent and warm nestled safe in her mother's arms.
Was that me?
How could it be I feel so much fear deep inside of me?

A little girl, laughing and bright.
When darkness came was afraid of the night.
To laugh by day and cry by night,
needing to be loved with all her might.

A teenager with charm and grace, dresses of satin, silk, and lace.
On the surface things look bright.
Deep inside is the little girl afraid of the night.

A wife, loving and warm, seeking protection in her husband's arms.
Finding none, to her alarm.
The loneliest lonely there can be is the little girl deep inside of me.

Looking deep into my soul,
I begin to wonder, can I ever achieve my goal?
Can the reflections of the past be erased from my soul at last?

Can the fear that hides beneath the surface
ever come to any good purpose?
Will the loneliness disappear?
Is someone going to hold me near?

Gladienne Hartzler

Time Passes

Time passes. Seeds spring
Into a greening flow
Across the fields and up the hills
Like mossy fur.

Time passes. Birds sing
And swoop and dart,
Proclaiming from the highest wire
Their vibrancy.

Time passes. Ocean slings
Itself upon a widening shore,
Repeating a tidal roar
Forever more.
Time passes.

Page Rappaport

Through the Clouds

I know not why the sky is dark
And covers like a shroud.

I only know my God controls
The thunder and the clouds.

I know not why the days are filled
With heartache and with strain.

I only know my God controls
All the weariness and all the pain.

I know not why sometimes the sky
Is not so bright for me.

I only know my God controls
my life and its destiny.

It matters not that I can't see
The "wherefores" and the "whys."

As long as God is in control,
I will be satisfied.

For I'm His child, and He's my God,
He knows the reasons why.

So I will trust until he leads
Me on the brighter skies.

Willie McNear

My Vow to Her

I dedicate this to Emmai—
distance only makes me love her more.

The blister bliss cried a vow
The vows carries till next life
To love her forever, till ever
No matter how far we apart
Her love will chase my solitude

I look afar, far away
Across vast ocean-
And tall mountains
To that island my angel rests
Knowing someday she will come

I close my eyes and imagine
With silk grace she walks to me
She, the gift of my life

I spread my feelings, show my heart
The only way I know how
The gift from heaven she's to me

She's to me that honeybee
She's that rose without thorns

And only time defines my love,
For eternity seems just right

N. X. P.

Michael, My Friend

Michael, I could never explain
how grateful I am to have you for a friend.
Just knowing you're always there with a sympathetic ear,
an encouraging word, and an understanding heart
gives me a feeling of peace that I wouldn't know if it weren't for you.
And to know that you can count on me just as I count on you
makes our friendship one of the most valuable gifts
I've ever been given . . . and I wouldn't trade it for anything!

Susan Strange

The Cat

As I looked around, I saw a cat. I love her.
She is my friend. I pretend I am a cat and play with her.
Ears alert, eyes sharp, muscles tense, and nose scanning the air,
I am a lion. I am the tiger in the jungle,
roaming with the beast itself, the cat.
I am quick and sleek as a cheetah, glowing eyes on the African plains.
Tail twitching and moving gracefully, I spend my time with her,
acting as she does, rolling on my back, pouncing, chasing, running.
We are wild cats in the jungles. We have fun.

Nicole Fryar

I Love You, Mother

I am so sorry you have MS,
but I'll take care of you the way I know best.
I'll pick you up if you're on the floor,
help you to walk and open the door.
Help you to transfer from one chair to another,
all because I love you, Mother.

I'll take you to the doctor when you need care,
and be there for you when there are things to share.
It was a hot summer day that wasn't so fine when you got diagnosed in 1989.
It took quite a while before you became confined;
I was far and away and totally blind.

I can't change the past as neither can you,
but I'm here now, and there's a lot we can do.

I'll fight for your cause and for millions of others,
all because I love you, Mother.

Danette M. Zieman

Miracle Babies

I'm going to have another baby our daughter said,
smiling so wide nodding her head.
This will make pregnancy three. Total joy we felt, happiness you see.
The day of the ultrasound came very fast.
Now we would know your due date at last.
And Oh, the surprise when you came into view.
You're not just one, God gave her two.
We laughed and cried from surprise and joy
now the long wait, is it girls or boys.
It's two little girls exactly alike identical twins, Oh, what delight.
One morning early when mommy awoke
she felt real wet thought her water had broke.
Only 26 weeks not far enough along but she knew by her pain something was wrong.
The trip to the hospital was very bad. Mommy was crying 'cause she was so sad.
The doctor said from what he saw you both were in trouble no weight gain at all.
It was decided the doctors must take both of you now before it's too late.
You both were starving each minute each day so off to delivery without delay.
Jenna was born exactly one pound upon delivery you made not a sound.
They rushed you into NICU where doctors and nurses were waiting on you.
They worked real hard giving you life,
once you began breathing was such a delight.
Hanna was born one pound three point five,
so small and tiny, hard to believe you're alive.
They rushed you into NICU where doctors and nurses took care of you.
It's been hard watching you grow 'cause pounds and ounces go on so slow.
But Miracle babies are what you are, God watched you both.

Debra Jean Eddy

The Sweetest Harvest

The harvest grows
Especially the wheat
But the harvest is not sweeter
Than a Mom so sweet

S Franklin

Lost

I am the lost child
Of the universe.
No family, no friends,
No one to cry to.
Moving into oblivion.

Jean M.

Alice

A time's gone
Like clouds past
In which I've done,
Crying, you go fast
Ending from me to none.

Noe Pereira de Campos

Untitled

You are my angel.
When you appear,
All of my troubles disappear.
You must been sent
From Heaven above.

Gail Morin

Dark Mystery

Dark mystery beyond the seventh sea
Why do you seek me?
From some forgotten yesterday
Dreams of the golden years gone astray
Or maybe of a distant memory.

Meri A. Anthony

Beach

Blanketed with sand and shells
Everything can be seen miles away
Awesome things to find
Creatures are unbelievable
Houses by the ocean

Amanda Elizabeth Peck

It's Time!

The leaves are falling, it's Fall.
The snow is falling, it's Winter.
The flowers are blooming, it's Spring.
The sun is shining bright, it's summer.
It really is something isn't it.

Sarah Tirado

Media

Launching the invasion,
With words of great persuasion,
Entering our minds ever so slow
To lead us to sea, of false reality,
One by one drowning in perfect harmony.

Steven E. Schubach

Searching

Staring up at the ceiling, I look all around
not knowing what exactly I am searching for
However, I can't understand why I am feeling what I am feeling
It pains me to see how dreary life can seem
However, I know life is what I choose it to be
Through my struggles I find my strengths
destroying the pain and making them blank
My eyes become filled with such high hopes so I test myself to climb up the ropes
I guide myself to follow my dreams, by knowing that in the end I will succeed.

Neelam Raju

It

From beneath the window seal it crept,
It was silent, it was so strong, it was quick,
It was so unexpected.
I closed my eyes expecting to wake up,
I opened my eyes to find it staring me in the eyes,
I turned my head in shame as it was so beautiful and I was so obscure,
I wanted to run and hide in a corner, until it went away,
I found that the more I resisted the stronger it became,
So I gave in to its demands, and here I am,
In love for the first time

James Allen Laurent

The Falling Spring

The leaves come down.
The running river bank stays, but higher and faster will tell it lives.
It has life like Mother Nature and movement like the wind.
It's nice and quiet like a feather coming down.

There is still more to come.

The animals love nature in the water.
People and kids come to play and splash.
All the tree's leaves fall into the river, floating away.
Will you see the falling spring someday?

Tabatha Johnson

An Angel Who's Earned His Wings

Mommy's little angel has gone to Heaven,
for he left this world without sin.
He left this world having done no wrong.
Now he's where he truly belongs,
With God, where he'll meet no harm. Where he is safe and warm.
I used to be scared of you being alone.
But I'm sure you've made a new home.

They say everything happens for a reason.
God had his when you were chosen.
Now you're a true angel, you've earned your wings.
To fly as you wish, you're free.
Just promise me that once in a while, you'll look down at me and smile
You'll always be with me in my heart, no matter how far we're apart.

I just hope you know how much I love you!
I pray every night that you do.
No matter how much I wish this could be erased,
I know you're in a better place;
Never again, can anyone hurt you.
Only God knows what you went through.

But, now, you're protected eternally.
You're as safe as anyone could possibly be.
And though I wish I could go back in time,
and once again make you mine.
I have to believe that you were chosen,
for whatever unknown reason.

God can protect you better than anyone,
better than the job I had done.

Chere Shores

E

Unwrap your mind with me,
Blast through time with me,
Travel the galaxy.
Am I you are you me,
Tell me what do you see,
In that black odyssey?
My eyes do perceive atomic
Energy, released!
In that black odyssey I see
You, me!
This ecstasy enthralled in me
Is heavenly, feel our bodies
Transforming into vine leaves
So divinely, finally,
God sent you to find me
Blinding, the lighting
Of our love's lightning
Makes the night sing!

William Thomas Busch

The Ocean

The ocean is my place
to flee the human race.
To sit upon the sand
and sieve it through my hand.
To look upon the waves
that the little creatures brave.
To see the perfect mass
shining like does glass.
The pain and sorrow I felt
quickly starts to melt
As my find is finally free,
and I am who I wish to be.
My mind is clear of what I fear,
and, of joy, I shed a tear.
When night begins to fall,
closer I do crawl,
As I strain to see,
through the dark, the shining sea.
The waves curl and bend
from a thing that never ends.
And, through the dark and light, I see
the mass that means so much to me.

Donald Clayton Walters, Jr

Every Passing Day

Dedicated to my very special friend, Dana Thomas.

Sometimes I sit and think of all
the special times we've shared
Of all the hugs and special smiles
to simply show you cared

You always seem to know just how
to clear the clouds away
And when my skies are dark with gray
you turn them back to sunfilled days

You've always been a special friend
and held a special place
You've left footprints in my heart
while others leave without a trace

So how could I began to thank
God for this special love?
How could I start to thank Him enough
for sending you from above?

So while no words could ever tell
or even start to say
Just know you mean much more to me
with each and every passing day.

Mary Ledford

Falling Stars

I had never heard of falling stars, 'cause no one could ever be worth it
I had never understood the reason behind the love people shared
But then I finally met you and I understood it all
It was because of you that life was no longer a dream
But the dream turned into a nightmare when you became a threat to me
I had never in my life met anyone quite like you
Because in my twisted so-called world, death was all I knew
I never smiled before or showed any affection
Unless it was when Death came knocking and took the souls away
I had never intended on death to take you
But you had become an obstacle that I just couldn't handle
You're the only one who had ever seen me smile
But then again,
It was because of you that life became too difficult
My job was to bring death and that's the only thing I ever knew
So when I felt love for the first time in my life, I actually felt alive
But that was a problem that I was trained to deal with
I knew I would regret it, and I wished the stars would fall
But they never knew you, and now, they never would

Marina Raynis

The New World

Cheer up, things soon will be much brighter, the skies above more blue.
You'll find the ones who love you, and you'll find you love them too.
Then things will run more smoothly, like a peaceful flowing stream
And you'll have lots of children, lovely as a dream.
For we know the Psalms are no fable,
And they tell us we shall have children, like olive plants around the table.
You and I know why, dear, they'll never need to fear.
They'll run and play by the silvery stream with nothing harmful near.
They'll play with lions and lambs and things, and a beautiful turtle dove,
With a lovely new world beneath their feet, and happy new heavens above.
So if we strive on, and with God's help endure,
The trials from this old world, which soon will be no more.
Then this world, has never seen or heard
The things God has promised through his word.
For those who seek him, and they will have no sorrow,
Only the joys of a glad tomorrow.
This is no pipe dream out of the blue.
God's word told them write! These words are faithful and true.
So let's forget the old world, and work for the one that's good.
Then our hearts will overflow with thanks for blessings from God's love.

Jessie Cherry

Jennifer's Foo-Foo

With all my love and memories forever, Mama

Dear foo-foo, my one and only foo-foo,
Oh, how I did love thee, let me count the ways;
I loved you in the morning and I loved you all day long.
I loved you especially at my nap time,
Since that was when I would always fuss and whine.

At bedtime you were my finest comfort,
As you always helped me to fall fast asleep.
Oh, foo-foo, my dearest, cherished foo-foo,
No other foo-foo would ever do, than just you.

My Mama and Daddy sneaked and tried to fool me,
And slip me other new foo-foo's in your place.
But I knew they were impostors and simply were not you,
After one taste, I would open my mouth, and throw them out of my face.

You bare my little baby teeth marks,
When I would bite you as they broke through my sore little gums.
You eased my pain and helped me to get through,
Until my teething was over, gone with, and done.

Of course I used you much longer than I really ever should,
And as I got much older, the braces corrected my teeth and bite as they could.
Oh, foo-foo, dearest foo-foo, I may now be 27 years old,
And yet, I still have you with me, and I should have you plated in gold.

Gwendolyn Lucia Browning

Lampposts

Useless by day
Leading dogs astray
But at night
They bask their soft yellow light
Guiding cars their way.

Charles A. Sanders

Kittens

The newborn kittens
with different color mittens
scampered out to play.
They played all day
until dismay
when the sky had turned grey.

April Marie Myhre

Guess I'll Fall in Love Again

Love, is such a fickle thing,
With all the sadness it can bring;
Lonely times and all those tears,
A thousand heartaches and many fears.

Love can leave you sad and blue,
Love can make your heart untrue;
Still, I know I cannot win,
Guess I'll fall in love again.

Broken hearts, mean empty rooms,
Love can die before it blooms;
Leaving souls, stacked row on row,
Guess I'll give it one more go.

When your heart aches, deep within,
Love has flown, you've lost again;
Still, you try and play the fool,
For you're just love's helpless tool.

Yes love is just a fickle thing,
With broken hearts and broken dreams;
And though I know I will not win;
Guess I'll fall in love again.

Bob Bearden

A Hug Is a Hug?

Inspired by & dedicated to Yaser,
a wonderful man, whom I love dearly

A hug is a hug
And a hold is a hold
This is the truth
So I've been told

But a hug is not just a hug
And a hold is not just a hold
They can be so different
And feel so warm or cold

A hug can say I love you
A hug can say I care
Or a hug can even say
Hey, don't worry, I'll be there

A hug can say good morning
A hug can make you cry
Or a hug can take the tears away
And bring a smile back to your eyes

A hug can say good-bye
A hug can say we're friends
Or a hug can even say
I'm sorry, you know this is the end

Debi Bosisto

The Pathway

We walked along the pathway under trees where branches meet,
The golden leaves lined the archway and made a carpet for our feet.
The tunnel sheltered us from cold, outside the chill winds blew,
But safe inside the canopy's gentle rustling waved us through.
Our steps were soundless as we strolled on moistened litter ground,
A magic scene, perfection, tranquility profound,
Just two of us with nature's autumn garden wrapped around,
So hand in hand, enthralled by all, a loving kiss was found.
At times, a leaf would flutter like a golden butterfly
And dance and twirl to settle, waiting next to come from high,
And diamond drops of moisture saved from early morning dew
Would splat on nature's carpet and then disappear from view.
A few more steps and pathway gently curved, the end was seen,
The outside world is waiting to engulf us back from dream.
We pause and say, "I love you," with the message understood
By all the living cells contained within this alpine wood,
And then with sigh we step outside to stark reality
Prepared to face life's daily tasks with renewed energy
And thankful of the time to pause and feel so reassured
That though life's pathway may be rough, there are parts that give reward.

Celia Johnston

A Tribute to Our Ancestors

They came from mother England, far across the ocean wide,
As free settlers to Australia, to live in Sydney side,
They dwelt in down town Mosman, built a stone house by the sea,
Overlooking Middle Harbour, with a view so grand to see.

The family were all builders, the sons experts in their skill,
Built homes all over Mosman, most standing sturdy still,
The town was young and growing, it was a long, long road to hoe,
There was vacant land all over, times were different then you know.

The old man owned the quarry, for they needed stone you see,
To build the famous first Spit Bridge, still in its infancy,
Horse and carts were used those days to get to and from the job,
The men worked so hard, long hours too, just to make a bob.

We are grateful to our ancestors, for they paved the way for us,
It was they who knew the heart ache, as they toiled in sweat and dust,
The old and young depended too, upon the workers pay,
No help from others in those days and you had to pay your way.

So rest in peace our ancestors, out in the great beyond,
Although we did not know you well, of you we are still fond,
For you had a vision long ago, and we carry on your genes,
And those of us you left behind, are living out your dreams.

Gwen Ablett

My Best Friend

She was always there for me and I know she'll stay by my side for life.
Thick and thin, we've been through it all. . . . together.
When one is upset, so is the other.
I can trust her with all of my secrets because I know she will not tell.
We go everywhere together; we're never apart.
We are very similar to each other—like sisters;
Hand in hand and heart in heart.
Whenever my spirits are down I know
I can count on her to listen to how I feel.
She knows me inside and out,
My deepest thoughts and my hidden fears.
She knows secrets no one else knows but her and I.
She can read my mind like no one else can and she knows
What I am thinking without me even telling her.
Whenever no one else is there for me,
I know I can count on her to be waiting for me.
During hard times that I know I cannot get through by myself,
I don't have to worry because she'll be there for me no matter what.
We'll be together for life, together until the end.
One may ask, "Where do you find such a friend like that?"
The answer I always reply is, "I find her in my mirror."

Tasha Trodden

Life

When sickness befalls us
and we lack our health,
we cry and we say we
will promise our wealth.
In fact it should be,
fall down on your knee.
His blessing we ask—
for him it's no task.
The spirit of God is very near;
His love for you was always clear.
Our bodies may crumble and turn to dust.
It's with the Lord we place our trust.
It was he that intervened,
Not just a person, but the one,
the supreme being.
Even with the fading light,
you still put up a heartfelt fight.
But the battle was lost, my loving wife,
with that fragile thing called life.

Dennis L. McGaffee

Pain

Pain is a part of life.
Sometimes I wonder if
it isn't the other way
around.

Love, having, waiting
wanting, or losing,
tears whole even in
the strong.

Loving you, such as pain.
Like that of a hundred
paper cuts, that never find the
time to heal.

My heart is set aflame,
by your presence.
Only to be burnt by
your absence.
So now answer me this:
Is pain a part of life,
or is life a part of pain?

July 24, 1999

June Petersen

Time . . .

For Matthew

I thought I'd have more time.
Eighteen years have flown by.
I'm not ready to lose you
Watch you strike out on your own.

Wasn't it just yesterday
Your very first day at school?
I drove you there myself.
You walked in without a care.

I remember your first date
And when you got your car
I was afraid for you to leave
And stayed awake until you came home.

I spent your whole life
Getting you ready for this day.
I gave you the tools you need
But forgot myself to prepare.

Now I have to look up at you.
You've grown into such a man.
It's time to live the life you planned
But remember I'll always be here.

Denby L. Stutz

Wind Cries in Autumn

Could you! Remind me why?
I was there, to stroke your hair, to wipe
your tears, to comfort your fears.

The wind cries in Autumn. In a heavy
rain of leaves. Which were once full of
life, love, hope, promise, bringing beauty
to the world.

The leaves now dead to the world are cast aside, dumped, and burned.

My eyes are tired of watching their every
movement, looking into a void of nothingness.

My ears are tired of listening to the cries of the wind,
in my heart, rustling the leaves, which remain intact.

My heart is something interesting. Through time, this life,
has not known love,
but can feel it, can sense it, in your eyes,
in a few unspoken words,
in your beauty burning from the inside.

The wind cries here in my heart.

Thomas Richard Jennings

Soul of Colors

Life again was aquamarine.
I stood facing the mighty mass: the sea dancing to its orchestra.
Those white fringes, lace-like, overlapping one another,
That whoosh, that treble, whispering,
"I see you reflected. I see you captured in me."
Suddenly today, dunno why, my soul feels restless.

Life again was saffron. The sun spread across my cheek.
Slicing the light, the silhouette of a stork waved by.
Those elegant flapping wings, the majesty, and the hollow call,
Saying, "I see you reflected. I see you captured in me."
Suddenly today, dunno why, my soul feels charmed.

Life was mercury. I stood on a pool upon boulders and pebbles,
My reflection beneath undisturbed, duplicated, yet orientated.
Outstretched, nudging limits and boundaries.
Life was emerald, lilac, crimson. Life was a kaleidoscope!

Within the profoundness, I then heard it: sonorous, flawless,
A chanting voice so bathed in colors, a voice so fragrant, so female.
And life became sienna, earth-like.

Suddenly, in that soul-stirring voice, I understood myself.
Suddenly today, I now know why my soul feels restless.

Mohammad Jannatul Haque

The Unspoken Message

Every shift I work there is a ritual that occurs
I spend time with Dee as she's the only resident who won't talk with me

While we play our game of cards with the house cat looking on
I notice the dark brown eyes of my partner staring at my dark green eyes
As I carry on a one-sided conversation, hoping to achieve a bond

Dee is seeing scary images and hearing frightening voices
Her world right now offers her limited choices
You see, paranoia is the cross she has to bear
And I know I must keep trying to reach the caring woman I know is there

A remarkable event takes place as our card playing progresses
I am a student again and Dee is my coach
She teaches me how to find comfort in silence
Without speaking, she shows me how to listen and hear

As I was getting ready to leave the house one final time
I quickly glance in my mail slot to find one last note
Upon unfolding the paper I read, "I am really going to miss you. Love, Dee"

I tearfully observe our deck of cards lying on the desk
As I thank Dee for these lessons for which I'm forever blessed
In silence and with perseverance, the message can be clearly heard
For I now understand the meaning of the unspoken word

Becky Bemmes

The Light of Hope

I know not
what today will bring
so I await the sunrise
before I sing.
In hope to discover the truth
that today, everything is new.
I awaken my mind
to feel the rhythm of life
and let it become part of my soul.
Wiping the blindness away;
I can see a much clearer day.
Now I can respond to life.
Strive to approach with a deeper insight
of what is right in my life.
With my dream and a vision in mind;
I know I will find
the light of hope.
With each sunrise
there are new beginnings to behold.

Antonietta M. Maienza

Lost in the Desert

Lost, lost in the desert
where to go, I do not know
sand in my face, very hot

Sun setting, lying in the sand
almost buried
when will the night end

Morning comes
another hot day
when will I find water

So hot, so hot
I am dying of thirst
my throat is dried out

Walking down, long sandy hills
looking for water, will I find it
no one knows

I think I see it
or it's just my mind
I am walking toward it

It was just my mind
playing tricks on me, dying, dying, dead

Nicole Dauphinee

The Shining Star

There is a special person
Who plays a special part
Beyond the ocean,
Through the trees,
A place that's called my heart.

Throughout the years it was locked shut
Like a bathtub with a leak,
But then my heart it opened so,
To take a little peek.

And what it saw was like a star,
Shining bright into the sky,
And when I looked at you, I knew,
I've found that special guy.

But when I thought and thought a while
About this shining star,
I knew someday he would be gone
To a place long and far.

So now I mourn and cry all day
When I look into the sky.
I only wish I could have said
Just one long, last good-bye.

Chalynn Pertuz

You Are

You are my highest aim
Higher than the depths of my heart, you make flicker like a flame
The words you speak to me are real
Enfolding myself back on me to forge me of the strongest steel
And sharper than the sharpest blade

And when I look to the heavens' section
I see you, telling me it's important to look the other direction
To me you do convince
you can sum a life of happiness, love, fear, pain in a single sentence
The sentence that empowers me

You persevere in the battle of right
You have solved the riddles Satan has bestowed to blind your sight
You are the hero I look up to
Because there is no one taller, stronger, or prouder than you
The truths I see in those opalized brown eyes

Time and time again, I can't believe
that you wish to love me, to listen to me; I guess I am a little naive
To me life you are larger than
as I expand my mind to learn from you to its extent of span
But most importantly, you make me feel like a man

Jason Marshall Garner

I'm Sorry, Son

His father lay in a hospital bed sick and very weak.
He looked up at his son, and slowly rubbed his cheek.
His father knew how near he lay to being close to death.
He didn't want his son to know for fear he'd lose his breath.

He wanted to spend the little time to make his son a man.
He struggled onward day by day with his trembling hands.
He knew the day was soon to come when he no longer would be seen.
His son would be alone and thinking of how things could have been.

He thought of his son getting married, and to whom these vows would be.
He thought of his future grandchildren; those whom he'd never see.
He thought of the beautiful memories, his childhood and his youth.
He thought of raising his only son, teaching him to tell the truth.

He dare not shed a tear of pain for fear his son would know.
His father feared his only son would see his dad was dying slow.
He loved his son so very much yet couldn't tell him so.
The doctor stood by his father's side, there's something you have to know.

"I'm sorry son, your father's dead." Kept ringing in his mind.
He thought of all the happiness his father left behind.
He looked up into the shining sky, and smiled away his frown.
Five little words came to his mind, "You didn't let me down."

Darlene Lessard

A Poem from Your Angel

When the clouds turned black in the midday sky
Evil brought you to your knees and forced you to cry.
Why it happens, I shall never know why
But still, I lifted you up and the sorrow passed by.

The men of the thrones deprived you of your wealth
And with your money, you soon lost your health
But I witnessed it all and when I came down in stealth
I lifted you up and you were back to yourself.

Grieving is what time and the fates brought
You lost faith in me and an answer you sought.
You left my side and pain was what you got
But fear not my child, for I shall leave thee not.

Fear not, my child. You shall never pay.
Fear not, my child. Your heart knows the way.
Just keep faith with you and you'll hear me say
From the minute you were born, to this very day

I have been there for you. In your darkest hours, I'll see you through.
On the toughest of trails, I'll carry you. And only when you're mighty
will I leave you but remember, though you may not be aware like the Father
in Heaven, I shall always be there watching over you.

Michael Ross

Beauty

Daisies in a cracked coffee cup
beside my keys
wink as I walk by.
And the dry
butterfly
catches my eye.
You don't treasure beauty much.

Melanie Freeman

Ode to My Unsung Hero

Because you are important to me,
I pray blessings and peace be with you
now and each day.
And I will ask my angels to tenderly
watch over you and me,
so we may endure tomorrow,
and finally win.

Peggy Snyder

Sunshine

The first light of the day
shines warmly through my window
and gives me
life . . .
and the first thought of you,
shining warmly in my heart,
gives me the desire to live it.

Timothy Sullivan

Bearing Witness

She went her way
and who could say
she was unholy!

Did she not cast out daemons
with a good word
and prophesy for free?

As he was tried and persecuted
she stood aside
suffering his confusion.

Some say
it was her curse
changed the seasons.

K. A. McMahon

God's Stress Busters

A peacock with tail feathers spread.
A male cardinal so brightly red.
A hummingbird who is so small.
An ostrich looking clumsy and tall.
Once an ugly caterpillar,
Now a butterfly on a flower.
A roadrunner looking so funny.
A cute little cottontail bunny.
A precious family of gambol quail,
Going on a single file trail.
Birds both great and small, flying free,
Or nesting on the limb of a tree.
The sound of a cricket on a quiet night.
A coyote howling at moon so bright.
Sit and listen to nature's music,
It is relaxing and amusing.
A symbol of peace is the dove.
All were created by God with love.
Just sit and watch them at their best,
It's God's own way to relieve our stress.

Carol Cline

Today I'm Thankful

Is anyone listening out there?
Can anyone help me?
I would help myself,
But I don't know what's wrong.
I strive so hard to perfect every aspect of my life . . .
that I forget to live.
And in trying to perfect all aspects of my life,
I forget how perfect my life already is.
I work so hard to help perfect my child's grades,
his attitude and manners,
that I forget how lucky I am—he has his health.
I work so hard to help him be his best
in basketball, baseball, and soccer,
that I forget how lucky I am that he can even play.
Tomorrow could change everything I know today.
Tomorrow my child may not run jump or play.
So, if anyone's listening out there and feel your life's in despair,
sit back and be thankful for who you are and what you have today . . .
It could be gone tomorrow.

Angelia Michelle Gautney

The Ending of the World

That night, when I saw your face
I nearly died.
The sweet honey dew devoured your lips, and I knew I could not have you.
It was the end of the world.

I knew I could not have you as my own because you were someone else's.
You were the forests, you were the flowers, you belonged to the faeries:

I wanted to stand with you on the top of a mountain, where time would
Stand still, so I could just catch
One glimpse of your face and the smell of your skin.

But I couldn't.

You were too beautiful.
You weren't mine to have
And you weren't mine to keep.

I could never compete
With what they offered you.
What did I have?
My love, and that was all.
How could that ever have been enough?

The night was a night when the world nearly died.

Melissa Merry

Fear, but Do Not Doubt Me

My eyes are open wide, but I see nothing but fear.
I try to close them, but control I'm unable to steer.
I've learned of a problem deep within me
that lingers over like a dark cloud.
What must I do to bring this fear down?
Many people say, put your faith in God; he'll show you the way.
But I can quite do that now.
Finding myself in doubt for the pain I so deeply feel each dreary day.
I have a better idea; simply pointing the finger of blame,
while suddenly having an urge of going mentally insane.
Why should I be the unlucky one, I ask? A small voice answers,
"Luck—no such object." You have been blessed with many things,
even a talk show speaking on many topics. Yeah! That's right,
I give people hope each and every day;
why can't I make that hope do a reverse replay?
Wait, why aren't my eyes closed yet?
Everything seems to be clearer.
An unexplainable force pulls me to my knees.
Suddenly I'm shouting, the words aren't clear.
I feel the weight of my heart begin to lift.
These words must be about my deepest fear.
A smile began to form and lights up my face.
At this very moment, I realize in his hands, there's no safer place.

Sharlene Burris

Slow Death

Dying are those who deserve to cherish
Living are those who deserve to rot
The best ones are picked up,
The rest find the berth . . .
Is it just luck
that the meek inherit the Earth?

Swathi Dhoopati

love

we often hear that love is kind
love is not selfish
love endures all things . . .
but I say to you
love isn't love
until you give it away.

Victoria Ekanem

Watercolor

If it rained on my picture,
and the vividness fades . . .
is it gone forever ?
. . . Or has it softened its shades?

If it rained on my picture,
and the colors would bleed . . .
is it gone forever?
. . . Or will my heart's eye intercede?

Sarah Binderberger

Girl with Overcoat

I may, I may find you
Giving out pamphlets on
some street, incomplete.
Dressed to complete
As the moon shone bright,
through the night.
Tonight, tonight.
In small grass huts
the bats keep us awake,
but they keep out the mosquitoes.

Mark S. Smith

God's Garden

My world is made of many people,
Formed in a garden of colored faces.
They sit in their own garden lot,
Until they are mixed in a certain plot.
These people try to bloom and grow,
But the outside world wants control.
The flowers reach for sun and rain
To feed the blooms that do remain.
Why can't we grow and be beautiful,
The way God wanted his garden to grow?

Betty Rose

Stranger

Deep, dark eyes blazing with desire.
Within them I see a pure soul with
as many hopes and dreams as the rest
of us but also in the eyes a
hint of loneliness I see also fear
as I gaze deeper into these mysterious
eyes I, realize these eyes belong to
no ordinary stranger they belong to
a stranger of my heart, they belong
to the real me inside.

Christina Wilson

Open the Door

Open the door with the key, and you will find the best part of me.
For if we don't grasp for life, sometimes we may smother deep inside.
For I can be your strength when you need an extra hand,
For my heart, dear love, will never break.
For you are my strength.
Open the door and let me in.
Life together will teach us to stand side by side through thick or thin
Till death do us part and our journey has come to an end.

Sharon Whitmire

Mountain of Life

Today is the first day of the rest of my life.
What should I do—go ahead and enjoy it, or let someone else enjoy it?
I am at the crossroads of life.
Which way do I go? Is it my decision, or leave it to fate?

Should I grab the brass ring or be chained to a link?
The circle is overwhelming, never-ending.
Should I conform or break the chain?
Damned if I do and damned if I don't.
There is no sadness, there is no gladness.

Should I be a pessimist and be led on a leash,
Or be an optimist and take the lead?
It's a mad, mad world.

It's a long, hard road, filled with stones and boulders,
Stumbling along, climbing, climbing ever so slow,
Hoping one day I can reach the top,
Before I fall off this mountain we call life.

Sharon V. Calahasin

The Verdict

McAdams Golden Age Club had its Christmas dinner,
but I'll tell you for sure it wasn't a winner.
The veggies looked all old and rough,
the crust on the potato pie was tough,
and the filling looked a little like snuff.

The gravy was thin, thin as water, they oughta have bought
some jars of Heinz, really they oughta.
Folk began to shout "hey, the food is out" some were hungry as a wolf,
no turkey, left, not anything on the hoof.
Not one bite did I eat,
I wasn't going to be a part of that feat,
from that I did retreat.

I hate to say, I told you so,
but next time you will know,
go to a place with lots of class,
where everybody will get plenty of food, and be served fast.

Clara M. Powell

If I Could Bring You a Rainbow

If I could bring you a rainbow

If I could bring you a rainbow, I'd color your world with vivid hue.
Your dreams would all come true.
A ribbon of fantasy to design whimsical realm—
Through the clouds, stormy skies subside
And your eyes—
They bring the dawn
Lucid, blissful, in all ways perfect.

And the glass of shattered hopes—
Each splinter would be replaced.
To reconstruct elegance
A renaissance of your spectrum within.

If I could bring you a rainbow
All the world would be envious
But no one would ever take it from you
For they, too, find zeal in your bliss.

Miss Linzzy Linzzy

The Crude Art of Alienating

Put your head up to the screen
Tighten choke hold on your brain
Media's lies substantiated
Loving all the things you hated
Censorship and conservation
Soul and mind manipulation
Legalized soul prostitution
Spoon-feeding mind pollution

Andrew Mark Seymour

Posted

We've both been around some time
with you being so very kind
Can't you see my signals flashing
on and off like old fashion
But some things will never change
It's only time that turns the page
and it's back at our old ways
like before in an endless maze

Brendan O'Mara

Children

Young faces,
round and sweet,
touched by innocence
and endowed unique.
Souls-a-caring,
love's a faring,
when all the while,
there is the child.

Kermite H. Bristow

Sanctuary

A soul with a torch
In a flammable vapor
Searches for a haven
To glow unthreatened.

Found with luck another,
Whose stone bubble
Holds for her
A universe unquestioned.

Michael Moore

Our Land

From east to west,
North to south,
This is our land.

The buffalo,
The deer, the crops,
This is our land.

We use our animals
For food and clothes.
This is our land.

Our animals,
Our people, all belong to us.
Because this is our land.

Our trees are used for
Homes and boats.
This is our land.

We believe in many things,
Like masks are for disease
And our ceremonies are very special.
This is our land.

And everyone else's

Serena Matson

Colors

There is a pale moon hugging the lavender hills
Where scent pervades, pursues me, and then spills into golden Morning.
Strewn dew leaves arrest my eye and pause a while,
A sigh of contentment to touch my depth of solitude meant for Learning,
And to have learned what? said the pale moon.
Then dawn is up with color, which pours across the land
Like honey and spreads to paler edges of light,
Where it whisks into peaks of blinding white; the day begins.
Pale and soft, the bluest tint of ink,
A tone, a hint on hint to pardon dusk for creeping
Over this all too pale by light emitted to be forfeited by night.

Juliet Ward

A Better Tomorrow

As I stand decorating my tree, I ask the Lord, why me?
Why is it I have such pain and sorrow?
Lord, I have been so sick, why not let me have a better tomorrow?
My sons are in Heaven, my health I do fight.
Oh, Lord, please let me have a night
where I can be free,
From all the pain I have within me.
I know you are beside thee, for which I am glad,
Reach out your comforting hand, so I feel not so sad.
While I ask for comfort for myself, I ask comfort for all who grieve,
I know you will give peace to all who believe.

Marjorie Magill

Sleeping with an Angel

As your eyelids close, I watch you sleep,
Wondering what you are dreaming,
if you are dreaming of me.
Watching your every movement as you lay in my arms.
I look upon this angel of beauty sleeping in my arms,
and think to myself about how lucky I am to have found her.
I wonder if you know you are the one for me,
that you are the one I need, so I, too, can fall asleep.
I live for you, I truly do. Your love is what completes me;
it is what makes me whole, it drives me.
You are my guiding light in a world of chaos and confusion.
As I lay in your arms and you sleep in mine, my eyelids become heavy.
I pull back to catch another glimpse of my angel at rest.
You look so peaceful lying in my arms.
Until the moonlight is berated by the coming of the sun,
A final kiss I give to my angel.
Till the morning light, I love you, good night. . . .

Simon Ly

Blessings

I try to remember every day to
thank the Lord each time I pray

For all of the blessings that
cover this Earth, and most
of all for the saviors birth

For the angels he sends to
be our guides, to share and care
as we learn to abide

With hope one day mankind will
know, all things were made for
God's love to grow

Joyce E. Schobloher

My Prayer

Free me from condemnation,
help me toward my destination.

Give me strength to guide the weak,
give me patience to help the meek.

Guide me through the hurt and pain,
show me what there is to gain.

Let me help those who need,
with my love, I'll plant the seed.

I'll show my scars from deep within,
to show my strength, my will to win.

Wanda Borgs

One Sweet Smile

Anytime I feel downhearted
Or I'm feeling kind of blue
All I really need to do
Is stop and take a look at you.

You always have a ready smile
To share with all you know
If ever you're discouraged
You never let it show.

You lift me up and make me smile
To have a friend like you
Because I know you really care
By all the things you do.

My sweet friend remember this
In whatever you say or do
Nothing more could mean as much
As one sweet smile from you.

E. B. Mann

Janice

Sitting here thinking,
yes, next week
buy a birthday card.
For whom? My best friend.
Will I find the right one?
It must relate my feelings.
Decisions, decisions, so many cards.
Do I buy
  To a special friend
  Thinking of you
  For "Old time's sake."
Will one say what I feel?
No.
I know why.
My feelings for you, my friend,
belong only to me.

Agnes H. Scott

The Audition

Do I have what it takes?
Do I have the talent?
Determination? Stamina? Energy?
Yes. I love it. Yes, it makes me feel alive.
Yes, I believe, but do they?
When I appear, will they know I'm the one,
Or will I be overlooked for the "plain girl"?
Will they think, "Oh, what talent!"
Or will it be, "Oh, (yawn) next!"
How do I know? Impossible.
How do I cope? I dance.

Hanna Elizabeth Stiens

Wealthy

To be wealthy is to be happy
To be wealthy is to bring children into this world and care for them
To be wealthy is to be satisfied with who you are and what you project to others
To be wealthy is to live life flawlessly, yet understand your mistakes and mishaps
To be wealthy is to have knowledge and respect for others
To be wealthy is to be honest and true to yourself
To be wealthy is to be one person and only one person
To be wealthy is not to complain
To be wealthy is to appreciate what you have
To be wealthy is to realize what is never going to be, yet never stop reaching for what you want
To be wealthy is just be. . . .

Thomas J. Horton

The Little Things Matter the Most

When we are together, all of my dreams come true
It is all of the little things that matter, when I am with you
Things you wouldn't think of, that happen every day
Things that I would miss the most, if you ever went away

It's the smell of your hair, as I caress your face
Thinking of your love, which I can never replace
It's the everlasting happiness, when I look into your eyes
A feeling of completeness, that I can never deny

It's the way you laugh at a joke, someone will say
Your witty banter in reply, that I hope will never stray
It's the way you smile, whenever we meet
Your desire and passion, that can never be beat

There are so many things that I love about you
These were just some and I hope they will do
The only way I can explain all the things I feel when you are with me
Is if we were together forever for eternity

Jeffrey A. Sobieraj

It's Easier to Forget

So, I'm not the same person you used to know,
my life has changed, you see.
I used to love to shop and help anyone in need.
But now I sit impatiently,
Waiting to be brought life's necessities.
My freedom is gone, no more long walks,
There are walls all around me now.
They're afraid I'll get lost, they say, although I can't imagine how!
I don't understand what's happening to me,
Or why I'm treated so differently.
I know I don't do things just quite right
I like my music very loud and leave the doors open at night . . .
Is this why you don't visit me?
I'll try harder, I say. We've been friends and family from so long ago
Now it seems I'm someone you don't know
They say I have a disease called Alzheimer's
It doesn't make sense to me, 'cause I feel fine, you see!
I'm sorry you can't face me, or give me a call;
I still get lonely, after all.
Maybe you can help find a cure for this disease
But I guess it's easier to forget.

Linda Crabtree

Field of Bright

Millions of stars
All so bright,
All so beautiful.
All of these stars
Are shun by the light.
The bright, harsh lights
Of the city mask
This beautiful, bright field
Some never have the
Opportunity to see
Such beauty, simply
Because of one thing,
Man's invention of light.

Richard Galaway

Life Is a Gift

Death is a mystery
and life is a gift,
An enigma, a joy,
an everlasting bliss.
Take a moment, a fraction,
one breath to give praise,
To honor, adore,
and hear Him always.
Count each day a blessing,
fertile ground to discover,
Listen to the Lord, have faith,
and love one another.

Brian L. Price

Home

The four walls of this home
Have a strong, sturdy lock.
I'm safe and I'm comfortable
But galvanized in shock.

For only just yesterday
I could gaze out on my lawn,
To the flowers in the border,
Now everything is gone.

The house needed fixing,
I'm just too old to mow.
Four generations of family,
And now I must go.

But forever I'll picture
That home in my heart;
And wait upon Jesus
My Heavenly Home to start.

Annette Mates

Perpetual

Tomorrow is dawning
On the horizon afar
The call of the wild
Echoes in the breath of air
The waves crash
On a fire that burns
Looking all around
With every single turn
Finding you still
In my heart
Chasing sunsets ever so soon
Sad faces reflected to the moon
Now is the time to claim
How shall I explain
Shedding no more tears
No more fears

Sherrie Lacy

Torn between Two Places

Sitting alone, her head in her hands,
She looks at nothing, digs her toes in the sand.
Her shoulders are slumped, her posture, dejected,
In the glass like surface of the ocean, her misery is reflected.
Torn between one place and another, she doesn't know which to choose,
But surely, either one or the other, somebody has to lose.
So much is at stake, her heart, her hopes, her dreams,
She doesn't know if she should make the leap, silently she screams.
The fabric holding her thoughts together, is wearing very thin,
She's almost at her breaking point, hoping everyone will win.
She's just a child, yet a woman too, about to set out on her own,
Hoping that one day soon, she too, will have a place to call, "Home."

Heather Reaska

Another Day

Thank you, Lord, for another day.
It is hard to put into words what I want to say.
We must always keep a positive attitude,
Even when you have a disability and people that meet you are rude.
What will it be today, walker or wheelchair?
At least I have a choice; I look in the room and they are both there.
So whenever life throws you a curve,
Keep your courage and your nerve.
It is easy with support of family;
With their help you can be the best you can be.
So thank you, Lord, for another day,
And all the people you sent to help in their special way.

Joan Hargrove

The Feeling of Guilt

I walk into a room and in the corner I see him.
He sits there with a face of innocence as if he knows my purpose.
I walk toward him as I stare into his endless black eyes.
It's almost as though he is waiting to be noticed.
I pick him up and carry him with me as his power flows inside my body.
His unbearable strength has bathed me in sin.
His pale confessions slip away as his pure mind turns to hate.
He holds onto me tighter and grasps every breath I try to take.
Heaven's hope has left my side and my innocence has been robbed.
No longer am I free to run, for I have been captured.
I have been buried in his eternal darkness.
Ashamed and suffering, I stand here, praying for some return.
I begin to think of past experiences and future chances.
He promises that no peace or salvation will greet my damaged soul.
He's taken all of my love and faith which once held me with security.
I realize that my destiny remains in this prison.
I lie here trapped, unable to make a victorious escape.
He has left me faceless and conquered forever.

Lindsey Patricia MacDowell

The Hall of Doors

Here I find myself standing, standing in a hall.
It's a hall of doors and I can't help but ponder, ponder the meaning of it all.
Which door leads forward and which one leads back?
Which should I choose, the choosing of my life's track?
Forward awaits the future while behind fades the past.
It really is a decision I cannot reach that fast.
Which of them are good, which are bad?
Which will make me happy, when so many make me sad?
So many choices, the choices of life.
Careful of your choices, they can cut like a knife.
So here I still ponder, ponder it all.
I can find no meaning, nothing at all.
I stand there beside you. No, not there, but inside you.
My spirit has long since fled. Now I suppose I must be dead.
Long since forgotten. I stand here rotting.
In a hall. A hall of the heart.
Still pondering, pondering it all.
Never having once thought to try them all!

Donnie Meade

There's Nothing I Can Say

There's nothing I can say
and nothing I can do
to show you how much
I really love you.

I wish I could show how
much I care.
I search for the words,
but they're just not there.

But until you know, I'll
just do my best,
and maybe my heart can
show you the rest!

Christopher Harville

Behold the Majesty and Power

Dazzling sunshine,
Swaying trees,
Sparkling snowflakes,
Whispering breeze.

Twinkling stars . . . and
A bright . . . silvery moon,
Soft, springtime showers and
Destroying typhoons.

What man on Earth
Has powers such as these?
To quiet the rolling thunder or
Calm the roaring seas?

Cecelia M. Hall

Leaves

Fall, leaves fall.
Every leaf speaks bliss to me,
fluttering from the autumn tree.

Its leaves are fragrant,
feathery, showy in their colors
beckoning with sexy shrug to come over.

Wreaths of leaves blossom and glow
in the Indian summer sun.
Streams are trilling and frothing
in a mad dash to escape the summer calm
taunting the leaves
for their climax of color
a shade of red, caught in the act.

Fall, leaves fall.
When night's away
ushers in a dreamier autumn day.

Carol Merolla

The Possibilities of a Dream

Dreams are made of sunshine,
And the tickle of a breeze,
They fill your heart with laughter,
And put your mind at ease.

You can open a world of wonder,
The moment you close your eyes,
You could dream of sweets and candies,
Or Grandma's apple pies.

You could find the sweetest love,
That lasts forever more,
You could dream of smiles and laughter,
You could make the winning score.

The possibilities are endless,
The sky's no limit now,
So compose the finest dreams,
Then step back, and take a bow.

Jessica Jean Pool

No Signal

It makes my body boil with the thought that turns my head.
It looks to me, what seems to be the end.
Reality shattered by the dreams that seem to click.
Shame should keep me quiet. But I am never going to quit.
It makes my body boil with the words that burn my mouth.
I need to see the benefit of all my doubts. I'm telling you the truth.
But my hands are sold, and I can't show you the proof.
It makes my body boil with the touch that stings my skin.
I fight with you all of the time, but I never find the words to win.
Can't you give me what I want, and get out of my way?
Because the bursting of my body will have you laughing all day.
Here in isolation, I lose myself to my own insanity.

Elizabeth Carranza

Storm of Purpose

Sailing in a sea full of constant waving days,
A ship floating aimlessly struggles to gain its way.
Blind to the unseen and deaf to storms of wrath,
No guidance swaying farther still, until a light shines the path.
But shine is the only thing this lighthouse was built to do,
To show the way, all but pray—the rest is up to you.
Will you turn out to sea when rough waters tide comes in,
Or hold fast and wait out the storm until visuals come back again.
If it comes to that night when my light isn't all that bright,
My only hope is you're not that far to take care of me, your shining star.
I need you ship, as you do me, and remember not to blame the sea.
If it weren't for dark rain to fall, there'd be no reason for a light at all.

Shelahna L. Jenkins

Never

As I wake from restless sleep, I find a brighter day.
A greater hope in knowing in my heart you choose to stay.
I never thought I'd find the one about whom I'd feel this way.
Never a happier man was there, than when in your arms I lay.

Some say I'm a sap . . . maybe so, but I don't mind.
I'm your sap, no one else's, not chopped liver or onion rind.
Our hearts fit like the puzzle piece all people want to find,
Never were two souls more meant to meet
than yours and mine in kind.

As I gaze out through the window at the falling shades of green,
I drift off to a special cabin . . . you know the one I mean.
There a happy couple lives with two green chairs and lots of dreams.
Never, forever, in all of my life, would you have I foreseen.

And with a thought like that in mind, pretty well I think I'll fare.
Only you can understand how much about you I really care.
I've not lived a long life, but for this love I'll dare,
Never will I or anyone else, 'cause your heart to need repair.

Jacob Donovan Libbey

Light at the Edge of the World

In a time where people are searching for escape,
there's a light at the edge of the world.
It glistens and glows; a band plays in honor of our escaping.
There's little or no peace for the one who searches for it.

The good suffer along with the bad under a system
bent on hunting the fair game.
But the light at the edge of the world gives hope,
as the band plays in midair in front of the Aura Borealis;
lights blue, red, and green tell a story.
The light it gives is a spiritual one that only one seeking it
can understand.

The band playing gives one a sense of inner peace never felt before.
Unraveling the mystery of time and space itself.
Traveling at a distance greater than the speed of light.

Yes, this light at the edge of world takes one away
from all the evils that plague this world,
and gives back the peace and harmony lost in the beginning.

David Johnson

Stardust, Starbright

Stardust, Starbright
Twinkling stars I try to grasp tonight
Hoping and wishing
On the sky tonight
Thinking and thinking
On the perfect wish
To request on stars tonight
Comets and Meteors
All whirling around
While on this Earth
We are Safe and sound
Stardust, starbright
Please grant my wish tonight

Janna Elyse Arrant

A Beggar's Lace

There is a time and there's a place,
When I am sure we all must face
A Judge Supreme, who'll hear our case,
Where matters not our rags or lace.

And if you're quick to pass with scorn,
A soul whose clothes are frayed and torn
Who has no home and is forlorn,
Take heed, he's too, of purpose born.

That riches make is without base,
Though great wealth now may win a race;
When in the end we state our case,
A beggar's soul may be his lace.

Louis J. Mazzochetti

No Time?

You say that you don't have time to talk
Because you have so many troubles.
You say that you are sick with grief,
And your stomach's in a rumble.
You say that life has passed you by
Even though you've really tried—
But what about those who cannot talk,
Even those who cannot walk?
What about those who have never sung
Or even those in an iron lung?
What about those who have no home,
Those of us who have to roam?
You say that you feel better now
And you are going home?
You say you'd like to see me sometime?
I'd like to see you too,
But you see, I'm blind.

Patricia Anderson

My Love

For Ron

I love you in life
With each and every breath
And I will love you forever
Beyond my death
I will love you in Heaven
If the good Lord is willing
And I will love you in Hell
While the teardrops are spilling
My love for you is as endless
As the ebbing of the sea
And no dark and filthy pit
Will contain my love for thee
Hear me shout from every mountain
Writing your name across the sky
Now and forever I am with you
Our hearts forever intertwined.

Arlyn Rosa Pipitone

My Daddy

My daddy is a wonderful man. He gives from his heart all that he can.
If I ever need a hug, he's always there to give,
so why does he have to die, why can't he live?
My daddy I will forever love, whether he's here with me or with God above.
Mama's calling him to Heaven for a pair of angel wings and to be with her for now,
we'll all meet up again someday but only God knows when and how.
He's seen mama in his dreams and when he talks of them being together
there's excitement ion his voice it seems.
The only times I've seen him cry is when he's telling me who's in Heaven
in his dreams and his father isn't there. I think my father feels as though
his father never really cared.
My father is my hero, he's the strongest man I know,
but now I guess it's time I share, it's time I let him go.

Tami L. Stork

Vision

Looking in your eyes, I see a vision,
A vision of you making an important decision.
A decision of love and hate!
One that could even decide your fate.

You have to decide what's right or wrong,
Or whether to this society you want to belong.
A society filled with hate and rage,
One that discriminates because of your race and age.

To them it doesn't matter if it's one or the other;
Nevertheless, your sister or your brother.
Nothing's going to change, unless we make up our minds
By taking the time to realize who are our enemies and who are our friends.

Carie Dominoski

War for Love

It's hard to say what love is really worth.
You never know which love it will be—second, third, or fourth.
So many people sit and dwell on when they'll find their love,
And some don't even know what the word love is made of.
Is love really worth it? Some wait to just get hurt.
And then where does love leave them? Often in the dirt.
You see the smiles of the couples, wishing you were one,
Dreaming you were there with your girl having all the fun.
And then there are ones like me who have it but are scared,
You want to spend a lifetime with them without a second to be spared,
And 'cause if you lose this love, when will the next one come?
But that won't matter, 'cause the one you lost is really the right one.
So do your best to win the battle and remember, this is war,
But the heart of the one for you is what you're fighting for.

Mark Michael Francis

Thoughts from the Road

Like the drivers of the great trucks
I stride swiftly across this fair land
It seems so fair to be eternal
A land for heroes never less than free.

What cruel magic causes men to search for power
and call it protecting the poor,
Helping the weak, the disadvantaged?
Supporting the drifter, the drop out?

Seek out the libertarian
and he will say,
Beware the politicians bearing gifts
Those relief checks, your ticket to a socialist agenda.
I see the forests, the fields, the farms, and wish this stuff of freedom
Could be a part of every soul,
A song for every heart.
There is no gain in spirit
When what is given is ripped from another;
Nor are there any accolades in Heaven
For those who tax one to give another.

Clay Janecky

For My Carolyn

You're the apple of my eye
You're the whipped cream on my pie
You're the sunshine in my morning
You're the beauty in my sky

You're my soul mate and my true love
And I hope that you can see
That all these things I've written
Are what you are to me

William G. Sturgeon

Longing for Amina

I watch the waves as they come in,
the sound they make on shore.
The gulls cry out, soft breezes blow,
how could one wish for more.
But oh, to have you here with me
and love your soothing voice,
would more than anything I know
fulfill my dream of choice.

Mary Mansour

Womb of My Age

Womb of my age . . .
Is there a light at the
End of a tunnel so dark
That none can compare?

Room of my age confines me
To perimeters snug and comforting,
Sustenance emanating from sources
As yet unknown, nurturing blindness,
Floating in wait . . . for what?

Womb of my age . . .
When will I see the light
At the end of this tunnel so
Dark that none can compare?

Room of my age confines me
With years of living condensed to these
Few treasures, just this space,
Sustenance coming from strangers, pills,
Withering in wait . . . for what?

Womb of my age . . .

Susan Drake

Never Know

For You Momma; I love you.

I'll never know
Know the pain you're in
I don't know how to help you
Don't know what to say
Is there anything I can say or do

I do what I can
Be there for you to talk to
Or just be there if you need me

But how or will
I ever know
Know if I am helping you
Or if I'm not

None of that matters
As long as you know
Know that I am here
And I love you

I hope you know
Know that I'll always be
Right here, if you need me

Crystal Bollinger

Waiting

Waiting is all I do.
You have changed through and through.

We all go through changes this I know, but I can't let you go.

There are many things I want you to know.
There are many feelings I want to show.

You left me out in the rain, but raindrops can't wash away the pain.

I love you, can't you see?
I need your warm embrace, come back to me.

Tracey A. Timian

Before the Father's Throne

As I knelt before the father's throne I realized I was not alone.
The angels gathered around the place as I looked into my father's face.
He said "my child I know why you are here,
I want you to know you have nothing to fear."
"For I have always been by your side.
From me there is nothing you can hide."
I know what you've done and I know where you've been,
but when you came back to me I absolved all of your sin."
"So go now in peace and follow my ways for I will fill you with love,
hope and joy the rest of your days."

Melissa Bratton

God Is No Respecter of Persons

Many people ask, "Why did this happen to me?"
God is why it happens to all of us, even me.
People make life miserable and unrewarding
for themselves and everyone in their lives.
God has the power, holds the key to make things
happen for us to have joy in our lives.
As long as people continue to worship the devil instead of the Lord,
There will never be any lasting happiness or peace in their lives.
People don't stop to think, there is no promise of tomorrow.
That means, "Make the most of each moment."
One day we're fine, the next we are old and alone.
It seems we sit and wait to die,
because the world is scared of death.
Were it not for God, old people would be completely alone.
The only way to overcome anything in life is to turn all your troubles over
to Christ who holds the power over your life.
If something is wrong in your life, don't be afraid.
Pray and read the Word of God and He will guide your life.
Anything you ask of God, through Jesus will be done.
Proof of this is in the fact that God had Jesus to shed His blood.

Cora W. Moore

If I Could Do It Over I'd Do It Right

I was looking at the old photo album today
And I felt I had some things to say
I've been wishing I could turn back time
So many pictures of that little boy of mine
I found my heart aching looking at pictures of you
Because I never took the time to enjoy the things you used to do
I wish you were younger I'd do things differently
I'd spend all my free time with you, and do so willingly
I wouldn't leave you with grandma like so many times before
But it's too late, time is gone my chance I have no more
I never meant to hurt you by pushing you away
But here I sit alone now, and it is the price that I must pay
I was so busy trying to grow up myself that my memories of your childhood are few
How my heart hurts for missing the important years with you
I look at you now, you have come a long, long way
Life has been hard and you've had a price to pay
But now my boy's a man and there's no going back
And you have yourself to thank for staying on the right track
Stephen, you are a good man and I'm so happy and proud that's true
I only wish I had another chance to have been a better mom to you

Karen M. Foy

Sunny Side

I worked with Pete, who could not speak,
Sue, who could neither hear nor swallow,
Jose, with two stubbed arms and feet,
and those with swollen heads
just soft enough to squeak.

From them, wet tears would seldom flow,
though my heart owned tears a-plenty.
Yet, from children never to grow,
there came a loud guffaw
when awkward me would show.

Now past this work at aging stage,
I live among the senior folk,
and those who meet me often wage,
because I smile a lot,
I've not known inner rage.

Someone steps from our heated pool.
With unmatched gait and flaying arms,
he keeps his long-determined rule
to show his sunny side.
We joke; Paul wipes his drool.

Florence R. Ehlers

A Smile on My Heart

When we're together
On your heart my love rests
I can only see forever
Can't accept anything less

Nobody lives up to you
In your arms I've found home
Couldn't ever fill your shoes
From your love couldn't try to roam

Honey, your love is my love
And I don't know where to start
How many ways I can tell you of
That you put a smile on my heart

So many speak out wrong reasons
Of how we two came to be
And I can't imagine a season
That you and I wouldn't be

Too bad all people aren't like you
For all the Earth would love dart
And for me your burning love will do
Forever put a smile on my heart

J. Stephanie Rose

Just Came By

i just came by to say hi
it's been so long since you died
growing old, starting new
i just don't know what to do

hopes and dreams, flies it seems
i promised i'd never let go
laughs and tears, all my fears
i never got to say "bye"

i wonder what you do all day
or if time is endless where you are
are you trapped between heaven and earth
or are you really not that far?

sometimes i wonder why
you chose the road that you did
sadness or heartbreak
how could you, i was just a small kid

looks in eyes, long drawn sighs
standing here at your small grave
i just came by to say hi
but i'll go on, at least i will try.

Bree Culnan

Uncontrolling Tears

It is never easy I've heard, to lose someone you love
But even harder still, is when they leave for up above.
You know they will be happier, in that heavenly place
But, there is no controlling tears that come streaming down your face
Sometimes when it's a grandma or grandpa up in years
You feel as though, they fulfilled all their dreams and fears.
But then, as little children lose their life sometime
You wish, the Lord could have spared them, if only for a short time.
And, even though death is a reality we all must face
There's no controlling tears that come streaming down your face.

Stacy C. Cooper

A Farmer

To a man who helped give me life that stood tall and proud of his heritage
Never going against his conviction or his dreams,
Showing me honesty and integrity each day of his life
Giving me a wonder of nature and all living things
To a man with rough hands and a heart for the land
Tilling the soil by summer's light
And caring of animals in the cold of winter nights
To a man that showed his love by hard honest day's work
And just a smile and a look of his eyes
Letting me know that my life was for a purpose

Carol Beemer

Restless

When night hits, darkness devours the sky.
I sit here RESTLESS,
Pondering all the things to come and all the things that have been.
The memories that lie in my head flash every second of my living day.
Feeling like a vampire in the night,
Sometimes I even yearn for that little taste of blood.
The sensations going through my body wanting more anxiously.
Blood of PASSION, blood of RAGE, the thirst to taste love once more.
Clouds of smoke go in and out of my body waiting for that final
Moment when my eyes shut and I enter this dream state,
Where all my dreams of happiness start to come true.
Just as the song goes, "It's 3 a.m., I must be lonely."
Actually, it's 3:30 and I am lonely.
I lie here, RESTLESS, hoping soon that my other half will come to me
And tell me everything will be all right and just hold me in their
Arms till the sun goes down for all eternity.
RESTLESS, waiting for that true moment in time when my world
Is filled with everything I believe in my mind is true and right.
RESTLESS, waiting for that final moment when my eyes shut
and the DREAMWORLD I so long for BECOMES REALITY.

Angela D. Capps

He That Hath Ears, Let Him Hear

Written by the inspiration of the Holy Spirit

Let's gather together like animals in the ark,
What Mathew speaks is seen through the eyes of Mark.
Jesus is supposed to be our heart,
But we part from his will,
Described as a lamb during the kill.
He told one of his disciples at the last meal,
You're going to deceive me,
I'll be crucified but resurrect in three,
No weapon formed can harm me.
Seek thee for comfort, you stubborn like Israel, in Exodus through Numbers,
A new creature in Christ emerging,
New revised, living, King James version.
I'm just rehearsing until I walk through those gates,
Think Philipians, chapter four, verses seven and eight, not hate.
Give me a plate of the tree of life,
Not lose my life but have it everlasting,
The peace of GOD passeth all understanding,
Enhancing faith and fasting, casting out evil sin,
Jesus said, follow me and I'll make you fishers of men. . . .

Charles Edward Andrews, Jr.

God Loves a Comic

God has a sense of humor, it is said.
I hope he doesn't test it out on me.
Not that I can't take a joke,
But I'd rather not be the "bloke"
On whom its refinement rests.

If the Lord came to me and said,
"We have a need for mirth,
Can you oblige us with its birth?"
I'd have to say, "My Lord,
Pleasing you is my reward."

It seems the need to be comical
Outlasts the need to be practical.
My joy may be chronic.
I try to be laconic
When my solitude turns funny.

We know our Lord is humorous.
He spreads glee throughout the universe,
Collecting grace in every place.
He gives each one a chance to be
Keeper of the merriment key.

Margaret Hockran

Pity

So . . . you didn't get what you want,
it didn't turn out the way it should.
Well . . . welcome to my reality,
everything's as twisted as it could.

You can pray for hope,
you can pray for truth.
But you shouldn't waste your time;
hope for you died long before youth.

You ask for your wants,
you ask for your dreams.
Even if they seem to come true,
it's not as good as it seems.

Welcome to my world,
welcome to my life.
Even when you feel "happy,"
you're still doused in strife.

And then when you're doused,
all it takes is a flame.
'Cause then it's fire,
nothing's left but shame.

Ryan Lee Maynard

In the Mirror

I look in the mirror
who do I see?
I think I should fear her
who can she be?

A cynic
A freak
A critic
But weak

The look in her eyes
They burn red with anger
Many despise
Perhaps they should hang her

But those that do love her
She pushes away
She does it to cover
The fears that won't sway

How can I help her
And who can she be?
'Cause in that reflector
I only see me

Crystal Pribble

Lake Lanier

Oh! What a "heavenly" sight
That suddenly appears majestically, almost magically,
Whether arrived at by day or night.

Lake Lanier must be one of "God's" most secretive,
Wonderful places here on Earth built by "His" great powers and might.

Today, of all places to be found,
There is entertainment for everyone in abounds.
If you can but imagine,
You may find your haven
On one the lake's playgrounds
Or in one of the nearby towns.

Victor J. Futral

I Will Remember

We should all remember the day our soldiers fought,
Yet some of us forget it, though we should all be taught.
Imagine if someone you loved went to war and died,
Then you received a letter back, I'm sure you would have cried.
You might even be a soldier, who loved our country dear,
That you would go and fight for us, though you were filled with fear.
Or maybe you're the child, and your father passed away,
Of course you had a father, but that was till today.
Or imagine you're the mother and your son was gone for real,
Then you would have to eat alone every single meal.
Maybe you're the grandma and your first grandchild died,
Wouldn't you feel terrible, you just would have to die.
So remember to remember and make sure you don't forget,
You wouldn't want to say something later on you will regret.

Monique C. G. Regnier

Princess Remembered

While walking in the mall on an afternoon in May,
I stopped to watch the animals in a store display.
A ball of fur was tightly curled among the paper shreds
Gently sleeping, perhaps dreaming of the life that lay ahead.

On the window lightly tapping, this "fur" awoke and seemed to say
"Take me home. I'll be your friend forever and a day!
By your side I'll always be; your wishes and commands to learn.
I ask only that you care for me and love me in return."

Through all the years, both thick and thin, it was a promise kept.
In the day, close by she stayed; at night, beside my bed she slept.
Her coat a shiny white and sable, around her neck a little bell.
She frolicked in the summer sun, barked with joy when snowflakes fell.

To one and all life comes full circle, a beginning and an end.
With wholehearted pain and flowing tears, I bid farewell to my friend.
In a shaded window her ashes remain, along with her collar and bell.
With this poem and heartfelt love, my Princess, I remember you well.

Eloise D. Vincent

Mama

I was the early age of seven when God cut short our Daddy's time.
We all looked to Heaven, 'cause we were left without a dime.
Thirteen kids all ages from me to twenty-nine.
All in different stages; it was hard to keep us all in line.
We'd trip on life and stumble, but Mama would catch us before we'd fall.
'Cause when it comes to mamas, she's the daddy of them all.

If Mama was a fighter, she'd win her weight and size.
If Mama was a writer, she'd win a Pulitzer prize.
It was a real true thing of beauty, the way she made us realize
that she'd always do her duty above and beyond the call.
'Cause when it comes to mamas, she's the daddy of them all.
Mama had her hands full; she always did her best.
She'd use some of God's pull when we put her to the test.
In no way were we wealthy, just rich with Mama's love.
Thirteen kids all healthy; we were blessed from up above.
We'd trip on life and stumble, but Mama would catch us before we'd fall.
'Cause when it comes to mamas, she's the daddy of them all.

Stan Farris

Letters

Reach out to the never-ending darkness
Learn to feel the warmth
Near the time of love
Make the best of everything
Perfect the rights
Strengthen the fall
Lose the fear
Call for help
Die of hardship
Holler the pains
Mend the scars
Direct the light
Fool the stars
Scream the night
Try to hold it in
Make everything right
Leave the angry soul
Join the fall, grasp reality
Justify the moon
Resolve the differences.

Laura Hinkeldey

The Memory

Gone so many years now
Soon, you said you'd be back
With all my despair, how
Do I keep my life on track

Visions come back to haunt me
A soft kiss you left my cheek
The presence of you to be
What my longing eyes still seek

Fighting to gain
Left tattered and torn
Crying in pain
Left families to mourn

Searching through dust
On the battle zone
No sign of my lust
I shall live alone

With the passing of time
Debts have been paid
Memories in mind
A wreath has been laid

Tansy Lee

Longing of the Five Senses

I use my eyes to look into yours,
so you see how much I yearn for you.
And no matter who you are with,
they will never love you like I do.

Afterwards, I smell you,
and the scent is burned into my memory.
You really just don't know
that you are the heart and soul of me.

My mouth comes into play.
Tells you that I love you,
I wouldn't mind being yours forever.
Wants to know do you feel it too?

I can't hear you clearly,
it almost sounds like gibberish.
I understand what you're saying,
you will not grant my wish.

Then my hand reaches out
as you look to the one above.
Suddenly, you realize,
all I ask for is your love.

Kaleetia Shenae Griffith

Get Involved

There's no excuse not to get involved,
MS is the riddle that must be solved.

People with MS desperately need a cure,
For they are the ones that suffer and endure.

There's no excuse not to get involved,
everyone's efforts brings us closer to resolve

More research is needed to find a cure for MS
So what's your excuse, get involved, please say yes.

Step up to the plate, before it's too late
If you don't get involved, you'll wish you did
The next victim of MS could be your sister or brother, parent or kid.

What's your excuse? Get Involved!

Jim D. Watson

I Am a Thug

The one who good little girls grow to love,
while her parents assume I sell drugs.
I am a thug.
The voice, life, and character of the street.
The cause of fear in America's heartbeat.
I am a thug.
The type that works for food and hustles to pay rent.
The playa who feels all his problems are more reason to stay bent.
I am a thug.
A lover of hip-hop and my sworn enemy is a cop.
And I know cocaine is poison but I'm literally forced to slang rocks.
I am a thug.
Since 1619 America has swept me under her rug.
First a King, later a slave—turned panther, and now I am . . . a THUG.

Jerry Franklin Little, Jr.

I Can Breathe

You ask me what brings me here.
The only reply seems so self absorbed.
Sadness and confusion I say.
Out of sight now, and you have drawn me here.
Why is it that the bad things are what give us the most intrigue?
Not the bliss times, which are often forgotten soon after course.
But the bad is what will be talked about for eternity.
Now I can't help but to feel like sadness is no longer my air.
I can breathe with out the pain, and I can smile when I feel the love.
I feared that letting go of the past meant
letting go of me, But how can you lose
something that you never had . . . until now?
You can't.
So I won't.

Amy Lea Jewett

Life's Uncertainty

I woke up one night in a hallway made of towering, dark walls.
I looked behind me and saw nothing.
I looked in front of me and saw a light,
And as any person would have done,
I chose to walk towards the light.
As I walked towards the light, I started hearing
sounds of joy and happiness.
I walked closer, and as I walked closer, the sounds became louder.
After hours of walking,
I reached the light and the sounds stopped.
I saw an object of shimmering beauty,
A beauty unmatched.
As I looked closer at this object, I saw a boy surrounded by darkness.
This boy had a frightened look on his face.
His facial expressions and his surroundings told me
he didn't know his place in the world.
As I took a closer look at this image of a boy,
I realized this object was a mirror, and I was that boy.

Marshall Despain

My Life

I sit and watch
Never to play,
Everyone leaves
And here I stay.
Shadows of the past
Loom ever so low,
Forward progress
Timely and slow.
Trapped in a shell
Wanting to fly,
The door is locked
A tear I will cry.
Clouded mind
Of pain and quilt,
All defences up
A wall I have built.
I can believe in you
Doubts for myself,
Just another picture
Sitting on the shelf.

Anthony Spansel

Fiftieth Anniversary

Grandmother, Grandfather,
fifty years it's now been,
since you met a glance down the aisle,
sharing that lovers secret smile.

Grandmother, Grandfather,
fifty years it's now been,
since you said those words,
promising each to the other.

Grandmother, Grandfather,
fifty years it's now been,
since you shared the first kiss,
of your wedded bliss.

Grandmother, Grandfather,
fifty years it's now been,
since your wedding night,
and all it's delight.

Grandmother, Grandfather,
fifty years it's now been,
since you started this family,
and all the love within.

Angela Jonnie Bailey

Is Love Real

In all of my years
I've never been sure
What love really was
Was it simple and pure

Do we fall
In love way too fast
Not knowing or caring
If it will last

I've been in love
Or so I have thought
But never too long
And so it has brought

Me here to ask you
Is our love real
Will it last longer
Will it help heal

My negative thoughts
Of love that's not pure
Of simpler times
Of love that is sure

Bonnie Gail Cunningham

In Our Heart, There Is a Yellowstone

In the heart of the Yellowstone, in the stone burns a fire
Forget all that you thought was known, let your mind wander higher
In the heart of the wilderness, where there is no control
Rising spirits in the dawning mist, rediscovering your soul
In the heart of the Yellowstone, in the stone burns a fire
Realizing that you're not alone, reach out, touching your desire
In our heart is everything we dream, we perceive the passage of time
Question, is it what we think seems, free the oneness of our minds
In the heart of the Yellowstone, in the stone burns a fire
In your heart, mind, soul, in the stone, scent your visions are inspired
In the Yellowstone, in those open spaces, close your eyes and you will see
In the center there sacred places, where you feel all that is free
In the heart of the Yellowstone, in the stone burns a fire
In our heart there's a Yellowstone, reach out, touch your desire

Steven C. MacNaught

My Husband Cycles!

We met in nineteen forty-eight, he was a friend of a friend of mine,
He asked me out on a dare, to date and we were married in forty-nine.

Cycles! Cycles! Run! Run! Run! For years he played the game,
our life completely turned around, and was never quite the same.

Oh! He rode them in the sunshine and he rode them in the rain,
and every muddy hill climb, just to gain a little fame.

Cycles! Cycles! Run! Run! Run! Let me at 'em, I'll buy some,
and while I watched in bitter awe, he tried to buy each bike he saw.

Richmond, Catalina, Shasta, Big Bear, even twice
he rode them all with gusto, and damned the sky-high price.

He's older now and calmer, at least, that's how it seems,
but he still riding cycles, if only in his dreams

Joanne Hearth

My Forever Promise to You

I lay my head against your chest and listen to the rhythm of your heart.
The bond we share is pure and true and to keep it strong I will do my part.
I promise to hug you, I promise to kiss you,
I promise to have faith in you in times of doubt.
I promise to trust you, I promise to love you,
I promise you that this is what our bond is all about.

You wrap your arms around me tightly and you kiss my lips so sweet and true.
I want our love to last forever and that is why I make these promises to you.
I promise to touch you, I promise to hold you,
I promise to let you know exactly how I feel.
I promise to talk with you, I promise to cry with you,
I promise you the love I give is and will be real.

I promise you.
Forever.

Katherine Paonessa

Life

The colors of life comes masked with many faces.
Some say disease, some say pain, some say sadness,
and some benefit from happiness and success.
When we find ourselves in these states, we must look
toward the bright light sometimes called faith, sometimes
called courage, sometimes called opportunity, or maybe even tenacity.

The power that we all have been blessed with comes
from deep within our heart and soul. The spirit is the only
answer for dealing with adversity and achieving spiritual
happiness and true success.

So when physical things, mental things, and emotional
things invade our bodies, we must reach with grace deep
within for spiritual understanding. Its wisdom is the only
medicine of life!

Lamont Holliday

The Warmth of the Season

When the snow is crisp, beneath my feet,
I feel the heat in my heart,
knowing that the world is gathering together
for the same kind of thing.
The spirit of the season glides through our hearts
like an eagle soaring in the morning skies.
The lights displayed is like the light of love,
and we all gather we don't feel the cold.
For when everyone feels the warmth inside,
we seem to forget our problems,
we just let them slide.
For the season is one to remember.

Bobbi Johnson

Rainbow of Life

You've given me joy in life;
a rainbow to call my own.
Emotions called, "colors of light,"
inside my heart they've grown.

You gave me pink—as a little girl,
orange—a sunset's delight.
You gave me red for my anger,
pale yellow my full moon's light.

Purple was for my fickleness,
and gray for my sad days.
You gave me green—for it is serene
and white for frostiness.

Black is for my demise;
bleak and scariness.
But blue is for the eyes
and gold for holiness.

For the last, words are lost . . .
indigo—deep maroon.
It represents all the cost
of life—your return is soon.

Kimberly Hamilton

The Sun

Bright and sunny,
I'll bring you the day.
Early every morning,
Without delay.

Children without me,
Outdoors they can't play.
Plants without me,
There shall they lay.

When adults see me,
They are glad and gay.
Especially when they
Get their pay.

People at the bay,
Pushing through their way.
When I give them ray,
it is always in May.

I'll just stop here now,
I got nothing else to say.
I've been saying so much
For the whole of today.

Tiffany Chao

Fallen

I Miss You my Love . . . Deep within my Soul . . .
For a time You were the Glue that held my Tender Heart Together . . .
Where would the Earth . . . Sun . . . and Moon be without Gravity . . .
Like the Stars . . . I have Fallen from the Sky and burned away . . .
Don't know where I am in the Dark . . .
Haven't seen where I've been headed for days . . .
Just very aware of these empty spaces where laughter once Lived
and Darkness has come now to take its place . . .
Your Place

Barbara Ann Hannett

What Do I Want from a Man

I want a man, a real man, to love me
because of all the pain I've suffered.

I want a genuine man to respect me because
I am a lady and need to feel reassured.

Admiration, good times, laughter, tenderness.
Respect, loyalty, not too tall an order for Superman, I guess.

Real romance, not just sex, and intelligent speaking—
that will make me love the man I've been seeking.

What do I want a man to do for me?
Treat me like the queen I am, how hard could that be?

I will no doubt treat you like my king,
but don't think I'm materialistic because it doesn't depend on a ring.

I want a king with a royal heart
and a reign that makes us never want to part.

Vivian Eloise Ennis

Mansion on the Hill

There's a mansion on a hill and it sits in paradise.
To be there is such a thrill it makes my spirit rise.
In the distance there's a hill that frames the setting sun,
It's God's way to say, "Be still, this blessed day is done."

Then comes night in all its splendor with sparkling stars so bright,
shining beauty they surrender, as they light up the darkest night.
As you wake up to the dawning morning and see the rising sun
it is a sign, it is God's warning, a new day has just begun.

Hear the buzzing of the bees and birds singing in the trees,
flowers down beneath send a fragrance through the air we breathe.
As you look up to the blue, blue skies, you can see the butterflies,
a spectacular display, like shooting stars across the skies.

No, this mansion is not made of gold; it is just a humble cabin
but the joys within are sevenfold. It is my home, my piece of heaven.
Before my days on Earth are done, I wish my heart's desire you fill
that soon you'll come to share the thrill at the "mansion on the hill."

Fidelia Valdez

A Daughter's Compliment

Seeing you and me in pictures of how life used to be,
Makes me realize the truth of what you mean to me.
I find myself to be more like you every day,
Thinking the way you think, loving the way you love, and saying the things you say.
With just one look and a smile, you take away all of this world's
hatefulness,
Words would be too small for expressing all of my gratefulness.
Kissing away all of my hurt and blowing out every fiery pain,
You complete me like a link in life's continuous chain.
Brightening up my life with your gifts and your love,
You're my tangible angel from Heaven above.
Never overly judgmental or critical of my strange ways,
You always bring a light of hope into my dark days.
For all your years and to this day,
I am a stronger woman, just like you, but in my own way
So when I look in the mirror, down the road, and you are what I see,
I hope that I can mean half as much to my daughter as you mean to me.

Patsy Williford

My Love

Dearest love,
The stars above
Never outshine your smile.

And even though,
I love you so,
My visit may be delayed awhile.

For you, my love,
Are up above
And live a dimension away.

And all this time,
I've written rhyme,
Sitting where you lay.

We'll open doors,
Sincerely yours,
Your loving admirer

P. S., I know,
You love me so.
I'm your only desire.

Mandi Hawk

He Has

He has a quiet presence,
this obvious even as a child.
Thoughtful, gentle and caring,
with a manner that is mild.

He has a lot of talent,
with vision in what he has made.
Good at building, good at creating,
he's a carpenter by trade.

He has a sense of humor,
always subtle, clever and wry.
Seeing humor in most instances
with a twinkle in his eye.

He has an abundance of family
and friends who band as one
All loving and supporting him,
all proud of what he has done.

He has a ton of courage,
with strength you can feel and see.
Understanding and accepting,
with faith in the Holy Trinity.

Carol J. Carroll

My Dear Phyllis

I thank you so for loving me,
these many years now to see
why else, your whole life be,
if not devoted just to me.

With this I say to you today,
Just after God took you away,
As I found there where you lay
only heartache and dismay.

To look upon your lovely face,
I would gladly take the space
for the journey from this place,
you, now in this final race.

Look down on me, dear sweet wife,
as I struggle with the strife
now so lonely in this life,
cut apart as if by a knife.

I truly love you, Phyllis dear,
my words of rhyme I pray you hear
to me you'll always be so near,
to brush away that lonely tear.

David Stratton

Thief of Mystery

One morning, like a thief on a dark and dreary night,
like I was an open window, you crept into my life.
You've stolen my energy and most of my strength,
but still, I will not let you be a restraint.

Now as the days go slowly by, it's so hard for me to get out of bed,
and because of you, there are so many times that I've wished I were dead,
but my family and friends, say that I've come too far
to let you end it this way, so with their love, prayers,
and support, I will face you, through yet, another, painful day.

Doctors, to this day, still don't know what causes you for sure,
but we all pray that someday soon they will finally find your cure.
Yes, you've changed a lot of things in my life,
but M. S., you have not yet won this fight.

Tammy Payne

Cancer

Cancer is an obstacle that many people face.
My grandma died of lung cancer last May with so much grace.

She fought against the odds for two very long years.
She knew her family, in this time,
Shed many, many tears.

My other grandma fought a different form of cancer too.
She is doing fine now.
In her life she has so much left to do.

Sports people, famous people, and common people, too,
Learn they may have cancer and don't know what to do.

I hope that in my lifetime that a cure for cancer can be found.
Then, in my opinion, our world would be a place that is safe and sound.

Tommy LaCalamito

Daddy Helped Save the World

Daddy earned medals in World War II, I still don't know what for.
Even as an adult, I don't know, what that brave man did in the war.
Silent is he after 56 years, only his nightmares full of fright.
Battle of the Bulge and D-Day too are visions in the dark of night.
My brother went to Vietnam, and he could have been excused,
for Daddy was on the draft board, but he felt duty, so he refused.
You see, they fight for all countries. It's freedom they desire
so you say good-bye.
You fight for unknown persons hopelessness, and pray that you will survive.
The American Flag is a piece of cloth, but can bring, tears to a grown
man's eye.
When it passes by, you stand and salute, for that cloth you dignify.
Daddy brought home a war trophy, a center piece of cloth from a flag,
from a dead Nazi's hand, a swastika, for this flag you would never brag.
Some medals he earned never were awarded, no memorial did they deploy.
This, the man, who helped save the world, was only a college boy.

Susie Lunsford

Teacher

Teach me what it is like to live in this world you speak of often,
Where feelings don't change from day to day, and cold, cold hearts do soften.
Teach me what it is like to trust a love that is honest and caring.
Show me how people can have two lives, but it's really one they're sharing.
Tell me how it is to live without fear of consequences.
Where conversations don't have to be held dodging invisible walls and fences.
Where a hurried step means excitement, and not anger about to unfold.
Where words are never used as weapons to cut, and to wound . . . to scold.
What is it like to share a love where words are only spoken
To warm a heart, to bring a smile; not leave hearts damaged . . . and broken.
Teacher, please be patient with me when I speak of fears and sorrows.
Please understand . . . my world does not Hold promise of bright tomorrows.
I have so much to learn about a love, a life fulfilling.
These walls of silence are much too loud, this atmosphere is chilling.
So, teach me what I need to know to stand strong on my own.
Teacher . . . you have opened the door, don't leave me out here . . . alone.

Karen Sobiesczyk

For Chaunta, My Dog

We were rovers,
We ran and played together
You shared my dreams here

You almost made it

You saw my pain and cared

Just now, what kind of passion stirs
inside of me I cannot say.
I feel for you
and it's as much as love,
but whether it's because I feel
you leaving, slipping from me
day by day
or because I depended on or want you
I have no way of knowing

But as you are scattered
over the crashing
waves I will remember

you were important
I loved you.

Susan Kaplan

Our Yard

Our yard is such a peaceful place,
It's where I love to be.
To see the birds and butterflies
And squirrels up in the trees.

With a large flower garden
Spread out across the lawn,
In the shape of a half circle,
Measuring eighty feet long.

And behind a row of lilacs
Is another special place,
We call the "English Tea Garden;"
Roses grow within its space.

Then looking out the window,
In the fall, we often see
Two little white tail deer,
Eating crab apples off the tree.

It's such a quiet, peaceful yard
With wildlife all around,
We could never ask for more,
You don't find this in town!

Gayle Hunter

People

There is a bamboo
So fragile and small
There is a sycamore
So big and strong

Here comes the wind
Here comes the rain
Here comes the sun
The day becomes gay

Still . . .
The bamboo looks fragile and small
The sycamore looks big and strong
Nothing has changed

Then . . .
There comes the storm
There comes the thunder
The day is gay once again

But alas . . .
The bamboo still looks fragile and small
It stands gracefully
The sycamore fails to keep growing

Nia Fitrasanti

A Crohn's Farewell

To be whole again just like new.
To not feel in the minority or one of few.
I should be grateful it could be worse.
This cross I bear, this intestinal curse.
It will beat me yet if I'm not strong.
God tell me what I did so wrong?
I will trade my soul for a healthy hour or day.
why won't this illness go away?
you are worried and scared.
You love me and are there for me you have always cared.
You don't know how to help or what to say.
You would give your life for me, no price you wouldn't pay.
For you I fight each day stand tall smile and laugh the pain away.
You give me courage, strength to fight reminders of the hope in sight.
You support me when I am weak, provide the courage that I seek.
Thanks to you life has some good a few days of health as it should.
If I leave I did not give up the fight.
God just decided to make the bad right.
Don't be sad, fear you failed to do your part.
It was loving you that gave my life battery its start.

Lisa Patrice Galatte

I Dreamt

I dreamt that I was beautiful, sensuous lines and full of grace.
My skin was delicate ivory. Striking was the beauty of my face.

I dreamt that I was lovely. My smile would fill the room
With sunshine, youth, and warmth and would chase away the gloom.

I dreamt that I was greatly loved. My heart was gentle and true.
Kindness mixed with modesty, passion alive in every breath I drew.

My fragile dreams were broken by the footsteps in the hall.
I awoke and found just me. I was not beautiful at all.

My lines are not sensuous. They are not curved and full of grace.
My skin has lost it youthfulness.
There's nothing striking about my face.

In the mirror was no loveliness. My smile was ordinary and plain.
It sparked no inspiration. It could not stop the rain.

But I knew that I was greatly loved and my heart is gentle and true.
My passion for life knows no bounds. I am modest and kindly, too.

I thought I had to be beautiful to be considered worthy of love.
But beauty is just a picture in which a good heart stands above.

Sonya Deliyannis

And

It's been an eternity since I watched your eyes move over my body,
Since I felt your gentle hands caress my skin,
since I kissed your soft, comforting lips with my own.
It's been a eternity since you held me in your arms,
since we watched the hours pass together,
since I've heard your soothing voice.
It's been an eternity since my ears have heard your secrets,
since my heart has opened up to you,
since you've seen inside my thoughts.
It's been an eternity since we've slowly danced together,
since I've cried on your shoulder, since you've whispered my name,
And in this short eternity, I've felt such trust, such pride, such love.
In this short eternity I've felt such deceit, such sorrow, such pain.
In this short eternity, I've made a new friend,
fell head over heels, lost my whole heart and some self-respect, too.
In this short eternity, I've spoken many truths,
cried many tears, unmasked many secrets and who cared?
I thought my new friend would.
But he didn't!
And this is one life experience
I will never forget.

Wendy E. Howard

Sunset of Life

Days and years pass quickly by
We pause and wonder with a sigh
How long will we live?
When will we die?

The Prince of Life comes riding by.
We fall in love, and then we try
To live our dreams of make believe
Even though sometimes we grieve.
The only things that really lasts
Are memories borrowed from the past.

Dreams of crystal chandeliers
Golden treasures from the years,
A stolen kiss, a child's toy,
Among the thoughts that give us joy.
Memories good, memories bad,
Sometimes happy, sometimes sad.

Trinkets and body we leave behind.
We can take with us only our mind.
Some things good, some things bad.
Some things happy, some things sad.

Opal Kafer

Lost or Found

What do I say to faith?
Can you have too much?
Or is too much not enough?
It is sometimes not easy to believe,
especially when you fall short
of what you want to achieve.
Has anything ever happened to you
to make you lose your faith?
Something that happened,
made you feel out of place?
When you wish upon the Lord
and it doesn't come true—
Now you feel lost; what do you do?
Have you ever given trust—
in the end it is broke.
Your mind feels all cluttered,
blinded by the smoke.
Being rejected by love—
Suppressed by your own thoughts—
Is it real or is it fake?
To find it once more
is a chance I'm willing to take.

Ryan Acosta Flock

Fear

In all that you see,
you wish all that you could be;
was just like anyone there,
or there, over there, right here.

You think? Could they be me?
Your minds says, that is too mean!
your heart says, what do you mean?
Constantly your body is saying, Why me?

Through it all, you make it every day,
but, really at what cost do you say:
Think it impossible, it is possible.
Think it probable, and it is improbable.

Why does it always come down to this?
you, your friend, your life, or sex.
It always ends, all of it,
but still, you never quit.

You keep it going, you let it go.
you know that you can never say 'No!'
So, it grabs a hold, never lets go;
until, finally, You are all alone!

Keith Cozart

This Is the End

I'm tired of all your secrets, I'm tired of all your lies.
I'm tired of all the little things, that you keep inside.
I'm sick of how you treat me, I'm sick of all my frowns.
I'm sick of all your rudeness, You always get me down.
I'm tired of being so grateful, And getting nothing in return.
I'm tired of your never listening, It seems you'll never learn.
You're sweet when we're alone, You make me very glad.
But when you get with your friends, You always treat me bad.
I don't know why I've stuck around, I've been blind not able to see.
But now I know your true self, It's not someone I want to be.
You never call me on the phone, Or ask me to go out.
It's always me the one who's reaching, And you the one to pout.
You are not a very nice guy, I just want to be free.
Everything you say is hypocritical, You're always trying to fool me.
I don't understand why you're so rude, A lying selfish man.
Please get your life together, Put your actions in your own hands.
I don't know why you are like this, Why me you're trying to offend.
I'm sick and tired of this treatment, I'm not sorry, this is the end.
I'm out of your life forever, It's the end of our love dance.
No sorries will be accepted, Last time was your last chance.

Julianne Helen Davies

Grizzly

With scars about his face, and arms made of steel
His crooked walk would tell, of wounds to never heal
For a name he's known as Grizzly, for the bodies he would leave
Victims without life, scattered amongst the trees.
Grizzly was drafted, in the spring of '69
Sent to Vietnam, till he stepped upon a mine
They offered him a discharge, but he refused to go
Death he learned to give, killing he loved so.
The war came to an end, Grizzly was sent back home
He lives out under the trees, he wishes to be alone
He brought the death home with him, buried deep inside
He could not leave it there, many times he cried.
They say he'd never fallen, as the record shows
How many men he ravaged, no one may ever know
Many a man has ventured out, Grizzly they would kill
Few of them ever returned, buried up in the hills.
So for those of you who believe, this story not to be true
Just sit upon those hills at night, and see what happens to you
They say that Grizzly lives today, the mountains are still his home
So if you ever go there, you better beware, and you better not go alone.

Joseph E. Neidhart

Deah Season

Ole' Joe sat, cleaning his gun
Maw was watching, 'cause he had more than one
"Joe," said Maw, "Take me hunting, please."
Ole' Joe laughed, pretending to sneeze.
"Now Maw," said Joe, "Let me told you one 'ting:"
You don't know a Deah from a hog's nose ring."
"Well! I'll show you," said Maw
"We'll go tomorrow, see who has the last hee haw."
They got up early to be on their way.
Maw found a good spot and said "I'll got one today."
Joe left maw by that big oak tree
He walked a half a mile and let out a big hee hee.
All of a sudden he heard Maw shoot!
"May," said Joe "She must have got one, that or her foot."
Joe ran all the way to where he left maw.
He nearly dropped in his tracks at what he saw.
A game warden was backed up to that big oak tree.
His hand was raised in the air and he was begging, "Lady please don't shoot me."
If you say my horse is a deer, so let it be:"
"My horse is a deer, lady, I do agree:"

Dottie N. Bonner

Whispers

To my husband, Kevin

Whisper a song
of time gone by
Whisper a song
that makes me cry
Whisper a song
I long to hear
Whisper a song
quietly in my ear
Whisper the song
sent from above
Whispers of time
and truth and love
Whisper no more
say it out loud
let it be heard
strong and proud
Then Whisper again
soft like a dove
now and forever
I know I'm in Love

Jacquie Manworing

Take My Hand

Our lives seem worlds apart.
Our differences, there are many.
Will our love survive this test?
Will we conquer this rift of life?

You give to me your love so freely
You bring a light to my lonely heart,
When you hold me I feel contentment.
When you kiss me time stands still.

Our love grows every day
And every day I wonder how
You continue to love me all the more
Even though we seem far apart.

My love for you fills my heart
Giving to you all I have
My heart, my soul, my dreams.
Take care with these and I will respond!

We struggle with our identities
To understand and accept.
Take my hand my love,
Together we can conquer all.

Kathryn Dobson

I Promise

I Promise to take a closer look
At all the different ways,
That I can stop to help someone
And turn their night into day.

I Promise to take an elder's hand
And let them lean on me,
As they tell me things of long ago,
Things they want me to see!

I Promise to give a child a hug,
No matter race or creed,
For soon that child will stand up tall,
To represent you and me.

I Promise to love the animals,
Whose purpose is so sweet,
Not be slain, and traumatized.
So that we can gloat on meat.

I Promise to always listen more
So that I can hear His voice
The One who gently whispers to me
That I always have a choice.

Carrie R. Owens

Good-bye Letter to Drug of Choice

One day when I was about the age of 13
I decided to take a walk down the street
I bumped into you, you bumped into me and at that moment I knew.
It was you I was longing to meet
You loved me like no one ever before, you helped me survive in the world of war.
You were my life, my everything, I needed you, you needed me
For the next five years my companion you were
You took over my life for you were sure
You thought that our love would never die you thought I would never leave you behind,
you started to take over, my life was in your hands
You started to scare me with all your demands
Then one day I started to cry, because of you I wanted to die
I tried to run, I tried to hide, but I couldn't you were everywhere even inside.
So I decided to face you. I decided to stand up and be strong.
I knew if I didn't, life would be like a black time bomb.
So now I am here and I want you to see
I wasn't meant for you. We weren't meant to be.
And now it is time to say good-bye, I need to learn to love, I need to learn
to cry, I no longer allow you to take over my life.
I no longer allow you to bring my life strife. Good-bye!

Mandy Crane

Today Is Mine

The true heart will only reveal to us what needs to be
A gift, the miracle of life given us from birth till infinite time
Allow your heart to feel, your soul and spirit to live life free
The courage to change, make a difference; today is mine.

Do not allow this moment to slip by, taking life for granted
Cannot get back what is gone, live for today,
for each day is borrowed time.
Tomorrow may never come, so follow your heart's true intention—
not to abandon
The courage to change, make a difference; today is mine.

The empty quiet space in your soul has hidden messages to reveal
Learn to listen, trust your heart, for if you don't follow,
lost you will be in time.
The courage to change, make a difference; today is mine.

Free your spirit from within and allow God to do for you in your heart
Surrender, do not forsake Him, for He will give you immortality in time
Believe He cannot ever forsake or abandon you,
from the universe never part
The courage to change, make a difference; today is mine.

Urszula Gawle

Needing More

I have no explanation why so much time went by
and I have not become all that I can be
fate does not matter—I have my heart to follow—
to bring out the best of me—whatever time relates
for the need for more accomplishment is reality that time itself creates
in rhythm like an eagle to conquer mountains and hills galore
I am taking on the challenge to spread my wings and soar
holding the key to the end results—the approval commitment makes
unlocking the door to fulfillment is the range of what it takes
chasing desires through winding roads—changing time
my tune becomes way off key—then again my tune will rhyme
focus—I am in need to restore to master the course
I go on needing more
Whatever may befall this will—this guide
belief in my soul must abide
for loved ones—for friends—for the public to see
before the day comes to share my dream come true
I must prove myself to me
with rhyme like an eagle over mountains and hills I am going
with great anticipation I am spreading my wings and soaring

Katherine Hagans Clark

When I Spell before I Think of You

It was back
in the years that my mind reflects upon
with joy
I loved you
your eyes had a charm so specific
they drew me in
with an unwilling hunger
I followed
bewitched like a soldier
and the soldier ensnared
sweet song of the seductress
sweet
but undesired
you captured me
and all the years have rolled over
first love
polished like sea glass
emerging more precious than
but I can't let it be like
before . . .

Dominique Parris

Lisa, My Bride to Be

Written for my wife, on our wedding day

Lisa, my bride to be,
your love gives so much joy to me.
Our bond is that of steel,
only our hearts can truly feel.
On this day our wedding bells ring,
we can softly hear the angels sing.
As we join together as husband and wife,
I hereby pledge the rest of my life,
to love, honor and cherish you,
to have and to hold,
through sickness and health,
from this day forward,
till death do we part,
until we rejoin in Heaven,
as one eternal heart.
Lisa, my bride to be,
today and forever,
you are a part of me.
I love you,
your groom to be, Robert

Robert Abner

A Rose in the Garden

I saw a rose in our garden
That took my breath away
Its fragrance and its beauty
Caused my mind to stray

Am I a rose in His garden
For others to observe
Do they see an inner beauty
With a willingness to serve

Is there a sweet aroma
That comes from deep within
Does it reach out to others
To help their souls to mend

There are hurts we encounter
And pain that we must bear
Can we put aside our suffering
And show others that we care

Like a rose showing forth its splendor
Down deep I'm sure it mourns
For in spite of all its beauty
It bears its own painful thorns

Darlene Mae Moser

'Tis Love So True

To my sweetheart!
'Tis Love for you, honest and true.
'Tis warm your touch can be, mean so much to me.
Touch of your hand can stop the land,
the warmth, the gentleness, makes me feel so grand.
'Tis your life be broken, your love a token,
a gift to be given, a gift to receive, Oh, Dear God let it be me.
'Tis a love I feel, ever so real, so clean, so strong,
anything we do could not be wrong.
Tis beauty I see, beauty I feel, 'tis my darling, I love ever so real.
'Tis a pit so empty, so deep without him, I cannot sleep.
'Tis my darling I need in every way,
so Dear God help me pray, that I may have another day.
'Tis your timing my Lord as to how long I have, don't make me sad.
Give me the time to build that home,
for the only family I have ever known.
'Tis what I want, 'Tis what I must have,
to fill my heart with joy, grant me a little time to raise that boy.
Forever my love you will have. So make me ever so glad.

Ann Hepworth

My Grandmother and Me

We are so much alike,
My grandmother and me.
Not in looks, but in the way we think and feel.
It just gives me a thrill
To think that a part of her has become a part of me.
She touched me in a special way which will forever stay
In my heart, in my thoughts, forever and a day.
Never did I think that when I was grown there'd be a link
between my grandmother and me.
She must have sent a little elf to spark the rhymes I hide within myself.
Since never before did I feel a need
To put my thoughts and feelings on paper to read.
So today I think, as I sit here all healthy and pink,
That one day we will meet to enjoy and share this great treat.
This poetic link that has joined us as kin,
And erase the space of time—our enemy has been.
As each day goes by I see more clearly why
We are so much alike,
My grandmother and me.

Penny R. Simmons

Mommy's Little Angel

He's Mommy's little angel, Mommy's pride and joy,
Mommy's little angel, for he's my little boy.

Early one morning about the break of down
I heard a baby crying, crying for his mom.
I ran to the kitchen to warm up some milk,
But when I got back with it, I was suddenly filled with guilt,
The room was so quiet and cold I could just feel something in the air,
I didn't know what it was but something was there.
I suddenly froze I couldn't take another step I started crying I got so upset.

He's mommy's little angel, Mommy's pride and joy
he's mommy's little angel, for he's my little boy.

He was just laying there with his little hand touching his brothers.
I knew then God wanted my little and no other
It just wasn't fair it just wasn't right,
The way God took my little boy away that night.

Well, I guess God knew what He was doing when he took my little boy away,
For if there is a Heaven above my little boy is watching me today.
For now he's God's little angel, God's pride and joy,
He's God's little angel, for he was my little boy.

Angela Nocero

The Wind

The wind's
power
amazes
and devastates.

Wind
dances
trees, leaves, flowers.

The wind
destroys
our most precious gifts
we love.

Wind
enriches
and haunts our very being.

The wind—
wonderful,
mystic,
quick,
fearfully strong.

Bruce Charles Robert Smith

First Thoughts on Kristen

Curious like a monkey
The green-fresh scent of spring
Brilliance like the morning sun
An independent queen

Her life is lived in private thoughts
She laughs and plays her games
Fickle spontaneous autonomous
She remains untamed

This mysterious vitality
Frustrates my selfish pain
Wondering can I keep her
Knowing control is vain

Seeing beyond my years
Uncommon insights true
Consistence responsibility
Peace for wild in lieu

While introspection illuminates
Unknown remains her mind
I passionately tap my senses
To know if she'll be mine

Aaron Peterson

Memories

As the years go by
And older I've grown
My thoughts go back
To my childhood home

Our memories are precious
Time can't erase
We hold them so dear
In a very special place

Wouldn't it be wonderful
If we could turn the page
Back to where we once were
And we would never age

But life is wonderful
A gift from above
We grow and learn
Best of all how to love

But we all walk together
Never say what might have been
For the best is yet to come
Just around the bend

Grace Craft

The Home

I am a house. I am made of wood, brick and glass.
I am a shelter from the rain and cold.
I have four walls, a floor and roof.
I am sturdy. I stand up through all kinds of weather,
Because of the strong foundation upon which I stand.
My windows let me see out, and others to look in.
There are doors to enter, hallways to walk through, rooms to occupy.
Within my walls, life is sustained, babies born, children run, parents love.
Dreams are dreamt. Happiness is found. Sorrows endured.
Within my walls, I keep many secrets, and hold many memories.
I see all, absorb everything, and say nothing.
I am a source of safety from the outside world. A haven.
A place where love is grown.
People will come, and then someday will leave.
More will come in their place,
But I will never forget those who have come before and dwelt within.
For I am a part of them, as they are a part of me.
I will never change in basic structure, for the basics will always remain the same
Love lives and is nurtured here. I am a home!

Karen Taubenheim

Schemes and Dreams

How wonderful to have lived and gathered memories so dear
To know how to be light of heart though our winter years draw near!
To be able to live your years with dignity and be an important part
of life's scheme, to know you're able to hold your head high
while your heart shows you how to dream!
To be thankful for gifts of life, whether big or small
For no matter how much we seek the treasures, we may not collect them all
It's the treasures of caring, of giving and sharing,
that is a sign of wealth; of knowing we're winning in life's game
when granted the wealth of health.
And though there are times when those near and dear leave us to stand alone
in the end; let's not forget the greatest gift of God
is the gift of love of family and friend!
For happiness is counting our blessings, making the best,
of whatever we've got, building hopes, dreaming dreams,
striving for things we have not
It's knowing the importance of waking each morn
and beginning each blessed day, by holding dear the memories
we've gathered as we walked through life's path way!

Irene Bortolot

Buddy's Theme

We thought we would have tomorrow.
To talk, to laugh, to play, to share.
Don't be sad because we did have my lifetime of yesterdays
Of the memories and the laughs,
The talks, the special times, I will never forget.
I know you'll love me always and forever.
Mom,
When you feel the sun . . . it is my heart to warm you.
When you feel the rain . . . it is my tears to remind you I miss you also.
When it thunders . . . it is my anger, I had to leave without . . .
Your hug, your kiss, your touch, your voice saying good-bye.
When you see the moon . . . it is my love and my soul to warm your heart.
When you see the stars . . . hey, mom, I'm the biggest and brightest,
Remember you told me I could be the best.
When you see a rainbow . . . you are the beginning and I am at the end
And soon we will meet again.
To feel your touch, to see your smile, to hear your laugh
I know you'll love me always and forever
And I will love you forever and always!

Dari L. Lee

The Rug Room

They call it the rug room,
the room in special Ed.
You can check in, any time you want,
but you can never leave
is what these kids believe.

We'll never get out of this place,
so they think.
Wonder what it's like
on the outside
beyond these walls.
Why can't we be
with the so-called "normal" kids.

Out in the halls,
no one likes us,
they think we're dumb.
We need someone
to understand us.
Can you be that one?

So what if we can't sit still,
what's the big deal?

Geri Egan

The Day

The silky darkness
of the fading night
Slowly gives way
to the day's first light.

The brilliant hues
of the awaking sun,
The sweet singing of birds
signal the day has begun.

The laughter of children
engulfed in their play,
Another sure sign
of the brand-new day.

The blooming of flowers,
The deep blue of the sky.
The slow drifting clouds,
a soft murmured sigh.

As the light gently fades,
one thought seem to stay.
I have just had the joys
of a wonderful day.

Gary Smith

I Watch This Child

In memory of Heather Lynnette Pendleton, 6/24/79-5/4/97

I watch this child as she grows.
Oh, what a joy to behold,
And only one day old.
I watch this child as she grows.
What the future holds,
Only Heaven knows.
I watch this child as she grows,
With curly hair and freckled face.
Can't hold back, must win life's race.
I watch this child as she grows,
Infant, toddler, child no longer.
A young woman with real life dreams
and heartaches like a river flows.
I watch this child as she grows,
A beauty to behold
The prom dress bought with such pride
hangs beside her cap and gown
never to be worn.
But now all we have are memories,
FOR THIS CHILD GROWS NO MORE.

Joy Pendleton

Running Rivers of My Mind

The rivers twist and turn without knowing where they will go,
never having any specific destination.
The current can be strong, or breezy like the air on a spring day.

The sound can be as loud as thunder on a stormy day or
it can be soft like a honeybee singing through the air.

Running Rivers have freedom to flow anywhere.
There is nothing that can restrict the way to freedom.

Running Rivers give life to the great forest that surrounds them
and restricts the way to freedom.

Running Rivers give all life to the great forest that
surrounds them and supports the very life of the majestic trees.

Running Rivers give a home to the Lord's smallest life form creatures;
they are a resting place to nestle and to be warm and free.

Running Rivers are free to conquer any obstacle that
may be in the way of the pathway to freedom.

Running Rivers are like your best friend, always there on time for peace, love, support.
You can express your thoughts with trust, that of the freedom
of your mind with the "Running Rivers"

Running Rivers forever flowing in my mind, and listening to the constant
flow and music of each twist and turn of the fate of the "Running Rivers."

Lynda S. King

The Life We Choose

To live is man's greatest joy,
But if told to him this fact he would ignore,
To pick the way we live is not God's choice but ours,
But to choose our path in life is a gift from God above,
The way we live is how we are seen to the world,
And the world will judge us all, be us boy or girl,
To take a life or ruin a life we sometimes foolishly choose,
But no matter what when we are engulfed in eternal flames we will pay our due,
So choose the path of life wisely for the one you take,
You will not like the consequences of your actions when your eyes open
and you are forever awake

John Lennon

The Diligent Student

For those who study diligently, there is a miracle.
With sonorous sounds, they are educated.
With dancing letters, they are cultivated.

For they uncover and discover the smoothness of knowledge through their eyes
Matching letters decrypt in their brains, causing delight without pains.
And what a pleasant surprise when,
with their hearts, they touch the skies.

For they will open the lustrousness of knowledge through their ears.
Mating sounds decode in their minds,
bringing joy with exclusive signs
with plenty happy tears, their hearts transform in finest pure spears.

But, do they know when does it all begin, as they become great unique earls?
When do they enter those nacreous shells of beautiful pearls?
Discovering lyric similes sealed in written prose
or epic metaphors shielded in spoken verse.

Do they know when does it all begin?
Those who still make spume gum
when their rough edges become softer than cotton balls,
bouncing on or climbing moons, stars, suns
without feeling impotently small or blindly tall.

Then, there is the miracle gift for those who study diligently
becoming masters and mistresses of a fraction of knowledge,
for they digest knowledge that polishes and molds them very gently.

Luz Algarin

Finding Out

So you are the one who died for me and
Shed your innocent blood
I've read of how you took their assault
And didn't say a word.
You could have easily said not for them
I'm not giving my life.
But because of love you stayed there
So we could have eternal life.
If I refuse you as my Savior
I have no chance to win.
Thank you, Jesus,
For bridging the gap
Between God and men.

Wayne A McCullough

Winter Wonderland

The world becomes a winter wonderland,
With chilling winds and icy, frozen ponds.
A blizzard blew some flurries all around,
Which showered snowy blankets on the lawn.

When all is finished, a peaceful hush remains
As nature's beauty is beheld by all.
The view outside my window is not plain,
And white has covered all things, great and tall.

Corice Thornton

Memories

Memories are made every day
in deeds we do and words we say.
Be considerate and kind;
then happy memories you will leave behind.
Treat all people like a brother.
Get rid of hate and love one and other.
Once your memories are made,
they can never be replayed.

May S. Varkala

Parents

In the journey through time that we call life
The roads we travel are paved with strife
We try to stay on course each day
But sometimes fail and lose our way

The road of life is seldom clear
If we but knew which way to steer
When we are lost and sometimes stray
You're always there to point the way

Donald Seebold

Dark Skies

Dark skies and dewdrops on leaves,
all I see is my past surrounding me.
What can I do to make my past slip away?
I can't change it; it's still here to stay.
Every time I think about it,
it feels as though a black sheet has covered my head,
and the harder I try not to think about it,
the harder it is for me to breathe.
People say, forget about your past, it's the present and the future.
What they don't understand is once it's there, it stays there.
And that is why dark skies and dewdrops on leaves will
always surround me.

Taylor Ayres

The Party

I sat in a room full of people yet I was alone.
I watched them walk by and smile yet I was alone.
I sat as people stopped to talk to me. I am alone.
I don't fit in here with these people.
I don't fit in with anyone, I am eternally alone.
They rush past, caught up in their own lives, as I sit and wait for you.
I sit lifeless, waiting for you to come.
You came so briefly, and I was no longer alone.
But as fast as you came, you left.
As quickly as I lost the emptiness, I gained it back.
You were my last and only hope, but you stand by,
pushing me into loneliness.
Why did I trust you? I wouldn't have let myself fall if I had known
you would leave me alone and hopeless.
You are now just another passing, smiling face.
I am alone until you pass again, and my dreams smash like glass.
You walk by and smile with countless others, yet I am alone.

Emma Meyer

Come Home to Me

We wait for someday to come.
We both have a glow about us like the rising sun.
We cherish the time we have together.
It's like the calm between storms of uncertain weather.
We agree that the time line was way off.
But now that we have found each other, we can't get enough.
We long for the day when we are in each others' arms.
Knowing that being together is certainly not wrong.
Our ideas, our thoughts, our likes, and dislikes are one and the same.
And people all around us seem to notice; it's just that plain.
We hope, we pray, we want, we need
that the bond between us will flourish like a well nourished seed.
When I see you, I get a feeling inside.
It warms my heart so much, it's something I cannot hide.
My feelings seem obvious to all the world to see
that they know I long for the day when you
Come Home to Me.

Robert F. Stanislow

Missing You

As I sit here in the shimmering candle light,
Wishing you were with me on this lonely, winter night,
Thoughts of you are racing through my head.
I spread my body out to fill this empty bed.
Outside the snow is falling from the sky,
A gleaming, white blanket, appealing to the eye.
But a sight more pleasing is that of you,
The one so kind, sweet, gentle, and true.
I lay here dreaming of what to do if you were here,
Kissing you softly from ear to ear.
We could stay up all night talking and having fun,
Almost to the hour of the rising sun.
But at the end of the night, I'd look deep into your eyes,
And sing you to to sleep with my soothing lullabies.

Steve Kiddy

Home

Home is where I live, home is where the heart is.
I love my home.
It's comfortable and full of wonderful things
that are needed for the purpose of living.
It makes me feel happy when I am glad,
and brings joy to my heart when I am sad.
Home has everything, and full of God's love.
It's where I belong when I come home from a long tired day from a job.
It may have changes, but God is sent from above
to cleanse it with his love.
I am thankful for the knowledge he gave man
to build this great home.
We are here to take care of it,
because home will always be home, sweet home. . . .

Pauline McKay

Soul of a Thief

Why am I here?
When I should be there?
To fill in the blanks—to fill in the spaces,
To ease your conscience?
Why did you do those things—How do you sleep at night? I can't.
And didn't. Did you? No.
When you look in the mirror, do you soothe your own soul because
you have stolen someone else's?
Do you tell yourself you're okay and everything is going to be all right?
I'm not all right—why should you be? Do you pray for forgiveness?
Do you pray that your soul won't be stolen like you have stolen mine?
—Do you think I am all right?—do I sound alright?
—No. You can't stand to look at me
—So go back to the mirror and pray that in the middle of the night
my soul doesn't sneak over to yours
and take back what you have ripped from me
—Pray that I won't tell—Pray that I am going to be all right—and
maybe someday—you will just die.
Then I will be all right.

A. Payette

One Last Moment

I'm alone; I can already tell your not being
here is going to be hard.
From the moment they said you were never coming home again,
I've felt lost, afraid, hurt.
How could you leave me here?
Every time I think of you, it makes me want to die, too.
Last night, I don't know why, for some reason,
I already knew the whole story.
The look of horror on your face stunned me in this nightmare of mine.
And it felt like a thousand knives stabbing me from all sides.
My dreams have been smashed along with you,
and your love for me . . . .
Now, when I'm alone, I can still hear your voice
as if your standing right behind me,
whispering in my ear, calling me your girl again.
And every time I close my eyes, I see you, and it hurts me so bad.
I just wish I could have one last moment to say I love you.
One last moment to hold you, kiss you.
One last moment to say good-bye.

Angela Harter-McBride

Reality

At first glance when I saw you, my heart had skipped a beat.
My mind had raced with thoughts of you, but would we ever meet?
I watched you walk around the room, oblivious of my stare,
I longed for you to notice me, but you were unaware.
For months I recalled your beautiful smile
and the sound of your gentle voice,
but circumstances surrounding us left us with no choice.
You wore her ring, I wore his heart; there was nothing I could do,
but sit around and dream of someday making love to you.
Now a year has passed from that first day
and things have changed since then;
broken hearts and shattered dreams have brought us close as friends.
We share each day together, each moment I hold dear,
when we're apart as life goes on, I yearn to hold you near.
To smell your skin or to feel your touch is not just fantasy,
no more late—night thoughts of you, you're now my reality.

Robin DeAndrea

Deep

As I sit in a room and think about life
things that appear to me are now all I see
you see life games to me are somewhat shared tears
Throughout the world with no fears; think deep with me for a second
Time, would you believe that we are in a world of a dying breed?
All the pollution and man-made disease make us wonder
who's the real enemy
Time lost is time blind in a world of illusion brought to us by mankind
someone asked me do I believe in an afterlife.
I ask, do you believe in what's wrong or right
who to judge if he steals to feed his family at night
or if a young boy having to do what he has to do
because his parents on drugs and having no food
So I ask if another life really exists, then why are we going thru all this? Worldly things
I'm not trying to be perfect because I never seen this
but all I know is how to survive and exist so I pray and pray
and maybe one day I will understand
I won't fall for nothing but die as a man.

Negre Marad McKenney

Downpour

As I start to drive off down the street,
raindrops drizzle lightly on the windshield, and
the wipers brush them aside as if they were invisible.
I glance up at the semi-cloudy sky and think about everything.
As I progress towards my destination,
the clouds begin to twist and twirl and form a giant clumps
like massive gray marshmallows slightly burnt on the outside
but still soft and sweet on the inside.
The rain comes pouring down, trickling into the window that is cracked,
and slowly forms a wet place on my arm,
yet it isn't pouring so hard that I should pull over.
Driving on, the rain only becomes worse.
Thunder rolls and lightning sparks directly in front of my car.
I consider pulling off to the side of the road now,
but after struggling to decide,
I realize that every storm must come to an end eventually.
So, I continue driving, but a little more carefully,
so as not to lose control.
And just as I expected, the clouds disintegrated, the rain stopped,
the sun came out and life handed me a rainbow!

Kim Hooker

Friendship Recipe

Take some morning sunshine; add a smile, some kind words, too.
Sprinkle in some happy hours, it's not very hard to do.
Add a little thoughtfulness, stir just enough to blend.
Serve it warm with loving hands; it's the making of a friend.
Blossoms need so much to grow, the earth and sun and shower,
But with a warm and loving thought, true friendship stays in flower.
Joys will keep on growing, like the flowers in the sun,
As friendship's ties grow closer, and thoughts become as one.
Love protects the helpless, love understands the small,
Love keeps the peace forever, with true goodwill to all.
We may not always reach our goal, but there's recompense in trying.
Horizons broaden so much more the higher we are flying.

Marg Roswell

Matt

Well, my time with you is over,
the clock has struck midnight,
reality has begun to sink in,
and my prince has become nonexistent.
Although we never made it to the ball,
we still had a good time.
You would have given me the world.
I could have had the guy I went to bed dreaming of
as a little girl.
You are one of the only good guys left,
and due to my insecurities, I drove you away . . .

I saw you today for the first time in weeks,
and the face I never saw as all that
attractive, seemed to have become perfect.
The voice that used to make me laugh,
now makes me cry.
The kiss I used to avoid is what I long for every time I'm near you.
The chance you gave me nearly a year ago,
is what I beg you to give me now.

Emily Weber

Listen, Christian!

I was hungry, and you formed a humanities club
and discussed my hunger . . . thank you.
I was imprisoned, and you crept off quietly
to your chapel in the cellar and prayed for my release. . . .
I was naked, and in your mind
you debated the morality of my appearance . . .
I was sick, and you knelt and thanked God
for your own health . . . thank you! . . .
I was homeless, and you preached to me
of the spiritual shelter of the love of God . . .
I was lonely and you left me alone to pray for me . . . thank you!
You seem so holy, so close to God:
I am still very hungry, lonely, and cold.
So where have your prayers gone?
What good have they done?
What does it profit a man to page through his bible or book of prayers?
What good does it do when the rest of the world
is alone and cold and crying out for his help?

Flo Craven

Aimless for Love

Written for one with much inspiring wisdom: dedicated to Joseph
in your search for absolutism
to heal your callused heart
you run into the arms of risk
to find the reassuring comfort of our unique exactness . . .
you are a gem of your own inner beauty

Jenna Lynn Louderback

Fate

A small rock chipped off from his brothers
lays on the ground in a pile of rubble

Not knowing where he had gone,
only hope carried him on

As time passes on, we see a future,
still blurry, thinking we can't go further

But life goes on and plants will die the seasons will turn,
we don't know why
That same little rock knows this too, he accepted his fate,

As we must do.

Serena Elston

Joan's Dream

There my monument of me stands in France
Although it has passed many hundreds of years after my death
Many citizens remember me because of my fight
My fight to keep my dream
My enemies fought to prevent my dream from coming true
They fought in an endless battle, but I did not yield
I fought back with my companions and friends
Each more loyal than the last
I fought back keeping my dream, my battle, my life
I fought and won but also lost
For although I accomplished my dream to save France
I too lost my life in the hands of my enemies known as the English

Jasmine Atay

My Wife

Some men take time, they search hard and long
Sometimes they are right, sometimes they are wrong
To find the perfect lady, and share in his life
A lady that's special, he can call her his wife
To find such a lady, you must be a lucky man
Like peaches and cream, sharing life hand in hand
I found this special someone, a long time ago
If I would ever lose her, I'd be lost in the snow
So I thank my lucky stars, and the Lord up above
That I found such a lady, like a hand fits a glove
She is one of a kind, I will treasure all my life
I Love this special Lady, and I call her my Wife

James (Jay) Lee Aristidou

Dear Mother

You were always there for me,
whenever I would fall and hurt my knee.
when you would smile and look my way,
You would make all the hurting pain go away.
For all those times that you were there,
To praise me with all of your loving prayers.
you will always be the one I adore,
Never be the one that I could ever ignore.
I will always love you in my own special way,
Sorry I don't let you know this every day.
But no matter what I might ever say,
I know you'll always be there to show me that special day.

Kimberly Ann Hudgins

We Must

The violence and anger are all around us
Every day peace in this world is slipping away
People fear every day what will happen next
We must take a stand for our peace
We must come together as one
We must bring unity to the world
If not for us, then for our children.

Holly Anna Kosnik

Just One Kiss

I hold a vision in my mind
That reappears from time to time
A whispering breeze
By shimmering seas
Strong shoulders and eyes of jade
Against blue skies they never fade
Hands and muscles that appeal to my desire
Controlled by a mind that I admire
Chills run up my spine
To think that all of this is mine
And I am surrounded by ultimate bliss
Waiting . . . waiting for just one kiss

Christy Scott Buckalew

Two

Two paints on my palette, one black and one white.
If I painted a sky would the sun be as bright?
Two paints on my palette, I've started my day.
Oh! The white kissed the black and made a wonderful gray.
Two paints on my palette, I have stories to tell.
Of moonlit north woods, of sand, sea, and shell.
Two paints on my palette, no yellows or greens.
Yet the tree that I've painted seems so real and serene.
Two paints on my palette, as right as the rain.
No color for Bogart or Citizen Kane.
Two paints on my palette, two eyes on my soul.
Two hands that hold meaning, one bell that may toll.

Francis Thomas Lunetta

Woman

HE doesn't make mistakes.
we get lonely too easily
HE made her just for us
more beautiful than any sunset
more precious than any gem
HE made her soft
HE made her eyes as clear as the sky
she has a scent no flower can match
and a voice that calms restless nerves
the perfect being to love
us, second to their beauty without compare
HE doesn't make the same mistake twice.

James Cottone

Lost in Your Memory

I'm lost in your memory and I'm floating in bubbles
Each day that passes my love for you doubles
I see a reflection of your face in my eyes
and each day that passes I'm hoping your memory dies
I don't want to feel this pain in my heart
How can I forget you, I need a new start
I'm lost in your memory and I'm crying inside
My love for you I just can't hide
I often wonder if you think of me
When you close your eyes is it me that you see
I'm praying for your love to come back around
I'm lost in your memory and I'm hoping to be found

Irene Gonzales

Renewal

Let loose the Dogs of War and Hounds of Hell
Ravage the World and Silence the Land
Let the Lambs come to Slaughter and the
Generals to Honor
For in their Death and ours will the Land be
Reclaimed
And Mother Earth will start again

Robert McMakin

Appreciation

Today is a day of beauty and majesty beyond belief. Even with the bitter cold bowing outside, the sky opened up and the sun shined on me. The aura of colors were unspeakable, with the bluest blue, and the brightest magenta flowing along the horizon. However the most beautiful part was waking up and having another day to call mine, to see the smile on my kids' faces, and to realize that this Thanksgiving there is so much to be thankful for. Especially for the gift of life, family and people who love you just the way you are. So on this day take time to appreciate everyone and everything around you however good or bad, with a thankful outlook.

Liz Kennedy

Thief in the Night . . .

You invade my soul at the most inopportune times, I can't seem to get you off of my mind. Like a thief in the night, you entered my dreams, with a smile in your eyes and a kiss from your lips. Is this for real or are you playing a game? I have looked for something all of my life, will I find it with you, my thief in the night? Or will you just smile as you walk away, to leave me alone for another day? Ah, but I'll see you again when I close my eyes. Come to me soon, my thief in the night, come to me soon and hold me tight. Hurry! Before the sun touches the sky and wakes me with the morning light! I must see you one more time, touch me, hold me, my thief in the night. . . .

Becky Elaine Hoffman

Peace

Peace, peace,
We all need peace
The world is a beautiful place to live,
If we all share, take, and give.
Great is its necessity,
Should be there in bounty.
No wars, conflicts, tensions should arise,
And make us think, or too much wise.
Peace is a nation's food,
It should give us bliss.
We all should join hands together,
And make it a better place for our welfare.

Yasmeen Fairooz

Cry of Innocence

Mother, I am something more
Than just a child—please listen close.

I need to tell you about my cloak;
It is wet and I am soaked.

Not just from the rain, but from my tears.
I've been hiding something for many years.

It's about the one you call your spouse;
He drinks and molests when you leave the house.

I can't stand his demented ways;
It has to stop or I'll end my days.

Laura J. Laughy

The Snowfall

Let the snow make a snowman in your backyard.
Let the snow fill up the sky with white jewels.
Let the snow fill up your mind with happiness.
The snow covered my neighborhood with white magic.
The snow made the lake a frozen diamond.
The snow fell as soft as a blanket,
and I love the snow.

Jennifer Cassandra Albina

When Dreams Come

Sleep,
sleep comes over me.
It comes slowly,
as if to creep along the beaches of another time,
to scoop up the sands of rest.
I love to dream about life,
and worlds beyond our own.
Kings,
dragons,
a sailboat upon the waters of youth.
Sleep,
sleep comes over me.

Katheryn Elizabeth Middleton

One Young, One Old

One's very young, one's very old
Nothing in common, so I've been told
The old one may sit and stare
The young, she doesn't care
The young one doesn't realize
The age and wisdom in the old one's eyes
The old one knows when something's wrong
Tells you, sing the young one a song
No words ever need to be spoken
A bond of love never to be broken
The young one loves the old one like no other
The old one's the young one's great-great grandmother.

Doris Lee Louise Barlet

My Secret Bottle

Inside of me is a secret bottle full of thoughts and feelings.
It holds long lost stories of loves gained and lost.
It holds pictures of games and lust.
No one can get to my bottle—sometimes not even me.
My bottle is never empty, some times it just has less than others.
My secret bottle is now overflowing with secrets and feelings.
I try to keep a lid on it, but putting a lid
 on it is like putting a closed can of soda
 in a freezer; eventually it will explode.
Trying to empty my bottle is like trying to
 find water in a desert; hard, but not impossible.
If only I had that water, I would be almost empty and ready to refill.

Ashleigh Nicole Rice

Just Another Day

While sitting on a cold cement step, watching my neighbor,
A heavy set woman, standing on an unsturdy chair,
Almost killing herself trying to hang Christmas lights,
The lights are burning my eyes.
They are so bright.
People can be so plastic.
Yes, it is a Glorified Holiday.
You spend way beyond your limits.
Max out everything,
Then spend the next 12 months whining about the payments.
While the world is busy making Christmas wishes,
Here I sit, wishing it all away.

Brenda Johns

A Dream

A dream is destined only by the dreamer.
Who might look in a sea of stars and be
Broken in doubt because of a black hole.
To be destined on by a mirror of courage,
There are many obstacles.
As many stars as there are, a dream is bright,
But when I go to sleep there will be none tonight.

Joel Otis Hopkins

My Day

My friends and I are talking on the phone
While eating a small ice cream cone
It is such a beautiful summer day
I tell them to meet me at the park so we could play
I brought a basketball so we could shoot some hoops
Me and my friends spotted a snoop
He is studying us from the slides
While we are looking he pretends he is going down like a glide
We ask him if he wants to play
He said sure isn't it a wonderful day
We ask him if he wants to play 2 on 2
He said yes and he was pretty cool for being new

Tiffany Earle

Lonely Moon

Cautious feet shuffle across a vacant floor,
Old, wrinkled hands reach for unwavering walls.
Shadows of the past are hidden in the darkness,
The spirit of life is lost in the stillness.
A room where old memories lay
Reveals what has been desolate for so long.
To the cracked window, gazing out at his lonely moon,
One lost tear falls.
A sigh rolls out from his heart.
Youth went by so quickly:
From boy to man—
Soon from man to memory.

Andrea Rose Collins

Things I Never Had

I never had a dog . . . but I wanted one
I never had a cat either
I have never seen the ocean, or Greece
I never had a date, or a father, or long hair
I never had long love either
But if I died today, short love would be enough
I never had a new car
I never made over minimum wage
I never rode a motorcycle or drank wine in Paris
I never had a baby, or a husband
But I had a good mother
And if I died tomorrow, I would die happy

Jill Dakis

Into Eternity

Sometimes we stop and wonder why?
God lets those we love die.

It's not His fault you must know,
Life is a river that must flow.

When our loved ones leave here for eternity,
Remember in no more pain will they be.

Let me tell you this my friend,
together we will be in the end

So dry your tears and try to smile
together we will walk eternity's miles.

Susan Bernal

Society

Screams of pain and anger
are mixed with cries of pleasure
as we, a people, try incessantly
to be more civilized.

In the end
we really just become more efficient . . .
in our savagery.

Dustin James Fay

Turmoil to Freedom

I use to be scared of the fate which you gave to me.
My mind was always back there.
You forced awful things upon me, and I willingly obeyed.
I was desperate for love and affection.
I am now grown, and those days no longer control me.
I have learned to accept you as evil and myself as a victim.
I now look into your eyes, and you are the one who is defeated.
You are embarrassed, and I merely want to laugh at you.
Your life was so meaningless.
I have gained the power back,
and I will continue to use it to beckon your apologies,
of which I shall never accept.

Katie Schwabe

A Fight for Peace

It is dark, wet and very cold.
Everyone killing people.
Dying.
Blood gushing all over everyone
and everything.
A lot of yelling and screaming.
Men drowning in their own blood and guts.
Bombs falling, exploding.
Guns firing and killing.
Battle over.
Home.
Men, women, and children can go in peace.

Tammy Walsh

Fight for Life

Here's a little puppy that needs a little home.
See I found him at a store, sitting all alone.
He needs a little love from someone who
Has a lot of love, someone like you.
So if you are afraid, well, so he is a little afraid too.
So if you are in some pain, you can hold him tight.
With all your might.
He will feel your love, and help you sleep at night.
You can give him a little name, and he will be all right.
So if you need some love, well, you both will be all right.
Hope you like my little poem, so I will be all right.
See, we love you very much, and we will help you fight.

Debbie L. Mulkey

Blue Road

Going down the blue road that I've been down before
Leave me be, girl, don't come knocking at my door
Don't have time for you, get it through your head
Going down the blue road and play it till I'm dead
This music is in me, it's keeping me in control
Have to play the blues, don't need that rock and roll
The blue road is a long, long way from here
I love you, but not enough to keep me near
Don't cry, girl, you've got to find another man
One who'll be there, not a "catch you when I can"
Got to know, girl, I can't love you like before
Going down the blue road, don't come knocking at my door.

Nancy Plourde

You Don't Know

Some say happiness is just a dream,
That I don't believe.
Some say you won't, no matter how hard you try,
I believe that you will try,
and most times, present yourself victorious.
Some say there is no meaning to life,
Others say, sure there is; you just don't know it yet.

Sarah Ruth Peabody

The Wind in the Willow

One morn in my cosy warm bed,
The wind in the willow put these thoughts through my head,
Memories of my childhood,
The fun I used to have.
Should life have to change?
Should I let go of this past?

I listened a moment. . . .
The wind whispered to me,
"Keep the memories of your childhood,
and, no, it doesn't have to be.
But keep this a secret between you
and between me."

Patricia Oldford

Heartache

I wish I could get a break
From this constant heartache
I wish the pain would disappear
So my heart could be free and clear
I wish I had someone at last
To help me forget the past
Someone who is interested in forever
And a life of love and laughter together
Someone to be there through the good and bad
Someone to brush away the tears when I'm sad
Someone who would love me for me
From now till eternity.

Meshell Smith

Found

A child was born into the world without love,
She was sent from somewhere up above
She knew something was not right,
So she looked into the night.
She asked the stars for someone who cared,
Someone she knew would always be there.
Somewhere else not too far away,
a woman wished to have a child someday.
She hoped and hoped and prayed and prayed,
until that one fateful day;
They found each other and their world's changed forever,
They would never be apart, for they were finally together.

Alexis Broadhead

Never Say

Never say I love you if you don't really care.
Never talk of feelings that aren't really there.
Never say you're planning if your not willing to start.
Never hold my hand if you could break my heart.
NEVER SAY FOREVER IF FOREVER IS A LIE.w
Because those nevers that were once forevers
COULD MAKE MY LOVE FALL AND DIE!

GOD WILL BE WITH US TO SEE OVER ALL THESE THINGS . . .
HOPE, LOVE, AND FAITH.

February 23, 2000.

Debbie Burris

Treasured

So many happy memories
I have in store to keep.
No one can take them
From me, not even when I sleep.
God is the only one
That can make the memories that I make.
Then only that He sees it is better for my sake.

Nina McDaniel

Happy Birthday

Kiss the 20's goodbye
You'll turn 30, oh, my

Some say it is all downhill from here
Of course, it is not that bad if you like beer

But since you are not into that
Just stay the way you are, you will be better off by far

Funny, inspiring, helpful, and kind
Are only a few things that come to my mind

So don't worry about getting older—you will be just fine
After all, it is only a matter of time

Ute Feierabend

Christmas Is Near

Christmas is near,
so let's start spreading the holiday cheer.
Take out those lights,
put them at great heights.
Go get a tree,
and decorate with me.
Everyone loves cookies, pies and cake.
So get to work early on all things that bake.
The stores are open early, and some even close late.
Buy all those gifts; there's no time to wait.
All this planning and doing is all in the fun,
make Christmas special for everyone.

Jay Eichner

I Love You

I got your back you got mine,
I'll help you out any time.
To see you hurt, to see you cry,
Makes me weep and want to die.
And if you agree to never fight,
It wouldn't matter who's wrong or right.
If a broken heart needs a mend,
I'll be right there to the end.
If your cheeks are wet from drops of tears,
Don't you worry let go of your fears.
Hand in hand love is sent,
We'll be best friends until the end.

Lora Waters

A Poem for the Northwoods

As summer leaves and autumn steps in,
With the wheel of the seasons continuing to spin,
The low plants and trees shed their versions of green
In self-preparation for weather more mean.
But they try to remember summer sun's golden rays
As the dress themselves up for fall's cooler, short days
By putting on colors warm, vibrant, and bright,
For one last fling 'ere winter's long night.
Then they'll shed their bright garments, leaving gray limbs bare
To rattle and creak in winter's cold air.
They'll sleep until spring knocks at their door,
Then they'll dress for summer and the seasonal cycle once more.

Susan K. Blumerich

The Schedule of the Week

Sunday's bliss and Monday's kiss
are like boisterous wonders
Tuesday's face and Wednesday's embrace
lie among silent thunders
Thursday's are, too, loud and true
Fridays are a time to expect something new
Saturday is high and low
Another week to plant and grow

William Szany

The Last Survivor

He stands with a face of steel
He is ragged,
But you can see the depth and knowledge in his icy blue eyes
His belt holds two ancient revolvers with copper wood handles
The cut on his lower lip bleeds down his rough chin
He sees you staring
He grins, for
He has seen things you will never see
He has felt things you will never feel
He has gone places you will never go
He is the last survivor

Melinda Victoria Hine

Unknowing

To not be nervous would be foolish for the first time;
everyone is in need of education.
Through the eyes of dawn,
could you only see the truth
and through the ears of dusk,
could you only hear the world die?
The Heavens know its fate,
but only you can write the pages in its book of endlessness.
The most sensitive touch
and only the sweetest taste of everything
is saved for this joy.
To be brought love is to set adrift on an undying, blissful memory.

David Edney

Living Thoughts

As I climb the mountain,
I am in search of my destiny.
I dream that the many stars above will
lead me.
Clouds cover the stars
and bring me back to thoughts of reality.
As I descend the mountain,
I return to the center of emotions.
I follow my instincts and let my heart lead
the way.
With honest and sincere feelings,
I live day by day.

Patrice Grundhauser

The Moon

Who glides in air on silvery nights,
While stars are out in full bright,
Amid the clouds that roam the sky,
High up like birds that glide and fly?
What is the globe that shines so bright
Far above the Heavens to show its light,
And roams the sky in lighted air
Amid the view of glittering diamond flare?
Oh, celestial light that lights the Earth,
Only from the hand of God gave birth
To rid the sky of darkness during the night,
And to add the brilliance of northern lights.

William J. Auger

Night Wish

I wish I knew what to do.
I wish I knew how to do it.
I wish I knew where to put it.
I wish I knew who to give it to.
I wish I knew when to do it.
But most of all I wish I knew why sometimes.
And other times, I just think to myself,
"Nah!" or "Who cares?"

On second thought, I'm just to tired to
think. Good night!

William Shepherd, III

Infinite Silence

Silence.
Solitude. The inexplicable feeling of
complete and utter destitution. Feelings of
remorse, sadness, and torment begin to
unfurl. Silence. Silence. A slow trickling
of memories lost begins to overtake my mind
and not let go. Silence. Silence. Alienation
from mankind and those we take for granted.
Silence is what strikes fear in the heart of man.

Fiona Kouka

He's Gone

As I gazed across the deep blue sea,
I felt the distance between You and me,
My heart ached to once again see Your face,
To know Your loving kindness and Your grace.

I thought of the years I wasted so much,
When all you asked was to stay in touch.
I loved You Lord, and now it's too late,
I left Your guidance and sealed my fate.

If ever You want to know God's love,
Just truly obey Him.

Patrisha Goodwin

Unexpected Love

Not once in the snow filled days of winter could I see
That Valentine night would be brighten by my lover to be,
The gentle glistened snow had stopped just moments before.
To let the moon shine on the world's white splendor once more.
While drinking all this beauty into my memory,
An angel was sent from Heaven straight to me,
A kinder, sweeter man I have yet to meet,
Fascinated by all his charms, I didn't retreat,
His warm smile and nice manner thrilled me so,
Did create in me and after glow.
Two souls so near, so excited.
Did in marriage become united.

Mary E. Noller

Three Gates

If you are tempted to reveal
A tale to you someone has told about another,
Make it pass,
Before your speak, three gates of gold.

These narrow gates first; "Is it true?"
Then, "Is it needful?" In your mind, give a truthful answer,
And the next is the last and narrowest, "Is it kind?"

And if to reach your lips at last
It passes through these gateways three,
Then you may tell the tale, nor fear
What the result of speech may be.

Stephanie Sharp

Independence

Take off your mask of severity
Focus on this task of sweet charity
Like angels in waiting you all mourn
With memories fading and new ones born
all of the things You must be joking
look who you are provoking I said I would do
unrealized because of you
big mouths small brains
just to plow through your pain
without gain without knowing
and never hope of growing
you do not know what you had it is so like me
everyone else is mad just because of you
you never ask my opinion

Ashley R. Cole

Kosovo

Are you going to Kosovo?
Partly saved, yet dying in time.
Remember them and the child that lived there,
They once were just like you and I.
Cover the ashes with sweet falling rain,
Partly saved, yet crying inside.
Remember them and the tanks that live there,
They still are just like you and I.
Gather the masses with no place to live,
Partly saved truth hiding in lies.
We'll meet again
When the bombs are all done,
The truth will win
And stand tall in the sun.

Robert Kastle

The Telephone Girl

The Telephone Girl sits in her chair,
And listens to voices from everywhere.
She hears all the gossip, she hears all the news,
She knows who is happy and who has the blues.
She knows of our trouble, she knows of our strife,
She knows every man who talks mean to his wife.
In fact, there's a secret 'neath each saucy curl
On that quiet, demure looking telephone girl.

If the telephone girl told all that she knew,
It would turn half our friends to bitterest foes.
She could sow a small wind that would be a big gale,
Engulf us in trouble and land us in jail.
In fact, she could keep all the town in a stir
If she'd tell the tenth part of the things that she knew.
Oh, really now, doesn't it make your head whirl
When you think what you owe to the telephone girl?

Jewel Bruce

Eyes of a Child

A hand clasped tightly in mine,
the hand of innocent youth.
A child in body and in soul,
unaware of any untruths.
A laughter at life, a small puppy to love,
a look of love unrestrained,
a trust in all that surrounds their world,
a soul no evil has stained.
To see a cloud and gaze in wonder,
envisioning worlds far away.
Fearing nothing for the world is theirs,
so only one small thing do I pray.
Father in Heaven, give me the knowledge
to know the reasons he smiles.
Help me to see the world that I live in
through the innocent eyes of my child.

Michael Everette Andrews

My Love

My love for you is like the virgin snow
That embraces the land with its winter glow.
The birth of my love for you,
so precious and rare just like a
diamond solitaire.
If you were a mountain, I would be
the breeze that lovingly surrounds you,
whispering amongst the forest trees.
Like the waves that softly caress the
sands, I extend to you . . .
my heart, my soul, my hands.
If I could wish upon a star,
it would be to love you . . .
even if only from afar!

Odette Love

My Cyber Love

Not strikingly appealing, but Oh, so
alluring. Beckoning for mounds of my time,
And commanding loads of my attention.

Possessing a soft and mellow hum, and a
sweet sophistication. Easily accessible,
And an unrelenting companion. Responsive
and attentive to my very interest, graphically
and boldly keying into my senses.

Sometimes quick, sometimes not, and granted,
not always predictable. Ever-changing and
rearranging, sharing ups and sometimes downs.
Still, unequivocally, simply sends me,
fondly providing the ultimate satisfaction
to my click.

Sherry M. Nash

Game of Love

Your tender touch
feels so good
that's all I can remember about you
that was good
you never loved me
you never wanted to be with me
it was all just a game
a game that never should've been played
you say you never meant to hurt me
but I know you did
one day you'll fall in love
and she'll play the game
the game that will hurt you
then you'll understand that it does hurt to
play the game of love. . . .

Erin Renee Radabaugh

Cycle of Life

We are but leaves on the true of life,
Our frailties exposed by the winds of strife,
A leaf that has blown into the throws of a world
With wonders beyond belief about to unfold.
We pass through each season the spring with its glow,
Awaiting the warmth of summer when things flourish and grow!
Then comes the autumn when we all succumb
To the cold winds of winter making us numb,
With each passing season we struggle to live
So we can perpetuate life and continue to give
Back to our creator and this beautiful land,
A new bloom which will continue to develop and expand
This the cycle of life which nurtures us all!
Through the spring summer winter and fall.

Elaine W. Ostroff

True Patriots

When you salute the flag,
Reflect on its meaning,
Because it isn't just another rag.
For our forefathers, amidst great strife,
Fought and died while their families cried,
So that they and the generations
To follow would not be under
The rule of another country
And have their bitter pills to swallow.
Taxation without representation was
One of the events that led them to
Fight with all of their might,
So that we are able to have freedom
And enjoy such a good life.

Margaret Kolter

Kisses of Dew

For a moment in eternity a short season,
I will be with but memory of my quenching rain.
The rays will not dry the veins of my life;
I remain protected by the strength of the trees.
I shall curl up and pass through the darkness,
Warm in the Earth to find delight with my memory.
As the light returns to the forest within,
I will uncurl with joy and stretch forth in the morn.
I will be covered in the moisture of memory,
And I will know my love, my life, is yet with me.
I will dance about and stand but even taller,
Singing praise and waiting the pouring rains.
For my thirst again is quenched and life filled,
By my beloved's kisses of dew.

Alecia Ping

Night for Day

An August night as I lay in my keep,
lunar tears rained down high above my bed.
I went out to view the source of the dread
and found the moon in a remorseful weep.
Her love for the sun ran recklessly deep,
but time had pushed him twelve hours ahead.
At night she prayed for the dawn but instead
of greeting his smile, she fell asleep.
She longed for warmth on her porcelain skin
from his beams of indescribable hue.
Dreaming of when he'd seen her crescent grin
as she slid across a background of blue.
And when day broke to signal night was done,
I witnessed tears on the face of the sun.

Beau Harmon

Soul Mate

Oh, gentle hand touch my face,
take me to a far away place.

Lay your head next to mine,
share with me this special time.

Take my soul but leave no trace,
make my blood boil, my heart race.

Like the wind above the sea,
take not a part, but all of me.

Explore the savage within the man,
oh, bountiful woman, make it grand.

Let there be passion, an absolute must,
let there be a naked trust.

Byron Whitney

The Death of Love

Disturbing shadows
Seen through teary eyes,
Desperate thoughts
In the night I cry,
And on this night,
The stars refuse to shine.
The pain becomes stronger
When life and death combine.
And my eyes search again to find comfort above,
But as the moon disappears.
I feel the death of love.
And now this hope is gone.
So I must sacrifice my soul.
If all the love is gone
Then death is all I know.

Jamie San George

Directions to the Cross

When things don't go as you had planned
When life seems to have dealt you a bad hand
Remember you were chosen just for the task
When hope is a long forgotten friend
When you can see no end in sight
Remember His ways are not our ways
When others say there is no chance at all
When there are no tears left to cry
Remember, He too was condemned to die
When silence is a close companion
When you have been tapped completely dry
Remember He came to give us life
When sadness has overcome your smile
When laughter no longer has a sound
Remember He will never forsake you

Kelly Theresa Northington

Glass Tears

Tiny glass tears
Stream down my broken face. Broken
Faced, broken hearted—empty-souled. So hollow.
Blind rage—blackout. Such angry words.
My black eyes are no longer forever, but
They are never. I am angel. I am devil.
Horns and halo. Anger boiling up inside me.
Hatred, blind, fuzzy remorse. Can't shake
This feeling. Can't shake you. Ugly emotion.
Ugly, stupid man/boy. The tear of sin. The
Year of hell. 370 days of burning sensation.
Empty words. I hate you. I hate you. Eat my
Pain. Digest my agony. Explode into flames.
While I cry tiny glass tears. For you.
Forever.

Ashley Snowden

You're Gone, But Your Memory Lives On

In loving memory of Zack, my friend

When the sun comes out and you're not there
Your memory will be with us
As the days go by and you're not there
Your memory will be with us
As times goes by and we make new friends
Your memory will be with us
As we pass the fields where we use to play
Your memory will be with us
As we think of you we won't cry
We will continue to ask why, why
We know that God had a job for you
We know you'll know just what to do
We know you're gone and life goes on
But your memory and spirit will be with us forever.

Julious Alvin Grant

Every

Each step that she takes
makes me wonder how long she will walk.
Every morning she gets up
makes me wonder if she'll ever get up again.
Every day that goes by
makes me wonder if she's afraid.
Every stumble, trip, and fall
makes me want to reach out and take the pain away.
Her struggles make me want to hold her,
and say, "It's going to be okay,"
even though I know I'm probably wrong.
Every time she starts to cry
because the pain is so strong,
makes me want to dry her tears,
and makes me wish this disease was all gone.

Calah Jeanne Crutcher

Here and Gone

And here again, I'm being dragged away—
away from here, from where I long to be.
I see your smiling faces in the pictures of my memory
and think of the good times, the tears, the joy, and the madness.
I hear the wheels on the steel tracks as I go and I see
the brown, orange, and bright fire of the leaves
as the train sweeps me away.
Everything beside the tracks seems so still and lifeless—
the only other things moving, for as far as I can see,
are the almost toy-like cars on the streets below.
The billboards and the people standing at the stations
seem part of the scenery,
and I, seeing only sunlight and shadows
in the mists of this dream
become, at once, entranced.

Sara Arienta

Untitled

Dawn arises, stars recede, what will the day hold?
The present speaks of new beginnings, wounded spirit, oh, hear!
The cry, morning glory, tell that heart that he does care.

Morning into day, here we go.
Deliver that back into thine eyes.

I ponder what, my love, you are thinking, lips of sweet honeydew,
Kiss of all kisses tells it all.
My heart given to ecstasy over your thoughts of me.
Spirit wounded knows of joyful news into the souls of another day.
Return your spirit into thoughts of me, souls dance
To rhythms of beats, praise glory, hope, into days ahead.
Summer of my heart begone into the night, cometh not into thy heart.
Never into thy wounded spirit will you speak,
Disappearing of thy love, oh, broken spirit.

Carol S. Jackson

The Immortality of War

Bombs drop, guns fire,
screams heard in the distance.

Men march in groups,
preparing for battle,
blood and death.

They pray, pray for their lives to be spared,
their souls to be saved.

Wounded, carried off in stretchers,
sick and dying lay in trenches.

Bodies, lay in piles,
surrounded by thick pools of blood.

Letters return home, a son is killed,
a father lost, a family begins to grieve.

Astra Rose

This Little Step

I've taken my first step,
The one to hope and success.
I am ready to become the me I see . . .
not anything less.

I want to be able to feel good
whenever I shall fail;
To know I have done everything
possible, my best . . .
never once had I bailed.

Because of this,
I know I want to live my life
as happy as I can,
so when I die, it will be all right . . .
to have lived my life as planned.

Alisa Brooke Adams

Observances of a Nomad

Ignorance, in the form of men
in little blue suits, with stars and guns
who envision, in their minds, themselves as kings
Ignorance in the form of men in robes
who, in their minds, envision themselves as gods
Ignorance, in the form of men in expensive suits
who, in their minds, and the minds of masses
envision themselves rulers

Ignorance, in the minds of people
who, in themselves, or in others
envision greatness
when therein only lies mediocrity
and still the lonely
and the hungry
and the children, cry

Mick Walker

Leaving

It's times like these, I feel like fleeing—
take you with me and watch the sun set,
and rise.

Too many obstacles, no hammer when I need one,
and there's no sun to set
or rise—
all the time.

Maybe you and I will run, drink 'til we get drunk,
and when we finally get there, we can hid and sleep.

Rest, take a deep breath, close our eyes
until we are dreaming the sweetest dreams.
Our minds
can mold
so deep.

Stacy Stout

Megan

Lying in the glow, staring into her eyes
ever so softly, brushing back her hair, our thoughts intertwine.
Talking and laughing, the hours pass by
Smiling at each other, her hand kisses mine.
Gaining much more than an acquaintance, a true friend she be
every impression revealing this to be right.
Tomorrow I only hope she will agree
that something special this will ignite.
Oh, This would be nice if it wasn't a dream
great it would be if I were to awake
even though how perfect this seems
thoughts blinded by the ability to partake
Her disposition so sweet, she must be true
every day thinking about her, these thoughts I must pursue
real this must be:

Brent Joseph Seibert

Reflections

As I walked through the sands of time
A crystal showed me the reflections
Reflections of good and not-so-good times
A small gypsy woman, countless nickels and dimes
Could not show me the way
The future, I asked?
It tried to be told
Predictions and stories were bought to be sold
As I searched deep inside
Could the stories be true?
Then I realized one thing, which I already knew
Live in the present
Don't dwell on the past
The future is vast, it is made to explore
Fate is the key that unlocks all doors

Jennifer Porter

Mireya

Whenever I need sunshine in my life,
I will look at your face.

If on a cloudy day I wished for clear
blue skies,
I will look in your eyes.

When my spirit is restless, and I need
to find peace,
All I want is you by my side.

And when I'm feeling mellow and tender,
I will lay by your side, and within you,
I will find all the comfort I need.

If anyone ever asks me to describe love,
I will give them your name.

Barbara Trueba

Candle Thoughts

When I sit here at my desk and the candle burns away,
I think about a lot of things, like am I heading the right way?
I think about all the dumb things I've done,
I've endured a lot of pain and had a lot of fun.
I've met a lot of people on my path through life,
I've dated a lot of girls, but still I've found no wife.
I remember all those people who've influenced me,
They said to be myself, they said to live life free.
I remember the girls who broke my heart
And the boys who bruised my skin.
I buried it all so deep inside, I thought that's how I'd win.
But now years later I feel the pain, but have no one to blame,
Now when I pass a mirror alone, I bow my head in shame.
I want to breathe and be myself and let my spirit free,
I want to stand tall and say, "This is the true me!"

Tyler Ray Sauve

Beauty

a hot beautiful day
watching the sun set by the bay

yes it is a pretty sight
and seeing you is such a delight

my love for you is so strong
please don't do me wrong

i'd climb the highest mountain, swim the coolest sea
i'd do anything for you to be with me

i want to be with you under the stars
you can be venus and i can be mars

together forever
forever together
nothing could be better

Craig W. Denbraven

A Rainy Vision

I watched and I wondered, as the clouds and
sky thundered and the darkness fell over my
head. Amazed and perplexed, at what I
witnessed next as I lay under covers in
bed. The light danced around, without
making a sound and disappeared right out of
my sight. It appeared over me, Then
outside on a tree and floated in the air
like a kite. As the rain fell outside, I
felt I had just died as I watched my house
from high in the sky. I watched and I
learned, as I tossed and I turned while the
light flew me into the sky. I watched and
I wondered, as the clouds and sky thundered
and the darkness fell over my head.

Jesus Gilberto Vergara

The Beach

As I look across the shimmering blue
I am reminded of eyes a shining hue
Gigantic arcs slam the ground
Wham . . . Wham . . . Wham
The foam sizzles and pops
As the water slowly relaxes its grip and recedes
The sound of gulls is silent over this deafening roar
As the water slams more and more
Sand slips slowly through your fingers
So that only your happy thoughts linger
You're remembering a mystical time,
A mystical hour
When you relied upon your relaxing power
When all you did was sit on the sand
And watch the water gently lap the ground

Alice Vincent

Rest

It tears at me, when I try to sleep.
I tried to count, but only killed the sheep
the wounded mind is full of pain
I'm almost sure I'm insane.
Peace is what I search for
lights out, close the door
Thoughts are cluttered, got to get straight!
a messy mind is what I hate.
turn it off, I wish I could
stop! I wish it would
Peace is what I search for
lights out, close the door
darkness imprisons me in my tomb
I cannot see, the final rest
that I really need.

Bill Price

Life's Travels

We've both been down this road before;
So familiar yet the scenery is constantly changing.
A path we travel till the ground is worn,
in hopes that the search we've been on will finally be born.
The traveled path is so well known,
we continue to stroll unsure of what's to be grown.
It's a part of our life we hang onto,
afraid of making a change for fear of losing our way
on another road less traveled.
The one sure thing that life has given us is a choice;
We can continue to travel that familiar path we've been down before
or we can choose to take another road unsure of what's in store.
Whichever path we decide to take,
be sure to plow your road for it's the life we make.
Don't travel it alone, it wasn't meant to be.

Cindy Naczynski

For John Denver

He was nature's true companion. He could tell you what she wanted, tell you what she needed, and only she could understand him, and she knew just what he wanted, knew just what he needed. So she took him out to Denver where he had to climb the highest mountain tops. He watched the eagle and the hawk fly free, and he knew down deep inside of him, that she would be the one to take him home.
Then she introduced the ocean on the spirit of Calypso.
He did sail the changing waters and he learned of her emotions, felt the freedom of a wind swell and the calmness of the harbors.
Then she took him toward the heavens where he flew over the highest mountain tops. He felt the eagle and the hawk fly free . . . and he knew down deep inside of him that she would be the one to take him home.

John Caputo

Nothing, Not to Me

I'm the predator to your endangered dreams
I'm who smothers your little schemes
I'm the novelist of your precious themes

I'm the breath to your gasping lungs
I'm the thrust behind your frail hearts
I'm the crimson river to your needed parts
I'm nothing like the good book talks

I'm the figure of your blind faith
I'm the gentle kiss you call a breeze
I'm the mind behind this terminal tease

I'm the intoxicating light you call hope
I'm the smuggled story of endlessness
I'm the dull point to this numbing mess
I'm the mother scheme of commonness

Ruben Ortiz

Time

Time it comes and then it goes.
It brings the sunshine and the rain.
It brings us smiles along with pain.
Time brings the daybreak with the morning light.
It brings the darkness and the stars at night.

Regardless of what time should bring,
One does not have a minute to waste.
So do not rush through life in haste.
Take time for those who mean the most,
whether they be young or old.

When time brings sadness,
You'll still have cheer,
'Cause you spent your time,
With those you held so dear.

Norma Harris

Today

Today I woke and reality was there,
Deep in my bones, haunting me.
I love my family, yet a burden they seem.
How much do I sacrifice for thee?
What do I want to be today . . .
Mother? Teacher? Wife? Slave? Lover?
Prostitute?
Today will be cold, hard, and uneventful.
I will seek distraction to ease the pain,
To prevent the dread of what I have chosen.
In the past these feelings would pass,
Now they fester in my heart.
Who shall pay for my freedom?
Today I woke and reality was there,
Deep in my bones, haunting me.

Lisa Smith

Confused

I am so very confused today.
What shall I do?
I need to make a decision
to make this confusion go away.
My heart says try to love him
once more.
But my head tells me
you've lost this game before
If I don't attempt, I will never know
what his true feelings are.
Then again if I just ignore
no pain shall I endure.
Maybe one day my feelings will just fade away
Until then this state of confusion
will my heart and head stay.

Shannon Elizabeth Cline

To My Death, Be My Truth

Amidst my fading desires
hidden among shadow stricken alleys,
in kissing cafés and wondering hours.
Upon wicked scented words,
falling into soft little lies
and fluffy facades,
with thoughts near candy-floss but motives tasteless.
Filtering happiness,
echoing pretentiousness.
Alive and well on borrowed dreams, forgotten morrows,
and gilded hopes.
There in the cities, shifting into . . . and out of.
Bless me into sheltered hollows,
that I may suffer no more from cold unyielding winds,
but rather, complete my only truth.

Jason Turnbull-Jackson

My Happy Mask

As I open my eyes, and arise from my bed
thousands of things swirl around in my head
Meetings, deadlines, what to eat, what to wear
I catch a glimpse of my worries in the mirror and I stare
The lines are deep as I check in a hurry
and no amount of makeup can hide all my worries
But I know this face will soon go away
as soon as I emerge and face my day
My neighbor said "good morning" as I went past
she was the first to see my Happy Mask
I put my Happy Mask on every morning without fail
come rain, sleet, snow or hail
When I return home at night
I lay my Happy Mask right there,
alongside my worries, frustrations and cares

Eva M. Cotton

Oblivion

It's what we're all seeking
A time away from life and its problems
We try through drugs, sex, and alcohol
Even sleep
But it's something we're not quite able to achieve.
But still we seek it
Because of loneliness
We all have it
No matter the crowd of friends around us
The music, the chatter, the hustle and bustle of everyday life
We're still alone.
Yet we move on
Waiting
And wondering
Is this all there is?

Bonnie Lou Hayden

Released

Released
And my soul screams with the noise
of pure freedom.

Released
And my soul floats lighter than the air
which cradles it.

Released
And my soul drifts over the velvety clouds
of joy and tranquility.

Released
And my soul knows of the inevitable
return to reality.

Released . . . if only for a moment.

Lisa Davila

Tears Fall

When the tears stop falling, that's when you feel like it's through.
But when they don't stop falling, what do you do?
The pain in my heart, I thought was done.
But the power of the pain has just begun.
I wish it was all just a nightmare,
Just a prank or a scare.
But the loss of the laughter is so great and deep.
Sometimes at night, I lose sleep.
I try to carry on and fight the fight.
But at night, the pain blinds my sight.
The tears just won't stop falling,
And my fears won't stop calling.
The emptiness in my soul I was so unaware of.
But my relief comes from up above.
All I can do is open my heart up and love.

Warren Nicole Audra

Thoughts

Walking across the woods in a late afternoon
Walking under a delightful blue ceiling
Surrounded by peace, by harmony
Surrounded by trees, by silence
Touched by a soft ray of light
Touched by a gentle wind
Thinking what is wrong
Thinking what is right
Seeking for the truth
Seeking for wisdom
Wishing the day
That joy and
Innocence
Prevail
In us

Javier Humberto Venturi

Mister Reaper, Sir

Mister Reaper, sir, please lend me your ear—
Please move on, sir,
Far from here.
A grandfather and then an aunt,
Please take no more—
You just can't.
I beg of you, Mister Reaper, sir,
Please, oh, please,
Leave my family alone.
We've grieved so much,
Enough is enough.
When are you satisfied?
When do you have enough?
Please, sir, just leave,
Please, sir, please.

Jessica Lynn Stokes

Feather on the Wind

How did I succumb to be a feather on the wind?
A will had I as strong as stone,
my heart had never sinned.
But now I'm thrown and tossed about
by your emotion's gusts,
Thrust and tumbling,
will my tattered soul ever again know trust?
Denial, to despair, to anger—
How, why, do I stay afloat?
My unforgiving love for you keeps,
"The storm's over," in my throat.
Will your breezes ever calm?
How can I hear a silent fate?
It's time to shed my final tears.
This feather must know her weight.

Jossalyn Thiel

Something about You

I can't explain the way I feel.
It seems like a dream, yet so real.
You reach me like no young woman has ever reached me before.

Your uncanny beauty I can only adore.
I care for you. I cherish you.
Yet I don't say a word, hoping you'll get a clue.

So how is it that I always pull through?

I guess it's that fear of losing you.
So if you're wondering why
I sometimes don't know
what to say or do,

It's just that I can't get past
that something about you.

Anthony Dwayne Williams

He Kissed Me

He kissed me in the garden,
beneath the big willow tree;
His lips warm as the summer,
he eyes blue as the sea.
He kissed me in my father's den,
behind the big oak door;
Hungrily he held me close,
always wanting more.
He kissed me in the kitchen,
beside my grandma's stove;
eventually a love web around my heart he wove.
He kissed me in the hallway,
before my mother's vine;
But when he mentioned my bedroom,
that's where I drew the line.

Roberta Carmela DeCaprio-Lemke

Snowfall

Last evening I sat,
Both observer and historian,
and watched legion upon legion of snowflakes
descend on this "City of Big Shoulders."

First silencing the rumbling of railroads
and the chatter of air hammers.
Then bringing to a halt
millions of Henry Ford's finest.

The masses cursed the skies,
but all to no avail,
for snowflakes only speak
to children and poets, softly whispering:
"We've only a short time.
Can you come out and play?"

Paul Lindenmeyer

Remember

shadows like faded memories
lie scattered amongst the pages of my life
the trees beside me are growing still
over me

they become my dreams
trying to make their ways to Heaven
only to be stopped by death.

now what has become of these bodies?
turned to soil
now where the earthworms play
once lay my dream
and the tree of new thoughts
has been born
this one will make it

Lindsay L. Rowinski

Life

Life is a precious mysteries everyone
questions, why? When? What if?
Yet no one appreciates what beauties,
and treasures we take part in . . .
Like the brand new beginning of life
when your children are born
Or a seed that is planted and grows
into a beautiful tree.
We watch as the Earth evolves and
begins anew, and yet we struggle for peace.
Jesus died for us, and yet we are
still ungrateful not realizing how
precious every moment is
There's a plan for all of us, if you
haven't guessed what it is yet, it's called life.

Valerie Wietrzykowski

To My Husband

A magical beginning with love and at first sight,
Only to grow into more love of incredible height.
Each day, each memory, more grand than the one before,
Both of us letting each other in, opening up a new door.

New doors that have never been journeyed by another,
Only to lead us through new feelings, new experiences together.

At times, although there was great love, there also came heartache,
In the depth of our souls great strength and will would awake.

Through each twist and turn our commitment grew stronger,
Our passion and love made our relationship continue longer.
Both of us falling in so deep that at last,
We joined our souls with God and although it was fast,
The feelings we shared seemed like a lifetime or two,
Bringing us to today, where my darling, I'm so in love with you.

Angela Poor

The Land of the Forgotten Lovers

The wind blows with its soft caressing fingers
The love in our hearts to some forgotten land
The land is of peace and beauty
While our hearts are empty and cold
The love will never be given to the person it was meant for
That person was shallow and cold
And yet the warm side was hidden beneath it all never to be shown
His eyes were the essence of his love
And only there could it be seen
I have seen that love, but it is lost now in some darker place
My love is now in that land where some day it will be mine again
The wind is my friend but at times like these
I do not understand its reasoning
That love was my own, meant for someone dear to me
And now it has flourished to the land of the forgotten lovers.

Nancy Susan Strother

My China Doll

My mother left me to be with the Lord,
and left me no dolls,
So God gave me a baby girl, to love,
to hold to teach and care.
When she grew up, she decided to see what was
on the beach, thinking, "why am I here."
You came along, "Tony" looking of her, so pretty,
so refine, thinking would she be mine
"Yes", she said, "Please don't hurt me,
for I am my mother's china doll."
"If you do, same free,
for my mother will take me back, you see,"
"Together we will sit on the beach to mend
the broken pieces, to laugh to sing, to pray again
and thank our God for her china doll.

Carmen B. Gorsuch

Sacrilege

I remember the first time that I recognized him.
Sitting in his corner in the dark—just
drinking in the smoke and rising above
the fumes of the Vodka. He walked right
through me-with those pupils of pale
glass—An Irregular Albino. That's right—
I remember now—my spirit ached like the
pain of a thousand delirium tremens. And
when that subsided, I stirred from the
nightmare—cleansed and pierced through and
through in a rift of deep blue.
I am those unfeeling, unseeing ivory eyes.
I am the Death-Head's Moth that you pinned to the mattress.
I am the sweat of your breath that shall taste no more.
Father, forgive me, for I know not what I do. . . .

Noelle Marie Raelson

Thanks to You, Lord

The fall of darkness is as quite as the splash of the sun
When it sinks to the ocean afar.
The singing of a bird is as sweet as the taste of candy.
After a rain, the air is as clean as a newborn child.
A woman is as pretty as a rose.
The sun coming in our window in the morning is the Lord's
Way of letting us know He's watching over us.
The wind is the Lord's way of sweeping off his trees and flowers.
The rains are for the watering of all plants, gardens,
And to keep the Lord's lands from drying up.
Most of all, we were given the 25th day of December.
Even nonbelievers take notice
That this is the day we set aside for our Lord.
For all He's given us, Christmas is all we can offer back,
along with love and thanks to Him for watching over us.

Thomas M. Greenlaw

A Question Unanswered

Each day goes by and still I cry.
I weep because you left and I didn't say goodbye.
All your life I've loved you so why,
I wonder, did you have to go.
They say it's God's will, it was his way.
If that were true, you'd be here today.

Evil was loose looking for prey,
For a fresh little soul to take away.
You stepped in his path as he hit you with pain.

God would not have let you hurt how you did on impact.
No pain, no trauma, that is a fact.
I felt all your pain when I saw you that day.
Your bruised, lifeless body strength in my head
Every day when I ask my God, why did he take you, Jose'.

Aida Torres

I Miss You

I am feeling blue;
because I'm missing you.
My skies are grey because you're not with me;
and that's where I want you to be.
I've wanted to tell you how I felt;
but every time I wanted to tell you
my heart would melt.
I wanted to tell that, "I loved you,"
but I didn't want your response to make me feel blue.
Please, come back to me;
and I'll make things the way they use to be.
I remember the happy times that we shared.
because that showed me that you cared.
So, please stop me from feeling blue;
because I know you miss me too.

Michelle Williams

Fly Away, Little Soul

Fly away, little soul, free from all harm,
To a far better place so safe and warm.
Fly away, little soul, to the Father above
For you, dear one, were conceived in love.
Fly away, little soul, to the angels on high
For this is not farewell, it is not goodbye.
One day soon in Heaven we shall meet
And again we'll see that face so sweet.
Fly away, little soul, from your place on Earth.
Heaven above will rejoice in rebirth.
Fly away, little soul, though you'll be missed.
You're covered by the angels' kiss.
The dear Lord's purpose we do not know,
Yet His blessings will continue to flow.
Fly away, little soul, fly away.

Mary Ann Green

A Father's Pride

He watches from across the room.
A bride like a rose ready to bloom.
A young man ready to be a groom.
He sees a church of family and friend filling the room.
A brother stands at the side of the bride.
A mother watches with pride.
And a father who cannot be seen watches from the side.
And on his brilliant wings a father shall glide.
So he can stand at his daughters side.
And with a kiss on the cheek he shall give to show his pride.
With the blink of an eye to the side he shall glide.
Knowing that through their lives he will watch and guide.
And though a young bride cannot see her father by her side.
He shall always be there to help and guide.
That is the promise he makes as he stands by their side.

Michael John Ogden

Sister

One day I awoke in my hospital bed.
My back hurt I was ready for dead.
Then this face, a lady dressed in long white,
came into the room.
She told me not to worry, everything would be OK.
She smiled, and took my hand, and then sang a soft tune.
Soon my sister walked into the room.
She gave me a hug, and I felt at that moment,
my sister really loved me.
Soon after, more family came in, but it didn't matter.
All I knew was that my sister loved me,
and that I loved her more than anything,
and I also knew I would give her my life if she needed it.
When we grow up we may grow apart,
but never in my heart.

Lisa Beauchesne

Life

Life is cruel,
Life is kind,
But why do we commit such treasonable crimes?

Life is love,
Life is lust,
But why must some be prejudiced?

Life comes fast, forgetting about the past,
But no one knows how long we will last.

Life may change in many ways,
But let's not forget our merry ways.

People live and people die,
But we must all learn how to survive,
Because that, my friends, is the meaning of life.

Melissa A. Collazo

I Miss You

I will miss your laugh, I will miss your smile.
The time we had was well worth the while.
Thoughts of you still fill my mind,
Lots of treasures you left behind.
Moments of bliss, full of love and tenderness.
Diamonds nor gold, not even a pirate's treasure trove
Could ever compare to the love that you and I shared.
Fire and passion.
Our love was more than a fashion.
It was real something that very few will ever feel.
The closeness was unique; we hardly needed sleep.
Love was our food sent only from Heaven above.
Nourishment was just a touch, oh, how it meant so much.
So as I journey on, you will always be in my heart,
Meaning we will never truly be apart.

Michael Judkins

I Love You, Mom

I know your fears now that you know I'm here in your womb.
I feel your pain and turmoil.
I am touched by your every tear.
Aborting me persists in your thoughts.
But please I beg you "let me be!"
Hard times await you and me but we can work it out.
I already love you as my Mother.
And given the chance you will love me too!
I have no rights, no power in my present state.
My life is entirely in your hands.
I need your loving care now.
The same as I will need it after I am born.
Believe me, Mom, my first smile will be my "thanks" to you.
And I will be at your side for a lifetime.
Please Mom, "let me be!"

Kathleen Beilman

Love Never Forgotten

To one in a million, "Sonny."
Suddenly, you walked into the room, unexpectedly.
I saw your face and heard your voice,
my heart pounding, I was weak all over,
I still remember many times before,
this happened, and I knew; I always loved you
from the start and felt I loved you in my heart.
A love I felt for many years I could not
really have; it's sad to say, but true.
The love so deep within, I loved for you,
Many years have long gone by, like the twinkling of an eye.
The feeling's deep within my soul.
If only we could be made whole. What fate this is
to lose you now? Without God, I just don't know
how? Good bye, my love, Claire

Claire Battis

Poem for Peace

We all are from a fine land,
not far from a Finland.
A land of peace and love;
fulfilled as sea turtle and dove.

A clean breath for all to endure.
Harmony, serenity, tranquility, of us pure.
A defined gesture of kindness any of day,
will the blood of life flow through any of bay.

Melvin A. Zamora, Jr.

The Wonders of Life

As we grow older we realize how fast Life can pass you by.
We ponder about many memories and wonder
what we missed out on yesterday.
A miracle of having and holding and creating a life
is so precious to us all.
How sad life can be when we lose a loved one
so close to our world.
As our world turns and spins about.
Our fondest memories are so precious to us.
Even though we strive to be the best we can be.
We all are so lucky to have beautiful memories
to ponder and wonder what is in store for us.
Perhaps that is what God made Life to be.

Connie Sue Kyle

Life

Life is a thing, every thing you should love,

Life is what brings us laughter, excitement,
sadness, love, and everything in between.

Life is something that doesn't always make us happy,
Life doesn't always go our way . . .

But we should love, cherish, and enjoy each
and every day of life . . .

Because if we don't life could be gone as
fast as it got here, and we don't want that
because . . .

Life Is Everything

Amber M. Terry, 12 years old

Passenger of My Brain

Driving to Phoenix the steering wheel of my Thunderbird
is firm, powerful
Highway 10 predictable
with the feel of smooth leather
and cruising to raucous but comforting sound,
sensual accelerating and braking.
Distances are emulsified,
casually connecting points in my plan.

I remember my 1994 silver Skylark
careening into an unexpected Plymouth
lung contusions and pain, gradual healing.
Even then, I was master—
directing my bird to nest in the roadside mesquites.

But now—I, who have been called brilliant,
am no longer sure of my thought vehicle.
My brain can operate apart from me.
I cannot be sure of driving it expertly.
Simple rational act does not quiet it.

The brake instead, 400 milligrams of red and white capsules.
At any moment it can betray me
can pulsate wildly into confusion.
I am no longer the driver
but the passenger of my brain
my only hope—a new and flaming highway to Phoenix.

Margaret Louise La Due

A Faded Love: Sonnet I

Tomorrow's faded and unclear, the colors of the pale
Blue ocean and waves upon which the toy boats sail
Ever so carelessly. I waited for you to call to me
But your soft voice I did not hear and your face I did not see.

Tomorrow's love has disappeared much like you, my love.
Where did you go? Where did you go, sweet love?
The silence between us parts our souls.
And tonight it looks as if neither of us knows our role
In this far-from-perfect world. I shall think of you
Tomorrow and wonder where our love became untrue.

Sarah Ann Branson

What Is Love?

Love does not speak a language of color,
Love does not plant any field of lies,
Love sees neither hate, nor knows any spite.

What love does speak of is peace in life,
Growing pastures full of promise,
Revealing truth from above.
Love erases all sorrow blessed with the grace of God.

Fragile in flight, this hope of harmony remains to be.

For only in the presence of His love is where we each become free.

Kimberleigh J. Smith

Multiple Sclerosis

Multiple sclerosis will
Someday be a disease
To say with a lot of ease.

So please, drop to your knees,
And ask the Lord to conquer this disease.

Believe in Him and yourself
And than it shall all come to an end.

So don't frown, the cure
Is sure to be found.

Linda Sager

Naomi

Although I know you are going.
I cannot say good-bye.
Knowing that the oceans tears
will touch your graceful feet
and the wind that stirs your flower of being,
will bring to you the feeling
that stars are guiding you through the midnight sky,
the southern cross will remind you of love that never dies.

The Southern Cross is a constellation of stars
in the southern hemisphere and God's love never dies.

Baxter J. Dye, II

My Mother

To Mother, with love

You were always there for me in my deepest, darkest moments.
You were always there for me when I felt so much gloom.
Through many loves, lives and losses,
Your heart always maintained for me plenty of room.

You are my heart, my soul; you are my energy,
You are my reason for living.
You even had triumphs and struggles of your own,
But no matter what, you never ever stopped giving.

You created my life, my strength and my foundations,
You made me the woman who I am.
Torn between a husband, a job and three other children,
You would give your precious self to me whenever you can.

Sarah Wardlaw

Crystal

Shattered crystal as it be my heart

Tearing on my knees
I construct beauty back with spirit hands

And to banish its commission it must saturate
in impenetrable forces

And so it should lose all sensitivity
And still love so strong for love
will suckle from the fruits
of that which should throw crystal again.

Michelle Thomason

Did You Know?

You've blessed so many along the way,
With your gentle smile and what you had to say.
Leaving footprints on the hearts of a chosen few,
I was such one at my wits end till there was you.
It was one such as you who showed me how to feel,
You put meaning into my crazy world and made it real.
People like you are far and few it's true,
Receiving little recognition for all you do.
So today I salute you my diamond in the rough,
For mere words and thanks are just not enough.

Carmen Robinson

Nonstop

Stranded in the desert,
The camel moves continuously without a stop.
The Arabian knight drinks occasionally without a care.
The helpless camel moves up and down over the hilly desert.
Civilization grows nearer.
The townspeople come and greet the restless knight.
And the knight bears gifts—
A magic lamp, golden coins, righteous rubies.
For he is the knight of gift, power, and generosity,
Continuously without a stop.

Celine Alexandra Aubert

Reflections

You say your feelings
have grown stronger,
but there's no feelings
in your hugs any longer.
You say you still care,
but that feeling in your hug isn't there.
Have you ever loved a
glass with blonde hair?
The person I thought I
loved was never ever there.

Shawn Paul Short

Friends Forever

A friend is always there
well the ones who care,
There always around
You'll never have a frown,
They don't talk behind your back
Or give you any slack,
Telling each other which ones better
trying to write you an unfriendly letter,
Those are the ones you should look for,
look for the ones you can adore,
so you can be glad
not stressed out and sad,
I hope this convinces you
Don't let the ones you care for be sad and blue.

Jene Massey

Friendship

Friends are those whose care for each other
This is a relationship like no other
Some last long, some are short
But while they last, each other you will support
Some say forever while others do not
But ones that do tell a lot
Some are sweet, some are sour
But friends have a special power
They usually last and stay strong and true
I have no other friend like you

Megan Pilcher

Sea

The sea is blue and dark like a stone.
The sea is calm.
I look, and what do I see,
Beautiful, blue waves filled with dolphins and whales.
The sun now sinks in the sea,
And makes a new day somewhere else.
The sea is all that I see.
The sea is the master of the water.
It carries the life of the water.
The sea is the sea.

Nicole McGinnis

I Used to Be

I used to be an animal, locked up in a cage.
Now I am a bird, free of sorrow and rage.
I used to be a rain cloud, on a sunny day.
Now I am a ray of sunshine, to guide you on your way.
I used to be the hate, that tore people apart.
Now I am the love, deep within their heart.
I used to be a weed, that you would pick or you would pass.
Now I am a tulip in a field full of grass.
I used to be a hurricane, that ripped through the sea.
Now I am the gentle breeze, that blows through the trees.

Jessica Moore

Childhood Lost

Where have the years gone?
What have we done?
Yesterday we were children yet today we are old.
Chattering, running, playing in fields of gold;
Innocent, invincible, searching for the unknown,
From babes to teens to adults we have grown.
Life becomes reality as the days go by,
Leaving behind the simplicity of earlier times.
Confidence and trust in mankind disperse,
As we live out our years upoh this earth.

Donna Courson

A Moment in Time

I close my eyes
I see the rainbow
The sun is shining
The birds are singing
There you are standing
The sunlight makes an ethereal glow around you
You envelop me in your strong arms
I hear music, soft, sweet, and beautiful
The wind whispers around us
To shield us from tomorrow
Today, yes, we can have today
A moment in time
That will build a memory
To last eternity

Cybele Renee Torres

Death Do Us Part

Death do us part was a phrase I thought would never happen.
But it did; you were gone, and I was alone.
You died, and I was alive.
You left with the spiritual world,
and I was left with the human race.
To figure things, to do things, to see things, to be things,
to hear things, and to live with things.
Yes, death do us part was so true.
Until death comes to me
and I would be with you.

Lilian Cirino-Highsmith

to understand

the words of life are never understood
from living to love to all in-between
we all try to speak well, usually meaning good
never interpreted as, always comes out mean
esta la vida, as some may say,
but as some would do,
never in this day
for life is not a word, or thought of
life is an action
of which words are prescribed

William Kearns, Jr.

Grandpa

Grandpa brings back memories so fine,
A tall stern man with no defeat.
A bucksaw and an ax was his way to build the log cabin
And hunt the prey for a food-filled day.
Living off the land nestled deep in the woods,
Raising nine children the best that he could.
This was his haven for years to pass;
Plowing and cropping, he made it last.
A chew of tobacco, a string of the guitar,
A song sung and the Northern Star.

Vickie Owens

Conscience

In loving memory of my wonderful dog, Tipper

What is a conscience I did ponder
Out my window I did look
Two dogs I did consider

As a wave of revelation it came to me
That the conscience is two dogs that war within me

One is good and one is evil
Depending upon which one is nurtured and fed
That is the deciding factor in who will prevail

John Bret Harrington

Daddy's Lullaby

Little baby, don't you cry.
Love to see your smiling eyes.
Your laughter always brightens up my day.
I wouldn't want it any other way.
See the carousel—it's turning 'round.
Listen to its happy sound.
Each time I hold you my heart starts to sing.
I hope you realize the joy you bring.
As the days they quickly turn to years,
Through the laughter, through the tears.
The world you'll know will be a world of love,
Shining brighter then the stars above.
Little baby, don't you cry.
I'll sing you Daddy's lullaby.

Jason Gilbert

I'm Gone

I sit in there scared. trying to close my ears
they say I'm rotten, she must be poor. I'm gone
I think I cannot hear but deep inside I
clench my teeth . . . they follow me home, she is,
she is. I know it myself, why don't they think.
I'm gone, I'm gone, I wish to myself, I'll
disappear within myself. I can't hear I will
not hear . . . but now I know that I did fail.
The hurt is deep I try to heal, I'm gone, I'm
gone within myself.

Monica Scherer

Crucifix on My Wall

I had this crucifix on my wall
Cold and hard as my thoughts
I took down that crucifix from my wall
Not because I question my own faith
But because there was a sad man on that
Crucifix on my wall
He'd count my sins one by one and wait for
Me to fail . . . I couldn't bear it, couldn't stand it
Couldn't help it
So I took down that crucifix from my wall

Nicky Borson

Night Calls

With it's infinite magic all of mother nature began its
final call to the day.
Twilight crept across the forest floor with advancing
shadows of the night.
The mood was set as faint beams of filtered light
streamed down from the star filled sky.
With the moon on the rise, all of nature sang in their
chorus song, which lulled the world outside into slumber
and tranquility.
Once again the world became at peace.

Julie Himes

Vampiress

Darkness falls all around,
for I am a child on the prowl.
I go into the night looking for a bite.
I am the shadows you see
and the shivers you feel, but don't fear me,
for the time is near; so take my hand.
You will feel no pain.
Let me take you to my domain.
'Tis I, the vampiress of the night,
so come to me and you shall be free.

Lara F. Whittaker

His Love

when I look into your eyes I know you tell me no lies
your eyes' gaze leaves me in love's maze
when you hold my hand my feet don't feel like they're on land

I dream of you saying I do
I can still hear those three words I love you
when I'm with you no other guy can do
what you have done

you are my life and I hope to be your wife
when we kissed I know I missed
the chance to say this no matter what may come your love
leaves me numb

your love reminds me of a dove that flies above
and spreads its love

Cassandra Cannon

Ashley

A very friendly person.
A big flirt.
Someone you can count on.
Someone who tries to be nice to everyone.
Someone who doesn't like to fight.
Someone who needs somebody to be there for her.
Someone that is fun to hang out with.
Someone who I always laugh with when together.
Someone who has a shoulder I can lean on.
Someone who needs to think more highly of herself.
Someone who doesn't give herself enough credit.
Someone who is pretty.
Someone who cares.

Chantal Pagni

Daddy

Why did you leave me?
Why did you have to go?
Why did you go to Heaven,
When I was only seven?
Don't you know I miss you so?
I wish you could see me grow
into a beautiful young lady.
I miss playing with you in the pool;
I miss seeing your smiling face when I get
home from school.
I miss you giving me horsy-back rides;
I miss having you by my side.
I wish you could come back to me, Daddy!

Diane Patricia Di Bisceglie

Cooperation

I'm the rock, solid, steady, and true.
Just plug away, both night and day.
I never quit; I'm never through.
Just go along, day after day.

But I know a little butterfly who
Flits around from flower to flower,
Bringing sunshine and happiness, too.
She's small and light, but full of power.

However, it takes the two of us
To make this old world go around.
I'm looking from the ground; she is free.
Together we see all there is to see.

LaVern L. Clark

Waters Cannot Quench

All of Hell tried to stop me.
They stood against me as a wall.
I walked through the fiery flames.
I didn't think twice, neither did I stall.
My blood has been lit.
The heat is on,
And waters cannot quench.

I run the race of love;
Setting ablaze the paths that I take.
Stumbling blocks and evils tempt,
But I shall not be subdued,
And waters cannot quench.

The zeal of the Lord burns in my soul.
It's just like fire shut up in my bones!
My mind is made up.
My heart is fixed.
I am totally consumed,
And waters cannot quench.

Eli

Grandson

To my grandson, whom I love,
and who is handsome as a dove.
He makes my heart burst with pride,
Just to know he's on my side.
Even though he does some things
Not too shabby, just spreading his wings.
Grandmas try not to criticize,
Nor stand in judgement otherwise.

June F. Herrick

24

Linger daylight to kiss the moon—
Two passing lovers,
Who share this boon.

They breathe the wind, and dream the sky,
And how they remind
Of you and I.

Such passion as is seldom seen,
And yet that's how it's
Always been.

And so, my moon, I'll chase you, too—
As my daylight's dusk
Turns crimson blue.

David Abbitt

Life

The winds of age
move inexorably
With purpose and
presumed finality
Through life's stages
and endless cycles
Planned and spontaneous
ever progressing
Impatient in youth
fleeting in old age
Too often interrupted
by life's frailties
Savor each day as
if there are no more
For we are but temporarily
given a slice of time
God's gift for
one ride on the carousel called life. . . .

Jerry Post

Well, What Do You Know?

Well, what do you know about yourself?
Yourself is all you know about when it comes
to the inner soul of your inner self.

Well, what do you know about your life?
Your life is all you know about when it
comes to living, loving, and learning, and
when it comes to giving, glowing, and growing.

Well, what do you know about yourself and
your life within the self and life of God?
Yourself and life is all you know about when
it comes to being it and living it with joy.

Well, what do you know about?
Well, what do you care about?
Well, what do you feel about?
Well, what do you cry about?
Well, what do you smile about?
Well, what do you know?

Rhonda E. Carroll

Unknown Hero

Though it was fourteen years ago, and I have no memory of it,
I believe my birth mom was so strong to take a risk.
The risk of giving me to a family of strangers,
That I think was the best thing, she could have possibly offered.
Though she was only seventeen, just a child herself,
She believed she knew, the best thing she could do to help.
To help give me, the best future I could have,
And though she must be happy for me, I know her tears must be sad.
If only she knew how much she's given, to me already, so long ago,
I wish I could tell her, that she is a true hero.

Alissa Yeong Smith

Placid Agony

The ocean like a window
Into my bitter thoughts
A mirror to reflect
The cool blue sky as the
Silent noise around me brings back the painful truth
The wind, a cold kiss on my naked cheek,
A sour way to bring me back
All is quiet and still,
The roaring silence enough to
Paralyze you where you stand
I wait. I cry.
The streaming tears destroy the happiness left behind
I scream as sand whips past my face
Like the dust of my forgotten memories.

Courtney Nicole Boyd

Why?

Why won't the one I love, love me back for real?
Why can't I have you dear?
Why can't my dreams come true?
At least the dreams I have of you.
Why is it that you and me can't be together?
Why won't you believe I'd love you forever?
Why won't the one I love, love me back for real?
Why Oh, why can't I have you dear?
Why can't I just get over you?
Why is that such a hard thing to do?
Why do you have to be so funny and kind?
Why do you have to have such an adorable smile and wonderful eyes?
Why won't the one I love, love me back for real?
Why can't I have you dear?

Katie M. Betts

Blossoming

Through the eyes of a child,
sometimes what we see is not so clear.
The true knowledge of our world
opens up with each passing of a year—
Explaining how it is . . .
Changing ideas for the better,
for the worse, or still, as a mysterious quiz

As I grow older, I wonder what was
real, and what I only saw as a child.
Does it truly influence my actions,
my looks, my hope, my style?

The boy must grow to become a man:
yet if time remains still, the boy he will stand.
The girl who carries the sadness
of a child with her each year as she grows;
Just as the boy, adulthood she never know . . .
Sometimes adults remain emotionally as children,
needing another to give them a hand.
He helps her to know womanhood.
She helps him to become a man.

Lollie Cotten

A Time in Life

Chasing the sunset, running from the storm
Following a dream, trying to get it to form

Where am I going, where have I been
Pushing to be better, wanting not to sin

Getting thoughts straight, new ideas to find
Learning more concepts, opening up further in my mind

Only knowing to help, but how to do it right
Communication is dim, sight of knowledge is bright

Consciousness is all, ignorance gets none
Keep a hold of hope, care until living is done

Finding my way, the biggest adventure yet
A journey 'til the end, walking that line without a net

Pamela G. Ratliff

The Friday Night Rush

Living slowly, unfocused and confused
From days of being worked, drilled, and abused.

I try to do my schoolwork but say,
"Leave it away for another day."

Coaches preach—focus, work, and dedication
But all these lead to my misdirection.

My blood and sweat are bringing, it seems,
Vast arrays of hopeless dreams.

I sacrifice every day, right and left,
Bone and sinew are gone by theft.

Why put myself through this miserable hive?
The game time rush makes me finally alive.

Derek Benson Breier

The First Time I Kissed You

I lay here and start to reminisce
I can't stop thinking of our first kiss.
We were alone together, I never expected what was to come
We began to kiss, our passion was as hot as the sun.
We put our arms around each other, is what I'm feeling true?
I never imagined I'd be kissing you.
We pulled away, looked in to each other's eyes.
Why do I feel this is all a lie?
As I think back, it seems so far away
Yet I remember the date and the day.
It was a Tuesday, October 28th, 1997
Standing there together, we were in pure heaven.
In my heart that day will always be true
I'll never forget the first time I kissed you.

Megan T. Gaul

Nature, No

Grow a summer garden and watch it die.
Some people do that, I don't.
Raise a lovely bird just to let it fly.
To suffer that grief, I won't.

There are queens and there are worker bees.
To rule or work, I shan't.
Useless bees shunned from the hive, I see.
But fly with them, I can't.

If left to me to plant the seeds.
To toil so hard, I couldn't.
Don't wait for me to do good deeds.
If I were you, I wouldn't.

Perhaps I will endeavor to—no, never mind.

Geraldine E. Murphy

Tell No Tales

Speak no tales of opulence to my ears,
No fables of the glimmer of Solomon's gold,
Could reach my mind,
Falling short and paled by a vision,
Spin no yarns of creamy jade,
Deep green like a dragon's eye,
Silence the bard to still his tongue,
For I have been to Gethsemane,
I stole a brief glance to the edge of temptation,
Seeing the genie in her eyes,
The color of gentian after rain,
Doomed to a pilgrimage to lose my soul,
My heart now as spar,
It will soon fade to nothing and be gone,

James Robert Neubaum

Commitment of a Lifetime

I've spent my life searching, for what I don't know.
So many choices, which way to go?
Good or bad, wrong or right?
I don't want to feel the darkness in my room at night.
I need Your guidance, love, and protection.
I need You to show me my direction.
Give me a sign of what I'm to do,
and how I can bring more glory to You.
You gave your life and You died for me.
You loved so much, for all to see.
I'm so thankful for how much You've cared,
but I do not deserve this love that You've shared.
Lord, unto thee I commit my soul;
mend my wounds and make me whole.

Tyler Alan Travitz

Image of You

Through Your creations,
I can see an image of You smiling with joy.
Through Your word,
I can hear the image of Your voice quietly whispering.
Through the light,
I can imagine You and I walking in Heaven together.
Through what I eat,
I can feel You fill me up with unconditional love.
Through the colors of the world,
I can feel the happiness that You shower me with.
Through the water I drink,
I can feel You rid my soul of evil and fill it with right.
Through everything in this world,
I can see a picturesque image of You.

Matt Ryan Kennedy

Dreams

There is that dream that we all have,
that makes you cry, that makes you sad.
It is about that one lost love.
The one that resembles an angelic dove.
You may think his heart is pure,
but the question is, do you know for sure?
Is his love for you or her?
Something that can't be taught,
yet one must learn.
Is it his devilish smile that you adore?
The one that you have constantly seen before.
So have you had this dream before?
If you haven't, you will,
in nights that bring more . . . dreams . . .

Victoria Geller

Babylove

Maybe one day you'll know inevitable
Inside my heart you've been from the start
Chances and fate brought us to date.
Happy and smart are your best parts.
All that you are comes from afar.
Existing within but a touch of your skin.
Lips are divine when they touch mine.

Open to me, thank God you could be.
Time will but tell, the moment within when
The one who was beating my heart had appeared.
Instinctively, it came to be
Another had changed but a part they couldn't see
No one can say why it's this way
One must but know when touched by the soul.

Monice M. Richards

Free Will

The light dims and the angels mourn.
Can darkness snuff the flames of enchantment
or merely cast shadows to prevent us from seeing clearly?
Tears fall from Heaven as another child is led astray.
Hell's army celebrates in victory.
Homes broken and lives in disarray.
The blood of the lamb has no power when it is not welcomed.
The gates are open, wide and welcoming.
Yet we choose another way, our own way, the way of destruction.
Pride keeps us from choosing the answer which is already given.
We see the light but close our eyes to it.
Choosing to be blind when sight has been offered.
Choosing to be lost when the direction is clear.
And pretending to be dead when life has been granted.

Jason Mikeal Johnson

Dreams Come True

Do what you can do
To make all your dreams come true.

Step into a fantasy,
See all the things you can be.

Imagination can bring you far
To what you really are.

Find that place inside of you,
That special something that won't make you blue.

When you find it, grab it and go,
Then it's time to start your show.

You found that something, now it's up to you
To make all your dreams really come true.

Lindsey Nicole Smith

In the Marsh

I love sitting in the marsh
Especially when the weather is harsh
Sitting motionless as ducks and geese pass
My worries and cares never seem to last
Waiting with just my dogs, father, and me
I ask myself, how much better could life be?
Everything is calm as sunrise nears
And as daylight is upon us a flock appears
They pass over with no intention to land
I believe these birds deserve a hand
See the outdoors to me is a special place
Just seeing the sights puts a smile on my face
There is more to hunting than just the kill
Just being able to go is most of the thrill

Jesse McGuire

Willow

To my Willow

While branches caress the moonlit brook.
Fairies dance in every nook.
Flowers placed upon its feet.
The magical place where fairies meet.
To play and dance.
Sing and prance.
Beneath the willows loving glance.
While braiding ribbons in her hair.
Laughter like bells tinkle in the air.
As the fairies cast their wondering stare.
Upon the willows silent tear so rare.
All loneliness cast away to night.
Happiness brought by this mystical sight.

Melody Lynn Larson

Wishful Thought

Looking out in the distance, I think of you
sometimes. Oh, how I dream to be yours
and you to be mine.

Gazing at the sky above, to wish upon a
star, but still none have falling down
and I wonder where they are.

So looking in the distance among the crowded
stars, I see your image within the darkened
sky. So full of life, hope, and love are
shown within your eyes.

If I had one wish to make for my perfect
man, I would look no further, you'll be the
one I'll be wishing for . . . .

Yamilek Buck

Successful Illness

Hold your nose and swallow hard, the medicine is bitter.
How do you feel today? Tomorrow, will you feel better?
You've been dealt a hard blow, but you can take it!
Keep the promise of faith, try not to break it.
Time is not yours alone to waste.
Fill the seconds, and the minutes, but not with haste.
Bribe your stubborn body to do your wishes,
With little rewards on fancy dishes.
A hand painted goblet with a lemon slice,
Make taking the pills almost nice.
With a little joy here and a big smile there,
Show the world around you that you still care.
There's time enough for the funeral dirge to play.
Begin the second half of your dreams today!

Agnes M. Pont

Limitations

I cannot make the sun to shine, however strong I'd be,
I cannot fill the sky with blue, nor still a rolling sea!

I cannot make a rainbow, nor wash the trees with rain,
I cannot make a bird to sing, nor ripen fields of grain!

I cannot usher in the dawn, nor warm the day at noon,
I cannot make the sun to set, nor hang the amber moon!

I cannot light a firefly, nor catch the early dew,
I cannot build a mountain with peaks of purple hue!

I cannot measure up to that which God would have me be
But I can shout about His Love! He gave His Son for me!

God's world is filled with many things that I could never do,
But I can build a bridge of love to reach from me to you!

Ina Murray

Fall Has Come

Fall has come

Cool winds flush shadows of summer heat from
the withering grasses

Fall has come

The days fade to early twilight and invite
all souls into the glowing warmth of home

Fall has come

A wandering mind will tease the heart with
visions of the first snow

Fall has come
The season is changing and so am I

Darin B. Crisman

Love

Love should not be betrayed
Love is more than we made

It felt like the morning's dew
Like we never knew

In the day we meet
At night is always sweet

I wake up to your voice but you're not there
It makes me wonder . . . where are you?

What happened to the love
We cared about so very much?

The love we shared
Was it ever there?

Amie A. Strait

Though Sightless, I See

A wretch am I, who needs for sight a dog.
How sad it is that I may but in sleep
Behold the world! The Earth is but a fog.
I must depend upon my pooch, else creep
About this realm. I am, must think the girl,
A clumsy boy who waddles like a duck.
Despite my eyelessness, I see a swirl
Of things not seen by those with eyes! My luck
Is not so ill! Of lovely blooms my pass
Is full. I do not see an ugly tree.
Shines brighter than a summer's day my glass.
From shackles bounding those with eyes I'm free!
So now I shall not frown and bawl and cry,
Nor wish that I would shrivel up and die!

Monica Esmeralda Ahmad

Terrified Tears

The face of an angel is all that is here.
One beautiful freckle equals one terrified tear.
Not ready to leave but has to go.
Wants to go back but God says no.
Leaving your life is a scary thought.
I guess it's something that can't be fought.
A mother, A father, A sister, and friends.
A meaningful life that suddenly ends.
An angel is what he was meant to be.
Now just think of all he can see.
Looking over his family night and day.
Saying I love you in his own special way.
In the night we sleep, In the day we cry.
He watches us all from his star in the sky.

James William Higgins

Super Excellent Xylophone

Dance among the souls of the restless night,
Victims of a worthless tragedy.
Sweating skins squirm like the serpent,
Don't think of love, I don't want to regret.
Feel no shame, your guilt is for the grave.
Make me tonight, your fear ignites my senses.
Pushed inside of a dizzying dreamscape,
Pulling out your own hair but feeling no pain
Made like a golden heart shaped box.
My fingers like keys open your locks.
Taste of the sex, the salty sweat lick.
Smell in the air is getting quite thick.
Bloodlust tremors falling down like rain,
Shaking your body like a runaway train.

Joseph D. Kwoczka

His Turn

When I heard he was gone,
I was sure everyone was wrong.
As I saw all my friends in such a terrible state,
All I could feel was a strong sense of hate.
People hugged me and said "Don't cry,
at least you got to say goodbye."
Now it's been half a year,
and I still shed a painful tear.
For my friend that I will always love,
his soul will be in the hands of the above.
Even if there's no one to blame,
I will never feel the same.
The one thing that I have learned
is that I will wait until it's my turn.

Jennifer Dawn Smith

Revelations

I cannot understand   Anything.
Life   Love   Infinite in perverse secrets,
Every action   wrong;   Every word   mistaken.
Harm, Spite   Boundless in the imagination of GODS.
Comprehension   like sand between my weak fingers.
I want,   I Need   to learn what causes the delicate   Pain.
My actions, my words, our very thoughts?
Two gaping wounds   a Single strike.
Countless tears   Flooding the world.
How can we heal the tender, Red flesh?
How in man's limited wisdom can one hope to prevent them?
Forgiveness,   Balm for the perpetual ache of Love.
Acceptance and hope,
Infinite perverse secrets.

Jay A. Moore

Everything

These things we speak of are feather soft and fleeting
they should be whispered barely louder than the
rustle of summer leaves
and spoken only from one's eyes.
By these things may you come to know
that your voice is as lovely to me
as the laughter of a newborn babe to a weary
mother who has just given birth
your scent envelopes me like sweet jasmine from
the Garden of Eden
and your touch so divine
that a mere flutter turns my skin to gooseflesh and
I want nothing more than to be pressed into the
security of your warmth.

Kelly Dassow

Legacy of a Woman

She stands tall and erect,
A statute of her gender.
Slow to raise her hand, yet quick to correct—
No man dare offend her.
Her voice as calm as wind,
With words as sharp as a sword.
Knows nothing of the word sin—
Fears no one but the Lord.
Loves her children like only a mother can;
Disciplines them and loves them the same.
Teaches her son how to be a man—
Shows her daughter that with sunshine comes rain.
She is the woman all women wish they could be,
The woman inside all of us—a legacy.

Laticia Chandler

Hear Me, Lord

I have a son, his name is Rodney.
All he thinks about is money.
I pray one day he'll look up and see
that you Dear God is the one he needs.
He's a grown up man and yet so small.
He doesn't think he needs anyone at all.
I love him so but he brings such sadness.
In his mind there's all this madness.
It's hard for him to sorts things out.
Will you tell him what this life's about.
Will you let him know that You are there.
That he doesn't need to live with his despair.
With arms wide open on bended knee
I pray Dear God you'll hear my plea.

Beverly Mattos

So Alone Now

Why do you have me alone in the park
And why do I sometimes cry in the dark,
Because I love you so much
And I need you so much that my mind goes blank
I can hardly think about life without
So alone and so cold with out you here to hold
You left me, no good-byes
I think of your soft brown eyes
Your warm breath on my face.
I've loved you my whole life.
More than my best friend
More than my heart
You were my dog, my pet
And I will never forget you.

Lisa Moore

My Reflection in the Rain

To those that are lonely and hurting

I was standing by a pond, talking to a friend
When it seemed like I was going on and on with no end
She stood there and listened without saying a word
But I was wondering, am I being heard?
I told her about my problems—well, that's all she knows
I looked at her face—sadness is the only thing that shows
As time passed, we had a laugh or two
At that point the rain began to dry
Just like the tears from my eyes
The sun began to shine
The sadness wasn't there anymore—no more was it mine
You know, she's always there when I'm in pain
That friend of mine . . . my reflection in the rain?

Marquita Lenear Hughes

That Reflection I Never See

When I look in the mirror, what do I see?
A reflection of a man looking back at me.
I wonder what my reflection sees.

Have I taken time to look at myself,
Not from within, but from without,
Without the image that I see,
But from the image my reflection sees me to be?
I wonder what my reflection sees.

Can it be that my reflection sees what God sees?
What is the link between what God sees and I see me to be?
Can Jesus Christ be that reflection I never see,
That is always looking back at me?
I wonder what my reflection sees.

Howard B. Reed

Your Love

You'll never know what you've done for me.
How your love has cured me.
You carried my torch when I was weak.
You were the voice when I couldn't speak.
You were there when no one was.
You gracefully wrapped me in your haven of love.
You were the rain to my dry fields.
You gave me the strength to heal.
You were there when I couldn't stand.
You helped me up with your giving hand.
You are the warmth that burns in my soul.
You make my life feel so completely whole.
Your love gave me the power to succeed.
Because you are my everything.

Ashton Nicole Byles

That Horrible Day

In honor of Stephen Forestal, my father

Boyhood to the start of my manhood.
My life is stained from that horrible day.
November 11, my heart fell to pieces in every way.
My mom started crying.
My mind started flying.
What has happened?
As we sat there playing war,
My grandmom walked through the door.
She told me what had happened.
It was so sudden.
All the sudden, my heart became sore.
My mother had nothing to be said,
As I found out my father was dead.

Norman S. Forestal

Dreams

Gladly I close the doors of day, and turn
To night's dim, nocturnal blues. No noon
Has held the beauty of this shadow-moon
Creating ghostly patterns on my soul. Burn,
Oh, heart, brimming with fantasy dreams
Never close enough to fill the caressless
Spirit drowsing silently in weariness;
The splendor song of opal screams.
Soft is the touch of purple glimmer
In silver starlight, rainbow-moons sleep
Awaiting loveliness, so cool and deep,
Melting magical moments of music-shimmer.
And well I know the shadows from the past,
Tomorrow's dreams a spell will cast.

Mychele Owens Taylor

Daddy's Gone

Please do not cry and shed another tear,
For I have been happy through all of my years.
Please do not think of everything I will miss;
A hug, a smile, a loved one's kiss.
Please be not burdened of things left unsaid,
Just whisper them to me, all the thoughts in your head.
Please never forget all the memories we shared,
and always know how much I truly cared.
Please understand that you have touched my life forever,
And keep in your heart that we will someday be together.
Please always smile when you remember me.
God eased me from my pain;
He finally set me free.

Love, Daddy.

Kristin Humes

Gramma

Gram, you had a kind word for everyone you knew.
You made this world a better place, just for being you.
Gram, you're like an angel with all the love you gave,
Taking care of others first while you chose second place.
Gram, you were my lifeline, connected at the heart.
No matter where you are now, we'll never be apart.
We'll always have our good times, no one can take away.
We'll never forget those biscuits you made Thanksgiving Day.
Gram you know I love you, more than words can say.
Although you're time with me has passed, in my heart you will remain.
So now it's your time Gramma, to take a little rest.
God has bigger plans for you, he would only chose the best.
I know at a later time we will meet again.
So save a spot for me up there, dear Gramma my best friend.

Julie Kendall

The Narration

It's over yet never began, it's constant and
never started, so many times retired and keeps
going like a broken chant whispered so low and
can't be understood like the man who punches
the wall until he bleeds just to know the
narration of passion, to feel pain.
To him passion is pain and love is passion, not knowing the
depth of his passion but it being so deep
he'd need not know to believe in it, just the
narration of the surface is too deep of an
emotion and the depth of feeling this emotion
is to extreme to express at the surface, that
pain is passion and passion is love, in order
to love with passion we must narrate pain.

Ramon Garcia, IV

Life

As each day turns into night
I'm still wondering where is the light
For, the days they pass me by
no time to dance, no time to cry
work all hours late into the eve
missing the life I was taught to perceive
raising a family in the world today
is more frustrating in many ways
try to live as my father before
waiting my life away, the excitement from this bore
Would money make it less painful
Capable of affording the house, car, and travel
I may never know for the years have added on
Soon my time here will be gone. . . .

David Lord

Terrified Tears

The face of an angel is all that is here,
One beautiful freckle equals one terrified tear
Not ready to leave, but has to go
Wants to go back, but God says no
Leaving your life is a scary thought
I guess it is something that can't be fought
A mother, a father, a sister, and friends
A meaningful life that suddenly ends
An angel is what he was meant to be
Now just think of what he can see
Looking over his family night and day
Saying I love you in his own special way
In the night we sleep and in the day we cry
He watches us all from his star in the sky

Kourtney Goff

Hidden Angel

Mistaken for a human,
An angel slid right in.
Reached and touched a thousand hearts,
So he could have his wings.
He graced us with his presence,
And then out the door he flew . . .
Leaving echoes of his laughter;
Leaving imprints of his smile;
Kept us here to realize,
Life is a short while.
Every day is like a gift, don't overlook its worth.
Make rainbows out of raindrops, that's why we're on this Earth.
Memories he took with him, leaving lessons in return.
This angel taught us about love, and how from love you learn.

Lisa Anne Gregorich

Morning Prayers

With a gift of tobacco and arms stretched wide,
He chants his prayers to the morning sky.

Three days of fasting, he can hardly stand,
Yet he still dances in the morning sand.

His prayers unanswered and his head hung low;
He leaves a trail as he drags his bow.

He looks across his once great land,
His future is now in the white man's hand.

His forefathers sang to the spirits out loud,
His children now are just one of the crowd.

He weeps as he stands like a weathered tree, and wonders,
Will my great-grandchildren remember me?

Ray D. Powell

Deliverance

You planted your heritage in my womb,
And I killed a nation; for sure I am doomed.
Only your Son's blood can set me free,
I thank you Lord for this gift you gave to me.
Because your forgiveness came so easy it made me strong.
The chains that once bound me are broken and gone.
I don't deserve your generosity of love,
But I have it because of your grace from above.
No going back to change the past;
I can hold my head up now and let go at last.
Before all I knew was anguish and guilt,
But now upon your Son's blood, my life is built.
I am no longer imprisoned by my sins of blame,
Thank you, Lord, for delivering me from my shame.

Denise J. Morgan

I Am Who I Am

I am a boy who stands tall and proud.
Some may say I am a little loud.
I am a person who loves to learn.
I am a person who never runs.
I am sweet.
I am kind.
I am a person with my own mind.
I can think.
I can read.
I do believe I was born to lead.
My mom says I am a great lamb.
I say, I am who I am.
Who am I?
I am Robin, a shorter version of my father.

Robin Matthews, Jr.

Six Blessings from God

I looked out my window and asked myself,
what will it take to fill life's shelf?
Then God whispered, "Don't fret,
good things are coming yet."
Just be patient and wait on me
and soon the little trinkets you will see.
Oh, how true He was to His word!
The next day was wonderful the news I heard!
Now I have Blake, Wade, Ryan and Josh,
David and Jade to fill that spot!
Now at 50, I look out my window and reply,
"Thank you, God, you didn't lie!"
Six faith testings,
Six wonderful blessings!

Glynda H. Abraham

Alone

I look upon myself, even though I am not fully grown,
and yet every day I find myself all alone
But now, where shall I go, and what about tomorrow
I cannot even express my depression and sorrow
and yet I have to believe, not only in myself
I have to think about everyone else
and now where do I go
I was always so scared, so full with fear
and it used to be fuzzy, but now my destiny is clear
for now I have found my only limitations
and now I know my only obligations
I have been so blind, for I did not see
The cure to my disease, the remedy
that I am not alone

Anatoliy Vasiliy Kulbanskiy

Brat

You tease people
You laugh at people
You make people want to die
But really,
You're the one who's shallow.
The one with the knife
Inches from your aching heart
So why take your pain out on us?
You brat.
Afraid people will see the truth?
Afraid people will see you in your own light?
So you pretend
To be a brat.
Lame.

Rachel Ford

Twister

you start as some clouds and some wind in the air
then silently turn and start forming up there
with the lightning's crackle, and the thunder's cackle
you unleash your funnel, towards the Earth it will tunnel
and chaos erupts in the midst
your winds faster turning, destructive forces are churning
and the fear can be felt from your hiss
you take what you want and toss it around
flexing your forces, tearing up towns
then you silently fade and reside to small breezes
and mother nature has warned us
she'll do as she pleases
when are you coming, when will you be there
as you start as some clouds and some wind in the air

Joseph P. Haley

Seduced by the Wind

Did you ever stand outside alone
When the wind began to whistle a song?
Shhhhhh, be still, relax, and see
What it's like to be seduced by me.
My strength you'll feel enclosing you tight
But you can't see me even at night
I'll seep right through to your deepest parts
I'll touch you gently, caressing your heart.
Close your eyes, give way to see
What it's like to be seduced by me.
You'll find no feeling to compare
What you will feel when I am there.
So stand, still, relax, and you will see
What it is like to be seduced by me.

Darlene Monhollen

Loving Skies

Walking, walking, to a place unknown,
Swiftly striding, in the valley below,
Across the rivers made of sky,
Reflections are what caught my eye.
My beautiful face has shone bright.
I get a rush that fills my might.
Running along the weeds and grass,
Crossing the streams with a hefty splash,
Looking for a friends in the sky,
Only made me start to cry.
Knelt down with tears of grace,
Filled my lonely, empty space,
Looking for a place called home,
As I realized I was all alone.

Aaron M. Kubicina

Questions

You don't ask me questions about my day
You don't ask me questions come what may
Questions they are the key to understanding
Questions they are the key to handling
So if you don't care to ask
Then forget the whole task
For I am worth an ask
I have not a mask
So you may ask
For no questions is the loneliness of life
For I did not ask for it all to be over
Then again I did not ask for it all to begin
For that is the way it is with questions
From beginning to an end

Gennifer Marie Montoya

This Love

Will this love last forever; how long will it endure?
Or will it simply fade quite quickly, how can I be sure?
Will it be like the great river, always flowing past?
Will it be like the ocean, in its endless expanse?
Will it be like the mountains, whose peaks rise so high?
Will it be like the stars that twinkle in the sky?
Will this love last forever; how long will it endure?
If it grows quite sickly, will I know its cure?
For even rivers lose strength, and sink into the Earth.
Then oceans dry up, awaiting their rebirth.
Great mountains often crumble, shrinking their vast size.
Stars sometimes fall, a streak of light shows their demise.
Will this love last forever; how long will it endure?
For nothing ever stays the same, of this we can be sure.

Tim Hendrickson

On the Mend

Have you ever fractured a bone?
I don't recommend it—Groan!
For eight weeks I laid around,
Unable to put my foot to the ground.
Friends and neighbors came to look,
Some offered to clean and cook!
Patience, patience, I had to remember,
As September turned into November.
Doctor said: I can start to weight bear,
Slowly, slowly, I will get there!
I'm looking forward to the day—
I can throw my boot and crutches away.
Then I'll walk along the street—
So happy to stand on my own two feet.

Patricia Anne Reppucci

My Dear Friend

We have shared laughs, dreams, goals, tears,
Ambitions, crushes, opinions, and fears.
The problems we've shared, the secrets we've told,
Our times were precious, our memories gold.
The advice you gave, the wounds you have mend,
Thank you, thank you, my very dear friend.
Someone once said friends are angels from Heaven above,
Carrying gifts of friendship and packages of love.

So thank you for the time you spend
With me my very, very dear friend.
Thanks for always lending an open ear.
Though we'll be apart, in my heart you'll be near.
Remember, this is not the end,
But good-bye for now, my very dear friend.

Rachel Katherine Griffin

Still

Time stands still when u are by my side
My feelings for u I just cannot hide
Without u all I see is shades of blue
Without u I'm lost, I have no clue
I drift into a world of my own
I'm completely lost, I'm here all alone
I need to hear the sound of your voice
Your sweet melody makes me rejoice
The time just lingers and drags away
I have to suffer yet another day
U will still remain deep in my heart
The memories of your love will never part
I'll wait for u just for u I will
I'll continue to love u still

Timothy White

The Sky

The sky, on a warm, summer day
Creates wonderful sunshine so we can play.
Those puffy clouds of pure white cotton
Do not look dirty, stiff, or rotten.
See the planets, far away,
We'll never reach them in just one day.
These two planets, Mercury and the Sun,
Are way too hot and not much fun.
In the night, see the stars,
They look so close and yet so far.
Our galaxy, the Milky Way,
Looks bright and starry from far away.
The moon sets a glow in the sky.
See it shimmer over the rooftops high.

Joan Ling Xie

Special Angel

Today an angel showed me courage,
Today an angel showed me love,
Today an angel gave me the gift of
compassion,
Today she gave me the gift of patience and
understanding,
Today this angel may be unaware of what she
gave me,
But most of all today this angel showed
friendship above and beyond.
God made angels for a special reason, each
one has a different assignment.
Today this angel prayed very quietly for me.
This special angel is my friend.

Delores Robinson

The Shadowed Side

Clouds overshadowing a resenting mountain
Purple, dark, and heavy on the bottom
So heavy
It's about to explode
Into a defying steel-cold rain
However, rain is not without its purpose
Rain's water reminds the dark mountain side
Of its little springing-forth sprouts
Of its pretty-smelling flowers hidden in its dirt
Of its forgotten trees
Rain's water reminds the dark side of the many strong roots
All over the mountain
On this side of the mountain
The shadowed side

Michele Brady

Can I

Can I hold on in this day and time
Can I be strong, can victory be mine
Can I be thorough in the work that I do
Can I be calm and be courteous too
Can I be wise in the choices I make
Can I not pass judgement in things I partake
Can I be just, can I be fair
Can I be knowledgeable, can I care
Can I speak freely about the way that I feel
Can I pray for forgiveness, can I do God's will
Can I be selective about the things in my life
Can I survive my toil and strife
Can I dream, can I be free
Can I be acknowledged for just being me?

Yvonne Broadus

Lost Love

Now that I am old and grey
I think back to a bygone day
When we were young, and love was all
Your kisses did my soul enthrall
I loved you then you were my life
But I became another's wife
Where are you now? I wish I knew
Was your life good? Are you old too?
Or do you lie beneath a stone
And leave me here to dwell alone
On what our future might have been
Had fate not deemed to come between
But the thought that will not set me free
Is did you ever think of me?

Barbara A. Jones

Wacko World

As I turn around and look
All I see is selfish people surrounding me
Some consume intoxicants and inflict their disease upon others
While some are busy squandering their coins on nonsense
Meanwhile the world is on the verge of self-destruction
I scream and yell
Waiting for this madness to stop
For people to realize their everyday wants shall obliterate us all
Then surprise drops on them like a bomb
If they just came up for a fresh breath of reality once in a while
They would not be astonished
By the fact that we are no more than just selfish creatures
Destroying and giving away what was not ours to give
We, the people of today, are creating the monsters of tomorrow

Myraida Ortiz

Friendship

Friendship can be a strong or weak bond between people.
Friendship seems so hard to gain but so easy to lose.
It can change every day like an endless rhythm,
But why do peers take over a emotion so much?
When you lose friendship, it feels like an endless spike
going through your entire body.
When you gain friendship it feels like a huge,
extreme sunshine in your heart.
Friends are always there for you when you need them the most.
Friendship can be like a blinded road trip;
you never know where it could go.
When you work together, it feels better than if you were alone.
Mostly it's like a cosmic knowledge between people
that nobody ever knew about.

Dustin R. Pohll

The Jealous Moon

The sun soon sets with darkness to abound,
O'er the distant mountains he takes his leave,
And as a weary traveler he eases himself down,
Not in the least aware what others of him perceive.
Following in pursuit, anxious for his turn,
The moon rounds a corner to proudly wear his worth.
And as he travels further he feels as though a burn,
For where are all the welcome wishers come to share his mirth?
As true for the sun, their duties have come to end,
They close their eyes and block his light from view,
The moon, once grand in heart, now knowing to descend,
Saddened again by spending this eve without the likes of you.
It's time for the sun to rise again, praise to be granted.
The moon now faded, leaves the sky, once more disenchanted.

Rachel Gallagher

The Answer

His body was ravaged by that deadly disease
And on a cold January morning
He left us with such ease.
A few months later she is
diagnosed with MS
And my faith was put to a great test!
I asked my God on high, why?
Why? Why?
My answer finally came
from the Holy Ghost
Just when I needed it the most!
I was told,
"Quit trying to second-guess me;
Just let me be God."

Sarah Nesbitt

Trials

We all have trials, just like you
And just like you we sometimes are Blue,
But there's always a hope of someone greater
Who says maybe not now for your cure, but maybe latter.
We look and want things to happen today.
But we have to realize it's only God's way
We just have to trust Him and look above
And know that God's love is as pure as a dove.
White and clean and never wrong
and always having a sense of where He belongs.
Just remember to keep smiling and not give up.
Remember even Jesus wanted to give up the cup.
The fight is hard and sometimes long,
But if you'll trust in God He'll show you where you belong.

Debra Tootle

My Desire

How long can I wait? I fear no longer.
How long must I wonder? I can take little more.
I look to You to see my fate. It is not clear my current state,
Am I in Your will? Do I follow Your call?
Or do I choose the path, knowing well,
It is not right, it is not true,
I step from the law I have built my life on.
I look to the sky, I ask for Your help.
I know not what thy heart desires.
Shield me, oh, God, from the constant fires.
I look to the book for a guiding hand.
I lean on it, unwavering it stands.
I am searching my life to make it much more,
To make my each step closer to Yours.

Nathaniel Thomas Taylor

A Beautiful Waterfall

A lovely waterfall is truly
something that is so very enticing
to see while that flow of that rushing
water helps one's heart and mind,
to ponder, and relax.

As that sparkling water comes rushing
down into the mouth of the receiving
river, true and ongoing beauty
is continuously abiding,
and it seems to get greater.

Yes, indeed, a rare sight for anyone to see,
and to behold is certainly this creation of his,
a beautiful waterfall.

Mitchell Miles

To Know You

To know you . . .
Is to know of your strengths
And your determination to persevere
And overcome obstacles

To know you . . .
Is to know of your imperfections and weaknesses

To love you . . .
Is to talk to you, to listen and to understand

I love you for the person you are
Good, bad and everything between.

My love is constant, unconditional and forgiving,
Take it for what it is worth, nothing more, nothing less.

Guendolynia Davis

How I Feel . . .

Until you've walked at least a mile, in my very shoes;
Until you've cried an ocean, until you've sung the blues.
Until you sing sad love songs, and know just what they mean;
Until you look into my eyes, and know just what they've seen.
Until you feel such pain, you think that it won't end;
Until you feel so broken that you think your heart won't mend.
Until the world has beat you, and held you to the wall;
Until it's taken everything and made you feel so small.
Until you've held a baby, to smell its sweet, soft skin;
Until you play a childhood game for fun and not to win.
Until you've seen a sunset across the ocean surf;
Until you've seen such beauty, and know how much it's worth,
You cannot say you know me . . . or know my wounds will heal;
Until you've seen inside my soul, you can't know how I feel.

Jeauxdee M. Spang

Can You Hear the Rainbow?

A sunrise, a sunset, a rainbow or two.
A thousand angels in harmonious tune.
Listen yonder, listen far,
Listen for joy beyond the stars.
A peaceful calm, a tranquil endeavor,
The voices are heard on and forever.
Where is this, you ask?
Where can it be found?
The quiescence of time is yet all around.
Can you hear the rainbow, the sunset, or sunrise?
Imagine you can, it's just disguised.
Conquer the range of what you hear,
The sounds of the rainbow are very near,
Like the words of God we so often hear.

Merlin Sellard

Loved Ones

Remember my loved ones
When I am gone
For I will always be around Spiritually
I will always be by your side, in your mind and in your heart.
When you see the sun shinning so big and bright
Just think of me being there by your side.
When you see a kite flying high in the breeze
Just think of me and I'll throw you a kiss.
When you see raining and it's heading your way
Just think of me telling you that I am Okay
If you see a Butterfly by your side
Just think of me because I'll be right by your side.
And when you see a rainbow so colorful and bright
Just think of me telling you that everything is all right.

Jeannette Baylor

Dreamer's Sonnet

Oh, Dreamer, I have wondered who you are
Your presence now begins to make it clear
You come to me from yonder falling star
And show your face to calm my rising fears.
Your shining light leads lonely trav'lers home
Across the sands of time and winds of change
You've come to let me know I'm not alone
The chaos of my life you'll rearrange.
The truth about my life is almost here
The power of your beauty I will see
Unrealistic will be all my fears
The beauty of your power will be me.
Oh, Dreamer, you have come to set me free
Your servant always will my heart song be.

Zarah Walker

Dreams

As I lie on my bed looking so lifeless,
so still, so dead,
patiently awaiting the thoughts and dreams
that pop into one's head,
I pray to God in the Heavens above
that he will watch over me in the Heavens above
like a Dove that flies high over a rainbow
in the Heavens above.
For my thoughts and dreams carry so many emotions.
This is why they need the protection, love, and strength,
of the Almighty God in the Heavens above.

Elizabeth J. Friedly

On Raven's First Birthday

I was filled with joy this time last year
My precious baby girl was finally here
You've grown so much since that day
And brightened our lives in every way
Your eyes and smile could replace the sun
Every day with you is more and more fun
Your wisdom has grown as well, my child
And instead of lying still, you now run wild
My love has grown with you every day
I thank God for you each time I pray
One year has passed, with many more to go
I will love watching you as you grow
Stay smart and sweet and keep God near
For He loves you too, He sent you here

Andrea Sullivan

A Father Dearly Missed

The life of a man who was always so dear
Ended before I even said good-bye.
I loved him so, but he was lifted high
Above until he was no longer near.
Even though he is gone, he is still here.
It pains me that he is so high.
And so many people would try to die
But I know that I am too needed here.

It's still hard but we are getting through it
With lots of love and support from each other.
It's been two years past but the love shared
Was real and I know it will always fit.
He was my father and he loved no others
Like he loved us, now he knows that we cared.

Marti Quay Triche

The People Cry

Life is like the sun, so fiery bright,
It can blind the eye and scar lovely souls.
Why so harsh on hearts so open and light?
Earth's people are like a bucket with holes.
People cold and hard, problems in our lives,
A shame it is that people do not care.
Pain searing in, feels like a thousand knives,
Why don't people care, why don't people share?
Many people hunger, countless a night,
No place to call home for many masses.
Beings fight neighbors just to grab a bite,
Struggling each day, hoping it passes.
But a select few care enough to learn.
People who care give part of what they earn.

Michael Daniel Danto

Kiss

Each thought in my mind moves my body so much,
The warmth you will find with each gentle touch.
As your fingers run down each side of my face,
Moving onto my shoulders then onto my waist.
Feeling this sends chills up my spine,
An exotic feeling, lasting quite some time.
Suddenly the heat of my body starts to rise,
As the touch of your hands move onto my thighs.
The strength of your fingers caressing my skin,
Emotions in my body come from deep within.
After this it's coming to a close,
Feeling the side of your face touch my nose.
As this happens I'm waiting in bliss,
For the happiest moment with that sweet gentle kiss.

Shauna Ware

Butterfly

Butterfly, listen to the silence of your wings
as you drift into altered states.

Fly among your dreams as they are real
and become one with the universe.

Tie the colors of your wings to the clouds
in the sky for there, they become you.

Fly to mountains far beyond the universe
and touch the cords of gold that string along the path.

Fly to me and let me become you just for a day.
For your body will leave you soon,
your soul will drift along its paths.

But the memory of you will last and last.

Cynthia A. Thiessen

Vita

Upon Nature's bosom rests man's predestined fate.
All his strength and vigor, his fortune and his state.

He enters a race unknowingly and he runs the race alone.
Bolting and sprinting erratically, for things he cannot atone.

He rumbles into the first turn, not jockeying for position.
Where he should have gained momentum, he stumbles to submission.

In the far stretch he ponders, "Why didn't he take command?"
When the early opportunities had been so close at hand.

He struggles for determination as the far turn rears its head.
To mold his "win" decision before his strength is bled.

Into the home stretch he gallops, when the hour is in its twelfth.
Not knowing the race he's running is only with himself.

C. L. Murray

Heavenly Love

As I look at the stars, in the heavenly sky
I see so many wonders, that catch my eye.
I see sparkle of your eyes, in the darkness of night
And feel the wind in my face, as love reaches new height.

The moon, the sun, all the planets above
Could not compare, to our wondrous love.
Tho' time passes by, so swift, Oh, so fast
I know in our hearts, true love eternally lasts.

Margaret Dennison

The Power Within

The power within lies inside
The strength holds with a grip stiff, motionless
The power within is energy's pure beauty
All sorts of colors and shapes
Worked into a sculpture of life
Holding deep secrets of the world and future to come
The power within is all around
It moves silently, swiftly, quickly
It is always moving like Earth itself
That's why no one knows were the power within lies

Marie Elyse Hamm

A Spiritual Prayer

When my spirit leaves me, where will it be,
High up in some lofty tree or, maybe out to sea?
On a ship bound for some far off place,
Or wandering around in empty space?
It may tuck inside some other being
Could be someone old, with not much time to spare,
Or perhaps a new life will share.
Wherever or whatever I may be,
I pray my spirit will live with God
Eternally, amen.

Aloha R. Miller

Untitled

I love; I don't get loved
I sacrifice; no one sacrifices
I care; no one cares
I speak; no one answers
People say love is blind; love sees
It sees me for what I am not
Wish and wish for a love to touch
All I touch is pain, runs deep
I have no one, no one to call my one and only
Soul mate

Justin Matylewicz

Falling in Love

It is a warm, colorful autumn.

With each floating leaf that touches the ground,
I am touched by your voice-simply the sound.
With each light breeze that blows through my hair,
I find that your breath is lingering there.
With every bright color and every bold hue,
I become lost within visions of you.
With each setting sun, and each glowing moon,
I am wrapped in your smile as I waver and swoon.
With each passing bird in the blue sky above,
I helplessly fall even deeper in love.

It is a warm, colorful autumn.

Jaimee Tyler Severa

The Fairy Tale's Ending (for Michael)

I see
in his eyes the longing for me
I know from his smile
his love for me
I long
for his hand to reach out and touch me
In my mind
I feel his arms wrap around me
I need
his love to set me free
I adore this man
who patiently waits for me
I trust in his heart because I know
as one we will be
I wait
in longing for him to come and be with me
I want the fairy tale's ending
happily ever after
that which is destined
to be . . .

Vickie L. Lawrence

Out of Control

Out of control,
it's a scary feeling.
Out of control,
with what are we dealing?
How can we put out lives together
when sometimes bad thoughts last forever?
Every morning we resolve to change
and every day we drift from that range.
We propose new ideals, we try to conceal
the pain and inadequacy we feel.
What is it like to be normal?
To wake up without all this turmoil,
to live life to the fullest and accept all our faults?
If negative thoughts we could halt
before they become conscious reality,
Why does it all seem so clear? How do solutions seem so near?
And yet we have shown through fault of our own
that we are still
Out of control.

Shannon Dowd

Chris, the Panda

Chris, the Panda,
My homeland is a wonderland.
The monkeys swing from tree to
Tree.
Birds fly like the wind over the
Dancing flowers.
One of my favorite places to lie
Is under a canopy.
The weather is not as . . .
There are plenty of leaves to eat
And a wonderful lake.
Chris, the Panda,
Then, I am awake, and
I'm not in the
Heart of China but
Instead I'm in this prison.
Then I cry myself back to sleep
And Pray that someone has the heart
To save me from this terror.

Chrissy Mcdowell

You Know Where to Go from Here

Broken faces falling against the floor . . .
Broken places, cracked like Hell's closed
door . . .
This is where the rain rushes in,
Where fire burns the house we live in,
And you know where it goes from here:
Here is nothing to fear.

Broken hearts hatched open like an egg . . .
Broken darts where we lose our leg. . . .
The wind that drove us on has died,
The war cry has sighed,
And you know where we go from here:
Here is nothing to fear.

Broken dreams shift into the whole. . . .
Broken lives lead pathways to the soul. . . .
This is where we learn and relearn to trust,
And you know where to go from here:
Here is nothing to fear.

Rebecca Pierce

Thrust with a Secret Mission

A close one visiting smelled a rat . . .
Built a castle on surmises,
founded by hitherto overlooked
grouses and complaints could well be
the strongest and most authentic structure!!
Hapless, I got an inkling of the mess, but
soon volcano erupted—heart-wrenching cries.
Charges—"Unbearably casual," "Insensitive . . ."
fired cutting-edge over a length of time,
communication cutoff, holocaust revisited.
I came scorched and lonely, destiny's hand?
Loss of loved ones and the pain opened senses—
Do I see two traits clearly now?
So full of self, hurting, and ignorant majority
and rare, sensitive larks, sacrificial to core,
their cursed love or hate selective, intense.
I experience also fleeting, wholesome,
enriching moments of compassion and love
so healing, I'll never spoil or fritter away.

Luxi Krishna

Whaas Up?

She did it all so right;
She grew up straight and strong.
Homework done each night,
All things where they belonged.

She was nobody's fool.
She studied hard at school.
Mistress of physics, math, and art,
She got the fastest start.

She declined the "mommy track,"
Made it by the sweat upon her back.
The pretender to the throne,
When she found herself alone.

Alone with three kids, one dog, one cat, two cars,
One spouse, and, of course, a trendy house.
Yes, she'd done it all so right,
Counseled in the day, called on God at night,
To explain in burning bush, in stone or song,
How could she be so right and end up, oh, so wrong?

Nancy Grasiani

Remembered Flames

These dying embers now around us
Lay the fading fires of passing day.
Yet in the heat and moment
was no thought
As we watched, as they danced.
Whose the will, whose desire fulfilled?
Now this remaining glow
but a spare memory
Against the gathering chill.
Shall we drink one last draft of joy
That some kept faith and did not quench
But gave full vent and not-yet tempered zeal?
These coals then, do they token,
When our tongues (and the silent tongues),
Cloven, merged and lapped,
Were unmuted and one voice?
And when some who gathered,
with the circling flames,
Uttered the cry of witness
and unloosed the seal?

Stanley Holt

Grandma

When I think of you I start to smile,
I'm off in a daydream to reminisce for a
while, to think of the joy you brought me
as a child. I can remember the things you
would say and how we would sing songs to
make the rain go away.
We would eat soup to see the pictures
at the bottom of the bowl, lay on the
ground and watch the clouds roll.
You would put prickly rollers in my hair,
see Grandma, the memories are so clear,
though you've been gone twenty some years.
I have a sweater that you once wore, it
hangs behind the closet door. When I put
it on I can feel you near, I can still
smell the perfume you would wear.
I think of you and start to cry, how could
the Lord take you, please tell me why.
I know you send Angels to help me through,
I love you Grandma, and I miss you too!

Theresa M. Watral

Mama Loved the Flowers

Mama loved the flowers, she grew them everywhere.
Once she even had one tucked up in her hair.
Flowers are not for the rich, nor are they for the dead.
Flowers are for the living, that's what my papa said.
Mama loved the flowers, it was plain to see.
For every time I went there, she'd show them to me.
Mama had them in every room, on every window sill,
She even had tulips planted out by the windmill.
"How do you get them to grow so good?" I asked her one day.
"That's because I water them on every Saturday."
Papa would bring her wild flowers he'd found along the way.
They made her very happy, it always made her day.
Mama so loved the flowers, that was plain to see.
No matter where they came from, she was always pleased.
Her favorite was the yellow rose, she liked them the best,
But I always got her red ones, they stood out from the rest.
No matter what you brought her, she was happy as can be.
She always set them out for everyone to see.
Yes, Mama loved the flowers, that's all that I could say,
Now she is surrounded by flowers, every single day.

Judy A. Lee

Confusion Runs Deep

Goddess drawn forth from the blood of this
tattered society,
I hoped I would never see the stain.
Echoes of days gone by ring loud in my ear,
trying to outlive what's already been done.
Healing wounds already healed,
hurt me just the same.
As I look into the cloudy mirror,
trying to find the way,
possessive destiny keeps holding my hand,
and a teardrop blurs my vision.
Thoughts.
Thoughts can bend safe perception.
I hear questions but I don't have any answers.
These repressed thoughts don't lie well in
an unstable mind.
CONFUSION? !
Losing myself to the lure of destruction,
I throw myself into the flames,
and now I burn, only thinking of you.

Peter Vincent Mazurkiewicz

Winds through My Fingers

Wearing my loneliness like a drape,
Over my soul, inside a pockmarked shell.
Trying to stop it from peeping out
Like dirty laundry in a laundry bag,
As I keep waiting in a dark corner,
Like an old hat stand, gnarled and cracked.
Waiting for a hat to feel complete.
A letter from you.

I keep waiting in a dark corner, always alone.
You said you would be there for me, forever.
Send me the only letter I receive, comfort.
I keep waiting.

Why is it that every time I try to feel for you,
All I feel is the wind rushing
Through my empty fingers, rustling memories.

I keep waiting in my dark corner, alone.
For the letter from you.
Fear. Loneliness. Sadness.
Rushing wind, rustling memories.

Praveen Nirmalan

The Fireman's Legacy

The morning alarm clock rings,
He sits up and wonders what today brings.
His uniform is cleaned and pressed,
Wife rolls over as he gets dressed.
"Do you have to go in today?" she asks,
Lately leaving home seems to be a task.
He arrives at the engine house still quite groggy,
Not knowing in ten minutes he will be sooty and soggy.
The fire burns in a furious rage,
Reports come in, there are people to save.
He and a green rookie rush in,
But only one comes out again.
What went wrong? Why here? Why now?
He knows he must go on, some way, somehow.
It's so hard for him to even imagine,
That this pair will never talk or laugh again.
This is the worst fear a fire fighter has
"He hasn't lived long enough to pass!"
Back at the station, it is quiet and glum,
The veteran sits and cries, "I'll miss you, son."

Anthony Beurkens

Dreaming

When I go to sleep, I dream.
I dream of many things,
like I'm flying on a cheerful cloud.
But then the cloud turns dark and gloomy
and it starts to rain.
It rains harder and harder,
because I'm getting angry.
Then I find a castle and I dance with the princess.
And I get happier and happier
until the rain is a light spring rain.
And we dance on and on
until we float to the clouds and dance very lightly.
I get so happy, the rain almost stops,
and a light yellow sparkle glitters on us.
And then we both are dancing with light
glistening color on us,
because of a little peeking rainbow.
Then it bursts out all its color,
shining a big, full rainbow
right on us.

Zoe Davis-Chanin

Fall Is Here, Thank the Lord, for He Is Still Here

Fall is here,
the trees are bare that stand there.
No birds there for me to stare.
The air is clear that life is not fair,
but I continue to care and want to share,
and that's because I know You're still here.
Sometimes I become sore because I am poor
but I strive for more by opening doors.
Share the wealth to keep all in good health.
I know the Lord is mightier than the sword,
but when it rains, I know it's God's pain;
we must not play greedy games where only one gains.
Is there no shame for our being so lame?
Who's to blame for our being untamed?
Not the Lord, for He forgives,
We are blessed and don't confess.
Spread the word that should be heard,
before it's too late and we meet our fate,
by the Lord's roar and will be no more.

Dominic Marcus Herron

What Makes Me Mad

What makes me mad
Isn't that you kiss me
Or hug me, or hold me ever so tight

What makes me mad
Isn't that you care about me
And like to see me happy
So you always try to make everything right

I don't get mad
When you stick up for me, or buy me a gift
Or make me smile, or give me an emotional lift

What makes me mad
Isn't that you love to spend time with me
Or you rather be with me then your friends

What makes me mad
Isn't that you think
That I'm the girl or your dreams
It's that you do all these things for me . . .
And you really don't know me at all

Michaelene Francis Wiktor

Light after Dark

Deep down Dark Avenue in Africa,
glistening eyes, pain in my heart.
Freedom songs echoed from the plantations
that one sweet day, these chains shall break.
Deep in the slavery waters
sailed terrifying merchant ships.
My ancestors, sold less than a dollar!
How they worked the cane fields;
they toiled, sunlight to moonlight.
Till I saw sweat, blood and tears
roll down their weary faces.
They pleaded with their deaf masters
to stop the whippings.
One day our tears will be for happiness,
sweat for victory, they sang.
Though we shed blood for liberation, children,
There must be light after dark.
On my knees, praying for departed souls,
I saw the sun shed light upon a people,
I saw freedom coming.

Francis O. Juma

My Mother's Quilt

In her youth, her color was vibrant.
She conquered her task of life's quilt
with grace.
She stitched into it, humility, with strands
of purest spirit.
Embellishing her plain work with laughter,
she made it entirely rich.
She asked for little.
Faded recognition for hard won victories was
a banquet for her soul.
Her time was neither one of gilded grandeur nor
gaudy praise.
She was embarrassed by such fluff, but snuck
a bit into her apron pocket to enjoy alone.
She lived for love and nurtured it well,
gathering pieces of comfort and tenderness,
and knotting them with sacrifice.
When death did take her, the threads of her
lovely quilt did not break, but bound my
heart forever.

Lois Jean Halldorson

Cupid's Arrow

Where is Cupid's arrow?
Why has it done me wrong?
It shot me up
and laughed at loveless dawn.
Where is this Cupid's arrow
that has left me sad so long?
Pain has overwhelmed me.
I believe it true to be the Devil's spawn!
Why is Cupid's arrow
always such pleasureless fun?
It left me unassured,
now from everyone I run.
Why is Cupid's arrow
such a disastrous one?
I can't seem to erase
all the brokenness; the harm that's done.
Where is Cupid's arrow?
All I want is one last chance!
Upon all this misfortune
I'll make it right this dance!

Annette Gail McCullough

The World As I See It

The world is almost like a battlefield,
in the sense that it is blood stricken with pain.
People everywhere are crying in despair
for their lost ones or even for their new.

The sight of our world is almost depressing,
for we have taken a kingdom and made it a shack.
We have destroyed a dream from God,
only to make it whatever we wanted.
I can't understand why some are rich and some are poor,
because we are all human, aren't we?
We have taken more then we need to live our
lives in happiness,
while others are just grateful for even being alive.
Some of us however, the ones that I admire,
have taken their lives and dedicated them
for others in need.
These are the heroes of the world, those whose
hearts are righteous.
Be thankful for them, because they are holding
this world together.

Paul Michael Hilborn

Phantom of the Night

Along the deep, dark hall she creeps,
Shimmering lights upon her cheeks
—they're tears.
A phantom of the night in gown of flannel
white and little toes so bare—
See her standing there?
She stares within the darkened room at forms
reclining back to back.
A silent plea, a prayer perhaps, "Tell me what I lack!"
The hell which forms her days can't hurt her
now in slumber's peaceful ways.
Yet restlessly they turn as if to staunch the
flow of love that in her tiny breast does burn.
A bird calls out to warn: 'tis time to go,
'tis time to greet the coming of the morn.
Her hunger not assuaged, she sighs and turns,
and back along the deep dark hall she creeps,
Shimmering lights upon her cheeks—they're tears.
As wistfully she passes by the fading shadows cry, "Who can she be?"
I know, I know her well—she's me.

Antoinette Harris

Silent Disaster

It all came crashing down before me
without a siren bell
It didn't knock or turn a lock
before it made me yell
Neither telephone call nor buzzing
Nor beeping on my "comp"
No music song to sing along
or a slightly sneaky stomp
I turned around and there it was
lying on the ground
A slap, a clap, a sickening snap
would've been an all together welcoming sound
Along with a swish of a rattle
or the ringing of an alarm
A warning shot, a clanking pot
or a soldier shouting "at arms!"
A whisper or a repetitive tap
The bouncing of a ball
But it's hard to hear with a silent ear
any sound at all

Heather Gross

What I Have Lost

I have lost someone I can never get back
I have lost love for a lot of things
Someone I have seen for many years
I will never see again
I will never feel at ease because of this
I have lost one man who has taught me
right from wrong
I have lost the one man who has taught me to love
I have lost the one man who has taught me
not to change for anyone else
The person I have lost is my father
William Leverne Vereen, Sr.
Now my unborn child will never see the man
I called dad
She will never get the opportunity to call him grandpa
He is not here, but you know what,
my daddy knew I loved him
And it's safe to say he left me knowing by your side I will be

Danielle Vereen

I Thought I Noticed Everything, What Did I Miss

Sometimes you barely noticed me but I noticed you
I noticed your smile
I heard the words you spoke
I noticed your group of friends
I noticed your kindness
I enjoyed our talks
Even though no one knew we talked I still enjoyed talking
I noticed every thing but not what I should have
We talked about everything but what was most important
And now that you are gone I can't stop wondering what I missed
Did you act different
Did you sound different
What did I miss
Was there a sign
I'm sorry if I missed your cry for help
Everything is different
Without you nothing will ever be the same
The world will still turn
It does not seem fair

Janel West

I'm Incomplete

Mother, Father,
Look at your little monster
I'm a hero, I'm a zero
I'm a prayer without faith
A city without a door
I'm a bad word, a wink, a nod, a shiver
An untold story, sex without fury
A creeping grey memory, I'm incomplete
Doctor, cure me, what caused my condition
This madness shoots me like bullets
Smashing glass in a silent movie
I'm a temple without a god
A word that never
Rolls off the tip of your tongue
I'm a broken promise, an un-mailed letter
A deck of cards without jokers
A naked obsession, a good intention gone bad
I'm Incomplete,
Incomplete,
Incomplete.

Jackie Marie Cunningham

Untitled

Make the world go away
Take away all this pain
I don't want to be here
Save me in space.

Make the world go away
I can't take the pressure
They're all pounding on me
I can't reach their faces

Save me, I know.
I'm not as synthetic as it goes.

Pull me up. Out of this mess
Grab my hair, or grab my dress.

Please, make the world go away.
Issues get harder every day
The fight to stay alive.

Make the world go away
The shame of myself is too constant to bear
Please go away. Listen to me say.

Mary Wells

I Am Judas

I am Judas, the traitor,
I gave you more than all the others,
I gave you more than love.
For the others the mercy of heroism
And faithful docility to you,
because they never faced your gaze there in Gethesemane.
Would that you had said:
"I understand, you're doing well, courage, Judas!"
They sailed in ships saved by wonder from wild tides,
I sank to this abyss of being human and remembering.
They all saw the nails and wept.
I sacrificed you so that you could bring dawns again.
Many were called to take part in this passion,
Caiaphas, Annas, Herod, and Pilate.
Why also me? I loved you.
Why would they mint the coins and make prophesies?
Why the doomed tree like a feral eye accusing me?
I am Judas, the traitor.
The one who filled his sorrowful cup to the fullest.
The one who handed over one he loved, out of love.

Ester de Izaguirre

I Am Love . . .

Cast me out
Throw me away
Not usable any longer
A disregarded piece of paper
That has lost its use for transferring feeling
Ignore me tonight
As you have done before
Many times the same game
Fill me up then
Just empty me all over again
Forget me quietly
A gift that you seem to have
Making a distant memory
Of things happening to you now
Not even batting an eye
Casting me out
Ignoring me tonight
Forgetting me quietly
Will not release me so easily
I am here for all eternity with you

William J. Larrin

Just Another Statistic

I go outside,
where blackness envelops the land
and greet a dear old friend of mine.
The moon's glassy surface,
shines down on me.
It's radiant light seems to pierce my soul.
I can not hide anything from him.
Tears roll down my face,
in the silence of the night.
I confide in Him,
as the whispering wind
brings words from my delicate lips
to his understanding heart.
People are too anxious
to gaze upon their Creator.
Why can't they look
through the moon's eyes
and see how precious life really is,
maybe even find
Hope!

Lisa Ann Erdman

A Mother's Peace

Everywhere I turn I see her face
Her little red dress with trim of lace
I hear her voice underneath the crowd
Soft and gentle, but I hear it loud
Hello Mommy, she says with a smile
I've been sent to Earth to guide you a while
You've been chosen to teach others
Little children and especially their mother's
I've seen my future and I know the past
Life is precious, a gift that never lasts
A child's love is life itself
A gift from God the greatest wealth
Although not healthy from the very start
My little Desiree was exceptionally smart
She gave me wisdom and knowledge I never had
Showed me love and for that I am glad
Sent to heavens during holiday season
No good-bye, not even a reason
One day we will unite
Until then I pray and to all a good night

Tera K. Triplett

Think Positive

any time you're feeling low
or you're feeling sad,
every time you have a problem
or don't feel good about yourself,
think of all those people
all around the world
who die of hunger and misery;
those people who don't have
nobody to think about them
and tell yourself that you are lucky
because you have friends who care about you
always try to think positive
because in all the universe,
you don't even represent a dust
so your problem can't be as big as you think.
after every storm, the sun shines.
so anytime you're feeling low again,
just try to smile and look up in the sky
in the search of a rainbow, a sign of happiness
and harmony on mother nature

Nancy Leconte

Untitled

aggressions, suppression
your self made depressions
you'll never be worthy to hear my confessions
you're lost, you're found
you're stuck in the ground
you're high, you're low
it's moving too slow
your sun, your sky, your life is a lie
you stand up and fight
just to lay down and die
you're scared, you're running
you can feel my wrath coming
it's clear, it's confused
doesn't it hurt to be used
you're seeing, you're blind
trying forever to find
is it gone, was it here not hope only fear
your love, your hate don't try it's too late
your pain and your sorrow
will live still tomorrow

Kimberly Dawn Rolland

Journey Ahead

Through all the pain and tears
We've endured these two past years,
Fighting and cheating are just half the trouble;
For all the love you shared, I gave double.
Your family dislikes me and that's okay,
I hope now they can see me in a different way.
I can go back to being me,
Well, maybe I can't; we'll just have to see.
Life will be different now that's it's over,
you won't be there to lend me a shoulder.
I'm sorry for all the mean things I've done,
But you have to admit, we did have fun.
I tried so hard and you did too,
But that's just not enough for me or you.
It'll be hard to let you go;
Maybe we'll end up together, I guess you never know.
I'll keep you posted on how things turn out,
If you need me, just give a shout.
And if I need you I'll drop you a letter,
you can tell me it's okay and make me feel better.

Denise Marie Bertzyk

Poeappith

She is like me, I know what she felt
When she laid there that day,
She couldn't stand the pain
It was too much to bear
She knows the truth about the world
Shadowy floods cloud her mind
Happiness she cannot find
So lovely was the loneliness
Upon her, upon us all
Murmuring in the melody
Is the terror of this poisonous fall
In visions of the dark night
My mind and body fight
For a life so right
She finds her soul alone
With Mid'Dark thoughts of the tombstone
Her night though it is clear, it shall frown
With horrible creatures staring down
Her life is a burning fever
With warm blood that will soon leave her

Aaron Strichartz

Miraculous Insight

Driving home at the end of the day
I stopped in for dinner at the local cafe.
The line was moving very slow
And my agitation began to grow.
Grumbling, I sought who held up the line.
Then I saw the white cane, and the man who was blind.
In a second everything changed for me,
Realizing the miracle of all I could see.
The slow-moving line full of strangers became
A colorful picture, though I knew not their names.
The noisy chatter was soothing to my ears
When I thought of those who cannot hear.
And the voice of each stranger became so sweet
When I realized there are many who cannot speak.
At home that night I fell on my knees
Thanking my Father who is so good to me.
I was sorry for never taking the time
To appreciate the miracles that are truly mine.
Let me not take for granted ever again
The gifts I've received from God's gracious hand.

Robin L. Dyer

Unappreciated

He gets up for work while I make him a lunch.
He is rude, the jerk; just let me get in one good punch.
He leaves a little kiss while I clean up his mess.
Him I will not miss, for the baby is now a pest.
I clean all day, I cook all night.
He is on his way home so we can't fight.
Under stress all day, I can't take anymore,
And he comes home to say his feet are sore.
I ask about his day while I rub his feet.
He never asks what I have to say in the evening when we meet,
So I put him to bed sobbing and saying,
It's now 3:00 a.m., and the baby is crying.
I want to ignore her, but I can't.
I have to go feed her, so I get up and pant.
Half an hour later I'm back in bed.
Then I hear a voice say, "Is the baby fed?"
I roll back over with a pillow on my face.
I want to run away, I'm sick of this place.
Now it's 6:00 a.m., time to awake
To do my unappreciated work and get another headache.

Tabatha Carlson

Harbor My Soul

My soul is a harbor anchored by emotions,
Which endlessly find their way in, never to escape,
Infinite thoughts of jubilation, love, lust, longing, peace, sorrow.
Any conceivable emotion, experienced infinite numbers
Of times, have fastened themselves to my being as
A barnacle would to the face of a rock.

But alas the once resilient shades of color which
was the make up of my anchored soul,

Have now become void of any color.
Shades of grey surround my inner vessel as I have
Become consumed and defeated by all that I feel,
As there is no release for this all consuming being.
There will be no loosening of the well practiced
Knots clutching the harbor docks.

For my soul has entered into a demanding existence,
So void of expression, so accepting of this charted course,
My ship has sailed as it were.
I will remain adrift through eternity,
Filled with love, empty of hope.

Heidi Plangg

You Are to Me

It has been a while now
In life we met, in dreams we shared
You told me your story, I told you mine
In thoughts we made love, in friendship we found comfort
You opened your heart to me
In return you made it easy to open mine for you

In times I have often reflected what you meant to me
I looked inside, around and above
I realized I could not be me
If it weren't for your love

In your passion I find the courage
To do all the things I do
In amazing ways you have supported me
What would I have done alone I just don't have a clue

Like pebbles in a stream life shapes us as it flows along
The future comes to us, like raindrops from the sky
The past fades away, like mist on a new summer day
I do not know the rest, nor do I care
For I love you now, and I will love you then

Kiran Rao

Survivor

My name is Jacob, and I was a happy Jew,
Living in Germany, something I never knew.
They wanted us dead for so very long,
They wanted us to leave, they wanted us gone.
I was petrified when they took me away,
I remember that moment still to this day.
The trucks rumbling was thunder on the road,
They stole us away, load after load.
We wanted to escape so badly we did,
Some tried to run, but others just hid.
Many were shot, as I was told,
They killed the young, weak, and old.
All the others were forced to work and labor,
We had little time with ourselves to savor.
Although harsh, I refused to shed a tear,
What they had against us was very unclear.
So this is my story, as I tell again,
I'm a survivor, grateful how it's been.
I never thought I'd get out of there alive,
but I held on to life, and I surely survived.

Ashley Suzanne Denney

Dance

He thinks he'll save me.
"Take it slow," he says when my nail splits.
He knows it's not my fault, but he needs someone to blame.
He says he'd take me to a land of purple diamonds, if he could.
Let me twirl in my jelly shoes among moonstones.
He wants to see me run. He wonders what it's like.
I wonder, too. In the meantime, I can concoct my mythical potions.
I will cast a spell on you, Daddy.
I will make it so you don't cry anymore.
Dance with me among the purple diamonds;
hide with me from the ripples of fluid within me.
I don't want to be a window watcher, Daddy.
The cracks in the ceiling are converging into little shapes,
and they scare me.
Let's go catch some lightning bugs.
Tie that red ribbon in my hair and we will dance among them.
They will electrify your skin.
I will prove to you that I am well.
My fluid will become a spring and it will nourish me.
I'm not scared, Daddy. Come with me and let's dance.

Jill Carleen Balota

Rejoice This Day

Somber boredom fills the temple;
Silent emptiness . . . our fault.
People stare and criticize;
Envy rules our thoughts.
What's wrong with song? And laugh? And play?
What's wrong with pure delight?
Birds are scared to sing today;
Butterflies afraid of flight.
Economy now owns this Earth,
Showing nature no respect.
The pollution of technology
Has ruined our intellect.
Think, people, of the stars
Set in dazed designs.
Look, people, at nature itself.
See what you've denied.
Feel, people, the little things;
Like love and truth and dreams.
Fight, people, for a life.
Listen as it screams.

Adea L. Humphries

A Lover Like You

Six months ago I never could
Have imagined a lover like you
Oceans are broken when our love is spoken
laughter is heard Without saying a word
Imagining you I always would
Six months ago I never could

Encouraging glances you touch me gently
Each day to moisten my heart as it cries
And with tears of joy I desire to be
The man you see when you look in my eyes

With every night passed you've comforted me
From love spilling warm from the depth of Your soul
In you I now see how a lover should
Six months ago I never could

And now dreams dance effortlessly
From your lips to mine
As Reality sparkles to our place in time
Creation somehow joined the two
Who could have imagined a lover like you

Damon A. Boucher

Marriage

Walking along a moonlit path
As one we walk into the grass
Upon the bench we sit you and I
Together forever, side by side
We started this walk fifty years to the day
Neither would have it any other way
Holding your frail hand in mine
I'll love you forever, till the end of time
And though we know that our time is near
We won't waste our time, shedding one tear
Looking back at all that we've done
At our beautiful daughter, and our son
Good times and bad, we've shared them all
Took turns picking each other up, after a fall
For richer, for poorer, in sickness and in health
The love in our hearts, our measure of wealth
So when the time comes, that it's our turn to go
When the Angels appear, I want you to know
We have no regrets, we've lived a full life
Remember us always, as husband and wife.

Michael Robert Hildebrand

Love You Forevermore!

You are the one for me,
Days gone by and all you are, is on my mind.
In my heart the pain is great.
Where you are I don't know, but in my heart you will stay.
The sky still blue with big white clouds and
the days are grey my heart to see.
there is no more you and me.
I will love you forevermore 'cause you are
the one, no one has ever put this straight
to me that feelings could last so long.
Years gone by and no calls and no show the
sky still seeing you the clouds are your
name and the blue is for the feeling I've been feeling for you.
I will love you forevermore, God has shown
that one day you and I will walk together
again. And the clouds that are so beautiful
and bright is where we will be walking together.
love you forevermore, my sweet love that
lives in my heart and soul by the grace I
feel feelings of you. . . .

Eugenia Guarino-Yenchi

Nights of Giving

As night comes for the last of my rest,
Dressed in white to look my best.
As I take one last peep at my home,
I go to take care of those that are alone.
Some would say "I wouldn't work that shift!"
But each patient I tend to is like a gift.
I punch in at the clock at the hour of ten,
Clearing all outside matter off my mind then,
For Mr. Jones' call bell starts to ring.
As I answer his call, I hear Mrs. King.
One by one as they settle in for sleep,
Someone hollers out, "I'm ready to eat!"
I check Mrs. Hall to see if she is wet.
Mr. C. wants to know, is it time to get up yet?
All gets quiet around one and two,
Recording in the a.d.l. charts I have to do.
Morning has come as the night has wound down.
I check from room to room on my last go-around
I smile as I say goodbye to all,
For the love is worth, it great or small.

Clara Thrash

The Special Girl I Love!

On the coldest days, and darkest nights, I
see you in my dreams. I think about you all
through the day and feel a sense of security.
My heart warms my body when we are together or
when we are apart. I've been looking for you
all my life and have only found you now. Your
eyes are beautiful which match with your smile,
leaving me in a world of Fantasy! To believe
that you can make me cry, with tears of happiness
instead of sorrow. Our love is like a powerful
unstoppable force. I love everything about you,
there is nothing that I would want to change
or could possibly change. I love you for who
you are and not for what others want you to be.
When we shared our first kiss on top of the
mountain, I knew you were the girl I would
love for a long time. I will always protect you
from what I can, you are too special to me. I
can't imagine not being by your side. A tear
forms as I write, but will eventually fall.

Tim Malone

If I Had a Star

If I had a star it would be as bright as you.
A star is loaded with five corners.
The first point is beginning a new life with you.
The second corner is sweet and loving
like you. The third corner is open and
honest and keeping your word. The fourth
corner is always be open and talk about your
problems never keep them to yourself that
will never help you. The fifth corner is
coming together with you as our chosen
family member to spend time growing and
learning with you. Stars are as bright as
you and they are great to look at and dream
of loving stars and learning things
together. God choose you to be my son and
God never makes mistakes. I will enjoy
being your mother and growing with you and
learning new things with you. Love and
kisses and lots of hugs. Love your mom and Jesus.

Nancy Underwoodm

The Fool

I gaze at you across the room
and close my eyes.
I hear the aria of your voice
echoing in my mind.
The rush of hands push me down,
the pointing and cursing
at a condemned body of crystal and ice.
I break through, unaware of the footprints
I've left in the sand.
Hollow hearts follow the path
to live inside my soul and
breed their anger and
weave their hatred into me.
I thought you cared, I thought you
wanted the way things fell into place.
I lived with it
and wished an imagined state of mind,
teetering on the edge of insanity,
leaning on the brink of love,
and falling off.

Chelsey Michelle Nulle

Welcome the Joy

It may have been just a chance,
To perhaps give this ol' heart a dance.
It also may be, that we don't normally see
Just what it is He has for thee.
For the joy that comes from up above,
Will give us all a Heavenly love.
And it will never fail to bring,
Just what it is we need for these hearts to sing.
You see, Jesus came to die for us all,
And through this death there was a call.
A call for us to believe in Him,
And that He was sent to die for our sins.
Three days later He rose from the dead,
A jubilation for the blood that was shed.
This is where my joy comes in,
For He has risen and is alive again.
Thank you God for sending Your Son,
And thank you Jesus for all you have done.
Thank you for the joy you bring,
And for the love in my heart that longs to sing.

Brenda Johnson

Lizard Love

I have two lizards, Bonnie and Clyde.
Under the wood chips, they like to hide.
They are a lovely little pair,
Even though they have no hair.
I feed them crickets every day.
I find them in a bale of hay.
Most of the time, they just sleep
Under the lamp in the nice, warm heat.
They don't talk or make a sound,
But they like to wiggle on the ground.
They are not big, they are not small.
They are very short, they are not tall.
They do not run, they do not play.
Put a finger in their mouth, and you will pay.
They have big nails, they have sharp teeth.
They have long tails, they have small feet.
Bonnie is expecting, a mother she will be.
Then they will be a big family.
I love my lizards, oh, yes, I do!
And if you knew them, so would you!

Travis J. Horwath

Some Thoughts for My Child

When does life begin?
At conception or birth or when you are Loved?
If this is true, then you have been alive for quite some time,
Even though I will never get to know you
Or see the kind of person you would have grown up into.
You will always be a part of me.
I must admit, I sometimes question God's ways.
If you were here, my life would be very different.
Mainly, your sister would not be my daughter,
But would belong to someone else.
And because of your death, I cherish her more.
Thank you for that lesson.
But, losing you tore my life apart.
Slowly, with the help of loved ones, I put my life back together.
But, the piece that is you will always be broken.
Now, I keep your memory up in the back storage closet
Of my mind and heart.
On certain occasions, I take it out and breathe you in.
I will pack your memory up for another time.
You will always be a part of me.

Sharon M. White

Polaroid

The camera flashes, chemical reaction.
Instant images jerk me into reality.

Is that me?
Where was the woman,
beautiful and proud,
full of life? Sharp.

All I see is this
old, lifeless woman,
trying to get used to this body,
breathe life into it.

The beautiful one
peeking out from beneath the shadows. Dull.

The flashes continue as I scream
wait a minute—let me compose myself.
Sit tall; hold that head up high.

Pretend for a moment
until the picture
develops.

Kathleen Kubik

Dream

What was it?
A mist—faint but cool?
A web—which I had woven
and got entangled into?
It wasn't either.

It was a colorful thread intricately woven
with beads of emotion
which kept on lengthening day by day.

It turned later to be a chain—
which tied a knot so tight
that it made me swirl and twist.
Later—
it pulled me deep into an abyss.
Lost forever.
Deep down, there was total darkness.
I could see—a flame
shimmering and flickering,
opening up a new horizon
totally unknown to me!

Amita Hegde

The Moonlight Night

So far in the heavens above
Shining down, white as a dove
Casting light and shadows on us all
Upon this tiny, little ball
Up in the velvet blackness of the sky
Looking over us like an angel's eye
Sister Sun not out to play
But daughter Moon is out, out to stay
You share your beauty on this cloudless night
For me and my lovers delight
Her body cradled in my arms, head upon my chest
Playing who loves who best
A warm glow upon her cheeks
In her hair, moonlight streaks
As we stare into each others eyes
Thinking, what if's, how's and why's
The embrace grows tight
Both of us wait for the moment right
Closing our eyes, both turning our heads
As our lips match our warm embrace

Keith Flaherty, Jr.

Retired

In days of old he came here often,
to meet the dragon's fire
But now those days have gone forever,
his time come to retire
For one day prior he met his foe,
the last one of its kind
His might was strong his courage fierce,
his reason out of mind
The dragon fought for his own life
and those who went before
But the dragon's cause was lost that day,
against the knightly lore
And so, the dragon vanquished,
the knight returned to home
To find his life now empty,
no reason left to roam
And so he stands here one last time,
to face his terrible deed
He understands the awful truth . . .
The dragons filled his need . . .

Daniel Berry

An Autumn Encounter

I felt His presence on the porch today,
As I left to go on my usual way.
He gave me a gift; a majestic morn!
I thanked Him for a new day born.
The crisp, cool feel of the autumn air
Wrapped around my skin and hair.
The piercing blue of the cloudless sky
Took my breath, momentarily, and drew my eye.
Leaves sailed swiftly to their bed below,
Soon to lie under a blanket of snow.
He whispered softly, that He believed in my dream.
He encouragingly lifted my self-esteem.
He reminded me He'd planted dreams in my soul,
And together we could accomplish any goal.
He said dreams needed tending, as gardens do.
I saw the dream from a new point of view.
He gave me tools, said we'd work side by side . . .
My dream could blossom, if in Him I'd abide.
He got my attention in His masterful way . . .
This time, through the artistry of His stunning autumn day.

Barbara Sue Daniels

Wishes

Have you ever gone to wish upon a star,
And realized that you had nothing to wish for?
You can wish for anything you want,
Realistic or not, at least there's something.
But what if you realized one day,
That you've lost all faith in make-believe?
Wishes seem so unimportant, but they're not.
Life is meaningless without wishes.
If you have nothing to wish for,
Then you have nothing to dream for.
If you have nothing to dream for,
Then you have nothing to hope for.
And without hope, life is worthless.
Have you ever looked up at the stars
And realized that no matter how hard you wish,
None of your dreams will come true?
Wishes are important, but reality hits hard.
Dreams are our break from life.
Never lose your wishes,
For they are the base of all creativity.

Amanda Rorick

Loneliness

As I sit here and wonder
what I did wrong
I find comfort here in the grand silence of my home
the memories I have will stain me forever
and when I die, I hope my body to wither
because in death, there is no pain
and you won't be able to get to me
through my stone walls, I will be protected
my loneliness will comfort me
and keep my secrets safe and warm
I can't wait to be buried
and take all the secrets and treasures to my grave
I long to be with the sky and stars
among the heavens, where I can look upon my loved ones
and so I cut my wrist with a sharp knife
and lay down
and as my soul creeps from me,
I forget why I chose this . . .
but then I remember you
and realize that I'm finally safe

Karen Lisa Fernandez

My Forbidden Love

The love that I felt,
I thought it was gone,
deeply buried inside of me.
I thought it was no longer there. . . .
Out of touch, out of bounds,
that was our love.
But one look at you and I know
the fire still burns deep inside
steadily . . .
it had never stopped burning
and it burns . . . still.
How can I tell you, could I tell you
do you know what I felt for you
what I still feel for you
for I still do love you
and I do.
But
I could no longer tell you
My secret
My forbidden love.

Asma Mohd Fauzi

Thoughts of Her

Thoughts of you

My Love, when I am with you,
Never once I feel the blue.
Your smile lights up my face.
I have everything, nothing left to chase.
The happiness I feel burns my very soul,
You are the last thing, my ultimate goal.
But I cannot help to think
If this boat is ever going to sink.

If these thoughts of you and me

Will ever turn bitter and cold,
Or will my heart ever be sold?
Will you turn your back on me,
And my precious love, can you not see?
Will it be easy for you to forget,
And pretend that we never met?

If it is like that and life is so,
I really need to know, for I must learn to let go.

Arif Gilany

Back to My Roots

From the cloud covered hilltops
to the bottom lands below
Around the curvy narrow roads
that guide us gently home
We're raised here and then we leave
but not before we learn
instilled in us a heritage
from which we'll never turn
Many years we may travel
many countries we may see
But in the end we turn toward
the place we'd rather be
The peaceful morning dew upon a spider's web
The humming of the bees around a farmer's sweaty head
The laughter of a little child skipping rocks in a creek
A sleepy afternoon in a private woods retreat
The baying of a coon hound upon a fresh new scent
The blessings being said at dusk as we sit down to eat
As lights begin to fade and shadows slowly creep
We bank the fire together and then we go to sleep

Connie Elaine Haddox

Internet Friend

Eyes appear through a grey sky
With hand waving to the world
Happiness is coming again
As I search for the perfect girl
Women come and women go
Breaking hearts along the way
Thank you for your friendship
It is special to me today
My pride was lost, I had fallen from grace
You have helped me to regain my place
Embarrassed by sorrow I ran to you
Friendship everlasting I will always hold true
You have comforted me in time of despair
Picked me up and showed you care
You have produced a smile from a face unknown
Your heartfelt friendship is worth more than gold
You have helped me in a time of need
A loving heart from a stranger indeed
If your heart is ever in strife
Remember this, you have a friend for life

Larry Weston

I Will Wait

So sad . . . so mad . . . yet all due to fear.
So deep in the hole of emptiness.
No grace seems sufficient . . . though it is.
Now with time, time only, on my side,

So much pain . . . relentless pain.
With the fire of Hell burning on my spine.
How long must I suffer?
Who really knows?
Not I . . . so I will wait.

Sleepless nights . . . endless days.
With people all around,
Yet I feel so alone . . .
So far removed from earthly things.
I suffer in silence . . . so I will wait.

If one day I cannot, what shall I do?
I pray for relief onto what seems like deaf ears.
God does hear me pray, yet he is not ready to answer.
Am I willing to stay? Can there be a way?
I know not for sure . . . so I will wait.

Sue Ann Vick

Pass Through

The Ghost of myself wanders blindly amidst
The throng and the crowds—amidst life.
Life flows by, life flows away.
Life never flows through,
Like a river cleaved in two
By cold and empty desert.
Nothing resides in translucent chest;
Only an echo of some heart's beating
From long, long ago.
No friend to memory, no memory to friend;
Not forgotten,
Only unremembered and unremembering;
Untouched and untouchable.
And it passes through blood and bone,
Wood and stone.
Never knowing once, never passing twice
Anyone at all.
The Ghost of myself stands silently still
Amidst the crowds and the throng—
Amidst life.

Lloyd Aquino

Yesterday

Years of laughter, years of tears—
together we have been through many fears.
Fights and furies, rage and hate,
love and caring, hopes for sharing.
Good times and bad times,
together we've seen,
friends melt away into the distant
light of our pasts,
love grows strong
even when we thought
it wouldn't last.
Confident smiles line the
walkway to your life,
so you'll give a firm handshake
and be done—
I'm sure you'll remember all the fun.
With amazing grace
you'll walk with pride
into the light of tomorrow
leaving yesterday behind.

Jamie Ann Bunt

Stormy

As the wind howls,
the shutters smack and swing.
Rain pounds the cold pavement.
The clouds grow darker and closer
moving quickly, as if they were trying,
trying to trap the village looming far below.

A girl sits in a corner crying, silently.
She worries no mother, makes no sound
she just cries,
cries because of all the wrong
that has been set upon her.

Her tears of salt soon stop,
just as the rain and storm did so.
The ground outside is moist with fresh rain,
her pale cheeks salty wet.
She wipes them dry as she walks away,
away from all the wrong, away from the pain
and away from the village
where it was so often stormy.

Becky Cassidy

Fun

Take time to laugh and play
Not sometime, but every day,
For laughter fills the soul with smiles
As innocent as a little child,
Open up your heart to shine
Then gentle pleasures you will find,
There's always time to work or worry
But in the future you'll be sorry,
If the time you have not taken
For peace and joy you'll be makin',
The wonderful memories you will cherish
Will be yours forever, never to perish,
The things we hold dear to our hearts
Would take the scale clear off the charts,
For when you take time to have fun
Trophies of treasures you'll have won,
So enjoy each moment the best you can
Making them multiply as grains of sand,
Life is too short to not have fun
So make the most of it before day is done.

Betty LaVonne Sargent

Little Boston Terror

Born in the early morning of 1997,
in March of '98 I'd meet Noel, a gift from Heaven.
Quite literally I mean that,
she arrived on Christmas Day !
Could I go home without this pup ?
The answer there—no way!
Puppy adolescence is tough, most people say.
The price tag for her love I know, in furniture I pay.
Pillows shredded, futon unstuffed, the coffee table's toast.
Separation anxiety? " Just curious," she boasts.
I say, "Bad dog!" then feel remorse,
when regretful pout she shows.
Despite this stage of "devil dog,"
a loving friendship grows.
Enrolled in doggy college, where discipline is sold,
I'll stop destructive habits before she gets too old.
She excelled at everything she learned,
now that her goal was set.
She'd "sit" and "come" and "heal" for weeks,
at the end, first prize she'd get.

Rochelle Peterson

Mixed Feelings

I don't know what I am feeling,
could it be love?
I thought he was my one and only
I thought he was my soul mate.
But what I thought was only a dream,
a dream that was so untrue.
I hurt so bad inside, I don't know what to do.
Should I tell him how I feel,
how my heart beats for him every day.
Or should I keep it inside,
if fear of my feelings scaring him away.
My heart tells me,
these feelings are so strong,
Not telling him would be wrong.
So I will take a breath,
and tell him of my love.
I will tell him that it is him
that I am always thinking of.
If he pushes me away in the end,
I know some way, somehow, my broken heart will mend.

Amber Nicole Robbins

A Babe

Warily I came into this world,
Screaming and crying with all my might.
Born of woman. Creation of man.
The earth my home, as long as it can.
Without a care, peacefully I sleep.
Unaware of disasters I've yet to meet.
Unaware the world's a funny place.
Full of scorn, full of hate.
Yet to understand
Why God put me on this land.
I am loved and cared. Oh, so much.
Their voices music to my ears.
In an abyss all my own.
Unaware of what is yet to come.
My soul is clean; no wrong can I do.
For to this world I am still new.
My actions are honest, my thoughts sincere.
I am still a babe without any fear.
The young are meek; the meek are mild.
What will happen when I'm a child no more.

Maria Upyr

Wake Me from This Dream of Mine

I had a dream about this life of mine
Winding roads and crooked paths
Down the path no Y did I see
Just arrows pointing up and down
What is real and what is not?
Ringing circles spinning round
Which way do I go? I can't seem to find a road
I have known many things in this life of mine
Nothing compares with this
Wake me up from this dream of mine
Knock three times so I can't hear
Although I'm only 29 I feel like I'm 99
Double the trouble, double the fun
when does life stop and start
I'm doing triple time
can't stand to watch the time
Lights are blinking red and green
should I stay or should I go
All I wish is to wake up
and end this silly dream

Melodie Mahaffey

Personal Highway

Sun-baked blacktop cradles me softly
on my own personal highway
Reflections dot the edges
Keeping me on course
Resurfacing with an angry rumble when I
stray, speeds steal your breath.
Winds, swirling thoughts in my mind.
A chaotic dance.
My journey. My highway.
Stillness allows me to look deeper.
Reflections of meaning of purpose.
Entering my personal highway, they journey
with me on this blacktop experience.
Soon they exit, unwilling? Unfulfilled?
I continue on hopeful of many things.
The highway soon will narrow.
My journey soon will end.
Now only the rear view mirror holds
proof of my journey,
and of my personal highway.

John Provost

What's Inside

As you look into the mirror,
You see a figment of yourself.
It's like a picture on the wall,
An image of oneself.
It's only just a mimic
Of who you think you are.
You should look beyond that face
And search for something more.
If you think what matters most
Is perfection on your outside,
You, my friend, have got it wrong
And will run into trouble as the years go by.
You will never have what it takes
To be someone great.
All the future holds for you
Is a downhill path of fate.
So if all that's ever on your mind
Is how you look outside,
Look beyond your flesh and bones
Deep down to what's inside.

Jessica Donna Reinhardt

Fireflies

Nights grow longer and the wind starts to blow,
The moon is as white as snow,
Fireflies start to twinkle and whisper when they glow.
Little kids begin to laugh and play,
Dazed by the night and tired from the day.
The night brings smiles aimed towards the sky,
The fast firefly sparks a twinkle in their eye.
One of those moments you stop in your sight,
A classic example of pure delight.
The bug so bright, the moon so white,
A wonderful sound rings in the night.
It never brings fright but a whole lot of joy,
Like a child on Christmas with a brand new toy.
Staring at bugs who glow and glisten,
A chirping sound just to stop and listen.
A moment to be called a limited edition
Like a Grandpa and a young boy fishin'.
All of this happiness and pure delight
On a calm and mellow night
When the fireflies take to flight.

Joel Antone Christensen

The Day You Were Born

The soft orange sky
chilled the air that day
I could see my icy breath forming
on the way to the hospital
Go back, I thought,
remembering Valentine's Day when
I gave in to
passion lust chocolates
a diamond ring and your father.
Now you were fully formed
perfect and ready to emerge
breathe push breathe push
blood placenta tears screams
You—beautiful,
pure you:
mine
You changed me:
loved to loving
child to woman
woman to mother.

Cortney L. Hodges

Letting Go

As I look at the moon on this starless night
I replace my thoughts with daydreaming
my sporadic consciousness keeps me to
reality, though I start believing this fantasy
I turn and see her, him, it
I feel the nervous anxiety
I want to speak of how I feel
Then I awake and find this not to be real
He slowly returns to my thoughts
His face I can see through a series of lines
Again I want to speak, nothing will come
The words start floating from my mouth
He seems to understand
He touches my hand and I feel relief
A new mind set replaces my grief
The past is what made me
The future is what will break me down
and build me up
So I will grow and I will learn at this time
abrupt

Michael Kreplin

Tomorrow's Child

MS is very serious
Even if the cure is unknown
Maybe I can help a little
By writing this thoughtful poem
Teach tomorrow's children to reach higher
Have expectations and goals
Help them recognize friends and prayer
Are important for their souls
Take all their guns and weapons
Throw them at their feet
Say no to drugs and violence
Keep them off the street
Be there when you're needed
Listen and understand
Take the time and enjoy them
Education is the plan
Montel, tomorrow's child
Depends upon us a lot
So I thank you from my heart
For letting me share this thought

Dirk A. Marple

Enigma

I see with my soul
I hear from my lips
I feel with my heart
I speak with my eyes
I smell not the fragrance of flowers
I see not the colors in the petals
I envy not the dreams in my eyes
For I do not dream
For I live not to cherish my life
For my hope left me long ago
For I am a widow of my dream
Conflagration is what exists in me
Avenge is what I seek
Of the death of my love
The storms have dried my body
The deserts have quenched my thirst
The pain has given me pleasure
A puzzle is what I am, the pieces scattered
He will come and join the edges
He of whom I am a widow.

Sheheryar Hafeez

What Is Love . . .

Love—
the worst thing about it
is the harder you try understanding,
the more confusing it seems.
  Love is misleading;
    it's a few-minutes feeling,
    but when you least expect it,
    it blossoms,
    like a rose on a hot summer day.
  Love is complicated;
    it gives out mixed signals,
    but worst of all,
    it could end up in disaster.
  Love is unpredictable,
    one day you think you're in love,
    the next, suffer from a broken heart.
Love—
the best thing about it
is that it is an emotion,
one that makes you feel special!

Tania Chevalier

My Life

My goals and ambitions: clouded with hate,
Trapped by evil, it's a fool's fate.
I constantly sin and have lost my way.
When I need something, then I pray.
I know it's not right; I've lost all hope.
I think I'm damn near at the end of my rope.
I want to do something to make Mom proud;
Instead I walk around with my head bowed,
Longing for a girl to call my own,
But how can you love, with a heart of stone?
I used to care, until I got hurt.
It seems like girls treat me like dirt.
There's only two girls I've truly loved,
And right back at me, my feelings shoved.
I need to get away for a couple of years,
Find myself, shed some tears.
My life is hard, but I let no one see;
Many would think I'm always happy.
This is my life—what would you do?
Would you overcome it, or just stay blue?

Keith Bryant

My Garden

In my Garden
The flowers bloom,
The children play,
And the sun shines bright!
Not all Gardens start out this way.
In each Garden there's a rainy day.
In mine it rained
And rained and poured some more.
Then the day came when the sun shone through.
A fine ray brought a world brand-new!
A tiny bird started to sing
And made me realize a little something:
The sun shines everywhere;
To enjoy it, you have to be there!
Feel it in your heart,
And it will follow you along the road!
Every time it rains,
You know that tomorrow
There will be a bright rainbow!
That's why your Garden is so beautiful!

Janie Michaud

The Picture

Here I am Brothers, Sisters, and Mothers,
the sometimes forgotten images of others.
Frame me hang me on a wall,
make me dominant first one in the hall.
Images past and present captured in Ink,
printed on paper eyes never to blink.
Faces of people who love you a lot,
vivid in color and sometimes not.
Time may fade their colors as you know,
years passing dictates this to be so.
But as the years pass and people grow old,
within this frame are memories you can hold.
Newer pictures arrive, and this they must,
but don't hide me away to gather dust.
Look at me often, but don't shed tears,
think instead of many memories we share.
In dark of night when thoughts turn gray and bleak,
when life hands you more then you seek.
Turn your mind to images on the wall,
listen hard you hear timeless faces call.

Marvin L. Cole

The Color Symphony

Color swirls all around me,
music drifts in and out of my mind.
I dance through the colors and sway to the music.
The colors change with the music and slowly they turn
from bright to dull,
dark,
dreary.
The music slowly changes from cheerful to
sad,
low,
depressing.
I slow my movements to match the music and make my dance
more graceful,
elaborate.
My mind is flowing with the color and song, as suddenly
the song ends, and I come out of my reverie.
The dream is over.
The color is gone, the music has died, but remnants are
left behind.
The dream is over, for now.

Krista Pattie

Wendy and Peter

Peter Pan—a child who found my heart
Or, rather, I found his shadow
Through an open window
Waiting to awake my sleeping eyes.
They opened; I found a sparkle in his ways
Through his soul.
Every night he flew to my side
The window was always wide open.
I could even see his shadow before his presence arrived
And my heart dropped when I saw him standing
Before me waiting for a last kiss good night.
With one twitch and a move of his lips, he always fell asleep.
One morning I awoke to something I had never known,
As I looked through my window I saw a sadness in
Peter's soul, he had closed the window the night before.
He left with no reason at all.
I grew up from then on with the glass pane shut
Tight and Peter stayed a child with Wendy by his side.
I can't release my good-bye's through the window of my soul,
And he'll stay a child alone forever more.

Nikki DeRusha

To All the Mothers

Who have lost a child that was killed
We all have something in common
We share a certain kind of pain
And sometimes it makes us feel insane
We go through the emotional distress
Now let's continue with the rest
With the pain of our lost
Now the tears and the chills
Oh, Lord give us the will
When the Birthdays and holidays roll around
And we want to hear the sweet sounds of their voices
On solid ground we have no choice
But to deal with the pain that will always feel the same
So it's time to get down on your knees
And pray for you and me just talk to your Heavenly father
Because he always has the time to be bothered
And Lord send us a sign
So we won't scream or holler Oh, Lord teach us to pray
So we can live safer through the day
We love you Lord in so many ways

Betty L. King

A Birthday Wish

A day of joy turns into a day of pain
How I wish you were here living again
My day would not be filled with torment and sorrow
Only hopes of a better tomorrow
Though your presence is felt through God's grace
I would much rather prefer a warm, felt embrace
Reminiscing on the times we were together
Thinking, how could this ever get any better
The answer to my question is simple and sweet
Only if you could have overcame the fire and rose above defeat
Ultimately, God has a divine plan
We, as a people, are just simple man
The life you lived was not in vain
You helped plant, nurture, and provide for a grain
The grain, which has developed into a blossoming tree
Unmistakably, that would be me
I shall finish where you left off, when life was pure
Praying to never go through what you had to endure
I am at ease, knowing you are protected
With you in my heart, I will never feel neglected.

Aisha Toney

The Light beneath the Door

When a room in our life becomes empty
And the door is tightly closed,
And the only entrance permitted
Is that of memories of joys and woes,
Then faith directs our vision
To see the light beneath the door
That spreads its rays of hope,
And leads us to seek for more.
Like a beacon in a raging storm,
The search for a cure prevails,
So the millions who suffer from MS
Will be freed from the cell where they're jailed.
We wait with tear-stained faces
And hearts that bear great grief,
While time escapes around us
And fear guards us with no relief.
Yet strength and courage come to visit
Each time faith holds the key as before,
And points from the wall of compassion
To the light beneath the door.

Emily Ann Dean

A True Gift

I love God's creations, Mother and Earth
I'm going to compare them, for what it's worth
You always find a way to cure my pain
You are my cover from the rain
I know I'm at the moon
It won't be long, I'll be home soon
If you look at the brightest star
We can see each other from afar
You smile at me like a blooming flower
You give me light in my darkest hour
You shine on me like the sun
Wait a minute, I'm not done
It doesn't matter how far away
In my heart is where you'll stay
I know the past has been more than rough
I've seen you cry, I've had enough
You're the best thing that's happened to me
I found the way to let you see
You gave me God, God gave me you
We'll just pray to make it through.

Bret Galvin

Painless Love

Oh, how my heartache
Is this scene of my life real or is it fake
Often I think back on how I gave you my all
But you were not the man I thought to catch
me if I were to fall
Sometimes while I'm reminiscing
My heart tells my mind to just listen
There are times the past can be so devastating
To say that least I find the past to be very much so aggravating
I gave birth to your baby boy
I feel like you took my body for a toy
You can only dream about how he has brought me so much joy.
If you wouldn't try to cause me so much trouble
Maybe our friendship could seem to just bubble
I can no longer hold onto the past
Heartaches and pains are not made to last
I have learned my lesson, only God I trust
In the first place this should have been a must
Now I know the reason why at so many weddings they release the dove
To capture the moment of painless love

Vivian Holder

Faith

The evil flows through her veins, the heartache and pain,
the scars that remain, a life of insane.
He takes her away to the street, all the strangers she will meet,
a life of crime and defeat, all the pain with no relief;
that life of bittersweet.
No place to sleep, no food to eat.
No Satan, you will not win the life of sin.
She belongs to my Lord, Jesus,
who covers her in the darkness of night with his light.
My Jesus sends His angels to watch over my child
and I know she will be back to me in a short while.
I will hold on to my faith, no matter how long I will wait.
I will never let her go because I love her so.
She is a part of me that I will never set free.
The ache in my heart I could no longer bare
if I did not have Jesus there.
The nights are long, the dreams that take me far away.
I always need to pray that Jesus gets her through another day.
If she were taken away from me tomorrow,
my heart could never bear the sorrow.

Debra German

Athena

In memory I see her beautiful face,
The deep sapphire of her eyes,
The long, soft curl
Of her glorious light hair,
Her skin like alabaster—
Alabaster, yes, yet with the sheen
Of exquisite French porcelain.
The moonlight brings
Her enchantment nearer;
The starlight brings
Her enchantment dearer.
No man ever loved a woman more.
My wife, my bride,
But alas, alas she died
Too young, too young, too young.
Twenty years ago she was in my arms
Unto this day with all her charms.
Though from the grave she rules my heart,
She rules my heart, she rules my heart,
Athena will forever rule my heart.

Ethel Mae Zarr

Metaphysics

In this day and time, I find myself refine,
Possessing a mind, one of a kind divine.
And there is no difference with what you possess,
We are all from the same source of consciousness.
It's just which of the unconscious chooses to use it,
I choose to use my gift through music.
We all have faith, it's just some of us lose it,
Nike summed up life best with the slogan "Just Do It."
Know that God is not beyond the sky,
Crush this lie, He resides within you and I.
The inner eye knows and it's all fundamental,
Each of us holds infinite potential.
Let go of your self-doubt, throw the earth shades out,
Learn what life is all about as you stroll the route.
Of the spiritual, yes, it is metaphysical,
So every day to me is a simple miracle.
It's so habitual to know my good is here and now,
That's why I walk around with a big Kool-aid smile.
Nobody can bring me down like gravity,
For I have the spirit of God in me.

Eric Franco

Misconception of Love

A misconception of our love,
Confessions, secrets, no one could think of
The reality of life, it is such a sight
Communication, passion, honesty
The facts upon us
His heart beats in pain
Such wonder, such shame, who is to blame
Is he in love, or is it a fling
Doubt it there's too much pain
Reminiscent of love
A mystery to be found
A misconception of our love,
To be fonder, than thrown away
Love we say,
May that be the actual solution
Love should not be an excuse
Nor a monopolization of the mind
It should be a relationship, to defeat
A misconception of our love,
That is what the conclusion shall be. . . .

Katishka Dioone Brown

Do You Remember?

Do you remember, lest we forget,
Their wives wiping tears and whispering, don't go, not yet?
Do you remember the ones who fought,
Too young to be called men, too old to be taught?
Do you remember the stiffening silence,
Amongst all the terrible violence?
Do you remember the blood curdling screams,
And deafening sounds of war machines?
Do you remember the blood-drenched clothes,
The sickening stench of dead man's bones?
Do you remember the thousands of graves,
The names and the medals of those who were brave?
Do you remember the doctors trying
So hard to keep each one from dying?
Do you remember the ear piercing sounds,
And the bodies of soldiers littered on the ground?
Do you remember the poppies that grew,
Between the crosses, two by two?
Do you remember on this eleventh day, month and hour,
Why we pause to say thanks with a little red flower?

Kristen Lister

The Real Me

I wish I could take off my mask
show you the real me,
how I wish you could see.
People make me laugh
people make me cry,
the part of me you see
is not the real me
I have a fragile heart
you'd never believe
inside I'm falling apart
I just wish you could only see.
I'm afraid you may not like me
if I decide to wash the paint from my face.
You may think I'm stupid,
and find a new friend to take my place.
I'd love to free my thoughts,
not keep them locked up
but the clown inside me
won't let it happen
he always interrupts.

Teresa Hogshooter

A Birth Mother's Story

Years ago I held you in my arms,
So small, so sweet, with all your baby charms.
I cared for you for six, short weeks
With many a kiss on your little cheeks.
Then a stranger took you from my arms,
"It's for the best," they all insisted.
"Go on with your life, forget he existed."
Life went on, but the memories lingered—
"Where were you? Was your life good?"
Then one day a letter came,
Call this number; tell us your name.
You had searched for me for nine long years.
We've talked and wrote, so much to say.
All those years are slipping away.
We decide to meet, time goes so slow,
Then two days of hustle, meeting me and mine,
Talking, hugging, meeting me and mine.
As each other we get to know,
My "mistake" is no longer a shame.
I'm proud to say, "son," when I mention your name.

Mary J. Perrault

What Is Love?

What is love?
Maybe something from up above.
You think of them constantly in your mind.
Every second you may find.
If your love is true, it will last forever,
No matter what problems or defeats you may endeavor.
If your love is going to last,
You may have to set aside things from your past.
You may have feelings from deep within your heart
Hoping that you never part.
Everything they say carries you away.
Every time you hear their voice,
Your heart races bearing no other choice.
What is love?
Love is something to be cherished by all,
Anyone slender, tall, or small.
The first time you see their face you'll know you have found love.
It must have come from the stars above
When you stare at the stars above,
Ask yourself, what is love?

Jeffrey Carlyle Overton, Jr.

Homeless No More

I found an old coat, but it was badly worn
It was dirty and the sleeves were torn.
Oh, it wasn't so bad, but I knew it was all I had.
I put it on and walked down the street,
Now all I needed was some shoes for my feet.
That's when I met you.
You said come with me, 'cause I have an extra pair or two.
I thought, My I'm well to do,
A coat and shoes, and I thank you.

Now the weather was bitter and cold
And I really had no place to go.
Then I saw an old building with a do not enter sign.
And I thought to myself, this will do just fine.
I pulled back the boards and climbed right in,
I huddled in the corner and thought of my new found friend.
I got warm and drifted off to sleep,
Because I didn't have any food to eat.
When I woke up everything had changed.
And I felt so odd and strange.
My body felt all nice and warm.

Julia G. Harris

Ego Trip

I dreamt one day
Fame came my way,
Oh, would it could be true!
I'd be content before life's spent,
If I could prove to you,
My life on Earth was full of worth
A worth beyond compare!
A song to write with lyrics bright
A poem for all to share.
Oh, would one-day fame come my way
So all the world could know,
That I was born to toot my horn
Before it's time to go.
An ego trip, Oh, please equip my very heart and soul
With talent oozing from my lips,
Sweet fortune be my goal!
One last request, just tell the rest
No need to compromise.
I am the best in this contest,
Deliver me the prize!

Martha Buckley

To Someone Who Cares

To someone who cares, Zachary moved far away.
I wish he'd come back if only to play to someone who cares.
I often wonder why but whenever I do that, I sit down and cry.
To someone who cares, I can't be there to watch my son turn six.
Maybe I'll go to the doctor so my heart he can fix..
To someone who cares, I have a really deep pain.
A lot of that comes from watching him leave on the plane.
To someone who cares, Zachary has a step-daddy named Drew.
I wish things were different so I was the only daddy he knew.
To someone who cares, we talk on the phone,
But the phone doesn't help when I'm sitting alone.
To someone who cares, I can't take him to school.
The feeling that brings, I must say is cruel.
To someone who cares, I wish I could see his little face.
But pictures are all I have, at this time and place.
To someone who cares, he'll be back, but I'm not sure when.
I hope it's real soon, because I've lost my best friend.
To someone who cares, I try and keep my emotions inside,
But that rule about men crying is hard to abide.
I hope we'll be together when he's old enough to decide.

Sean David Leary

Mourning

Early in the morning, out of bed I rise.
Waking up from dreams, I open my eyes.
I focus my mind in, and back on reality.
But something's amiss, and out of normality.
An image is there, a picture of a dream.
Something important, as so it would seem.
I remember it now, it's coming back to me.
I see myself dead! How could that be?
I read a note, clenched in frozen hands.
It tells years of sadness, a soul drifting in sands.
My tears swelled up and rolled down my cheeks.
No one has noticed I've been dead for weeks.
I turn my back to forget my nightmare.
I look back one last time. Someone is there!
I try to focus, try to see a face.
It's covered in black, it's covered in lace.
A woman kneels down and whispers to a cold ear.
I try to listen, but I cannot hear!
She is crying now, she is weeping.
I want to tell her I'm only sleeping.

Steve Wemus

Sea of Wonder

Sandy shores, sandy seas,
Water flows up to my knees.
My hands glide across the sea
It touches back tickling me.
Below I wonder what is near,
Water whispers in my ear.
Quietly I step away
I wonder if I want to stay.
The waves pull me right back in,
They flow up to my knees again.
Seashells prance across my hands,
My toes dig deeper into the sand.
Deeper the floor, the deeper the thoughts,
Water trickles down in dots.
I stare out to the bright daylight,
Waiting till the dark of night.
The sun sets lower on the sea,
Making darkness ahead of me.
Sandy shores, sandy seas,
The water flows up to my knees.

Kelli McNeilly

The Me That Nobody Sees

Living in a world that does not care for me
To be what I was meant to be, not
a drug dealer, or thief. "Hu"
Maybe doctor, lawyer, Indian chief
that's what I see for me.
Crime, I don't have the time
educated, that's what I see for me
not what society has deemed me to be
Yes, standing tall, staying strong
to be free to be all that I must be
so don't let the world tell me
what I must achieve
I'm not a thug on the street corner
doctor Malcolm plausible so,
Not a dealer selling my soul
Just give me a chance, don't judge
from a glance,
for he is he,
and I am me,
shining for the whole world to "see."

Marlena L. Odom

Wings

Like a bird that has no wings I could not fly
Seeing everyone else soar high above the clouds
Left me empty and feeling alone
My heart was vexed and needed to be repaired
I was losing confidence because I had no wings to fly
Watching in a distance hoping that I could be like everyone else
Not realizing I was unique and going through a making process
Oh, if I had wings I would fly so high
High above the trees and looking down at the valley below
But I couldn't I could only see what was in front of me
It wasn't until words of encouragement where spoken unto me
"I know you can do it I want you to do it"
I understood at that moment what I didn't understand then
It wasn't actually having wings to fly
It was just believing that you could soar!
Believing that you could reach the unreachable
And still be able to see the valley below
Today I have my wings and know that I can fly
Thank you mother for giving me my wings
I can fly because of you and believe me I'm going to fly!

Stephanie McDowell

The Great Highland Bagpipes

Over rocky shores
Through snow capped mountains
Somewhere, someplace, the bagpipes are playing

Whispering a gentle hymn
Proudly displaying a Celtic tune
Somewhere, someplace, the bagpipes are playing

And deep down in those air filled pipes
Comes a friend that brings my ear delight
My soul finds it difficult to decipher what they're saying
But I know somewhere the bagpipes are playing

Emotionally singing of the Scottish Highlands
Using a mellow tone
Tragedies, trials, and tribulations too
Passed on from the pipes to me and you

Over rocky shores
And through snow capped mountains
Somewhere, someplace, the bagpipes are playing
Sowing the world with seeds of inspiration

Christopher Warren Jones

Dreams of a Dancing Soul

Shades of gray are the colors of my soul.
Ebbing out from somewhere deep inside.
These shades are the reflections of lost loves
and betrayals unimaginable in my younger days.

Once my soul held vibrant colors and songs
Golden sunshine yellow and ruby reds.
Dancing joyously together with the promise of
true love, peace, and bright tomorrows.

A trusting soul I was, believing in the good of people.
Tricked by the promises of others who knew me not.
A heart that is true to the end, once given cannot be taken back.

And so my colors were replaced with grays,
my songs no longer sung. Then you entered my life and
brought your truth. Clearly reflecting in your eyes so blue.

My soul begins life anew and looks forward to the day.
When my soul is no longer gray but the brilliant colors
of yesterday. This is the soul I wish to share with you,
the brightest colors and unending truth.

Christina Therrien

A Walk in the Park

As I trudge along my way
Through a golden and burgundy sea
Frigid gusts of wind
Whip through the naked trees.
The gray clouds block the sun
Preventing any light
From warming up the hearts and minds
Of those blessed with its sight.
The air is heavy with sorrow
And things that were never said
Doubt, regret, and disbelief
Are swirling through my head.
My thoughts are milling over
The hundreds of loose ends
That people wish had been tied up
But now might never mend.
And then a beam of heavenly light
Burst through the clouds like a golden rope
Pulling me out of my dreary thoughts
And handing me back over to love and hope.

Lara Suzanna Rodriguez

COBOL

In nineteen hundred and seventy-five,
a language was created and made alive.
It seemed the best language to make a report,
because compared to zeros and ones, it was very short.
In nineteen hundred and eighty-two,
This language was updated by the COBOL guru.
It was made a lot better, but could not compare
to the new languages out, so nobody cared.
In nineteen hundred and ninety-nine,
COBOL programs were running and everything seemed fine.
But the language would crash at midnight, January first.
The world needed COBOL programmers like a really bad thirst.
Everyone was scrambling, and running about,
so that no company on this day would do without.
In the next few years, until two thousand and three,
The guru will strike again, to make COBOL free,
From the constraints of the millennium, and the languages of today,
that beat out COBOL in every way.
But COBOL is doomed to be the language gone awry,
That no one can get rid of as hard as they try.

Jason D. Berlin

God's Greatest Gift

Christmas is such a special time,
When hopes go soaring and spirits climb,
All too often we forget the reason why,
We celebrate as time goes by,
On Christmas we celebrate our Savior's birth,
God sent His Son down here to Earth,
That's why it's such a special day,
A beautiful star showed the wise men the way,
In the city of David the new king would be,
An angel told the shepherds to go and see,
No greater gift will you ever receive,
All it takes is you have to believe,
So remember throughout this holiday season,
That the birth of Christ is the real reason,
He was sent here for all mankind,
No greater gift will you find,
You need to show everyone that you care,
Love is something one has to share,
Give Thanks to God for all that He's done,
For the reason for the season is He sent us His Son.

Brian Shields

Tonight

There's no easy way to say this,
It's just something I have to do.
I've loved you for years and years,
But you never even knew.
Tonight I will speak from my heart,
Telling you just how I feel.
Laying it all on the line for you, How can all of this be real?
I set up candles galore,
And I've rehearsed this a thousand times in my head.
You're sitting right in front of me,
And this is what I just said.
Tonight I will speak from my heart,
Telling you just how I feel.
Laying it all on the line for you, Finally this is real.
I love you and have for so long,
I just didn't know how to say.
You are the one thing that keeps me going,
For forever please, please stay.
Tonight I spoke from my heart, Telling just how I feel.
Laid it all on the line for you, Yes this is real.

Ashley Kenion Hart

Watch the Slow Rain

Walk with me and watch the slow rain
and listen to the far whistle of a train.
Touch the shimmer of any light
in night reflections that exist.
Put your fragile hand in mine
let your thoughts wander and realign.
Let the fresh rain moisturize your face
each drop that falls to leave a retrace.
Catch the strange fragrance of the ground
hush, keep the quiet without a sound.
Listen to the harmony that calls
the enchanted dream that rises and falls.
The rain will go on until the dawn
and then the sun we'll look upon.
Tired and weary, wet and cold
but breakfast here is always sold.
I shall remember the rainy night
with all its glitter, diamond bright.
You came not watching, and so it seems
a dream was lost among the dreams.

Jim Gharib

The Women

Look into her eyes, and you will see the hurt
and the pain that life sometimes brings.
Feel her hands, and you will feel the roughness of them,
which are a result of taking on the role of both woman and man.
Taste her lips that have turned from sweet to bitter,
because of the men who never cherished them.
Hear her voice that cries for someone's loving arms.
Smell her sweet scent of fresh flowers.
Listen to her heart, as it plays a song longing,
to experience true love.
Feel her feet that have helped her stand through the test of time.
Embrace the arms that carry the weight of the world.
Behold the legs, which have walked through all kinds of storms.
Take a trip through her mind, to see all of her hopes and dreams
Put your fingers through her hair for it is her glory.
Once you have done all of this you have truly
discovered a divine creature. Made of so many different things.
Instead of always using her mind with her heart she thinks.
She roams the Earth in search of understanding. So often taken for
granted but if she did not exist life would be meaningless, the
Women.

Leah Smith

Mother

The greatest gift that you can receive
is the thoughts of one who always believes.
At times, life seems hard with its burden to bear;
all it takes is a call and she'll always be there.
As I try counting gifts too many to confess,
by just knowing this women, for that I've been blessed.
For you've done for me when unable to do for myself,
sacrificing well being, sometimes even one's health.
So don't ever believe God knew not what he does;
the gift of a mother could only be sent from above.

Michael Jackson

Christ in Christmas

Jesus help me carry your name through the
darkest night and to the other side of the
fight. For if we can hold your name close to
us we together can support each other.
Let us be able to put you ahead of ourselves
so we can reflect on you instead of the
deceptions of this world. Let us seek the good
of others instead of ourselves, as you gave to us
on that solemn Christmas.

Evan Colin Smith

A Valuable Lesson

Why mind the color of my skin,
when there is so much goodness within?
No need to hold my head down nor shed a tear,
I will lift up my voice, sing loud and clear,
For I have so much to be thankful for,
the life God gave me and so much more.
Yes, we all are equal, so let us just be glad,
for if we were not, it would be so sad.
Let us give God thanks for our blessings,
and let Dr. Martin Luther King's dream be a valuable lesson.

Joan Waring

Probing Fingers

Back in the corners of my mind
Where only shadows dark and cold,
Those insistent, probing fingers long to go,
Those fingers longing to make me remember
Things only time can forget.
My heart guides the fingers, wanting to find you again.
My mind strengthens the shadows,
Not letting the uncaring fingers in.
I hope never to see sunlight,
For those shadows will go and the probing fingers will then know.

Jennifer Cobb

Darkness

Mommy, when I fear the dark, what do I do?
I reach out to the darkness, and Mommy's not there
With ghosts and goblins in the air, only darkness is there.
I saw, Mommy, with my eyes of royal blue—I turn to you
And say what do I do?
Don't be afraid, but then I say it's okay to fear
Mommy's afraid today, turn to the darkness of night,
TJ, and turn on the light.
So my little hero, be brave. Mommy wants to come home today.
She'll take TJ's fear away like she did yesterday.

Dawn Olson

The Sun, the Moon, and the Stars

The sun is bright yellow.
The moon is white.
The stars are shining bright tonight.
The sun is round.
The sun is gold.
The sun goes up and down.
The moon decided to go in the light.
And disappeared out of sight.
The stars are bright at night to shine.
They are lights from Heaven, to sparkle at night.

Shannon Dunkle

God's Love

Be happy
Don't be sad
Just 'cause you're sick
doesn't mean you have to be mad.
God thinks you're beautiful in every way
And fills you with that beauty day by day.
Everybody loves you
and you are beautiful in the world's eyes.
I can just say you're a strong, beautiful and loving person to me
and the world that loves you.

Teresa M. Gaggens

A Special Love

A special love that comes down from above,
A special touch as gentle as God's love.
A special bond that is always there,
A special look to show she cares.
A special talk to show her true love,
A special prayer to reach above.
A special person to show her devotion,
A special feeling to show her emotions.
A special mother is a great treasure,
A special love that can't be measured.

Sherry Roman

Jesus, Give Me Strength

Jesus, give me strength to endure all the devil throws my way.
For the more he throws, the more I will pray.
Let each passing day that I am blessed on this Earth
Be filled with your love for which I thirst.
Jesus, give me strength to teach your word and do your will
until the end of my days.
Jesus, give me strength to love and not hate.
Jesus, give me strength to smile when there should be a frown,
until the day I am honored to set eyes upon you.
Please, Jesus, give me strength in all that I do.

Rashina Price

Life

One way
Any kind of road
You can make it any way that you desire
You are the one who makes the one way
Pretty way, hard way, wide way, narrow way
If you want, you can make any branches
Also you can take a break whenever if you feel like it
No one make you hurry
Because it is your way
Just don't forget, you only have one way

Hiroko Beltz

Man

When man has doubts about God and all,
I say, send him to the country in the fall!
Moon so bright and full
Lighting mountains and lakes
Tho' trifle cold
Serene warm days, with golden aspens to behold
Sunrises and sunsets for which we are so fond
Clear brooks and streams and blue-green ponds
And don't forget our frisky friends, the trout.

How can any man have any doubts!

Marylou Melton

Daddy's Eyes, Mommy's Skin

Every time she opens her eyes, it's you I see
But you choose your skin over me
Afraid to love outside your race
Ashamed of people, staring in disgrace
It was only right when the lights were out
It ended there for you; in my mind, there's doubt
She has your eyes and I know that smile
What am I to tell my child?
Is she to feel that she's a sin?
'Cause she has her Daddy's eyes and her Mommy's skin?

Jennifer Losey

Bad Day

Let me hold you
Let me hold you close to my lips
Let me taste you only a sip
I need you in me hot and warm with that tingling feeling
that will make everything be gone
You go right through me like a pick through ice
You make me feel oh, so nice
A couple of you is all I need
Bottle top open because without you
I feel I cannot breathe

Romina Caporrino

Moon Shine

You came to me in a dream
Through a wispy, autumn mist,
And I followed you in the waving
Branches of a willow.
There among the leaves we played,
Under the cover of your intoxicating breath
Until the dawn changed into its early yellow,
And in the morning's final hour,
Armed with the embrace I carved,
I awoke as you handed me a flower.

Kim Kacoroski

New Beginnings

With every End comes a new Beginning,
And with every Beginning comes a new Challenge,
A Challenge to accept this new Journey,
A Journey full of new Wonders,
Wonders that will spark new Ideas,
Ideas that will give birth to new Thoughts,
Thoughts that will give a new Meaning,
A Meaning that will touch a new Life,
A Life that will someday End,
And with every End comes a new Beginning.

James Paul Sanchez

Dreams

The room gets quiet,
No words are spoken,
Suddenly . . .
Screams pierce the silence.
The look of deadly fright on everyone's faces,
Breathe . . .
This is the first time this
Has ever happened to you
And yet it seems all to familiar.
You finally find the strength
To find and take in air,
But somehow, it doesn't seem to help.
Tears start to form, and you hold them back
With all your might.
It's simple . . . so simple.
Soon enough, everything goes dark,
And you realize you are somewhere else.
Some dreams . . .
You just don't want to come true. . . .

Jennifer Tabitha Dodge

Sojourn for Peace

We come from many nations; to gather
Here at this location.
We come from many lands and many
Places, of many colors, and many races.
We are of many heights, and many weights,
of many beliefs and many faiths.
We have met to compete, to show good
Sportsmanship and to win our heats.
All of us will do our best, when we go
Up against the best of the best; if we
fail to reach our goal, we go back home
For a four-year's rest.
As it was in the first olympiad, the laurel
wreath wasn't all there was to be had.
So, bringing home the gold isn't all that
matters, it's things like: diplomacy,
friendship, love and chatter.
When the Olympics roll around again,
We'll be back with another plan.

Henry B. Porter

The Garden

A throng of renegades
Has surrounded the garden
Holding the tranquility hostage
And feeding on the sun

They squat amongst the foliage
With the juice of my precious sweat
Dripping through their teeth
And gobbling all that grows to give

Sinister smiles armed with spades
Digging here and cutting there
Pulling up what they may
Leaving the fallen to dry in the murderous heat

But here I hold a fistful
Of squirming serpents anxious for release
And setting them to the grass pleases them
As they find their way into my garden
And they fed well on those who would violate there

Edward Randall Arriaga, II

Untitled

It profits much to scorn,
So sullenly to sulk.
Beating them down to bear your grief.
You speak of them only to derogate
Their ethics, their morals, their ambitions.
They play in the sand and you wish to fly.
Ay, it profits much to scorn
Where you do not fit in.
To pity yourself for striving to succeed.

For to pity yourself in loneliness
Is folly indeed.
It is not loneliness wherein you bathe,
But ambition, experience and hope.
Dare not scorn that which you are not,
For behind such actions seethes the serpent jealousy.
Remember them for what you are not,
And sacrifice not what you are for them.
For it profits, ay, to be alone,
How else would'st thou find inspiration for such a poem?

Farah Razack Moti

You're Never There

There are always people around me,
Yet I feel so alone.
I've shriveled up inside;
My heart's turned into stone,
Because you're never there.

What hurts me the most
Is when I stand out in the rain
With open arms calling your name,
You're never there.

I don't care why you left me,
It was beyond our control;
I just miss you, I love you,
And I want to go home,
But you're never there.

No one can replace you,
I know that for sure,
But deep in my heart there's an open door,
For someone who will be there.

Irene Thalasselis

Forever Forbidden

My heart yearns to reach out for his
Alas, he is not free
We shared something
Though never truly expressed
His tender caress
Touching more than my skin
My soul cries out
I want to hold him near
He knows not the sorrows
Hidden so well within my smile
An agony so pure my body screams
I need to feel his lips again . . . his touch . . .
His tongue
Trembling in fear
I lift my eyes to his
Finding nothing more than an empty shell
I accept his cold caress
Knowing that which I long for
Is forever forbidden

Cinnamon Paget

Mary

For Karl

Of late, I have come to find
from friend and acquaintance
with all states of mind
that they know not the extreme responsibility
of a mother,
a father,
a teacher
or friend.
Think.
If
a butterfly,
a bee,
a tree
or a smile
did not exist, would you be here
holding my hand in this eternity
as in this pain,
I give birth to our only child?

Leah D. Moretz

Requiescat

Who will wash my body?
Who will close my eyelids, and clothe me in my shroud?
Dear strangers, be gentle with my body,
The miracle that carried me through this life.
It encased my heart, my soul, my spirit.
It bore my children and gave comfort to one.

Have you noticed that I am dying?
Have you noticed how easily I tire?
Have you noticed how slow I have become?

Dear strangers, be gentle with my body.
Lay me down in the place of my birth.
Lay me down in the red earth that stained my childhood feet.
Lay me down where I first learned
of the love of God and to pray.
Lay me down with those whose bloodlines I bear.

Dear strangers, be gentle with my body.
Let me give it back to that sweet earth
From whence it came.

Joan Patricia Panton

(dis)Honesty

Just a label
One single word
An entire life summed up in three letters
The truth will hurt you
But the lie is killing me
I wish it didn't matter
I hate you because it does
You don't see the fear in my eyes
But I see the fear in yours
Why are you so afraid, it's not a disease
I'll still be alive tomorrow
Or maybe that's the problem
Is it something so terrible
That you'd rather I take it to my grave
I try to tell myself I don't care
All that matters is that I love myself
But loving me isn't something you taught
I hate hating you
But I despise hating me.

Chris Pulaski

Legends

Legends are made, not born, and they never
die. They live on in the hearts . . . and
hopes . . . and dreams . . . of those who follow
their paths to greatness. Their spirits set
a pace that only your hearts can follow.
Run with all you have and you will pave the
way to glorious triumph. Run every race as
though it is your last. For if you don't,
you may never get a chance to prove it to
yourself or to God—and you will never have
what you once held . . . never grasped for what
you once reached . . . Citius, Altius, Fortius—
Faster, Higher, Stronger. But not
necessarily Faster, Higher, and Stronger
than who you are competing against—just
Faster, Higher, Stronger. You must hold
yourself to a higher standard than winning.
You don't run a race to win, but to test the
limits of the human heart. Godspeed.

Jon Jungwirth

Wondering

Raised by my mother, I have no regret,
but things would be different with a father, I bet.

I can't really fix things, don't know how to fish,
I want my own children, that's my greatest wish.

Am I really ready? I don't know the rules,
Do they come with instructions? Do they require tools?

Will I teach them well? In these thoughts I am mired,
Because their emotions come stamped "some assembly required."

I know I shouldn't worry, I'll put away my doubt,
I'll have my wife, Becca, their mom, to help out.

With our combined love, everything will be fine,
This woman, our baby, their hearts held in mine.

Her hero? His idol? What will my child see?
I wonder what kind of daddy I'll be.

I see my sweet baby, snuggled at my wife's breast,
And think to myself, I'll be the very best.

Christopher Aaron Hollins

I Am—Anne Frank

I am a Jew who sees good in all mankind.
I wonder how all this suffering could be true.
I hear the cry of loneliness.
I see the light in the souls of Nazis.
I want peace around the world.
I am a Jew who sees good in all mankind.

I pretend the war is over and go on with my life.
I feel the pain of other Jews.
I touch the light at the other end.
I worry of nothing but the life of my father.
I cry at the thought of my father's death.
I am a Jew that sees good in all mankind.

I understand the slaves of Hitler.
I say my love will not die.
I dream about the better life.
I try to make the best of things.
I hope my father and I survive.
I am a Jew that sees good in all mankind.

Daryl Dawson

The Girl on the Other Side

As I step in front of the cool smooth glass,
The girl on the other side follows.
I raise my hand up to brush my cheek
And still she copies my act.
I look deep in the mirror. Deeper.
Until all the hidden secrets break free.
I look in the mirror to solve all my woes,
To tell me that I look great,
Yet hidden inside are the secrets it keeps.
Such as the "Kick Me" sign on my back
Or the mud someone put in my hair.
All of these things are just out of eyes reach.
But the mirror sees it all and never reveals,
How ugly we are under the cakes of makeup,
Or how beautiful we are
Under the tangles of greasy hair.
No, the mirror doesn't tell its secrets.
So, bored, I walk away.
And the girl on the other side follows.

Lynsey Gooding

Making a Journey

Strolling through the countryside
Mountains, hills, and plains
The sounds of nature coming from everywhere
Footsteps sound on the beaten path
Calm breezes bend the trees
Two travelers making a journey

Strolling through the countryside
Mountains, hills, and glades
Streams flow past, adding to the joy
Wildlife watches as time moves forward
Marking each passing
Two travelers making a journey

Strolling through the countryside
Mountains, hills, and valleys
Avians fly across the sky
Watching and wondering at the scene below
Waiting patiently
You and I, making a Journey

David L. Kilpela

Endless Love

I am the light
That you see in the night
And I have come from a place faraway
Though my journey has just begun
I have seen a thousand suns
I will see a thousand more before the end of the day

I have witnessed your face
From across the endlessness of space
Seeking answers from the universe above
But I tell you what I bring
Upon the chariot of an angel's wing
Replaces hopelessness with endless love

For I am the light
Neither wrong, neither right
My purpose for being, yours to explain
Thus, the brightest star you see
Can be yours for eternity
For I am truth, I am love, without pain.

Cory Michael Woodward

My Insane Devotion

There are days when the sun doesn't shine,
and days when the rain doesn't pour.
There are times when my heart is high,
and times when it is low.
There are sleepless nights
when I have appalling nightmares,
and tranquil nights when I dream of you.
There are places where I can unwind
and deem about the beauty of my love for you,
and there are places as gloomy as agony
where my affection for you
feels like an unwinding kaleidoscope.
There are instances when my
blissful thoughts take me to an outlying distance above the clouds,
and there are circumstances
when my wretched ideas block my mind
from the content universe.
But truly, the best moments
are when I'm thinking of you. . . .

Farrah J. Abbas

This Chair of Mine

This poem was written for a friend of mine.

My body, confined to this chair made of steel;
On either side is a big worn wheel.
But my spirit soars through the cold night air;
Going where it likes—be it far or near.
It soars across silky skies at nights;
Alas, dear friends, I have no plight.
Oft' times did I fight against the tightening of these ropes;
A prisoner in this body—yet I still have hopes.
My very being, though kidnapped, still fights
Against the constrains, of my soul in plight.
Oh, to be released from these pitiful chains;
To soar like an eagle—but here I shall remain.
As I look around at the people who abound
Do I lust for their freedom, like a hungry wolf hound.
But alas! As I open my eyes do I see,
Another beautiful day has dawned for me.
Take heart, let your sorrows be finished;
Life is too beautiful—to allow it to diminish.

Marlene Bridget McMurchy

Search for Me

Be still my child and search for me, I'm hidden in the mist.
Of life's wild dreams and empty schemes,
cast aside through thoughtlessness.
The self-indulgent world suggests our way is truly best . . .
If you proclaim and play our game, we'll accept you as our guest!
To them, the measure of your worth is a dollar and a dream . . .
Or scheme or scam or any plan, leading on to their promised land!
The lonely hearts within this land, where avarice is king,
would fill your heart, from the very start,
with the joy of owning things . . .
You MUST be the best; OUTDO the rest;
social status your brass ring!
Compete and beat; now you're the elite,
in their land of empty dreams.
I'm here inside the mist today, awaiting your return;
an easy play, just a prayer away . . .
Then together the mist, we'll burn!
I've always been near, no more darkness to fear . . .
Be still . . . and search for me.

DeeNae Jensen

Split

Why is it that I'm always at
That road which bends and curves?
The 2 paths have always been
So alike to me.
I have often believed
That with you, there was a third path
In the center of it all.
Why do you think sacrifice
Is the price for gaining speed?
Why can't we reach that through the middle ground?

Finally, I have paid the price
Of a friendship so dear.
That is one gift that
I have gained from you.
Yet you believe that the gold of friendship
Loses value with intimacy.
Why do I have to choose between my best friend
And the beauty I adore?
Can it be that they are not the same person?

Gillie Bilson

God's Promise

To Letty Bell—Davy's "Angel" Mom

It's impossible to rejoice while we're
encompassed in grief, when grief is the thief
that will heal, God gave His only begotten
Son; He shares in the pain that we feel.
The promise of eternal life is hard to keep
in sight, when we have to walk through the
darkness, before we can see the light.
The selfish creatures we can be will keep us
in our pain, the mighty and powerful irony
is, our loss is truly God's gain.
How can we deny the Lord what He so freely
gave from the start? Our loved ones are
truly gifts from God and will live forever in
our heart.
When we're all called home to the Father, and
the Angels light up the Heavens above, what
an awesome family reunion, fulfilling God's
promise of His eternal love.

Star Rae Geib

The Window

I sit and look through a window that looks so inviting.
The birds chirp, the sun shines brightly,
and the flowers grow strong and beautiful.
The only problem is I cannot reach that side.
I am stuck on the other side of the window.
My head aches from the thought of this place.
In here, it is cold, dark, and lonely.
The only birds heard here are the crows
that scream their angered cries of sorrow.
The only light comes from the lightning
that sparkles off the heavy rain.
No sun for me, storms are all I see.
The only plants are dying weeds.
In here, this place is a sorrowful pit of agony.
I used to be on the other side, but now I am not.
I wish I could go back.
Oh, Lord, help me to go back,
or I will forever be stuck . . .
in this black hole of death.

Sharon McClelland

Little Boy Baby Blue

I lay you down and you close your eyes,
And the stars dance on the far horizon;
And I thank God for the joy I've found in you.
And the sun rises in a clear blue sky,
And I wake with thoughts of you on my mind.
Sweet dreams and lullabies and little boy baby blue.
Such joy since you've been in my life.
I often wonder how I used to survive
Without your sweet smile and clear blue eyes.
I am so proud that I could cry.
I often wonder how it will all turn out;
You know a father can get so filled with doubt,
Because he's learning as he goes.
So he prays for guidance from the Lord above,
And thanks Him for every bit of your love,
And every day his love for you will grow.
Then the sun rises in a clear blue sky,
And I wake with thoughts of you on my mind.
Sweet dreams and lullabies and little boy baby blue.

Chris D. Keith

The Differences

Though the ground we tread may vary,
Though the cold we feel may be odd,
Though the air around us is different,
And the scene we take in is strange,
Though the people around us are different,
Though the times on our watches are changed,
Though the shivers we feel are odder,
There is one consolation, you know.
When you look into the sky,
You see endless Heaven,
And through its colors we see,
Dark for you is my light—
It's just one Heaven we see,
Not separated by oceans,
Not split up by territories.
So though everything differs and varies,
From weather down to attire—
At least when you look up at Heaven,
It's the same one that's over me.

Sheharyar Haider Malhi

Tree

To look back, you were so small
branches young, thin, pliable.
Vulnerable, to the children playing by you.
Over time you matured, growing
buds change into splendid leaves.
Your branches reached to the sun,
moving upward, proving life.

Why they want to damage you, most don't know.
To use you in the world
as something to write on or with.
The ax wanted to wound precious bark,
Stripping you down as if there is no feeling.
Some wanted to mangle you,
never looking back to survey the damage.
Life runs on through your aging branches,
spared from certain death.To watch you grow still is fascinating
Observing
There is safety, peace of life.

Amy Page Elkins

Self-Pride

Look at me having fun
Just like an young man in the sun
But then I realize how it really is
In the young man eyes he does not care what others think
But now as I realize I have gotten real weak
My self-esteem use to be as strong as his
Now look at me full of so much pride
Scared of what the other think or say
That young man does not hide
So why do I hide my face
I admire that young man for what he has
Something that I put to waste
I will change my life to carry myself
As that young man although I will keep certain standards
To be in a respectful manner
And I will be
Me who I am and who I will always be Myself
And nobody else
Then and only then I will have Self-Pride

Corey Oliver

Reflections: The Winter Knows . . .

Life lies beneath fallen snow
Waiting patiently for winter to go
It doesn't need a calendar to know it's "Time"
Suddenly it's spring with no reason or rhyme
Life lies incipiently within a frosty tree
Knowing from past times gone what it is to be
As the sun melts the ice of its winter bed
The seeds within know what lies ahead
Images of green inside a bud's memory
Are all recalled, even a bird's melody
It hears whispers of leaves rustling
Within the winds of its mind
Calling it to believe that spring knows—
It's "Time"
The winter hears the voice of spring's song
It disappears as the days get long
Sunshine is its friend: melting snow and ice
Revealing the gift of life within
Springtime feels, oh, so nice!

Faye Mary Lee

Riding a Dream

I have traversed this land and climbed its
mountains in search of this magic I dream.
It's a spell of freedom, purity, and riches that
is sought in the hills, trees, and streams.
I have seen the beauty of the picturesque and
tasted innocence in the huckleberry fruit.
I have cleansed in the waters of the great
divide and stood on the battlegrounds at Crowheart Butte.
I have felt pain, loneliness, and times of fear
at night when the wind howls and the sky is clear.
I wish upon the first star I see for this magic which I dream.
I have heard the songs of the morning dove
and had strangers greet me with their love.
I have cursed at the hills for them to be over
and found luck in a four leaf clover.
Luck and dreams are a lot alike,
it's a wish for at least one night
but a dream is more permanent. It lasts forever
like the gift of a friend. It's something you shall always treasure.

Ryan Adam Siebert

Making the Person

In the distance I see
What I long for.
Although, as much as I want,
Everyone tells me it's wrong.
What should I do? What could I do?
When it's people that make the person.

In the distance I hear
What it is people say.
Although I don't agree with it,
I go along to please them.
Who am I? Who was I?
These are the people that make the person.

I long for the distance
That I see and hear.
Although it goes against everything I know,
I know that I must at least try.
What will they say? Who cares?
I am the person that makes the person.

Brian Youngberg

Thus It Be Written . . .

Dedicated to Jance "Aller-Jancer" Versheck

Ah, so it has been written, another chapter in my book,
as well as another day of life you took
a hand held dear, close to my heart
a mind that's clear will never go far
standing close to my heart and my mind
these memories will last till the test of time

fighting for that song, to play once more
fighting for things to be like before
play for me, minstrel, play; don't let these songs end
play for me, minstrel, play; don't let this feeling end
continue on this path you lead, I will sing right by your side
and I will learn to lead myself, with my very own piece of mind
Stand beside me, traveling friends, these paths we travel are true
Fight beside me, traveling friends, this life you live is for you
show not your fears, but to yourself
explain your loves, but only in stealth
and stand with me, and see how I care
As we walk our paths to a Renaissance faire.

Cody James Noren

Promise

In the years to come
we'll walk the ups and downs
We'll fight the battles
and laugh with the clowns
We'll wipe the tears from each other's eyes
and we'll lend a shoulder until the crying dies
To say I do is to say I will
and when our youth is gone
I'll love you still
Promise
I've feared the walk of life alone
but with you I'm twice as strong
I know I'll cry I know I'll weep
but with you close my sanity I'll keep
Sleep in silence and know you're safe
because I'm always near and I'll never stray
I'll lift you up when the tide rolls in
and lay you down when the night begins
Promise

David R. Scherb

I Am You, You Are Me

Young woman learning to be strong,
NEVER FEEL the NEED to have to belong.
We all have our place,
a name put to a face.
The attitude will take you far, if YOU take care of YOU . . .
Learn what you really need, not what you want.
Seek out your happiness well thought out within your heart . . .
Step aside and take a look at the you, you submit to,
mind your words, and feel committed, too.
Take another look to see who you want to be.
Take another breath and make it reality.
The struggle is just what it is.
The outcome is the piece you play.
My woman, you are me today.
As I grow and learn, hurt and pray
that the Lord will lead the way someday . . .
but what I notice not is his subtle guide!
Because my life is His written word . . .
and to him I subside.

Jacqueline Astet

Old Woman

There sits an Old Woman, quite lonely it seems.
Should she have my pity? Would that be extreme?
Was her life successful, or crushed in body and soul?
Were her people kind to her, or were they very cruel?
Was she gay and lovely and always bell of the ball,
attracting suitors everywhere, with beaus so handsome and tall?
Or was she a tart or strumpet, who really didn't care, who drank
and smoked, and carried on, with bright red dye in her hair?
Are those furrows in her old face, a road map of her dreams,
or are they scars of an evil life, and nasty little schemes?
Were her young dreams shattered or reached with great aplomb?
Did she experience adventure, or was she a very sweet Mom?
The lines in her face, her story of life, a design I try to read.
Her self-etched soul, untouchable, which one cannot perceive.
What do I think when I look at her? My questions I want to yell!
Was yours a life of triumph, Madam, or simply one of hell?
She suddenly turns and looks at me, I feel she can see me within.
As if reading my inquiring thoughts,
she struts away with a sly little grin.

Ann M. Colegrove

The Fire

Blood courses not through my veins
It does not fuel my soul and desires
Nor does it drive my passion
There is only the fire
A flame eternally grows strong in my mind
Tiny and flickering at birth,
Steady through to the end
This is the flame of my one enlightenment
Twenty small and fortified matches are lit
Insignificant, almost, at birth
Now burn intensely to the end
These are the lights of my nurturing nature
In my heart therein lies a bonfire of
infinite fervor
It has always been from the dawn of time
Through many lives it has been; strong and
growing still
This fire is the depth of my soul and the
pedal to my passion

JoAnn Burke

Whitnea

i looked destiny in her eyes today
and how i feel is hard to say
i've prayed so long for this day
now gods blessed me
and how i feel is hard to say

i'm floating, lost in another world
mesmerized by the magic in her eyes
my feelings i try, but i cannot hide
i feel there is nothing left to find

i'm used to this world rolling me
i've come accustomed to the agonies of defeat
but still i poured my soul out at her feet
with all my heart i feel this is fate
i pray i'm not setting myself up to be raped

i looked destiny in her eyes today
and how i feel is hard to say
i've prayed so long for this day
and how i feel is hard to say

Jeb Butlerm

Beautiful Thing

If I could
I would take from the sky
The star with the brightest magnitude
And hold it gently in my palms

If I could
I would show you
All its beauty and glory
In shining, shimmering, wonderment

If I could
As the rising heat emerges
Like the breaking of darkness into morning
I would toss to you this brilliant star
So that it would slowly singe
Everything that is you
What a vengeful, burning, insanity!
And then upon you a startling realization:
What ugliness such a seemingly beautiful thing can cause
If only I could

Brittany Anne Brockner

A Piece of Mind

as i, live my life
i see why, so many are blind
tellin' lie, after learnin' 'bout trife
so why, try bein' kind
mind as well, sell
your soul, to the devil
get out the hole, price is settled

a piece of mind, from jai
let it shine, one time

some say, while we lay
asleep, our soul creeps
but if our soul creeps, why does the body
still breathe, in our dreams
full of deceit, and mysteries
gives us the belief, of inner peace
and psychic abilities, so what is reality?

a piece of mind, from jai
let it shine, one time

John Yer Yang

Grandma

Our time we shared with you we treasured,
having you around was more than a pleasure.

To try and express our love words could never say,
all the favors and things you did for us
words could never repay.

We showed you love and even more you returned,
the titles mother and grandmother
were titles that you earned.

The memory of you will stay burned deep in our mind,
because of you the words "I love
you" will never be hard to find.

Now you look down on us from above,
watching over us and blessing us with your love.

Rest peacefully knowing you have the love of
us all, know there is a special place for you
in our hearts, you, our mother, our sister,
our grandma.

Michael Gaietto

I Am

I am thoughtful and caring
I wonder what is the meaning of life
I hear the sounds of angels singing
I see them coming down upon me
I want them to take me away to the Heavens

I am thoughtful and caring
I pretend to fly around with the wings they have given me
I feel the soft touch of their wings
I touch their colorful, silky hair
I worry they won't let me go back to Earth
I cry because they are so beautiful and loving

I am thoughtful and caring
I understand why they are there
I say the prayers to God
I dream I have their wings
I try to be just like them
I hope they love me with all their hearts inside them
I am loving and caring.

Stephanie Marie Thome

Parting and Departing

Sleepless so I roam
So far from a discomforting home
Beyond the night and through the day
So eager to run away
Recklessly into someone else's novel arms
From that familiar, secure ground
Yet so scared not to stay.
Dancing upon a rhythm of desperation
Beaten by your heart
Directed by togetherless
Constant disharmony, at best minor chords to pull,
In each other's company or apart.
Time to fish for happiness once more,
To stray upon the whim of unattainable love
I recklessly depart.
Baited by
An obvious white lie
But more so the truth of our incompatibility
That I've tired of trying to aimlessly deny.

Farrah Jane Tate

ME

This is dedicated to my mom, Diane.

It is a picture, it is mine . . .
It is me . . .
There are clowns dancing, mysterious masks smiling . . .
is it a nightmare, or a dream . . . ?
It is a bright light, in a dark room . . .
Mad and mean . . .
Nightmare on Elm street . . .
To me, a game . . .
To you, reality . . .
To me, a war . . .
To you another daily thing . . .
Lonely and vast like you and me, are there . . .
It's the devil . . .
It's God . . .
Don't worry, be happy . . .
It's meaningful, I am unique, in ways . . .
I see a creepy man, that man is . . .
ME

Robert Ramos

Gathering of Friends

We are all gathered together here
Meeting for the last time this year.

The bond between us seems to grow
To help us all when we are low

As the New Year will come and the old will go
God can make us all as white as snow.

For all of us to do good whenever we can
For us to bring love to our fellow man.

To show the world we are sincere
As we stand at the gate of another year.

The New Year and whatever it brings
We'll face it together right into the spring

As summer approaches our moods we hope high
There will be a few more to whom we'll say "good-bye."
For we'll never forget the bond that we share
Because we all know that every one of us care.

Carol Minch

Mission Statement

I will live each day as though it is my last.
My words will be bold enough to shatter glass;
yet so delicate, I could calm a room
full of tyrant children.
I will be the confidant for my close friends
and the backbone of quarrels.
I will strive for excellence in all that I
do and I will never look back on a step once taken.
I will not waiver in my belief that there
is only one God and He is known asJesus Christ.
I will be versatile in my career and
successful to the means of infinity.
I will be the daughter my parents have
always known and continue to give them praise
for guiding me along my journey in life.
I will be a leader and I will make it in
this unsettled world we all live in.

Amber Michelle Schoenfeld

Racism

What am I that you step on me?
We both came here the same way
We breathe the same air, eat, sleep and drink
We go to the bathroom the same
We cover our bodies, sit, talk and walk
We are made of the same thing.
We are dirt, so why act as if you are not?
Or am I the most dirty dirt you can find?
The most dirty dirt of color and kind?
Why is your dirt any different than mine?
Dirt is Dirt
We came from the same stuff
None any better.
Alive we are clay
Dead we are dust
Dust, dirt, ashes, what makes you different?
In the end we will all pass away.
Ashes to Ashes
Dust to Dust.

Alice Grate

Is God in My Life?

Do I see God?
In every hue of the perfect arched rainbow
In the colors of the springtime flowers
In the birth of every new creature
In the beauty of a star-filled sky
In the magnificent color of changing leaves
Oh, yes, I see God.
Do I hear God?
In the cry of each newborn
In the laughter of a child
In the song of every bird
In the gentle breezes and falling rain
Oh, yes, I hear God
Do I know God?
Because he gives me life each day
Because he gives me eyes to see,
ears to hear, and a heart to feel
Because he gives me the ability to love
Oh, yes, I know God.

Roberta Woodfell

Ask to Be Heard

Wonder what makes God happy
So today let's all make his day
Everyone of us sit down and say
We have fault and illness too
We have so much that you can do
Heal the sick oh, Lord, make them clean
For we ask while awake and even in dreams
We love you Father as mother to child
You taught us to love so tender and mild
So help us to heal all sickness and sorrow
Make it soon Lord today or tomorrow
Bring down your mercy stretch out your hand
Heal us all oh, Lord, we know that you can
Make the lame walk and the weak strong
Then we shall praise thee as the day is long
For we are but human and know not all things
So we ask for mercy to see what it brings
Thank thee oh, Lord, I know that you heard
For we ask in your name and believeth your word!

Nelson Eddie Weyandt

Love Is Dead

I sketched a portrait of love in my heart
before I met you

And I keep walking alone through the
uneven pavement and mistaking you
as my love

I called your name a million times in my
dreams and felt a reptile's magnetic power
grabbing me inside his mouth, pressing me hard
to stop my breath

My heart bleeds, I am mistaken again;
reptile ripped off my sketch by his
harsh, cruel nails

Your eyes, lips, and shoulders were phantom;
a bloodsucker reptile was sleeping underneath.

An empty deep down inside my heart,
love is stone-dead in
the ripped-off portrait!

Ayesha Meher

Depression

Depression, heavy blanket over soul
sinking, eternal woe
How can I keep my chin up high
when even the sun seems to sigh
Rain filters through with a fiery blaze
lending a subdued murmur to my days
Days without number pass by my face
I'll never finish this race
Blessed be he that finishes last
the world is going by too fast
At this rate I'll be first
and then I'll thirst for another chance
Scorching thirst to be free of sorrow and join in the dance
Don't let life pass you up
Some days joy will overflow your cup
Days will seem to drown you with tears
Relinquish all your fears
join our eternal search for silver linings
You'd be surprised at what we're finding

Shanon R. Stanford

Petal by Petal, Our Family Flower

In memory of Coyt Anderson, Cecil Anderson, and Crystal McCracken

It seems so long ago, Daddy, since you went away,
God picked one petal from our family flower that day.
You were the strongest petal we had,
You were our preacher, our teacher, our dad.
Little did we know what was to come,
in only nine months God called your son.
Three petals have gone now to Heaven above,
asleep in Jesus and all of His love.
Wait, sweet petals, on Heaven's shore,
Wait for the others, there will be more.
Then our family flower will be whole again
with Jesus Christ, family, and friends.
Wait for us, Dad, Daughter, and Brother.
Wait for us, and wait for Mother.
Wait for us on Heaven's shore,
Where no petals will die anymore.
"To God the Glory"

Brenda Anderson McCollum

The Camp

Barbed wire and machine guns
Rotten meat and muddy water
Searchlights and hungry canines
These are the images that haunt my mind
Children crying for their mothers
Husbands searching for their wives
Women lying in the road, breathless
These are realities I thought we left behind
Bullets pierce my flesh, flames sear my soul
And finally the gas, yes, the gas
The gas that choked my life away
The gas that stole my son
The showers from which I would not return
These are the horrors caused by mankind
Dachau—Mauthausen—Auschwitz, genocide
Words to describe the past
Bosnia—Kosovo—Rwanda, ethnic cleansing
Words to describe the present
These are the truths to which we are blind

Joseph A. Cantor

Blarney but True

It happened on Sunday or Monday I guess, the day is not clear in my head. I awoke in a daze and shaking my head I realized it wasn't my bed. I lay in a meadow all covered in green with a sparkling haze on the ground. I heard a strange sound and looking around, you'll never believe what I found! Just six inches tall with a green suit and all and a smile as bright as could be. He lay on his back with his hat cocked way back and I wondered just what he could be! When he said with a laugh "You're not going daft, I'm a leprechaun plain as you see. One wish you can have 'cause you've caught me, me lad, so tell me now what will it be?" "No question about it," I said with a grin, "The wish that I want is your best!" With a wave of his hand and a flash Oh, so grand there before me the treasure did stand. In a chest covered gold I couldn't wait to behold what the little man had given me. Opening the lid and looking within, my heart filled with joy you could see. For there in the chest with a diamond-like shine was the image of my wife's love for me!

Herbert Hamilton

Tiger in My House

There's a Tiger in my house,
he lurks in every room . . . sitting . . . waiting . . .
for me to be alone.
A hollow Hell encased in black and gold,
green eyes shining with lust.
Fangs dripping rich with the semen of
unrequited love,
waiting to rip away the warm flesh of
security
and expose cold bones of loneliness,
to be gnawed upon by the jackals of
night.
There's a tiger in my house,
sitting . . .
waiting . . .
for me to be alone.
I am afraid,
I am alone.
Please . . . help me kill the Tiger.

Charles (Chuck) Schumacker

The Optimist

"Am I an optimist," you ask, "who views the glass half full?"
I usually never stop to notice as a general rule.
I'm watching silver spirals and how the moisture bends
the light rays into colors that flicker, streak and blend.
So details often sidetrack me from seeing bigger things;
Can't see the forest for the trees; the outcome for the pain.
So, then, am I an optimist? Well, judging from the past,
I always take life's handouts and try to do my best.
And if the glass is full, I'm thankful for the fact;
But if it's only halfway there, it pays not to react;
that even if it's empty, there's still something you can ask;
And that would be a refill—but until it comes along,
just learn how now to be content and learn how to be strong.
Keep looking at the rays of light that's always shining through,
with hope so wonderful and bright, with all that's good and true.
"Am I an optimist?" you ask. I really do not know.
I think sometimes I try to be but never let it show.
It's difficult to stay that way each day and not give out;
One simply just cannot afford to yield to fear and doubt.

Mattie Lobato

Chance

Smiling, I watch you pass my way
Thinking of you, not knowing the words I long to say

A somber summer's day that I do recall,
Listening to a laugh so wonderful,

We exchange memories, laughter, even slight loving consent
Glance at one another, yet never allowed a moment.

A friendship kindles like a warm winter's fire,
An innocent romance longing to transpire.

Honesty begins to bring a sad good-bye,
Never knowing where this friendship's future may lie.

Time passes and hellos be said,
Yet this friendship's life does not end.

Now these two continue their humble innocence
Is it fate, destiny, or mere coincidence . . .

Friends, lovers, or lovers and friends in one another, we may find
I breathe, wake, and live each day with time.

Charles Neil Snetsinger, II

The Dying Smile

I cannot fathom.
My companion cried and wept till dawn.
She was dubbed the cancer's spawn.
She shined in her last bed like a crystal beacon,
though I rather her not, why—that was her sickness.
Though nearly quarter a century seemed hardly worthwhile,
she handed me life in a garden of smiles.
I have my whole life ahead, forced to leave hers behind,
wishing I could live my life in rewind.
She made my day, my nights and my years,
only to turn them to heart-pounding tears.
She left my life with a smile on her face.
As she lived, she died with grace.
I cannot fathom a smile on my face,
wishing I could be put in her place.
I cannot fathom loving again,
not until I see her when I am a hundred and ten.
When she was born, was the only one crying;
as she died, she was the only one smiling.

Ryan Boyce

Calling My Lover

May the sunflowers bloom and the daisies dance
The breeze of love's exchange from west to
East and east to west
A soft exhale of love's contentment
A deep breath again and again
As many thoughts prance deep inside my head
Underneath its cover
To and fro, calling to my lover
My beating heart, panting for another
So I close my eyes to be with you
Our love's gentle breeze swallows me
Like a vine I wrap myself around you
All my emotions ebb to the flow and there it is I belong
In the soft summer's breeze
I wade at the sweet taste of our love
Tonight as my eyes begin to shut
May they dance as they see
That we're together and our dreams touch
Once again my thoughts calling to my lover

Lafayette Armstrong

All I Worked For

Across icy Jordan, I shall never take
one trinket of gold or silver I make
All that I hoard and cherish today
after I'm gone on Earth must stay
tho' I should toil for an object rare
to display on a table
I'll leave it right there
Alive I can brag and boast my worth
but I'll give it all up
when I leave this Earth
So often I wonder just what will I own
when I cross that cold river alone
what will the master see
in the soul that answers the call for me
will the master say when my journey's through
that my soul has gathered a few riches too
or . . . in the end . . . will it be mine to find
that all I worked for
I left behind

Jesse Joseph Reynolds

Upon a Step at Night I Stood

Upon a step at night I stood
I looked across the narrow street
Where wondrous wealth did meet the light
Reflecting diamonds, dropped from Heaven's
Mine—the Horn of Plenty.

So delicately cut, so frail
The diamonds seemed to sail
Through calm, but chilled and wintry air
Upon the many there already.

I slept so soundly late that night.
The diamonds peppered white the pane,
While blue their brilliance entered clear
Through the window near my bed.

On waking—Daylight? thought I.
Yes. Morning came—Or had it come?
There was no sun—just diamond light—
Oh! Sparkling still, the riches fell and fell and fell!

Judith Hrycenko

Faith

On our trip back from two weeks
of seafood and sand castles,
I remembered.
"Mom!" I shrieked from the back seat
so loudly that she swore,
"I forgot to feed Max!"
Mom sat straighter and promised he'd be fine.
I prayed anyway, all the way
from the gas station to McDonald's,
then from McDonald's to the pet store.
At home I dashed upstairs with my bag
of bugs and released them inside
the aquarium on my dresser.
I pressed my face to the curved glass.
My lizard lay spiny and lifeless
as a seashell while spared crickets
preyed across his body.

What if God forgot about His dinosaurs
like I forgot mine?

Cathy Murphy

My Aunt

For Valerie, my favorite aunt

She is my aunt,
the one I love the most.
How frightful for her,
that she found out she was a host.
She is a person
like no other.
No one could even come close
except, of course, my mother.
We live far apart,
and nobody in my family agrees with that.
She has the biggest heart,
not just some mean old bat.
Even though she's sick,
she can still keep up with her beautiful grandchildren.
Nothing would be sadder
than to see that come to an end.
So let's keep fighting to help cure M.S.,
and not let this disease bring other people to an end.

Cara Elaine Hendrix

The Question

Yes, this is another poem from me to you
So, this will make poem number two.

There is a woman who has entered my life
Whom someday I hope will become my wife.

Do you remember "You Are Not Alone," our song,
That you are always in my heart, do you belong?

You have touched me with your gentleness
With you around, I feel pure contentedness.

We have prayed upon our hearts to the Lord
He has found it in His time to now open our door.

We have both known our true feelings for a while.
For me, it began when I first saw you and your smile.

So to let you know, the question will be asked in time.
Will the answer be yes to toast over a glass of wine?

Now this is the end of my poem.
I can't wait for you to move into my home.

Mark Hertz

Do We Long to See Jesus?

Do we ever look up to the Easter sky,
and wonder if Jesus might be night?

Will we really be happy to see
Jesus arriving for you and me?

The lilacs says he will come as a thief,
Will we be fearful or feel relief?

Will we lose our patience and turn away,
Thinking that He surely won't come today?

We must be prepared for we know not when
From the Heavens alone he will descend.

So be not afraid and trust to the end
Though some may fail us, he is our dearest Friend.

When we confess and believe His holy will,
He forgives us our sins and loves us still.

Then no longer on Earth will we roam,
For Jesus is coming to take us home.

Edna Reeves

The Gift

A day of loneliness and rejection
Afforded no pleasure
For the long road ahead
Praying for enlightenment
Ending with the Lord's Prayer

Suddenly a blinding storm
Covered everything in sight
Prayer more immanent than before
As fast as lightning the rain disappeared
A spiritual beauty of Heaven unveiled
With colors in a rainbow
Colorists would embrace
Reflecting in the bayous
Joining Heaven and Earth

When the road ahead darkens
I will always remember
The gift our Father gave to us is
Locked in our hearts

Louise Coviello

Poems

In youth I had a dream so high.
Life intervened; busy years flew by.
The dream lay dormant.
Is it too late for dreams to come true?
At my age could I try something new?

I wrote stories, quite a few.
It proved a struggle to get through.
Then I tried poems.
I love the rhythm and rhyme.
They bubble in my head like sparkling red wine.

Beauty, pain, life, love, sun, and flowers.
Poems remind us of rainbows and showers, of life being lived.
Sunshine, rain, gardens, and trees.
Poems sing of things like these.

They can remind us of sorrow and pain.
Sunshine and flowers can be followed by rain,
But poems lift us, give us hope while we endure the pain
And wait for the sun to shine forth again.

Inger Simerly

Night Freedom

Moored in a backwater harbor,
Swaying and pulling against roped constraints,
Windsong feels her lines now taut, now loose.
Moving fretfully, she grumbles and sighs:
Not the song she wants to sing.
An outgoing tide slap-slaps her hull; begone, begone.
Windsong may, on a moonless night,
Break free from lines too carelessly tied
And slip away to her own dark freedom.
Vessel of night flight, let me board.
Vessel of night hope, take me with you.
Let me, a moving shadow on your deck,
Loose your sail ties and let up the main,
Turning you into the quickening wind.
Take me away from slap-slap words,
From hands that tie knots too tight.
Take me away from roped constraints
That moor the spirit.
Let us begone, begone.

Peggy Eastman

Legacy of Love

Do not for me weep.
I am not dead, but rather instead
I sleep and live
When in your heart you have love to give,
For the greatest gift you'll ever earn
To simply to love and be loved in return.
This, my legacy, to you I leave:
To live, to love, to soar, to achieve.
Do not weep for me, for I am not dead,
But celebrate my life.
That whistle of the wind is my voice,
A song to rejoice.
That soft rain upon your cheek is my touch,
To reassure, not to fear or dread,
That still I care so much.
I am with you always, with eager heart and mind.
Call me; I'll be there, you will find.
This is my legacy.
I give with humility.

Jack Compton

Till the End of Time

I take this walk across my mind
walking until the end of time
Vivid images that haunt me
Words that taunt me
I did not choose to walk this walk
But I have lost myself
So I must walk, walk across my angry mind
till the end of time
Faces that blame me
People that hurt me
All the things I see here
are a part of me, I know this now
This is how I made it here
As I cross the path of my memories
Walking across my mind . . . till the end of time
I must say my good-byes now . . .
As I walk deeper into the dark nothingness of the unknown
I have walked across my mind . . .
Until the end of time.

Erica Latoya Sip

Time Is Perfection

As the sun rises above the horizon,
A young boy and his tired father
Get all their fishing tackle and bait ready
In anticipation of a marvelous time together.
The canoe is slid into the shimmering water.
The two jump gently into the bobbing canoe
And start the search for the perfect spot.
At last the precious spot is found,
The lines are baited and lowered down,
And the serene and quiet waiting game begins.
The boy gets a strike!
The large trout is reeled in slowly.
The young boy is ecstatic,
His eyes are glowing with excitement.
The father seems even more excited.
Their luck continues all day.
They return home jubilant and tired.
The colorful sunset is spectacular across the water,
And the perfect end to the perfect day.

Karol Hyland

The Darkness Doesn't Answer

Darkness black with despair
Her heart cries
The blackness deepens with dark
Her thoughts sink in the well of sadness
Life's hopes fade with the wearing of souls
These Spirits need souls to ride with joy
Where is the Joy?
Will it come with death?
Will the darkness turn to light with the
sun's ray?
Light imprints dreams
Is darkness a dream, or is it the light?
Her thoughts sink in the well of darkness
Dreams fade with the wearing of souls
Light calls the darkness, the darkness
doesn't answer
Where is the Joy?
Will it come with Life?
Light imprints dreams.

Francine Sterud

The Moment

No longer in the days of the year
A specious child to the sympathetic ear
She crossed over to the sleepless darkness
You will always be a simple princess

Growing out of the moon's mysterious light
He screamed the names of the gallant that night

No longer in the hours of the day
A spectacular sight was once twenty-twenty
She danced the spells for the stars her crystals
You will always be the queen of onyx

Growing out of the moon's mysterious light
He shed his red-eyed blood for everything right

Never again in the minutes of that hour
A lifeless soul in the arms of a maiden
A pale face stricken for what had happened
The laughter of fate shown on her hands.

"My love, what have I done?"

Heather Paiser

In the Mirror

In the mirror I am a wolf
With light blue fur and light blue eyes,
Deserted in the moonlit desert.
I travel to find other wolves
But cannot find them,
Only stopping for sleep,
Growling at everything that crosses or comes beside me.
I'm trying to yell for my family
But I wind up howling.
Eating scorpions, spiders, bugs, lizards,
In my mind I think wolves are wild, old living, vicious.
When I am sick, I just lay there and howl at the moon.
I start to change into something else,
A dragon in a cave wrapped in chains.
I'm trying to burn my way out of them.
I'm cut up, bitten up really bad from a battle.
I notice another dragon, my best friend.
Next I see me and my friend are put on a cross together.
I stare and stare and I smile, knowing that I'll be fine.

Patrick James Newton

Rain

She gazes out at the blistering rain,
Feels suffocated by the confines of her life.
"I've lost control of everything," she explains,
Shedding bitter tears of sorrow and strife.

She extends her hesitating hand to me.
I reach out, try to save her from pain.
For a brief second our fingers meet,
Before she slips and falls again.

As her weeping eyes search mine,
Down the swirling vortex she sinks,
Lower and lower into her binds,
Surrounded by flaming reds and pinks.

I try to clinch her reaching hand,
Relinquish the victim from danger's lair.
But she disappears into the quicksand,
As my searching hands grasp thin air.

The rain continues to pour.

Meng-meng Fu

Cote

My special one,
God's gift to me:
My beautiful son.
His hair of gold
And eyes hazel green,
If he were any more perfect,
He would have to be a dream,
When he says, "I love you,"
All words, honest and pure.
His big hugs fill me up inside
And as I watch him grow smarter,
He builds on my pride.
The closeness and understanding
Is so very true, to think
Of a life without him . . .
I'd be lost without a clue.
So together forever, always side by side,
I'll try to make his life wonderful
For making me feel this way inside.

Carriann MacDonald

You Whom I've Never Met

I have longed to touch you
To be held by you, to smell you
To know you, my heart has yearned for you,
You Whom I've Never Met
I've missed you all of my life
I've cried for days and many nights
Although, I've never seen you face
to face, I know your resting in an
eternal place, through God's love,
his mercy and his grace, he has lifted
me above all the agony and pain, of not
having you here with me every day
Through him I have found the way,
to live without you and just pray, that
someday, he will join us together in
his special place, and I'll be able to
tell you face to face, all the things
I've longed to say, I love you, I've
missed you, Daddy can I hold you

Mynida Roxanna Williams

Start with One

Looking for a way, means, or sign,
Guidance for what can be done.
Where to begin before the end,
Some mark on accomplishment to leave behind.
So many questions in the world today,
Answers we search for in vain.
Trying our best to help so many,
Giving and loving without condition.
Trying to press our limitations,
Wearing down our bodies and minds.
Wanting just a little inner peace
But settling for some realization.
Caring for one or a handful if lucky,
Family, friends, or a special loved one.
This could be just as fulfilling,
Rewarding and touching in this finding.
Laughing, crying, the sharing of life,
Knowing we are making a difference.
Heaven on Earth for those whom partake.

Gary L. Wessner, Jr.

Whole

You fill my empty space with an easy beauty
and chase away the skeletons others have
left behind with understanding in your eyes.
Holding you, I could sleep forever
knowing you are close by,
the sweetness of your breath just inches
from my heart.
I can see you there etched in my mind,
like the melody of some ancient love song
played for only us to hear.
You whisper your secrets
(all the hidden treasures of your spirit)
allowing them to echo in the hollow cavern
of my soul.
You bring your heat to me and radiate it
off my skin that aches for your touch.
We are like two separate puzzle pieces
locked together to become two halves
of a love that makes us whole.

Christy Marie Schmalfeld

Marriage

Jenn, my love, I want you to know,
on the mountain top tomorrow I'll show.
So don't you fret, and don't be tense,
for on the morrow there'll be no suspense,
I'll be there just to marry you,
It's something I really want to do!
For when we're together, I feel complete inside and out,
happy together we'll be,
of that I've no doubt.
Our times together, they seem so great,
for more time with you, I just can't wait!
I know it's not all peaches and cream,
but it all works out good,
with you it does seem.
I'm looking forward to our life together
of having kids, being married
and in love forever!
For you are the love of my life,
and tomorrow you will be my wife!

Curt A. Jordan

Grief

It's hard to breathe
Not because you can't
But because you don't want to
Yet, not even because you don't want to
Because you don't care
Nothing matters much anymore

People talk around you
You don't listen
You don't hear them
You hope they don't talk to you
Yet you dread being alone with your thoughts
Oh, torturous thoughts

You hate those faces
Faces that stare
Faces that smile
Faces that don't understand
They don't have a clue
They try to understand and fail

Jennifer Joy Maloney

Little Girl

Little Girl, Little Girl. The center of my world.
Little Girl, Little Girl. I knew the minute I saw you,
you'd be the center of my world.

You wasn't a mommy's girl or a daddy's girl,
but you lived in your own world.
I loved you at a distance, but in an instance,
Little Girl, Little Girl! You were the center of my world.

Watching you grow up, has filled my cup,
with proudness and pleasure,
the child I'll always treasure.
Little girl, Little girl, the center of my world.

People say you're smart, but they could not begin to start
to know you like I do, 'cause I see me in you.
Little girl, Little girl, the center of my world.

The day is here for you to walk that aisle,
no longer a child, but you'll always be to me,
Little girl, Little girl, the center of my world.

Marilyn Henley

My Dog

My dog is very weird.
He eats anything off the floor, even foil.
If there's gum, he'll chew it.
If there's candy, he'll eat it.

When he hears something outside,
He'll go out there and bark,
The whole night.

If he doesn't know you,
You better watch out,
'Cause he'll most likely bite you.
Trust me, he's done it before.

If you have food, watch it
'Cause if you turn your head,
It's gone!

So if you come to my house,
Keep an eye out
For my dog!

Evan Spellman

My Star

You are the star that shines at night
Your glow is here and everywhere
You fill the dark with light.
I see you and I touch you and I love you . . .
But what's more . . .it's good to know
the love I give is in your hands
You make me live . . . the woman I adore
You're lovely and you're beautiful and in your shining eyes,
reflections of the dreams we share . . .
contentment in our ties . . .
What can I say . . . you make me go.
You lift me to these heights, I know . . .
I have your love; thank God for this . . .
Your tender touch, your wondrous kiss.
And in the end, what is my role?
To love and have you as my mate.
To gain your trust, that is my goal.
To love you is my fate,
for you have touched my soul.

Richard Procop

Waiting . . .

Alone he sits. Waiting for what he does not know.
Maybe a taxi, or a friend,
or maybe he just sits . . .
The vastness of the night sky provides a
canvas for his colorful mind to paint upon.
The pouring rain hits relentlessly against
the ground causing a warm sizzle.
The same sizzle of a cozy fire,
like the one back home, but still he waits . . .
Ahead of him stands his only acquaintance—
a slender street lamp, giving light only to
his immediate surroundings . . .
He gazes past his visual limits wondering
what is in this vast darkness waiting to be found.
With every sigh, steam is sent into the air,
only to dissipate in an ocean of black.
The night chill consumes his
unprotected face as water to an empty vase.
His countenance unchanging as he waits. . . .

Geoffrey Stephen Smith

Just before Dinner

Juan Carlos Jobim croons sweet Portuguese
Diaphanous clouds pepper the Mediterranean sky
Alix tells me, "Life is tough, quite tough"
He also says the moon makes people crazy
Then howls, to prove it
Above an ellipse of borrowed light spreads
itself thinly into the magnificent air
White oleander drop themselves exhausted
after days of bloom onto the terra cotta
tiles around the pool
Philippe and the boys have finished
their tennis match (all sweat and smiles)
The noise of revelers is carried even
over the well groomed juniper and sycamore
Genevieve places a bowl of white peaches
on the long wooden table
The air suddenly seems cool
I think I will finish my wine
and take a warm bath

Sarah J. Forman

Passing It On

Dear Son,
This world is so big, so full of things I want to share with you.
The bugle of an elk on a crisp October mountain,
the songs of rivers, and the music of shallow creeks.
I want you to see a moose up close—close enough
to see his nostrils steam in the morning air.
Let's hike far above the tree line where the wind owns the horizon,
and I'll show you where the bighorns have laid among the flowers.
And you need to see the Northern Lights and mountain constellations;
stars stacked so close together in the night sky,
that you can't believe your senses.
I want to show you grizzly tracks in the river bank mud
and wolf tracks in the snow.
And when I'm old and my eyes and ears are weak,
I hope you will say, "Dad, look at this," or "Dad, listen!"
And most of all, I hope to be around long enough
that someday, I'll hear you say, "Son, come and see this."
And hear the excitement in your voice
that you must hear in mine.

Mike Moutoux

Friendship

Listen to my thoughts
Listen to my prayers
Since you are my friend,
I know you really care.

People need guidance
Through life's big maze.
And you never know what it will give you,
Until you finish that phase.

I'm not always the one
To let my feelings show.
But you've been through it with me,
So you know
How I feel.

I told you all of my life
And I know that I can trust you
With everything that I have said to you
We're growing up,
And we'll go through it together.

Christine Gee

Grandpa

The G is for great, because Grandpa is the
greatest man I know. The R is for rare,
because he is one of a kind with a very
loving soul. The A is for awesome, because
I know my grandpa is the most awesome of
all. The N is for the never ending love he
has for us all. The D is for delightful
because he brings delight to all who know
him. The P is for powerful because of the
power he has to make you smile, even when
things may not look so glim. And the final
A is for authentic because, boy don't we all
know, God broke the mold when he made him.

Suzanne Peace

Mama's Boys

Mama's boys grew big and strong
Nourished with love flows deep from my heart
A day will come they'll have to leave
To put in practice the morals and values that once were taught
Without that voice that seemed to nag
I will have to let them go, as they say,
They must go
I will pray to God to be their keeper
To their success
Arrogance, they must do without, but humility
And appreciation is a must
Embedded in my heart are
Mama's boys

Cecilia Malele

Let It Speak

Spinning around, with my arms straight out,
as fast as I can, twirling about.
Looking up at the sky,
completely vertigo, as I begin to fly.
I am weightless, spinning around,
faster and faster, I can't slow down.
This is it, it feels like this.
This is love, I can't resist!
Let me spin, let me fly.
I don't want this feeling to start to die.
My heart is racing, my knees grown weak,
love is talking, so let it speak!
Let it speak!

Joseph Mentor Nichols

The Process of Becoming

As I watch, the fields are turned over,
a wave on the ocean;
rich silt kneading through mechanic claws.

I suppose long ago, bison roamed; tread steadily across
that very field—or a wagon plowed noisily, hopping from rut to rut
but no matter

For today it is in the process of becoming—
Over a cup of coffee, steam curling gently like a spirit
rising from a grave,
my eyes lock with yours—a moment shared
And I become the churned field,
wondering exactly where in your heart I stand.

Derrick Penner

Pain of the Unknown

I kiss away your tears, and all I seem to taste,
is the hurt and pain you hide beneath your bright smile.
Look into my eyes, see the love I yearn to show.
Please let me comfort you, and wipe away the sorrow.
It seems like all you do is worry and fuss over me,
when truly you're trying to hide
your own disappointment and agony.
Tell me I can help you. Let me pray for you.
Show me your heart, let me try to mend the hurt.
Don't hold it all inside. I need to know you'll be all right.
You can smile all you want. You can bottle it up inside.
But when you're ready to change the cause,
know I'll be by your side.

Audrey Mae Booth

Shellbound

Please don't walk away when I'm trying to
convey, I have things I want to say. I'm not
done yet, I have drool on my chin, please
don't look disgusted, for I can't ask for a
towel because I cannot speak. Please
understand my needs, for I cannot tell you.
Please understand that I had not intended to
be this way, sometime when you reflect upon
your work, maybe you can think how you would
feel if you were like me. Don't ever begrudge
yourself your freedom, for it can be taken
away so fast, and forgotten and betrayed is
your everlasting past.

Teresa Rose Cummings

Forgiveness

Where would I be,
had your arms not been waiting;
had God granted desires
my deceived heart was craving.

Foolishly, we seek pastures which appear
greener than our own,
yet you were the one to hold me
when the walls came crashing down.

Please don't ask me to explain.
My passionate heart escapes all reason.
It is said there is a time and purpose
under Heaven for each season.

Rebecca L. Harris

Life

Life, such a wonderful thing.
But do we take it for granted?
We go along thinking we are invincible,
That we are Superman.
But the end is always just around the corner.
Why are we so afraid of Death?
Why do we make it such a bad thing?
What if we never died?
Seeing the same people every day,
The monotony would be staggering.
Why can't we just accept that Death
is just another part of
Life.

Greg Johnson

Untitled

I have found my thoughts suspended in time,
As I am drained of the energy I once possessed.
Trying in vain to recall the memories of my past,
All I have left is the will to surrender.

I have reached this point with my life long companion,
Who has never once left my side.
I have questioned his loyalty on many occasions,
But at no time have I received a reply.

I look around and find no one there.
I cry out loud hoping he will hear me,
Only to be answered by a familiar silence,
I know he is still there, my loneliness will never leave me.

Leone Vukelj

Trees

Trees like life are varied in size,
Some like twigs, tiny and easily bent.
Others like boards, rigid and spent . . .
If they could tell stories what joy they would bring!
Tales of gentle breezes and birds that sing,
Seasons passing year after year . . .
Life ever changing, laughter held dear.
Tears of lovers staring out to sea,
Children playing, climbing towards God's sky.
Storm winds blowing death's gentle sigh.
The chattering of squirrels as winter snow
gives way to the newness of spring and all
of the glory that each day brings.

Deborah Powers Holloway

Precious and Few

Our time together is few and far between
It almost seems like a dream
Just to hear your voice makes my day
But your touch is the only way.

Inside of me you create such a fire
There is no doubt you are the one I desire
My love for you is real and undying
A never ending bond that is there without really trying

You are and will always be special to me
Your tender, caring way is how you need to be
Even tho' our time together is precious and few
My love will always be there for you!

Jan Roberts

What Is Life?

Life is an ever changing cycle.
There will be mountains and there will be valleys.
Everyone is afforded the chance to love,
And sadly, everyone will have lost a love or loved one.
Just remember!
Everything happens for reasons we may not see right away.
Every day isn't sunny, neither is every day gray.
Deal with the cards you're dealt, no matter how unfair.
It's part of life's ups and downs that everyone must share.
So keep your head up, remain strong, centered, and optimistic.
So when your ups revolve 'round again, you're not so jaded
that you miss it.

Cynthia McKoy

Thankful for My Life

To all who knew and loved her,
Farah was a heart so sweet.
She'll never know how much
She touched the ones she'll never meet.
We'll never forget your smile,
Your sweet angel face.
But we feel better now
That you're in a safer place.
A child so small and helpless
Should never know such strife.
Farah, thank you for helping me realize
I should be Thankful for my Life!

Love, Natasha

Natasha Marcoux

Mirror Image

When I look in the mirror,
the image I see is a picture of me.

Sometimes I know the image of me and
the rest of the time, I see the world's
judgement of me.

The image of me is forever changing and
has many faces for the world to see.
The mirror is a picture of me that I hope
someday to understand, so that when I look
in the mirror and see the image of me,
I hope that one day, I will be able to see
the picture image that is of me.

Mary Kathleen Patrick

Tracey

Tracey is a friend of ours—you couldn't ask for more.
Coming from Brazil to our fine shore.
She was adopted, and it opened the door.
It should have been easy forevermore.

Tracey needs a kidney and that's for sure.
Having lupus is all Tracey should fear.
Unfortunately it's her life from year to year.
Dialysis every day isn't easy, my dear.

Twenty-four is too young to be dead.
Living in a hospice plays with your head.
We hope a kidney comes instead.
Lupus is awful, but it doesn't make you dead.

Patricia Poore

Cracked

To all former users

There come's a time when we must see
Our world is not all it's cracked up to be
When you're all alone and down and out
our so-called friend's show us what it's all about
No time to live
Plenty of time to die
Nothing left to give
No where to get high
When this time come's we must simply say, Good-bye
Look to GOD, for he truly never lies
Can anyone break this down to size?

Donna Reinhardt

Thank You

Courage is a quality rarely found in a person
Faith in one self even more
Strength and the ability to stand alone in this world
Is a quality least found of all.

I have the courage to fulfill my dreams
And the faith in me is true
But the strength that runs through my heart and soul
Is powered by friends such as you.

Life is a miracle, death is inevitable
No-one can change what will be
So as I say farewell to you my friend
I thank you for setting me free.

Kellie Lorraine Chivers

Two Become One

When two people with loving hearts meet
They are given a chance to touch each other's heart
When this happens, a wonderful thing takes place
They fall head over heels in love with one another
There are those that try to find a special love
These have tendency to fall short of their expectations
Yet, when God brings two people together
That's when you know your love will last forever
The love we two share is just that
A gift from Our Lord God
A true blessing from Heaven
It is a love that will endure all the tests of time
May others find the love we found in each other

Antonio Manuel Fernandez

Compassion

I prayed for you today.
Boldly came I to the throne of grace.
Angels sang and shouted praise to the most high.
With a piercing, loving gaze that asked, and I answered,
Nay, Lord, I bring no iniquity, and yea, Lord, I come in your name.
I prayed for you today.
Boldly came I to the advocate with my petition,
And laid it at the master's feet at the throne of grace.
Spellbound, I watched as the king of kings presented the request
To the father who replied,
"Anyone who honors you, my son, honors me; thy will be done!"
I prayed for you today at the throne of grace,
and mortal met immortal in peace and pardon.

Furman J. Smith

Don't Give In

When the weight of life seems unbearable,
close your eyes and imagine yourself like that of an eagle.
If darkness appears to never end and
suicide feels like the only way, then find
a window, for the sun will soon be rising.
The rain spell is not everlasting.
And if you look towards the clouds, you'll
see a rainbow radiating just for you.
Avoid the traps of self-pity.
Life is an experience.
There will be days when you feel you can't cope.
In essence, seek the strength of your inner spirit
and in time, you will overcome.

Rebecca M. C. Vaughns

It's Love As Sure As I Am

As we look back at this moment
We wonder just how it began
Our whole life led up this moment
And it's love as sure as I am.

We just got lost in each other
It's so good it's hard to believe
Our whole life of searching is over
and you're here as sure as I am.

The life in this body expressing itself
Like blossoms when springtime comes 'round.
is you in disguise when you look in my eyes
and see that it's really just you.

Pateh

King of Kings

How much more can we take from Him?
First we're up, then we're down,
sometimes we're laughin', sometimes we're frownin'.
One minute we're up, one minute we're down.
Then it's this, then it's that.
We're always complaining about this and that.
How would you like to listen to that?
He does it every day.
Think about that!
He's the king! He wears the crown.
Still, He's listening to us here on the ground.
Do you know another? So high and Holy?
That will listen to you solely?

Vivian M. Brandon

Julianne

I once knew a girl with straightened blonde hair.
I would catch her entranced in deepened stare,
For there was this boy who caught her head over heels.
But later learned he had other appeals.

She looked at him with glowing eyes.
But little did she know she would have to say good-bye.
He talked to her at lunch and walked her to her door,
He lead her on, then said "No more!"

For there was another girl who entered his life,
Which hurt her so and caused much strife.
So if you see this girl with straightened blonde hair,
Know she is strong, but handle with care.

Kelly N. Pierce

The Man I Am

Because my clothes are torn and need some mending
My hair grown long, my feet are bare
I'm still the man I claim to be
Trust worthy and sincere with worthy principles
My cloak of truth I'll proudly wear

I care not if my status shows a lack of worldly goods
If a good name I can claim
But far be it if wealth and fame be yours
To think you're not as good is not my aim
Yet if I can look at life squarely in the eye
And face my God with love not shame
What matters what I wear outside
If I can be the man I know within!

Aurora C. Nicholas

In the Mind of a Teacher

I am a teacher who is always stressed
I hate it when I try to talk, but the
students do not listen.
I have good days when everyone participates.
But most of the time all they want to do is sleep.
I go home and wonder . . .
Why don't they like me?
Am I a bad teacher?
I can't just let them do whatever because
the county has certain expectations.
I try to make things fun so that it sticks
in their mind,
I guess I have to make it more interesting, so they will enjoy it.

Donna Lynn Gibson

Life on Earth

I never thought it would be paradise,
I walked a rigged pathway from the start,
No ugliness was hidden from the start,
No ugliness was hidden from my eyes,
Nor was life's pain a stranger to my heart,
And yet the earth sprung firm beneath my feet,
And summer winds were gentle to my hair,
I know gray moors where shadow mist lie curled,
And sun bright streams and night skies rich with stars,
For all its faults, I so have loved this world,
And found it beautiful despite its scars,
Though angels sing of glories greater,
Still, I leave in sadness much against my will.

Donna Carnwell

God Help Me

Help me today so I can be like you tomorrow . . .

Help me see light . . .
when darkness is all around
Help me to smile . . .
when I feel I want to frown
Help me be brave . . .
when my mind tells me to fear
Help me show the world . . .
how much I really care
Help me be kind to everyone I see . . .
Help me show the world that you live inside of me
Help me with my choices and everything I do . . .
Help me show the world we can all be like you

Donna Marie Fanning

Welcome

I welcome you—
To the beginning of the end.
For to be born is not to be given life,
But to be given death.
Because once you are born,
You begin to die.
So look upon what has been give to the world—
Another story which saddens the sky,
And brings tears to the soul.
Another story in which I know Oh, to well—
Another story that makes Earth seem like
Hell.
Another story that must be told.

Nicholas Rogelio Perez

Pearl of Heaven

Deep in the sea where Atlantis lies
and the Manta Diablo (or devilfish) flies
quickly through the murky depths
guarding the Great Pearl of Heaven
no one has ever found it
because of depth and monsters around it
no one's hand has ever obscured
its sleek black surface
its sole purpose to please Madona
the goddess of the sea
its only flaw is that it brings death and destruction
to all who insult the sea
and the Manta Diablo

Cassandra Lee Guernsey

Innocent Victims

Small and defenseless with nowhere to run
Marching to the beat of one woman's drum
Unable to determine their paths in life
Lives cut short with a single-edged knife

Not asking, but desiring so much to live
To experience the love that only she can give
Stuck in the struggle between life and death
Praying and wishing for just one more breath

Seeing the knife and realizing the time has come
Nowhere to escape and nowhere to run
Soon this life will be no more
The innocent victims must travel to a different shore.

Corey Bu-Shea King

My Love

Thoughts wander, what does it mean?
Night after night you fill my dreams.
I stare into the starry midnight sky, your face appears.
I find myself living in future memories.
Why are the obvious things so hard to see?
Because I need you?
Am I blinded by your gentle smile?
If you were to ever disappear, would my heart be left empty?
Without you near, why do I feel incomplete?
I can't seem to reach you . . . why?
I ask myself, I find, still no answer.
Searching my ocean of thoughts, the only words I find are . . .
I love you.

Stephanie Laura Piscopo

The Summer Resurrection

The sun shone high in the afternoon,
as the children died by arrows and pistols.
The dead rose like angels in the sky,
as the sound of a magic bell called to their souls.

They flew on the wind and clouds,
and sailed on the sky, as the enchanted castle
rolled to a stop in front of shoe-shod feet.
"Chocolate faces for two-bits!" cried the ice cream prince.

Back to the battlefield the dead return,
their faces and hands covered in a sticky coating of joy.
Once more in the grass they lay,
as at peace as the Cowboys and Indians of old.

James G. Kovachik

When Harkness Tolls

So he wished to give me his jaded pearls
All over again. Sequential madness.
I'm supposed to treat them like holy beads
Of just his semi-physical entity.
It's all right. It's okay. It's even good.
As long as he says, "Umm . . . I am sort of here."
Suicide attempts? What he thinks of them?
No. Those are mine . . . mine alone. Cannon balls.
Lethal. Relativistic. Finally . . .
Ready to explode. Like cracking, splitting guts
Of war-weary detonated ghosts.

This is to you, my love, half-there and yet
Only never quite . . . never quite . . . when Harkness tolls.

Sabrina Afroze Sadique

Beyond the Horizon

As I gaze out to sea,
A perfect line forms in the distance.
This point where sky meets earth,
Forms questions upon my existence.

What lies beyond the water and the Heavens?
Do I owe my being to pure coincidence?
Or I am product of divine creation?
I wish someone could ease my inner turbulence.

I cannot be of both origins,
Therefore I must stand to consider the two.
Somehow I must find the one answer
Beyond dueling hues of contrasting blue.

Luc J. Miron

I Am No Stranger to Pain

I am no stranger to pain.
I, the one that God forgot about.
When he looks down from his throne on high,
he doesn't see me.
Sitting.
In a puddle of my own tears.
Crying for the life I wish I had,
the one that others take for granted.
He fails to acknowledge my loneliness,
my depression.
It's not that he doesn't care, it's just that he
doesn't see.
You can't care about what you don't see.

Willard Allen Vaughn

The Dreamer

Like a tortured soul I struggle on
Night turning into endless night
Daylight is shrouded like a mournful sigh
Droplets of tears wrap my troubled mind
Will I ever know the springtime of joy
Or the pleasant dew of a new morning
Or will I spend my life in winter's discontent
Time, like a heavy load, hangs upon my shoulders
With each passing moment, consuming life's moisture
I must perish then only can I find sweet repose
Oh, death, whose sensuous arms beckon to me
I must resist for surely hope will meet me at dawn's horizon
When I awaken to that perfect day then paradise will be mine

Rose Warren

"I've Been Sleepwalking"

Where has my life gone? It seems like
only yesterday, I was young and care free,
and now it's twenty years later.
"I've been sleepwalking."
Why does my mind lose track of time and
only remember highlights from my past?
"I've" been sleepwalking."
Why did you and I, who were once so close,
drift apart and become strangers?
"I've been sleepwalking."
Why is it the harder I try and make sense
of it all, the less I understand?
"I've been sleepwalking."
I'm not sure about anything anymore, what I
thought was the way turned out to be a
dead end road, which leaves me scared,
lost, and confused.
"I've been sleepwalking."

Linn Rey Menzie

Rain

Rain falls down,
cold as ice.
You think that it feels nice.
Against your skin,
raindrops splash,
and now they're turning into ash.
Your mind wanders,
dark and renewed,
the shapes are shifting fast.
You look around
at the world and it is different now.
You see things a way you've never seen things;
you feel a way you've never felt.
You do not recognize anything.
The Earth turns and you come about.
You see things once again.
They are normal, reality.
Is the lost world gone forever?

Kayla Sue Hartsock

Nature

How is nature a wonder,
too much to hold.
Is there any more yonder?
For it is as good as gold.

The prowl of the lion at night,
and the antelope running is a sight.
Is there any more yonder?
For it is as good as gold.

When the butterfly comes from a long stay bright,
it makes a sad face cheerfully right.
Is there any more yonder?
For it is as good as gold.

When I came to a conclusion,
I told myself it was all an illusion.
But still, is there any more yonder?
For it is as good as gold.

Nabil Perwad

The Invisible Race

What powers does a cloth possess?
When draped in finery, one is blessed.
What securities does a household bring?
It seems to give them everything.

A job, good food, and friends who care,
But still they stay so unaware.
And if they should fall from glory and grace?
A new member's brought to the invisible race.
And one by one, the friends slip away
And leave you to struggle, day after day.
The clothes become soiled and torn with age,
And all we are left with is a heart full of rage.
You blame us, you scorn us, we're lazy, you say,
But we've looked for work, day after day.
Still, no one would help a dirty old bum.
Would you? If you had the chance to help one?
And you, when you're safe, in your comfortable place,
Forget all about the invisible race.

Shondelle Arcand

First Impression of a Rose, Mayqui (May Quay)

Rosalie, beautiful flower. Protected from
frigid winds and monsoon showers. Eyes that
run deeper than the Nile. A woman with
charisma, elegance, style. Golden compassion
neither bought nor sold. Stress reliever of every
day LIFE. Definition of a perfect WIFE.
Recipe to open up Doors. Immense World not
explored. Sweet apple to the core,
conversation never bore. Call 911, get me the
Dr., healing sore scars that trespassers
left on your heart. With me you will extend
your wings Angel and SOAR, Love Lamoure'. We
will score. Haven't we met somewhere before?
Reflections from my mind, like floating on
cloud nine. Thoughts deeper than the
oceans, soothing mental potions, quiet
devotions. Blink, whisked away to remote
lands. Long, intimate walks, on the soft
Caribbean sands, as I exhibit a True Man.

Samuel M. King

Addiction!

Parents! What is your quest?
To protect your siblings from harm, yes?
Why do so many have harm befall them?
No poor excuses! Not a soul to blame,
But you and friends.
Don't shrink away! Must confront them now!
Or forever hold your peace.
Siblings' lives are at stake. Don't you give a hoot?
Help them! Free them!
Or forever hold your peace.
They feed themselves increasingly each day.
They're in jail with the key disappearing.
Must grab it before it sinks to an endless pit!
Siblings will bear a ball and chain till forever comes.
Stand up! Take them by force!
Do what is right. Don't let them ruin lives.
For you are their protector,
Before they forever hold their peace.

Daphne Ann Chapin

Too Young to Cry

Her smile lit up the sky
Her eyes shown with pure delight
No pain would she share
She was too young to cry
The pain was hers and hers alone
She shed no tear, she cried no name
She just smiled with the sun,
Then smiled with the rain
She was too young to cry
No one knew the secret she kept
She would not share her pain
She would not stand for sorrow in their eyes
To her they were too young to cry
She bought her own grave
She bought her own tomb
And on it she had said,
"Mommy and Daddy, even with death
I was too young to cry!"

Penny Marie Thomas

We Are Here

We come in many sizes, colors, shapes and forms.
To reach God's children
To reach into every home.

We might look likes bums or heroes
dogs or humans
Special visions do we form.

To reach the huddled masses,
lost in drugs, wars and forlorn.
Lost of hope and dreams, lost in pain
and anger, lost in grief and guilt.
Too deep to pull themselves out.

We reach into your dreams, hear our
voices, feel our love reaching out.

Feel our Father, feel our joy, feel our
warmth that wraps around you, when
your heart is opened wide.

Melody Haidsiakm

How I Love Thee

Lord, I have to say how I love thee
for what you have given me.
My loving parents watching me grow,
Teaching me to always depend on thee.
My best friend trustful and true,
and never makes me feel unwanted or blue.
My children of good health and undying love,
watched over by your beautiful white dove.
My grandchildren you gave your brightest star for their eyes.
Their smile is the joy in your heart.
Your gentle touch is their hearts.
For anyone who saw them, their day had a new start.
As I grow older I have no fear, even when my death is near.
For I read your words and you said, now listen here.
Be kind gentle and true to heart.
Your new life with me will be a joyful start.
How happy we all will be, for the LORD was so clever.
He promised us we all will be together someday forever.

Catherine M. Wakefield

Amen

I see in my heart a special place

The wind's in your hair
The sun in your face
The peace in your eyes
And a moment of faith
I hope you can find in one another place

Look into my eyes
Put the wind in my hair
The sun in my face
and teach me your faith
Take me back to that special place
I need to know that moment of faith

I'll open my heart so you can come in
I don't need a lover as much as a friend
Till I learn how to believe and love again
I'll give to you my trust within
The key to my heart to restore, amen.

Pat Robertson

Wishes

I wish that every child could know
The joy of a yard, watching things grow.
To frolic with barefooted joy on the grass,
As soft and green as lad or lass.
Each child would be near a stream
To splash in, fish, or just dream.
Free of lessons and "No, you can'ts"
In loose-fitting shirts and dirty pants.
And oh, each child would have to be
Near a woodsy spot to sit under a tree.
Every child would be near a grassy plain,
Where flowers grow to pick or to chain.
Kids need a sidewalk with bugs and ants
To watch them at work as though in a trance.
And then a close friend to confide in,
Confront, whisper secrets as horizons widen.
Most of all, a child needs,
Time alone to plan great deeds.

Angie Hall

Spring's Magic Show

Dandelions, you popped up fast
Dressed in your coat of conspicuous green.
Are you ready to do your magic now?
It's the most amazing show I've ever seen.

First, you exhibit a yellow round shaped dollar,
You hold it up for all to see,
Then you flip it over very fast.
How you do it is far beyond me.

But suddenly all the yellow's gone
And in its stead is a silver ball,
Clearly changed from flat to round.
How did you make it stand up tall?

Then, while I stare in wonder and amazement
Poof goes the ball into the wind
Only now it's a maze of parachutes
scattering all about.
What a show! See it. I heartily recommend!

Celestine Pettrie

A Man with Remarkable Blue Eyes

As I close my eyes I see a man
A man with remarkable blue eyes.
But as he stares at me they seem to be
dark and droop with sorrow. As if they
were a pair of eyes that cried forever.
His appearance is healthy and strong
But his walk is weak with a twisted slant
As if his legs can hold him up no longer.
When he stands, he stands tall with a bold clean cut look
But deep down inside I notice the scars.
The cuts and bruises left from lost battles and
challenges he faced throughout his life.
When everybody looks at him they see a man
with no worries in life.
But they are too blind to see the sadness he holds inside.
As I continue to stare at this man I realize
that my eyes were never closed, but that
they are wide upon, staring into a mirror.

David Pouler

Thank You, God, That She Is Mine

For years I dreamed of her—
The perfect little angel sent from above.
Then one day God smiled upon me,
Answering my prayers above and
Beyond anything I could wish for.

She is the sweetest and most beautiful
Child in all the world.
I hold her and can't believe
That I am so blessed.
I don't have the words to express
The love and joy that I feel when I kiss her.

God, did you really love me this much
That you would entrust me with something so precious?
I can only express my gratitude
By loving her as you have loved me,
And by saying to you,
Thank you, God, that she is mine.

Shelia Skinner

Nothing's Too Hard for God!

Look how far you came
Look back and see you're not the same

Can't you see what He brought you through
I know there's nothing He can't do

Since He doesn't make mistakes
He won't put more on you than you can take

He'll give you strength when you have none?
remembers he gave His Only Son

Every day I pray for you all
'Cause I know He won't let you fall

If sometime you get weary
being human your eyes get teary

You must already know, he knows your feelings
before you feel them

Keep seeking God with Him there's healing

Deatria Freeney

Faces of Courage

There are those who have lost a loved one dear
And those who gave up a home to come here
A devastating illness has stricken some
And they are trying to valiantly overcome
The faces of courage we all can see
If we just look around us, you and me
Just look around and understand
The courageous artist with the stricken hand
Arms and legs that are no longer steady
Weakness in muscles that once were so ready
Faces of courage remembering too
When days were not lonely and sad and blue
Faces of courage that give us a smile
Through pain and frustration all of the while
Faces of courage keep going along
Showing their faith like a happy song
Yes, those faces of courage we all can see
If we just look around us, you and me.

Margaret C. Dayton

A Little Wisdom

I thought I had not, I wondered why things were so dim.
I couldn't feel, see, touch, or smell the joy around me or within.
The doom and the gloom, they were sucking me in.
This is easier said than done, I know, but here I will begin:
There is joy all around you, don't you know
God has a plan so let him lead.
Stand united and don't be deceived.
As the child trusts the parent, as it should be,
give your worries and woes to God and please don't resent it
Don't worry what you have not,
count the little things you have forgot.
Find a little piece of joy each day,
hold it and cherish it the rest of the way.

When you look back on days gone by,
you'll see yourself now stronger and wiser,
but still wonder why.
God will take care we only have to trust.
Know in your hearts, he really loves us.

Deb Hines

Tear of Pain

As I fall asleep, a cold breeze brushes
gently my cheeks
and it unleashes eternal tears of pain
that penetrates straight through my soul
and heart and into my chest
I look around and emptiness and sadness rule my life
and without putting up a fight
I fall into a bottomless pit
and experience the suffering
in my own flesh
and I know then what a tear of pain is

I saw her
I look at her right at her eyes
and turn around and walk away
now that I know what a tear of pain is
I ask myself,
"Would I turn around and walk away again
or would I kneel and kiss her feet?"

Juan Manuel Samayoa

how would you describe me?

am i like a butterfly with many things to say,
am i like a unicorn peaceful every day,
am i like an angel perfect in every way,
am i like a puppy when it starts to play.

am i like something you can make out of clay,
am i something you would find near some hay,
am i like a sun rise that you can see from the bay,

am i someone who likes to argue,
am i someone who likes to fight,
am i someone who likes to hurt you,
am i someone who likes to make you mad,
am i someone who likes to make you sad,

am i someone who likes to make you happy,
am i someone who likes to see you smile,

am i like time moving all day long,
am i like a bird trying to sing a song,

Jeremy Kyle Goff

Mixed Emotions

My, Oh, my! Woe is me.
My body is consumed by nervous energy.
From the crown of my head,
to the soles of my feet,
I feel joy, I feel doubt, I feel uncertainty.
I feel hot, I feel cold,
I feel a yearning in my soul.
I run here, I run there.
This heavy load is hard to bear.

Stand still and see the salvation of God.
Every road that you're treading, He's already trod.
He says, "If you're heavy ladened, come unto me.
Don't be consumed by nervous energy."
You'll find rest, and peace,
and joys that never cease.
If you just hear His voice, and make Him your choice,
what a glorious change in your life,
there will be!

Lillie C. Varner

Divinity and Me

Within every breath I take in Your essence
Your spirit surrounds, envelops my totality

Inner calming, peacefulness settles upon me
As a soft enclosing mantle, Your protective shield
Embraces me gently, yet firmly staves off offenses
With a repelling force fueled by Divine grace

My aura is magnetized with your Divine energy
Compelling only positive response, insights, actions
Leaving the negative ions scattered to the wind
Where they can be recharged once again

Turning negatives into positives
As easy as taking in a breath
Inhale the goodness . . . recharge
Exhale the negative debris . . .discharge
Stand tall and confident
Filled with new found positive energy
Divinity and me

Charlene Hatton

The Journey

Set the compass, mark the course, the path that You would make.
Steer the ship, hoist the sail for the journey I should take.
If the night is dark, and no stars light up the sky,
Lead me through the darkness 'til the morning cometh nigh.
If the day is dreary and the sun does not appear,
Lead me through the gloom so the way I do not fear.
If my ship on rough seas, reels from side to side,
Lead me where the seas are calm, where my fears will then subside.
If I come on rocky ground, and no longer can I sail,
Lead me safely to the shore so my courage does not fail.
You Lord are the captain, the navigator and the mate,
You decide the course we take, it's not left up to fate.
You decide the day, and the moment for each hour,
You are Majestic, Holy, as you display Your awesome power.
My life is like a journey on a ship around the world,
I don't know where I'm going, but Your Kingdom has unfurled
Before my very eyes, Each day I can be assured
That You're in control of everything You promised in Your Word.

Nikki Jane Dutton

Reflections in the Sand

To a love that wasn't . . .

Along the shore one evening we roamed,
together in neither step nor soul.

I stopped often to pick up a shell or two,
and once in my hand, threw down very few.

Broken or whole, rough or smooth,
'twas no matter to me; beauty still ensued.

I took with me a pocket full of gems,
he with him merely images in his head.

He sent many glances into the sand,
but found nothing fitting of his hand.

I am one of those shells, not beautiful and whole,
slightly flawed from a journey to places untold.

Oh, what an overwhelming misconception,
he should give himself to nothing less than perfection.

Lindsay R. Mannelin

Feelings and Dreams

Under the full moon and a sky full of stars,
You are close to me and yet so far.
There are so many words I'd like to say,
And yet, silent I stay.
To you I may not exist,
As I hide myself in the mist.
To me you are the light in my heart,
Of which I'm sure you will always be a part.
Nobody knows how I feel inside
As to some obligations I must abide.
But sometimes I've been close to letting you know
That I've never felt so much love before.
Though yet silent I stay,
I look forward to the day
The day I see you, talk to you, tell you how I feel.
But as beautiful as it is, it is still a dream,
A perfect dream of you and me,
which might always remain unseen.

Sherin Hani Radwan

Picture of Perfection

When I see her standing there,
I just can't help but stare.
Her looks make me drift away,
Like the wind on a summer's day.
Her eyes are like a raging fire
That burn intensely with desire.
Her lips are perfect in every way,
And they say the words only lovers dare to say.
Her body itself is a picture of perfection,
And her arms are like steel, made just for protection.
Her soul is like a lake, very calm, very cool,
But it can get very powerful, so don't take her for a fool.
She is very creative, very talented and smart.
Her touch is very warm; so is that of her heart.
Her love is as deep as the deep blue sea,
And she gives me chills just by the gentle way she looks at me.
Our love is very strong and it will never part,
But even if it does one day, she'll always be in my heart.

Harold Stevens

Tears of the Forgotten

Alone and forgotten.
They sit and cry aloud.
Feeling, needing, begging pleading,
up into the clouds.
Asking for another chance.
Another place to start.
Children forgotten across the land.
Crying silently in their hearts.
A tear caresses their gentle cheeks.
Falling slowly to the ground.
Dropping silently, oh, so quietly.
Making not a sound.
One day hope envelopes them.
Warm, soft and sweet.
As a gentle loving hand takes theirs,
Soft and warm and fleet.
Showing them to endless love, laughter, life and peace.

Trenton Lee Howeth

Remember

Do you remember when we said "I do" and I
really did and so did you? Do you remember
our first kiss? Do you remember all of this
The loving, the laughing, the touching, the
promises we made. Do you remember all the
fun we have shared? The hopes and dreams and
schemes? Do you remember me?
I remember our first kiss; the night you
first loved me; your gentle caress. I
remember how you held me when I cried or
just needed your touch; your silver tongue
when you convinced me of your love. I
remember the promises, the dreams, the
hopes, the fears, the loving, the laughing
and yes, the tears. But mostly I remember
the joy, your loving touch, our dreams and
our love. I remember, I remember, I remember you.

Jeannie Schupman

My Angel

Yes, you fell from the clouds above
With a broken wing, my dove
To try and mend my broken heart
Think I loved you right from the start
My darling, my angel, my only love
The only one I'm thinking of
Yearn to have what I can't possess
I'll do anything just to caress
Your supple neck and each tiny toe
Just one touch would make you glow
Stoop down slowly and whisper in your ear
That I'm with you now, you've nothing to fear
You pull away and start to shiver
Lost without you, my tears like a river
Rained down on our heads from above
Collect on the ground and start to flood
The world I know, and wash away
All my pain I hope and pray.

Anthony Keith Ham

Time

Twelve more months have come and gone
the days flew quickly by;
we cannot slow the hours down,
though some of us do try.
Age matures the body and time ferments the mind;
what of all the loved ones we leave so far behind?
Our life is just a cycle that goes from birth to death;
the time that counts is in between
while we still have our breath.
We want to leave something good for those
that would remain; to be remembered is a goal
that does not bring us shame.
Some will be remembered for things they may have said;
others are remembered for things
that brought us dread.
Live each day to the fullest, each hour as if the last,
show love and understanding because
time does go too fast.

John Campbell

A Stolen Moment in Time

A Stolen Moment in Time
Two heart that beat as one.
Two minds that think alike,
but are different.
Two bodies that intertwine and become one.
A Stolen Moment in Time
Like the Earth needs the sun
Like the grass needs the rain
Like a baby's first breath.
When two bodies of water meet,
they run as one.
A Stolen Moment in Time
The boyish grin on his face.
The light that gleams in her eyes.
When the two meet, they anticipate
The stolen moment in time.
What was once shared
will never be forgotten.

Sabine Gallant

Thank You, Mom

Since the day I've been born,
You've done nothing but give.
You've given me love, peace and happiness
And many other reasons to live.

From day one—late night feedings,
Taking care of me when I was sick.
Fixing me breakfast and lunch
And getting me off to school quick.

Being so patient when you wanted to shout,
You've always been there for me, without a doubt . . .

Listening to my problems when I got older and never complaining,
Even though at times, I know it was very draining.

So many times you've done without to give me the things I need
And it was your giving out of love and never out of greed.

For all these things I'm extremely thankful and many, many more
Your my mother, my best friend, whom I'll always and forever adore.

Diane Cope

The Light Within

A candle is much more than wax and string
A lovely glow of light it'll bring.
The wax gathers upon the strand;
Patience is the key,
Once you understand.
When complete,
The candle will shine bright;
Once lit,
It'll cast a soft, delicate light.

Life can be like that little string;
Patience and understanding it'll bring.
Every day,
Life throws us a different strand;
With love and guidance,
We give each other a hand.
Though a candle give us light;
What inside of us,
Is what makes us shine bright.

Kristi M. Slusarski

The Key to My Heart

The key to my heart lies in the sparkling
waters on a mountain's side where the birds
sing and the bear cubs play.
The key to my heart lies in the scent of a
rose in the morning dew where all is still and calm.
The key to my heart lies on a deserted
stretch of beach where the wind cools my
brow and the gulls cry above.
The key to my heart lies in the forest where
the blue morning glory still grows wild and
the sharp smell of pine surrounds me.
The key to my heart lies in a wind swept
field where the sunflowers dance and the
jackrabbit tends to its young from down under.
Considering all this, I give the key to my
heart to my husband and best friend.

Tamberlyn Sharazota Sykes

Cry . . .

When there is nothing else to do
When you feel like the world hates you
Just sit and cry . . . ask, keep asking, why?
Just sit and cry . . . when you feel like you want to die
Feel so lonely, this hurt, this pain
Then you see your life, you're so ashamed
One more touch, your petals fall
The world around you, it's now so small
Petals on the ground, you start to arch
This is the life of yours you must now part
You have falling and can't get up
You are neither loved, nor pretty enough
Say goodbye . . . no more tears
Say goodbye . . . to all your fears
This is the life that felt so long
You failed at everything, you are always wrong
Now it's just not enough to cry
Your thoughts came true, it's time to die . . .

April Lynn Lewis

Phoenix of Love

Awake, bleeding a river of sorrows
Internal shards of red scattered like wild horses
The incestuous union of love and lust
Bears a wretched offspring

Where are the roses of passion
Only withered roots tossed on the heaping pyre
Darkness drowning the depths of the heart
Fires of yearning dashed by an icy night wind

Crush me, tear at the flaming seams
Ignite the dull ache of remembrance
Desert me to burn to ashes
Alone to be abused by memories of days gone by
One day the ashes will rise again
Again to wander the sizzling streets
Cut down, rebuilt, emotion full tilt
The Phoenix of love

But not today

Joshua C. Magee

School Is Like A . . .

School is like a cycle,
Repeating, rotating and going 'round,
Tutoring the children they have found,
Intelligence and knowledge that is their name,
Try to put fun and games to serious shame . . .

School is like a running track,
Set the pace with no going back,
Whizzing past the excited crowd,
Breaking the rules is not allowed . . .

School is like a rolling pound,
Rush for the vendors before homeward bound,
Whatever the price we would grant the fare,
Into the wrappers we wildly tear . . .

School is like an ongoing cartwheel,
End of the day waiting for the piercing drill,
And right at the end after homework club,
Get home and relax in the soaking tub.

Ben Hughes, age 12

Options

Options
Plan A
Don't smoke
Don't drink as much or as often
Get fit
Accept responsibility
Never give yourself away cheap
Do the things you need to do
Get a life
Be happy
Plan B
Smoke
Keep drinking as much and as often
Don't get fit
Run away from responsibility
Always give yourself away cheap
Don't do the things you need to do
Don't get a life
Be miserable
Choose
Options

Peter Faulkner Stanford

Mark

The way I feel inside,
I could never tell you,
How do I explain,
That I love you.

It started as a joke,
But it turned into something real,
I didn't want to love you,
But I can't help what I feel.

I know by loving you,
That I will get hurt,
I try to keep my heart protected,
But it's impossible.

You got to me,
Like no one has before,
What am I supposed to do?
Just close the door?

I know now what I must to do,
I have to push you away,
And it's only because . . .
You're gay.

Phener Marie-Louise Hines

dream

Dedicated to my niece who has lost two sets of twins in the past year

i see it in your eyes
your sorrow and your pain
to lose a never ending dream
over and over again
to hold one so small
that completely fills your heart
so soon taken away
to tear your world apart
but in all of your tomorrows
one dream does come true
no matter how far the distance
they will always be with you
they touched all of us
in just their short time here
and all we can give them now
is the purity of our tears
they want now to grant you peace
one your heart never had
although they may have left you
forever you will be . . . mom and dad

Christie Michelle Eagle

Every Morning, Every Day

Roll. Stand. Walk. Pee.
Wash. Rinse. Repeat Again.
Lather. Cut. Burn. Soothe.
Gel. Comb. Brush. Spit.

Left sock on. Right sock next.
Pants ride up. Shirt tucks in.
Shoes noosed tight.
Tie noosed tighter.

Wait in line. Wait some more.
Train, bus, car go slow.
Friends you have none around
You just impede their gaining ground.

Pushed for an inch.
Scolded for foot.
Hungry for a seat
They crush your feet.

Every morning, every day
This is how we wake up.
This is how we pay.

Timothy Burke

Show Me

If you love me then show me
I need to know without question
A life without passion
Is not a life worth living

In a world uncertain show me
In a life of no guarantees
Let what you do assure me
That what you say is true

In a day of lofty promises
Let me not feel cheap
Wrap the arms of love around me
With your presence the promise keep

In this very moment show me
With your breath upon my lips
With your soft voice so close
Let the distance between us vanish

If you love me then show me
Let me know the worth of my years alone
That solitude is far better
Than to live a life of lies

Charles W. Hastings, Jr.

Life

What is this life
What does it hold
To some it means love
To others it's gold

But what is love
If you must be alone
When for lust of gold
Your spouse has flown

All the gold in the world
Will not bring happiness
Will not buy you a friend
Nor ease loneliness

Why is it that fate
Will match up the two
The one that loves gold
With the one that loves true

Yes, what is this life
Fate has brought our way
Will we find happiness
Before Judgment Day

M. L. Holmes

Confusion

So many questions
So little time
Sometimes I ask
"Am I losing my mind?"
So many decisions I know I can't make
So much criticism I just can't take
I can't please everyone
Though I always will try
Sometimes I'm discouraged
But I don't know why
I hate all the pressure
That's brought upon me
Too many decisions
Than I'd rather there be
I just can't stand it
I don't know what to do
To feel what I feel
If only you knew
I'm not looking for sympathy
I just wish it will end
I feel it's a battle I never will win

Antoinette Marie Kelly

Three Little Words

There are three little words
That mean so very much.
They can lift the weary heart
Like an angel's soft touch.

There are three little words,
But, oh, what they convey!
They can say so much more
Than a hundred words can say.

Please often say, "I love you."
Say it again and again.
If the day is bright and sunny,
Or if it's pouring rain.

My heart longs for the words
From lips of one so dear,
Words that will lift my heart;
Vanquish all my fear.

There are three little words
That should often be said.
Please tell them to me now,
Don't wait until I'm dead.

Bernice Marrs

Louise

I knew her well, Louise
Struck down at twenty-four.
Too young for this disease
But then who's keeping score?

Diagnosis didn't come quickly.
Many doctors were confused.
One suggested a psychiatrist,
In my mind, she was abused.

Seven years went by and guess what?
Louise is really sick.
To the hospital she is taken.
MS finally, the verdict.

Fourteen years spent in a wheel chair.
Trying hard to do her part.
But exhaustion overtook her
And she died, it broke my heart.

Oh, for answers, we are looking.
What to do to ease the pain?
May M.S. one day be conquered
And the world will stand to gain.

Lorraine Bohlinger

A Butterfly's Journey

In memory of my beloved cousin,
Roslyn D. Ards

You were like
enraptured sounds of a violin string
a butterfly's wing
Flutter to the towering faraway hills,
pause while your soul fills
Gaze,
the intricate pale blooms
Look at the light on a leaf
the delicate tracing,
frail interlacing
of sun interwoven on shadow
Sand and shell
orchestrating a string of pearls
Listen, a symphony of psalms
gently strumming the sea
Fly up to the Heavens
on a glistening sunlit rod,
A destiny with beauty,
A destiny with God.

Glynis Kaye Miller

My Grandmother

What picture could be sweeter?
As we travel along life's way,
Than a grandmother,
Whose hair has turned to grey.

Her cooking was the finest
I though no one could beat,
Her house was always shinning,
It looked so clean and neat.

Her hands were always busy
For others she would do,
Piece quilts, make rugs,
Knit socks, and mittens, too.

She always loved her neighbors
She gave to those in need,
Gave help in time of sickness,
Clothes, food, or garden seed.

She loved her home and family,
Her heart was big and true,
She could make you happy,
When others made you blue.

Bertie Waugh

The Hand of God

Butterfly, butterfly
What do you see?
Floating your way through your life
Much like me.

Butterfly, butterfly
What do you think?
The changes you've gone through
As quick as a wink.

Butterfly, butterfly
Where will you go?
When life's gentle winds
Turn to harsh cold of snow.

Butterfly, butterfly
Please teach me to fly.
I stand on the ground
But I long for the sky.

Butterfly, butterfly
I now understand.
It takes nothing more
Than the touch of God's hand.

Vince Miller

Trickle

You trickle into my mind
And form a puddle.
It becomes so big
It fills my soul.

It overflows,
And I feel tears form.
They start to pour; my body shakes.

You rain and storm
From inside my soul,
From inside me.

You finally become a sprinkle
And now a trickle,
Falling to my trembling lips.

You taste sweet, but sour.
You are bitter, yet dulcet,
And I can't decide which is better.

I cry until you're drained.
My mind is dry of you.
I'm tired; I have to let go.

Charity Marie LeGrand

Country Road

Today I walked down a country road
To see what I could see.
Tall grass was growing there, and
Beautiful flowers were all around me.

I heard the birds all singing
High up in the trees.
And stopped to watch, at work
The busy little honey bees.

I turned my eyes to Heaven
To see the beautiful blue sky.
The sun was shining brightly
And soft white clouds were floating by.

I saw the crops all growing green
Across the rich and fertile land,
I knew as surely I stood there
It was all a part of God's great plan.

A lovely thought came to my mind
As I was standing there.
That no matter how far I wandered,
I was never beyond God's love and care.

Josie Tarpley

Special Blessings

Merry Christmas, Merry Christmas!
It's the time for lots of fun.
Please, dear Santa, bring me presents,
And I hope there's more than one.

You remember each December
The excitement drove me wild.
Though I'm older, much, much older
Still at Christmas, I'm a child.

It was Christmas, yes, 'twas Christmas
When the Holy Child was born,
And we thank Him for appearing
On that blessed Christmas morn.

How He came to Earth from Heaven
Was a miracle, you see.
Now He reigns once more in Heaven
And He waits for you and me.

Merry Christmas, Merry Christmas
And a Happy New Year, too!
You're wished joy and special blessings
For today and all year through.

Dorothy Higgins

Praise and Glory

Oh, Lord, I thank you
For all that you bestow.
You give me love and friendship;
You keep my life aglow.

Your Holy Spirit is in my heart;
You fill my every need.
Dear God, keep me pure
In thought, word, and deed.

Protect me Lord, and keep me;
Bless me with your might.
And use me, Lord, I plead to you,
And hold me in your light.

And Lord, please keep me humble;
Take away my pride.
And Lord, when I stumble,
Please stay by my side.

Lord, I give you praise and glory.
Show me, Lord, your way.
I ask this every day.

Valerie M. Knott

Truth

You seek the elusive Truth, child.
From this quest you should not part.
Your journey will not end, child.
You must know this from the start.

Remember your birth quest, child.
It's deep inside of you.
Feel it re-awakening, child.
To your cause you must be true.

Learn your lessons well, child.
Learn all you need to know.
Keep your lessons close, child.
Were forth out thou go.

Are you at your peak, child?
The spirits are all around.
Hear the angels speak, child
The guides are on the ground.

Cast the despairing seed, child
far away from you.
Let your spirit soar, child.
In the sky so blue.

Susan Anderson

My Gift to You

I cannot give you Heaven
I cannot give you gold
Some things can't be given
And some you can't hold

I have shared my happiness
I have kept my sorrow
But sometimes I wish
There would be no 'morrow

No heartaches, no troubles
How happy life would be
To see when each morning breaks
That joy and happiness are free

But what would life be without troubles
And what would you do all day
Would dreams vanish like bubbles
Or would they be here to stay

No matter what is given
And no matter what you do
Love is the reason for living
That is my gift to you.

Judy Carpenter

The Heart Is a Wonderful Thing

The heart is such a fragile thing,
Subject to earthly pain.

Still one must not complain,
Nor hold in emotional disdain.

The heart is a loving vessel,
Capable of handling life's hostile.

It may be twisted as a pretzel,
Pained as though hit by a missile.

The heart is a marvelous thing.
It's rebounding so inspiring.

Where there is beauty—glorifying;
Where there is love—gratifying.

The heart is a wonderful thing,
Filling life with meaning.

With joy and happiness to bring,
Rejoice and hear the heart sing.

Gerald Giuffra

Words to Live By

Through all your changes
Down all your paths,
you've lasted this long;
It's time to relax.

Look forward to tomorrow,
and go on with life.
Remember the memories,
but forget the lost times.

Make every second count.
Make every day worthwhile.
Cherish what the future will bring.
Happiness is the way to be.

Depression is not the answer!
Stress is not allowed!
Smile after smile,
thoughts of flying proud.

Get a job and settle down.
Make a life for yourself somehow.
Forget most things you left behind,
make new dreams, strive to survive.

Angela D. Foreman

A New, True Friend

My friend is nice and he's handsome,
he's also an attorney—so smart.
I knew from the day that we met
he'd always be close to my heart.

It was his second year in college
and he really impressed me so much.
He spoke so fondly of family and home,
his brother, his horse and such.

Now he's a deserving young fellow,
not the ordinary sort you meet.
He will always be there if needed
and knows you out on the street.

I pray God's richest blessings
as he pursues his place in life,
with a busy career, decisions to make
and sooner or later, a wife.

Now as he finishes law school,
the hardest part of life thus far,
he's headed in the right direction,
so hang in there, Curt, pass the bar!

Vivian Bray

Who Art Thou, Love?

I look and look.
every day, every night.
Searching for the one,
The one to bring me light.

Everywhere I go
I wish I would find
That very one.
But he never seems
to be where I am.

Who, who, who is he?
How will I know
who he is?
What does he look like?
What is he like?
I do not know.
All I know is he will
brighten up my life.

Who is he? I will know.
It's a feeling
I can never miss. It's "love."

Stephanie Lengel

Old Glory

Thirteen stripes of red and white
Fifty white stars on a field of blue
A symbol of our 50 states
We're proud of her through and through

She's waved o'er many a battlefield
And o'er thousands of dead men
From Gettysburg to Iwo Jima
I'm sure she'll make again

She's been frayed and burned and torn
I'm so proud as she goes by
I get goose bumps when I say the pledge
It brings a teardrop to my eye

God gave us this great country
That Old Glory does symbolize
Let's remember those brave soldiers
That guarded her with their lives

July 4th comes once a year
It's a very special day
It gave us Independence
To whatever we have to say

Patricia Wike

My Family's Love

I look into my heart
and what do I see
All of my family's love
burning inside of me

I see my heart
overflowing with love
I'm thankful for what's
been sent from above

I live for my family
and what they provide
They provide a place to grow
and not to hide

In my family is where
I belong
and in my heart
I can hear a joyful song

I know this love
is all I need
Ever since I was born
This love has been a flourishing seed

Laura Jenny Olson

Dark Moon

I look out the window,
At the cold and desolate sky.
The sky is dark,
There's something wrong,
A moon that should be there.

I look into the sea,
To try and find myself.
But when I do,
I want to run,
From those that aren't so rare.

I sink into the black,
Of a life I have not lived.
The things I want,
I think I need,
If only I could share.

The moon is dark tonight,
I can't see the sea.
So all I see,
Is dark to me,
And nothing's really there.

Mat Lindholm

Marriage

It starts so beautifully with "I do"
The sight of you takes away my breath
On the day I said I will love you
Until we are parted by death

As the many years go by
Some harder than others
Filled with lows and highs
Becoming Father and Mother

How will we make it
Through the hard times
When it would be easier to quit
And forget the good times

But we must stay together
A promise we once made
In front of God to each other
Our love it will not fade

Our love is true and deep
So special we are together
Something in our mind to keep
A love to last forever

Angela J. Dehring

A Carnation's Wish

In a field full of flowers
my tender stem stands.
When I felt near me
sweet tender hands.

Your touch is like rain
cool, fresh vibrant and free.
Your voice is like the wind
with calm tunes from the sea.

Prince of the flowers
if you could only see,
this lovely carnation that's
been waiting for thee.

King of the Heavens
grant me a wish
before I grow old,
before I cease to exist.

That this little carnation
will soon receive
sweet kisses of honey
that comes from her prince.

Lillian Rivera

never

walking through a narrow street
my soul is what i cannot keep
stuck in my own nauseating daze
full of anger and vile ways
but i won't let heart escape
i won't throw away the key
there is someone that keeps fighting
someone inside me

heather fankhauser

Summer School

Alone in a jail cell.
No, you may not climb the trees!
We planted them here
To impress your parents
Because they have money.
We knew you'd be trouble
After the first week.
You did not go shopping,
You tried to save energy,
You actually recycled!
So now we look at you weird.
If you will not give us your money,
You must remain
Alone in a jail cell.

Nissa Hennessey Fowler

Make a Plan, Take a Stand

MS has got to leave
this land.
Multiple Sclerosis get out of town
Thanks to research, you're
going down.
I would like to join the fight.
To knock out MS and do it right
Montel, I'm glad you took my advice
Poetry.com will suffice
This is a fight that we will win
Let's all stand up and pitch in.

A cure will be found in your lifetime,
just wait and see,
you'll feel just fine.

Montel, you won't have
much longer to wait,
God bless you dear,
And keep the faith!

Tamara Oliver Eaddy

My World

In my world
there is no sorrow
In my world
there is no sadness
In my world
there is no death
In my world
there is no pollution

In my world
the lion lies down with
the lamb
In my world
there are only tears of joy
In my world
children play and laugh
In my world
my beloved dogs wait for me
I long for my world
Some people call it HEAVEN

Patricia Shields

When Christmas Comes

When Christmas comes,
cold air begins to numb.
The season warms our hearts,
it warms all our inner parts.
If only for this one season,
we relish love and dump reason,
until the season comes to an end,
when the sun forces us to again bend.

Carrie Urban

My Angels

From where, I don't know, they came
They were, a gift to me
And all, know their names

I hope and pray, that my angels
Never go away,
'Cause, I would be all left alone,
Me and my mind, would go astray

Through trials and drama, we made it
Not I, or any of my angels can be faded

Keep on looking, for those sun rays,
And continue to work . . .
For those, we dream of . . .
Those precious days.

Twanna Swinton

I Am Free

I am free at last . . .
No more suffering
No more pain.
I am free at last.

Now I am free to speak,
Free to run,
Free to live,
Free to fly
I am free at last.

No more planting,
No more picking,
No more slashes,
No more cooking.

I am who I am,
I am not a slave.
I am not a maid
I am me, who is free . . .
I am free at last.

Jaimie Lynn Myhre

Mercy

Hanging
Upon a tree
With thieves
Took
The nails
[Mercy suffered]
Blood was spilt
[Mercy died]
Lay in
A borrowed tomb
Out of pity
Condemned
Fire in the soul
Darkness
All around
Three days . . .
[Mercy rose]
Alive
[Mercy lives]

Stacey Aleita Higdon

Love

In an ocean of blue sapphires
I found a diamond.

Carla De Kelaita

Little Things

It took some time
to make me realize
that all things
must surely have to end.
When I reach it,
I will be no more . . .
heart will shatter;
mind will explode;
body will split.
And perfect they'll forever stay,
secured in that place in the Sun.
It will happen so easily,
so slowly,
like a fire burning out
as we, the matches,
help you burn faster.
Soon you'll slowly fade . . .
to become . . .
Little Things.

Kristen Agro

Iron Mask

I sometimes wonder who decides
When it is time to cry
We've all been taught
To wear our masks
Never letting the light
Of day slip behind our
Iron mask
Never exposing our pain
But what happens if
A single drop of rain
Slips behind our masks
From the storm
For which we have strived
So hard to master
Into nothing more than rust
One day when all is safe
I hope we will be able to
Crumble our masks to the ground
Maybe one day

Megan Elise Carey

A Flower Unpretended

Please don't say I didn't care
About you, when I did,
Nor think I sought to veil my fault
In secret from you hid,
For nothing I withheld at all,
But gave my heart to bid.

No other gift had I to bring
In silver'd chalice, fill'd
With blossom'd hope and dreams to share,
Than love's completeness will'd
And trusted full within thy care,
Though purposed joy were still'd.

Please don't say the tears I shed
Were not for you intended.
Say but this: His hurt is mine,
May his sorrow soon be ended.
Still all my love is none but thine,
A flower unpretended.

Oscar Vincent

Haiku

One row of field peas
With a dozen vines reaching
Out bearing pea pods.

Frieda Smith

July Morning in Victor, Idaho

Dew glistening on the
Pillowy grass like stars glistening
In a clear summer night sky.

Hear the birds singing
Their song to wake up
The farmer and his wife.

Cluck, cluck, go the chickens,
Waiting to be fed, across the
Path, the porcelain and smoke-
Colored goats wait to be milked.
Mmm . . . this milk will make
A great ice cream.

Hear the giggles and laughs
Of the little children
Playing in the yard,
Waiting for a new day to start.

Stephanie Hutchinson

I Love You Always

Flashbacks of the past
That we once had
I hold you here
On the ground wondering
Why you have to leave
We have everything
You are my world
You are all I need and all I want
And I know that it's the same for you
My friends always tell me
That you're the one
The one that will always be mine
Please don't leave me
I need you here
I know you'll be safe
Where you're going
Just remember
I'll always miss you
I love you always and good-bye.

Amanda Elizabeth Bigley

One Last Gift to Mom

This urn is very special
I painted it myself
This represents a daughter's love
For a mother who is now above
I hope this makes her proud
As she looks down from the clouds

There is a Kokopelli
(Boy, she liked him so)
For each of us she left behind
Four to keep her safe
One is on the inside
And that is just for her

So when you gaze upon this urn
Just remember one thing
This was made of lots of love
And we will never be the same
For when someone so special leaves
We are left behind with hearts that grieve

Megin L. Goetz

Mother

How do you thank your mother,
for giving you life,
for teaching you values,
for mending all those scraped knees,
for being there no matter what?
How?
Like this:
Mother, I love you.
Look what a great job you've done.

Kirt C. Suominen

The Grape

The Grape!
Come Bacchus, fill the cup!
 For what have we to do—
 but drink the grape?
We have but little time to live
 And even now—we must escape.
What joy is there, but be it in the cup?
 All that we are is contained therein.
We drain the cup—
 And never pass this way again.

Raymond Burghen

Our Garden

On the day that you were born
I planted our garden
With the love that you brought
I carefully tended it and it flourished
The years flew by, we both matured
The seedlings of love blossomed forth
Then one day you said
I need a garden of my own
Tearfully we uttered our good-byes
The stones between our gardens
Span the many miles
Our smiles are the sunlight
Our tears the rain
Walking through the winding paths
I recall the many flowers we have
Grown and outgrown
If birds and bees could stop and rest
They would never sense the love
That grows so strong
There is no season, nor reason, it just is

Gladys Marie Cormier

The Ireful Spark

Teary face
Gets slowly red
Heartbeats hammer
Heavily in temples
White knuckles
Shine on fists
And the heart
Slowly twists
Black eyes
Ignite sparks
Clenched teeth
Behind mouth suppressed
Blood boils
In narrow veins
Captured energy
Fights to get free

A primal scream

Then silence

All tensions are released

Elisabeth Vera Ekornes

plans

our love opens the day
just as the sun rises
and lights the way,
for a journey through life
till moonbeams soften the path
as wonderful husband and wife.
we will no longer be you and me, but
lovingly tread as only "we."

Mel J. Malkove

Breaking Away

You knew the time would come.
You knew the time would come.
You knew the time would come.
You knew the time would come.
You knew the time would come.
You knew the time would come.

Oh, why does it have to be me?
Oh, why does it have to be?
Oh, why does it have to?
Oh, why does it have?
Oh, why does it?
Oh, why does?
Oh, why?
Oh!

Mary R. Cargo

No Reason

When you come back from your
beautiful, pleasant season
and I from a season of cold snow
what's left but, a broken family
for a reason we'll never know

Like the trees that lose their leaves
during a change of season
so was your decision to change our
lives for no reason

How so unimaginably strange
maybe even necessary, for you
this change

In some respects it can be
considered treason
to disrupt the security of family
for no reason

Richard Serrano

Reflections

I am still a young man
Full of zip and pep.
I am still a young man
Up to date and hep.
I am still a young man,
But please help me up this step.

I haven't aged a single bit,
Few others make that claim.
I haven't aged a single bit,
My memory is the same.
I haven't aged a single bit,
But again, what is your name?

I have the health I had when young,
Body, mind, and spirit.
I have the health I had when young
I am not old or near it.
What's that you tell of being young?
Speak up so I can hear it.

I haven't changed since twenty-five,
For a younger man I pass.

Harold S. Knight

Time

Time is such a precious thing
we take for granted each day,
but wouldn't it be something if
time could go the other way?

Gene Patrick Damiano

True Love

I turn towards my inner eye.
I see you and the sky.
Glimmering in sunshine,
gloriously divine.

The remembrance of heady days,
when both life and love were full.
Now there is nothing left to say,
for others a simple fool.

Although you are far away,
with you my heart shall always stay.
There is no need for you to be
forever beside me.

For true love is that which sets free,
the cost of which is me.
Gladly it is to you that I give,
the reason why I live.

Regina Maglanoc

Abandoned

It's hard to believe you're gone
It didn't take very long
This day came so quick
I felt as if I was tricked
I knew this day had to come
But why did you have to be the one?
The one who left me alone
Tell me it's not over,
Tell me you won't go
Please talk to me I need to know
How am I suppose to go on without you?
You were my life,
You meant everything to me
O' no, how can this be?
Please God, don't let my love walk
out on me
I should have said the words that
were meant to be spoken,
But instead my heart is broken

Nicole Elizabeth Boesch

Down

Some call it love
Some call it addiction
Some people hate it
Some people pray for it
Call it what you want
it still has a price,
and you're still going to pay it.
If the side of the coin is heads,
you're a winner.
You won't ever see tails,
so don't think you can lose.
From the top of the deck
till you hit rock bottom,
There's something for everyone—
Just sit down and drink.
The sight and the feeling
will help you unwind
until you make the decision
not to go home alone

Bryce Trapier

Promised Land

The sky is bright
My heart is light
I pray my Lord is coming tonight.
To see his face
To touch his hand
To finally see the promised land.

Di Watson

Homeless

Where shall I go?
No one wants me, Lord
No even the sidewalks.
Help me Lord, my master.
Tell me, where do I belong?
Help me find a bed
Help me find bread to eat
I want to live.
I must go on but
Each day a piece of me dies.
I'm listening, Lord
I'm waiting for your help.
Please do not fail me
Give me your hope and peace
Most of all a place in your heart
A place where I can come and stay
A home where I belong.

Alice M. O'Toole

Piece of Mind

Cast out the evil
The fire in your soul
Take out the heat
and leave a warm glow
No need for pain
No need for a fight
Just take that flame
and switch off the light
Could be so calm
with peace in your mind

Now I am calm
What will I do?
I have no drive
and nothing to say
Bring back my fire
to light up my way
Lost in this peace
my minds drifting away

Samuel Peter Uithol

Ribbons and Lace

Ribbons and lace. A little girl's face.
Fingernail polish and lipstick.
Her boyfriend's name is Rick.
Wedding gowns and high heels.
Happy is how she feels.
One child was born.
It was early in the morn.
Her daddy has passed away.
She feels sadden each day.
Her husband soon might die.
Now she will always cry.
Her heart is filled with sadness.
Her eyes are filled with madness.
Her second child is here.
Now she has no fear.
Her husband has now died.
She has never lied.
Ribbons and lace. A little girl's face.

Michelle Ann White

People

People are
Every where.
lOok and
sPeak to
eopLe and love
Everybody.

Valerie Michelle Mok

Final Chapter

To Kevin, the man of my heart and of my dreams

Whispering winds surround me
Thy comfort echoes deep
Life's changes are abounding
The highest mountains, not steep
I hear your voice is calling
To me, I wait below
I hear my children's laughter
Seems a lifetime ago
My days now have a number
They were once too high to count
This, my final chapter
Time to lay the good book down
The unknown holds a story
Of life I've yet to see
Oh, yes, I think I'm ready
To start a new book with thee.

Kathryn Widmer

A Night to Remember

I woke up and couldn't sleep.
I started to weep.
I was thinking of my long past.
The scenes flashed by fast.
I went to take a midnight walk.
I couldn't help but talk.
I found an old house.
I saw a bloody blue blouse.
I tried to walk by,
but I started to cry.
I walked past the shirt.
I went through the dirt.
I opened the door.
I couldn't go any more.
I saw more blood everywhere,
Over here, over there.
I ran out screaming.
I then realized, I was only dreaming!

Heather L. Juranek

Walk of Life

To walk with you I cannot,
For you are there not, in my world,
To hold my hand, I know.
For away from the world I stayed
To keep the devils of the world away.
For a part of the world you were,
To part it, you could never;
For me you let it all go,
To live a life away from the World.
For a walk you took my life
To the place my heart had always longed.
For to walk alone, I knew not;
to walk together we learned in life.
For the world grew jealous in mind,
To take you away, it did.
For to walk alone, I can't do.
To stand through this life, I can;
For to walk with you in Heaven, I hope.

Shalu David

Think about It!

I think, that I shall never think,
a thought that no one else has thought.
But if I thought a thought,
no one else had ever thought;
that thought, I thought,
would truly be worth thinking about.

Evelyn Charlene Gaetjens

Next Winter, Maybe

hey, supernova eyes
when you took off those glasses
did it feel like surrender
did I taste a promise on your lips
of warmer days to come
and sunshine
what was that
I felt
and then you look
and ask, hey,
what about New Amsterdam
in those now-fading daylights
and with the leaves falling and all
and I think
it's not that I don't want to go
it's just
I still haven't made it
to Baton Rouge

Carsten Thomas Titlbach

Now Forever

It was errant spring
so blossoms crinkled for cover
beneath the boughs, between the leaves.
But the balm slipped,
making way in the wind.
Tied on different edges,
we gaped through the season
until he said, what do we do?
Nothing, I said.
The luxury of an odd stroke
undesigned, so undemanding.
No next thing to do,
no rush hour snarls,
nowhere to reach, no morrows, no then.
It's now, this, here.
The present continuous is perfect.
We don't live grammatically,
we live happily herein.

Jayanthi Dwarakanath

Listen to Me

You say you will listen
When I have something to say,
Yet every time I begin to speak
You jump in with your own problems
And I get not a word in edgewise,
Then you ask why I am so quiet?
I love you too much to tell you
That I have many problems and concerns
Also, and I need someone to
Talk to that will listen to me as
If they understand me and have
Had the same problems themselves.
Only if I could find someone
Like that, like me truly.
I have always listened to
Everyone else's problems and
Never have anyone fully listen
To mine.

Tim Snell

Deceived

Smell the rose
touch the thorn
your finger will start to bleed
the scent of the petal
the pain of the needle
are very quite different indeed.

Susan L. Fiala

Her Eyes

Her eyes,
they are my eyes,
and they scream at me
even when she is sleeping.
And I love her so completely,
so serenely,
and they follow me,
wherever I go.
She knows me,
because I am true to her,
because I am myself with her.
She is life,
and I have made her.
She screams to me
some kind of answer to all
my confusion,
even when she is sleeping,
safely in my arms.

H. Leigh Feldman

Love

I don't believe in love,
The whole thing isn't real,
It's a temporary happiness,
That pulls you deep inside.
You can't imagine what's overcome you,
Until you feel it leave.
It comes and goes like night and day,
Or as quickly as a breeze.
There are many shades of "love,"
Right now, I know but one,
The unconditional real love
from a mother and God's Son.
But other shades of so-called love,
Come and go in just a blink.
That's why I don't believe in love,
It's not to be this way.
Love is long, and lasts forever,
This way, shall it remain.

Tatiana M. Horton

Under His Banner

Am so weak
and not able to speak
and look my face
have you not read the
flame of suffering I live?

There's hurricane of spirit—
I ache, I ache. Of this life.
Behold—I do wonder, wonder
if His word is true—
when I read, will live.
Eyeing, His love for me
glowing, burning
once and for all.

He's my beginning and my end
for His love keeps
firing
and waving till end.

Leo Persigas Udtohan

My Pillow

She walks along night breezes
To haunt my dreams and
Swim in the dark waters of my soul.
I awake. She's gone.
Her scent is on my pillow.
I will hold it forever.

Robert Kirkland

My Angel

You are an angel
The very thought of you
Brings joy to my heart
And tears to my eyes
When I lay alone at night
I dream to myself
Thoughts of you
Being there with me
You make me feel
Complete and loved
When I am with you
The world will seem
To be a better place
And all my cares will slip away
To make room
For your presence
In my heart and soul
Which is where I cherish you the most.

Kenny Eugene Koons

Life

Sunrise and sunset
Two polar realities
Between them is Life.
Life lies in darkness
Life is waiting to be born
Life is from the sun.
Soul faces the sun
Awaiting her conversion
A living fountain.
The Spirit breaths Life
Glory of Heaven and Earth
The vessel is filled.
In the Beginning
Those who have, have more Spirit.
In the filling is Life.
Creativity.
Male and female He created them.
Between them is Life.

Louise Bradbury

Searching

Dedicated to my cousin, Nita

I'm trying to find myself
Have you seen me anywhere?
I've searched a long time, high and low
Looking here and there

Is my searching all in vain?
Will I ever find one that shares?
Will I ever find one that shares?
I'm not lost; I can be found
I know I am somewhere

Do you see me yet? No! Not over there
You'll find me if you really try
My clues are everywhere

Still searching, trying to find myself
Have you seen me anywhere?
Open your heart to one last clue
See me now? I AM YOU

Diane Edmonds-Vitashoka

Funny

You loved me so much yesterday;
And now, yesterday's gone . . .
In that moment of love,
Was a lifetime of me;
Now love, overtaken by time,
Is once again free.

Cynthia Murray

Hush

Don't say a word, don't speak
Just listen, she sleeps

All of her, naked, calm
Her body
Rests

Her shoulders, so soft
Her womb, so tender
Breathes

Her chest, protects
That part of hers
I want to kiss

Her eyes, closed
Dream secrets

Her lips, her mouth
Those cheeks, all her face
At dawn, smiles

Tomas Luis Cubillo

The Reflection

The clarity where the
Rooted reed can be
Seen—thick with
The life of water, mud;
Promised, strung and pearled,
Anciently, organically—
Stern shallows,
Treading, wavering, rustling—
Summer, fall, silver,
Green, an eternal season.
The random, hardy
Reed shadowing the
Rippling tracers
That fall between his clinging
Fingers, greedy
Narcissus, aches;
For the clarity of the water
Is dependent upon its mudded reed.

Jane Crown

On the Carpet

At the hour of indulgence,
I approach you, trembling.
Your voice is but a whisper,
yet it cuts like a knife.
Your eyes are somber,
yet ferocious as a tiger.

We hunger for his love and approval
as lust sneaks in the door.
Within the room I see demons from below;
you see angels from above.
I call this fear.
You call it answer to prayer.
Death is knocking,
can't be seen or touched.
The voice in the wind is calling;
rain offers no protection
from the fire within.
WE SHALL BE CALLED ON THE CARPET.

Laurel Baker

Wife's Birthday Limerick

To Jeanie, the Angel of my life

There once was an Angel above
Who descended to Earth like a dove
February 3rd was her birth
Her arrival on Earth
Happy birthday, my Angel, my love

Gary Gene Brown

My Best Friend

As I sit here alone
thinking to myself,
I have no one to talk to,
until my friend
shows up.

I suddenly feel his
presence all around me,
I feel His love wrap around me.
He is letting me know
he is always with me,
no matter what
the situation may be.

He is my best friend
who died for me
one day upon the cross.
He is my friend, Jesus,
who loves me so.

Marcey Hoffert

I Have a Hero

One day I was down and upset.
I thought that
no one loved me.
Everyone acted like
I wasn't there.
So, I thought I would make it true.

But when I almost did,
I got a phone call
from a girl.
She told me that
she liked who I am,
and that I was her friend.

She saved my life that day,
with just one little call.
Now I know someone
cares enough to say,
"Hey, you're not that small!"

Kelly Ann Morgan

Pianist

The music floats through the air
The pianist raises her hands
Loud and soft
Emotions pour through the music
Fingers gliding gently across the keys
Head and Body swaying in time
Now bouncing, faster and faster
Slower now the fingers glide again
Motionless the pianist plays with ease
Gliding, bouncing, gliding again
Up and down
Loud, soft, loud and soft
Softer and softer it goes
until at last the pianist no longer goes
The music stops
The pianist sits still
Finally a sigh of relief escapes
She has achieved her goal.

Amie Marie Simonsen-Starr

Fly Free, Fly High

Fly free, fly high
Soar out to the universe
Where helping hands are waiting
To take you to the pinnacle
As you lay down to rest
Spread your arms to encompass
All you love, and all who love you
Keep us in your heart
As we keep you in ours
Fly free, my son, fly high

Ann Pert

Another Bad Day

It can't be true
It's just not fair
Why does it have to happen to her?
She's been so good
She's been so kind
But still she seems not to mind
Why does this have to be so hard?
Isn't there an easier way?
I'll pray and pray
That she's OK
Wherever she is after today

Stephanie Ross

Character

What is built in you
are your reactions.
The darkness sometimes
is only a shadow.
Take a step away
and you will see the light.
Your reaction of character
will be in place.
But please don't act like you care
if you're only an actor caring.
That is not a good character! ! !

Lisa Jan Biggerstaff

Deathly Beauty

Her beauty transcends time
Rain in Paris is her voice
Swiss snow is her skin
Hells fire is her hair
Her body is from above
She knew Lenin before John
Stars before stripes
Pain before the Hammer
Vodka before grain
Hate before love
Death before life

Todd Roche

Equilibrium

sometimes you have to get lost
to really find yourself.
sometimes you have to reach out
to heal within.
you can only begin,
after an ending.
and sometimes the rules
are meant for bending.
sometimes fools
don't really realize
life . . . is but a circle.

Alex D. Holdren

Rainbow

Heart is red.
Nay, not mine.
Mine beats onyx
And pulses azure.
She communicates in prisms
And bleeds translucent
Through not the ventricles
As much as the eyes.
Her skin turns yellow and green
And she screams in purple,
But then beats onyx and azure again.

Betsy Jo Henry

Morning Star

You are my Morning Star
Guiding my way, when so far
Far from the dreams I once had
Of a love that would make me glad
Glad to have met someone like you
Someone so honest and true
True to the feelings of love
Looking to him who is above
When I was lost, you guided my way
Hoping someday that you would say
I'll never leave, I'll always stay

Robert E. Walters

In a Dream

In a Dream
  My hope and my desire
  My kingdom for your soul
In a dream
  You standing a pool of blood
In a Dream
  Killing myself is my only desire
In a Dream
No hope for cure, NO desire
As the wind blows darkness whispers
In a Dream

Jeff Nightmare Dionne

a-void

stop screaming in my head
there are so many doors slammed shut
right into my face
the expressionless goes forth
to subdue the masses a
wanting of my time, my concern
well, I'm tired now and
lying down beside me
the great void of being
that which has/is/never will exist
to me, it's forever unknown. . . .

Charles Fleis

As

As the storm howls outside,
As my mind rages with
  questions long since unanswered,
As my heart aches with
  pain long since diminished.

As my dreams echo through
  the still night
    long since fulfilled,
As my memories drift on the
  breath of ghosts
    long since forgotten.

Jonathan Adams

Dreamlessness

Into my eyes
  what eyes?
I see
  what dreams?
No dreams
  reality?
Into your eyes
  your eyes?
I see
  your dreams
Dreams

Tim L. Ambrose

Misguided Female

I'm a spare sex with soul,
Understanding sacred love.
I chant to Buddha,
Nirvana is not ignorance,
Be still.
Many abandon precepts,
Existing in spirit everywhere.
Masses awaken,
Realize truths.
An enlightened nothingness between me
And fools!

Jamie Raabe

Emma

Did she ever see the reason in my face
beyond the hospital scrubs
the longing for her innocence
unconditionally
even without her name
I love her
knowing the forbidden joy
longing
maybe one day I'll be graced
graced
with the beauty of my daughter

Jamie Marshall

The Sun Is the Color of Yellow

The sun is the color of yellow
Like birds are the color of blue.
Trees are the color of green
And sometimes orange, too.

The sun is the color of yellow
Like the sky is the color of gray.
Lakes are the color of sea-green
And could be the color of a bay.
The sun is the color of yellow.

Aleah Niemczyk

Fall

We fell fall,
never, as nothing at all,
you and I.
We know the world's winter
is undercoming,
and our time, double-duty
to seek its spring.
Let's us two revel in these restful,
restless falls; changing youth,
heed the call, before our work, yet joy
must come to be done.

Chris Moneypenny

My Best Friend

Angel guardian, my best friend
You are ever at my side
You will stay with me until the end
And all my footsteps guide
You lead me on life's journey
And help me find my way
You are truly are a gift from God
You taught me how to pray!

Ann Williams

Her

Soft pale skin
Tall and thin
Deep green eyes
Quietly her heart cries
Shimmering silver wings
Beautifully her dress clings
Small is her stride
Such beauty is hard to hide
Sweet is her voice
Listening is your only choice
Her lips so elegantly red
By her faith she is led
Her head held up high
So gentle is her sigh
As she quietly stands before you
your heart she begins to coo

Jennifer Nicole Becklund

My Pumpkin

Waking up early
No need for that
Thought you were here
As a matter of fact
Sat up in bed
And looked around
I shook my head
But not up and down
Want you to know
I miss you much
Even if
It's only your touch
I guess it's time
To start the day
Just wanted to say
That I love you, Schae!

Steven A. Weber

At the Edge

Strange as it seems
Comfort slips in
So soft and kind
Only once in a while though
For a split second it comes
It's a Hell all the other times

A little while longer please
Don't go away
Let me hold on to it
A little more while

Why do I linger on
Why not call it quits
Why not right now

Was it worth it though
I should know that
One second before I go
At the edge

Shinichi Ichikawa

Christmas

Can you hear it?
Can you see it?
Bells are ringing
Angels singing
Everything in array
As we celebrate today
"Merry Christmas!"
We will say
As we scurry on our way

Anna L. Newman

Who Am I?

I sit down and wonder
Who I really am.
What I am doing here?
And why was I chosen to live.
As free as a bird I think . . .
As slow as a turtle I wander . . .
Where am I from?
What shall I do?
Shall I sit here my whole life,
And wonder who I am?
Should I sit here and wait,
For the one with the warm arms?
What will happen towards the end?
How long might I live?
Who am I really?
No one but a kid.

Danielle Roach Martinez

Winter Cold

Winter cold is coming
Gone is the summer heat
Brisk cold days that wake you up
And liven up your beat

Scrape those windows on that car
So driving, you can see
Get out the coat and slacks
So comfortable you can be,

Keep the flowers growing inside
Outside ones, gone with the winter frost
All the fun of summer is gone away
Though not all of it is lost

Memories still remain
Of warm days of fun and sun,
But that's all that's left of summer
'Cause winter has begun

Richard Dottery

Amorous

If love is blind
Guide my eyes strong
For what I believe in
Together we belong

The vindictive encounters
Often we have faced
Leave us longing for love
That many times, we misplaced

Finding the right answers
We search so deep
Hindering most precious time
Forever ours to keep

As my eyes rain
My heart thunders
He strikes me like lightning
And my mind ponders

Michelle D. Kromm

Heartbroken

Once upon a time so sweet,
a time one day we all will meet.

It was one very lonesome night,
a man like we has seen the light.

We saw him lying on the ground,
seeking something he never found.

When his life comes to an end,
we know his heart we cannot mend.

Amanda Dianne Hawley

Near Death

A figure lying so still,
I can barely hear her breathe.
Pale, so white, under her natural skin,
Oh, my lovely one, don't accept death.

I stand here beside you,
Giving you the strength you lack.
Holding your hand within mine,
Guiding your way back.

All the wires, attachments and such,
Still, I feel your life drifting.
But wait! A flicker of a smile, I see.
Sweetheart, my hopes you are lifting.

Time for a moment stands still,
A thousand prayers are sent above.
God answers as you open your eyes,
Sending me back my own true love.

Karen Rose Faison

Broken Flowers

A rose is a rose,
A heart is a heart.
Each like the other,
Can be torn apart.

Uncaring fingers, tearing, shredding,
Without a sense of guilt.
As the heart or flower's brought
To its inevitable result.

The fingers shred down to the stem,
Cutting away the life.
They then move on without a thought
For the trail of unhappiness and strife.

The flower wilts, the heart goes cold,
Despair is left behind.
Old memories play on and on,
In the recesses of a mind.

Roxanne Melanie Gentle Taylor

For Her

My life I would give
For your tender touch,
I can feel your emotions
Sadness and such,

A warm smile
With eyes so bright
I still get butterflies
When you're in my sight.

Soft lips
I wish to kiss,
Being with you
Is purely bliss.

So if you need a hand,
Someone to pick you off the floor
Just remember,
I'm always yours.

Ryan Donaldson

Promises

You made me promises
Promises I believed in
Promises I thought
That you would keep
And make come true
But what I found to be true
Was that your promises were empty
And full of lies

Nicole Frare

Poet's Demise

Upon the parchment
Of one's heart,
Words penned
Forever stay.
Amongst the tempest
Inked in swirl,
Thoughts bend,
Emotions sway.

When I, not pompous
In my stride,
Stroke quill,
Allusions rise.

Lament not writings.
Closed eyes be
In peace,
Soft falls demise.

Bonnie J. Duckworth

Necessary Steps

I have struggled to be right
I have danced within the night
I have juggled ancient fright
so will you publish what I write?

I have challenged highest height
I have tortured all man's plight
I have scaled the fortune's fight
so will you publish what I write?

I have taken heroes' might
I have fallen through the white
I have courted evil's knight
so will you publish what I write?

I have lied to sordid sight
I have cried to candlelight
I have tried to hold on tight
so will you publish what I write?

K. M. Robinson

Winter

I hate to feel alone,
then nights hold forever pain . . .
There is a hole within my soul
my eyes are full of heavy rain.

Clouds are bright compare to my face
no heart is broken as bad as mine
Leaves are making for snow more space,
it seams for me no sun will shine.

Grass was green and I had a smile
my passion was larger than planet Earth,
Now is time to sleep for a while
until Spring gives a "new love" birth.
Let the rain out, blow off the clouds,
magic of trust can do all of that . . .
Give life to leaves, rise up the sun
pain is behind, no love its death.

Branislava Petar Lazich

I Have Always Loved You

For Timothy C. Asper

I have always loved you, my darling,
From the moment we first met;
My heart and soul had been searching,
And with you completion had been met.
I have always loved you, my darling,
From the moment our eyes first met;
My life I give only to you as a small
Token of love's great debt.

Debra S. Hasbrook

When It Will Happen

When it will happen
If your eyes are torn away
By the priests of time.
Never, never again!

Will you still be there,
By the sea of forgiveness
To handle my ripped soul
Giving me time to forgive me.

At last, I forgive me,
Because I have sworn
That your heart is my gospel
And my fire will prevail.

But, stop! I am not crying
Are you still there?
Never mind, I will continue
Wandering through your veins.

Nicolas Albert Rovegno

I Thought

I thought it'd matter
For what I said or where
Now only rains' pitter patter
Shines on this window I stare

The turning of hands
Counting the moments that had past
Flying a dream land
Thinking this moment would last

But that's the story of yesterday
A memory in the wind
If words could have made you stay
Tomorrow would have another spin

I thought it's matter
For what I said of where
But now I realize it only matters
To say it when you were there. . . .

Steve Leslie Essex

What You Did to Me . . .

I have searched the depths of my heart
For the happiness that has parted,
The one who guided my fate,
Is now the owner of my hate.
I have lost my soul and all I control.
My tears are now dry
From all the years I have cried.
The trust I once knew
Is all gone because of you.
The life I had lived
And the LOVE I had to give,
Did not matter to you;
You wanted something new.
So now I sit in sorrow,
And wait till the day we call tomorrow
To take away my fears,
And bring happiness back to my years.

BreLea Williams

The Next Heartbreak

His touch is fire,
it burns me deep.

The thrill is higher,
I dare not sleep.

His voice is a choir,
don't make a peep.

Kisses full of desire,
it's only deceit.

Krissy Banzet

Sarah

My baby girl . . .
You came early one year.
Would you lose your life?
Was my greatest fear. . . .

Daddy and I Prayed,
For fifty-five days . . .
That the Lord would spare you,
Not take you away.

You went to our Father . . .
One late, lonely night..
Your battle was over . . .
You had won the fight.

I miss you, my darling . . .
I wish you were here.
I will always hold your hand.
I will always have you near.

Melanie Anne Russell

In the Heart

you're not my sister
by blood or birth
but you're my best sister
in all the earth
we're not sisters
by family or name
but we're sisters
just the same
you've been my dear friend
through all the years
through joy and sorrow
laughter and tears
no, we're not sisters
from our start
but in our deepest part
for we are sisters
in the heart

Patricia O'Brien Parker

Angel Forever

I do believe God above
created you for me to have
He picked me out from all the rest
because He knew I'd love you best

I once had a heart and this is true
but now it's gone from me to you
Take care of it like I have done
for you have two and I have none

If I die before you
I'll go to Heaven and wait
If you are not there on a certain day
I'll know you went the other way
So I'll pack up all my little things
and give the angels back their wings
And just to prove my love is true
I'd even go to Hell for you.

Becky Martinez

Of All the Things There Are to Be

Of all the things there are to be,
Lawyers are like a money tree,
Veterinarians are awesome heroes,
And a fortune teller always knows.

Of all the things there are to be,
And the choice is always mine,
The best I'll ever be, is just being me!

Brittany Zeller

Dreams

Our mind is full of wonders,
With darkness at its edge,
But lights shine through to glory,
And dreams that never end.

Our lives seem to change,
As we go through our life,
Bringing joys and sorrow,
Yet keeping dreams in sight.

For no matter what we wish for,
And doubts that we share,
We always find no matter,
Our dreams are always there,

So no matter where we travel,
Or what ever crosses we bare,
Our mind harbors its wonders,
And our dreams are in its lair.

Susan Frazier

My Love for You

Since the night our eyes met
I knew you were the one
I feel hopelessly in love
And my heart comes all undone.

Now my love is stronger
It grows stronger every day
You make my life complete
There's more I have to say.

I grew into a woman
From the teachings that you taught
Every second of every day
You are in my every thought.

You're my world and my life
Without you I'd be blue
So don't you ever doubt
When I say that I Love You!

Tammy Merwarth Weikel

The Camel

Today I saw a camel
He was walking in the sand
But as he walked away
His feet turned into hands

He was grabbing at my person
For what I could not say
But as I'm thinking back
Maybe he was showing me the way

The distance seemed so far
But I could feel him touching me
Fingers in the sand
I pretended not to see

Darkness closed upon me
My soul began to rise
Held captive by the grains
Death came as no surprise.

Alana Boehmer

Sara's Poem

Listen to your heart.
It speaks loud and clear.
It is a voice inside that
no one else can here.
If you listen to your heart.
It will always be true
Because it's the closest
you will come to the most
authentic you.

Kristeen Kradle

God's Armor

Together we fight our battles here.
We are as one, there is no fear.
But what about your judgment day?
Did you learn to love, to pray?
I gaze to the Heavens.
The answer is there.
My last glory, I do not share.
Heart and soul,
I begin to shake.
The ultimate warrior,
He decides my fate.
Pearly gates open wide,
My happiness, I cannot hide.
I stare in awe
As I look down to see
I wear God's Armor . . .
His cross and wings.

Vonna Rose Harrison

Time

Have you ever thought?
How time passes
Faster than lightning
Quicker than sound

Have you ever stopped?
To glance at your watch
Or waited around
For the six o'clock news

Have you ever watched?
The birds in the sky
Fish in a stream
Or people on and on

Do you have the time?
To stop and think
As you read the last line
Time will have past you by

Leslie Cain

God Is in All the Parts!

God is in all the parts.
We look for Him . . .
We search our hearts.

In the sky, we glance for His eyes.
We look for Him . . .
Will he see our cries?

Out to sea, we search for His ears.
We look for Him . . .
Will He hear our tears?

At our home, we seek His face.
We look for Him . . .
Will prayers find us grace?

Our family brings us all His love.
God is in all the parts . . .
In, out, at and Above!

James David Hagan

Happy

Help us to be happy
Over the years.
Teach us to be happy
Away from fears.
Happy counts in most
Of our lives.
By doing what makes you happy,
Open up your heart.
Happiness is a tremendous thing.

Virginia Viers

It's Morning over There

As we come to the end of life
To lay our burdens down,
We may think our future
Is an eternity underground.

But nothing's further from the truth,
As God's word declares,
'Cause when it's evening over here,
It's morning over there.

And when it's time for us to grieve,
A time for us to mourn,
We look into our sunset,
So weary, tired, and worn.

But friend, there is a hope in God,
So let us not despair,
For when it's nightfall over here,
It's morning over there.

Joel H. Tilley

Karla . . . My Endless Love

I shall think
many thoughts of you—
and our love . . .
will grow forever strong
through our dreams,
and our love . . .
will escape the chains of these times.
We must be strong—
until we can be together
and draw strength from
the nourishment of our souls.
We'll make plans then—
for our own special world . . .
for our time—
and we'll think,
only thoughts of us.

Michael Sergio Gilbert

Love Me

Love me tomorrow
as much as today
Always love me
as much as you say
Love me in laughter
Love me through tears
Love me for hours
Love me for years . . .
And I promise you
I'll love you tomorrow
much more than today
And I'll always love you
more than I could show or say
I'll love you in laughter
I'll love you through tears
I love you more each hour
I'll love you for years!

Debi Mahoney

Nature of Love

A fire burns in your summer breeze,
A cool rain, your warm embrace.
Enchanting smile, a longing kiss,
Your lovely smile I will miss.
A mountain glow as the clouds shine,
The sun warms as the moon shines.
All this means is I love you.
Running stream, ocean flow,
To be with you, anywhere I will go.

Byron Jackson

A Child's Visit

One last time
One last call
One last cry
I stand here looking
Copper turning old,
After two years
Cold silence
Eerie breezes
What do I do now
With this rose before me?
Nothing to hook it on
Nothing to claim it yours
Gently falling, slowly
Caressing the white blanket
Above your grave
Freezing
Into You.

Denice Marie Burns

A Nightly Rise

Nightful gleaming soothing sight,
Glittering brightly among all night;
Lightful beaming waking might,
Clearing lightly along with fright;

Gleaming brightly rising high,
Breaking darkly an unknown cry;
Doubtful seaming rising brows,
Silently sleeping frequent howls;

Starlit glazing eyes of wisdom
Unknown presence, presence shown;
Glowing brightly forth with coming,
Tearful lingering mournful rise:

Last becoming lowering gleam,
Losing slightly leaving dream;
From time becoming once before,
Time relieving come once more

Errol Coder

Pain

Pain, it's from the inside.
It's internal,
Never external
People think of pain as a cut or fall,

But that is only the throw of the rock.
The distance the rock goes,
That's Pain.
What is thought of as pain,

Is only the light of the dynamite,
The explosion, that's pain.
The one that eats the insides from you,
That's Pain.

Pain, is really hurt feelings.
Because pain, it's from the inside.
It's internal,
Never external.

Dien H. Pham

Finding a Toy

My eyes can't reach the highest shelves;
It's terrible you see;
But what most other people miss;
I can easily see.

I see the crannies and the crooks;
Where a person never looks;
And what do you suppose I see;
Sad old bears and bunnies;
Waiting just for me!

Stephanie Josephine Maas

Drowning

Retiring for the day,
we went down to the water,
and heard the waves sing.

The young one was forgotten.
He raced for the waves of Heaven,
diving into the arms of his murderer.

The eldest raced against time,
never forgetting about her mission.
There was a life in need of help.

The keeper arrived at once
and destroyed the taker of life,
remembering the evil it had caused.

The youngest was set free.
The keeper kissed his mouth,
and the youngest then breathed.

Lee Courtney Thomas

If's and Or's

If I found something so perfect
For why would I let it go
Is it the fear of getting attached
Or just unreadiness to grow

If I found love for a person
For why not give her my all
Is it the fear of pure rejection
Or is it walking before I crawl

If I realized that you're so special
For why am I not by your side
Is it the fact that you're too good
Or is it the fear of swallowing pride

I know that if's and or's
Don't do much more for you or me
But I don't know what to do
Because I'm just too blind to see

C. D. Edward Harris

Me

I once had a back,
But it ran away with a potato sack.
I once had feet,
But they ran away with a slab of meat.
I once had hands,
But they ran away with the band.
I once had legs,
But they ran away with beer kegs.
I once had arms,
But they ran away to some farm.
I once had a tummy,
But it ran away with a mummy.
I once had a chest,
But it ran away to a bird's nest.
Now all I have left is my head.
WAIT! It's running off with the bed.
Now there's nothing of me left.

Gina Verderico

Madness

When you worry about
The meanings,
You lose the feelings.

Worry not
Of the Whys and Hows;

Only remember
The Whencesoevers and
Whereabouts.

Jason M. Orso

Heaven Sent

A torch of light
begins to shine
on a lonely heart
as dark as mine

I walk the streets
with my head hung low
sadness spread on my face
as it begins to show

A change of events
A word that is said
can hurt you forever
make you wish you were dead

but getting past it
is the new main event
because I'm starting to think
that this was all heaven sent

Jonathan Schwartz

Heart Strings

My heart is broken.
Don't bother pokin'.
I won't feel it much.
Oh, to know the touch,
of unconditional love.
It's a gift that's like a dove.
It makes your heart soar so high,
It can never be mistaken as a lie.
My heart is in a bad zone.
My son doesn't want to come home.
My love for him doesn't matter,
Because he wants to be on his own.
I will always love him,
He is my gift from God.
So I have to let him go.
Oh, God watch over my son.
He is the only one.

Sharon Kragelund

Normal

Normal is a state of mind,
Mine is clear.
Mellow being perceived by others
Explodes in my mind.

Extreme to the limits,
Dreams that can't happen.
Memories rushing through,
Disappear with quickness.

I am not who I want,
I want what others have,
Beauty and personality,
Or rather just plainness.

The ability to speak,
To listen and to be spoken to.
I wish I could be normal.
But who really knows what normal is?

Elly Motloch

My Angel

There's a light shining on me
A force a field that keeps me

This is my "angel," my freedom
From my troubles that surround me

My angel's not white
My angel's not black
My angel's of no race
It's my angel of grace

Rachel Simms-Thompkins

The Chase of Glory

Attention! Attention!
We're looking for reaction;
Our own satisfaction,
By stepping on you all.

Creating our own power,
Denying our own father,
Betraying you with laughter,
Diabolical when you fall.

Resist if you want.
Stop us, though you can't,
Glorified, our human hunt
To heed the Master's call.

Here, we'll be forever,
Our forces bound together
In control we will be ever,
By stepping on you all.

Joe Gregonis

The Legacy

What will you leave behind
When your body's dead and gone
Will they remember how you smiled
Or even know that you are gone?

So it takes a calculator
To figure the money that you made
But what did it ever buy
That doesn't rot away and fade?

I know you really tried
To do the best that you could do
It really doesn't matter
When death treats us all so rude.

So enjoy all you do
The moment's not too late
For the only thing you ever leave
Is what you didn't take!

Richard Allen Payne

Wolf

Wolf, majestic in composure
And swift in run.
The soft fur is a parka
And the sharp teeth are daggers.

Wolf, carnivore of the plains,
Hunter of the forest.
Feared by caribou and elk,
The rogue is like a killer coat.

Wolf, one of the pack.
Like a howling kettle,
Every lament is heard;
Nothing audible is unwished.

Wolf, beast of the ages.
Timeless in thought
And unknown in action,
The assassin is alien.

Philip Alden Selmer

WanTinG

LeAves FaLL.
The SnoW ThreAteNs.

The FraGilE FielDs oF corN
SwAy iN thE BreezE.

my mind has become restless

likE th CriSp LeaveS of FaLL.

WintEr TeaSes my WaTerIng MouTh.

Nikki Head Kinsley

Flickering Candles

Candles flicker in the wind
messages from Heaven
dancing light of the gods
whispers in the air . . .
The call of loved ones
whom we feel are near us
The never-ending flames
continue to burn
full of life and energy
Not like the petals of a flower
which fall to the ground and die
Spirit lives on
in the life and breath of others
The hope and prayer that one day
we will be reunited . . .
and the candles will continue
to flicker in the wind

Kim Louise Steeves

Sonnet Poem

When men begin
Seeing you as nothing
And you are alone,
Know this that is truth—
You shall see me hurt.
Though the fire is gone,
The passion remains—
I that loved you before
You lost your desire.
My faith keeps you replenished;
The world will know
That love can still be
Even when all is gone,
And from that
You will see what
I have seen in you,
And I will forgive you for it.

Kacey Blaire Bryant

That's Why I Watch

I'm a child who needs to learn
I don't know right from wrong
That's why I watch

Today I watch in silent awe
Tomorrow I mimic what I saw
That's why I watch

Everything you do I see
Everything you say I hear
That's why I watch

I look for your guidance
I look for your love and
That's why I watch

I want to, no I need to
Look and learn from you
That's why I watch

Katherine J. Lindner

Where Was I?

I know how Jesus
raised the dead.
What it's like to have the
spirit leave the body,
hovering above, dancing 'round
the foyer of an existence,
while the body walks in
and out the door,
imagining that this is real life.

Kate Rander

Time

Time—passes by so slowly
Since you went away
Taking with it a part of me
Each and every day

Time—they say is precious
As we found out that night
One that we thought would live forever
Was taken from our sight

Time—I hope will ease the pain
Of the loss we have endured
To give us the strength to carry on
In the life that we have ensured

Time—I know will surely pass
To heal our broken heart
To put the smile back on our face
But how and where do we start?

Debbie Hatfield

Nature's Paradise

The wonderful waterfall
Gushing down to the stream,
Flowing into the lake,
Looks like a dream.

The silent lake,
Glistening in the sunlight,
Where owls fly
Only in the moonlight.

The owls soar
Up in the sky,
Seeing other animals around them
Flying up high.

A frog jumps into the lake,
It is silent no more,
But listen carefully,
You'll hear the waterfall's roar.

Jessica Palmer

Dark Knight

My heart aches,
This is true,
And I don't know what to do.
My dark knight,
I love him so
But he is a fantasy I made up long ago.
The conversations we have,
Are not real at all,
He doesn't catch me when I fall.
He doesn't hold me during the night.
Or comfort me when I get a fright.
The "I love you's" are not there
There is no one left to care.
My dark knight,
I love him so,
But he is a fantasy,
I made up long ago.

Tabitha Arnold

Nobody

Nobody pays attention to me.
They walk by and just be.
I walk around the school all day.
The teachers say, "Are you okay?"
I say, "Ya, I'm on my way
to a life, a life far, far away.
It will be long and hard, but we'll see"
Nobody pays attention to me.
They walk by and just be.

Nicole Marie Papike

Dreams

Oh, these dreams aren't made for you
And these dreams aren't made for me
These dreams are made for the amusement
Of those we see each day

And these dreams are made of laughter
These dreams are made of sorrow
And these dreams are made of a love
That graces each tomorrow

These dreams aren't for the old
And these dreams aren't for the young
These dreams are made for those who are
Of each and everyone

These dreams aren't for the boys
And these dreams aren't for the girls
These dreams are made for every person
In our dying world

Heidi Lynn O'Dell

Make Me a Child Again

At times I have so many doubts
That have yet to be erased.
No one should have to be put through
The problems I have faced.

It's a matter of finding a remedy
To stop the flow of tears,
To keep me company when I'm alone
And to comfort me from my fears.

I need someone to tell me
It'll soon turn out all right,
Someone to say it'll be okay,
And someone to hold me tight.

I know it's all part of growing up
But if I must go through pain,
Please put me back into my mother's arms
And make me a child again.

B. Wray

Pack away Your Troubles

Face your day with a happy heart
and end it with a song.
You'll find the hours in between
can't go far from wrong.

A smile is sure contagious
than a dreary frown,
and nicer to remember
when the sun goes down.

Don't miss out on happiness
by looking towards the ground,
but keep looking skyward
that's where the rainbows found.

Just pack away your troubles
for some other day.
And before you know it
they'll all have slipped away.

Wayne C. Quinn

Cats

Tiger, tiger burning bright
in the shadows of the night
Running, running, without rest,
trying, trying, to past the test.

See the lion hunt its prey,
See it get its own pay.

Dogs and cats all have pasts,
now I'm finished with this task.

Pilar Ortiz

Daughters

I think every time I blink
my eye they become bigger,
smarter, cuter, and only if
they'd stay so young and naive.
Life gets harder,
so many problems,
too much danger, and all the worry.
I want them to be strong.
They've always worked hard to teach,
My beautiful girls will grow
as wonderful as they can,
I was sent two sweet
angels to help me find
myself, and what they
taught me is what being
a mother really is.
To me they're God's greatest conquest.

Jennell Chilson

1-800-Heaven

Hi God,
I'd like to talk
To my Dad
I'm calling
From Earth
Please Mr. please
Don't hang up
I know he's there
Please put him on
The line . . .
I'm missing him
Real bad
I just want to hear
His sweet voice
To know he's okay.
Please Mr. please
Don't hang up. . . .

Endora Smith

A Castle Stands atop a Cliff

A castle stands atop a cliff
That bends beneath the skies
And leads you to an open door
With wonderful surprise

The mountains, out beyond the reach
Look proudly, up above
And stare at me through wondering eyes
That make me fall in love

When you're up there you won't believe
What lies far out of reach
You'll see the world as tiny toys
But beautiful and rich

The golden rays shine down on me
And make the dull ground shine
And everything seems magical
And all seems to be mine!

Ann Panteleev

I'm Listening, Little Bird

"Hello, I'm Buddy Blackbird.
I exist for your delight,
Trilling tunes of amity
From early morning light.
Pray dismiss my tiresome antics
Since I broke out of my shell,
Pecking plastic clothes pegs
And pinging on the bell.

Your garden looks presentable,
No need to toil all day,
Planting, weeding, mowing, raking,
Down tools—come fly away."

Adela Graham

Acquiescence

The damp oak leaves rot in tune
To the phases of the moon
Organic matter life's substrate
With sand and clay bear the weight
Of everything that stands or falls
Or held within predatory claws
One by one the forces toil
To return us to the soil
Sweet dreams await those who yield
Becoming flowers in the field
But those who cling and grasp and mourn
Become not flowers but the thorn

Gene Zizis

Genuine Laughter

Genuine laughter bubbles up
From the depths of the soul
It takes the most humorous moments
Magnifies and releases them all at once

It resists pretentiousness
It celebrates blissfulness
It proclaims realness

Flooding the ears
It brings tears
Of unadulterated cheers
To those blessed enough to hear

Laughter from a hidden place
Ricocheted into outer space
Then boomeranged back
To its hideaway
Awaiting the chance
To do it all over again.

Deborah Whiting Bentley

I Woke up This Morning

I woke up this morning,
I heard a sound say,
my children are lost,
they've wondered away.
I looked around to see
who it was speaking to me,
Jesus was crying, tears
in the sand.
Down in the valley,
lay fallen man.
Touched by his mercy,
raised by his mercy,
up came the man,
off of his face,
his blessed appearing,
just around the bend.
We don't have long
to be gathered in.

Margie Monroe

Ryan's Tattoo

I hear the needle buzzing, buzzing
Driving blue ink into my skin.

I am disappointed.

It doesn't hurt as much as I remember,
Not as much as I think it should.

I wanted it to hurt.

I wanted it to hurt like I hurt
The moment that I knew you were gone.

I know now it could never hurt enough.

Lisa Patrick

Carving Treasures

My heart is but a treasure chest
Overflowing with priceless gems . . .
Treasures carved from the laughter sweet
Of a friend I met and liked this week,
A line from a song I learned today,
The fun we had in our hour at play.
Treasures carved from the lilting rhyme
Of a poem read at vesper time,
Useful things we learned at crafts,
Knowledge gleaned from this and that.
God made my heart so high and wide,
To store the treasures I carve inside.

Ernestine Riley Ullum

Clear Outside

It happens when my eye is still
That everything, everywhere
Becomes a drink
In which the great
Majestic Eye
Nourishingly drinks.
Not for any purpose other
Than to see; to gaze; behold
And to drink
And outside the realm
Of ordinary sight,
To lead to the place of clear hearing
Where even thoughts raging in
The subconscious realm
Become pristine!
And I
With the help of "Eye" . . .
Become clairvoyant.

Krissi Edwards

Memories

The memories of loved
ones will always be
in the hearts of all
people.

Whether memories are
good or bad, happy or
sad, they will always
be there to show

that love will always
live on through the
years in the hearts
of all mankind.

Love is the greatest
thing you can give
to somebody in their life
to have the greatest memories
from their life.

Jessica Ondracek

Cloud

Why do things happen the way they do?
How did we get here?
What for?
Why am I here?
And why is it a secret?

Alexandria Marshall

The Garage

Some people have their mansions,
And others have hillsides.
My garage is my salvation
It's where I go to hide.

Now whenever I am tired,
Or my life is filled with haze.
I just go to my garage,
It's where I spend my days.

I have food and entertainment,
I could live their for a week.
The convenience of the outside world,
Does not appeal to me.

So if you need to be enlightened,
Or when you feel you need to flee.
Come on over the garage,
That's the place that I will be.

David Schwem

I Loved You

We met each other at a bar
I never thought it would go far

We connected from the start
We never did part

We stayed together for three years
The day I walked down the aisle
I saw my father's tears

My parents knew then that you were
not for me
I guess I just had to see

Well, we had a son to complete our book
I delivered him and you had the look

In your eyes
I was at your demise

I will carry on
you are finally gone

Mary Ellen Ferrer

Senescence

Forlorn leaf; wrinkly retiree,
Watch and wait—the final exit.
Sixteen lustrums survived,
Weary, worn out for tots.
Age-mates detached,
Next of kin deem millstone,
Hopes—hearts to lend hands.
Ganders back: winner or loser?
Hankers fruitful golden years,
Elbow grease chores—never again,
Hindered by ruthless time.
Frozen tears; chronic desert.
Moribund old timer, past best days,
Glances up!
Knock out!
Streams in the desert;
'Cause none turned empty handed.
Touched and healed—Happy Meliorist,
Peeks anew: full marks or naught?

Anand Victor

Infestation of the Heart

Deathly sleep
Thoughts captive in me no longer
Out of the darkness of night
A dream
Horror of horrors
Heart aching
Monsters raking
Insects shaking
My soul
Now fleeing
No more?

Candice Neavill

Untitled

Tick tock
Tick tock
acid rain
burning rock
tick tock
says the millennial clock
why worry
says the inner man
because nothing in life
is so bad
only our thoughts
make it so
I'm not ready
to go
tick tock
says another millennial clock

Noeleen Delamore

Carlina's Birth

Welcome to this world.
You bring happiness and hope
to your parents,
grandparents, and friends,
Carlina, Carlina!

You'll have in this life
your parents' protection and love,
and the blessing of God
in this promising land,
Carlina, Carlina!

I wish you to become
a happy, successful star
in whatever you desire
throughout your life,
Carlina, Carlina!

Luis Alejandro

Endurance

Along the borders of the Hudson's Bay,
Fort Churchill is the spot.
We are doomed to spend our lives here,
in this land that God forgot.

Down with the ice and snow,
up where men get blue.
Thousands of miles from nowhere,
hundreds of miles from you.

We swear, freeze, and shiver—
it's more than a man can stand.
We are not a bunch of convicts,
but defenders of our land.

When we get to Heaven,
St. Peter will surely say,
"They are from Fort Churchill, dear God;
They have spent there time in Hell.

Dall Beninger

When We're Together

To the one I love

When we're together
My life seems so perfect.
I forget all my problems,
And the pain inside me is gone.
I never want to lose you
I don't know what I would do.
I hope that day never comes
That I have to find that out.
You're my best friend,
And the love of my life.
I love you with all my heart.

Jennifer Elnor Gibbon

Hello, Old Friend

We stand in awe and wonder,
Watching you hang on to life
Why?
For family and friends?
Do you really enjoy us?
Do you hear the joyful laughter?
See the starry smiles?
We know you feel our presence.
We love you.
We have loved you.
Now the time has come
To let you go.
Go to the Heavenly Father,
Who awaits your arrival.
God loves us all
Till death do us part.

Phyllis Allen

A Sad Branch of Tree

Morning's sun
Brings morning sun rays
But as the evening falls
A dim light spreads all over
And after a while
Everything goes under the dark
In such a time
The moon sometimes shows on the sky
And sometimes the stars shine
To make their appearance known
Either it's morning or night
This tree in the back of my house
Is always standing there
With its branches spread
And I remain looking at it
As a sad branch of its.

Shalini Deoghoria

Love Is Forever

Love is meant to be forever,
even through the toughest of
times.
Love can say a thousand words
in every heart and mind.
Love sometimes brings troubles
and sorrows, but if we keep
that love in mind, there's
always a brighter tomorrow.
And when that love begins to
fade away, always remember the
vows you made, and the love you
promised one another 'til death
do you part.
All because you found that love
within your very hearts.

Barbara Alice Fondren

Untitled

I fail at life
So full of strife
I'm sad until the end.
Now this knife
Will end this life
Death is my final friend.
He awaits my passing
Never asking
just why I want to die.
He accepts my conviction,
My stern addiction
Then gives me leave to fly.

R. Briggs

Completion

You completed me,
From the moment we met,
You woke up my soul,
My heart rose from the dead.
When I looked in your eyes,
I saw myself,
I loved you before we even met,
I'll never love anyone else.
The day I confessed,
My love to you,
I saw shock and surprise,
Then happiness too.
Since that afternoon,
Loneliness has gone,
Our love will last,
It will go, on and on.

Sasha M. Bowerbank

My Special Effects

I wake up early, in the mirror my world
engulfed is twisting, turning, and
spiraling. To look away I am having an
earthquake, hard to focus.
There is no escape from the dizzying
kaleidoscope my eyes now see, my
face transformed to a grotesque mask.
Everywhere I turn, nothing looks
the same. My legs have turned to stone,
the heaviness coming form the
depths of my soul. I am a walking,
talking Hollywood movie, "Special
Effects." No, it's M.S. I reach out for
my Lord and feel comforted.
Waiting, ever waiting, for the "Special
Effects" to pass till next time.

Sandra Lee Emfinger

Angel, I Do, I Do

Dear Angel, sweet and soft,
Going somewhere at the moment?
Angel watching over me
As I lie down.
Not a word do I hear,
Nor a single sound.
Stories are told about you,
About the way you watch
Over me my whole life through.
I thank you—I do, I do.
I hope to see you someday
In the Heavens above.
I know, dear Angel,
That I am loved.
I know you love me, Angel,
And, Angel, I love you, too—I do, I do.

Brooke Danielle White

Life vs. Death

Death will battle me often,
And it may win the war.
But how many battles will I win,
And what of my score?
In each battle that I am defeated,
Where the war is not yet won,
My life will be a little depleted
And then will I die some.
But what of my victories?
Where by life, death is defeated.
Can death some decease
And life, in death, be seeded?

Jennifer Lynn Prowell

Learner

And I often believe in fairy tales . . .
that everything can be a fantasy
I dream of dreams that never come
wishing that someday they'll be.
Perhaps naive
in the game called life
Always searching for ways,
that leave sensibility aside
A student I am
and certainly I admit
that everything is first
learned, taught then, did.
So I leave things as they are
Like an empty cup I'll be
keeping a fresh perspective
on everything that I see.

Tiara C. Rigor

Wrinkle

Time has stopped yet I remain.
Everything stays the same.
Nothing happens anymore.
Existence is a bore.
I walk through the pale passageway.
A frozen man bent down to pray.
Everything fell into decay.
Everything—yet I remain.
Barren wasteland of shelter lies.
Broken and empty in my eyes.
Hunger grips my aching thighs.
Cuts through me like a thousand knives.
Exhausted and tired I remain.
Struggle to contain
What still is here to keep me sane.
Time has stopped yet I remain.

Joseph Barnabas Manske

Your Love

Your love is like a mystery to me.
I can't always see it,
but deep in my heart, deep in my soul
I know I'll always feel it.
Your hands are like an elevator
that lift me when I'm down.
Your smile is like the warm sunshine
that cures me when I frown.
Your heart is like a shield
that gets me through the day.
Your love is like a sweet piece of candy
that in my heart will forever stay.
Your eyes are like the twinkling stars
that brighten up my day.
Being with you is everything,
so promise me you'll always stay.

Deanna Harrison

Prison

Escape from this tomb
An impossibility
My thoughts
They keep my sanity
My heart beat
The only indicator that I yet still live
I cannot see
I cannot move
I can only hear
Familiar voices calling
Please have mercy
Release me from my body

Armando Lambaren

The Best Kind of Frustration

In the beginning things are great
A classroom smooth and polished
Students are curious about the day
Wondering what rules they'll abolish
They know that they're a special class
Their behaviors put them there
They go to recess, they go to lunch
While the other kids just stare
My job is to work one-on-one
To help him gain control
Sometimes he listens, sometimes not
Sometimes my eyes just roll
When my patience starts to wear thin
I always find this summation:
I love my job, love what I do
It's the best kind of frustration!

Lamon Theus

The Garden of My Mind

My mind is but a garden
I must uproot the weeds
Imagine all the roses
And nurture all the seeds
The seeds are metaphorically
What is planted in my mind
Some thoughts require rejection
And replacements I must find
The good seeds I will harvest
After imaging is through
Manifested in my environment
The old makes way for new
The laws of attraction
Have always been the same
Persistence is the key
To achieving every gain

Maureen LeFanue

If I Could Turn Water into Wine

If I could cause the sky to rain,
I'd wash away all hurt or pain.

If I were a saint in disguise,
I'd dry any teardrops in your eyes.

If I could give sight to the blind,
Clear blue skies are all you'd find.

If I were sent from the sky above,
I'd make certain you'd find true love.

If I had power enough to heal,
I'd mend any hurt so you could feel.

If I could turn water into wine,
I'd have your love and you'd have mine.

Sam Logan

Grandpa

When I had a lesson to learn
Those answers I had to earn
You meant so very much to me
You passed away, how can that be?
You fixed my bikes and wiped my tears
You wiped away my childish fears
So sweet, loving, and very kind
You're one of the few that I would mind
You didn't lecture or yell at me
You were always calm as could be
This comes straight from my heart
My feelings for you won't ever part.

Kamilla Walters

Iris

An Iris is a small purple flower,
but my Iris isn't.
An Iris is a sweet-smelling flower,
but my Iris isn't.

My Iris is a lovely, happy feeling
that will never die.
My Iris is a pool of sunshine
on a rainy day.

But my Iris is gone.
I never showed all my feelings
to this happy one.
And now I'm sad that she
will never know.

I'm sorry, my Iris,
my lovely dog.

Kelly L. Stavrides

Whispering Winds

The field was abandoned,
No one in sight.
He walked though the shadows,
Led by the moonlight.
He searched for the spot,
The spot where they lay.
And knelt by their side,
just like yesterday.
He said "Guys, I miss you,"
And started to cry.
The whispering winds,
Brushed right by his side.
Tagged with a message,
Just like yesterday.
"I'll always be with you,
My son, every day."

James Buonconsiglio

Truth Within

When science fiction
Becomes science fact
All things become white
Which once were black
There is Truth

When books of fantasy
Become very real
Many questions arise
Answers yet to reveal
There is Truth

When all lies learned
Have been erased
All hearts cleansed
Our souls embraced
Within we find Truth

Lory G. Prescott

Cards of Life

You play the cards you're dealt in life.
I was dealt them too.
Every hand is different,
But there's one that matches you.
If you could see the cards
And every hand that's dealt,
You'd know God's plan exactly
And how every person felt.
But if you can find that matching one
And help each other through,
Then you will know part of God's plan,
The part that's just for you.

Nikol M. Goretzke

Stars

Stars
Nocturnal pavement
For the wandering young dreamer.

Constellations precariously hanging
On the dark firmament.

Maturity
Unhooks them, one by one
On a free fall.

The years extinguish their light
The adult sky has fewer stars.

How many dreams are today's realities?
How many fantasies have been discarded?

Oh, my soul! How much you have grown
Oh, my soul! How much you had to forget.

Percyvaldo Wendler

The Wet Rose

The wet rose
Each petal bathed in morning dew
Some more than others,
some not at all
The wet rose
In a field full of daisies
Dry daisies . . .
The odd one
when all the daisies die
the rose will not be lonely anymore
it will then be accompanied by
the dark sky, the grass, the rain,
and the clouds
and it is then
that the wet rose
will be happy

Alyson Louise Barrow

Glass Tenki

i'm not hurt
i don't miss him
why should i
i never cared about him anyway
i've never felt anything for anyone
so it doesn't matter that he's gone
i like being alone
you may think i'm sad and angry
but i'm perfectly fine
i don't need any more friends
i don't want to be loved
i'm strong
no one can ever hurt me
i'm happy with my life
. . .
you see through me don't you

Courtney Joyce Brewer

La Vie (Life)

Life is hard
But give it a try . . .
Living is death
We all must die . . .
Life is strain
It gives off pain . . .
Death is life
It ends all strife . . .
Love is a flower
It's dying out . . .
Give that flower more water,
enough for it to sprout.

Joy Thierry-Chamber

A Treasured Friend

I lost a treasured friend today,
my little dog who used to lay
his gentle head upon my knee
and share his silent thoughts with me.
He'll come no longer to my call,
Retrieve no more his favorite ball,
for a voice far greater than my own
has called him to his golden throne.
Although my eyes are wet with tears,
I thank God for those grateful years
He let him spend down here with me,
and for his love and loyalty.
When it is time for me to go
and join him there, this much I know,
I will not fear the silent dark,
for he will greet me with his bark.

Judy Bruno

Loved

Your love moved me
touched my soul
reached deep down inside me
made me whole
it was the greatest thing
I ever had
it was my joy, my everything
it made me glad
I never had
a better day
when you were here
and your love stayed
you made me feel
like no one could
your love for me
was all that was good

Nathaniel Vincent

Michael

Michael Ziller
that is his name
He was taken from us
things are no longer the same
At his funeral
they played a great song
His classmates were there
I was singing along
but I was crying too
the pain hurt a lot
June second was the day
it'll never be forgot
We miss you, Michael
you were and still are loved
We'll never forget you
your life wasn't long enough

Stacey Marie Billmeier

Don't Pity Me

Please don't pity me
Because it's hard for me to speak
Please don't pity me if I can't play
For some reason, God made me this way
I can laugh, I can cry
Please don't tsk, tsk me as you walk by.
My body may be crippled that may be true
But I have feelings, just like you
So talk to me, I'm not a freak
Play with me, I'm not that weak
Remember this, and if you do,
That I am human, just like you.

Carl Gallub

Rag Doll

What about me?
Don't I mean anything?
Oh, wait . . .
I forgot . . .
I'm just a toy.
A ragged old toy,
Just sitting in the back of your closet.
You never take me out . . .
Unless I'm lonely or depressed.
Then I come alive.
It brings joy to my heart
Just to know you still care.
But that quickly ends.
And I'm left once more
With another broken heart
In the back of your closet.

Rayna Nicole Witt

Friends

Lose one friend
Lose all friends
Lose yourself,
Make one friend
Make all friends
Make yourself,

Hug one friend
Hug all friends
Hug yourself,

Love one fried
Love all friends
Love yourself,

Friends are everything
so treat them with respect
and don't take them for granted.

Santiago Joseph Rosales

Ever After

Scars run deep
Time honored blood
For all to see
Wounds open up
Unbidden

The Beast Unleashed
My Forever After
Comfortable Friend
Pain, My captive
Uninvited

Into the Night
My Second Self
Bloodlust Driving
With a Killer's Stealth
Unfettered

Stacey Freeman Hart

Falling Love

It was young and falling
But going so slow
It had to sometime end

Down past the clouds
That were once our goal
I was losing my best friend,

And sailing by our tree of past
we thought we would never climb
Now look at us
our love has crashed
the pieces lost with time.

Monty Moore

The Ghosts of Lovers Lost

I walk beside the graveyard
of lost and shattered dreams.
Thoughts of forever put to rest
love that fell between the seams.
If they had fought as allies
to win the peace and not the war,
perhaps their broken dreams
would have lived on forevermore.
But pride became a teacher,
and fear became a friend,
so that left truth, love, and honesty
out in the cold again.
They roam throughout the headstones,
the ghosts of lovers lost,
that never found the reasons
but they all had to pay the cost.

Scott Sosebee

Just Me

A new girl
In a new world
trying to figure out
What this is all about
Kiss me hug me
that's all they do
but tell me one thing
can this be true
am I here for real this time
or am I just dreaming of my mom
so tell me tell me tell me now
why is everybody saying wow
can't you see
I'm no one important
no one special
just me

Candise Lynn Wyrembelski

Christmas Time

Do you feel down and out,
Christmas on the way?
Kids want this and Dad wants that,
Oh, God, how do I pay?
This to do and that to do,
So much I cannot bear!
Am I the only one that feels
Like pulling out my hair?

If you feel like this, my friends,
Unloved and not worth much,
I, too, have had the pressures
But then I felt God's touch,
For I asked Jesus to be my friend
And His peace He gave to me.
'Cause He loves you all, yes, everyone
And He died for you, you see

Kathleen Patricia Sinclair

The Promise

Ebony hues across the sky,
dainty lamps stand trimmed to guide.
Look for me against the tide
and I'll come to you.
Silent creatures rise to prey,
weary heads seek where to lay.
Look for me though dim the way
and I'll come to you.
Sing ye languish? Sing ye numb,
mournful tunes of love undone?
Hush now. Look, for lo I come
and I come to you.

Alundreatta Louise Nichols

June 30th

I know when it happened,
I know just the day.
Someone ripped my heart from me,
and simply walked away.
So I stumble through the rain,
in the shadow of what once was.
Looking for some answers,
but I guess everyone does.
My life is so much different now,
spinning softly through the gloom.
Spent searching for some meaning,
a candle for this tomb.
Yes, I know when it happened,
I know just the day.
Someone took my soul, you see,
and simply walked away.

DJ Abraham

Life

I lifted up my eyes to see ahead.
The mist lay silently on all.
I trudged on.
Unseeing,
Trusting in the Lord.
He knows where life is taking me.
I stayed close to His footsteps.
On and on I journeyed.
Not knowing where,
or how rough the way ahead would be.
Following Him.
Knowing that
at the right time,
through the mist,
I will see a rainbow.

It is enough to know.

Sylvia Marie MacGregor

Alimentation

I say not need a word
A tool of potent precision
Of undying compassion
From her I am touched
I lay here broken glass
Untangled the knotted
Until I am heavyhearted
To deadweight inanimate . . .
She came to me in feathers
Exceeding hopes and dreams
Gently fabricate through her
She reassembles, gratis offer
A sheaf of nonsense, a puzzle solved
Her touch is only healing
Sometimes it's all I'm needing
Sometimes I feel I'm dreaming

Sean Galaviz

Light in the Night

It looks down on me
I look up on it
it fills the night with light
but it's only a mirror
a mirror in the sky
the sky of the night

It gives some hope
hope in the cold of the night
to some it is a symbol
a symbol of evil
the evil in the night
but to me it's just the moon

Christopher Hes

Lonely

What do you do when everyone slips away
Going on to live much happier days
You are stuck with no one there
Feeling as though they don't care
The one you could turn to
Starts to ignore you
How do you react to the cold shoulder
As life seems to be getting harder
Who do you turn to when you need to talk
When you feel everything is your fault
Pressures creep up on you
What do you do
When being lonely is all too familiar
When you have no idea who you are
When you feel trapped, you are not free
How do you deal with being lonely?

Chastian Jeffers

Let's Get Together

It sure would be nice
To get together with you.
Just to sit down and talk,
And have a cup of coffee or two
It's been so long
Since we been together,
A lot of years have passed,
It seems like forever . . .
You went your way,
And I went mine,
But it's mine we get together,
And have a good time,
Ya, it sure would be nice,
To get together with you,
Sit and laugh and talk,
And have a cup of coffee or two!

Marie Sherill

Broken

My heart is broken
My trust is gone
For what I had is forever lost
Shadows of night have taken the place
With fear sadness and disgrace
For what I feel cannot be true
The lose, the pain I have to endure
The love and trust for which I lust
I will fill when I am dust
High in the sky the suns so bright
Above me the shadows of night
The warmth is gone
The cold is here
My heart is bleeding with fear
Please help me God understand the truth
For I do not know what to do.

Shannon R. Hanners

Useless Circles

I think I'll just drown my sorrows
in this bottle of whiskey,
but where will that leave me?
Tomorrow, when it wears off,
I'll wake up alone and cold in my room,
wondering how I got home.
Then the tears will run down my face,
but I'll just wipe them away
and put on a fresh smile
so I can go out later that day,
only to drown more of my sorrows
in more bottles of whiskey,
to start the whole cycle again.

Heather Johnson

Orion

On the run from loud neon,
bright noise that blinds
and freedom chained to chaos—
—a rip-off package deal—
I seek sanctuary.

My fortress of taught thoughts
that survived sieges is sand now.

A mist of dreams is rising.

He stands above me alone,
ageless, flawless . . .
In a shy wordless whisper
as with a lover I plead
"Orion, take me away."

Marija Jovanovich

Son

My son, I miss you so
I hear your voice
When I awake each morning
But your chair is empty
My tears fall down my face
I know you don't want me to cry
But you were my only child
And you were so young to go
Your life not halfway finished
I had so many dreams for you
And I know you had dreams too
Nighttime comes, I hear your voice
Saying, I'll be home soon
I cry again, I miss you so.

Audrey Malone

Smokey Robinson: The Storyteller

Smokey is a people's poet.
He writes words for songs
That move the heart.
He tells us how to go on
When our world falls apart.

Smokey is smooth.
He puts us in a groove.
His music strokes us
Like a human hand,
It gives us the strength
To try again.

Listening to Smokey's music
Is an experience we always remember.
It helps us to remember our youth
And reflect on our declining years.
Smokey's music can help us face the
Future without any fear.

Frances M. Johnson

Fall Is Here

Red leaves glowing,
Warmth is going,
Wind is blowing,
Almost snowing,
The leaves are bright,
There goes the light,
Much longer night,
Poems to write.

Jameson Murphy

Hope

Don't weep for me my days have passed
I've had my share of trials to last.
I started out with dreams of hope
to show my Lord my love would last
but in his sight, I saw myself
I was but dust upon a shelf.
He called my name and I did hide,
you see, my heart was black inside.
He called again, I turned to see
that a lamb of love had stood for me.

Bucky Jewell

The Morning Walker

Take a walk with me
Down the streets marked homeless
Shine the light down the alley
To their meaning of streets.

Express to me your fear
Your meal of life
As you enter your door
Wake the shivers on your spine
As children play with needles
And adults play on their needless minds.

Speak to me of changing times
Convince me of attitude
Giving way to prejudice
Answer to me about equality
The understanding of empathy.

So let us go for that walk
As the sun shines brightly on your life
And listen to those who talk
Who'll tarnish your thoughts slightly

Eileen Sheridan

Angels

He said I was an angel
Sent from the Heavens above.
An angel of light and mercy,
and most of all of love.

An angel that will look after him
each and every day.
An angel that would be there for him
to wipe his tears away.

An angel to erase his doubts and
ease away his fears.
An angel that will be with him
throughout all his years.

I believe that I am that angel
sent from God above.
But I am not the only angel
sent here to love.

There has always been another angel
that has been waiting patiently.
For he was also sent by God
from Heaven just for me.

Michelle Kimberly Eberlein

My Inzane Day

Well, my zany family is always
in a crazy mood
and they seem to never think
what their thinking about,
whether their losing it,
or really a pain in the neck.

Rebecca J. Macfarlane

Old Love

Your name is sweet,
as sweet as rain.
Whenever I say it,
it takes away my pain.
You are always on my mind
and in my heart.
I'm sorry for the things I said,
you probably wish I was dead.
I will love you through thick and thin
I just wish you were mine again.

Austin Cole Weems

Forbidden Love

As I lay here in bed
Thoughts of you are in my head
I know our love can never be
But somehow I want you here with me
Although our hearts belong to another
All I want is you for my lover
If it's only for just one night
This whole world I'm willing to fight
I know it's wrong to feel this way
But I love you more each and every day

Shannon Suzette Smithers

My Box Is Empty

In the yard I search to find
the treasure I left far behind.
It lies some place I cannot see
now my life is like my box—is empty.
I hold my box near my chest
as I pray above to pass this test.
Where did it go, I ask myself,
for it left its place upon my shelf.
It lies someplace I cannot see
still my life is like my box—is empty.
Mom is calling and I have to leave
so my weary heart is left to believe
The treasure that I held so dear to me
is lost forever and eternity.

Taylor Jason Everett

Endless Possibilities

Angela, because of our love
I have something to believe in.

I am Endless
Possessing the strength and power
to change
Path
my Destiny
my Life is my movement.

I am Alive
For I Live
with Feeling
with Meaning.

WE are the lucky ones
For we have felt the rain.

Gerald Lee Fisher

Grace

Heavenly Father in the name of Jesus
Bless this food you made to feed us
All good things come from above
Thank You for Your grace and love.

Sarah M. Webb

My Children

Children
Children are the heart of it,
Children are a part of it,
Children don't grow without it,
Children can't go without it,
Children are a gift of it,
Children get a lift from it,
Children know the magic of it,
Children feel the tragic of it,
Children really live for it,
Children really give of it,
Love

Mark James Morton

Let the Candle Burn

Let my burning heart
Dry away my tears
Let my tormenting mind
Create new fears

Let the time of my life
Run faster than the world's
Let fate's lashing tongue
Snatch away my words

Let nature force its will
The Pain may return
But don't blow my life away
Let the candle burn

Bushra Tayyab Hassan

Pink

Pink is the icing,
On a five-year-old's cake.
Pink is the sun,
Reflected off the lake.

Pink is a sweater,
Warm and fuzzy,
Pink is the flower,
On which bumblebees go <buzzy>.

Pink is love,
That comes in a heap.
Pink is the cloud,
On which angels sleep

Hilary Anne Fleming

boyz

i thought you were my angel
sent from heaven's sky
i thanked god for your presence
and now i wonder why
you took a bow and arrow
and aimed at my heart
you let it rip through out my soul
and left me torn apart
i tried to work out what went wrong
i loved you without fail
but you helped me figure it out
you're just a typical
MALE

Deanne Glassford

Beyond the Pain

You suffered pain;
You would not show.
It was so hard to let you go.
We held your hands and stayed close by;
When God eternal took you home on high.
And now you have everlasting life;
There is no pain, there is no strife.

Darlene Hazel Webb

The Seasons

Winter, spring, summer, and fall,
Are the best seasons of all,
Summer is happiness,
Fall is leaves making a mess,
Winter is snow, all around,
Spring is tears on the ground,
Fall is angry, with leaves so red,
Winter is warm blankets on your bed,
Summer is your face, full of pride,
Spring is everything you feel inside,
All of the seasons put together,
Symbolizes now and forever.

Nicole Elaine Chambers

Why Are You Mad at Me?

Why are you mad at me?
I love you, can't you see?
If you don't love me, too,
I'll cook you in a stew.
All I do all day
Is sit around and pray
That when you reappear,
You'll want to hold me near.
So why don't you be nice
And buy our friends some rice,
To throw upon our heads
Before we both are dead!

Kay E. Tealer

World in My Room

Taj Mahal on folds of curtain
England over glass
Grandma near the firelight
Rocking in lavender
Her little parlor still snugly
Ticking in my heart
Saintly Dyfed's monkly figure
Over *Burton's Row*, standing
Under *The Illiad* and *The Robe*
Some passages of Dante
Set apart among
The gilded willows

Beth Patterson

With You

You are my light in the darkness.
With you I can see
A rainbow in the sky, a promise
of what is meant to be . . .
A life filled with laughter,
a life filled with love,
Walking side by side
with God's blessing from above.
Never again to be lonely,
never again a broken heart.
With you I can see forever,
never do we part.

Glenda Hall

The Sea

If only I could see
A sea of tranquility
What a pleasure it would be
to be a bumble bee
I could then soar ever so high
as I would fly by
my sea of tranquility

Howard Solomon

The Time Will Come . . .

I am a bird in flight,
With wings gently swallowing the wind.
My parents raised me young and proud,
To get me through this ancient world.
The sun beats upon my head,
To tell me time is getting close.
I must spread my wings some more now,
And leave the nest I call home.
They tell me things will get tough,
That I'll want to come home,
But to stick it out,
And grow!

Jaime Lynne Rettig

If You Could See

The way I walk, and what I wear
I feel your thoughts
I watch you stare
Prejudge this, and anti-that
Open your eyes
The heart's where I'm at
I'd rather grow up alone
And be myself
Instead of a clone
Can I ask of you just one thing
A simple deed
Don't judge what the heart can't see

Adam Gregory Golden

Do Owls Dream in Color?

Once an owl in his bed
had a dream in blue and red.
From his nest he saw a light;
music flew through the starry night.
Inside a garden with colors of peace,
summer, winter, fall, and spring.
Love and magic in twirling pink;
it's funny what an owl can think.
A bursting glow whipped by his wing;
a mystical drizzle started to sing.
But that was on a summer's moon,
for that was where an owl flew.

Jessica Kijowski

Kittens

Kittens are fun.
They love to run.
They're all different colors.
They love their mothers.
Take a kitten home.
Don't leave it alone.
Don't make them mad,
Or you'll get sad.
When they grow,
You'll see it slow.
They won't be as much fun
As a kitten was.

Rosemary Levesque

Cruel Intentions

this world is a cruel world
fighting over a simple piece of bread
for survival, hope or family
over a thousand people die every day
this world is cruel in every single way
children dying from a simple fever
no one seems to care
over every child dying
one could've saved the world
this world is a cruel world

Arielle Lloyd

Peristalsis

Confronted by the
bolus of human life I
wish to be an owl.

Small mice could not be
too harmful, hindsight of bones
so enlightening.

And flexible neck,
feathered fingers might suit me
more than this weak flesh.

Kathlean Brooke King

Thank You

What I want to express
are words full of meaning
their elegant origin had come at a price
paid to someone who chose to make the
world's first selfless sacrifice

Passed down out of love
bore tradition of pure simplicity
spoken in gratitude with respect
and deep humility. . . .

Thank You.

Cynthia Rey Russell

Humor

Humor me is all I ask
Do you feel up to the task?
I ask in faith, this of you
Beyond love I feel it too
Take the care not to choke
Create a life that is not a joke

Humor me is what I want
Alone I walk with my thoughts
The reason behind it never clear
Somehow I find myself standing here
Is this real, is this the time?
Serve the sentence of my crime

Steven Williams

A Unique Day in the Life of the Girl Who Left Her Boy

Eggs over light
What a way to start the day
Bacon and home fries
A coffee with one cream
A conversation
Two hours with a new boy
Different from the old
He eats his eggs scramble
His coffee has two creams
He salts his home fries
But he loves her all the same

Josh G. Cacopardo

Brook Trout

Gentle Spring Breeze
Blows through my hair
Wish that I was with my girl
The most wonderful place in the world
She weaves her spirit
Plays with my soul
She is my Lucky Charm
She's worth more than a ton of gold

Ray Stio

Truth

Heart, Body, Mind, and Soul
Come together to make you whole
You see the Obvious
And fear the New
You need to see that's not true
True to me . . .
True to you . . .
Open your eyes
To the dew
And feel the morning embrace you

Robert Jacob Yeager

A Pallbearer's Story

Carrying the Casket,
I was Dying.
Carrying the Casket,
I kept Crying.
Carrying the Casket,
I laid Dying.
Carrying the Casket,
I kept Crying.
Carrying the Casket,
I Died.

Jason Alan Hamman

Friend

To love is to know that
One's alive, which comes
From deep down inside.
What stirred this feeling
From one's heart:
The love of a dear friend
That never departs,
Who's there with you with her
Love and tears, helping you
Calm all of your fears.

Marian K. Lewis

The Fears and Hopes for M.S.

Why, oh, why in this big world
Our people suffer in quite despair
M.S. is just so hard to bear
It ravages people beyond compare
Someday I hope that we will find
The cure for all in this great land
My hopes and prayers for one and all
Especially you, my dear Montel
I watch every day and I can say
Your eyes fill up as you speak out
A cure must be found real soon, you say
So no more suffering, no more pain
I just thank God in Heaven's name
My family has never had to see
All the pain M.S. can cause
So as I end this poem for you, Montel
God Bless you and we love you

Elizabeth L. Troupe

Love

The warmth of days gone by
Leaves me no alibi
To show you are mine

You were such a wonderful sight
We'd make love each night
My heart is full of sorrow
To me there's no tomorrow

Justin Ebrahim

Victim of a Holdup

My legs are tired and frail,
I continue to walk some more.
Below the bridge I go.
Her lips were blue and cold,
the knife was sharp and shined.
My money is gone and spent,
my legs are worse this night.

Nick Elliot Cossa

Wheel of Fortune

I bend my ear to the wind,
And I hear a symphony.
I make the notes with my pen
As best I can;
For there are those among us
Who cannot hear,
But can see.

Maria Sauter Furby

Tomorrow

beneath a blazing sky
once majestic peaks rise
above plains black and hard
empty seas cracked oceans
mighty forests laid to rest
amongst the ruins of a broken world
a spot of green appears
maybe this time

Micheal Blaise Strahan

Moments

A moment may be too soon
Or a moment may be too late
It depends on the situation
That will govern our fate
Life is so uncertain
It hangs by a string
So value each moment
Before Heaven's bells ring

Ethel Saulter

Elation

Stars
Floating
Circling
Melodies
Embracing
Piano
Chopin
You
Me
Together
Dancing
Fermata
Elation.

Shelley Mariah Hussain

Remembrance

Lost pages of time,
now remembered in an instant.

Reality knows innocence, though,
and I am still lingering there.

Ruth A. Weatherington

Warrior

I know what all I've been through
I know where all I went
I didn't know how all I did it
Now I know it's God's grace that I am
through

Raghu Ram Rao Bhimrao

No Pain

What will you find in a broken heart
Burning hatred tearing it apart
Thoughts of suicide enter your head
The only relief found when you are dead

Anetta LaJuan Williams

The Window

The window was the warmest place
To sit and breath and warm the face
Close your eyes, look into the sun
Watch orange change from waves to runs

Carl Dawson

Me, Myself, and I

Laura loves lollypops
Always jolly
Unthinkable fun
Radiant smile
Always an angle

Laura Monroe

Ladybug

Ladybug, Ladybug fly away.
Ladybug, Ladybug come back another day.
Ladybug, Ladybug I love you.
Ladybug, Ladybug come sleep in my shoe.
Ladybug, Ladybug I love you.

Meghan Clarke

Brother

There was a time
When the sun always shined
It seems like so long ago—
But it was only yesterday
Yet it seems so long ago
Will the sun ever shine again?
Never as brightly as with you!

George Clough

Harriot

From the waters of the spring
Harriot took a drink
Spilling most of it in the sink.
Roaring thunder
Strikes a tremor
Harriot murmurs
Oh! what a wonder.

Andrea E. Morgan

The Power of Your Love

The ears may have heard
That your soul now soars like a bird
The eyes may have seen
Your mortal life disappear
But the heart still feels
The power of your love
Now when I think of you
And the love shared between two
The tears that I now embrace
The smile I put back on my face
Are from sweet memories
That cause me to remember
Why I miss you so
And the power of your love

Becky Weir-Smith

Solitude

A bird caged
Wings clipped
Hampered from flight
No longer free to roam
To spread wings and fly
In the open blue sky
Now there are limits
Where imagination and desire
Were the only restraints
Jailed without freedom
Optimism stolen
Depression set in
So now where will freedom be found
To put things back together
And be free again

William Roscoe Brown, Jr.

Wish

I wish I could make you love me,
Throw your insecurities away,
And take away your pain.
I wish I were beautiful,
But that would be a mistake;
I am ugly and unfake.

I wish,
On all my strength,
That you would love me.
I wish
I were so much more.
I have faith,
I can be all that.
Just wish
You would love me.

Zaira Shaal

Untitled

In the sea
I forgot my dream,
In my shadow
I forgot my light,
In my silence
I forgot my thought,
In my sleep
I forgot to wake.

She came out of her
courtyard, fake
lilies in her hand,
the smile out of
shallowness,
walked to her
master's land.

Sarah Elizabeth Lindsey

Right Away

Right away,
I knew I'd say
Yes.
He guessed the rest.

Tonight
Just before midnight,
When all is right
And no one's in sight,
Meet me.

Don't wake the dawn
We'll quiet the storm of the waves,
Caressing the shore.
You'll want me more
Tomorrow.

Paula Craven Edelstein

You and Me

Close your hands
like two palm leaves.
So as to imprison me
in your green melody.

I won't resist.
Promise.
Nor will I scream.
But please be gentle,
Not to wrinkle my wings.

Then, I will assure you:
2000 years later,
There will be a piece of fossil
with a butterfly and palm leaves
Pressed together.

Ruoyi Gail Gao

Unfailing Love

Unfailing love
We desire it from others
from our sisters and our brothers
But they can't give it
They don't know how to live it.

Unfailing love
We need some to share
with those for whom we care
But it's never there.

Unfailing love
When my supply is depleted
I find in Jesus love completed
flowing from the Throne of Grace
the source open to all the human race.

Edna Sherwood

Quest

Silence echoes in the heart of a void
Being is not thought
There is presence
Thoughts emerge

Wants occur
Actions happen
Right action perhaps
Movement is confused for consciousness

Right consciousness transforms
Thoughts are created then destroyed
Movement stops
Consciousness continues
Thoughts may be and may be not

Quester quest on

Terrance Stuart

A Visit with Friends

I dream of all . . .
the people I know at
least a time or two.
The morning brings annoying
sounds, that breech into my
world.
I do not want to leave . . .
My friends.
There are things to
be dealt with,
so much to be said.
So I'll just lie back
down awhile . . .
And visit with my
friends!

Pamela Rae Davey

Campus

empty skins drift
through brick walls
their faded shadows
reluctantly follow
these distant ghosts
the desires of the hollow flesh
of these apparitions
reside in material possessions
their weekend masquerades
their sexual obsessions
sightless to the life behind
every sunless morning
they march on like dragons in a parade
heeding not the warning
sent from above

Jeffrey Robert Strawn

What Can I Do

There was a time when I
Laughed with you Cried with you
Smiled at you Talked to you
Loved you Worshipped you

Now half the time you
Point at me, Laugh at me
Ignore me, Abuse me
Trash me, Hate me

What can I do
to keep you
from playing with my mind all the time
I look around
but all that can be found
is the memory of you and me

Beverly Burrell

Friends Always

Looking near—looking far
Fluffs and sometimes puffs
A laugh here
And giggles there
Camp outs, ghost marches
Games, skits and campfires
A precious time are they
A whispering pine
A summer breeze
Indian princesses with a sneeze
How precious are these
Love in God
Miles of smiles
In Daddy's little princesses
Friends always

Arch A. Costanzo

Granddaughter

Granddaughter, my little flower.
On this happy day,
God in his wisdom
created many things
one was the butterfly
which represents freedom
the second was flowers
which represents beauty.
On this day, October 20,
he created a one and only you.
As your grandmother
I wish for you on this day and always,
the freedom of the butterfly,
the beauty of the flowers
and the goodness of your parents.

Liz Maisto

All These Tears

As I sit here
With tears running down my face
Wishing I could hold you near
Wanting to have a place
We could call our own
These tears continue to flow
Even though I know
That you are my heart and soul
What could help
To stop all these tears
The only thing
I think could help
To stop all these tears
Is to be with you
For the next thousand years.

Jeff Suprenand

People and Me

People coming,
people going,
Never stopping for you.
Looking back,
Looking ahead,
But never looking through.
Never ending,
Never forgetting,
Things in life aren't always true.
Working here,
Working there,
taking time away to share.
Writing poets,
Dying for it,
People, We are all the same.

Josh James Talayka

Polio

Born of this sin I didn't make
Left my life forgot to take
Conjure the demons in my head
Picture that ghost lyin' in my bed
I walked past that empty grave
Looked down to see my name
Billions of candles light up the room
Billions of candles to light up the moon
Billions of candles light up my tomb
Still dark as hell
Still dark as hell
Don't know why I'm here at all
Every time up always fall
Put out the fire with your venom tongue
That burns a hole in my iron lung

Everett LaRose

Fisherman Boys

Two little boys
with fishing on their mind
probably don't know what they're doing
or even how to cast it right

They have their fisherman hats
their red shirts and blue pants

With their big puffy cheeks
and their little chubby arms
everyone knows they own grandma's heart

Kasey Peterson

Untitled

The wheels keep turning, inside my head,
There are times I wish that I was dead.
My landlord breathing down my neck,
While I sit home, awaiting a check.
With nowhere to turn, no end in sight,
My nerves on edge, both day and night,
What will happen, whom do I see?
My future seems so bleak to me.
To have faith in God is all I can do,
To show me a way, to make it through.

Kenneth P. Hardy

Morning Birds

I watch as the night
Turns to dawn.
Starry skies begin
To disappear.

The Earth renews,
As the sun comes up.
And birds begin
To blithely cheer.

Morning.

Andrew John Owen

From the Beginning to the End

God created love,
love created people,
people created unity,
unity created freedom,
freedom created respect,
respect created trust,
trust created hope,
hope created faith,
and faith leads us back to God.

Veronica Brown

Sweet Lies and Alibis

Trusting, believing you loved me,
dreaming of all it could be,
I gave you my hand and our love began
because of sweet lies and alibis.

You couldn't give what I needed.
I couldn't help feeling cheated,
so with heavy sighs, I closed my eyes
because of sweet lies and alibis.

You know I will always love you,
but now I see all the way through
with pain in my heart.
I know we must part
because of sweet lies and alibis.

Sylvia Seymour

Sunset Words

For Laura and Jessie

Two friends and I
Sat on a hill in the gold-dusky sun
And warm conversation
Flowed from our mouths like honey.
We let fly
With amber-colored words
Like "home" and "family."
Sweet words
Like "future" and "my daddy"
Bathed in the headiness
Of our own vocal prowess.
We fell silent and savored.

Leslie E. Ostick

Desolate

People laugh at his dirty face
People laugh at his different race
For he has no hopes or no dreams
He has no one, no friends it seems

People hurt him with their fists
No one wants to know he exists
He stands alone, without a friend
All he wants is for it to end

Every day is always the same
No one calls him by his proper name
He wants to tell them it isn't fair
Even if he did, who would care?

Priscille Belisle

Captured by Night

I sit alone
in a distant field
a drive-in of thoughts
made only of you
insecurity dances by
blown by wind
but dies of defeat
fog surrounds
you fade
captured by night
love grows stronger
and burns
the uncertainty away

Darci Penner

Time Is My Enemy

In a small town of Westmoreland
There live a man and a woman.
Wealth and riches they all have none,
But they always hold hand in hand.
He is very much old for her,
She is very much young for him,
But they're very compatible,
And they are really good people.
He works very hard all the time.
He thinks he doesn't have much time.
Soon he's going to leave her alone,
For in Heaven he's going home.
This really makes her very sad;
It makes her all the time feel bad,
But she doesn't want him to know,
Because there are much things to do.
He said, "Time is my enemy,
But I want you to be happy."
All she does is hug him and say,
"Both of us will forever stay."

Alpha C. Harrison

Sunny

The stir of life within me,
The wrenching gate to life—
The unknown,
Vast potential awaits the roll of dice.
Such fragile beauty awes me.
Each perfection brims my heart.
Fierce,
Savage Passion
For this tiny work of art . . .
My Sunny.

Cindy M. Cole

Innocence

Once what was lost,
is now found
laughter of children
all around
sweet thoughts of yesteryear
now only bring frowns and tears
Wish we could go back in time
to stay within our innocent minds
life so full of love and hope
now filled with despair
too hard to cope
family time and holidays
childhood crushes, fading away

Tangela Denise Martin

A Feature of Life

Adam and Eve were created
and then by some hated!
The hate came by fury of rain,
so that all felt God's mighty pain!
Only those who survived were few,
and animals each kind by two.
Now came land on a high peak,
man and animals Life must seek!
So the story is many times told,
and to the billions it is sold.
It often brings a question to mind
that keeps all thy thoughts entwined.
Life is made up of time,
man comes and dies.
He brought forth a world of crime
and left us bound with lies.
Why?

Robert G. Williamson

Love

All my life I've asked people
to explain love to me
To tell me how it felt
and what it meant
How I would know
and how it would show
Everyone said I'd know
Yet I never understood
And thought I never would
Until you came along and
taught me that I could
I never would of imagined
loving someone so much, it hurt
But If you asked me now
to explain love to you
To tell you how it felt
and what it meant
I'd be fit to tell you
'Cause I've learned.

Agnes Kathy Davenport

Your Heart Will See You Through

What comes from love in dreams?
Does it cause the darkness to fade?
It brightens your life, it seems—
This love your mind has made.

But on it can you rely?
Is it only in your head?
Don't seek some reasons why,
But ask your heart instead.

Your heart alone decides
What life can bring to you.
If love, in dreams, abides,
Your heart will see you through.

Anne Chapman

Whispered Voice

Life.
An existence you can enjoy or destroy
but, is it your choice
do they hear your
voice.
Among a crowd you shout out loud
but, do they not hear
what it is you fear, about being alone
with the only tone of your own voice.

but, just a voice among
a voice, among
a voice . . .
not a choice
whispered voice.

Jeremiah C. Morris

Daughter

The day that you were born,
My heart was so sad and torn.
Tiny you were—oh, so small.
Your life would be short—after all.
You finally left me—oh, the pain.
I cried, I wept, tears like rain.
The sun went down—no longer to shine;
A heavy load was on this heart of mine.
Peace for my heart I must find;
An answer to prayer eased my mind.
Daughter, you weren't with me for long,
But now an angel, to God you belong.
Happiness and peace I hold in my heart
Until the day when we are no longer apart.

Mary Adelia Tyler

Together As One

You've given me your heart
I don't know where to start
But loving you I will
I wish time would stand still
Never leaving your side
To you I will confide
And tell you just how I feel
Baby, my love is truly real
For eternity I will spend
In you I do depend
On a life filled with joy
A promise that will never be destroyed
Together our hearts are one
Now our lives have just begun

Judy Shaw

Feelings and Wisdom

Why can the wind blow through the trees
and through my aching soul?

Why can the fire devour the fields
and burn my heart like coal?

Why do the waters ripple so calmly
or rage like flowing tears?

Why does the Earth erode so slowly,
unlike my aging years?

The reason is growing
and the reason is dead,
like the young ones ignoring
what the old ones have said.

Douglas Hastings

Icy Journey

Fighting against the ferocious wind,
Trudging through the icy snow,
Blinded by snowflakes—
Which way do I go? !

Frozen body parts,
Runny nose,
Afraid of frostbite—
My poor numb toes!

I finally made it,
I found the right path,
All that winter Hell—
For what? ! ? ! ? ? !
MATH.

Emily Louise Kimmett

The Four-Letter Headache

A pounding in my brain
has developed once again
Made of simplistic cry
water returns to mine eye
What a vision I do see
draped in strange confetti
A view that's ever changed
results of lies remain the same
A hunter from the bush
for heads he does look
A monster full of gore
hides a heart that is tore
With a throbbing of the throat
take right hand and cast a "Vote."

Alexander Bonner

The Price of Freedom

The price of freedom is not what
I believe that it should be.
The price of freedom is that one
Named Jesus Christ so loved me.
The price of freedom is that he
Would give up his life willingly.
The price of freedom is the stone
That rolled away on day three.
The price of freedom is that he
Came back to life for all to see.
The price of freedom has been paid
For all who'll take it readily.
Accept this gift of life from Christ
Who wants you to, in Him, be free.

Jessica Surratt

Dream

I'm dreaming
But I know this feeling
It is always good
And when we die
We'll meet in the sky
As I knew we would
But before I go
I must let you know
Just how I feel
You've always been the one I love
You light my path from above
So I let go of the wheel
I feel that our fates are sealed
Our souls are forever healed

Darren Edward McIntosh

You

When I look at you, I see the sea.
You Always bring a smile to me.

When I look at you, I see the moon.
Hoping we'll be together soon.

When I look at you, I see the stars.
sporting around in your little cars.

When I look at you, I see a flower.
your heart is strong and full of power.

When I look at you I see the rain.
because together I feel no pain.

When I look at you, I feel the pride
Knowing you'll always be by my side.

Lance Johnson

Becoming

In the early hours of this waking day
I lay here bestowed upon myself
Searching for all the right reasons
In all the wrong places
In a world I thought I knew
But just a bunch of strange faces
Through the windows of pain
That I am staring through
True to what, not the world
Nor to my peers, but myself
No one said that this life
Is going to be fun
But the only way to have a friend
Is to be one.

Jeremy Zabinski

Shadows

Shadows dancing on the wall,
Some are short, some are tall,
Some are slim, some are fat,
Why just look at that cat,
Dancing, singing, playing along,
Until a cloud comes along,
But when that cloud goes away,
They come out to dance and play,
At night when your tucked in bed,
Out they come from under your head,
Coming from the closet and the wall,
Meeting out in the hall,
Planning something for the next day,
In a shadowy, sort of way.

Emma Pollum

Better Days

I'm looking for my inspiration
in not so quiet desperation
Now it can't be found at all
but it was there before the fall
It will have to be found again
to erase the traces of my sin
And I will do my very best
to lay these broken hearts to rest

I'm not sure what they will find
locked inside my troubled mind
But it's time for the pain to cease
so I can finally have some peace
And I know if I stay strong
I can fix everything that's wrong

Ronald Shute

Starless Shore

The ocean's surf upon the shore.
Perpetual, yet soothing roar.
The moonlight off the water glows,
A vision from the highest lows.
I walk alone upon the sand.
I'm weary so in heart and hand.
I journey on until I find
The place where I leave all behind.
Collapsing there, so ill at heart,
I wonder why I'm set apart.
I lay in pain beneath the trees.
My wound is such as no-one sees.
In vain, I search the seas and skies.
I long for hope to meet my eyes.

Peter James Friedrichsen

Snowball

He's white and puffy,
And so very fluffy.
He's not at all snappy,
Which makes me so happy.
He loves to go walk,
Without a balk.
He likes to lay around,
Making hardly a sound.
He loves a good bone,
Or an ice cream cone.
He sleeps all day,
And does not disobey.
He's my dog Snowball,
The best dog of all!

Christopher Hollis

My Yesterday

Tomorrow.
If only I knew
What tomorrow was,
What it would bring.
So many times I have
Despised you, Tomorrow,
Welcoming my Yesterday.
Because I knew who
Yesterday was,
Yesterday would not harm me.
But you, Tomorrow, you
Never assure me of
What you will do,
Only to grant me a Today.

Ana Anais Ramirez

Looking for Me

The sun shines through my heart
But the clouds hang over my head
The waves break softly in my mind
But the storm blows quietly in my soul
There are no tears to fall softly
Only the whispers of unspoken needs
I want, I have, I give, it's taken
What else is there

I see the flowers, I hear the birds
I smell the sea, I feel the breeze
Beauty surrounds me, I cannot stay
I know what is here
It's what is missing that I must find
Among the ruins of my life

Kathleen A. Fay

Play Me

Rough hands, gentled by the strings,
drawing sweetness from
your guitar—

Sweetness—whispering secrets
that echo my own
longing

Song bursting from my heart—
still silent on my lips.

I could sing it if you touched me.

Please let me sing it—
Beautiful music—waiting only for you
to begin.

Virginia Anne Ranta

Magic Spell

If I had a magic wand
This is what I'd do
I would use the wand
To find a cure for you

But I have no magic wand
You see,
It's hard to find a way
To ease your pain and suffering
That you endure each day

If we work together
Just think what we can do
Then we won't need a magic wand
To find a cure for you.

Magdalene Brown

For the Bard

I thought I'd write a piece of poetry
And enter it into a contest
My next thoughts were
Now just what would be its contents

I could write about trees
Like Joyce Kilmer
But that's already been published
Or about a kid I knew in school
But that's just plain rubbish

I think I'll settle for maybe something
That even the Bard would read
So here it is for the Bard and all
Have a nice day and help someone in need

Harry Davidson

My Type of Day

When my mom puts me to bed at night
I don't put up a fight
And so it seems
I always have good dreams
When my dreams end at night
I wake up to see the morning light
I have a breakfast every day
But it's not there to stay
While I'm eating it all up
I take some sips from my cup
When the time comes for school
My mom is off to watch at the pool
When I can't talk to my friend
I know my day has come to an end.

Mark A. Wesley

Get Over It!

I've seen the hurt,
felt the pain,
Get over it!
They say it takes time,
but how much?
Will the end come now,
or must I suffer for
many years?
I see my friend going
down the same path.
How can I stop her?
I don't want her to feel
the pain which
I had to secretly endure.

F. Mahi'ai T. C. Rossetti

All Mine

He caresses me with his hands,
and melts my soul like running sand,
I love to see his blue eyes shine,
for I know that he's all mine.
His loving touch,
I crave so much.
His understanding ways,
brightens my every day.
Although we're apart today,
I know soon the absence will pay.
For now his time is rough,
He says, "I make him so tough."
I know he yearns to return.
To ease the fire, in him that burns.

Kelly Christofferson

Up or Down

Noble angles at the pearly gates,
Eternal happiness will be your fate.
Vast and beautiful it will be,
Above all that we know and see.
Each one of us should do our best,
Hopefully we will be a guest.

If not,
Hatred, jealousy, greed abound,
Evil so thick that you could drown.
Lower and lower, down and down,
Lucifer's limbo lies underground.

And where would you rather be,
Heaven or Hell for eternity?

Margaret P. Scatchell

The Misdirection of a Broken Heart

If it were to cost
So much
To mend a broken heart
Would it be worth it to spend
All that time and pain
To fix it
Knowing how much
You would risk
And realizing that
It wouldn't be worth it
Because every mended heart
Eventually gets broken
All over again

Katie G. Smith

Endless Line of Petals

An endless line of petals,
Drifting over the sea.

Over mountains of ocean,
Coming to you from me.

I'll sit here forever,
Placing petals in the sea.

Hoping someday you'll
Send one back to me.

They travel for miles,
You cannot see the end.

I'll keep on placing petals,
Till I find the one you send.

Torrey Tomlinson

Doors

Standing
Staring down the hall
The walls of doors staring back
Wondering
What's behind them?
How do I choose?
Hoping
It will be everything I imagine
The choice I made was right
Wondering
Was I wrong?
How many chances do I get?
What happens if I was wrong?
Standing

Jenn Bliss

Time

Time, that elusive heartbeat
Time, what time is it?
Time, my hair is blond,
Time, must run now,
Time, everything to learn
Time, everything to do,
Time, I must run now,
Time, my hair is gray,
Time, haven't finished yet
Time, did I forget?
Time, running fast now
Time, my hair is white
Time, the sun is setting,
Time, I haven't much time.

Lillian Jenni

Soul Mate

Do you ever feel you are not complete
Walking through endless streets
Searching the faces of those you meet
Hoping soon your heart skips a beat
All the while your mate is there
Far from your thoughts
Or even your care
Searching too
Just as you
For that face
That smile
That charm
That tear
That one thing
No other can ever dare
To tarnish or taint
To forsake or shake
Your soul
Your mate

Stephanie King

A Grateful Thanks to You . . .

A spot to heart
To love as though I am reborn
Reborn to a life of love
A life to you to see the world
In beauty I see us in the sun
The sunlight of morning
As the bright light of day arises
Rises from the night to the sky
A love so deep in happiness
That a day can't go by
Without the sweetness of the touch
Of your hand on mine or
Your lips to mine
To the gentle touch of you
I give thee my heart and soul
To keep in safe
To save my heart from being in pain
A pain to crush my whole life and world.

Emily Suzzanne Weathington

No One's Listening

Dedicated to the souls of all who are lost

We try to solve the problems
Of our world today.
What's the point in all this screaming?
No one's listening anyway.

Children starve and we turn away.
People die and we look astray.
Why do we say we try to help,
When all we do is pray?

Time and again the needy reach,
Will they fall today?
What's the point in all this pleading?
No one's listening anyway.

We should stop and look around
And listen to their cries.
What's the point in even living,
When no one sees their eyes?

Anette Divjak

Heaven

Heaven

A perfect picture
hanging on a wall.
Still yet
moving.

Everything you've
ever dreamed,
plus lots, lots
more!

There's people
everywhere.
Or even no one
around.

Kindness and forgiveness
helps Heaven grow
to be as strong and
beautiful as people
think and dream.

Karissa Peterson

Now That You're Gone

You are gone,
I must move on.
Wishing to see you just once more,
Remembering those times before
When we would talk,
And go for a walk.
To the park we went,
Many times we had spent.
You always watched over me,
Always took care of me,
Always ready to do something,
For anyone, for anything.
Wishing you here,
Because you had no fear.
It was my turn to take care of you,
Before your time was due.
Never had a chance to say good-bye,
Now every night I sit and cry.
I have to move on,
Now that you're gone.

Liette Beland

What Do You See?

You see
the fold of my eyes,
the color of my skin,
the shape of my nose.
You see
the outer layer,
the label to use
the form God made.
You judge
based on stereotypes
and limited information.
You condescend
based on differences
with no remorse.
There are feelings
behind the exterior.
There is a soul
behind the eyes.
I am human.
You do not see after all.

Debi Smith

An Immortal Love

I dream
Of the touch of his hands,
The feel of his lips.
I imagine feeling secure,
So secure in his wonderful arms,
The feel of his body close to mine,
Illusions and promises of eternity,
A journey through eternity.
His beautiful smile I see no more.
His presence I feel no more,
The longing for his touch
And no fulfillment.
He moves gentlemanly,
Sole to crown.
I dream and long
For the slightest touch,
The slightest smile.
And then I wake up,
Swimming in pools of sweat.
He is immortal.

Titilola Ahmed

Immaculate Enhancements

Happy/sad; I'm going mad
Or am I just deluded?
Hyper/tired; hired/fired
Purity polluted.
Black and white; Day and night
Impossible to halt.
Sweet and sour; Weed and flower
Sugar, pepper, salt.
High and low; fast and slow
Opposing one another.
Cats and dogs; toads and frogs
Child, father, mother.
Over/under; through/around
A looking glass reflection.
Noisy/quiet; silence/sound
Mistakes without correction.
Up and down; left and right
I sail a single tear.
Wet and dry; Hello/good-bye
Omega now is here.

William Michael Fleming, Jr.

Solemn Dark

Through this world of misery
Have I past alone in times of fury
To find myself alone again
On this path of now and then,
Trying to forget the past,
Little joys that never last.
Nothing do I see above
But gleaming shadows from a dove
Flying over barren lands,
Places that are now but sand.
People come and people go
But never do they stay, oh, no!
Here I sit and watch the sky.
Colors fade away and die.
Darkness comes and sets upon.
Turn around and they're all gone.
I wonder how, I wonder why,
People always come to die.
Again I stand in loneliness,
Forgotten tales of happiness. . . .

Kojiro Silver Nytebird

Silence

Silence beckons me,
bids me follow,
engulfs me like antigens.
Her voice echoes
my name as an anuran
in the dead of night.
Silence haunts me
like urchins
invading my sanctum
as an eudemon watches
an infant.
Her caress lulls me
like a mother's lullaby
in the twilight.
The arms of silence
entwine me,
She eggs me on like an egret
On the sea of silence,
waves carry me across
sky-like waters to equinox.

Nolma M. Coley

To My Daughter

As I look into your blue eyes
I see an ocean of hopes and dreams
That I have for you
The corn silk that is your hair
Shows how delicate you truly are
I will never forget the first time
I held you in my arms
So fragile and small
Each night I lay you into bed
I am so grateful for the chance
To be your mom
Every second of every day
You grow more and more into a beautiful
Young lady
So full of hopes and dreams
And full of a love for life
That is why each morning
As I look into your eyes
I know the dreams you hold inside
Will one day come true

Jennifer Ruth Scroggins

Spring Belle Speaks

Color me like the rainbow
Where Cupid's bow has to show.
Paint me like the sunshine
Where the rays burst so fine.
Walk with me in my garden
Where jay greets the birth of the day.
Trail my path with flowers
Where blossoms merrily sway.
Swing me in the hammock of peace.
Let me sleep in the bosom of your ease.
For the wind brushes my sorrow.
The rain freshens my tomorrow.
Knight of never ending mystery,
Fill my garden with ecstasy
Where fairies live happily
Secure in the vest of reality.
Lo, meet the Guardian Lady,
Unfold her eyes of secrecy.
Leave thy footprints in her garden
For you, restore the Lost Eden.

Ma. Celerina Dulaca Halili

Nothing Left to Give

He demands her respect when
she hasn't seen his in years.
She can't see much at all now
through the falling tears.
She does everything for him
but he's never satisfied.
It makes me wonder if when
he said he loved her he lied.
She cares for the kids
he says he never wanted.
I hope one day she makes
those words come back to haunt him.
Somehow she finds strength
when she needs it the most.
But she's walking through life
as if she were a ghost.
Through all the years filled with pain
she's found a way to live.
But there's nothing left of herself
and nothing left to give.

Connie Lynn Barnett

To Bonnie at 40

We are the friends we are because
we come in so many flavors.
That variety has spiced our lives
and taught us love, forgiveness
and tolerance.
We've given each other the space
and respect we need to develop and grow.
We've allowed each other to Be,
without negating that Being.
We have defied the forces that have
tried to destroy our ties.
And through God's blessings
that friendship has survived
for over two decades.
So happy birthday, my old,
dear and true friend.
I love you.
Always celebrate yourself,
your womanhood and our friendship.
Forever Friendships and Freedoms.

G. Yvonne McLean

Our Own

Expectations set too high.
Why must we meet them?
Let's live our own lives
Together.
Let's live day by day
and side by side.
We follow our own hearts.
No one else matters.
We will decide our own destiny.
Reach our own goals.
Dream our own dreams.
We will break the rules
And make our own.
We will defy all laws of gravity
And search the stars.
Believing in ourselves
And in each other
We will travel far and wide
In search of happiness
of our own. . . .

Jasper Faith Johnston

Guidance

As I sit here in your basement
Of loneliness and greed
I wonder what keeps me here
Is it you or is it me?
You've changed me into someone
Who's really no one at all
How can I ever forgive you?
You were my only person to call
Now sitting in your basement
I think I see a door
To someplace far from here
So I don't have to be here anymore
I hate it here in this basement
It's dark and always cold
I need someone to save me
To give me warmth and something to hold
I think I've found this someone
He's a King without a sword
His name is Jesus Christ
My Leader and my Lord

Caroline Carter

I Had a Dream

I had a dream about a man last night,
It seemed so real it gave me a fright.
"Who are you?" I asked so clear
"What do you want from me in here?"
He answered the questions I had asked.
He told me he had to give me a task.
He stood there straight and tall,
He told me, "tell them, one and all.
I was a husband to my wife,
Whom I loved with all my might.
I was a father to my girls,
Each one I thought a precious pearl.
My grandchildren, loud and fun,
Gave me a twinkle as bright as the sun.
'My sons-in-laws,' I have said,
'You were brave my girls to wed
The pain is gone from my chest,
Now it's time for me to rest.
Cry not for me," he calmly said,
"For in your hearts I'm never dead."

Aleta Kennedy

The Ceremony

The day has finally arrived.
As expected, tears stream down my face.
I strive to make sense of things.

It seemed like only yesterday
Was the first day of high school.
Now, they announce my name.

My books are gone,
My locker is finally clean.
He hands me my diploma.

No more homework,
No more tests.
We shake hands with each other.

Looking into his eyes I see,
He is pleased with each one of us.
Finally, I return to my seat.

The finale is here,
The recessional begins.
Now, I must find my family.

Lynn Marie Przygocki

The Ghost of McBee

First came the laughter
Real haunting and deep
Then came a load moan
Enough to wake the dead from their sleep
As the creature began to walk
His loud footsteps one could hear
Coming out of his grave
The ghost of McBee did appear
Soon the graveyard was alive
With creatures of all kinds of fright
And the shrill noises they made
Carried into the night
With the first rays of sunlight
The graveyard was still
Not a creature was stirring
Except a crow on the hill
The moral of this story
My friend, is as you see
Never enter a graveyard
Wherein resides a McBee

Richard Gundy

Secrets

A secret is when no one knows . . .
The mysteries that the heart enclosed
The insecurities, the fears
That lie beneath one's selfish needs.

The need for what, no one knows,
Are you afraid . . . the secret grows.

Afraid that no one will foresee
How lonely that the heart can be.
Afraid to say, yet scared to keep
What's been inside, so long, so deep.

The secret grows out of control,
You're in a crowd, yet all alone . . .
No one to hear, no one to speak,
Who is the strong, and who is weak?

The secret dies when someone near
Goes deep enough to kill the fear
That someone then will hold the key
To your life's secret destiny.

Inna Gutnik

White Collar

Neighbors of four years
White collar workers
Mid-thirties, first child
Darling little girl
Chokes on penny
Daddy helping breathes life
One year old
Hospital exam reveals madness
Two broken knees
Two broken wrists
Two broken ankles
Twisted and tortured
Skull fracture
Three broken ribs
Old wounds, new parents
Almighty Dollar takes precedence
Family looked away
Life sentences for both
Saving our children
Real monsters in the dark

Lyn Patricia Waters

To God

To God I say
Even as I pray,
I know you've already
made the shaky steady.
Kiss my spirit
and make it shine.
I'll hustle till it's over
to make your grace mine.
Line by line.
All things in time?
"Sure. Stay pure."
I hope I can.
I can and will, for no other man
can keep my soul showered.
My spirit's empowered!
Catch it.
Feel it.
Breathe it.
And promise my father
to never leave it.

Suga Dlo

My First Love

When I first met you,
You smiled and said hi.
Now I can't forget you;
You're always on my mind.
I think about you every day,
You're often in my dreams.
When I dream of happier days
And times when you loved me.
I think of us together
In days to come or past.
I think of you and wonder,
Why couldn't our love last?
You were my first real love, dear,
Wish I could make you see
How glad I was to find you,
What our love meant to me.
For one year, you were in my life,
You showed me love that's true.
And I know in my heart, dear,
I'll never forget you.

Tiffany A. Gould

Breathlessness

I can feel it again
I'll never be free
It's all coming back again
Again beckoning for me
Why do they taunt me
Never soothing to my soul
Why won't they just leave me
Taking away that which makes me whole
I can feel them
Surrounding me, shrouding me
The darkness is all over
I can no more see
The life is sucked
Death is drawing
No time to think
No time for crying
I'm gone from the world
I look back and then
Head with them
So glad I won't be back again

Daniel John Zeigler

Grandma and Tweety

When my Grandma died
I was so sad I cried.
I will miss sitting on her lap
and watching her nap.
When I see a pair of doves,
I feel my Grandma's love.
I will miss her touch.
I loved her so much.
My birthday is New Year's Eve,
a day that in a way, I will grieve.
You see, the day I was born
my grandma was torn
because she thought she had
another grandson, a little lad.
She had been told wrong;
a granddaughter awaited her song.
She held me and sung to me.
She said I was her "sweety."
My mom and Aunt Connie nicknamed me "T,"
But Grandma's choice was Tweety.

Teresa Marie Phillips

Rhythm of Raindrops

One utter under stars,
my heart flutters.
Long lovers we are,
as in his car
we drive together.
I try to speak
a whisper.
His hand on my knee
squeezing slightly.
He turns to me,
softly, "Baby,"
as the rain drips
and the moon ever white.
"Where to tonight?"
Blue eyes shine,
dark waves of hair.
"I love you," I say,
"I'll follow you anywhere."
With a grin, he kisses my chin.
"How about Marcus Theatre then?"

Kelly Anne Tynan

Always Have My Love

Lying here in bed at night
without you I'm so cold
I need you to take care of me
I need someone to hold
It wasn't easy holding my tears
knowing we'd have to part
I'd wait for you forever
even if it tears me apart
I miss your gentle kisses
your fingers through my hair
but somehow in this lonely room
I can almost feel you here
You've given me your everything
and you're everything to me
I'll wait for that day
when once again we'll be
And the angels blessed me
with a piece from up above
no matter what we go through
you will always have my love.

Angie M. Alex

Vacancy in Neon Lights

Come, sleep, come . . . oh, I reach out
But never there is sleep, elusive
As the wind winding
Through the leaves and trees
Why? Surely not the cocktail
To whet my appetite; the sherry fine
Brought out winy taste in old, dull food
Bonded scotch and bonded rye
Kept the evening bright, so gay
Were witty we, all happy save
Some dolt who wouldn't drink
The brilliance of my thinking
The splendor of my speech
I laughed so well, I loved so full
I drank the most and was the best
After that I saw a rat
Only it wasn't there at all
The inner wall of this jaundiced pall
Surveys me, and the shipping tag
Reads, "HELL"

Jesse Jay Henry

Your Caressing Touch

Your caressing touch
Means so much,
The way you look at me
Fills me with glee,
My heart racing
As your hands are tracing,
My body so softly
My hair so swiftly,
Myself trembling with pleasure
As you measure,
Sensually kissing my body
Doing things so naughty,
The feeling of your lips to mine
Making me feel-OH-so fine,
Looking into my eyes
Hands sweeping my thighs,
You my dear
Making things so clear,
OH-your touch
Means so much.

Ann Leslie

Keep Your Head Up, Brother

Keep your head up brother,
I see you out there, making that money.
Did life treat you unfair?
Did someone take all that you had?
Was it your fault, their fault,
a deal gone bad?
Did you give to a woman who
did not give back?
Did she show you no love?
Compassion she lacked?
Did your momma mistreat you,
beat you, hit you, slap you,
whip you, tell you she didn't want you?
Did you drop out of school thinking
you could make it . . . without it?
Now you need it. Don't talk about it?
Well, whatever it is, my blessings
are with you.
Keep your head up brother,
Once again I see you.

Alicia Cherise Hunter

Forever Love

We say love's forever
Forever in our heart
Is it now or never?
Never we will part
'Cause you and I will stay
Stay in each other's heart
So is it now or never?
Have we seen the light?
The light that shines above you
It's all so ever bright
And we'll never see it fading
We will never let it go
Vanish from our existence
Be banished from our hearts
And love could be forever
Love can make you smile
So hold me now or never
Never let us part
'Cause, darling, you will always be here
Be here in my heart

Chris Mark Whittington

Open the Eyes

Follow the rules
learn the ways
pass the tests
PRACTICE
Remember the mistakes
devour the moment
accept the possibilities
GROW
Dance the steps
run the mile
complete the course
WORK
Budget the time
file the records
jump the conclusions
HOPE
Dream the dreams
push the days
live the life
impress the world and BE

Arielle Marie Smous

Trestles

A moonlit walk
Down a lonely road
But I am not alone

We reach the tracks
But don't turn back
Instead we venture on

Side by side they lay
Merging to one by light of day
As we will too one day

A single light
Pierces the night
Yet we take not flight

Instead two vessels
Under the trestles
I and my love

Thunder above
Realizing love
My Angel My Dove

Aaron Ceyanes

Angels . . .

Angels told me
How you felt
Angels told me
With what problems you dealt
Angels told me
That you loved me
Angels told me
I should still love thee
Angels told me
Of my angel
Angels told me
Then in love I fell
Angels told me
Everything
Angels told me
About you
Angels told me
A lot I didn't know
Do you know who my angel is?
It's you.

Kelly Dawn Taylor

The Lost Escape

The only escape that I see
Is so very lost within me.
I need to escape, my only escape.
When will I be free?
The pain, the torture
Deep within me,
Please set me free.
My only escape,
The forbidden escape,
The one you won't let me see,
Let me escape, let me be free.
The only escape,
The bad way out,
My life, My choice,
How do I choose to be free?
Life or death,
The forbidden way out,
I need to be free,
Why can't I go peacefully?
Just let me be free.

Liv Finch

But Where Shall I Go

I have arrived
With the names thou fears
Seven be the shadows
That now come near
Relinquish the taste
And absorb the fair juice
This wisdom is not too late
Less thine tongue hath broken loose
Thine mark has been left
The scars are so shrewd
Sins left behind
Now hath become sins renewed
Thou wanders and waves
Distant in the night
Relishing the movement
Dying for the light
But where shall I go
Is the answer they seek
But it is not a destination
It is a rise from sleep.

Ryan James Gleason

My Lonely Fear

I'm wandering in the fog
along a twisting, turning road.
I need you with me, sweetheart,
but my love I've never showed.
I'm afraid to let you in,
but I can't figure out why.
I want to tell you how I feel,
but I feel I need to hide.
I fear that you'll reject me,
that you'll laugh and turn away.
My fear is so strong that I
can't figure out what to say.
Deep down I know that you won't hurt me,
yet I'm way too scared.
I'm trying to understand this fear,
but I'm still so unprepared.
But, dear, I really do love you,
and I will always care.
And if you ever need help, please know
that I will always be there.

Laura Gene Keltner

Sunset Girl

A young man's dream
a beautiful girl
a tropical paradise
and sails unfurled
They talk about colors
the sky all ablaze
the winds of summer
the springs of change
As time goes by
the moon and its rays
see a young man grown older
and wiser in his ways
She grows more beautiful
with each passing year
each spring that renews them
each moment they share
In that last sunset
when the last sails unfurl
he'll see the true beauty
of his Sunset Girl

Gray Alan Porcella

Walk On, Lost Angel

Hooded, wingless seraphim
March the street in
Anticlimactic,
Head-to-the-ground
Monday morning
Of stale existence;
Having lost the craving,
And then ability, to sail
The seafoam sky
For fault of
The sharpshooting
Assassin, Boredom.
Momentary afterthought
Upward glances,
Longing for a sign,
Are sniped
Dead quickly
From the bell tower
Of the mind.
Walk on, lost angel.

Eric James Scharenbroch

Window Ledge

Sometimes I sit on my window-ledge,
Free in the gath'ring dark,
To look beyond the bordering hedge
And rid myself of captivity's mark.
All my life, here I've been,
To live only to serve,
The outside world, I've never seen
Past the horizon's sunkissed curve.
Here I want of nothing,
For there is nothing here to want,
Though I feel I lack of something
What, I was raised to know not.
For others this will be enough,
But never right for me,
And in time, I will be beaten rough
By the soul inside fighting to be free.
So here I sit on windowsill,
In the attic that is ours,
My body is here, as it always will,
But my heart is among the stars.

J. Reid

The Bloom

The color of ruby
On cheap glass
Connected by chain,
It is now broken.
We have broken it
Together.
Clasp tangled in lace,
Frenzied movements,
Need, Want,
Taking over all reason.
It breaks as does
My last vestige of
Innocence.
Once it was beautiful,
Pure, and unbroken.
Left alone with the bauble,
I am it.
Broken, Used,
The clasp still holding
Wisps of lace.

Jessica Carmichael

Empty Promises

You make these promises,
But soon forget them.
You tell me you will give me,
Many things of necessity.
But when I look to you,
You turn away!
Why do you promise me,
Things you do not give?
Why do you say things,
Which you do not mean?
You give me your word,
But it does not matter,
For what is the point,
Of these empty promises?
I give you things freely,
Without expecting a return.
Yet you promise to repay me,
For these objects of compassion.
However these debts can never be sealed,
For you are full of empty promises.

Darren Daniel Dreier

The Love of Friendship

I got your back, you've got mine,
I'll help you out anytime.
To see you hurt,
To see you cry,
Makes me weak and want to die.
And if you agree
To never fight,
It wouldn't matter
Who's wrong or right.
If a broken heart
Needs a mend,
I'll be there till the end.
If your eyes are wet
From drops of tears,
Don't you worry,
Let go of your fears.
Hand in hand,
Love is sent.
We'll be friends
Till the end.

Rebecca Mirzayan

Josh

I knew you little
I loved you long
Not very often
Does your dream guy come along
Holding your hand
You were all mine
Your eyes, so blue
They'd always shine
And even though
Your life is no more
In my memories
Your heart will soar
Your laughing made me dream
Your joking made me cry
My love for you will never die
When I close my eyes
I see you with me
But I realize
Now you are happier
Now you are free!

Brandi May Galloway

Soul Mate

When the others leave you
I will collect what remains
What nobody knows of you
Each time
that you wear the night
as a shroud
and seek to find my eyes
I'll have for you
a body like a greatcoat
When the others
pass you by
I will pick up your steps
and take them to the country
Where all the time
You were a little child
It is here that
I can talk with you
recognize you
and keep you
for me alone.

William T. Ryanm

Fragile

A hard outer shell
a soft inner soul
easily damaged by passersby

Gripping for love
grabbing only hate
trying not to fall into the pits again
needing to feel loved
actually feeling lost

Wanting to be free
wings clipped, limp within a cage
can't be grown again
unless there's a miracle

To forget the pain would be ecstasy
to lose the need even greater
longing for a chance
to break free
to fly again
to get out
to become unbreakable

Lesley Davies

Summer Breeze

I thought about you the other day
I heard a song, was swept away
It had your voice and had your smile
I closed my eyes, just for awhile
It touched my Heart, and swept my Soul
Cool yet hot, as if a coal
I thought about you the other day
The sun was warm, and gave its ray
It warmed my face, my neck, my wrist
It warmed my Heart, like we had kissed
It warmed my Soul, I wished you here
Our bodies warm, you pulled so near
I thought about you the other day
A breeze caressed, as on my way
It brushed my cheek and swept my hair
Like your hand, it shows you care
It cooled my skin and eased my brow
Soothing like you, I know not how
I thought about you the other day
As tomorrow, and as today.

David Laur

The Dream

Looking through the window
watching the sun come up,
What a warm and happy feeling
to see the day begin.

The sound of the wind
blowing across the trees,
Sometimes can sound
like the ocean in the distance
as the waves break upon the sand.

None of this compares to
waking up next to you
To having your warm, hard
body lying next to mine.
As your eyes flicker open
and they meet with mine,
A smile appears on your face.

The passion of our embrace
is stronger then we had imagined,
And we begin our day with love.

Dorinda Abendroth

To the Moon

Even though we are a world apart
it doesn't seem like it
because you are so close to my heart
You could visit me on the moon
and back
Sometime in the future
we could talk
What's a million kilometers against
a fallen heart
Just to be with the presence of you
is a start
We could watch the sunrise
and laugh till it sets
Memories we make
of loving days
only to leave back
Remember it all in your heart
Come back to visit me soon
because I love you
and we shouldn't be apart.

Martina Maria Sladkova

Look Inside

When you're searching for help
Look inside
You are your own Savior
You're certain to find;
Honesty is at your core
Kindness in your heart
Loving arms will hold you up
And help you make a start;
So take hold of your life
Find help as you reach
Pray to gain strength
As you strive to find peace;
Be your own parent
Be your best friend
Learn from your spirit
Don't let your will end;
Look deeply inward
And search for insight
See beauty in darkness
Find positive light.

Barbara Hass

Now I See

We were in love
But you had to go
I loved you my best
I hope I showed you so
I tried my hardest
And we were together
Something came up
And I flew like a feather
So many memories
That won't go away
I try to let them go
But in my heart they stay
I call you on the phone
And I cannot speak
With all the memories
My heart falls weak
I look at the past
And put together what I see
We can't be together
And that is how it is going to be

Jaime Puphal

Overcoming

As the sun rises
From its fiery depths
Of the unknown
Illuminating the sky
With streaks of gold and silver
Only to bounce off
The grey ridden clouds
Of sorrow
But the sun overcomes
The ebony clouds
With its glorious splendor
Filling the
Blue expanse of sky
In other words Jesus
The light of this world came
So that we could
Be saved
And in paying a heavy price
His like our sacrifice
Chases away the darkness

Tasha Weston

Words

Words flung out
Oh! so carelessly,
Bold and Bristly: "I hate you"
Whisper "I love you and I hurt."
Words diving helplessly
Deep into tissues soft,
Helpless to go back whence they came,
Like the hapless bullet,
Forever estranged from the gun,
Must now go and wreak havoc
Where it is forced to land.

Shadows on the wall,
Far removed but connected,
Rest fearlessly on the wall
Safe in the knowledge
That with darkness
They will return whence they came.
But words cry silently
For now they may not go back.
So, think, child, before you speak.

Farrah Melek

The Moment!

Lovely dark black eyes . . .
Darker than the night
So lit up with sparkles—
Trembling with joy . . .
For a moment—
Only a moment . . .

And then—
Like tiny raindrops
Wrapped into the ocean's bosom . . .
They went.
The placidity returned.

What had become of them?
Those fleeting moments of song . . .
I linger on—
To wonder . . .

While the ocean
Full with calm repose;
Thrashed with indifferent eyelids
And turned away from me!

Anju Vasudevan

Dreams of Life

Where does life begin?
In the heart?
In the soul?
In the womb?
Must be for all those
Who pursue their dreams.
Life starts out small,
Growing bigger each day.
Our lives become whole
When there is understanding,
When there is love, and
When there is life.
We cannot live without our dreams.

Barbara Gross

The City Beckons

The city beckons us to come
To explore her ins and outs
The city beckons us to come
To show us what she's all about

The city beckons us to come
To listen to her sounds
The city beckons us to come
To see and hear within her bounds

The city beckons us to come
To reach within her soul
The city beckons us to come
To share her richest gold

Benita Beckles

Mighty Tree

See the tree—how tall it grows.
In the breeze its leaves do blow.
The mighty tree, started from seed,
Up to the sun its branches lead.

Like human life started within,
Born to this world of mortal sin.
Grown to nurture and sustain us all,
The mighty tree we know will fall.

Fall from ignorance and neglect,
What's one life to regret?
Regret we will, the mighty tree's fall,
For when it falls, so will we all.

Debra May Raper

Sorrow

The battle field lay stretched ahead
The battle over—the toll is high
The ones who won are dead and done
nothing remains but one
The shadow on the plane moves
like a living being—it has life
it turns and views what it has done
The shadow laughs—its work complete
for it is the cause and end—
it brought upon this wretched place
a pain like no other
a pain of defeat—a pain of death
and the cause of pain is known,
known as the harvester of sorrow

Keith W. Mosgrober

His Gift

My life is His gift,
His blessing to me.
He fashions my heart
individually.

He is virtuous, honest,
righteous, and true.
He will lead me and carry me
all my life through.

He gave me the right
to choose and be free.
His word opens my eyes
and helps me to see.

I take pride and have confidence;
with Him I shall win,
For the Lord does not forsake those
who seek refuge in Him.

Kimberly Thygesen

Struggle

A light flickers in my mind
A feeling not of any kind
Suddenly I feel so calm
My life held within my palm
This seems to be a placid world
Free to fly as the gentle birds
No worries, there is just peace
A daydream's masterpiece
But all at once it creeps
These feelings carved so deep
Consumed by darkness am I
Peacefulness, I bid you good-bye
For a moment seems forever
Strong emotions held together
Seems I cannot escape the heat
Struggling only to defeat
Sometime this will have to end
Pacific come to me my friend
Now it is time for me to rest
For I have overcome the test.

Rosalyn Uy

Aging

My hair is getting gray,
Can't remember the day;
I must be getting old.
It's happening often.
May as well get used to it
Till I'm laid in a coffin
Or ashes to ashes—haven't decided yet.
Brown spots and skin globbies
Appear all over my skin.
Eyes twitch and dizzy spells
Are frequent now and then.
What is a person to do
As arthritis pain kicks in,
And it gets harder to write
Or draw or sew?
Try to remember what has been.
Toss the aging aside!
I'm going to fly . . .
Walk the beach in the sun
Till God calls me up high.

Donna D. Deiss

I Am Weary of Life

The sting of rejection
Is far too familiar
To my fragile heart
I am breaking down
Breaking apart. The tears flow
And they will not cease
I am overflowing
With the most desolate unhappiness
I am drowning in my own misery
Do you know how hard it is
To smile, to pretend everything is okay
When you are devastated and torn,
Your soul has been shredded to pieces
Do you know what it is like to wake up
And curse the day before it even begins
But that is what I do
Each and every day
And it is what I shall do
Until the day I die

L. Thompson

A New Horizon

When all hope is gone
we watch the setting sun
falling behind a new horizon
Trying to walk a path of hope and light
not looking back
staring at the setting sun
standing at the horizon
Waiting for the chosen one to come
With faith toward a better tomorrow
we wait for our hero
to guide us
and bring us a better tomorrow
In these dark times
when the sun sets
we hope, hope for a light
to rise from behind the hills
and the outer reaches of the world
bringing upon us
a hew horizon. . . .

Chris Linwood Abernethy

God's Grace: In Love Twice

Marriage is a union
of love, honor, and respect.
Remembering the commitment to
yourselves and to God,
Place God first,
for His will is perfect.
Rarely finding a love once,
but twice by God's grace.
Embrace God, help one another,
for it will bring you closer.
God loves you both,
knowing your hearts,
blessing your marriage,
wanting only the best.
So that
everlasting love that comes from God,
a gift that is given freely.
Grasping it and sharing it,
Your love will endure forever. . . .

Lori A. Zimmerman

Sheilagh

You're a beautiful person
A wonderful friend,
You're the rose in my garden
That I'm happy to tend.
xxxxxxx
Your radiance dazzles
As the love from you shines,
And the warmth of your being
Fills all that it finds.
xxxxxxx
As a mother you're perfect,
There couldn't be two,
The Good Lord blessed our children
When he gave them to you.
xxxxxxx
So at times when you're down
Or life loses its crest,
Just remember, my darling,
By all, you're loved best.

Steve Jones

True or False

True or false
False or true.
Which one
Is important to you?
Some believe in truth and reality
And some believe in false and fantasy.
Which one is you
And which one is me?
We see fantasy with our eyes
And reality with our minds.
So if you see with your mind
And not with your eyes
You'll see that the sun will never rise
And the moon will never shine
And you'll never reach
The full potential of your mind
So think before you leap
And dream while you sleep
Then your life will be less incomplete.

Casey Sawyer

Hope

If my heart could only speak
Thoughts of my soul be free

If my lips could only touch
The one who is meant for me

If the ocean's so vast
And the mountains so high

Could crumble or disappear
Into the star-filled sky

Then I would gain hope
To the one I hold so dear

As to think that we too
Would lose our salty tears

But alas the truth be found
That even the impossible can be

And forever the truth be bound
To those things I see around me

Gail Lorey

Love

Something that we make
Something that we want
Something that we give
Something that we try to find out
Something that we always talk about
Something that we always don't know how
to define
Something that we always feel about
Something that we always care
Giving . . . Wanting . . .
Comes to us without warnings
Comes to us without fear
Comes to us without lies
Comes to us without doubt
Been so high . . . Meant to be . . .
Cherish . . . Love . . .
Thank you!
P. S: I've been waiting for "this"
for such a long time.

Andy James Budiman Wowor

Loneliness

Loneliness is that deep
Ache in my heart
That is like winter all the time.

No spring ever.
Only the cold wind
Blowing through my clothing
Blowing through my skin
Blowing through my muscles
Blowing through my bones
Blowing through my soul.

I cover up with my clothing.
I cover up with my blanket.
I shake all over, and
my teeth chatter and crash
together, making their own dismal music.
No quilt is thick enough
To cover up that cold, empty, achy place
Somewhere in the center.

Nancy J. Coolidge

In the Distance

In the distance,
Far along,
I see an instance
For a song.
I will rejoice
When I reach it.
I have made the choice—
I must beseech it.
Long the weary days
While I travel on.
Many different ways,
Now my body is gone.
My soul shall travel on.
I do not blame it,
For if I could keep walking
I would go on,
And I'd keep on singing
And look on
In the distance.

Jessica Gray

Hide No Longer

Hiding is for cowards
you're not the hiding kind,
I'd wait for you for hours
Just to make you mine.

You've watched me, Oh, too keenly
And let your wishes be
When it is I who has chased you
As anyone can see.

Now that we have found each other,
Your fantasies can come true.
And now that you are in my arms,
All I want is you.

Michael L. Shore

God's Sea

I'm strolling by the sea tonight;
The starry sky is filled with light.
The ocean dark with waves of foam
Is gurgling out my song of home.

My sandy footprints are my past;
My empty heart is seashell cast.
Because my life of sin has been
A lamprey to my soul within.

I talk to God with salt-filled eye,
And with the wind comes my reply:
Pray on, my child, and you will be
As faithful as the tide to me.

Caron Lynn Nugent

A Blessed Penny

All of my life and time
I looked for a quarter, a dime
A penny, if found on tail,
I passed up without fail.

From a poem I recently learned
A penny found is a blessing earned,
Dropped by an angel true.
For me, Krissy, the angel is you.

So now I have changed my way.
I look for a penny every day.
The story often should be told,
A blessed penny is worth more than gold.

Gary R. Cooper

Shine

In the morning air
On a wing of a flair
Mesmerized by you
I sit and stare.

The time we spend
From beginning to end
We have a bond
My lover, my friend.

Forever this time
I'm yours, you're mine
Eternally grateful
Together we shine.

David Wayne Aguilar

Storm

Lightning through the ages
a chance of countless
whispered silences.

Rain falling from the sky
like shimmering silver beads
from ages far beyond.

Wind blowing through the trees
leaves falling to the ground
silently telling a tale of life.

The sun shines brightly now
flowers all blossom radiantly
everything is peaceful once again.

Katherine C. Olle

And the Baby Laughed

I tried to make her cry
The baby laughed
I gave her a lolly pop
The baby laughed

I gave her its teddy bear
The baby laughed
I tried to go in another room
The baby laughed

Knock, knock, went the door
The baby laughed
Her mother came in
And the baby didn't laugh

Samantha Mairie Ang

Someone to Love Me

To all disabled young people: May God lead you to your dreams.

Will I ever find someone to love me?
Someone kind and strong
Someone with courage
To shoulder the burden
To marry me

If such a man is meant to be found
He will send him
This love will be a rare gift
A gift to be treasured
A gift unlike any other
A gift no one yet anyone deserves

Monica Rose Uwajeh

Croaking Frogs

Croaking frogs critique
Fish that jump toward the sun
Yawning o'er the pond

Flying fish ignore
Seats of self-imposed justice
Floating lily pads

Diving with the sun
Bullfrogs forget their verdict
Having had some fun

Drifting quietly
Caressed by gentle moonlight
Sleeping fisherman

E. Lee Saffold

In the Stillness

In the stillness of the dark,
In the darkness of night,
In the night I have dreams,
My dreams are of you.

In the stillness of the light,
In the light of day,
In the day I have dreams,
My dreams are of you.

In the stillness of the silence,
In the silence of death,
Even in death I have dreams,
Those dreams are of you.

Belinda Carrie Knapp

Friendship

To lose a friend is a hardship
A long period of time
To wander all alone
In a stir of wonder
Is this the best or is it
A bad time
A friend is special
Something not taken away by any
Someone true to your heart
That will overcome many
To make you laugh
To make you cry
Someone to you that will not lie

Kyle Auch

Louder than Words

Ah, 'tis the smile of a lady
the joy of a child
the whisper of wind
the silence of sound

For in darkness we wander
in light we seek
in anger we shout
in sorrow we weep

For silence speaks loudly
Louder than words
So speak not lest ye disturb
the beautiful sound of silence

Tammra Jetton

Dear Friend

Dear friend

Do not harm yourself
You're harming me

Do not kill yourself
You're killing me

Dear friend

Do not pull the trigger
Pull it on me

Kill me to see your mistake

Dear friend

Artem Roma Babaian

Love at Home

Love at home
Is a sharing talk
About the day just passed;
A verbal walk
Through next week's plans,
A loving pat, or a captured glance.
Communion in bedside prayer,
A touch in the night,
To show they care
What tomorrow will bring
While they work alone,
And the night will ring with
Love At Home.

Chet Owens

Now

Are you looking for life?
It's not ahead.
Are you dwelling in the past instead?
The future can't be reached.
It's out of your grasp.
What happened before is too
long in the past.
Loss of time you must resist,
for the past and future do not exist.
Look inside of you
to find out how.
Look around you, for
the time is now!

Robert Prue

Those Apple Trees

The apple trees, the apple trees,
As I remember there were three.
Out in the middle of the nearby field,
As tempting as could be.

We were warned at an early age,
Not to pick till they were ripe.
But we'd sneak out there anyway,
While the floors, mama would wipe.

We loved them green, we couldn't wait,
Mama's warnings went right past.
Many a tummy ache we did suffer,
From what, you need not ask.

Connie Eagan

A Question

The clues are all around,
even in the miracle we are,
yet are the fragments playing
mind and thought reality?

If possible to completely end
the errors coined and stamped
in molded time-game metals,
is there any substance left?

Or will lost be finally found
as the shifting shadows
that hide and seek as life,
fade forever in light of truth?

Don Fay

Feather

She tells me it will all be okay
and this longing will end
I try to believe her
as you sink your nails
into my tender skin
pulling me closer
while pushing me farther away
someday I will throw you
into the wind
and watch you sway back and forth
like a feather
Until then I am caught
in the depth of your sarcasm

Lexi Marie Marciel

Fight the Monster

Fight the Monster,
He will hurt you.
Don't give him your life,
He will control everything you do.
He is strong and he hates you.
Fight the monster,
He holds down your ability.
Go and fight it;
One day you will see.
Fight the monster,
it will all become clear
Fight the monster,
he is only your own fear.

Dustin James Parker

In Search of Something Old

In the midst of the early waves
songs upon the boat
the sound of the pelican
circling like a moat

A far island sits on the horizon
so far, far away
trails of sunlight behind it
reminders of the days

Will there ever be a passing ship
that lands upon its beach of gold
and stirs its waters pure
in search of something old

Kevin Reid

It Is You

It is you I thank
my luck to find.
It is you I hold
deep within my mind.

It is you I carry
upon my heart.
It is you the one
right from the start.

It is you I pledge
to loyal stay.
And give my heart
in every way.

Henry A. Chisholm

Mother Sun

Mother Sun
Caresses me near
Unafraid
In a world of fear

Shivers with touch
Starry night loathed
Eros in clutches
With arms to unfold

Ethereal sage
Alleviates cold
Unwanted body
Unchartered soul

Uncluttered virtue
Mother to be
Lover Divine
My eyes burn to see

George Martens Stietz

Sunset

birds of prey
circle in the sky
birds of song
protect their children from the ground

red and yellow
pink and purple
bonds unbroken
above us all

passion and power
find each other
in ground and sky
in father and mother

winter storms
summer rain
never ending
life begins again

Deborah Anne Land

Overload

Searing heat.
Biting cold.
Flapping wings,
and days of old.
All of these and more
Beckon us back
To the days of lore.
Confusion it seems
Is the word of the day.
So much to do.
No time to play.
We're due for a change,
look and you will see.
How information overload
is affecting you and me.
So if you get a chance,
in your hurry-up pace,
Stop and smell the flowers.
It will brighten your face.

Patrick McCrohan

Do You Know?

Do you know how much I love you, my children, who are so dear.
Do you know I realize you've spread your wings and Mom will not interfere?
Do you know you'll always be in my heart and soul, whether far or near?
Do you know the proud mother I am through both the joy and tears?
Do you know Mom has faith in you, for that you'll never fear?
Do you know Mom's just a call away for words you may need to share?
Do you know that I am sorry for things that may not have seemed fair?
Do you know to put your Family first, for they will always be there?
Do you know to hold your partner close at heart and reveal the burdens that you bear?
Do you know how precious your babies are and that they fill my heart with cheer?
Do you know that you are strong enough for anything you may dare?
Do you know to take the time to laugh, cry, and play and keep your dreams always clear?
Do you know how many love you from Heaven and from here?
Do you know you have two angels watching over you?
Grandma and Grandpa won't let life became too despair.
Do you know Mom prays for all of you, each and every night?
Hoping God will protect, lead, and steer.
Do you know this is not good-bye?
Mom will come to visit, for this you can prepare.

Renee Tyler Hunt

Seeds

Seeds, seeds, seeds.
Strange looking little things, some brown, some green, some black,
some white, and even some you can't see.
How they grow and develop is so amazing to me.
The cattle in the field are grazing upon those that from the husks are set free.
A little, brown tear drop seed produces an apple tree.
Anyone can count the seeds in an apple, but only God can count the apples in the seed.
An acorn will in time produce a mammoth tree called oak.
That awesomeness is no joke.
A tiny, round, black seed can produce a green stem with brilliant-colored flowers on its end.
Another dark brown or black teardrop seed can produce a green vine with yellow flowers.
The flowers with age turn into a big, green watermelon with dark, red, sweet, juicy fruit inside.
Then there are the seeds of life called eggs.
Invisible they are, yet they form a brain, eyes, arms, and legs.
Seeds of faith, seeds of evil, seeds of kindness, seeds of love.
What type of seeds do you sow?
Will they be good or will they be bad?
And how will they grow?

Val Roberts

Poet Profiles

ABBAS, FARRAH
[a.] Beirut, Lebanon [title] "My Insane Devotion" [pers.] I believe that poetry is a special gift from God—an aptitude I am privileged to have. Nights when I can't sleep or days filled with extreme tedium are the times when my mind fills with intense thoughts and feelings that I translate on paper. My poem, "My Insane Devotion," talks about blissful moments in my life as well as gloomy ones. To me, love overwhelms reality and changes my mood—high or low—into a definitely better ambiance. I attend the American Community School in Lebanon. I enjoy playing sports, drawing, and writing in my leisure time.

ABBITT, DAVID
[a.] Hengelo, Netherlands [title] "24" [pers.] A native of Los Angeles, David continues to propagate his art through writing on a daily basis. He dedicates this work to his creator, who he credits with inspiring all of his work.

ABDEL-KHABIR, SHERIF
[a.] Giza, Egypt [title] "Silence" [pers.] I got a glimpse of how complex silence could be. I couldn't imagine how many actions, feelings, and natural elements could be bundled into such an ignored word. I was overwhelmed by how much I could put into the word, "silence." My poem is mainly an examination of the set of rules with which nature could be viewed as abiding. I think that silence could be regarded as a wonderful world of its own and not as an undesirable situation. I would like to thank Miss Harrington, my English teacher, and all my family for the support they offered me regarding poetry.

ABENDROTH, DORINDA
[a.] Oregon City, OR [title] "The Dream" [pers.] I love to write and dream, and the combination of both can sometimes produce the best feelings I have within myself. I have been doing both as long as I can remember, and being able to share this with others is a wonderful feeling. I would like to send special thanks to a very special friend who was my inspiration for writing this poem. Thank You, "Spike."

ABERNETHY, CHRIS
[a.] Brookeville, MD [title] "A New Horizon" [pers.] This poem is mainly about hope. Looking towards another day, towards the future. For me, poetry is a way for me to escape and to let out all of my feelings. I have known the power of words for a long time and I use it to go on day by day. Through poetry, I find my hope.

ABNER, ROBERT
[a.] Winchester, KY [title] "Lisa, My Bride to Be" [pers.] Poetry is my way of expressing the heart and soul of my innermost thoughts and feelings, in a form that can be shared with my loved ones. This particular poem is very special to me, as it was written exclusively for my wife and presented to her on our wedding day. I slipped it into her dressing room early that morning for her to read before she walked down the aisle. This poem captures our anticipation of our wedding and our growing love for each other as we prepare to unite as husband and wife.

ABRAHAM, GLYNDA
[a.] Apo, NY [title] "Six Blessings from God" [pers.] This poem is a tribute to my daddy, the Rev. Roy M. Hayes, who taught me to always believe that God gives what he promises in due time. He's is in Heaven today, smiling, saying, "See Glynda, you believed and received." Thanks, Daddy, I will always love you and never forget the values you taught me. To my mother, Mavis L. Hayes, who stood by us through the good and bad times, never giving up. To my children, Angela Thomas, and Jeffsenet, through whom God gave my, "Six Blessings," just when I needed them most.

ABRAMS, LIL
[a.] Nashville, TN [title] "The Black Granite Wall" [pers.] After visiting the Vietnam Memorial Wall in Washington, DC for the first time, I was left with an overwhelming feeling that finally the healing has begun. I wrote this poem in loving memory of Captain Richard Allen Kerr Kia Jan. 31, '68 RVN.

ADAMI, JOEY
[a.] Hicksville, NY [title] "Lady Blues and Windowpanes" [pers.] Words are just that—words are how they are meant to me; they mean what is true and truly felt. To write is to feel, without feeling, then I am not true to my ink. I am 25 years old and currently living on Long Island. Sweet tidings and peace to all that grace these golden pages.

ADAMS, ALISA
[a.] Columbus, GA [title] "This Little Step" [pers.] The majority of my life hasn't been the best for me. I'm tired of having it rough, so it's up to me to make my life better. I hope others will realize that, "if you don't like something, change it; if you can't change it, change the way you think about it." I'd like for this to make people think and for it to inspire many of you to be everything you possibly can. You have one life to live; live it well!

ADAMS, JONATHAN
[a.] Princeton, LA [title] "As" [pers.] Writing is more than a hobby for me, it's a way of life. Poetry has never been my focus, but after this I may change my tune. Originally from Spokane, WA, I live in Louisiana and I am stationed at Barksdale, AFB. I would like to dedicate this publication, my first, to Goldie, my single greatest inspiration

AGUILAR, DAVID
[a.] San Francisco, CA [title["Shine" [pers.] This poem is dedicated to my friend of five years who has recently become my lover. He has inspired me in many ways. Thank you for being!

AHMAD, MONICA
[a.] Forest Hills, NY [title] "Through Sightless, I See" [pers.] This poem is special to me because it expresses my personal belief that few things in life are one-sided. One should remember the "silver lining" behind seemingly dire circumstances. The young boy in my sonnet, "Though Sightless, I See," is literally blind; that is, he cannot see things in the real world as other people do. But he uses his imagination to create his own beautiful, vibrant world, a world without the cynicism and hard reality of the outside world.

AHMAD, NADIM
[a.] Birmingham, AL [title] "Nighttime" [pers.] This poem was written in a turbulent time while I was going through a divorce. I try to write poetry that people can understand, without having to squint their eyes and figure out what the heck I am talking about. God has blessed me with a talent that allows me to relate to people, and I can write poetry about any topic at a drop of a hat. If somebody reads my work and feels relief because someone on this planet feels exactly the same way they do . . . then I have done a good thing . . . and I am glad.

ALBINA, JENNIFER
[a.] Middlesex, NJ [title] "The Snowfall" [pers.] I am eleven years old and I love to read and write poems. One of my favorite poets is Shel Silverstein. I wrote "The Snowfall" because I really do love the snow and nature. I love animals. I want to be a pet sitter and rescue animals and write poems.

ALEJANDRO, LUIS
[a.] Alberta, Canada [title] "Carlina's Birth" [pers.] Luis Alejandro: is both my "Pen Name" and the name selected by my parents. I was born in Chile, January 10, 1940. I'm 29 years married and have three male children. Education: High School and technology, pensioned. I like to read, to listen to music, and to write poems as a hobby. I orient young people in peace and respect philosophic ideas. Note: Original poem has three stanzas. "Carlina's Birth:" Comes from a baby girl born in Calgary City on September 21, 2000, daughter of Tanya and Onkar—he has been our friend for about 18 years. Carlina is their first baby.

ALEX, ANGIE
[a.] Bothell, WA [title] "Always Have My Love" [pers.] I wrote this poem after separating with my first love. At first I was angry at him, but soon realized that in relationships, break-ups happen. I know most of you remember your first love, and some of you are still trying to find it. I cherish my bittersweet memories that I expressed in my poem. "When I met you, I liked you. When I liked you I kissed you. When I kissed you, I loved you. And when I loved you I lost you." Anthony, I will always have you in my heart.

AMBROSE, TIM
[a.] San Diego, CA [title] "Dreamlessness [pers.] Poetry for me is a tool, having that notebook and being able to express how I feel—it's a powerful thing. My father always told that I have a way with words, which has always inspired me. I wrote "Dreamlessness" for and about a certain someone who has visions like I have never seen. She has changed my life in ways I cannot begin to explain. That's all I am going to say about what this poem means to me. I feel that being able to interpret on your own is a significant aspect when it comes to poetry.

AMIAN, MARIE
[a.] Honolulu, HI [title] "Graduation Farewell" [pers.] What inspired me to write this poem are my peers with whom I've been through thick and thin since our grade school days. This poem is a gift to them on our graduation day. I dedicated this to my friends at W. R. Farrington High School, class of 1992. We made it and we are still climbing to reach the stars! Especially dedicated to the party crew of '92! I'm majoring in early childhood education and care. I believe that the children are the future so we must give them what they need to grow and develop to become what we hold them to be, the successors of our future. Early childhood education is the start, and we as the society must provide them the opportunity to have it. We need to show in our actions that young minds are a treasure and of importance in our society. We should give what we know will come back to us in multiple profits in the end.

ANDERSON, DOTTEE
[a.] Lowell, AR [title] "The Door Was Shut" [pers.] I wrote this poem, "The Door Was Shut," when I had recently moved and was facing many changes in my life. Wrongly, I blamed my best friend for my unhappiness! In many ways, my life has not become any easier, but thanks to the very person I had blamed, I found the strength to face them. One day I will write another poem thanking her! She is once again my best friend, the best I will ever have!

ANDERSON, JILLIAN
[a.] Norman, OK [title] "The Puppet" [pers.] I am currently a student at the University of Oklahoma. I am a visual artist as well as a poet, and this particular poem was inspired by a watercolor piece that I painted in 1997 (a still-life of a puppet). As I give the analogy of the puppet (and give my painting a voice), my goal is to illustrate simultaneously the simplicity as well as the complexity of life and to give a deeper purpose to the "little things."

ANDERSON, LORETTA
[a.] E. Orange, NJ [title] "Try and Understand Me" [pers.] This poem should open everyone's minds to understand that although you may have a strong and healthy body today, you never know when it could happen to you or a loved one. If something should happen, just love them. I have watched my healthy

daughters change to those not strong and healthy. All you can do is help them fight their battles and show them love. They had Lupus.

ANDERSON, SUSAN

[a.] Woodbury, NJ [title] "Truth" [pers.] My poem is an expression of my spiritual quest. Poetry has always been a way for me to let others share in my experiences, from spiritual experiences to the thrills of hiking mountains.

ANDREWS, JENIFER

[a.] Albuquerque, NM [title] "Black Dream" [pers.] Poetry dwells within me, in the depths of our inner being and flows out once there has been inspiration. I find that when I just sit back and take in the colors and textures and feelings of things around me, that there is a poem in everything. "Black Dream" was not an actual dream I have had; neither am I a morbid person. My purpose in writing this piece was to incorporate the idea that even when there is gloom and fright, there is beauty in the words to describe it.

ANENOGLOU, ELISEOS

[a.] Easton, PA [title] "Angel's Advice" [pers.] I wrote this poem while walking through the fog of love. Although I knew that nothing would ever happen, she was still the only thing I could think of for weeks at a time. Thank God, all fogs eventually lift.

ANSELL, CASEY

[a.] Moseley, VA [title] "Night" [pers.] I have always wanted to write novels but never had the chance. I found this contest in a magazine and thought it was a chance to show my teachers I could do it. I'm a twelve year old girl who got her poem published.

AQUINO, LLOYD

[a.] Chino, CA [title] "Pass Through" [pers.] I think that this is the most important work I have ever written. It's a very personal poem, one that I think captures the essence of the person I have always been, a person I don't think anyone really knows. It's always been a depressing poem for me personally, but I am more proud of "Pass Through" than anything else I've ever written. Poetry, for me, will always be a personal experience.

ARMSTRONG, LAFAYETTE

[a.] Flagstaff, AZ [title] "Calling My Lover" [pers.] The story behind, "Calling My Lover," is about a special person in my life with whom I fell in love. We both live on different sides of the United States, and one night before going to sleep I felt very fortunate that I had fallen in love but I missed this person so much since we are geographical separated. Never had I been in love before, and the feeling to me is deep ecstasy. The inspiration of my Love can almost be inexplicable. She is very dear to me. All I can say is, Love is patient.

ARNOLD, KIMBERLY

[a.] Stilesville, IN [title] "Even Me" [pers.] My poetry is dedicated to the spiritual questions and revelations that I encounter in life. This particular one reveals my search for a personal niche in the world. What would be my ministry? God's answer is the publication of the very poem that asks the question. Poetry can be an intense expression of the feelings and thoughts that race around and collide in the souls of all people. To be able to express these things is freedom indeed. My parents and husband have been the encouragers in my life, as well as my siblings. I owe them a lot.

ARNOLD, TABITHA

[a.] Selinsgrove, PA [pers.] I am a 14 year old with cerebral palsy and I feel that poetry is the only way I can really express myself. I wrote this poem about the loneliness I sometimes feel. I enjoy writing poems and short stories. I also spend a lot of time reading. I would like to thank my mother, Carolyn, for encouraging me to keep writing, even when I don't think my work is good enough. I would also like to thank the rest of my friends and family who read and enjoy my writing.

ARRIAGA, CHARLENE

[a.] Cocoa, FL [title] "Untitled" [pers.] Dedicated and written to my dad, Raymond R. Bearden, who passed away, March 25th 2000. Writing this poem helped me express and release some of the pain in me at a very hard time in my life. I love you, daddy!

ASTETE, JACQUELINE

[a.] Newark, NJ [title] "I Am You, You are Me" [pers.] Poet, Singer, Composer, Army National Guard. This poem, as well as the rest of my writing, is meant to open one's mind. I believe in projecting positive vibes and I think we all have different interpretations of what we read, hear, and see—as a result, having a special meaning to each one of us.

ATAY, JASMINE

[a.] Alberta, Canada [title] "Joan's Dreams" [pers.] I believe that poetry is one of God's innermost important gifts that anyone could receive. It has meaning which always leaves the reader thinking about the moral of the poem, whatever the topic may be. My poem, "Joan's Dream," holds the perspective of a courageous woman's view through her struggles to keep her dream alive. Joan has always been an inspiration to me, ever since I first watched a movie about her when I was seven years old. Her distinct characteristics such as courageousness and her free spirited nature are some of the things that I was proud to mention in my poem. I enjoy writing poems; it was one of the talents I was given through my mother. I always hoped to give a little part of me out to the world. I believe that this poem is the key to accomplishing that dream. I am forever grateful to the publishers of "True Reflections" and to my friends and family, especially my mother, for their constant support for helping my dream to become a reality. To you, readers, I hope you enjoy reading my poem which may relate to some of your heroes and heroines.

AUDRA, WARREN

[a.] Grant Town, WV [title] "Tears Fall" [pers.] I feel that poetry is a gift, one that my Savior, Jesus Christ, has blessed me with. My poem, "Tears Fall," talks about my sorrow over my brother's murder. I have always enjoyed writing poems and expressing how I feel. I hope that my poem enlightens people's spirits and touches their hearts.

AUDREY, REESE

[a.] Houston, TX [title] "As I Look at This World" [pers.] I have been writing poems since the age of 12. My poems derive from innovations. They are originated from the aspects of daily living. My inner feeling entwines with my emotions, and the words just seem to come together. I never know what I will write. I do know that whether it happens in an hour, day, second, or moment, the spirit takes control and I write. Thanks for hearing me.

AUSTIN, D.

[a.] Sevierville, TN [title] "Fireflies by Moonlight" [pers.] Dedicated to my "Beloved Buddy" and her girls. Someday 2-N-1-B Buddy, love Wayne—D.S

BAILEY, ALEXIA

[a.] Elberta, AL [title] "Christmas" [pers.] My name is Alexia Bailey. I am ten years old. I live in the Sunny State of Alabama on the beautiful Gulf Coast. Christmas is spectacular to me. My family gets together from all across the country to exchange gifts. Christmas is about giving to others and Jesus's birthday. I hope everyone who reads this knows what Christmas represents. I am interested in and enjoy writing music and poetry. Music and poetry can touch the hearts of people from many backgrounds.

BAIRD, JOCELYN

[a.] Marion, Oh, [title] "Heart of a Rock Star" [pers.] I started writing about four years ago when I was eight. Poetry didn't come to me until last year. My poem, "Heart of a Rock Star," is one of many I have written but it is my favorite. I wrote it based on the loneliness and sense of misjudgment that musicians and singers often confess to feeling. It is my dream and goal to become a journalist, and I hope that other people enjoy my writing and one day will be able to somehow relate to what I am saying.

BAKER, LAUREL

[a.] Port Angeles, WA [title] "On the Carpet" [pers.] My sister Cheryl inspired me to write poetry many years ago. I have three children, John, Christina, and Jennifer, that too are interested in writing poetry. My daughter Christina has also been published in a local poetry book, *Tidepools*. I have already had my novel published. My novel is called "Fragmented Recollection," under the pen name of Stephanie Queen. I have been interested in writing since I was 12 years of age when my grandfather's book, *Bill Bailey Came Home*, was published.

BALOGH, JOHN

[a.] Sydney, NS Canada [title] "I Thought about This Often, and Still Do" [pers.] I was born as the fifth and last child in Hungary in 1914. Brothers:Anton, Joe, and Frank and sister: Jolan. Sad but true, at present the Globe of ours is turning only with me on it alive. As a youth, I learned the baking trade. In 1950, I cut myself through the "Iron Curtain;" I risked it, to live or die. I loved my parents and I still love them. They were very good to me and they deserve, even now, the very best. Because of my DEAR parents, I wrote this poem for the contest. I have had only six years of elementary school and three years of trade school education in Hungary. I have bought books and have been my own teacher. I only had eight hours of English night school. I began writing poetry at the age of fifteen. I have written over 1,100 Hungarian poems, and have two Hungarian and one English poetry book in circulation. At present, I am known only as a "Hungarian Poet."

BALOTA, JILL

[a.] Fernandina Beach, FL [title] "Dance" [pers.] Often my mind and my soul are shredded into pieces. Creative writing allows me to reconnect those jigsawed pieces. I have found that poetry allows me to tap into moods and emotions that I can later use to enhance my fiction writing. I was recently asked to write a childhood poem for a class, and "Dance" is the poem that resulted. As a child I suffered from Juvenile Rheumatoid Arthritis. This poem became a way for me to reconnect pieces of myself and reconcile emotions which have been swimming in my head since childhood.

BANGURA, JAMIRU

[a.] San Jose, CA [title] "Love Sorrows" [pers.] Poetry allows me to express my deepest feelings, more than I could ever express through a journal, a letter, an essay, or any other form of writing. I feel truly blessed to have had my poem selected for this poetry book. I thank my family for supporting all of my accomplishments, and this accomplishment is something I will cherish forever.

BANZET, KRISSY

[a.] Coffeyville, KS [title] "The Next Heartbreak" [pers.] This is a dream come true, and I hope you enjoyed my poem. It's very dear to my heart. I want to thank my sister for talking me into doing this and my mom for all of her support throughout my life. I hope one day that you can again read more of my poems and will enjoy them as I have.

BARLET, DORIS

[a.] Cuba, MO [title] "One Young, One Old" [pers.] The inspirations behind this poem were my mother who is ninety-two, and my great-granddaughter who is almost two. She goes with me each time I visit the care center where my mom is. The love and kisses for an older one are great, I think. The words just came together as I was there one day visiting, watching the two of them. Also I have always loved poetry.

BAUCHAM, CURTIS

[a.] Sophcoppy, FL [title] "You're a Part of Me" [pers.] I dedicate my poem to my daughter, Renata Simone Baucham, of Kenner, LA, to whom this poem was truly intended. To my mother, Ms. Pauline R. G. Baucham of Apalachicola, FL and my Aunt Willie Morton as well as my Uncle Jacque Parker of Jacksonville, FL, I truly thank you for your spiritual support. To my brothers and sisters as well as their kids, thanks for your moral support. Special thanks to my girlfriend, Dianne Elizabeth Bell of Sopchoppy, FL who encouraged me to enter my poem in the contest. Last but not least, this poem is in remembrance of my brother, Charles Lee (Chuck) Baucham and my Aunt Mirian Parker as well as my dad, Mr. Leo James Baucham. To God be the Glory. Also in remembrance of Uncle Bill (The Biscuit Man).

BAUMANN, ERNEST

[a.] Twin Lakes, CO [title] "Comrades of the Mountain Snow" [pers.] This poem is inspired by the soldiers of the 10th Mountain Division, U. S. Army, who fought with distinction in Italy, smashing the Gustav Line, losing 999 of our finest. Our comrades of the mountain snows. My father was a ski instructor then; I am now. (Harvard '66-70) In 1962, I graduated as valedictorian of my high school class. I applied for and won a full scholarship to Harvard with an initial major in Astronomy and Physics. I graduated with the A. B. (Bachelor's) in Geological sciences. Worked at geology in several mines, underground, open pit, and then in the oil field as a petroleum geologist. Co-authored a book on *Toward a New World: Powerful Proof of the Existence of God.* Received a patent on a Collapsible Ski. We have five girls (the youngest is 20). I am currently retired. For the last nine years, I served as a security officer in armed towers and trained most of the Graveyard shift for six years, then transferred to shop supervision. I retired with injuries and disabilities. In October, I was voted the position of Grand Knight in Could #681 of the Knights of Columbus.

BAYLOR, JEANNETTE

[a.] San Antonio [title] "Loved One" [pers.] The loss of my loved ones inspired me to write this poem. I experienced such grief in so many ways. I understand that no matter how painful it is to go through, your loved ones will be by your side. My Lord God has blessed me with one son, Ralph Baylor, whom I love so very much. When my time comes to join my loved ones, I will leave this poem behind to comfort my son, family members, and friends. I know I will always be in their hearts. No matter how hard it is when your loved ones have to leave, you will never be alone.

BEARDEN, BOB

[a.] Oklahoma City, OK [title] "Guess I'll Fall in Love Again" [pers.] I write poetry as a personal release and for the sheer pleasure. I attempted my first poem at age nine. I have written more than one hundred poems since that time, including one dealing with the Edmond, OK post office tragedy, one about the Vietnam Veterans Memorial and about the loss of the Challenger Astronauts. I am a retired Union Officer with the National Association of letter carriers. I carried mail for the U. S. P. S. for 26 years and served in the U. S. Air Force during the Vietnam Era.

BEAUCHESNE, LISA

[a.] Merrimack, NH [title] "Sister" [pers.] This poem means so much to me and my sister, Caren. This poem was my first and hopefully not my last, and I would also like to say thanks to my sister Caren for the inspiration she has given me over the past few years, not only with my poetry but also with life.

BEAUREGARD, JOSH

[a.] St. Albans, VT [title] "A Dream Once Dreamt" [pers.] "A Dream Once Dreamt" was written for and about someone very dear to me. She has helped me realize the finer things life has to offer—the future, love, and never-ending happiness. And though we've been together for quite some time now, the feelings I expressed in "A Dream Once Dreamt" are stronger than ever. She is truly a Godsend.

BECKLES, BENITA

[a.] Lathrup Village, MI [title] "The City Beckons [pers.] This poem is a tribute to the city of Detroit. The city is working very hard to improve its services and image. Detroit is a great town with much to offer! I hope that others will discover its gifts and contribute to its success. Best Wishes, Detroit, on your 300th birthday in 2001!

BELAND, LIETTE

[a.] Ontario, Canada [title] "Now That You're Gone" [pers.] What inspired me to write this poem was the death of my grandfather. I was sad for weeks and one day I felt the need to write my feelings on paper. My grandfather was a kind and funny man who was there for anyone who was in need of help. For that reason I share this poem with those who lost someone very special to them.

BELISLE, PRISCILLE

[a.] Winnipeg, MB [title] "Desolate" [pers.] This poem was originally written when I was 13 years old. At the time, the poem was a reflection of what I saw around me and how people treated certain individuals. When the school held a special day on racism, I was asked to read my poem to my classmates and their families. The poem left an impact on a lot of people, and I hope it continues to reach out to others. I have kept this poem ever since, and at 20 years old, I still keep it close to my heart.

BELLINGER, KYLE

[a.] Ocean Springs, MS [title] "Why?" [pers.] This poem, along with several others I've written, came to me in a dream. I am a thirteen-year-old boy and I love writing poetry. Most people seem to think that writing poetry is not for teenagers, but it comes natural to me. I often lay awake in bed at night and marvel over how well organized nature is and how well the human body is built. I just figured I should write something about how truly amazing we really are.

BELMONTE, GONZALO

[a.] Rochelle, IL [title] "A Moment" [pers.] I first would like to dedicate my publishing to my daughter, Vanessa—R. I. P. I write whenever I need to get something off my chest. At the time I wrote this verse, I was going through a lot of drama and not feeling like myself. As soon as I wrote it and recited it to myself, it helped me feel a little better, or at least, it helped to let me tolerate my situation. Writing how I feel helps me to deal with life and now I hope that it might do the same for others.

BELTZ, HIROKO

[a.] Aberdeen, MD [title] "Life" [pers.] First of all, I'd like to thank my family and friends. I feel any languages are very difficult to use but the most wonderful way to express yourself. People get hurt by people. People feel happy through other people. As a human, I'd like to appreciate that we have such a special gift.

BEMMES, BECKY

[a.] Reading, Oh, [title] "The Unspoken Message" [pers.] Placing my thoughts and life experiences onto paper has assisted me immeasurably in my journey as a girl and now as a woman who is living with a disability. All of the events detailed in "The Unspoken Message" transpired while I worked as a social worker within a residential home, a setting that so vividly illustrated to me that communication possesses many forms. However, in order to truly and entirely integrate and internalize the message we need to receptively open our hearts, see with clear eyes not clouded by misperceptions, and listen attentively to what is and to what isn't being expressed.

BERMAN, LORETTA

[title] "The Man from Nowhere" [pers.] I put my heart and soul into my writing, and I get inspiration from my own experience in life. And from the dreams that haven't come true. I also write children's books and other stories. I draw cartoons, and take photographs of animals with my camera. I want to thank the people that selected my poem to be published in a book for people to read. Thank you for recognizing my talent.

BERNAL, SUSAN

[a.] Syracuse, UT [title] "Into Eternity" [pers.] I have always loved writing poems. This one I wrote after my mother died of breast cancer in March, 2000. I miss her very much but I know in my heart she doesn't feel pain anymore and I know we will be together again someday in eternity.

BERTZYK, DENISE

[a.] Wautoma, WI [title] "Journey Ahead" [pers.] For the last four years I've been writing poetry, whether it be about me or the events in my life. Poetry is just like a song—you can express yourself in any words you seem fit. This poem in particular is dedicated to a very special person whom I love dearly who's been a part of my everyday life for the last two years. His name is Ronnie. I love him dearly and I hope to never lose him, because everyone needs someone to pick them up every now and then.

BEURKENS, ANTHONY

[a.] Comstock Park, MI [title] "The Fireman's Legacy" [pers.] I wrote this because my father and I are both firefighters. When I was young, I would hear him speak about his day. The fires, the people he helped—I knew even then I wanted to be just like him. Thanks, Dad, you are my hero.

BHIMRAO, RAGHU RAM RAO

[a.] Hackensack, NJ [title] "Warrior" [pers.] I dedicate this poem to the almighty God.

BIAGAS, LILLIAN

[a.] San Francisco, CA [title] "A Wondrous Love" [pers.] "A Wondrous Love" is my search for that deeper meaning of love. Poetry for me is a release of all forms of emotion. My love for family is a form of "A Wondrous Love" in its depth, for my mother Barbara, children Shealina, Onezime III, and my Dad, Levian. I live in San Francisco, CA. Two years college, licensed cosmetologist, make-up artist. Poetry, painting, creative arts of all kinds—singing, teaching. I personally feel poetry allows me to touch others' lives in some way, to up lift their inner spirit; it's one form in which the Lord allows me to give. Please enjoy.

BILSON, GILLIE

[a.] River Forest, IL [title] "Split" [pers.] This poem is about every time that two people who care about each other have a hard time working things out. When I wrote this, I didn't know how it would turn out. I do now, and if anyone reading this is caught in this situation, work it out. It is always worth it.

BIRD, JACQUELINE

[a.] Elwood, IN [title] "I Still Believe in Thee" [pers.] This poem was written in conjuction with the other poem titled, "From the Heart." Both poems refer to the same person, Michael. I'm a working mother of two, married 26 years, a Creative Artist, and Over-the-Road Truckers Poetry and song writers run in my family.

BLACK, TAHNEA

[a.] Southfield, MI [title] "Why?" [pers.] I am a 13 year old girl who was raised in Detroit, MI for most of my life and I am also the author of the poem, "Why?" Poetry is a gift I have and something I am not afraid to share with the world. Even though I've only been writing poetry for a year now, I continuously receive compliments on my writing. I am very proud to have my poem published in the book *True Reflections*.

BLAKE, ERICA

[a.] West Columbia, SC [title] "One Magical Day" [pers.] This poem means the most to me, personally, because it's about my deceased grandmother and the wonderful impact she had on my life. I love her very much and hope she knows how much I miss her and I hope she's proud of me and my poems. I also hope that others can read my poems and feel the strength, passion, and love behind the words. Writing is an escape from the world for me, and I hope that other people have an escape as enjoyable and fun as mine.

BLUMERICH, SUSAN

[a.] Janesville, WI [title] "A Poem For the Northwoods" [pers.] All my life I've had poems running through my mind. When it "sounds" right to me, then I write it down. Poetry is how I express my emotions and perceptions of the world around me. "Northwoods" honors the beauty of Wisconsin's natural forests—an awe inspiring place where I truly feel in touch with God and nature.

BOESCH, NICOLE

[a.] Waretown, NJ [title] "Abandoned" [pers.] My name is Nicole. I am seventeen years old and a junior in high school. I enjoy all types of poetry and I was inspired greatly by the work of Maya Angelou. She is a very powerful writer. "Abandoned" is about a girl who has a hopeless crush. She wants so much to reveal the love she has for the man of her dreams. The time comes, and she wishes to tell her crush how much he means to her. Little did she know, his heart belonged to another. The girl's heart was broken and she felt she could never love again.

BOHLINGER, LORRAINE

[a.] Wisconsin Dells, WI [title] "Louise" [pers.] This is a true story. Louise, born in Greece, was made an orphan when she was a baby. The Greeks and Turks were at war, and her parents were killed. An American lady, teaching in Thessaloniki and volunteering in a hospital, fell in love with this beautiful little girl. She adopted Louise and brought her to the United States. In Louise's early twenties, she was showing subtle symptoms of ill health. She saw many doctors before a correct diagnosis, M. S., was made. At age 45, she died of complications of Multiple Sclerosis and cancer.

BONNER, ALEXANDER

[a.] Wallis, TX [title] "The Four-Letter Headache" [pers.] I discovered poetry at an early age. Then, I was mainly concerned with rhyme instead of intellectual content. As a disabled veteran and father, poetry has become relative to my existence. Poetry allows an individual the opportunity to present his or her views in a simplistic form containing an emotional position that is accepted by the listener as art. As a part of nature, I, as a responsible being, must give in some form. To the inquisitive mind, the understanding that we are joined together as one is poetry. God is . . . an echo.

BONNER, DOTTIE N.

[a.] Laurel, MS [title] "Death Season" [pers.] This poem was inspired by my family and friends from Ville Platte, LA. French Acadians or Cajuno, as they call themselves, have a lovely sense of humor. I simply take their stories about things that happen in their lives and put them into poetry. I try write the same way as their accent. For instance ,when they say, "thing," it sounds like, "ting."

BORSIK, MARILYN

[Evans, GA [title] "Evening Glow" [pers.] This poem was written shortly after my husband, Mark, passed away. He was my best friend, my pal, and the love of my life. It took me a long time to find such a wonderful man to share my life, and our time together seemed very short. This heartfelt poem is dedicated to him, with all my love. Fifteen years later, as I read this poem, I remember all the special times we had together.

BORSON, NICKY

[a.] New Ulm, MN [title] "Crucifix on My Wall" [pers.] Poetry is my outlet. I usually don't talk about what I'm feeling or going through; instead I write poems. Very few have gotten to actually read them, so sharing this poem with a lot of people is very special to me.

BORTOLOT, IRENE

[a.] Azus, CA [title] "Schemes and Dreams" [pers.] I'm a widow with a 46 year old Down's Syndrome daughter known as "my angel unawares," a meaning taken from a book written by Roy Rogers. I come from a family who knew the true meaning of loving and caring. My daughter was not expected to live beyond two years of age and in her muted ways has given me love and strength in knowing how life can be good in many ways. I worked 50 plus years in hospitals, and at 77, feel fortunate to have had the loving and caring relationships of family and friends. You have given me inner strength and the realization of knowing how to be thankful for those near and dear and the good life has to offer if we know the incite of loving and caring while coping and hoping.

BOSISTO, DEBI

[a.] Brooklyn, NY [title] "A Hug Is a Hug?" [pers.] This poem is inspired by and dedicated to a wonderful man, whom I love dearly, Yaser. During our relationship, I realized that something as simple as a hug can be so powerful and yet mean so many different things at different times throughout your life. I tend to write poetry as a substitute for a diary, when I have feelings, thoughts, or emotions inside me that I want to express or need to release.

BOSWORTH, RACHEL

[a.] Windham, NY [title["Castle by the Sea" [pers.] My poem is special to me because I love the sea and castles. I want to thank my dad, Rich, for encouraging me to do what I like. Also, I thank my mom, who read me stories about enchanted castles and magic. I have always wanted to have magical power. I do. It is writing poems.

BOTT, SYLVIA

[a.] Miami, FL [title] "Courage" [pers.] My love of poetry has existed since I was twelve years old. I wrote this poem in memory of my brother, Jerry. He passed away 16 years ago. He had more courage than anyone I ever knew. He had a rare skin disease which paralyzed his muscles. He was affected physically, but not mentally. He was the sunshine in my parents' and my lives. He had many friends. I loved and admired my brother a great deal. He was my hero in life. He touched many people's lives. "Courage" was for him.

BOUCHER, DAMON

[a.] Honolulu, HI [title] "A Lover Like You" [pers.] "A Lover Like You" was originally written to my girlfriend as a gift for our sixth month anniversary. As military musicians, we became acquainted with each other on a combined concert tour in American Samoa. I always quoted to April, "I wonder if anyone else knows that we're standing on the center of the earth." This poem reflects my appreciation for the way she makes me feel about myself. April is now my wife, and I'm very honored and flattered that others will enjoy reading an honest testament of my love for her.

BOYCE, FLORIAN

[a.] Brooklyn, NY [title] "Life" [pers.] I always believed that poetry was a window to the soul. However, I remember my ninth grade teacher, Ms. Reisin, made us do poetry, and at first, I hated it. Then I realized it expressed yourself to the highest degree, and on that note, I dedicate this poem to everyone who ever believed in me.

BOYCE, RYAN

[a.] Lakeland, FL [title] "The Dying Smile" [pers.] There was a time period in my life, when certain friends and role models of mine passed away. I had reoccurring dreams of a woman I loved, but the dreams always turned fatal as I awoke. I use this woman in my dream as a female entity to embody the emotions I had towards these people. When it is hard for me to express my emotions, I sometimes turn to my pencil and paper. I have learned it is difficult to express emotions with anybody if you can't first express them to yourself.

BRADBURY, LOUISE

[a.] Taus, MN [title] "Life" [pers.] Louise Bradbury has a natural ability to grasp spiritual and visionary matters. She can perform with the imagination and metaphysical matters like others' work with durable things. This aspects of study leads to a new way of seeing. She anticipates that she will soon be incorporating more of the unseen and spiritual world into her books and paintings. The unexamined life is what she champions. This writer/artist lives and works in Taos, New Mexico, that has been a haven for artists and writers for over 75 years.

BRADY, MICHELE

[a.] Antioch, CA [title] "The Shadowed Side" [pers.] My poem speaks to this: In everyone there is something called, "the shadow side." It is the side many turn away from. But I find that when I embrace my shadow side, these shadows and dark places transform my eyes to see new life and true beauty in the same world around me.

BRANCA, FRANK

[a.] Hudson, FL [title] "Vivera E' Un Arte" [pers.] I am an eighty-seven-year-old youngster. Because I yearned to hear the jingle of money in my pocket, I left school at the eight grade so that I could go out into the World and seek my fortune. Despite my lack of education, I was an avid reader. The library was my inner sanctum. Now that my third poem is about to be published, it will be another addition to my cup of life that is filled to the brim.

BRANDON, VIVIAN

[a.] Bentonville, AR [title] "King of Kings" [pers.] This poem is special to me, because it's a true story and a gift from God. We were having a very dry summer, and I had been praying for rain. So one day when I was working in my yard and it started to rain "hard" without warning, I started to complain. Then I had to laugh. That's when God gave me this poem.

BRANSON, SARAH

a.] Lubbock, TX [title] "A Faded Love: Sonnet 1" [pers.] To me, writing is life. It enhances my emotions, beliefs, and faith. Without it, my world would be somewhat empty. I've been writing since childhood. I was first published in eight grade. I wrote fiction and poetry to eventually have my own publishing company. Writing is my love, my passion. It's what I enjoy doing most. I encourage everyone to find something they enjoy, whether it's writing, music, or even collecting bottle caps, and give it your all. Everyone has talents. So strive for greatness. Not fame, but greatness. And have as much fun as possible.

BRAY, VIVIAN

[a.] Jonesboro, AR [title] "A New True Friend" [pers.] I grew up a farmer's daughter in Arkansas, the fourth child of nine siblings. I am the mother of two sons and twice a grandmother. I was inspired to write the poem by a young man who lived in my condo complex while in college and I served on the Condo Board. Curt is very intelligent, personable, and handsome. We became friends and kept in touch through college and law school. He inspired me with his charm and perseverance. Curt passed the Bar and was appointed Deputy Prosecuting Attorney in one of the counties served by my employer, the District Attorney.

BREWSTER, KELVIN

[a.] Tarrant, AL [title] "The Will to Go On" [pers.] I have always lo:ed to write poetry for about as long as I can remember. "The Will to Go On" was inspired by my own personal experiences and feelings through life. After losing my wife and kids to drugs, then the passing away of my mother, I gave up on everything good in life but I went back to church and brought the Lord back into my life. I began to pray and confess my sins. Now I'm blessed with my family again, I'm drug free, and the Lord has blessed me with the strength and the will to go on.

BROADHEAD, THERESA

[a.] Las Vegas, NV [title] "Found" [pers.] I was inspired to write the poem, "Found," because of the situation in my life. The woman in my poem is my mother, and the child is myself. I was eight years old when I was adopted and five when it all happened, so I tried to capture the innocence of a five-year-old when writing. I decided to dedicate it to my inspiration in most everything, my mother. She is truly my everything, and I'm glad we "found" each other. I love you, Mom.

BROADUS, YVONNE

[a.] Detroit, MI [title] "Can I" [pers.] My mother has been my inspiration to write, so religious and strong with her wisdom to guide me, I could never go wrong. I'm the third youngest of nine children and blessed with two lovely daughters of my own. I'm a college graduate and currently working as an "emergency service operator." I enjoy writing, skating, and dancing in my spare time. I choose to write because a lot of things are better understood read than said and I'm thankful for the air I breathe, the blessings I receive, and my freedom to achieve all my goals if I only believe.

BROCKNER, BRITTANY

[a.] Miller Place, NY [title] "Beautiful Thing" [pers.] Poetry plays a very significant role in my life because not only is it my favorite thing to do, but it is also the thing I am best at. I feel that poetry should be something that makes you think and leaves an imprint in your mind. This is my goal for all of the poems that I write. I will refrain from explaining my poem, "Beautiful Thing," because I believe that it is up to the readers to interpret the poem for themselves. I think that if you've gotten anything from this poem, then I've successfully accomplished my goal.

BROWN, KATISHKA

[a.] Silversprings, MD [title] "Misconception of Love" [pers.] My emotions guide my poetry. I wanted this poem to show people that love, and the misconception of love, can have a serious affect on a person's life. For me, it was a misunderstanding. I learned a lot, through my expression is this poem. I wrote it after a bad relationship. I am married now with two beautiful kids and another on the way. I know my husband doesn't understand my poetry, but he's there for me 110%. His high spirit keeps me motivated to write. I hope this poem can open minds and help relationships before it's too late.

BROWN, WILLIAM, JR.

[a.] Claremont, CA [title] "Solitude" [pers.] Poetry has been my escape from the everyday life. It allows me to become one with my creative mind completely. Poetry opens my innermost feelings and thoughts which others would never see. To read my poems is to know an intimate part of me.

BROWNING, GWENDOLYN LUCIA

[a.] Nashville, TN [title] "Jennifer's Foo-Foo" [pers.] I have been writing for many years. Writing is a wonderful, creative outlet for emotions and experiences. This poem is straight from a mother's heart to her only child. Jennifer is the love of my life. Through good and bad times, my unconditional love for her has always endured. On her 27th birthday, I gave her the baby pacifier named, "Foo-foo," wrapped in gold, adding baby photos I had kept all these years, along with this poem. This poem is a very special gift, a touching memory, to last forever, just as my love for Jennifer will.

BRUNO, JUDY

[a.] Somersville, CT [title] "A Treasured Friend" [pers.] I would like to dedicate my first published poem, "A Treasured Friend," to my son Ryan. Life's hidden lesson's open many doors, may you always walk through them. Your courage and wisdom has thought me the meaning of unconditional love. May you always have a dream. I would also like to mention my unconditional friendships with Cheryl, Marcus, Linda, Rod, Jennifer, Joe, and my family, for which I am truly grateful.

BRYANT, KEITH

[a.] Farrell, PA [title] "My Life" [pers.] Poetry to me is a way of expressing how I feel. When I'm writing, it's as if I'm in a whole new world, and there's no limit to the beauty I can create with my pen. My poem, "My Life," reflects on the bad moments that take place, but just because it get's rough you have to stay strong, hold up your head, and be proud.

BUCK, YAMILEK

[a.] Miami, FL [title] "Wishful Thought" [pers.] Even though the man who inspired me to write this poem will never know my true feelings for him, I do give him thanks for showing me that I can still find love in this world of betrayals. My poetry is me, from the ups and downs, to those around me who touch me deeply with their heartaches and pain, to the joy that we share each and every day. "In times we all have a thought or two to say and do, but in times I write my thoughts down, for then it will always remain."

BUCKALEW, CHRISTY

[a.] Meridian, MS [title] "Just One Kiss" [pers.] Poetry has always been an emotional outlet for me. Anytime I feel anxious or overwhelmed, I am immediately calmed once I've written down how I feel. Most of my work stems from love and the many perils of life. This poem, however, describes my husband, Brad, who has always generated passion in my life.

BULLARD, GRANVILLE (BUD)

[a.] Paducah, KY [title] "A Rose" [pers.] Bonnie is a thirty year career nurse, daughter, mother, wife, more precious than gold in each of these! To understand you must find (A Rose), not in full bloom, but perfect in form? Well, that is our daughter, Nancy. Have you ever seen a caretaker who looks at his flowers with amazement on his face? Well, that is my wife's father (James C. Phillips) who still lives with us at eighty seven. Reach for the stars? Yes! But I would rather reach for love and find it as I have.

BULLOCK, EVA

[a.] Fayetteville, NC [title] "Shadowland" [pers.] I am of Irish descent and inherited my love of poetry from my Irish mother. Poems can be of everyday life, or as in "Shadowland," about the nebulous and fleeting world of dream. In this poem I attempted to capture the misty images that oft are the components of our dreams.

BUMER, CAROL

[a.] Greencastle, IN [title] "A Farmer" [pers.] This poem was written in honor of my father, Warren Stutz, a third generation farmer, in hopes that our country realizes how dedicated farmers are to feeding our country with great passion of the land. It makes me, as a farmer's daughter, to feel great pride for every farmer in America.

BUONCONSIGLIO, JAMES

[a.] Shirley, NY [title] "Whispering Winds" [pers.] Whispering winds portray a sense of spirituality. This poem is very special to me because it symbolizes the presence of an individual after death. Whether the loss of a loved one remains in your thoughts or prayers, they will always remain in your heart.

BURKE, JOANN

[a.] Forked River, NJ [title] "The Fire" [pers.] I've always believed in an infinite soul: that when the mortal form dies, you live on as an energy force until you're ready to be sent back into mortal form for the next purpose. This poem expresses that belief through my current purpose: writing. Writing, whatever it is in—poem or story format, brings me happiness, and I hope that through my expressions, it brings happiness to others. Life is contradiction: accept it as is yet mold it into your "shape." J. C. B.

BURNS, DENICE

[a.] Lansing, MI [title] "A Child's Visit" [pers.] I write to express certain emotions that I am unable to verbalize. It is great therapy at no cost to me. This poem is in memory of my father who died not long ago. He was a very special person and always will be in my heart. The heart of Daddy's little girl.

BURRIS, DEBBIE

[a.] Ft. Worth, TX [title] "Never Say" [pers.] This poem is special to me, because I felt that my grandmother who died two years ago is with me. Each and every day. My grandmother felt that love is the true thing and it comes from "God." This is my first poem and I know that it comes from her. With all the love that she and the Lord can send at a time. I am going to start doing more with writing poems. I hope this will help others as my grandmother helped me. Maybe this poem will show others that true love is special, and if they let "God" in their heart, then anything can happen, and it will. Thank you all. God bless.

BURRIS, SHARLENE

[a.] Detroit, MI [title] "Fear, but Do Not Doubt Me" [pers.] Having my poems published has been like a dream come true. It's something concrete that my family can be proud of. I've found ability in me that I did not know existed until one day I was down and out and decided to write my thoughts down on paper. Some would call it a gift; I call it "Life." I dedicate my poems to Trenae Denayre, Brijae LaDon, William Burris, and my entire family.

BUSCH, WILLIAM

[a.] Valparaiso, IN [title] "E" [pers.] The highest point of inspiration can come at life's lowest times. When I was down, an angel named Kelli inspired me all the way to Heaven, and this is to her. To all the other poets, a thanks for your appreciation, and I leave you with a quote from King Theseus, "The poet's eye, in a fine frenzy rolling, doth look from Heaven to Earth, from Earth to Heaven, and as imagination bodies forth the forms of things unknown, the poet's pen turns them to shapes, and gives to airy nothing a local, habitation and name."

BUSHLAND, RYAN

[a.] Grand Forks, ND [title] "Remember the Brave" [pers.] I would like to dedicate this to my dad and everyone else who has served this country. I hope anyone who reads this poem is as enthusiastic as I am about honoring our veterans and our country.

BYLES, ASHTON

[a.] Natchitoches, LA [title] "Your Love" [pers.] I

have written this poem for the people I love the most, my mom, grandma, and my best friends, Indian and Joni. These are the people that have had the biggest impact on my life. It is remarkable that after knowing these girls for so long, they can still give me that feeling of laughter in my soul. Thank you so much for all of the amazing memories. I will love you guys forever.

BYRD, KELLI

[a.] El Paso, IL [title] "The Journey" [pers.] Poetry is special to me because it's a unique way to express myself. It can be used to show various emotions, whether it be in the trials or triumphs of one's life. Much of my writing is based on the experiences that have occurred throughout the years. The inspiration behind me is the love and support I've continually and unconditionally received from a special select group of family and friends. I don't need to write a poem to open my feelings towards someone, however I feel it's truly a special gift and opportunity to take a simple expression and turn it into a beautiful way of showing affection. If I've been given this ability or talent, I should take advantage, for it may help and hopefully bring happiness to others. If that be the case, then I'll truly be the one rewarded in the end.

CAGLE, DONNA

[a.] Lumberton, MS [title] "Unfulfilled [pers.] I never imagined that I would one day be considered a poet. My dreams and aspirations have always been centered around my desire to be a successful writer of suspense and horror novels. It's very ironic that the first recognition of my talent would come in so eloquent a genre as poetry. However, I am truly flattered. I embrace this sweet morsel of success, just as I do every other gift that life offers me.

CAIN, LESLIE

[a.] Ontario, Canada [title] "Time" [pers.] I would like to dedicate this poem to two very special people in my life: My grand-aunts, Margaret and Monica Dubroy. Poetry is a special gift, which can come from beyond, as this was from my guardian angels. I hope others can relate to these same feelings, which I have been sharing with family and friends and now with you, the reader. Thank you, Pete, Willy, and Thomasina.

CALAHASIN, SHARON

[a.] Alberta, Canada [title] "Mountain of Life" [pers.] "Mountain of Life" reflects on how we, as individuals, tend to let others live our lives; we forget about us until we wake up and find out we missed life altogether. We try so hard to please everyone else. We strive to reach the top through life's twisted turns and if we fall off, we die. Life is complicated; we need to take charge to get the most of it. Most of my poems are like my personal diary. Thank you for publishing my poem. It means a great deal to me.

CAMPOS, NOE

[title] "Alice" [pers.] Alice is a character in my second novel (to be published after "Good Night, Sweety!"). They will be available in English, Spanish, and Portuguese. Their plots have surprise, drama, adventure, love, psychology, and, of course, poetry.

CANNON, VIOLET

[a.] Como, MS [title] "The Storms of Life" [pers.] In life, so much pain is endured (mentally, physically, and spiritually). There are times when you need the strong support of loved ones, yet it feels they have deserted you or turned the other way. This poem depicts my life story from age 12, reflecting my survival of the storms of life and how they helped me to develop. I pray it will be a great blessing to others and encourage them to press their way through life. Three principles that will help are: Totally trust God in all things, form a solid foundation, and always count your blessings.

CANTOR, JOSEPH

[a.] Lowell, MA [title] "The Camp" [pers.] The inspiration for this poem comes from my family and my own realization of human nature. Having grown up Jewish, I became all too familiar with Nazi Germany. Like most people, I hoped it would never happen again, that we would not forget the horrors, but we did. One of my brothers currently serves in the U. S. Army and has spent many tours of duty in Bosnia. It was partially through him that I kept an interest in goings on and learned that, given enough time, humanity is doomed to make the same mistakes over and over.

CAPPS, ANGELA

[a.] Colorado Springs, CO [title] "Poetry in Life" [pers.] I will never forget the day poetry was brought into my life. I'd especially like to thank my seventh grade teacher, Mr. Swartz, who taught us poetry. It has helped me speak out in a whole new way I didn't think I could. Whenever something dramatic occurred in my life, my gift would come out and put all the feelings I felt onto paper. I now live in Colorado with my family. Poetry has done so much for me, and I thank you for sharing my art throughout the world.

CAREY, MEGAN

[a.] Rochester Hills, MI [title] "Iron Mask" [pers.] I think people who are able to write poetry are unique and special. The poem, "Iron Mask," is my most favorite poem of the ones I have written. It describes people's reluctance to show their true emotions. The poem uses the word, "storm," because our life is like a storm of good and bad that we endure while hiding our true selves. Sometimes I think we let a single "drop" of true emotion slip out and we are ourselves, but we quickly hide again behind our "mask" that is so tough, it's iron. Even though it would be a long hard journey, we still have our wish that one day the "storm" will die out and we will be able to be our true selves.

CARMICHAEL, JESSICA

[a.] Old Orchard Beach, MA [title] "The Bloom" [pers.] This poem is about innocence and the moment that innocence is broken, all explained by the presence of an incriminating broken necklace. This poem is very sad, it's about loss and desperation, and most of all it's about remorse. There is always hope though; maybe those wisps of lace can be mended again.

CARPENTER, JUDY

[a.] Springdale, AR [title] "My Gift to You" [pers.] I wrote this poem in 1963 when I was sixteen. At that time, I was thinking of the problems a teenager has and trying to help a friend through poetry. My aunt kept a copy and when she passed away a few years ago, the pastor read the poem at her service. This was a great honor for me as she was such a special lady. As the years have passed, the poem has taken on a more spiritual meaning for me, one of God's never ending love for each of us.

CARROLL, CAROL

[a.] Forsyth, MO [title] "He Has [pers.] This poem was written as a tribute to my son. It was written with a mother's love and respect. He is an extraordinary young man who has a great deal of faith and courage. The last line of the poem is . . . "He Has . . . M. S."

CARTER, CAROLINE

[a.] Free Soil, MI [title] "Guidance" [pers.] This poem means a lot to me because it represents everything I live for: Jesus Christ. Without Him, I wouldn't be able to get through my daily life. I hope my poem inspires others to believe in the one and only Creator and to try to turn to Him because He really does listen.

CAVALIER, KING, II

[a.] Loveland, CO [title] "Till the End" [pers.] My father was a Senior Master Sergeant in the U. S. Air Force who survived the Japanese bombing of Pearl Harbor, the Korean conflict and Vietnam. He passed away peacefully this year after 90 years of perfect health and vitality. As a tribute to his inspiration, I carried a rubbing of his marker on my Harley to "The Wall" over memorial day and escorted a gold star mother on my bike in the rolling thunder XIII parade through Washington, D. C. It was then that I realized my mission as a blue star son to make a difference for P. O. W./M. I. A. American Servicemen.

CEYANES, AARON

[a.] La Porte, TX [title] "Trestles [pers.] A professor once taught me that poetry is not the words on the page, but rather the way in which the poet perceives the world around him or herself. The moonlit walk was days before I proposed to my beloved Jennifer, and I completed the poem days after her acceptance. The poem was written to her, the one who saw in the faces of her students, hungry for knowledge, "Almond eyes filled with huge chocolate marbles." And for these perspectives on life we can only say, "soli deo gloria," (To God alone be the glory).

CHANDLER, LATICIA

[a.] Greeleyville, SC [title] "Legacy of a Woman" [pers.] Thank you, God, for blessing me with this talent. To my grandmother Charlena K. Chandler, I hope you are smiling down on me from Heaven, knowing that I am doing what you always knew I would. To my favorite teacher at C. E. Murray High School, Mr. Williams and Mrs. Jonte, thank you for encouraging me to find this way of expressing myself. Finally, but most importantly, thank you, Dante M. McCrea. Before I knew what love was, I knew I loved you.

CHAO, TIFFANY

[title] "The Sun" [pers.] The very first day I got to know about poetry, I began to like it. I truly feel that I have the talent for writing poems. This is a poem written when my friends wanted to test my skills of writing poems. So I was given a title and ten minutes. Finally "The Sun" was completed and ready to be read. From then on, I was a well known "Poem Star" in my school.

CHAPIN, DAPHNE

[a.] Fondulac, WI [title] "Addiction" [pers.] Poetry is a way to release yourself. You can write down about an event that has happened in your life or mind. Poetry is an open doorway to let people into a world that is uniquely yours. An invitation, "Addiction," was my feelings about the youth getting hooked on drugs. Nowadays, on TV and radio you hear about the different types of anti-drug. Here the anti-drug is the parents getting involved. It is their duty.

CHASE, BARB

[a.] Waterloo, IA [title] "Love" [pers.] I never knew I had a gift for writing poems. One day, when I wasn't feeling well and was on the couch, I decided to write poems. This is one of three I wrote that day. My "Love" poem reflects my life. I have found, in order to go on with my life, I had to forgive those who have hurt me in the past, including myself, and start loving again. This has worked for me! My life has improved in every aspect and also so has what I think about myself. To me, loving is the basis of living.

CHILSON, JENNELL

[a.] Horseheads, NY [title] "Daughters" [pers.] I just want to say thank you. My daughters are very precious to me; they are my life. I feel blessed to have Kaylee and Annahlise, my world would not be complete without them. They are not just children, the girls are my angels.

CHIODI, AL

[a.] Altamonte Springs, FL [title] "Invisible to Birds" [pers.] "Invisible to Birds" is one of my favorite poems. It is a true story. Any of us who takes time to stand still and breath slowly will see wonderous events. This poem and many others are available in Mr. Chiodi's first book, "The Watershed," ISBN 0-19663285-0-7.

CHIVERS, KELLIE

[a.] Perth, Australia [title] "Thank You" [pers.] Poetry for me is a magical world of words I can escape to. I have always found it hard to express my deepest emotions aloud so I retreat into my poems. I wrote "Thank You" for my good friend David who's ambition and dedication to his dreams has inspired my own. Also for my son Kalan, my true miracle, my source of faith and hope—without you, "Squid," their would be no me.

CHRISTENSEN, JOEL

[a.] Washington, UT [title] "Fireflies" [pers.] I'm a recovering drug addict and an ex-gang member. I'm fifteen years old and I live in Washington, Utah. Some of my hobbies are art, writing, and performing rap music. The reason I started writing poems is because of my English teacher, Bobbi. The idea for my poem, "Fireflies," was the fact that I have never seen a firefly. So I wrote my idea of what they would be like. I appreciate that you are publishing my work and I look forward to seeing it in the book, *True Reflections*. Thank you so much.

CHRISTOFFERSON, KELLY

[a.] Galesburg, IL [title] "All Mine" [pers.] My name is Kelly Christofferson, I wrote this poem because my husband got a new job and moved to MO. We were apart for about five months. I was really lonely one night and was laying in my bed thinking of him. I started writing this poem and it was just finished. I read it to my husband on the phone, and he was touched. He said, "The poem means a great deal to me." So when I saw the contest in a magazine, I entered it. I started writing poems when I was in sixth grade. My mother used to write poetry, so I guess she inspired me. I graduated from G. H. S. in IL and worked as a C. N. A. for a while. My husband is very supportive in everything I wish to do. I'm currently looking for a job and trying to have a baby.

CLARK, HEATHER

[a.] Eagan, MN [title["Tell Me How You've Bruised My Heart" [pers.] I wrote this poem after I saw a man hitting a girl in the mall I go to a lot. When I saw them I wondered why she'd stay with him if he was treating her like that. And then wondered what I would do in that situation. So I wrote what I thought she'd be feeling, hoping it would touch someone enough to remove herself from that situation. I don't ever want to have to go through that and I feel no one else should either. As Heather's mom, I have never been more proud. To see my parenting has paid off is a wonderful thing. I am so glad you chose my daughter's work for your book—you have made this mother very happy.

CLARK, LAVERN L.

[a.] Mesa, AZ [title] "Cooperation" [pers.] This poem is written about my daughter and me. Of course, I'm the rock. She has always been a little butterfly, flitting from person to person, bringing sunshine and joy to all. My name is LaVern. I was born, raised, and then married a wonderful man, Earl M. Clark, in Utah. We raised our family there. I have five children, 18 grandchildren, and 17 great-grandchildren. We moved to Arizona in 1972. Poetry and drama have always been a part of my life. I was always active in drama, from age three. I didn't start writing poetry till age 12. I never showed it to anyone because I had read the great poets, but I enjoyed my thoughts down. I sent my first poem in for criticism.

CLARKE, RODERICK

[a.] Provinciales, Turks & Caico [title] "For the Love of a Caring Mom" [pers.] This poem is dedicated to my beloved Mom. She struggled through a short life caring for six children to whom she taught sound values and the meaning of love. She is sadly missed by her children Fitzroy Thomas, Clive Clarke, Canute Clarke, Claude Dahl (deceased), and Sharon Clarke, my one and only sister. Mom did us good. It's our turn to lift up to her good name. Living the virtues she taught us will do her justice. To my beloved family: Odette Powell (spouse), Sequena and Seleena Clarke (daughters), I hope to be for you all what my mom was for me.

CLINE, CAROL

[a.] Tucson, AZ [title] "God's Stress Busters" [pers.] There is so much in nature that can relieve the stress that we so often find in today's society, if we only take the time to look and listen. This is the message I have tried to convey with "God's Stress Busters." With the stress of busy schedules and day-to-day problems, take a few minutes to watch and listen to God's nature. If it relaxes a person or brings a smile, that's not a bad thing.

CLOUGH, GEORGE

[a.] North Berger, NJ [title] "Brother" [pers.] This poem was written about my brother, Robert, one day after his death. The poem only took five minutes to write but includes a lifetime of love. If this poem is read by many and keeps my love alive for him, it will carry his memory to many. He was special, and I want the world to know it. The sun will never shine as brightly for me, but his memory will!

COLCLASURE, REVA

[a.] Elko, NV [title] "Escape" [pers.] "Escape" was produced in recognition of the incredible ability of the human mind to transcend the circumstances that sometimes hold the physical body where the mind does not wish to be. I was at work, and it was a very slow day in an office with small windows placed at the top of the wall. I could only look up and out at the sky, and "Escape" was born.

COLE, ASHLEY

[a.] Port Arthur, TX [title] "Searching No More" [pers.] This poem was written for my mother when she was found by her biological family. My mom had searched many years. And now since she must search no more, Ashley Cole.

COLEGROVE, ANN

[a.] Apo Ae, AL [title] "Old Woman" [pers.] My husband and I, the proud parents of seven and grandparents of twelve, moved to Europe in October 1996, because of his employment. I have always written poems for special occasions. With neither a TV nor a computer for entertainment, I bought a word processor at a thrift shop and began to write about people and places around me. I like my poems to tell a story and to be visual, in order for my readers to "see," and hopefully, "feel" what I am saying. I hope I have achieved that with "Old Woman," written about someone I saw on a train.

COLEY, NOLMA

[a.] Freeport, IL [title] "Silence" [pers.] I was born in St. Elizabeth, Jamaica, a community which, when I was a child, was known for it's silence, especially early mornings and at nights. I grew up in a family of nine, and with six siblings we could get really noisy at times. However, there was an unbroken rule that Sundays between 2:30-4:30 should be spent in silence. I have grown to respect and value silence. As an artist educator with a special interest in psychodrama, I view silence as time to be with myself to evaluate and reflect on self. Silence replenishes me and gives me the space I need to be truly alone with myself.

COLLINS, R.

[a.] Manlius, NY [pers.] Age 37. Resides in Manlius, NY; a graduate from Ft/ High School. Finished two semesters of Boces, located in Liverpool, NY. "Poetry of personal expression." Interest in writing poetry, freelance poetry written for a local paper. Many of my poems were edited in our local paper in Manliu, NY, the *Eagle Bulletin*. "The Whistling Grandmother" in *Treasured Poems of America* received editor's choice award for outstanding achievement and excellence in poetry. Got selected to be in *Poetry's Elite* of the best poets for the year of 2000! Thank God, for poetry!

CONDIT, ANNIE LLOYD

[a.] Willow Street, PA [title] "Morning Dove" [pers.] The origin of this poems was the visit of a Morning Dove, who sat on the railing of my second floor balcony, and looked at me with great interest through a pane of glass on the door! He gave his music and flew away but then came back to his railing another day. I have always listened to varieties of sounds around me, and their music and poetry always gave me the greatest pleasure, which many have put into words. "The Morning Dove" gave me a great gift of sound, and now I hear that Morning Doves are being hunted in many states in America. Can we give the Morning Doves a gift and save them?

COOK, TERRI

[a.] Sunland, CA [title] "The Thought of You" [pers.] I have always loved poetry, music, and paid close attention to the words spoken by those around me. This poem simply describes the feeling I had from being separated from my "other half," you see; I am one of the very few in this world who has been lucky enough to experience the "One True Love" that so many others only dream of finding!

COOLIDGE, NANCY J.

[a.] Richmond, CA [title] "Loneliness" [pers.] I've been writing poetry since I was ten, and I'm thirty-two now. Ever since I started, I've liked to write about deep feelings. I wrote this particular poem when I was down, and it made me feel better.

COOPER, JEFF

[a.] Des Moines, IA [title] "Angels without Wings" [pers.] Poetry is an excellent way to express your feelings. It brings to life something that you cannot see and you cannot touch, a part of yourself, hidden beneath a rough exterior, a side of yourself that only a few will ever see. This poem was written for my wife, a true angel without wings.

COOPER, STACY C.

[a.] Dudley, GA [title] "Uncontrolling Tears" [pers.] My name is Stacy C. Cooper. I am from Dudley, GA, where I live with my husband, Tim, and two children, Landon and Megan. This poem was written to touch the lives of all people who have lost loved-ones dear to them. I dedicate my poem, "Uncontrolling Tears," to my daddy, Jack Cook, with hopes that he is smiling down on me from Heaven. I love you, Daddy!

CORBETT, COLLETTE

[a.] St. George, UT [title] "Choice " [pers.] I am a wife, and mother of three incredible boys and one step-son. My children have always been my meaning in life and seem to always overwhelm my spirit with fulfillment. However, my inspiration for this poem came from three other beautiful children who have suffered abuse. I am a C. A. S. A. (Court Appointed Special Advocate), therefore I have been given the opportunity to witness a spiritual strength that I never perceived. These unfortunate children are proof of society's failure to prevent or help. These children will always be part of my heart. They are angels for those whose lives they will touch. I am currently a full time student hoping one day to achieve my
C. S. W. so that I can advocate on the greatest heights for all children.

CORMIER, GLADYS

[a.] Ontario, Canada [title] "Our Garden" [pers.] . I work as a teacher. "Our Garden," I wrote as a birthday tribute to my youngest sister, Shirley Iversen, B. C., Canada. God has blessed me with a loving family and many friends. I write poetry to express my inner feelings. It is my hope that my poems are an inspiration to others. Other works: "The Gift."

COSSA, NICK

[title] "Victim of a Holdup" [pers.] There is innocent life lurking in the long limbs of my body. Enraged at the justice system as they steal my rights and stain my clean hands with the darkness of blood. More innocent than those who prosecute me, I boil with stress and madness from wrongful accusations. Deep in a dreadful hole of destruction, I die from inside, killed by the persecutions of age. The justice system has unleashed angst in a kind heart. But as far down as I have been thrown, and no matter how hard it is to wash away these bloodstains, I will prevail.

COSTANZO, ARCH

[a.] North Royalton, Oh, [title] "Friends Always" [pers.] My love for life . . . with passing winds that reaches out, and so touches us and lies a window for all. "Friends Always" is that special window for all. Dedicated for Angelina and Marcella and all the dedicated, loving fathers and daughters.

COURSON, DONNA

[title] "Childhood Lost" [pers.] What an honor! My poem is a condensed version of a writing included in a talk I gave for a Christian Ladies Retreat. Music and writing are not only therapy for the soul, but they are wonderful ways to express yourself. When I lost my mother at the young age of ten, these were the things I used to deal with my life. They are truly gifts that I have been blessed with, and I thank you for the opportunity to share them with others.

COVIELLO, LOUISE

[a.] Ft. Worth, TX [title] "The Gift" [pers.] Please accept my genuine gratitude for giving me the opportunity to share my thoughts regarding reparations of the heart and lost souls who feel they have no one to turn to. I do hope, or rather pray, that my poems will be able to wipe away the tears and loneliness if they can understand that God centers the soul within each heart where life and His love are the cooperation of mind and body.

COZART, KEITH

[title] "Fear" [pers.] This poem expressed a lot of mixed feelings in my life. At the time I had written, I was down about my success I was having in school, or lack thereof. Also, on the happier feeling of the poem, I was inspired by the love in my life. She kept me going and kept me smiling, and if not for her, I would be alone.

CRABTREE, LINDA

[a.] Chicago, IL [title] "It's Easier to Forget" [pers.] "It's Easier to Forget" was written in dedication to my dad who was diagnosed with Alzheimer's at the age of 64, and to all other Alzheimer's victims. I am an only child by my dad, and my parents divorced when I was three, so when I married, my husband, Jesse, in 1977, my dad often lived with us. I had to put Dad in a Nursing Home but brought him home every week. He was still so active and loved life; the poem reflects on victims like my dad, that are "Forgotten," once diagnose with a disease others don't understand. He died at my home, in my arms, at the age of 69. My prayers are this poem will help others understand the importance of keeping in touch with Alzheimer's victims. I would like to thank my husband and children for all their help in keeping "Papa" happy, and my mother for her encouragement and prayers.

CRAFT, GRACE

[a.] Cedaredge, CO [title] "Memories" [pers.] I was raised on a farm and was the youngest of ten children. I entered a jingle contest and won first prize—that inspired me to write poetry. I'm married to my husband Carl, we both have the mountains all around us in this small town. Nature and Wildlife give me lots of subjects to write about. We have seven daughters and they love their birthday cards with my verses. Thanks so much for accepting my poem.

CRANE, MANDY

[a.] Mt. Vernon, WA [title] "Goodbye Letter to Drug of Choice" [pers.] I sit and think back to the time I wrote this poem and I remember how scared and alone I was. But just like I wrote in the poem, "I decided to stand up and be strong," I was able to do that and now I can look back and be proud of who I am today!

CRIBB, REBECCA

[title] "Aspects of Self" [pers.] "Aspects of Self" has been a significantly important poem in my life. Writing it has helped me understand my complex yet uniquely beautiful nature. Reading it regularly ensures I will never forget who I am. I believe everyone should have a list of their innermost characteristics, whether it rhyme or not—after all, we are all poetry in motion. It is only once we grow to appreciate ourselves and fully comprehend from where we come that we create true art.

CROCKER, STEPHANIE

[title] "Anonymity" [pers.] Friends, and those who were simply there are all who've turned this poem into what it is. It's about identity and how you can cloud the image you project to others. There's a lot of pressure to be and act a certain way, doing so doesn't apply to many of us. So be yourself; it's the simplest thing that you should know how to do. They say the pen is mightier than the sword, and now I can fully understand the importance of this quote. With the written word you can awaken thoughts, ideas, and dreams, and that is my ultimate goal. Yes.

CROWN, JANE

[title] "The Reflection" [pers.] New Orleanian, post-nihilist currently writing poetry in the midst of a third world setting, within a first world tapestry.

CRUTCHER, CALAH

[pers.] When I received the letter in the mail telling me my poem was going to be published, I was psyched! I wrote "Every" for my mom. She has M. S., which makes everyday tasks difficult. Since this poem is only loosely based on my mom, it's left open to your imagination; this way, it means more to you. I am on eighth grade student at Scott County Middle School. I am very grateful for this opportunity; I have always wanted something of mine to be published. My dream has come true! God bless you!

CUBILLO, TOMAS

[title] "Hush" [pers.] Singing and writing are two of the most important ways of expression for me. I am originally from Spain. I have been living in the U. S. since August '92. This poem was written first in Spanish and dedicated to a young woman from Argentina I deeply love. She knows who she is.

CURD, GARZELOUS M.

[a.] Sedalia, MO [title] "Bottled Tears" [pers.] I reside in Sedalia, Missouri with my wife, Jennifer. I met my wife in 1995 through a mutual friend and I have written her a poem every day since then. My wife has inspired me to pursue my dream of publishing a book of poems that would consist of every poem I have written her. I enjoy writing poetry, fishing, and drawing, of which poetry is my favorite. I always hope to touch the heart and lives of those who read my poems. I give thanks to God for giving me the talent and ability to share my gift of poetry.

DACUNHA, DENISE M.

[a.] Riverside, RI [title] "Your Voice" [pers.] In this world, the simple things get lost in the shuffle. We forget to look closer at the essence of people who are important to us. We miss their eyes, smile, handsm and in this case, the voice. This poem is very close and personal to me. It expresses the passions that are within and moved by someone important to me when they speak. Every time I need "Your Voice," I hear the echo of their voice deep within. I offer "Your Voice" to you to experience, and maybe it will allow you to find the voice in your life that stirs the emotions in you. Enjoy!

DAKIS, JILL

[a.] Beaver Falls, PA [title] "Things I Never Had" [pers.] Reading and writing poetry have always been very important in my life. Poetry is a way of connecting with an event of person. My family has always been supportive of my writing and the emotions behind each poem. This poem is special to me because it is a realization that although I have not achieved all of my goals quite yet, I have something more important, the love and support of my family.

DANIELS, BARBARA

[title] "An Autumn Encounter" [pers.] Since my youth, poetry has been my friend, a reliable companion fully engaged in the story of my life. It has given voice to my inner self, encouraging me to see with my heart. It has walked with me through joy and celebration, humor, pain, and sorrow. It has flowed freely from the wellspring of my soul, a gift that I have come to treasure as I grow spiritually. It has allowed me to teach children through song, entertain friends, share words of wisdom, and speak to the hearts of family, friends, and associates.

DASSOW, KELLY

[title] "Everything" [pers.] This poem was written while I was travelling in Europe and very homesick for my friends. How much I love all of them bring tears to my eyes and makes me feel very blessed. These words don't even do justice to how much they mean to me. I want the world to know what a lucky girl I am. I've found not one other half, but many.

DAVEY, PAMELA

[a.] Houston, TX [title] "A Visit With Friends" [pers.] I feel that poetry comes from the soul. It is your ultimate inner self. I love to write poetry. I dedicate this poem to my only sister, Patricia Louise Southerland, who passed away at a young age. This poem is in honor of her memory. I have dreamed of us a time or two.

DAVIDSON, HARRY

[a.] Chester, MD [title] "For the Bard" [pers.] Before you write anything, you must read a lot. My mother inspired me to read. I can still hear her reading out loud. But I still think it is a combination of reading and experience. I write about what I have lived, my experience as a hunting guide and working waterman. I have some poems and fifty songs copywrited. Some poems can be used as lyrics and music added. Some cannot. These ones must be read and enjoyed.

DAVIES, JULIANNE

[title] "This Is the End" [pers.] I wrote this poem during a personal revelation of self respect. I can't stress enough the importance of understanding and appreciating one's self. Hopefully my poem can encourage people to have positive relationships, where respect is held up high.

DAVILA, LISA

[title] "Released" [pers.] In 1998, at the age of 38 years, I decided to try and write poetry. I never let anyone read it until recently! As I left work one day, in the bright sunshine, I had a feeling of tremendous happiness and hence, these words came into my mind, so I wrote them down. My niece was very inspired by this poem—I hope others are too.

DAVIS, GUENDOLYNIA

[a.] Covina, CA [title] "To Know You" [pers.] Words have power. The power to communicate. The power to reach out and touch another individual. The power to relate feelings and thoughts, ideals and hopes, lies within the power of the word, written or spoken. In merely telling a story, I can relate facts or ideas. But in order to convey something more than information, in order for me to communicate the spirit behind my words, the listener must feel what I am saying as much as I feel it myself. To achieve this I use the highest form of the written word: poetry.

DAYTON, MARGARET C.
[a.] Chambersburg, PA [title] "Faces of Courage" [pers.] At 76, I am a retired NASA and Navy illustrator, mother of twin daughters Marcy Fahnestock and Cindy Shackleton, and living in a retirement village. Although I know many people everywhere are courageous, it became more apparent to me since I moved here that each one of these has something they are overcoming and seldom complaining about, whether it be illness, tragedy, loneliness, or whatever. I teach watercolor painting to many of them, and no matter what their lot in life, you'd be delighted to see their creative output. They all have "Faces of Courage."

DE KELAITA, CARLA
[title] "LOVE" [pers.] Creativity is a mystery, and compelled isolation may be a great incentive. My grandmother was a concert pianist, my mother an opera singer, and my father an operetta composer (Carlo Lombardo). I studied voice (Conservatory Guiseppe Verdi) in Milano, Italy. I never dreamed that what is coming from my soul may touch somebody else's heart! So, humbly, I thank you!

DEANDREA, ROBIN
[a.] Bellingham, WA [title] "Reality" [pers.] This poem has a sentimental value. It is a reminiscence of the first time I saw my husband's beautiful face. It portrays how changes in our lives can be a wonderful thing if we could only look beyond those that have lost at love, or have simply given up, to ever finding that special someone. It will happen when you least expect it. In closing, I would like to thank you, Joe, for keeping me inspired. After all, I could not have done this one without you. I love you, my "Reality!"

DECAPRIO-LEMKE, ROBERTA
[title] "He Kissed Me" [pers.] On 1950, I was born in Schenectady, NY. Because of a difficult birth, I was left with a walking disability. When you've been forced to take life in the slow lane, you notice people, colors, and sounds more. Because I couldn't be active, I read a lot of books, thus making me creative in writing. One doctor told my parents I'd be a vegetable and to put me into an institution. As of today, at 50 years old I have written two Native American Historical romance novels, self-published a poetry book, married, am the mother of two children, grandmother of two grandchildren, traveled all over the world, own my own home, drive a van, have a degree in Child Development, work as an After School Program Counselor, volunteer as a Chalain's Aide for a rehab hospital, sing, play the harmonica, and I'm a Born Again Christian who is a partner in Kenneth Copeland and Ministries, helping to spread Jesus words. "He Kissed Me" was written for my first love.

DELIYANNIS, SONYA
[title] I Dreamt" [pers.] Creating pictures, emotions, and ideas with words has always been a passion of mine. I write for pure enjoyment. I draw from my life and those around me to provide me with inspiration—a direction for my urge to create. I only hope it is a passion that I can pass on to my children.

DEMET, ALEXANDRA
[title] "Interlock" [pers.] To me, "Interlock" is almost a mystery story with clues that lead up to the answer of the question my poem asks. It tells of the relationship between the future, past, and present in symbolic ways. One of these three cannot exist by itself, so they must join together . . . they feed each other connected as one. Poetry is, for me, a way to express my inner thoughts.

DENNEY, ASHLEY
[title] "Survivor" [pers.] My poem is based upon the Holocaust, having always been of great interest to me. Ever since I first learned about it, I wanted to express my feelings on paper. "Survivor" portrays the life of one Jew among millions of others, striving to hold on to both life and heritage. Jacob is retelling his story, hoping to inform his listeners of the torture and hardships that millions of Jews had to endure, although many could not. Even though this occurred over sixty years ago, it is an important event worth remembering, possibly to learn from, and surely, never to forget.

DENNISON, MARGARET
[a.] Indianapolis, IN [title] "Heavenly Love" [pers.] I have been writing poems for many years. They have been about love and hope, trying to reach the heart of anyone who reads them. My children and grandchildren give me inspiration. My fiance encourages me and tells me to believe in myself. For my family, thank you for believing in me. If my poem can touch just one person's heart, then I am truly content and blessed in this life. Day to day living is a poem. Writing poetry is a gift and reading poetry is a love.

DERUSHA, NIKKI
[a.] Naperville, IL [title] "Wendy and Peter" [pers.] This poem might seem sad, but for me it was the beginning of my life. This piece changed my world forever and has brought me true love. He walked into my life, and we've managed to stand hand in hand for five years. I love you, Brendan. This poem is also dedicated to the people who have loved and encouraged me with my writing. I could have never done this without you. This is for you, Dad, Mom, Beth, Kelly, and Jenny. I couldn't have asked for a more loving, supportive family. Thank You.

DESPAIN, MARSHALL
[a.] Pendleton, IN [title] "Life's Uncertainty" [pers.] I feel that writing is a powerful way to express feelings of yourself and others. This poem, "Life's Uncertainty," is how a lot of people feel sometimes. I have sometimes felt alone and afraid, but there have been family and friends to help me through those times. The one thing that is most important to me is God's love, and He helped me write this poem. I am a Junior at Pendleton Heights High School, Pendleton, IN. 17 years of age. Lives with mother, father, and younger brother. Active in Choir and Radio.

DHOOPATI, SWATHI
[title] "Slow Death" [pers.] One may not be as lucid and clear a manner as possible in representing their thoughts to others. However, though, it is Mother Nature, the misery and cheerfulness that she brings along with her, that makes your innermost belief put into words.

DI BISCEGLIE, DIANE
[title] "Daddy" [pers.] I am a fifth grade student at Bayshore Elementary School in Port Saint Lucie, Florida. I wrote this poem in memory of my daddy who passed away from brain cancer when I was seven years old.

DIMITRIEV, HELEN
[title] "The Miracle" [pers.] She was born Helen Ann Brown. She lived with a married man for several years, but having born him four children, she left him because he was a chronic gambler. She then married a Russian Atheist and bore him twins. Their tempestuous marriage didn't last. She became a recluse and spent her time painting non-conformist pictures of Christ and writing mystical poetry.

DIZON, JEREMY
[a.] San Jose, CA [title] "Sublime" [pers.] Poetry never impacted me until recently as a senior in high school. Not everyone knows that eighteen years olds have so much pressure put on them: school work, college apps, social pressures, etc. However, among the hardships of life, I found a peace that can only be described through poetry. Like a snow capped mountain photograph, poetry can express emotions that are difficult to portray. I was lucky enough to realize the endless possibilities that poetry can bring. Please continue to keep poetry alive and never stop the endless possibilities for those who aren't afraid to run with their dreams.

DLO, SUGA
[title] "To God" [pers.] This poem is special to me because it is a daily conversation that I have with God. I love poetry because it is the purest way to express intangibles in the soul. I currently reside in Atlanta, GA. The air here plays music to my poetry.

DOHN, ARLENE
[a.] Eureka, SD [title] "The Lord and I" [pers.] This poem is the first one that I wrote and is in memory of my Mom, Dad, three brothers, and six sisters and for my husband, four children, and our eight grandchildren. They are my life—they are all very special to me and I love them all very much. And our three daughters-in-law and our son-in-law.

DOWLING, THOMAS
[title] "Innocence" [b.] December 14, 1978; Boston, MA; [p.] Richard and Kathleen Dowling; [pers.] I'd just like to thank everyone for their support, especially a wonderful young woman named Debbie, a girl who guided my pen and stole my heart.

DOZIER, SIEGLINDE
[title] "White Lady" [pers.] This poem was written for all the families that deal with the drug called "crank." A person using this staff thinks that the high is all there is to life. I lost my best friend because of an overdose to this drug. He was a very sweet person, and my kids adored him.

DREIER, DARREN
[title] "Empty Promises" [pers.] I am eighteen years of age and a student currently enrolled at Dallas Baptist University. I live in Fort Worth, Texas and am surrounded by a loving family. I enjoy to play sports, watch movies, listen to music, sing, advance my education, and attend my church. I also enjoy writing poetry. Poetry is something that I can always find inspiration and joy in no matter what the circumstances. Poetry is a gift that I believe I have been blessed with. I am truly thankful for this blessing and attribute it to my God, Jesus Christ, who created and strengthens me.

DUFF, HARLEY
[title] "Only Love Is Real" [pers.] Poetry allows me to touch those quiet places in myself that are filled with knowing and love. I feel connected when I write and time takes on a different movement. It's as though I am flowing in a vast ocean of consciousness where all of life flows and there my soul speaks to me. When I write, tears flow down my cheeks. The tears are not from a present day sadness, but a sadness from being away from home. A home that transcends this universe and is timeless and always full of love. It's the home of my soul.

DUPONT, JOYCE
[title] "Friends" [pers.] This was my first attempt at poetry. I made a card for a friend's birthday on my PC. Afterwards I was on the net, came across Poetry.com and asked, why not? Mother of two, Nani to five, married 37 years. A collector of Giraffes, "Liberty Falls" houses, and recipes, I like to feed the birds and try to grow flowers.

DUTTON, NIKKI JANE
[a.] Woodbury, MN [title] "The Journey" [pers.] This is one of many poems that I have been inspired to write in the last year. I believe that God has given me this gift to write as a means of sharing my faith and the gospel of Jesus Christ. I hope to publish all my poems in the future to encourage others in their daily lives and their walk with God. I am a wife, mother, grandmother, and nurse and I seek to glorify God.

DYER, ROBIN
[title] "Miraculous Insight" [pers.] I have been writing poetry since I was a child, and had my first poem published at nine years old. My rhymes tell stories of actual events that have taken place in my life and always portray my Christian faith and my belief in God. My writing is a major part of Single Sisters, the ministry I founded for Christian single women.

EADDY, TAMARA
[title] "Make a Plan, Take a Stand" [pers.] Special thanks to: My sister, my best friend. Teacher, Mrs. Faulkner, who voted me student most likely to succeed. Teacher, Mrs. Burns, who offered me a check for $10,000.00 when my mother became sick with cancer. My husband, Ed, who opened doors, pulled out chairs, and treated me. My mother, Erma, whom I rebelled against when she wanted me to get saved before she died. Better late than never. I finally gave my life to God.

EAGAN, CONNIE
[a.] Walhalla, ND [title] "Those Apple Trees" [pers.] Poetry has been such a wonderful release for me, writing about my childhood on our farm especially, as it brings back so many happy memories. I began writing poetry when I was in high school. Once I have a subject, the lines just seem to flow. I love to sing and have written a song that was also published. Being a mother of four and a grandmother, my life has given me many moments to write about, and poetry is a wonderful way to remember and cherish them.

EAGLE, CHRISTIE
title] "dream" [pers.] This is dedicated to my niece and her husband after the loss of two sets of twins. Sorry wasn't enough, but all I could say. As I began to write, the words seem to just flow. To the babies that are gone . . . I love you!

EARLE, TIFFANY
[title] "My Day" [pers.] I wanted to write this poem because I hung with my friends Brian, Spiras, Nickolas, and Lurian. They are always trying to make up words that rhyme, so I wrote this poem about me and my friends. Mrs. McCann, my teacher, read us lots of poetry. That is what gave me the idea. My mom and dad were the ones who got me a computer for me to type. I am eleven years old. I have two brothers, two dogs, two cats, and two birds. I am going to be a geologist when I grow up. I love to read and I'm a tomboy too. And I love to write even though it is not neat.

EASLEY, ANNA
[title] "I Hid You in My Heart" [pers.] God introduced Denny and I in 1980, but it wasn't our time. Twenty years later, after absolutely no contact, He brought us together again, and this time, we knew it was meant to be. We resumed our relationship with passion and tenderness. Poetry started to flow out of my heart. Suddenly, love songs made sense, sunsets were stunning, the world was more beautiful, and I found the love that I craved all my life. Somehow, I think I knew all along that he was the love of my life, so I hid him. I dedicate this to you, Denny.

EASTMAN, PEGGY
[a.] Chevy Chase, MD [title] "Night Freedom" [pers.] This poem celebrates the life of my loving, literate father, John L. Barr, Jr., who died in June 2000. Our family sailed *Windsong* on the Chesapeake Bay for many years. Only a poem could capture the senses of liberation *Windsong* gave us. Although my father declined physically with age, his mind sailed freely. He read poetry aloud to my brother and me when we were growing up. His favorite (and ours) was Tennyson's "Morte d'Arthur."

EBBOLE, ROBERT
[title] "Father" [pers.] I wrote this poem just hours after my father died. He inspired my words just as he did my life. I was recent and diagnosed with M. S. and the positive, fighting spirit he displayed and instilled in me will help me live a very full life. My only hope is that I can one day come close to being the man he personified.

EDDY, CELIA
[title] "Everything Is a Blessing" [pers.] This poem demonstrates my outlook on life. I had written this just after I accepted God in my life. The inspiration of my poetry is my mother, Crystal Eddy. She is the women who has raised me to always ask questions and to look for the positives in every situation. As I am conquering my teenage years, I write my thoughts on life in my poetry. For always encouraging me in everything I do, I dedicate this poem to my friends and family: Brenda Sanders, Dawn Varner, Pamela Stiles, Samara Cottrell, and last but never least, my aunt, Dorothy Hickman.

EDDY, DEBRA
[a.] Jacksonville, FL [title] "Miracle Babies" [pers.] Poetry is my way of dealing with life's joys and sorrows. I wrote "Miracle Babies" poem of my twin granddaughter's birth. It tells their story of their early arrival our worries and fears and the miracles of life. We thank God every day as we are truly blessed to have them with us. Jenna and Hanna turned two years old on January 4, 2001. Both are doing great as well as my lovely daughter. The three of them are living proof of God's wonderful work. I am the proudest grandmother of all and I'm glad I could share their story with you. I hope you enjoy my poem.

EDMONDS-VITASHO, DIANE
[a.] Decatur, GA [title] "SEARCHING" [pers.] I am a single female, born in Washington, D. C., now living in Decatur, GA. For sometime now I've wanted to write about my life's experiences. My trials and tribulations as well as my accomplishments. It is my firm belief that as human beings and "Children of God," we share a certain kinship. My voice of expressions come straight from my heart or soul and if I can reach just one heart or soul that understands and passes it on one to another, that "My writings have not been in vain." Thanking you for your time and attention, I remain forevermore, Diane Edmonds-Vitashoka

EGAN, GERI
[a.] Carmel, NY [title] "Rug Room" [pers.] This poem is very special to me. It is dedicated to the special Ed kids that I work with. Poetry has always been a big part of my life. My mother suffered most of her life from severe depression and poetry, and writing down my feelings helped me through it all. I am a teaching assistant in Special Ed High School at Western Conn. University finishing my B. A. degree. I love to sing, dance, act, write poems. I teach fourth grade CCD at St James Church in Carmel. I would love to be a talk show host because I love to talk and meet and be around all kinds of people. My philosophy in life is forever young at forty-one. I am a mother of two teenagers, Michael, 19, and Summer, 16, and married for 20 years to my husband, John.

EKANEM, VICTORIA
[title] "love" [pers.] This poem means a lot to me. I've been through lots of experiences and my only way out was to love. This poem is a reality for me, and I hope that all who read this might make it a reality for them too.

ELKINS, AMY
[title] "Tree" [pers.] I love the way that thoughts and feelings can come just from an everyday object that often gets taken for granted. I wrote this about a tree that has grown up in my front yard. One day while I was studying it, I realized just how mature it had gotten and how it has been through so much yet it still gets larger and is full of life. I hope that I will always be in awe with nature, even in its simplest forms, and continue to put my feelings to words on paper.

ELSTON, SERENA
[title] "Fate" [pers.] My name is Serena. I live in a very rural area in New Jersey. I think about this subject a lot and wanted to put some of my thoughts on paper. I finished my poem in one night after school and was very proud of how it turned out. I was twelve when I wrote this poem and plan to write more of this magnitude.

ENNIS, VIVIAN
[title] "What Do I Want from a Man" [pers.] Poetry is my blessing. With I. T. P. (a platelet disorder) and being unable to work, dealing with the deaths of my cousins, father, and grandmother (my Gram), expressing my life and feelings in verse is my testimony and comes quite naturally. My man tells me jokingly, "my help cometh from the Lord." If not for him where would I be? To thank him for blessing me, my gratitude is sharing my experiences for others, pay it forward spiritually. Let it be known God makes a way. Always. Plus, I'm thankful my mom is still here.

ESKELSON, ERICK
[title] "Fallen" [pers.] I'm delighted to say that this is the first poem I have ever had in publication. The story behind the poem itself has to deal with your own personal growth, living with all your faults, and who you have become as a result of your achievements and failures. I'm currently a student at the University of California Santa Barbara, play bass for the band (Backmask) and dedicate this poem to my loving parents Jim, and Marcela. Without your guidance and strength, I would not be the person I am today. I love you both.

ESSEX, STEVE
[title] "I thought" [pers.] This poem was written because of a shyness within and for one who stole the moments between reality. I've never been a forward speaker in life, but through creative writing, color has been added to the gray shades of my dream. Some walls can be breached, and the falling of the fortress sometimes leaves us alone in the cold . . . but the lessons of life are always better shared with others.

EVERETT, TAYLOR
[title] "My Box Is Empty" [pers.] I wrote this poem while looking at a picture. The picture was of a toddler sitting in the yard with a box in his lap. I was trying to captive this small child's emotions on loneliness, something that he would experience later in his life. In the end, the idea of the poem is not to be defeated but to search for another treasure. One not kept in a box or one that will never leave, but is with you in eternity, and it's only found, on bended knee. God Bless.

FAGUNDES, RUBIA
[title] "The Brave Ones" [pers.] This poem is my first attempt at writing poetry in English. I am from Brazil and am here in the U. S. studying literature at Brigham Young University. For me, Poetry is a supreme form of self-expression. In this poem, I talk about some of my heroes whom I consider to be, "Brave Ones," and who happen to be from the book of Mormon. These brave souls lived lives filled with faith even in anguish and trial, always following Christ's example. Reading about their legacy inspires me to be the best person that I can be, and I hope it inspires you as well.

FAIROOZ, YASMEEN
[a.] Sydney, Australia [title] "Peace" [pers.] I feel artistic talent is natural to me. This poem was, a moment's thought which flew so beautifully. I myself am a student of MCOM in Human Resource Management. Other than writing poems, I am much interested in music. Apart from singing on the stage, I would love to keep up my natural talent in writing. I hope this poem brings a special message for everyone.

FANNING, DONNA
[a.] West Haven, CT [title] "God Help Me" [pers.] Although I wrote "God Help Me," I can assure you, God helped me. This poem is about hope, faith, strength, and love, all of which are gifts from God if only we'd ask. Life is full of peaks and valleys; we should give thanks for both because it is the valleys that make us stronger. We should all love one another unconditionally, as God loves each of us. I'd like to say thanks to Mommy, Daddy, Ally, Paula, Kimmy, and Earl for loving me unconditionally throughout my life. I love you all. Thank you God! Always remember God loves you!

FARRIS, STAN
[a.] Petal, MS [title] "Mama" [pers.] The thirteen children in this poem consist of eight boys and five girls. Our daddy passed away in 1967. We're very fortunate to still have "Mama" and we all gather at her house at "13" Farris Drive several times a year. She was my inspiration for this true poem. I have written others about my three children, Aaron, Brandon, and Cheyenne, my oldest brother, "Pat," and other subjects as well. As a former truck driver, my mind would over-flow with thoughts for a poem or song while on the open highways.

FAY, DON
[a.] Oxnard, CA [title] "A Question" [pers.] I have made my living as an artist, designer, and musician. As my hair grays a bit, poetry, more than anything else, helps me aim adultward.

FAY, DUSTIN
[title] "society" [pers.] I was thinking of life and society when I wrote this poem and the four others I have written in the past year and a half. I'm a poet starting out and would like to publish a volume of my own soon.

FEIERABEND, UTE
[title] "Happy Birthday" [pers.] My friend Paula who turned 30 inspired me to write this poem. We are both nurses and work together on a very stressful unit. However our common interest in seeking new knowledge and laughter despite the stress is a pleasure in itself. She is a special kind of person and a wonderful addition to my life.

FELTON, BRITREE
[title] "Horses" [pers.] I like this poem because I like horses. They are my favorite animal. I have two horses. One is named, "Calgone," and my sister named the other one, "Sirlee." The beginning of the poem is about when horses are young and spry. The middle part is when they start getting mean and wild. The last part is when they die. I am a new poet and I like art. Art is a special thing for me. I have a beautiful mother and handsome father. I feel the same way about my brother and sister. Oh, by the way, I wrote this.

FIALA, SUSAN
[a.] Batavia, IA [title] "Deceived" [pers.] I'm 35, divorced, and love life. I grew up in the midwest and currently live in Southern Iowa, where I work for a utility company. I have no children but have a wonderful family—other, Linda, Stepmother, Karen and six siblings. My father David passed away in 1998 but remains in my heart. Finally my best friend, H. Wood, who is a treasure. I truly feel that poetry is a gift. It comes from one's heart. Poetry inspires me. I have always enjoyed writing. The meaning of my poem deceived is simple. No matter how beautiful something seems, it might not really be.

FIELDS, KIM
[a.] Walker, LA [title] "I Was But Now" [pers.] Most of my poetry is an expression of my love for God. He gives me the thoughts, and I put them in verse. I was never a vocal person, so poetry gives me the opportunity to say what is on my mind and in my heart. I receive a lot of encouragement from my daily and Christian friends, to whom I am most grateful. This poem comes from John 9:25. Just as Jesus gave the blind man sight, through our acceptance of His love, we are given spiritual sight.

FISCHBACH, BRANDY
[title] "I Always Wanted You" [pers.] This poem was written at a time in my life when my heart was broken, and I had lost hope. It was August twenty-eighth, and I had just lost my second child by miscarriage. I needed a way to express my feelings, and no one seemed to understand. Writing this helped me heal. My husband submitted this poem without my knowledge, and now it is the middle of December, and I have just found out that I will be published. It's the best Christmas present I have ever had. Maybe with my gift, I can help someone else heal.

FITRASANTI, NIA
[title] "People" [pers.] This poem was inspired by a friend of mine. She told me about the comparison of her and her friend. I made this verse to show her that it was not like what she thought it was. And I was glad that she could understand what I wanted to say to her when she read this verse. This verse made me realize that I can express my mind and my true feelings without having to say it in exact words.

FLAHERTY, KEITH, JR.
[title] "The Moonlight Night" [pers.] I deeply love philosophy, computers, poetry, and my girlfriend, Kerry Kerr, each of which takes up most of my time. This poem was written for her, to tell her how much she means to me. I use poetry to help me express the feelings I have better then just speaking them. Since I was ten, I have been writing poetry to express love, life, loss, and many other turning points of my life. Reading poetry has helped me feel like I am not alone in these feelings. My quote—"Life is a boat, shall we enjoy the ride, or rock it?"

FLEIS, CHARLES
[title] "a-void" [pers.] French. As an instructor of modern language, words are my passion. And the written word is a powerfully expressive too, and poetry is a greater challenge which I find extremely gratifying.

FLEMING, WILLIAM, JR.
[title] "Immaculate Enhancements" [pers.] I like poetry because it can be a radical expression of the simplest things. When I write, oftentimes things become dearer and are seen in a new light. The intended concept behind "Immaculate Enhancement" is that a more through understanding and appreciation of anything is gained through the understanding of its own opposition. You may have heard the phrase, "You don't know what you have until it's gone." "Immaculate Enhancements" reinforces that idea in my mind.

FLOCK, RYAN
[title] "Lost or Found" [pers.] This is the very first time the world will begin to see life through my eyes. I have gone through so many experiences, many experiences such as you. I have lived and learned from these experiences. My only wish is to give them to you. I have this yearning passion to speak my mind—worlds of wisdom, I wish to find. I watch and listen to all, follow me to help support, your mind I won't let fall. Knowledge comes in a surplus amount of energy. By all means, use it how you wish. What has more meaning, is when you use it to find your bliss.

FORD, RACHEL
[title] "Brat" [pers.] Poetry is a wonderful thing. I think that everyone can write poetry, only some can't find that talent yet. Some of the best poems have come from feelings. In this poem, I wrote about how I feel about harassment. It's so important to me since live been harassed most of my life.

FORESTAL, NORMAN
[title] "That Horrible Day [pers.] My father gave me that name because he felt it was a strong name—Norman Rockwell, Normal Lear, Norman Mailer, just to name a few. His wish is coming true, for I am artistic in many ways. My dad passed away from M. S., and this poem was written in his honor.

FOSTER, KERRI
[title] "Flower" [pers.] I'm in fifth grade. I love poems and flowers. I like animals. I'm ten years old. I'm glad that I'm a semi-finalist in the contest. I entered Poetry.com because I thought that I had a chance and I made it.

FOY, KAREN
[title] "If I Could Do It Over I'd Do It Right" [pers.] This poem was written for my son, Stephen Lee Moon, Jr.

FRANCO, ERIC
[title] "Metaphysics" [pers.] "Metaphysics," to me, is more than a poem. It's a way of living. This has been my way of living, since I initially wrote this piece four years ago. Actually, this poem wrote itself. At the time, I was, and still am, tuning my soul to the harmony of life. My motivation is to enlighten and uplift every soul who hears and now reads my poetry. Enjoy.

FRANKLIN, S.
[a.] Phoenix, AZ [title] "The Sweetest Harvest" [pers.] I like poetry because the imagination makes it so fun. You can be anywhere when you write poems. I am eight years old and I like sports. I wrote this poem for my mom.

FREENEY, DEATRIA
[a.] Dallas, TX [title] "Nothing's Too Hard for God! " [pers.] Poetry is a wonderful way to express what I'm feeling. This one was done for my nephew who has since passed from cancer; he was only 40 years old, married with three small children. I feel it was given to me to share with others how I feel—life is or can be hard but not for God. I'm a married mother of two special daughters. One just graduated from F. A. M. U. and one is a junior in high school. I have a loving husband—we are truly blessed and know for a fact nothing's too hard for God.

FRIEDRICHSEN, PETER
[title] "Starless Shore" [pers.] I wrote "Starless Shore" during a difficult time in my life. I felt alone and helpless. But as always, Jesus knew my heart. He soon brought me out of the pit of despair and renewed hope in my heart. To anyone struggling with the same despair I faced, I say that He can help you, too. Simply ask Him to help you escape from your prison of hopelessness. He is purveyor of my poetic gift. He is my Savior and my friend. He is Jesus and He loves you!

FRYAR, CHRISTINA NICOLE
[b.] December 19, 1986; Chattanooga, TN [p.] Christopher F. Fryar and Teresa J. Fryar [ed.] A student in sixth grade at Boyd Buchanan School; graduated fifth grade from McBrien Elementary in June 1998 [hon.] President's Award for Outstanding Academic Achievement 1998, Principal's Award 1998, Principal's Award 1997, Principal's Award 1996,

Principal's Award 1995 [pers.] This poem was written in honor of a cat that was very dear to me. Her name was Molly.

FU, MENG-MENG

[a.] Notre Dame, IN [title] "Rain" [pers.] As a high school junior watching many of my peers battle through depression, I often find that I am unable to help. When an anguished and saddened friend came to me with a problem, I struggled, not knowing what to say. Depicting the worst case scenario, this poem helped me release my frustrations and suggest to my friend to see the school counselor. Fortunately, her dilemma has been worked out. I hope this poem will inspire others not to follow the path of the girl in the poem. No matter how hard the rain pours, it will eventually stop.

FURBY, MARIA

[a.] Henderson, Nevada [title] "Wheel of Fortune" [pers.] My poetry reflects a spiritual development period of my journey in the human body during this 20th century on the Earth. This poetry was put into English-Tantamount Tone and verbally broadcast to the cosmic universe, following closely upon my being spiritually, mentally, and physically welcomed as an adult back into cosmic telecommunications. My creative writing talent welcomed through my female ancestry, including the Old English "Pearl" Poet, who was my incarnation. I trust that *True Reflections* will be a special guide to fellow travelers.

GAGGENS, TERESA

[a.] Belton, MO [title] "To Montel Williams" [pers.] My name is Teresa Gaggens. I live in Kansas City, MO. I just turned eleven and I'm in the fifth grade. When I was writing the poem I was thinking of my cousin, Jacob, because he has M. S. like Montel. I thought Montel should know how much God loves him.

GAIETTO, MICHAEL

[title] "Grandma" [pers.] This poem is very special to me. My grandmother, Maria V. Gaietto, passed away in April of 2000. I was very close to my grandmother and loved her very deeply. When we were making the arrangements for her funeral, I was given the privilege to present this poem at her funeral. I thought very long and thought very hard for many days to get it where I thought it was worthy of being read at this miraculous woman's funeral. This poem is in loving memory of Maria V. Gaietto, 1919-2000.

GALAWAY, RICHARD

[title] "Field of Bright" [pers.] Poetry is an art form that has been expressed in numerous styles over the years. Most people think that poetry must rhyme. Well, out of my 24 poems, only one follows a rhyme scheme. A lot of people have called me rebellious because of this; however, some of the best have done more extreme things than this. Take e. e. cummings, for example. He didn't even use sentences in some of his best works. So in short, it's time to change some of your views about poetry. It's not all rhymes anymore.

GALLOWAY, BRANDI

[a.] Roy, UT [title] "Josh" [pers.] The poem, "Josh," was written about my close friend who died in an automobile accident, October 1, 2000, when the car he was in drove off a cliff. I spent two wonderful years as his girlfriend. He was my first love and my love for him will never disappear. I am 15 years old and I live in Roy, Utah. I've found that it's easier to express my feelings in writing, through poems. I would like to dedicate this poem to the guy in my story, Joshua Theodore Morgan, 1984-2000. Josh, I love you, not to death, but forever!

GALLUB, CARL

[title] "Don't Pity Me" [pers.] I am a tour guide at a petting farm, and when I see the handicapped children in wheel chairs, my heart just breaks up. But when they touch the animals, their eyes light up and they try to smile. This is why I've written this poem—so that people can realize that every one has feelings irregardless of their appearance of handicap.

GALVIN, BRET

[a.] Tampa, FL [title] "A True Gift" [pers.] My inspiration to write poems comes from the deepest depths of my heart, mind, and soul. Introduced by the Holy Spirit, proceeded with a bond and incomprehensible love towards the queen of my heart, my mother. Concluded by the purest Adrenaline rush to become a true Galvin.

GAO, RUOYI

[title] "You and Me" [pers.] "You and Me" expresses the ultimate yearning for a harmonized unification of life and love. I came from an ethnic group in the Southwest of China called Hani. My grandfather was a lyric singer. During the New Year's season, he would pack up straw sandals made by grandmother and ride a horse to start his singing journey from village to village, from mountain to valley. People surrounded him by a campfire, dancing to his songs with the company of gourd flutes and string instruments. By singing the same songs about love and life for generations, we walked down the mountains, out of the jungle, to the urban civilization.

GARNER, JASON

[title] "You Are" [pers.] This poem is written to my fiancee, Sarah, who got me into poetry by showing me Rudyard Kipling's, "If." She said that I reminded her of the man described in this poem, her favorite poems are from Poe and Shakespeare, but I like Emerson very much. I think that he had the most beautiful perspective on life and reality. Anyway, I wrote this poem to her to respond to the "If" poem of how I see her and how she makes me feel.

GAUTNEY, ANGELIA

[title] "Today, I'm Thankful" [pers.] This poem signifies the happiness I feel every time I look at my son, Jacob. I've learned that behavior (attitude), grades, and small imperfections, are all parts of every day life. Overall, I have a perfectly healthy, normal child, and for this, I am very thankful. If we, as parents, would quit trying to perfect our children, we would have more time to see how perfect they already are. This poem is for my, "Perfect Little Handful," Jacob; may he always remember how important he is to me.

GAWLE, URZULA

[a.] Monroe, MI [title] "Today is Mine" [pers.] Thank you much, selection committee, for the certification and privilege of my poem being chosen amongst many to be published in *True Reflections*, as well as the entry into the finals. To the world, my children, John, Stacy, Kyle W., and a very special friend, Mark, who loves me the way I am just as I do you too. I would like to say, don't be afraid to follow your hearts. Always remain, "To thine own self be true." Don't allow fear and pain to rule, causing us to choose the wrong path. Learn to love again, for today could have been the day that life will pass us by.

GELLER, VICTORIA

[title] "Dreams" [pers.] I wrote my poem, "Dreams," for people to realize that love works in all different ways. I see love as a never ending dream, so that's what I wrote. Poetry is an extremely large portion of my life. Whenever something good or bad happens, I take a seat and write. My teachers, especially one, Mr. Buran, encouraged me to write a poem, "Dreams," to send in for a contest. I found out about this contest and entered. He influenced me in many ways, as well as my Grandparents, Mother, Father and Sister.

GERUN, LENORE

[title] "Btchin 2: The Sequel" [pers.] Poetry means everything to me. It's my heart and soul! I have always been told I have special talent; I just hope others feel the same. I use my poetry as an outlet of both good and bad. At the time of this poem, I felt unloved, unwanted, and sad. I had a normal case of teenage depression. By writing out my feelings I get through the hard times.

GIBSON, DONNA

[title] "In the Mind of a Teacher" [pers.] My name is Donna Gibson, and I am a sophomore at Robinson Secondary in Fairfax, VA. The meaning of this poem is that I talk to my teachers and I know they get aggravated a lot. If it weren't for my English teacher, Ms. Alexander, I would not have been able to write this great poem. One reason I wrote this poem is because I love English and I want to be a teacher. Ever since ninth grade I have wanted to be an English teacher because of my great teacher, Frank. Thank you, my teachers, for everything. I love you all.

GILANY, ARIF

[title] "Thoughts of Her" [pers.] I am a Kurdish migrant to Canada. I was born in the Northwest of Iran in the Kurdish high Peaks. My poetry mostly reflects my childhood hopes, dreams, hardships, and disappointments as well as my newfound life in Canada. I have a big family of ten siblings that have scattered on the world map like the autumn leaves. Four of my siblings live back home close to my parents, and the rest of us live in Sweden, Australia, Canada, and Turkey. In Canada, I have gone through a lot of new experiences and learned a great deal. However, my past has always been a big part of my life and often it has interfered with my life in Canada. The poem, "Thoughts of Her," was written when I was going through a hard time in my life. It was inspired when the cultural differences were causing a lot of insecurities in me.

GILBERT, JASON

[title] "Daddy's Lullaby" [pres.] This poem was originally written as a song and sung at the birth of my first son. It was written to express my hopes and dreams for him as he grows through life. Additional verses were added for the birth of my second son. My desire was to write a new song for parents to sing to their children rather than the traditional lullabies, while expressing my heartfelt emotions on becoming a parents. This is one of many songs I've written and one of my personal best over the years of songwriting.

GILBERT, MICHAEL

[a.] Reynoldsburg, Oh, [title] "Karla. . . My Endless Love" [pers.] This poem embraces the realization that the lady who captured the eternal affection of my heart may never be a part of my life except in the confines of my dreams. It is about the purest love a man can have for a woman, spanning twenty-two years of painful silence. My love was and remains so strong for Karla that I maintained my silence to protect her present life. It is only now, twenty-two years later, that I can no longer restrain my love for Karla. Before I journey into the next world, I must profess my undying love for her. Karla is the epitome of a lady, an excellent mother, and a socially conscientious individual. To this date, I have been unable to find a lady who compares to Karla's intellect, sensitivity, spirituality, or class. And although I kept my promise for over twenty years, that I would wait for the day we could reunite forever, I face the dark reality of only meeting her in my dreams to create our own world of perfection, magic, and eternal joy. Pleasant dreams, Karla, my love.

GLASSFORD, DEANNE

[title] "boyz" [pers.] Well, this is my favorite poem that I have written in a long time. It was written for the fact that no matter how much you love a person, you somehow always get hurt. My ex-boyfriend was one of those people who just didn't really care. Somewhere along the line, they're all the same, and that is the reason I named it "boyz." I think that, at one stage, he did love me, but not like I once loved him. He left me in a million pieces, thinking that it was my fault,

but in actual fact it was his. I'm so happy now I found my one true love and I shall never hurt again.

GLEASON, RYAN

[title] "But Where Shall I Go" [pers.] There comes a time when we all need to forget what we know. It makes anything possible, and the unreal becomes real.

GOETZ, MEGIN

[title] "One Last Gift to Mom" [pers.] This poem is part of my loving tribute to my Mother Sharon who passed away in July 2000, after a short, hard fight with cancer. It was written to go along with her last gift from me. I wanted everyone to know how much she touched the lives of her friends and family in her short time on Earth. I hope that by reading this poem, you can feel the love that I feel for her. Because she was not only my mother but my best friend. I hope she knows how much she's missed.

GOFF, JEREMY KYLE

[a.] West Valley, UT [title] "How Would You Describe Me?" [pers.] I am 17 years old. I am a junior in high school. Writing poetry gives me something to keep my mind off other things. It took me years to learn to read and write. I enjoy reading poetry. I enjoy writing poetry. I heard someone say, "life is like a jigsaw puzzle." Some of us are more puzzling than others. In 1998, I was diagnosed with Asperger's Disorder. Writing poetry can help me sort out of my feelings. Sometimes I need help from my family and friends. I express my feelings by writing.

GOFF, KOURTNEY

[title] "Terrified Tears" [pers.] I wrote this poem in memory of my grandpa, Barry Goff. I am thirteen years old and live in Michigan. I like to write poems and short stories, and draw. This poem means a lot to me and my family, because my grandpa was a great man and meant the world to us all.

GOLDEN, ADAM

[a.] Ft. Wayne, IN [title] "If You Could See" [pers.] These words are so fluent to me, because every day I feel that I am judged by my looks rather than my character. I feel that I am not accepted by society because I dare to be myself. I think the people in this world who feel that they must be like everyone else are trying to fill the void of loneliness in their lives. You know who you are. May Locale Machene keep rock alive.

GONZALES, IRENE

[title] "Lost in Your Memory" [pers.] Poetry, my definition: an open expression of heartfelt feelings. Writings has always been a hobby. I've always felt like I had a great deal of emotions waiting to be heard. One day,I put them all together and could not believe how the words just came together. This poem is dedicated to all of us who have loved and lost. In my case, it's easier to put my feelings on paper. Love does come back around—better. For those of you looking—you will be found. I have many poems and hope to share them all.

GONZALEZ, MANUEL I.

[title] "Nine Minutes" [pers.] "Nine Minutes" was written for my wife. The snooze button is important to most anyone. This poem tries to show that perhaps it is important to different people for different reasons. I have been writing poetry since I was sixteen. I hope to make a career writing films and novels but I will never stop writing poems. I am twenty-five years old and was born in East Los Angeles. I will graduate from U. C. L. A. in June 2001 with a degree in American Literature. "And, when you want something, all the universe conspires in helping you achieve it."

GOODWIN, PATRISHA

[a.] Stafford, TX [title] "He's Gone" [pers.] The poem was written as I gazed across the water, thinking about my dwindling relationship with God and the loss of my mother. Real life experiences inspire me to write. With his patience and dedicated love for me, Norman E. Reich, Sr. encourages in the midst of trial and disappointments. He taught me two great things besides how to laugh again: to accomplish great things one must not only act, but also dream, and every cloud does not mean a storm. All my writings I dedicate to God who gave me the talent to write.

GORSUCH, CARMEN B.

[a.] Marshalltown, IA [title] "My China Doll" [pers.] At nineteen I had Lisa, in IL. After graduating she moved to FL. She met my handsome son-in-law. Jogging, those precious words came to me. I believe God wanted to warn me that her marriage wasn't going to be easy. Then the years and two beautiful children later, she knows why God put her there.

GOULD, TIFFANY

[title] "My First Love" [pers.] I am a sixteen-year-old high school student. My hobbies include reading, writing, singing, going on line/internet, and handicrafts. I write poetry, short stories, and songs. In martial arts, I am a yellow belt. I am a positive thinker, sensitive, and caring. I believe life and love surround us continuously, and that to love is to live.

GRANT, JULIOUS

[title] "You're Gone, but Your Memory Lives On" [pers.] I feel that writing poetry is a gift that God gave me. I like writing poems to give to others to brighten their day. I wrote this poem in memory of my best friend, Zack, so I would have something to remember him by. His life was taken much too soon, but because of what he meant to me, I will remember him forever. I hope this poem helps someone to remember others they have lost in a fond and happy way. I'm happy to share my poem with others.

GRAVES, RA

[title] "Composer" [pers.] In words, I can only say this: Ragraves is an adopted pseudonym of Kevin Ray Graves. Here lies a man/boy, twenty five years old, becoming a god—there is contrast, from the first to the last. Light, to deathly night. I praise pen to paper, that I will not elevate myself above ink, but rather rest with night and shine yellow light till the blink of dawn. With a yawn, I rise today. Compose a love song, originally written while alone. She's what I was looking for then and have since found. Now I give this to Ana C.

GREENLAW, THOMAS

[a.] Atlantic Beach, FL [title] "Thanks to You, Lord" [pers.] Poetry for me is my escape from, all the bad that takes place among us! It's a form of meditation for me! Though I may be different, we are all the same deep down! When life isn't going my way, seek out a corner of this world to be alone with my thoughts and writing! For me, well, I'm happy if I can manage to bring a smile across other faces! Look into your watch or a clock—there's no end to time! At night look up to space—there's no end to it either! So be happy and put a smile on a face! Life's too short!

GREGONIS, JOE

[title] "The Chase of Glory" [pers.] It is my opinion that poetry should be viewed as any other art form. One piece can mean one million things to a million people. To define one's own poetry is to define one's own soul. This is the beauty that surrounds one's own work. I wish for my poem to make as large an impact as possible, but no more or less than what is written should be interpreted. One's own perspective will define this and every poem. I don't feel that my writing is a gift, but rather a style that is unmistakable, and therefore interesting. I enter a different mind set when I am writing.

GREGORICH, LISA

[title] "Hidden Angel" [pers.] Poetry, in my life, is a release. A release of the innermost thoughts which remain silent. This poem is a release of the heart, for it belongs solely to my inspiration, my fiancé, whom I lost this past year. For him and others, my writing will go on.

GREGORIO, GARY

[title] "Thirst" [pers] This poem is for my family and friends, both living and dead, and for all who seek a purpose in this complicated life.

GRILL, SUSAN

[title] "The Struggle of an Unknown Disease" [pers.] I struggled through the last ten years trying to find the cause of my severe abdominal pain. I have had so many blood tests, ultra sounds, X-rays, MRI's and CAT scans etc, but I never received an answer to the underlying problem. I have been in unbearable pain for many years, and the more time passes, the less help I seem to get from the doctors and nurses. When they can't cure you, you eventually become invisible to the medical profession. I have tried all methods of pain control—meditation, Eastern medicine—anything I thought might help. I try desperately to keep my faith alive so that there is some hope. Without hope you lose it all. During one of my attempts to relieve some pain and the pressure in my chest and to cling to hope, I wrote these words. I often feel since I have no where else to turn that writing is my only outlet.

GRONE, ASHLEY

[title] "One Night" [pers.] I am a high school senior at Wayne High. This is my first poem I had published. It means a lot to me and it is extra special because the poem is about someone I care dearly for.

GROSS, BARBARA

[title] "Dreams of Light" [pers.] I wanted to write poetry from my heart, and not just how people see life in general. Dreams are important. Without them, people would not have goals to guide them through their long journey of life, and the true meaning of life would never exist.

GROSS, HEATHER

[title] "Silent Disaster" [pers.] I've been writing since as far back as I can remember. It's a way for me to express my inner and worldwide views without stuttering with words. My poems don't always reflect something personal or of great knowledge to me, as my poem "Silent Disaster" speaks of a deaf woman, which I am not. It's tremendous fun for me, and I feel as if the words come out me. It's as if someone else is doing the writing for me. I feel this gift came from my mother, and she is my best critic. Writing is my true love, and shall continue to do it forever.

GROVES, JEFF

[a.] Odessa, MO [title] "Love Never Dies" [pers.] I have been writing songs and poems off and on since 1985. I've had several people say that they liked my writing and even had a friend tell me once that I should send some of my songs to a record company. Being that I didn't know how to go about doing that, I kept writing, hoping one day to be able to record my own music. However, just like most dreams, that kind of came and went. I still wrote songs and poems for several years, basically as a stress reliever and to give myself a sense of accomplishment. Then one day I met this wonderful woman named Tammy and I had a new reason to write. It was called inspiration. This woman inspired some of what I consider to be my best work. It is this woman that this particular poem is about. This poem and the many others that I wrote her were my way of expressing how I felt about her. She sent this poem in to share it with the rest of the world because it meant so much to her.

GRUBAUGH, SALLY

[title] "Left Behind" [pers.] This poem was my first, prompted by the death of a friend this summer. Suicide is so devastating to family and friends with very little written to comfort those left behind. This ironically was the beginning of a discovery that I

could write a poem to capture my thoughts and feelings on paper. More poems have followed, much to the amazement of my family, friends, and especially me. It is obvious this gift was given to me for a reason at this time in my life. Poetry is like finding my own wings to take me on a new journey.

GUERNSEY, CASSANDRA
[a.] Henryville, IN [title] "Pearl of Heaven" [pers.] I am a 14-year-old and I go to Providence High School in Clarksville, IN. I have a fond love for all poetry, especially Edgar Allen Poe. Poe was introduced to me by my third grade teacher Mrs. Thienamen. I have loved it ever since. I have read a little of every type of poem from haikus to 20 verse. But I like the free writing best. My best works are basic nature poems on things I see in my backyard. I also come up with my poems by daydreaming of imaginary characters and places. The best thing I can come up with for a closing is that literature is the best thing that ever happened to me.

GUERRERO, MATTHEW
[a.] Des Moines, IA [title] "Greenbriar Satori" [pers.] I'm 21, and already past my mid-life crises. I've reconnected with my parents, I've forgiven God for all his faults, I've tossed my desperation and possessiveness into the angry Pacific. And now I'm in Iowa which has pretty much triggered a brand new crisis. Oh, well. I was a California kid and will be again one day when the plants align correctly, coming back a conquering king. Until that day, I hold onto my memories. Greenbriar Satori;" is about one burning day in the fall of 1999 when the world whispered its deepest secret in my ear.

GUNDERMAN, THOMAS, JR.
[title] [pers.] I would like to thank my mom and dad who have supported me and my crazy dreams. Special thanks to: My family—Jim, Tricia, Jason, Judy, Larry, and Beth, my friends—Cindy, Jim, Kelli, and Terry; Colonel Dave and my writer's group—Michelle and Jeanine, who have all helped me in some way to write this poem. I must say that this poem reflects what I try follow when I do my soul searching. I hope that when others read it, they will reflect on their lives and find it helpful in their soul searching.

GUNDY, RICHARD
[title] "The Ghost of McBee" [pers.] I have been writing poetry since my senior year in high school. Life—I write about life. The average man on the street, a bird eating, anything I find interesting and can put more life into it—even a graveyard. "McBee" was written on Halloween in 1999. Halloween is a favorite holiday of mine. As a child I went trick-or-treating. When I grew up, I still dressed up but to give treats and, most of all, give life to the day. To create something is to give it life. That's what I do with poetry and writing.

GUTNIK, INNA
[title] "Secrets" [pers.] Sometimes we feel what is forbidden. Sometimes we say what we should not. Sometimes we act out of our nature. And sometimes we live as a matter of fact. What would be considered deviant or unacceptable in a "normal" frame of mind is "Poetry."

HAGAN, VANESSA
[title] [pers.] As a 19 year old college student, in Denver Colorado, I find my writing very inspirational. I love to write and love to express myself through my writing. I plan to write much more through my lifetime!

HAGINS, PRISCILLA
[a.] Simpsonville, SC [title] "A Second Chance" [pers.] Dedicated to my brother, Ernesto Carter, New Bedford, Massachusetts. He had a heart attack on March 11, 1990 and was blessed with "A Second Chance." He is now deceased and sadly missed by everyone, especially his children, Lindsay and Kristen and his wife, Phyllis. I stopped writing after this was written, March 15, 1990. With this first publication, it has given me the inspiration to write again. Love to Rich and daughters, Euleta, Ashley, and Richelle. Matthew 28:20

HAIDSIAK, MELODY
[a.] Des Moines, IA [title] "We Are Here" [pers.] The work that flows through me is of that of that creator. It speaks of healing the hearts and spirits of all mankind—red, yellow, blue, or white. To reach for the seed unseen with hope and faith. No matter how far we have fallen, the angels will guide and protect you. I am a Reiki Master Teacher who channels healing energy to others. Reiki is alternative healing for the spirit, body, mind, and soul. My goal is to reach and teach others. I have been a Law 17 years and a mother of three for 43 years.

HALEY, LISA
[a.] Findlay, Oh, [pers.] True friendship is a precious gift for all of us and one that should not be taken for granted. The love that you feel for a friend should always be something you give openly and share daily. My hope is that my poem will help express what others feel for their friends and give them the inspiration to share those thoughts, through my words. With each poem I write, I hope the words uplift and encourage each of us to treat others and ourselves better.

HALL, GLENDA
[title] "With You" [pers.] I have enjoyed writing poetry since a fifth grade assignment was given to write a poem. Everyone read their poem aloud, and I was the only one to receive a delightful response. I then realized I could express my feelings through poetry. The poem in this book was inspired by a special man that came into my life at a time when I couldn't find my way. He was my light. As God's rainbow in the sky, he was my promise of a new life.

HAMILTON, CAROL
[title] "September 19th" [pers.] After a decade of battling multiple sclerosis, Bob has gone home. He passed away on Tuesday September 19, 2000, at his residence. A loyal friend, loving son, brother, father, husband, and warm-hearted buddy who brought light to the dark, Bob clung to life and lived everyday like it was his last. He is survived by his wife and best friend, Carol and his children Amanda, Bobby, Ben, and Dewey. When someone you love dies, they live in your memories. Those memories become your treasures. Heaven has a new angel.

HAMILTON, DAWN
[a.] Hempstead, NY [title] "Sickness" [pers.] I was never a child that expressed my feelings, so while attending Independence City All Age in Jamaica, W. I., I found myself writing down the pain that I was feeling in a journal my mom gave to me; it became my freedom. Writing sustains me through difficult times.

HAMILTON, DAWN
[a.] Hempstead, NY [title] "Sickness" [pers.] I was never a child that expressed my feelings, so while attending Independence City, All age in Jamaica W.I., I found myself writing down the pain that I was feeling in a journal my mom gave to me; it became my freedom. Writing sustains me through difficult times. I thank God every day, for giving me a voice through my writing and allowing me to make a difference to someone along the way. I want to let others know that with faith and strong persistence, you won't lose your self-esteem but will build confidence within yourself. I have built my life on the philosophy that my corners of the world would not be the same just because I have passed this way, so in my journey I have decided to touch as many lives as possible and through my writing, I can touch more lives than I could through talking. I would like to let others know to believe in themselves—their goals and their dreams, because you become what you believe.

HAMM, MARIE
[a.] Simi-Valley, CA [title] "The Power Within" [pers.] My name is Marie Hamm. I am eleven years old. Poetry has been an interest of mine for about a year. Ever since my best friend Victoria and I started, it has been so interesting, the words you can put together make you want to just blurt anything that relates, and inspiring to yourself and others. I wouldn't have ever entered a poetry contest if it weren't for my Aunt Lisa. I also couldn't have done it without my Mom and my Dad's love. I give a special thanks to Victoria for all your strength and believing in me. Thank you and I love you lots. This is my greatest accomplishment, and I will cherish every moment of it.

HANEY, STEVEN
[title] "The Web" [pers.] I am one of few romanticists left. All I hold dear is my unique ability to see past the physical into the artistic.

HANSEN, KARA
[title] "The Crazy Ones" [pers.] Unfortunately my adolescence has not been an easy or enjoyable experience. I struggle daily with constant urges to cut myself and commit suicide. I have recently been diagnosed with Bipolar Disorder but I am stable with therapy and medication. Writing poetry has been one of the best outlets throughout these hard times. I am very fortunate to have this talent within me. I find it breathtaking how these amazing words can emerge from such an aching heart.

HANSON, TAMARA
[title] "Dreams of Hope [pers.] I have been writing poems and stories since I was a child. I'm home again in Arkansas, but at the time I wrote this I was living in Lynden, WA. My husband is from there. My uncle Gerald had just died, and my grandmom, Clara, was on her deathbed. I was already homesick, and it was too far away to just drive back. I love to sit for hours outside and just enjoy my surroundings. My poems just come to me in a thought or inspiration. "Dreams of Home" is for my uncle, grandmom, Mom, grandmom, Hogan—I love you.

HAQUE, MOHAMMAD
[a.] Chichiri, Blantyre Malawi [title] "Soul of Colors" [pers.] To me, poetry is like an interface with myself. It's always this harmonious closeness between inspiration and my soul that sparks off my poems. My poetry is usually about unique personal viewpoints and intense emotions. I simply write because I feel. I am lovingly observant towards nature and my love for visual qualities and imagery leads me to believe that nature and life speak through colors. Besides, the intense meaningful beauty in nature can be reflected in A feminine sense. In fact natural beauty is like a feminine thought. I wish to spread that colorful inspiration into every reader's soul.

HARGROVE, JOAN
[title] "Another Day" [pers.] I like expressing how I feel in the form of a poem. I have Multiple Sclerosis. I can be thankful for another day because of my husband, mother, sister, daughter, friends, and family. There really are nice people out there, and I am thankful for each and every one that helps me with another day.

GRATE, ALICE
[a.] Lamar, SC [pers.] My name is Alice Grate. This poem was submitted on my behalf by my Aunt Mamie Harkless since I do not own a computer nor am I financially able to afford Internet Access. It evolved out of my experiences growing up in a single parent home in the ghetto of Newark, New Jersey. I have been and continue to be a victim of poverty. The devastating hardships I have suffered in life, brain surgery, and a loss of my ability to work led to many hours of writing poetry.

HARRIS, JULIA

[a.] Knox, TN [title] "Homeless No More" [pers.] I would like to dedicate this poem to my late father who always told us as children, never turn your back on someone that is cold and hungry. You never know, it may be Jesus Christ himself. I thank my Daddy for all the lessons in my life that he taught me. So Daddy, I honor you with, "Homeless No More."

HARRIS, KATHLEEN

[a.] "Luminous Beverage" [pers.] Poetry is the reflection of spirit as expressed by the soul. The language of life that is lived to the fullest, the bitter and sweet, the truth and the victory, and the pain as we grow. For me, it is the reflection of the love I live, in joy and in honor of all that have touched me deeply. It is my gift to elucidate and to share in wonder, and in appreciation for the wealth I have received.

HARRIS, NORMA

[a.] Hyden, KY [title] "Time" [pers.] Poetry is my way of sorting out the situations of life. It gives meaning to the thoughts in our minds and the feelings in our hearts. "Time" is in remembrance of my brother, David, and my dad, William Harris.

HARRIS, REBECCA

[title] "Forgiveness" [pers.] The autumn of my life envelops a wide array of emotions, questions, and dreams. When I ventured into unknown waters in pursuit of myself, he waited, firmly planted on the shore. This poem expresses my love and respect for the man I'm blessed to call my husband.

HARRISON, ALPHA

[title] "Time Is My Enemy" [pers.] "Time Is My Enemy" is a story of my own life and is dedicated to my loving husband, Billy Ray. I was born and raised in the Philippines, and love brought me to the U.S.A. in 1998. I graduated as an Academic Excellence Awardee with a degree, Bachelor of Science, in Elementary Education (BSEED) and taught in the Philippines Public School for five years. Currently, I am working as a certified nurse assistance (CNA). I love travelling with my husband. We do things together most of the time. I enjoy gardening, growing flowers, listening to music, and playing the piano.

HARRISON, DEANNA

[a.] Elsberry, MO [title] "Your Love" [pers.] I'm from Elsberry, Missouri. I'm a student at Elsberry RII High School. I enjoy writing, acting, and playing sports for fun. This poem is important to me because I wrote it about my boyfriend. Poetry means a lot to me because it's fun, easy, and it's a way for me to express myself without speaking. Poetry is a gift that I got from my mother.

HARRISON, VONNA

[title] "God's Armor" [pers.] My children, Colton, Arielle, and Mariah, are my greatest gifts from Heaven. They are my heart and inspiration! My love for them, my family, and friends truly moves me to write special thoughts and feelings from the depths of my soul. God has blessed me with this precious gift to share. This poem is my tribute to those I have loved and lost in this life, my Grandpa Riley Harrison, my dear friend, Dreama, My Rottweiler, Sierra and all who have touched my heart and left a lasting impression. I know they are up in Heaven wearing God's Armor.

HART, TANYA

[pen.] Tanya Hart; [b.] 11 July 1975; Napier, NZ; [p.] Carolyn Hart, Ray Hart; [ch.] Joshua Lewis Fraser; [oth. writ.] Poems, children's stories, songs (not yet published); [pers.] My writing is inspired by life, love, and an active imagination. I deeply admire the writing of Jewel Kilcher and Nick Cave—their music hits the right note.

HARTMARK, BEVERLY

[a.] Phoenix, AZ [title] "The Light Beneath the Door" [pers.] Throughout my childhood, my father quoted poetry to me such as, "Flanders Fields," a reflection of his service in the army in WWII. Now I'm a soldier, fighting the battle of Multiple Sclerosis. Thanks, Dad, for planting the seeds of inspiration that will bloom with expression for a lifetime. Through faith in my Heavenly Father by His sons's eternal atonement for me, I've been given the strength and courage to seek the light beneath every door.

HARTZLER, GLADIENNE

[a.] Austin, TX [title] "Reflections"

HASBROOK, DEBRA

[title] "I Have Always Loved You" [pers.] This poem is dedicated to my three children, Jason, Nathan, Caylee, and Sarah for keeping me young at heart, and for the love and happiness they give to me; To my late mother, Ethel F. Hasbrook-Baker for always believing in me, and the encouragement she always gave me to follow my dreams, and to Philip Ryan Marschke for giving me all of his love unselfishly, completely, and with sincere loyalty. Who has stood by me through good times and bad, and with patience, loved me all the more. And most of all to God for giving me the talents that I do have, and the ability to share those talents with all of you. God bless you all!

HASEGAWA, YUSUKE

[title] "If You Disappear" [pers.] This poem is for the person I secretly admire. She's been in my life for so long, but I cannot push myself enough to say anything to her. I know she won't be around forever so I need to say something before it's too late. But what if she doesn't like me? The one question I'm dying for to be answered. I want answers but am too scared to ask. Poetry was the way I found that I could express this some way, but not all out, to her.

HASS, BARBARA

[a.] Pine Hill, NY [title] "Look Inside" [pers.] "Look Inside" is a poem inspired by a much greater source than my personal intellect. May its readers experience confirmation of inner strength. I look forward to ongoing opportunities to share my poems and songs as my life's devotion has become helping others shine their positive light.

HASTINGS, BETTY

[title] "To a Gone Friend" [pers.] Betty Violigal Hastings is a Brazilian writer, with reverse books published in Brazil and in Portugal. She is also an Arts teacher and writes in literary magazines.

HASTINGS, CHARLES, JR.

[title] "Show Me" [pers.] My best works seem to emerge almost spontaneously, as though the words and the emotions behind them are one and could be expressed no other way. In a few minutes, what must be said takes perfect shape, with little effort on my part and without that gnawing need to forever change it. And so it was in those few moments when "Show Me" came to be. Although the meaning brought true clarity, it felt more like a lump in my throat. The truth is that true love cannot be said, it can only be demonstrated.

HASTINGS, DOUGLAS

[title] "Feelings and Wisdom" [pers.] I wrote this poem on the eighth of June, 1991. I was planting trees in Northern British Columbia, Canada. There is nothing like spending time in the outdoors to get creative juices flowing. The written word has a certain magic, and poetry even more so. I am currently living in Kelowna, BC. I spend as much of my free time as I can enjoying the outdoors in the form of hiking, running, and rock climbing, as well as a myriad of other activities. Philosophically, I see that the world has balance. Sometimes the secrets are revealed in the quiet stillness.

HATCH, KAREN

[title] "Myself/My God" [pers.] This poem, I feel, describes me as a person that shares herself with God in a special way, as a special friend to myself and The Deep Beliefs within; about the beauty of everything around me, I enjoy my life and the nature of it. I thank God for it all.

HATCHETT, TAUNYA

[title] "Butterfly" [pers.] "Butterfly" was inspired by a romantic desire. A friend with whom I am very romantically attracted to always said, if I just stood still, the butterfly would come to me. After dating for several months, my impatience got the best of me. In an attempt not to be too forward, I masked my question through the "Butterfly" poem. The butterfly actually landed. I live in Chesapeake, VA, presently and I am a native of Mississippi. Forty-year-old mother of three children. I love music, the mountains, and the ocean.

HATTON, CHARLENE

[a.] Bangor, PA [title] "Divinity and Me" [pers.] "Divinity and Me" is a daily creed by which I do my best to abide. Life's journeying brings with it both adversities and joys. Lessons gathered from each have been the inspiration for my writing poetry. Being able to communicate, through poetic form, what the divine has placed in my heart is a true blessing. We all have our gifts that need sharing as a part of the divine plan which resides within us all, our own special love story.

HATTON, JEWLEA

[title] "Spoken Words" [pers.] I am an eighth grader at Lovington Junior High. I am in chorus, volleyball, and soft ball. I wrote this poem because I feel that the world puts "names" on certain people or races and when they do, it hurts the person being teased. I expressed in my poem how I think it feels to be a victim of this. I hope my poem makes an impression on some of these people who do this. Maybe, they will stop. I hope so.

HAURE, MARK

[a.] Berwyn, IL [title] "The Storms of Life" [pers.] I thank God Almighty for gracing me with my poetic and literary gift. This poem was written for my late grandmother, Mary, my mother, Marlene, my father, Warren, and my ex-wife, Linda, all of whom have shown tremendous endurance, patience, and courage to pick themselves up, dust themselves off, and start all over again. They have not let adversity stand in the way of what needed to be accomplished. My words also contain a message for my three beautiful children, my daughter, Dana, and my two sons, Michael and John. With God in our lives, all things are possible.

HAWLEY, AMANDA

[a.] Menomonee Falls, WI [title] "Heartbroken" [pers.] Amanda D. Hawley is 14 and has been writing poetry since she was six. Poetry.com has published a few of her poems. "Heartbroken" is one of her mother's favorites. The faculty at her school, even the ones that don't teach English, have commented on her literary works.

HAZELWOOD, JOAN

[a.] Henderson, NV [title] "The Day the World Cried" [pers.] I tearfully composed "The Day the World Cried" on January 16, 1991, the day the world watched the news coverage of the bombings in Iraq unfold . . . "Operation Desert Storm." My twin sister, Jean, inspired me write, more than 34 years ago, after she wrote poems as a tribute to our children, Dawn and Tom. I am now "Memory Maker" to our "Angels," (grandchildren), Sebastian, Alexis, and Briana. If I succeed in teaching them love for family and the human race, compassion, humility, a sense of humor about life, happy or sad, I will have spent God's gift wisely.

HEGDE, ANITA

[title] "Dream" [pers.] Anita Hegde, Ph.D, born 20th March 1971, Karnataka, India. Post-doctoral fellow in Indian Institute of Science, Bangalore, India. A poem is a way of expressing one's very own "self,"

deep emotions, and thoughts, which often go unnoticed and unsaid fall into words and make great impact. Poetry for me is one such way of expressing my views/feelings/emotions/experiences about a particular event/situation of life. Being a student of Science and surrounded by the modern scientific thoughts often leads me to "Nature." It is there that my ideas start flowing into raptures of a poetic river, and I pen down few lines!

HEISDORFFER, STEPHANIE
[title] "Mommy, I Miss You" [pers.] This poem must be a favorite, even though it was written towards the beginning of my writing career. My mother died when I was eight. I was severely overcome with grief for many years. In seventh grade I wrote the poem, "Mommy, I Miss You." This was written for the most wonderful, caring person I ever met, my mother. I hope this not only helps those who knew her cope with her death, but also anyone else who had to suffer through the loss of a loved one.

HENDERSON, BETTIE ANN
[title] "Stone to the Bone" [pers.] Poetry is a means of expressing my true inner feelings. This particular poem is a gift to me from the Holy Spirit to ease my pain. I dedicate this special poem to my Daddy, Eugene Siler, my son, Juan, my grandson, Julius, my daughter Denise and son, Bryant Henderson. I attended Southwestern Louisiana University in Lafayette, Louisiana. I was "Tutor" at Woodrow Wildon High School in San Francisco, California. My hobbies are writing, painting, and reading. I pray to God that my poem will inspire someone to improve his or her life and to stay sober!

HENDRICKSON, TIM
[title] "This Love" [pers.] I've only been writing poetry for a short time but have found it to be the best way to express my innermost feelings. My poem "This Love," in particular, expresses my opinion that everything is constantly changing, even people. I believe love can last forever, but only if you adapt to those changes to continue to satisfy your partner's needs.

HENDRIX, CARA
[title] "My Aunt" [pers.] My aunt, Valerie, is a very important person in my life. She has had M. S. for years and has to give herself a shot every day in a different place on her body. I hate shots so I feel bad when I have to watch her do it. When I heard of this website, Poetry.com, I felt it would be no greater honor than to publish a poem for her. I love you very much, Valerie, and I hope for a cure. I only can hope for a cure. I only can hope that other people have the same opinion as me. Thank you very much, and I hope that anyone who reads this poem feels the same way I do.

HENLEY, MARILYN
[a.] West Point, MS [title] "Little Girl" [pers.] This poem was written about my daughter, Brandy. She was the third and last child at home. She was about to graduate from high school, and as I was sitting on the sofa in my family room, thinking of what her life had meant to me and embracing the feelings of letting go, with pen in hand, I put my special feelings of her in words.

HERRICK, JUNE
[a.] Beech Grove, IN [title] "Grandson" [pers.] This poem is of my first born grandchild, a grandson, being the son of my son, named (K-C). Whenever I could get him, I sang him to sleep at night when he was with me. He was six years old when I got another grandchild, a granddaughter, his cousin. He lived with me for about a year at age 19, which inspired this poem. He is now married and is the father of my two great-granddaughters. My love keeps growing for them all.

HES, CHRISTOPHER
[title] "Light in the Night" [pers.] When I had first received Drew, my dog, we would walk around the school just before sunset. On some nights, I would sit on the bleachers, with Drew sniffing around, and look up at the moon. Each night that passed, I came up with part of the poem, "Light in the Night." I would change it just a little each night until I submitted it to Poetry.com. Since then I haven't changed it at all but I still look up at the moon.

HEYDEN, TERESA
[title] "Lingering Passion" [pers.] Poetry for me is an expression of my innermost feeling and visions. Most poetry I write comes from experience that has deeply touched my soul. Lingering passion is my expression of a man I met and thought I would never see again. Over the course of that following year, my life/my self went through a total transformation; he enabled my light to shine again. To him, he has no idea how his presence changed my life. To him . . . much love.

HIMES, JULIE
[a.] Lugoff, SC [title] "Night Calls" [pers.] In creating this poem, I realize what simple pleasure there is in the quiet of night. The peace and harmony of nature is a wonderful blessing all humans can learn from. May all who read it be inspired to live a peaceful, content life.

HINES, DEB
[a.] Neligh, NE [title] "A Little Wisdom" [pers.] Through the trials and tribulations we all experience in life, this poem is to remind us not to focus on what we have not but to appreciate even the smallest of blessings we have. If this poem gives hope or meaning to the reader, then God has fulfilled one of my dreams. We are all blessed, if we can only see. I wish to thank my family for all the support they have given me. Thanks be always to God.

HINKELDEY, LAURA
[title] "Letters" [pers.] Laura's poems often portray the essence of life's journey . . . a passage through the trials and triumphs, sadness and joy, fears and courage that are encountered throughout life. With compassion and keen insight, she illustrates these emotions by reaching out from her soul to gently touch her reader's heart. Laura lives with her family in Tabernacle, NJ, and is currently pursuing a degree in Psychology.

HIRST, LYN
[title] "A Time for Spring" [pers.] Door County, WI is a small peninsula jutting into Lake Michigan with Green Bay on one side, the Lake on the other. There are high rock cliffs on one side and great expanses of sand beaches opposite. I am a retired teacher and a voracious reader. I feel so privileged to have retired here. Every season inspires me. Rural roads, birch and pine forests, maples make unbelievable fall colors followed by trees and pristine snow; spring brings in a Daffodil Festival and summer flowers are incredible. How could I not write?

HIRT, MICHELLE
[title] "Just Me" [pers.] This poem is dedicated to my late father, John Di Alto. He suffered from a devastating disease, Alzheimer's. He also suffered from ignorance and intolerance from the medical community. I also dedicated this poem to my mother, Antoinette Di Alto. Although her speech has limitations from a stroke, she has so much to say. We need to treat everyone with respect and dignity, everyone.

HODGES, CORTNEY
[title]"The Day You Were Born" [pers.] This poem was written as an exercise to use my imagination. Having no children of my own, writing about motherhood certainly utilized my creativity. I saw a young pregnant woman and wandered what she would tell her unborn child when, years later, the little one asked about that unforgettable day. "The Day You Were Born" was the product of that image. I recently graduated from Virginia Tech. with a degree in English. At 22, I am seeking a career as an editor, but I will always remain a poet.

HOFFERT, MARCEY
[title] "My Best Friend" [pers.] This poem came to me as I was sitting alone in my home. For whenever I think I am alone in this world, a thought pops into my head, and right away I feel his presence. I know I am never alone; I believe Jesus is my best friend. I wanted others to know that Jesus is there for them. That he is their best friend, too, they are never alone. They just have to believe.

HOGSHOOTER, TERESA
[a.] Crocker, MO [title] "The Real Me" [pers.] My love for poetry just come to me as a natural obsession. I first discovered it through Edgar Allen Poe, who has been my favorite poet since the eighth grade. Not too long after my discovery of his poems, I decided I would start writing them myself. My poem, "The Real Me," is the most significant of all because it expresses all the beautiful people in the world that society sees as monsters. I feel there is good in everyone. Sometimes you have to understand their heart before you can see past their mask. My poetry expresses my life.m

HOGUE, CHESLEY
[title] "For Jesus I Would" [pers.] I wrote this poem to express my serious commitment to Jesus, that I made six years ago. I vowed to live a holy life that pleases God, no matter what the cost. I may not be perfect, as no one is, but I am sincere. I am excited about the opportunity I have to share my deepest convictions with the world.

HOLDER, VIVIAN
[a.] West Helena, AR [title] "Painless Love" [pers.] This poem is dedicated to my mother C. L. Holder, my children Ashley Nicole and Derand Devon. To my sisters and brothers that helped me through the heartaches and pains of growing up. Also to my Sorority sisters of Delta Sigma Theta, knowing that if we acknowledge God first in all that we do, we can make a difference in life's pains.

HOLDREN, ALEX
[title] "Equilibrium" [pers.] In our lives, we all have dark nights and bright days. Sometimes true character is revealed more during the dark nights. So we must always be thankful, because somebody, somewhere, has it worse off than you. Life is a game of give and take. But you must be careful what you give and what you take. Because it all comes back to you in the end. I love my niece, Samantha, (and the rest of my family too).

HOLLAND, DAVID
[title] "Ragamuffin Worship" [pers.] Ragamuffin and grace are two words that I've fallen in love with since coming to Christ. This poem was written at time when some people in my church had slammed others for the way they worshipped. How dare they think one form was more acceptable to God than others? The beauty of grace is that God loves the worship of his people, no matter how loud and charismatic it is, or reserved and calm. The key to worship is to remember that God wants us intensely. He by no means need us. Ragamuffin worship is sincere gratitude.

HOLLIDAY, LAMONT
[a.] Valley Stream, NY [title] "Life" [pers.] My inspiration for writing "Life" came immediately after reading Montel's "Cure for Multiple Sclerosis" Poetry contest announcement. The last time I picked up the pen to write a poem that was published, was in the year 1979, while attending Suffolk Community College. During my life, I have taken care of patients with Multiple Sclerosis. Life is very complex and it takes a deeper understanding and wisdom to fully comprehend people, life, success, and especially illness and disease. My hope is that "Life" will

offer a spiritual understanding of true happiness, health, and success.

HOLLINS, CHRISTOPHER

[title] "Wondering" [a.] Cleveland, Oh, [pers.] My poetry is inspired by events taking place in my life, both the good and the bad. It helps me express my feelings and cope with the emotional changes taking place. My recent poetry is dedicated to the love of my life, my wife, Rebecca Ann. Her support and love have shown me that I can be more than I ever thought possible.

HOLLIS, CHRISTOPHER

[title] "Snowball" [pers.] I wrote this poem as an assignment for English class. I'm only a senior in high school and I never expected to get my poem published. I guess that proves that almost anyone could get their poem published. I wrote about something I knew, which was my dog, Snowball. It was fun to write this poem about him. I love to write poetry. Sometimes I just write down a few lines throughout the day, and later form them into poems. I hope you enjoy this poem as much as I do. Maybe I'll write a sequel!

HOOKER, KIM

[a.] Chicago, IL [title] "Downpour" [pers.] There isn't a story or special meaning behind this poem, only a message to anyone who has ever felt like life was at its worst. This poem is meant to inspire in people with perseverance and determination to get through life's struggles and find their "rainbow." Yes, at times, life may seem unendurable but like I say in the poem, "Every storm must come to an end." I feel honored and privileged to be able to share my poem and message with anyone who reads this book.

HOPKINS, JOEL

[title] "A Dream" [pers.] Poetry is a major part of my life. I write all the time. I love to write. I am going to college in the summer. I have a sister that is a sophomore named Stacey. I wrote this poem when I was a freshman, and it explains how I was viewing my future.

HORWATH, TRAVIS

[title] "Lizard Love" [pers.] I am 13 years old and I wrote this poem when I was 12. I like to write poems about my pets. I also like to rhyme words. Poetry is not my only hobby. I play basketball, baseball, soccer, and I wrestle. I have a black belt in Tae-Kwon-Do. I play the saxophone also. I have also written poems about my bird, "Ode to Desdemona."

HOWARD, WENDY

[a.] Pierre, SD [title] "And" [pers.] "And" the story behind this poem speaks in deafening volumes to these who open their hearts enough to understand. It stands for those who have "loved" and been let down, to those who have given all they could in a relationship and then have been "tossed to the side." It goes out to those of us who feel like there is no one meant for us in the world, and a special person that we thought was "the one" could be someone completely different. Finally it's about the pain of heartbreak in life that we can never seem to forget.

HOWETH, TRENTON

[a.] Newcaster, OK [title] "Tears of the Forgotten" [pers.] Throughout my life I have heard of children who are mistreated and alone. Although I have never experienced this, I know people who have. This poem is a tribute to them and a way to offer hope for the future. Because I believe that if you hold on tightly, hope will always be there, no matter the situation.

HRYCENKO, JUDITH

[title] "Upon a Step at Night I Stood" [pers.] Returning home one Christmas Eve, I walked up the steps to my front door and turned to see the soft, light snowflakes heavily falling under a streetlight across the street. I inhaled the crisp air on that most important, silent night and felt my eyes becoming moist. At that precise moment, my entire being was totally immersed in that wonderfully peaceful experience called, "The Christmas Spirit." When I awoke the following morning, my room was angel bright. Such a perfect Christmas day!

HUDGINS, KIMBERLY

[title] "Dear Mother" [pers.] This poem is dedicated to my mother, she always made sure she was there. I'm from McKenzie, TN. I'm married to Matt Hudgins, and we have a little boy named Andrew. I started writing poems at the age of 17. They were a series of words to show how I felt. Each of my poems reflects some part of my life. This was a gift for Mother's Day. I know it is hard to tell the way you feel, so just write it down. I thank you and hope you enjoyed the poem.

HUGHES, MARQUITA

[title] "My Reflection in the Rain" [pers.] A domicile of West Helena, Arkansas, I'm an African-American female, born December 24, 1983. I'm an aspiring lyricist, poet, musician, song writer, and singer of most genres with other various potentials. I've always had strong ambitions to pursue careers in different fields of the entertainment business. Computers, reading, writing, singing, rapping, and playing the piano are a dominance of my time. A lot of aspects of my life deal with writing, and poetry is one of them. To me, poetry is a written portrait of life! It reveals the good and the bad.

HUMES, KRISTIN

[title] "Daddy's Gone" [pers.] This poem, "Daddy's Gone," is one that is very meaningful to me. I wrote this poem two days after my father lost his battle to cancer. My father was the most influential person in my life. My father had the strength and spirit to fight his cancer for two years. He taught me the true meaning of love and trust. This poem is seen through his eyes. "Daddy's Gone" is my father's farewell to everyone who has loved him. He will never be forgotten—he is my daddy.

HUMPHRIES, ADEA

[title] "Rejoice This Day" [pers.] After my son was born, I realized how much of life I had forgotten. I had forgotten how much fun it is to spin in circles until you feel dizzy. I had forgotten how neat it is to watch ants build their homes or to watch birds feed their young or to chase squirrels on sunny days. I forgot how to make pictures in the clouds and I forgot how wonderful the sunlight feels on your face when you're lying in the grass. I forgot how much it is to eat an ice cream or jump in rain puddles. I owe my life now to my son, Evan Humphries, who has helped me to stop and see the beauty of what God created. "This is the day the Lord has made; let us rejoice and be glad in it."

HUNTER, ALICIA

[a.] San Diego, CA [title] "Keep Your Head Up, Brother" [pers.] I was born in Cleveland, Ohio. I hold this poem dear to my heart, because people are precious, and these men and women need to know that people do love them. This poem is for my brothers, Calvin, Chris, and Curtis Carter. I love you very much.

HUNTER, GAYLE

[title] "Our Yard" [pers.] I think poetry is a nice way of expressing oneself. I like to write a poem when I give a special gift, or to a special person. My poems usually relate to that gift or that person, but I also write about my surroundings, such as "Our Yard." I write for the pleasure it brings, to myself, but especially to my family. I live in the country where I love to work in my yard and flower gardens. I enjoy working where I can see and hear nature all around me. I like the quiet, peacefulness, and privacy of country living.

INMAN, TORIE

[title] "Drunk Driver" [pers.] This poem is very special to me because I had two friends killed by a drunk driver in two separate accidents. I was trying to put myself in the parents' position, but I guess no one can really do that until it happens to them. I just hope this will bring some comfort to the parents of these children. I am a certified Nursing Assistant and live in a small town in Virginia.

JACKSON, CAROL

[a.] Detroit, MI [title] "Untitled" [pers.] My journey, started in Salford Lances, England, 1944, on October 23, where I was born the second eldest of fourteen children. This American soldier had met this British woman, Doris Sullivan, in 1943, and they were shortly married later, in the war torn country. In 1946, I was seriously burned in a fire in our home, which later, assisted my parents in coming to the United States of America. We came here in 1949 on the U.S.S. Washington and docked in New York City, coming eventually to Detroit, Michigan. I went to school here and graduated from Central High School where at an early age I developed a love for reading and desire for a creative imagination. This later came in the form of writing, and poetry was a love of mine. I married Charles E. Jackson, in September, 1974; he was a very unique individual, who later encouraged me and understood my love for life and the zeal for writing and creativeness. I currently work for Henry Ford Hospital, working on the Oncology unit, which has taught me a great deal about compassion and dealing with cancer.

JACKSON, MICHAEL

[a.] Sumter, SC [title] "Mother" [pers.] The poem is a dedication of a poet to present and future mothers. No one gives as much of one's self as a mother, as I know from the impact both my grandmother, the late Jarnie Sanders, and my mom, Mrs. Marie Jackson, have had on my life. Mrs. George Bradham showed me that she didn't have to give birth to me to love me just as much. With that kind of love, I am rich beyond riches and to God, thank you.

JANECKY, CLAY

[a.] Newport Richey, FL [title] "Thoughts From The Road" [pers.] Poetry should enlighten and enrich. If it does this, it will expand the horizons of its audience.

JEANNOT, JENNY

[title] "Autumn's Angel" [pers.] When I am going through hardships and obstacles, I turn to words to release all the emotions from my heart. To me, this poem is a homage to all the people that have made a positive impact in my life. Some came and some left. When things go wrong, they take me under their wings to dismiss all fears. I want all people on this world to know that we all have beautiful angels in our lives.

JEFFRIES, KAY

[a.] Knoxville, TN [title] "Recipe for a Mother's Love" [pers.] Recipe for a mother's love was inspired by my mother, who sacrificed so much and had so much love for all of her children. Thank you, Mother. I love you. Mother, Betty O'Dell, daughter Regina Jeffries, sisters, Terry, Tammy, Sandy, Fiance, Carl Smith.

JENKINS, SHELAHNA

[title] "Storm of Purpose" [pers.] This poem was written for somebody that got lost along the way, and about the long trip home. I can relate to both sides at some point in my life, and hope to relay my belief, "everything happens for a reason," should we understand it, or not, and people you care about most are taken from you too soon. I thank my mother, for reminding me to not only make a living, but to make a life! I finally see the road to happiness isn't always a paved one, thus, something worth having is worth fighting and waiting for.

JENKINSON, BRENT

[a.] Oshawa, ON [title] "Pogo Love" [pers.] Hi, I'm just a man, a renovator who never thought to write poetry till I met Mary whom I hold dear, unfortunately, she did not live near. So I started to write verses to express the feelings in my chest, to let her know she was the best. Mary encourages me to write every day. I'm glad she did, 'cause it gets easier to say whatever I want in any way. Everyone needs a Mary in their life; although we've never met, one day she will be my wife. A little about me? I don't know what to say, except I wish that everyone will be as happy as me hopefully one day.

JENSEN, ALLISON

[title] "What Beginning?" [pers.] My name is Allison Jensen. I live in Thorold, Ontario. There really is no story to this poem. I just wrote it one day. I enjoy writing poetry; it helps me express my emotions and feelings if I've had a bad day. I am enrolled in Thorold High, grade eleven. My hobbies include hangin' with the T.S.'ers (my boys), listening to music, TV, and just chillin'. I would like to tell anyone and everyone not to despair. Shoot for a goal, and you can make it. Don't let anyone tell you, you can't do it! Thanks to Poetry.com for this, and thanks for everyone for believing. (You know who you are and what I mean.)

JERVAY, SANDRA

[a.] Philadelphia, PA [title] "Day Dreaming" [pers.] I would like to attribute this poem to my son Tereen (Tony) Hart, 2/76-9/13, and to Rev. Wanda Henry Jenkins for being that catalyst in my life, by encouraging me to put my feelings on paper. To all my family and friends who supported me, I give thanks. God has furnished me with a gift, neither to asphyxiate nor to be suppressed, but to unveil and to be shared with others. For without God and some exceptional people, this talent may have never been revealed.

JETTON, TAMMRA

[title] "Louder than Words" [pers.] I find that poetry, for me, is a way to release emotions that otherwise would be left unsaid. It is a light into the heart of a person's soul. I hope you enjoy my light.

JOHNSON, BOBBI

[a.] Allenspark, CO [title] "The Warmth of the Season" [pers.] I live in the mountains, as close to the sky as I can get. I am 29 years old, with two sons, Wyatt and Garrett. I have a wonderful husband, named Tim, and I love to find the beauty in everyone I meet. Thank you for your kindness.

JOHNSON, BRENDA

[title] "Welcome the Joy" [pers.] This poem is very special to me, being the very first poem I have ever written. I am also very proud of it. I truly believe that this poem was a direct gift from the Lord. During a down season in my life, God reminded me of the true reason for joy and how to obtain it. In the thirty minutes it took me to write this poem, my downcast mood was changed to joy overflowing. My prayer is for the same reaction by those who read this poem. I also pray to be able to write more poems, giving God the glory.

JOHNSON, CHARLES

[title] "My Angel" [pers.] This poem is about a young girl I sat next to in French class. She was "My Angel," but I was too afraid to talk to her. It took ten years and the marines corps to give me the confidence to talk to her. I'm glad I did, she's still my angel, we've been together for a few months now. I guess what this poem is saying is that, I love you, Rachel.

JOHNSON, DAVID

[a.] Detroit, MI [title] "Light at the Edge of the World" [pers.] Poetry to me is an art of self-expression about the problems going on around one's society. I attended Wayne State University in Detroit, Michigan. I minored in film and music. My main goal is to get my book, entitled, "The Destiny of the White Steed," published. It is a collection of poems and song lyrics that tell, in story form, how film and music are related to poetry. My hobbies include collecting videos and music.

JOHNSON, FRANCES

[title] "Smokey Robinson: The Storyteller" [pers.] I am a Chicago native. I started writing poetry when I was seven years old. *A Child's Garden of Verses*, by Robert Louis Stevenson was included in a Christmas box, my family received. I read this poem and started to write my own poetry. I have been writing ever since. I am a self-taught poet. I write poetry as a hobby. It has helped me to get through difficult situations. When I write poetry, it can help me to put my life into perspective. Poetry is the "Wind beneath My Wings." No matter how difficult my life is, poetry can help me get through it. I thank God for this gift.

JOHNSON, JASON

[a.] Keerville, TX [title] "Free Will" [pers.] How many times have we known the right thing to do but have done the opposite? How many children must die before we stop parading ourselves in ignorant pride, and instead, humble ourselves? Why must we choose destruction when peace invites us all? He is calling. Will you answer?

JOHNSON, LANCE

[title] "You" [pers.] I was a sergeant in the Marine Corps, deployed to Okinawa, from Wakuni, Japan. During some down time, I wrote this poem to my girl friend, Kyoko, who is now my loving wife.

JOHNSTON, CELIA

[a.] Putney, Sydney, NSW [pers.] Born 02 September 1930, Sydney; Married with two sons; Attended Fort Street Girls High and Balmain Teachers College; Now a retired school teachers, active in Environmental Education; Honors include Life membership of the Gould League of NSW, fellow of the Australian Association of Environmental Education; Other writings include writing and illustrating Educational Material and Children's Books; I am consumed with the wonder of life, the interdependence of all living things, and living in harmony with the environment.

JORDAN, CURT A.

[a.] Clarksville, AR [title] "Marriage" [pers.] I wrote this poem for my wife-to-be the day before our wedding and sent it to her with a bunch of flowers, hoping to help relieve her of some of those "night before" jitters. She loved the poem, and we are still very happily married.

JORGENSEN, AMBER

[title] "Endless Cry" [pers.] This poem is dedicated to the most important person in my life: my father, Terry Jorgensen. His courage, intellect, and dreams have all aided me in the hard and complicated road of life. I know that one day he may die, but he will live forever in my heart, my mind, and through my words. I will never forget him, neither will I ever stop loving him. Dad, if you read this, never give up, the truth is there but only to those who wish to see it. I won't let you die in vain.

JOVANOVICH, MARIJA

[title] "Orion" [pers.] Poetry gives me freedom. I always try to look at the world with a slightly different perspective. My poetry is a way of sharing what I see with others. Ordinary words are never enough—the world is too beautiful to be transcribed into anything but poetry.

JUNGWIRTH, JON

[title] "Legends" [pers.] I have never been one to write poetry but am a reader and writer. I am deaf and read captioning on the TV and have read countless books from *The Lord of the Rings* to *The Scarlet Letter*. I believe that poetry and music are from the heart. The most important gift I have from God is prayer. Prayer got me where I am today. I can't imagine life without prayer. As a Roman Catholic and spirited runner, I must say we must extend our arms to those who need a helping hand and tighten our grip for those who can't hold on. My poem is about running giving you speed and strength for the final lap, the homestretch. "Run for fun . . . run for yourself . . . run for glory . . . run for God . . . run for life." Godspeed.

KASTLE, ROBERT

[a.] Pembroke Pines, FL [title] "Kosovo" [pers.] Poetry is like Steven Spielberg on a 50-cent budget. You can create a world with only pen and paper. In college in 1975, I took a poetry class given by a poet. Then I really learned how to write. I write from my favorite experiences: talking to people about God's wonderful promises, family, friends, astronomy, space travel, hiking in the mountains, and nature. Listening to music while driving alone in my van sometimes helps to get it out. After learning about Kosovo from radio and TV, it became a moving experience to me. Thus "Kosovo" was born. Truth awaits in God, above politics.

KEARNS, WILLIAM, JR.

[title] "to understand" pers.] As a 25-year-old, married with two children, society often places the stigma of "Carefree Adolescents." More times than not, a verbal argument arises, and the point I want to make never comes across. Poetry is a way to help vent frustrations, make ideas more lucid, and make statements louder than actually verbalizing them.

KEERTHI, RAHUL

[title] "Paint Me a Picture" [pers.] I began writing poetry at age ten and have never looked back since. Poetry has always had a special place in my heart, and I feel that it has made me a better person. Being a literature student, most of my poetry is based on themes I uncover in plays and stories. Love, hate, age, youth, religion, friendship, and family are examples. This poem is one I wrote to remind a close friend of mine to love and be loved, because I believe that love is a feeling that must be shared with all and everyone.

KEITH, CHRIS

[title] "Little Boy Baby Blue" [pers.] I have been writing poetry lyrics for many years, motivated mostly by events in my life. I have a suitcase fall of lyrics in my attic. I would love to collaborate with a musician and try to write some surveys. A carpenter by trade, a husband and a father, I don't have either the time or finances to propose writing full time. Thanks for this opportunity, I was flattered to have my entry accepted in this contest!

KELLY, ANTOINETTE

[title] "Confusion" [pers.] As long as I can remember, poetry has allowed me a way to clear my mind from negativity. This poem is an example of the negativity I sometimes feel. Also, the little suggestion has cleared away some of the "Confusion" that I was feeling.

KELLY, JILLIAN

[title] "I'll Meet You at the Moon" [pers.] I wrote this poem in memory of Kyle Birch and Patricia Mitchell. I love to write poems and I started the idea from my friend—thanks, Christi! I write poems when I am mad, sad, or upset. I have been having a tough two years dealing with the death of a good friend and a wonderful grandma. I also wrote this poem in memory of my godfather, Rich Kelly. The first poem I wrote was with my good friends. Their names are Brittney, Vicki, and Christine—I love you guys! I also want to thank my mom for always being there for me.

KENNEDY, BRIAN

[title] "The Girl under Glass" [pers.] I first discovered poetry a year ago this December. I wrote my first poem as a Christmas gift for a friend of mine, Kara Rochelle, and since then she has been the inspiration for many of my poems, including this one. She is also a talented writer, whom I highly recommend, and I feel she deserves recognition not only for her own work, but for encouraging me to write and remaining my continuing inspiration.

KENNEDY, LIZ
[a.] Madison, IN [title] "Appreciation" [pers.] There have always been important things in my life—writing, reading, family. When combining all, they make life great! My life is committed to learning something new each and every day, and to always taking in the beauty of life! What is more exciting than life itself?

KENNY, LAURA
[title] "Where I Live" [pers.] Born during the worst year of the Depression, I grew up in Los Angeles. As a child I was an "extra" in Hal Roach's "Little Rascals" (Our Gang Comedies). From three generations of teachers and writers, I wrote as soon as I could put pencil to paper. After University, I become a teacher for three decades. Now living near Death Valley, California, I write a weekly column for a small Nevada newspaper, am editing two historical journals, and will soon pen my own memories about growing up in Hollywood. Eleven years ago I had breast cancer, but am now a survivor.

KERR, MAMIE
[title] "I Understand" [pers.] Writing Poetry has always been a favorite pastime of mine. As I write, my soul and spirit venture into another place and time.

KESTNER, GENTRY
[title] "Club Love" [pers.] Gentry Luanne Kestner is a twenty-four-year-old college student from Greenville, Michigan. This poem was inspired by a nightclub, the Grotto, that she frequents often.

KIJOWSKI, JESSICA
[a.] Webster, MA [title] "Do Owls Dream in Color?" [pers.] I've been writing for about seven years now, putting some of my work to music, too. I absolutely love the arts and have won many awards on the topic. The poem, "Do Owls Dream in Color?" is a Picasso-like story, dealing with the rainbow and the senses—"Love and magic in twirling pink." I have written many other versions of this poem, much longer, and my hope is to find a good high school in which I can better my creative senses.

KILPATRICK, LOUEDYTHE
[title] "A Mother's Prayer" [pers.] She was a musician, artist, and poet, my mentor and best friend, she was "my mom." Though she is gone, her soul lives on in her talent, left behind. Talents have been around since the creation, but they may not show until another generation. She was a musician, artist, and poet, my mentor and best friend. She was my mom. Though she is gone, her soul lives on in her talents she left behind. Talents have been around since creation; they are likened to the wind, as you know not where they started or where they end. My mom passed away at eighty nine; she was aware of everything, although her eyes were blind. Her strong character and the "Bible" truth are my inspirations to keep our talents in line, because you see, I too am eighty-nine.

KING, BETTY L.
[a.] Bridgeport, CT [title] "To All the Mothers" [pers.] Betty King from Bridgeport, Connecticut. I work at Owens Brockway Bridgeport Plant. I had three kids, Faien, Londell, and Larise. One of my kids was killed—that is why I wrote this poem, to help others deal with their pain and lost. This poem is in loving memory of Londell King, deceased March 17, 1997. Love always, Mom.

KIRSCH, NANCY
[title] "A Tribute to Montel" [pers.] I, Nancy Jane Navy Kirsch would like to tell you about myself. My birthday is January 27, 1953, and I am an Aquarius. I love people very much. I enjoy cooking, traveling, writing poetry, short stories, and creating recipes. I work as a school aide and enjoy office work. Prior to this, I worked as a clerk for the Department of Finance for twelve years. I am married to a wonderful husband, Steve, and have a cute son, Aaron, who loves to sing. Also, this poem is dedicated to Montel Williams and my parents, Frank and Sally Ann Navy, alone with my brother, Ric, and my beloved grandpa, Dr. Morris M. Goldberger. Love Always, Nancy Jane Navy Kirsch.

KNAPP, BELINDA
[title] "In the Stillness" [pers.] I have always expressed my emotion, no matter what it is, through poetry. This is what it is, through the depth and wholeness of love.

KNOCK, BARBARA
[a.] Erlanger, KY [title] "Jesus Loves Me" [pers.] This poem is special to me because I love to tell others about the love of Jesus. I had many heartaches in my life and caused many heartaches. I felt a void and was always searching for love. When Jesus came into my heart, He filled that void. I now feel so loved and have so much love to give. He truly made a difference in my life, and I love writing verses about my friend, Jesus.

KOONS, KENNY
[title] "My Angel" [pers.] My name is Kenny Koons. I am a 16-year-old boy from Jersey Shore, PA. I am currently attending Jersey Shore Sr. High School. I am in tenth grade. Some of my hobbies are playing football, men's softball, talking on the phone, and writing. I wrote this poem for my family and friends, whom I care about greatly.

KOSNIK, HOLLY
[title] "We Must" [pers.] I would like to dedicate this poem to the people closest to my heart. My parents Chester and Wendy, my sisters Cristy, Mandy, and Kelly, my nephews Christopher and Dylan, my best friends, Holly and Matt, and the love of my life, Craig. They are my inspiration.

KOUKA, FIONA
[title] "Infinite Silence" [pers.] I'm a seventeen-year-old high school student who enjoys all forms of English and literature. Among my hobbies, I enjoy writing the best. I thought this contest would be a great opportunity for me to display my writing talents, which hopefully one day will lead to the publication of my own book.

KRADLE, KRISTEEN
[a.] Madison, WI [title] "Sara's Poem" [pers.] This poem is dedicated to my daughters, Sara Kristeen, who inspired me to write this poem, Heather Ann, and Fawn Beatrice. May you always find in your hearts, the answer to your prayers. Trust in God, I love you, Mom.

KRAGELUND, SHARON
[title] "Heart Strings" [pers.] I feel sometimes the only way to express myself is in poetry. Life seems like poetry to me in many ways. My son inspired this one. A mom letting go is poetry in itself because it is a lesson from God.

KRISHNA, LUXI
[a.] Nampa, ID [title] "Thrust with a Secret-Mission" [pers.] I had to cope with anguish and turmoil. Writing this poem, "Thrust on a Secret Mission," is a sharing of my experiences. Thanks to friends, I saw light, felt peace, and had a glimpse of "self," pure, strong, and happy. I have learned a great deal and can perceive change and growth in my near ones.

KUBICINA, AARON
[title] "Loving Skies" [pers.] My writings reflect the kind of mood I'm in, and the poem, "Lonely Skies," represents the subtleness of my mind. Most of what I am thinking goes into my writing. The first thing that comes to my mind goes down on a piece of paper. My poem is an example of a child that has run away from home. The child soon realizes he loves his family and friends and decides to return. I really like this poem and hope everyone who reads it will too.

KULBANSKIY, ANATOLIY
[title] "Alone" [pers.] This poem is very important to me. It describes me more than anything in the world. It is how I feel sometimes. My father was the one who led me to write the poem. It was at the time when I felt that way that I decided to write it. My father accused me of something that I didn't do, and I became irate and wrote the poem. Even though the problem between us is resolved, I think that teenagers like me can relate to this.

KYLE, CONNIE
[title] "The Wonders of Life" [pers.] This is the first poem that I have written since my high school days. I turned 50 years old this year and began reflecting about my life. Our son was killed in 1994 when he was only 23 years old. A deer jumped in front of him on the Interstate. He was coming back from going to the super center. He had bought his fiance birthday balloons and a present for her 18th birthday. I would like this poem to be a tribute to our son, Paul Michael Kyle, 1970 to 1994. He inspired me to write a poem again.

LACALAMITO, TOMMY
[title] "Cancer" [pers.] I am eleven years old. I attend Thomas Jefferson Elementary School in Parkstown Heights, NY. I enjoy playing sports and reading. I wrote my poem about cancer because both of my grandmothers had the disease. They both have a special place in my heart; they taught me many lessons about courage and dignity. I hope that this poem will honor my grandmothers and the many people like them.

LAFATA, JANET
[title] "Why?" [pers.] I am a wife and proud mother of four wonderful boys. Children are and continue to be an important issue in my life. Poetry is one way I hope to reach out to people on the important subject of our future in children. It is all of our responsibilities to help provide a safe and nurturing environment for these innocent children so that they can grow into loving, caring, and concerned adults. We should teach them through examples, help them learn from their mistakes, and guide them. Children did not ask to be born. God bless—Giuseppe, Orazio, Francesco, Angelo!

LAMBAREN, ARMANDO
[title] "Prison" [pers.] I wrote my first poem at the age of thirteen, and it continued for a short while after, then I stopped. Eleven years later, I'm back at it again. Careless in my youth, I missed an opportunity to have my work published. Nowadays, my wife does not wish for me to be that same careless youth. So somewhere in between my son's naps (where are extremely short, believe me!), I was able to write "prison." I dedicate this poem to them both, the inspirations in my life, and also to my grandfather, you are not forgotten and, Mom, thank you.

LANGSTON, JEFFREY
[title] "Special One" [pers.] This poem was written after the deaths of my father and grandfather. They played an important part in my life. They died the same year, ten months apart. Poetry is a release for me. I have a hard time explaining my feelings vocally, but I have never had any trouble using poetry; whether it's confusion, love, hurts, loss, or any other emotion, it flows out of me on to the paper, saved to reflect on and learn from by myself and others.

LAZICH, BRANISLAVA
[a.] Panchevo, Yugoslavia [title] "Winter" [pers.] Even though I'm only 19, this poem is mature. It expresses feelings of being alone and feeling lonely. That is what this poem is all about, when there is no one around you, and when feelings are frozen—totally different situations but the same emptiness. And even more, this poem is about how can life twist. It has ups and downs, and I saw it as nature within four seasons . . . one of them, which is the title of the poem, matches

the best with a feeling I had to share with someone, anyone. I'm not a native English speaker, but at the time my thoughts was in English, and so is my poem.

LEARY, SEAN

[a.] "To Someone Who Cares" [pers.] I am a 27-year-old self-employed carpenter from Milton, Delaware. I had Zachary when I was 20 years old and had to grow up along with him. I believe I did an excellent job and I'm a good father, and that's the most important thing in my life. When Zachary moved to Japan, it broke my heart, and it remains that way today. I hope people can relate to my feelings. Anyone who has been there knows how painful it can be. Anyway, thank you for reading.

LECONTE, NANCY

[title] "Think Positive" [pers.] This poem was inspired by my father. He always emphasized the importance of having a good frame of mind to achieve what we began. This poem is a way to keep in mind that I shouldn't let myself down about the things in life that go against what I expected. And that I should always look on the bright side of things, so I can always go on with my dreams, concentrate on my goals . . . and achieve them. It's also a way of saying to others: "Don't lose heart, look at the good things you've done, you can do more." That's my message to each and every one.

LEE, DARI

[a.] Eugene, OR [title] "Buddy's Theme" [pers.] "Buddy's Theme", was written days after the death of my nephew, Buddy Ray Biggs. I wrote this poem for my sister, Debi Winja—Buddy was her oldest son. Buddy was a Navy Seal. He died when he was 23 years old in a water craft accident when he came home. Buddy was a man who graced and made everybody's life better just knowing him. My sister lives in Nooksack, WA. I live in Eugene, Or with my husband Gary Lee, and my children, Melissa and Dennis Cuddeback. Life is so precious and taken for granted. I wish I could have "My Buddy" say one more time, "I love you, Auntie Dari." I love you, Buddy, and miss you so very much.

LEE, FAYE

[title] "Reflections: The Winter Knows . . ." [pers.] This poem is very significant and special to me as it symbolizes "my creative turning point." Basically, I believe we "create our own reality," which was impressed upon me during a somewhat painful time in my life. Furthermore, the late Jane Roberts, who created the "Seth Books," was influential in reinforcing this premises as well. Hence, I wish to dedicate "Reflections: The Winter Knows . . ." in honor of her memory, since her unique contributions have left a remarkable impact upon my life. This philosophy has been the impetus and inspirational force behind my poetical and songwriting endeavors: what a creative outlet!

LEEDOM, ANNE

[title] "What is God's Word" [pers.] This poem was born out of the unique perspective my mother, Maryann Mattos, instilled in me. I wanted to express what I consider the heart of all spirituality, the essence of all we call religion, as I see it. That the love of God and knowledge is a rescue to direct our lives and improve our souls is a perspective I feel is often lost in our extremist world. I hope this poem helps people connect God's love with the love we all have in our hearts every day.

LEFANUE, MAUREEN

[[title] "The Garden of My Mind" [pers.] God has blessed me with the gift of poetry that I might bless the lives of others by sharing it with them. This poem was inspired by ten years of chronic fatigue which rendered me incapable of working to take care of my son and myself. I prayed many evenings that I wouldn't wake up in the morning. But God, in his goodness, lifted me out of the endogenous depression which accompanied my chronic fatigue, and I have now been in full time employment for five years. All thanks to my Creator—the credit goes to him, the source of my life and my being.

LEGRAND, CHARITY

[title] "Trickle" [pers.] Good poetry should be cherished, and I am pleased that my poem is one that may be appreciated by all who read it. I hope and believe that many people can relate to "Trickle." I am sure that many people have experienced in some way the feelings expressed in this poem. "Trickle" is my way of signifying the feelings one may have about someone they love and how they can influence emotions.

LENGEL, STEPHANIE

[a.] Newark, DE [title] "Who Art Thou, Love?" [pers.] My nana, Lauretta Tennyson, and my mother, Laurie De Jesus, loved writing poetry when they were younger. They never really thought of sending them in and perhaps getting them published. I am the first one ever in my family to get my work published. So I feel totally overwhelmed with happiness and I hope in the future I'll get some more of my poetry published. Thank you so much for this opportunity.

LENNON, JOHN

[a.] Brandenton, FL [title] "The Life We Choose" [pers.] This poem is very important to me because it represents a life I used to choose and the life I choose now. I made a lot of wrong choices but finally I saw through the dark barriers and found the right choice. And that right has made me who I am today. This poem is for my mother, because I hope she sees the right choice too.

LESLIE, ANN

[a.] Sturgis, MI [title] "Your Caressing Touch" [pers.] I grew up in Ligonier and Scott, Indiana. After I delivered my wonderful son, Brett, I moved to Sturgis, Michigan. My son is very special to me. My life wasn't complete until I had him and Mike in it. I would like to dedicate this poem to Mike, for he is the one who inspired me to write this particular piece. He showed me a sense of feeling that I hadn't even been dealt. It was and is wonderful and fascinating. He's the bright star in my sky. Without him showing his passion for me, this poem wouldn't be published today.

LEVINE, MATT

[title] "Someone Else's" [pers.] For me, writing is a selfish catharsis different than any other form of self-expression. I've never written anything that didn't tell a truth or deal with the truth, even my short fiction "stories." No one's perfect, but truth does transcend virtually all else. And it's a great feeling to be able to see things for what really they are.

LEWIS, SALLY

[title] "Illness" [pers.] "Lewis Sally's Strength" gone but not forgotten. This poem is about strength for the one who is ill, also for loved ones who must help you endure your illness. In remembrance of my mother, father, sister, brothers, and sister-in-law.

LIBBEY, JACOB

[title] "Never" [pers.] All of my life, I have found poetry to be an outlet for my creativity. As a child, I was fortunate enough to have a father who often read to me from *America's Best Loved Poems*. For him, my only expression is one of profound thanks, for an enlightened and unequivocal childhood.

LILLMAN, ABIR

[title] "Written in My Soul" [pers.] Written in my soul is a very personal experience I shared with my soul mate. This poem is dedicated to my soul mate who made my life on Earth a Heavenly journey after years of depression. The visa card is in my husband, Daniel Lillumcan.

LINDENMEYER, PAUL

[title] "Snowball" [pers.] Carl Sandburg's "Chicago" is one of my favorites. The poem was written with his in mind, during a great blizzard while I was living on the South Side of Chicago in the 1970's. Hope you enjoy it!

LIPPA, KRISTEN

[a.] Rochester, NY [title] "Forever Mom" [pers.] In the past, I have written a variety of poems and thoughts of inspiration, never shared until now. This recent piece, "Forever Mom," is dedicated to my cousin, who at a very young age lost her mother suddenly. Through the years, we try to stay focused on salvaging memories and keeping them cherished as we go on through life. I hope this poem is able to touch others with guidance and inspiration.

LITTLE, JERRY, JR.

[title] "I Am a Thug" [pers.] The gift of rhyme is something that is very precious to me. I feel that whenever I release a verse, my soul expresses itself in a way that can only be explained by the words that are written. Where I'm from, poetry or any other type of artistic expression should always be a reflection of the artist. If not, in most cases the people will consider the material not real. Well, "I am a Thug" is not only a reflection of me but it also speaks for a lot of my peers. Some conservatives may criticize my art, but they will have little effect on my work or me. This is because I write for the rebels, hustlers, factory workers, desks aides, nurses, teachers, addicts, and everyone else that's trying to see brighter days in a world where the ghettos don't get too much sunshine.

LLOYD, ARIELLE

[a.] Fort Pierce, FL [title] "Cruel Intentions" [pers.] Poetry is living everyday life which is very special to me, as well as how our world seem to be perfect but cruel in every way. My love to my mother, Lanay Lloyd, Jimmy Lloyd, Dorthony Smith, Prince Jone, Kaylin Highsmith, Tijuana Jones, Bruce Whitehead, Gregory Smith, and Tommie (Ann) Broome. I live in the sunny state of South Florida, my hobbies are writing, dancing, and playing the violin. My personal note is to speak your mind and don't give up.

LOBATO, MATTIE

[title] "The Optimist" [pers.] I believe that the written verse reveals the innermost feelings and emotions of a person. Poetry is a way to release those feelings. My poetry tends to be about real life situations, things that have touched me deeply. What I cannot express in other words comes out as poetry. Some say it's a gift; I say it's a blessing.

LOGAN, SAM

[title] "If I Could Turn Water into Wine" [pers.] Love is sacred, and if I can intensify the feeling in a poem, I am gratified.

LOREY, GAIL

[title] "Hope" [pers.] Native of Des Moines, Oh, (although I have been told that I actually originated in California—some vacation that was!) I am a single mother of six wonderful children—seven including my son-in-law and two beautiful grandchildren. Plenty of room to grow. Writing has been a passion of mine, and sharing it is one of the greatest gifts for me. I hope you enjoy.

LOUDERBACK, JENNA

[title] "Aimless for Love" [pers.] In relationships, we all tend to be burned along the way, therefore causing us to place a shield over our hearts. Written for Joseph, this poem describes the way he ran into the arms of risk, chancing his heart, to see if he could find love again. In his will, Joe—poetry is a gift. I was inspired to write through seeing two of the most

important people in my life, put their lives into poetry: to my cousins, Chris and Larry, you are my inspiration!

LOVE, ODETTE

[pen.] Odette Love; [b.] 18 October 1961; Auckland NZ; [p.] Paul Otto Smith and Bertha; [m.] Separated; 17 July 1987; [ch.] Richard, Paul, Christina; [ed.] Kelston Girls High; [occ.] Nanny, part time correspondence student—writing school; [hon.] Finalist 1996 Telecom Art Awards; [a.] Sandringham, Auckland, NZ

LOZIER, LUCIENT

[title] "The Apology" [pers.] The poetry I write does not come easy for me. The reason for this is that most of my inspiration comes from a sadness deep in my heart, over the loss of a loved one. On occasion, I do write one about the woman who has given me new hope in life. One thing is certain though, all that I write comes from the heart. I realize that my punctuation and English are not the best, but if one person reads "The Apology" and has second thoughts about bringing someone harm, then I have succeeded in getting my point across.

LUKSCH, MICHAEL

[title] "Time" [pers.] I'm lucky to be able to walk through each new open door with my lovely wife, Teresa, and to share our happiness with my mother, Millie, in the Autumn of her life!

LUMPKIN, ANDRIA

[a.] Rochester, NY [title] "Time Gone By" [pers.] As I wrote this poem, I was reflecting on the past and the future. My husband and parents had recently become the past, reminding me how short time really is. My granddaughter, Jana, is the reason I wrote this poem. She is the future.

LUNETTA, FRANCIS

[title] "Two" [pers.] I awoke one day with an urge to paint. Having no canvas or paints to use, I found a few cans of white and black house paint, and the radiator cover in my bedroom was in need of a cleaning. With nature in mind, but void of primary colors, I had to use my imagination. I was able to produce a scene so real, it inspired me to write "Two." I attribute this to growing up with black and white television, when total imagination was needed to enjoy life. Gray areas can be a beautiful experience.

LUNSFORD, SUSIE

[title] "Daddy Helped Save the World" [pers.] The poem I wrote was in honor of my father on this 79th Birthday, and it was written with love and respect for a man who is a hero in every aspect of his life and mine.

LUTZ, LUCILLE

[a.] Saginaw, MI [title] "Memories" [pers.] Being a mother and a grandmother, love inspires me to write my poetry—so much love, so many words, and so little time to try to create from each of them. Soon I'll become a great-grandmother of a baby girl who will be named Halley, a celebration of a new life and another generation in the family and another inspiration for more poetry from me, to all with love. The cold winter's here in Michigan, providing me with time to work on my hobby, which, of course, is poetry. Blessings from me, to all who need them: I hope you enjoy the words I put together and maybe find something in them that you can relate to.

LY, SIMON

[title] "Sleeping with an Angel" [pers.] This poem was specially written for my girlfriend, Breyann, whom I love very much. She was the inspiration for this poem, along with many other things in my life. Without her, I don't know where I would be. She truly is my guiding light, helping me through a world of chaos and confusion. I wrote this poem to tell her how special she is and how much she means to me. My life is better, because I know she's there to love and support me, and so I thank her.

M., JEAN

[title] "Lost" [pers.] This is dedicated to my mom, who knew I was a sensitive child. But she could not relate to me because of her European upbringing and lack of a education.

MAAS, STEPHANIE

[title] "Finding a Toy" [pers.] I am eleven years old and have been writing poetry for about nine of these years. I entered this poem from a book I have been adding to since fourth grade. I got the idea while in an antique store, where I was too short to see the highest shelves but found treasures in the low places. I was so excited to hear it would be published! That letter meant so much to me, and I was really excited to receive it. This will be very inspirational for my future dream of becoming a professional poet.

MACDOWELL, LINDSEY

[title] "The Feeling of Guilt" [pers.] Poetry, to me, is a true blessing. It has taught me several things about myself and the world around me. Poetry has also helped me discover a new way of expressing how I feel about certain problems that surround us daily. My poem entitled "The Feeling of Guilt" was created on behalf of those who deal with guilt and suffering and truly believe that it is too late to ask for forgiveness.

MAGILL, MARJORIE

[title] "A Better Tomorrow" [pers.] My name is Marjorie, but I prefer to be called Marge. I live in Washington State. I am the wife of John, mother of Brian, and grandmother of Anthony. I do not work due to a chronic syndrome called fibromyalgia, and I am also a six year survivor of breast cancer. The poem I wrote, "A Better Tomorrow," deals with the pain and sorrow of losing two of my sons, Mike in 1988 and Tony in 1991. I have survived many trials and tribulations and I want people to know they can too with the help from the Lord.

MAHONEY, DEBI

[title] "Love Me" [pers.] I dedicate this poem to my two beautiful daughters, Angella Sue Keith and Kari Ann Mahoney. I love you! And special thanks to my dearest friends who have always been a big part of my life, Lori and Rick Palm, Angie and Kari, Kris Turner, and my family. Without your love and friendship, I wouldn't have had anything to write about. May you always be blessed!

MAISTO, LIZ

[a.] Secane, PA [title] "Granddaughter" [pers.] Poetry to me is one heart touching another. I am so happy that you picked my granddaughter poem to be in a book of poetry. I am honored and proud to share it with all the granddaughters in the world. I am sure all grandmothers feel the same way. Now my poem will be here forever because of you. Thank you so much, Liz Maisto. "Poetry is God's own tranquilizer to reach people's hearts and sooth their souls."

MALELE, CECILIA

[title] "Mama's Boys" [pers.] My two boys, Mel and Matthew, have been a blessing. I wrote this poem, or thoughts, because they have inspired me to be a parent. There's so much to say about them that it will take me a whole lifetime to write.

MALKOVE, MEL J.

[a.] Anniston, AL [title] "plans" [pers.] Born 73 years ago in Birmingham, AL. This was my first attempt at poetry, but there have been a lot of "firsts." Began my business career at nine years old. Lying about my age, I sold *Liberty Saturday Evening Post* magazines door to door. Left school in the tenth grade, went on to a few entrepreneurial endeavors. Retired in 1998. One of the "firsts" was getting a computer in August of 2000. I met the most wonderful woman on the Internet. We were married in December, 2000. The inspiration for the poem came from my thoughts about my Suzie. I still write poems to her at times, and she has saved them all. I may publish more or I may not.

MALONE, AUDREY

[title] "Son" [pers.] I have always loved poetry, and after the death of my only child in a tragic accident at 28 years, words were in my head that I needed to let out, so I wrote them down in this poem. I have loved reading books since I was a small child, growing upon on a tiny island in the Bahamas. Book supplies were sometimes limited, but we managed. Someday I hope to write a book or books of my own, and maybe getting my poem published will give me the incentive I need.

MANSOUR, MARY

[title] "Longing for Amina" [pers.] This poem, an expression of my deep love for my daughter, Amina, was written as I gazed out of my windows of Mobile Bay and felt the empty space she left after her summer visit.

MARPLE, DIRK

[title] "Tomorrow's Child" [pers.] I am 41 years old and have written different kinds of poetry throughout my life, sharing a lot with my wife Jane, 40 and with my children, Chelcei, 17, Dirk, Jr., 14 and Ben, 11. My grandparents had a large influence on my life by showing me that family comes first and raising your own family is difficult, so be patient and understanding. In "Tomorrow's Child," I wrote about some challenges that my wife and I deal with in raising our children. Poetry comes from my heart and from the many experiences in my life.

MARROW, JAMES

[title] "No Distance Is Far Enough" [pers.] This poem, along with others, was written to my wife while I was deployed on a military mission. Upon my return, my wife felt that I should write more poems or even greeting cards. I explained to her that the poems were written for her, and only her. Six years later, I am very proud and honored to have the opportunity to share this poem with others.

MARRS, BERNICE

[a.] Houston, TX [title] "Three Little Words" [pers.] I began writing poetry about four years ago. I write from my heart and from my life experience. I am happiest when working on my poems. The inspiration for "Three Little Words" came from the fact that there is so little love in the world, even among families—lonely, starving children, yearning for just a little bit of love, and perhaps some food. Three little words, often spoken, will gladden many a weary heart. Those three little words? "I love you."

MARSHALL, ALEXANDRIA

[title] "Cloud" [pers.] I know exactly who I am, yet I have no idea, so to sum up myself in 100 words or less is somewhat difficult, but I'll try. My poem is about those wonderful but sometimes frustrating thoughts that come to us at night when we can't sleep, and I love to write, because poetry is usually the only way for me to keep my sanity. As for summing myself up, all I know is that I'm destined for anything at all.

MARSHALL, CECILE

[a.] Phoenix, AZ [title] "Arms of Love" [pers.] This poem was written for my sons, Matthew and Marc. Giving my sons up for adoption was the hardest decision I ever had to make in my life. So meeting them 30 years later was by far the happiest day in my life. God gave me the words to this poem as I was praying. What a blessing to be able to have it in print as a reminder to Matt and Marc how much I love them and always will!

MARSHALL, JAMIE

[title] "Emma" [pers.] My poem, "Emma," is about the most beautiful thing I have ever felt or seen, my daughter. It expresses the way she opened my eyes to so much love and beauty that I thought didn't exist. It also tells of how hard it was to say goodbye. How I couldn't give her everything she needs or deserves. The publication of this poem is very special to me, because I am sending a copy to her and her family. My poetry is my infinite tie to Emma and perhaps when she reads this, she'll understand a little more just how much I love her.

MARTIN, DARLENE

[title] "Body and Soul" [pers.] I dedicate this poem to all who suffer in sickness and pain, as I do. I had an injection of silicone, and my body rejected it. I used to model and dance with paper and pen. I trust God and his angels and I thank my family: James, Charlene, Jaylene Sierrah, Christine, Kenny, and Paul, for being there in my darkest days, so that I may go on and write and share about life and love and spirit.

MARTIN, TANGELA

[title] "Innocence" [pers.] This poem represents to me the innocence that all of us are born with. Through life changes, we somehow lose that innocence. It can be anything in our past that we wish we could go back to and change and regain that feeling of hope. Through my own life, I have experienced these feelings and sometimes look back to try regain it. This poem represents a little part of me. I would like to dedicate this poem to my mother, Margaret, who passed away in 1994. I miss you. She represented my love and hope for life.

MARTINEZ, BECKY

[title] "Angel Forever" [pers.] I wrote this poem for a special someone. A special someone everyone has. You know, the kind that can make you laugh and cry. Make you thank God you're alive and even make you wish you could die. These special people make life what it is.

MATES, ANNETTE

[a.] Galesburg, IL [title] "Home" [pers.] Homesickness bleeds inside. For eighty years, I lived in the home my great-grandfather built in 1854. I never dreamed of leaving, except to die. Old and alone, you realize time is a traitor. Transplanting an old country girl into a city high rise is not natural. Praise the Lord, my Heavenly Home is next! It's a mansion on a golden street.

MATH, SUSANNE

[title] "Destiny" [pers.] I am a dreamer as well as agonizingly romantic. I think with my heart and dream the impossible. I am a poet whose life has been like a poem, sometimes magical and lyrical, sometimes tragic. I write because words are a resting ground for thoughts of the soul, thoughts I feel, that come wrapped in ribbons of blood and tears which are inseparable. Poetry is my destiny! It is also a reflection of the legacy of inner peace and integrity given me by my parents. What I write will hopefully always reflect the beauty of their soul and the wisdom of their hearts!

MATTHEWS, ROBIN, JR.

[title] "I Am Who I Am" [pers.] I am a seven-year-old young man, who lives in Anchorage, Alaska. I am in the second grade and I love to write and read books. I wrote this poem in order to express how I feel and love my father. I chose the word, "father," because it applies to my human father as well as my spiritual father. I found that when I am unable to say, thank you, it's better to write it. For without my father, I would not be here. Hobbies are reading, writing, and playing chess.

MATTICOLA, MELISSA

[a.] Doylestown, PA [title] "Tears" [pers.] Poetry has always been a positive outlet for me throughout my life. My mother has always encouraged me to share my gift with others. I feel that God has given me the opportunity to reach others using my poetry. I hope that there will be many more opportunities throughout my life in which I will be able to share my emotions and values with others.

MATTOX, VICKI

[a.] Zebulon, NC [title] "Mercy of Reality" [pers.] Writing serves as a release from frustration as well as a way to dream. I put on paper words that flow naturally, without thought given to it, as a form of poetry. It is a personal expression of emotions and desires. This is the first time I have shared my writing with others.

MATYLEWICZ, JUSTIN

[title] "Untitled" [pers.] I was in a near fatal car accident on December 3, 1996, and in a coma for three and a half months. I now have traumatic brain injury. When I awoke, I found people my own age no longer understand me. I first got into poetry as a release for my feelings. It has become very therapeutic for me. Things have a way of piling up in my life, so I have needed a way to release my anger. My poems reflect my feelings.

MAYNARD, RYAN

[title] "Pity" [pers.] My poetry is something that I hold dearly. It is my life. It speaks for me. Poetry is my life, and my life is poetry. Every poem has a meaning. All the poems I have written are about what has was happening in my life. My poems are my true voice, one that people rarely see or hear.

McCORMACK, CONSTANCE

[title] "The First Kiss" [pers.] A person's first experience with anything—death, love, friends, is the experience that will remain in your memory throughout your whole life. This poem is a tribute to the paper and significance of these first experiences, especially the profound first experience of love.

McDOWELL, STEPHANIE

[a.] Lockport, NY [title] "Wings" [pers.] As a little girl, I used poetry as a way to release my emotions. I could not express myself verbally to another person like I wanted to. So I wrote everything down. This poem is about my inspiration, my friend, and my mother. It is my way of letting her know that everything I am and who I'm going to be is because of what she and my father instilled in me. Poetry is a way of telling the one you love (for me my parents) that you were listening when they gave you that good advice.

McELROY, FELITA

[a.] Jackson, MS [title] "Humiliation" [pers.] This poem was inspired from my pledging experience in '87, and it is a feeling we all can relate to. For me, writing is a spiritual and social outlet. I believe everyone is gifted to write, once the inner self is discovered through pain or profundity.

McGHEE, EVERLINE

[a.] Tallahassee, FL [title] "Thank You!" [pers.] I want my readers to know that I believe in God with my whole heart. I am happily married to a wonderful husband, Samuel D. McGhee. We have four daughters, one son, and six grandsons. I wrote this poem, "Thank you!" after a few days of illness. I want readers to know that no matter what you're going through, God is there for you. He is closer than your kin, your friend, and even your skin. He's there! In all things give thanks.

McGINNIS, NICOLE

[title] "Sea" [pers.] I wrote this poem because in the summer of 2000, my family and I went to Ocean City, MD. I swam in the ocean every day. We were there! I love to swim in endless places! It makes you feel free! I love the ocean so much! That's why I wrote "Sea."

McGUIGAN, KEVIN

[title] "Reborn at Fifty-two" [pers.] "Reborn at Fifty-two" is not as it would first appear. I am in fact only 32 years of age, and the reason I made it to 32 was because of my "Soul Family," the Boylands, who lived at You Gussgo 17 #52. Thank you with all my heart.

McKAY, PAULINE

[title] "Home" [pers.] Pauline McKay, born in Jamaica West Indies and migrated to Brooklyn, New York in 1972. I love to read, write, sing, dance, and relax at home. I love to be around people and the joy of life to live and enjoy. I love poetry because it uplifts me in a way of reaching out to others, so that we can see how life can be beautiful in our greatest thoughts. I am the last of seven children and live in New York with my sisters and brothers. I am employed at New York Presbyterian Hospital as a call center agent. I give thanks to the father above for giving my parent the gift of life and the knowledge to learn as much as I can, to be able to choose wisely of the choices that I am surrounded by, being on this planet. The knowledge of accomplishing my dream, I kept in my mind from the first day I started to write in my first diary, which became my masterpiece. Thanks for giving me an opportunity to express my thoughts through poetry.

McKENNEY, NEGRE

[a.] Tulsa, OK [title] "Deep" [pers.] This poem is to everyone who has gone through something or felt someone else's pain. As for me, I write poetry through my experience and the pain I been through in life. I like to thank God for giving me that talent to express myself. I also like to thank my lovely wife, Garran McKenney, for inspiration, and my mom for believing by me. This is dedicated to my best friend, Dee Sells, and his wife, the Sells family, and to all my other family members whose names are not mentioned.

McKOY, CYNTHIA

[title] "What Is Life?" This poem is extremely special to me, because it helped to convey a side of me that few people have or ever will see. It was originally written to help a friend, Robin Mitchell, overcome a brief, bad period in his life. It was then rewritten when my dearest Uncle, Johnny Davis, passed away, and I started to question life's meaning. It is my hope that these few words will help others who may feel as I have.

I am a thirty-six-year-old native New Yorker, who is currently employed by the U.S.P.S as a customer service supervisor. I have been writing poetry and short stories since J.H.S. and will continue to do so, simply because it is what makes me feel free.

McMAKIN, ROBERT

[title] "Renewal" [pers.] I feel that if we continue to desecrate our world and each other as we are doing, this will be our undoing. I hope people will read this poem and see the possibility it describes for the future.

McMURCHY, MARLENE

[title] "This Chair of Mine" [pers.] This was my first attempt at poetry. I was inspired by my very special friend, Cynthia (Cindy) Dawn Caola of Florida, USA. Not only did she gave me ideas, but she is also a source of inspiration to those of us who think we have a heavy lot in life. She never complains about her burdens and gives me the courage to face whatever may come my way. Thank you, Cinds. We love you.

McNEAR, WILLIE

[title] "Through the Clouds" [pers.] I never claimed to

be talented at poetry, just always like to write. I brought it out in front of church and public and now I can't quit writing, God blesses so!

McNEE, MYKAL

[title] "Have You Seen the Wind?" [pers.] "Poetry is the observation of the world through the eyes of the soul." The soul reveals itself, free of its quiet solitude, in the confines which it dwells deep inside, and rises up. Between the eloquent lines, lies a deeper meaning of life . . . a yearning to understand and be understood. An image's reflection in water is a distortion of the natural elements abounding; everything affects something else—the wind to the leaves. A heightened sixth sense of higher awareness is a passport to wisdom on a road less traveled, a path of life's revelation and simple splendors of all God's gifts.

McNEILLY, KELLI

[a.] Corona, CA [title] "Sea of Wonder" [pers.] The gift of poetry was given to me by my great-grandmother. The inspiration was given to me from my grandmother's poetry book, which was given to me after she died. Poetry is a gift given to all, no matter what age. Take that gift, use it, share it. This poem shows how much I love the beach. Writing poems about the ocean gives me feelings I cannot explain. I enjoy having the opportunity to put those feelings into powerful words through my poetry. I enjoy writing. I am in eighth grade, thirteen years old, and live in Corona, California.

McRAE, AMANDA

[a.] Winnipeg, MB [title] "Long Far Away Cat" [pers.] This poem is in dedication to my cat, Misty. I'm twelve years old and from Winnipeg, Manitoba. I enjoy writing poetry and have written a lot. I also like writing songs. My other hobbies are singing, karate, piano, camping, drawing, and swimming.

MEADE, DONNIE

[title] "The Hall of Doors" [pers.] This poem is about the torture of indecision, being afraid to make decisions of change because of poor ones made in the past, the choice of holding on or letting go, the fear of being wrong. True, you may try and fail, but if you don't, you'll always fail. Writing has always meant a lot to me. Most of my interests lie in story writing. Poetry is something I've enjoyed and been inspired to write when flooded with emotions. It's almost a spiritual thing wherein you always seem to learn something of yourself. It's a beautiful gift to be able to share.

MEDFORD, HAROLD

[title] "clusters" [pers.] Harold Medford is a Steelworker who resides in Illinois. I have been fortunate to realize that every day we live is just like a poem. At 47 years of age, I have been blessed with the love of my life, and have two children. I also have one granddaughter whose name is Sarah. I dedicate this poem to her, as seen through my father's eyes. "Daddy's Gone" is my father's farewell to everyone who has loved him. He will never be forgotten because he is—my daddy.

MELEK, FARRAH

[a.] Brentwood, CA [title] "Words" [pers.] This poem was written for my nine-year-old daughter, Zara, whom I love far beyond the words. The subtlety of poetry soothes as it caresses. The reward of the writer is the opportunity to share a human emotion with others.

MENDOZA, ASHLEY

[a.] Stafford, TX [title] "We are Meant For Each Other" [pers.] This poem is very special to me 'cause I hope to feel like this with my boyfriend/husband later in life, with our love burning for each other every day for the rest of our lives, till we die. Anyway, I am 16 years old and I go to Stafford High School. I love to read and write poetry. Soon I hope to finish school and to be a fashion designer.

MERWARTH, TAMMY

[title] "My Love for You" [pers.] I'm 27 years old, the oldest of four girls. My sisters are Heather, Tara, and Gail. My parents are Isabel and Bud. I'm married to a wonderful man, named Donnie. I have three children—Crystal, Trisha, and TJ. I also have four step children and a grandson—Christi, Carly, Thomas, Nikita, and Deacon (our grandson). I started writing poetry as a child. I wish to have more published someday. I would also like to write a book. Poetry is important to me. It has a lot of meaning and is very powerful. More people should read poetry.

MESITE, J. T.

[title] "Lonely Thoughts" [pers.] Before I met my future wife, this poem told the story of everyday life. Through college, most people expect party and fun, but there's always that empty feeling, something missing. I am glad that I filled my empty spot. I love you, darlin' Heather.

MIDDAUGH, MICHELLE

[title] "'Til Death Do Us Part" [pers.] This poem was written for and recited to my husband at our wedding ceremony, December 7, 1996. It is very special to us, and however personal to us, it also seems to fit for any couple getting ready for marriage. Which is wonderful in case you're wondering, not always easy, mind you, but a wonderful gift from God. It was my pledge of love and commitment in all times, not just good. Also, it is my conviction that God has perfect plans for us and for marriage, but focusing also on our dependence upon Him to help fulfill His plans.

MIDDLETON, KATHERYN

[title] "When Dreams Come" [pers.] I believe that writing is what everybody should do, because it expresses your feelings. I thank my language arts and writing teachers who have always encouraged me and told me what they thought of my writings. They have encouraged me to express my inner thoughts and to reach above and beyond. My family also supports me in my talent of writing. I usually write to entertain, but sometimes my writing comes from my heart. I am very excited to be chosen to be published as an eighth grader and to share my work with others.

MIDDLETON, RACHEL

[title] "Day 09: Total Awareness" [pers.] For me, poetry has always been special. It's a beautiful way of expressing oneself and is a gift to be cherished. This poem is an abstract version of a personal experience, and I hope others can relate to it and enjoy it.

MILES, MITCHELL

[a.] Cedar Rapids, IA [title] "A Beautiful Waterfall" [pers.] I was inspired to write this poem as I was thinking about a lovely forest with a beautiful waterfall rushing down the side of a hill into the sparkling water below. "Oh, what peace and quiet one can receive and feel!" as I see this unique work of true art in continuous motion. As I continue to write my poetry, I always seem to be truly inspired by the Lord above.

MILLER, ALOHA

[a.] Pittsburgh, PA [title] "A Spiritual Prayer" [pers.] Poetry, like paintings, brings visibility to feelings placed in written form, to savor the moments of one's deeper expressions.

MILLER, PAUL

[title] "Josapp" [pers.] "Josapp" was written in memory of my friend, Joseph Michael, who took his own life on Easter Day, 1999. Months went by, but not a day passed that Josapp, as we called him, didn't come to mind. This poem helped to ease the pain, and I think, serves as a fitting memorial. There will always be a place in my heart, and I'm sure the hearts of many others, for 'Sapp. Mata Aimasho, my friend.

MILLER, VICTOR

[a.] Lisle, IL [title] "Favorite Son of America" [pers.] In April 1999, I had a premonition of a lady in a vineyard wearing a wedding dress. She was surrounded by flowers, and it was a sunny day. Suddenly it became gray; I was in an airplane with two women. I glimpsed into the window of the plane and saw a reflection of John F. Kennedy, Jr. He looks disoriented. The airplane splashed in the water, and everything became dark. A moment later, there was an unstoppable sunlight which rose from the water. In July, I remembered my vision of April and wrote this poem in August, 1999.

MILLER, VINCE

[a.] Park City, MT [title] "The Hand of God" [pers.] I was raised in Northern Minnesota, although I currently call Park City, Montana home along with my wife Deborah and our three boys Lane, Cody, and Tyler. As I have grown through the many changes which have occurred in my life, I have come to realize how many ways "God's Hand" has touched me through people in my life. One of the most influential to my writing was my high school English teacher, Bev Jorland. She was the inspiration for this poem, it is my tribute to her.

MINCH, CAROL

[title] "Gathering of Friends" [pers.] I like to tell things that are from my heart, for this poem was for very special friends. Sometimes I do poetry for special occasions, and if I have any gift for this, I owe it all to a very special grandmother who had many special gifts besides poetry. She has gone from us, but she is always with me.

MINNOWSKY, ALLAN

[a.] Brooklyn, NY [title] "People" [pers.] This is my second poem that I sent in. I'm very happy that this poem will be printed. My poetry helps me very much. It also makes people know just how I feel.

MIRZAYAN, REBECCA

[title] "The Love of Friendship" [pers.] Wow, I never thought I would be published! I am a fourteen-year-old sophomore and I attend Bonita High School. I would like to give a special thanks to my English teacher, Ms. Penner, for inspiring me to write.

MOK, VALERIE

[title] "People" [pers.] The poem, "People," was written for my best friend Christa Rebatzke. I would like to thank her for being there when I needed her most.

MONEYPENNY, CHRIS

[a.] Shadow Hills, CA [title] "Fall" [pers.] Poetry for me is a portal to the multi-dimensional reality just beyond, next to, or within the physical world, as it appears to be. This is the first poem I wrote in what turned out to be a fair-sized collection during my college and post-college years. It is meaningful to me that "Fall" has been published at this point in time. I guess what goes around, comes around, just like the seasons. Love to all those whose seasons I get to share in.

MONHOLLEN, DARLENE

[title] "Seduced by the Wind" [pers.] I thank God for the gift to write and for giving us such beauty to write about. I thank my mother for this poem, amongst others I have written. She is a very special lady in my life who has encouraged me to write since I was eleven. My mother never stood behind me but beside me. She taught me that it is what's within you that will bring your true happiness. I feel that nature encourages and excites that which is within us, if we allow it. I hope others find the same joy in nature that I have found.

MOORE, JAY

[title] "Revelations" [pers.] I crafted this verse for my fiancée when we were going through difficult times. Writing "Revelations" made me truly realize some-

thing of human nature—every time we hurt someone else, we also hurt ourselves. I have often made mistakes in our relationship and I have learned that the smallest transgressions can cause incredible pain when two hearts are as close as ours. I can only hope and pray that our love can endure for the rest of our lives.

MOORE, JESSICA

[title] "I Used to Be" [pers.] The easiest way for me to express my feelings is by writing them down, making them into beautiful songs of thought and feelings. Every word in poetry has its own meaning, and almost every poem tells a story. My poem is about how people change as their lives go on. They learn from experiences that have affected them and the people around them. With a little bit of love and hope, you can see the world in a new light.

MOORE, MONTY

[title] "Falling Love" [pers.] First off, thanks for enjoying some of my thoughts—I must be getting sentimental in my old age. I am a self-employed janitor with a tenth grade education who enjoys fishing and camping. My wife, Leslie, and I live about twenty miles east of Williams Lake, British Columbia. I have been putting my thoughts on paper for many years but have never expected any to see the big lights. This poem expresses my feeling for things, from broken relationships to death. It's nature's way. Like tossing love from an airplane and watching it drop, we have all experienced . . . "Falling Love."

MORGAN, ALOURA

[a.] Manteca, CA [title] "Good-bye" [pers.] I was ten years old when "Good-bye" was written.

MORGAN, ANDREA

[a.] Bronx, NY [title] "Harriot" [pers.] Not every poem I write is based on a true life experience like "Harriot," which actually happened and involves a moment when I was once with my sister. I love poetry because it allows me to feel and express all of the things I feel in life, especially the subtle things, and all of the moments between moments that people experience or might experience but seldom observe. Poetry gives life to those moments and reminds us how important they are, and why it's so much fun to just pay attention.

MORGAN, DENISE

[title] "Deliverance" [pers.] For me, this poem represents the past, when I walked on shaky ground, and the future, where I now walk on solid ground. I've attained an inner peace by simply accepting the greatest gift given to mankind and was inspired to put my feelings down on paper. A special thank you to my friend, Gina Legges, who encourages me to share this with others. To my husband, Robert, for all his support and the love he gives me unconditionally, I love you so much.

MORGAN, KELLY

[title] "I Have a Hero" [pers.] When I wrote this poem and my other poems, I try to put myself in other people's situations to interpret how they feel and express their emotions. In this poem, "I Have a Hero!" it says that even if you feel ignored, alone, depressed, and no one cares, there is always someone who cares and wants to be your friend.

MORRIS, CARLA

[title] "Twist of Fate" [pers.] This poem is special to me, because every time I read it, it reminds me of how fate has us all by the coat strings. And how ever so thankful I am, to be able to enjoy the beauty of earth, as well as the wonders of life. This poem takes me there. "Much Love," Carla.

MORRIS, MELL

[pers.] Irving, TX [title] "Word Song" [pers.] There are several people in my life who are battling terminal illnesses, and that was the genesis of my poem. I've had ten short pieces of fiction published and only recently turned to poetry which seems to be the ultimate distillation of creative expression. My son, Eric, has encouraged my versification; an accomplished musician, he has composed melodies for some of my poems. I live in a Dallas suburb with my husband, Gary, and two dogs, Lace and Buddy.

MORTON, MARK

[title] "My Children" [pers.] I am a Military Police Officer serving in Wiesbaden, Germany, and during a class I was attending (D.A.R.E.), we were asked to prepare a poem on a topic provided by the instructor, and my topic happened to be "Children." I have two children of my own whom I cherish, and due to my current military assignment, I only get to see them once per year. They are my inspiration, and I miss them terribly. Even though we are apart, I have not missed calling them every weekend in four years.

MOSER, DARLENE

[a.] Mohrersville, MD [title] "A Rose In the Garden" [pers.] I hope my poetry and short stories will be a living legacy to my loved ones. I feel God does inspire me so that I may bless others, and in turn, glorify Him. This poem was birthed out of a contest ad featuring Montel Williams, who has M. S. I have always felt that he does reach out to others in spite of his own pain. "Thank God for people who can do that."

MOYER, DAN

[a.] Rochester, WA [title] "The Passing of My Children, Ages Nine and Eleven" [pers.] This is my one of my many writings I did in memory of my children, Melissa Rae and D. J. Moyer, when they were tragically killed in an accident on Thanksgiving Day in 1991. My writing were the one way I could deal with the loss of my family.

MURDOCK, LAVONNE

[title] "Just a Child" [pers.] I am 62 years old and have been writing poetry for a lifetime. There is so much happiness in poetry and the message that it sends. One can open many doors of life and find the true spirit of the soul. I have found that writing poetry is a way to find love in verse. To make one person happy a day is my wish and if possible, more—this is one of God's great blessings.

MYERS, JUDITH

[title] "Heart Strings" [pers.] I dedicate this poem to the Lord, from whom I was inspired. He, himself, is my motivation to share the blessedness of life. Also, I dedicate this poem to my granddaughter, Robyn Nicole, who is unique and most talented. She is a ray of sunshine. God bless each life with inner beauty and blessings to bestow.

NACZYNSKI, CINDY

[title] "Life's Travels" [pers.] I was inspired to write this poem when I met a man who's life was in a state of disarray. He was alone and felt that all he had had been taken away. He was afraid to move on. Through long conversations and understanding the meaning of my poem, he has picked up the pieces and has begun living again, not alone. We will soon be married and begin a journey of our own.

NEFF, MATT

[title] "Election Time" [pers.] I have always enjoyed writing humorous poetry and giving poems as gifts. It's a great way to put special events and memories on paper so that they can be brought back to life with each reading.

NELSON, BARBARA

[title] "Today I Smelled the Rain" [pers.] As a writer since age nine, I have explored many avenues of the written word, but none touches my being as does poetry. For 20 years I have written a poem to distribute to family and friends at Christmas. This tradition has meaning to me, much more so that anyone can imagine. This poem, "Today I Smelled The Rain," was my first. Its philosophy sums up my life as in the words of my two favorite scholars, Thoreau and Jesus Christ. It is from the former, my goal to live a quiet, simple life. It is to the latter that I credit my gift and dedicate its use.

NESBITT, SARAH

[a.] McCool, MS [title] "The Answer" [pers.] This poem was written in memory of Mr. Thomas Ward and in honor of his wife, Dot. I watched him fade away in six months with cancer and watched her take care of him while in severe pain, thinking she had arthritis. Six months after his death, she was diagnosed with M. S. I had a hard time dealing with all of this until I attended a Bible study class. One of the lessons stated, "quit trying to second-guess me; let me be God." After that night, I haven't had any more problems accepting his death.

NICHOLS, ALUNDREATTA

[title] "The Promise" [pers.] I am the daughter of Alonzo and Laverne Nichols, and the eldest of four siblings. I believe that nothing touches a person's life quite like the power of words, and that power is a gift from God. I am grateful that I was chosen to be a carrier of the pen. My desire is that others would find that which they might hold to themselves in my writing. This poem is special to me, because it came about during a low point in my life. It was God's promise to me then, fulfilled now and always.

NICHOLS, JOSEPH

[title] "Let It Speak" [pers.] I love writing poetry. I love the way that I can inscribe all of my hopes and dreams onto paper. They're not just poems either—each and every one of them is a memory to me. I can read any of my poems and remember exactly how I felt when I first sat down to write them. Most of them are fantasy love poems above the one true love that I dream of finding someday. Others are playful poems about Christmas or Halloween, etc. Some of my poems are just school assignments that I couldn't bear to part with, yet they are all compiled together to make one big poetry notebook that I have carried around almost everywhere with me for the past two and a half years, though my love poems will always be my favorites. I just love the feeling that comes over me when I read them, especially when I read this poem, "Let it Speak," which is one of my favorite poems that I have written. I was astonished to hear the news that the first poem that I have ever entered into a contest had been published!

NICHOLS, KIM

[title] "The Journey" [pers.] In my early twenties, I took a trip to Shasta Lake. As I was lying beneath a tree, reflecting on my life, I watched a single leaf trickle down to the ground. It was a slow glide all the way down. It seemed that leaf had chosen a very peaceful path. I realized I wanted to take a similar journey in my life. That one simple leaf renewed my appreciation for life. I believe nature, time, and self-expression can help heal the soul.

NIEMCZYK, ALEAH

[a.] Marinette, WI [title] "The Sun Is the Color of Yellow" [pers.] Poetry is very special. I started writing poetry two years ago, when I was ten. I got a book of poetry and kept getting more. Poetry is a way to tell people how you feel in writing, and it just makes you feel good. One of my favorite books is called *World Poetry*. "The Sun Is the Color of Yellow" was inspired to me by nature. Nature is a fun and surprising subject to write about, and I enjoy it a lot. No one should miss out on this joy in life.

NOCERO, ANGELA

[a.] Elsmere, KY [title] "Mommy's Little Angel" [pers.] At the time I wrote this poem I was very depressed and confused. I more or less blamed myself for my son's death. My brother, Mario Nocero, who helped me through all of it told me to write down, the best I could remember, what had happened that night. And that's what I did. My brother passed away two years ago. I miss him so very much. I think of him also when I read my poem, for I wouldn't have wrote it were it not for him. He used to play Santa every year at Children's Hospital in Cincinnati, Ohio for all the sick children, and now they have a children's fund at the Hospital in memory of Mario Nocero.

NORGOAL, DAVIN

[title] "The Voice" [pers.] I'm not really a poet—I like to write rap songs, which are basically a form of poetry. I've been writing songs since I was in the seventh grade and still write to this day. I was known as "Mailman" in my old, underground group, BDB. Today, people still call me, "Mail." This "poem" is not just from me, but from every other young adult stereotyped as a criminal. It's something in life that my friends and I deal with every day.

NORTHINGTON, KELLY

[title] "Directions to the Cross" [pers.] I wrote this poem because I was going through some very tough times with my newborn son, Emmanuel. I wanted everyone to know that God is in control, no matter what the circumstance. He subsequently died as a result of a congenital heart disease, and this poem is a tribute to his memory. I hope someone else can be encouraged by the peace that I felt.

NOVOTNY, CONNIE L.

[a.] Sioux Falls, SD [title] "Time to Fly" [pers.] "Time to Fly" was written when my daughter, Jenny, was in her final year in high school. I could sense and see her struggle to either hang on or fly. I knew she had to go and I believed she was eager to go . . . and she did. I have another daughter, Amanda, who also has since taken flight. I have only dabbled in poetry over the years whenever the spirit moves me. Most of my poems have been seen by my eyes only.

NUGENT, CARON

[a.] Adel, IA [title] "God's Sea" [pers.] Over the course of my life, I have written many poems, over 300. Out of all those poems, "God's Sea" is the only one that I can recite from memory. It was written in remembrance of my dad, Forrest Lynn Robb. A God-fearing man, he did his best to teach me right from wrong and to live by the Golden Rule. I hope he is proud of what I have become. This poem has since been put to music, and every time I hear it or sing it out loud, I think of my dad. I miss my dad.

NULLE, CHELSEY

[title] "The Fool" [pers.] For so long, throughout my childhood, I couldn't find an outlet for my sorrows. I was an aggressive, great, big ball of pain. The hurt ran so deeply that it took every ounce of me to find a way to make myself happy. I found that in my creativity, a big way was through verse. I told the stories of losses, of joys, but always about life. Every day that goes by is nothing more than it is, unless it impacts your life, and only then is it worth being a memory and a poem.—Chelsey "Celsi" Nulle, age 17.

NYGREN, DOUGLAS

[title] "Crucified" [pers.] This is one of the first poems I have ever written, so it might not be the greatest, but I like it. Actually, I'm not even a poet, I'm more of a writer. Currently, I am working on a novella that will be somewhat like George Orwell's "1984." I hope those who read this poem will enjoy the brutality that is behind it.

ODOM, MARLENA

[a.] Petersburg, VA [title] "The Me That Nobody Sees" [pers.] This poem was written with one of my sons in mind. I am a mother of seven—a daughter Marlena and six sons Marcus, Malcolm, Mandela, Muhammad, Malik, and Myles. My husband and I have seven free spirits, each one a gift from above. After leaving New York to move to Virginia, our son was met with dislike and prejudice from students and some teachers. We feel prejudiced towards what we don't understand, dislike what we can't comprehend—a closed mind is a waste of time. Life is a puzzle waiting to be solved. There is so much more ahead if we only evolve.

OGDEN, MICHAEL JOHN

[a.] Glendale, AZ [title] "A Father's Pride" [pers.] This poem was a gift to my sister on her wedding day. I was honored to stand in my father's place and escort her down the aisle. I wrote the poem to show that even though he passed away twelve years ago, he is still by our side. Being a full time student at Arizona State University, poetry is my escape. Having this poem published is a step towards my dream of becoming a published poet.

OGLETREE, ALICIA

[a.] APO, AE [title] "Baby Santanna" [pers.] During the teenage years, I discovered I had the gift to write. My poetry gave me a positive outlet for self-expression. First, I would like to thank God for blessing me with the gift to write. Next, I would like to thank my husband, father, mother, brother, and grandmother (Sean, Louis, Linda, Tony, and Evelyn) for all of your love and support during the years. A special thanks also to my best friend, Drelin, who seems to know me better than I know myself. Thanks to all of you! God bless you all! You are my inspiration.

OLIVER, PATRICK

[title] "Band Leader" [pers.] In an age when we seem to spend more time thinking and less time feeling, more time consuming and less time giving, more time hurting and less time healing, "Band Leader" is a cry for mankind to become fully aware of and connected to his own heart. Perhaps then we can bridge the gap of "aloneness" we all feel and realize that we all ultimately want to love and be loved. I would like to thank the people I feel most responsible for helping me meet my heart, including Dan Gotlieb, Roseann Sellani, Karlene Lavelle, but most of all, my father, Karl Oliver.

OLLE, KATHERINE

[title["Storm" [pers.] I have been interested in writing poetry since a poem in high school was published. Writing poetry allows me to experience dreams and put them into words. "Storm" was begun as an attempt to write a poem; it was a challenge to find the words to complete it. But it is the joy of completion that inspires me to continue writing.

OLSON, LAURA JENNY

[a.] Chehalis, WA [title] "My Family's Love" [pers.] This poem means a lot to me. It's about my family and the love that they provide and give. I love my family with all my heart. I hope that this poem signifies the love from all families, and that hopefully they can share it with their family. I live in Chehalis, WA. I love to write and draw. I have three brothers and one sister. I go to W. F. West High School and I'm a Freshman. My sister's name is Karen. My brothers' names are Kyle, Lann, and Andy. I love this poem and hope others will love it too! Poems like this one come from the heart, and I hope that everyone will give it a try.

OLSON, STACY

[title] "Someday" [pers.] Throughout the past 15 years of my life, writing has been the only way I could express myself. This particular poem was written for the teacher that had inspired me to move forward in my life in positive directions. I want to thank them for all that they put into this world, asking for so little in return. Without teachers, the joy and pain in a poet's heart would remain there, for they would not have the precious gift of words to express themselves. So thank you, Ms. Shelly, Mrs. Albertston, and Mrs. Shirm, as well as all you other teachers that have given the profound gift of words to us that live by them.

OSTROFF, ELAINE W.

[a.] River Forest, IL [title] "Cycle of Life" [pers.] This is my legacy to my darling granddaughter, Melissa. I hope someday she will read it to her children and her grandchildren in memory of my love for her.

OVERTON, JEFFREY, JR.

[a.] Beaver Falls, NY [title] "What is Love?" [pers.] This poem come straight from my heart. I wrote it when I met the girl of my dreams. I then learned that in order to love somebody, you have to cherish everything about them, not just their looks. I thank everyone who has inspired me to keep writing—you know who you are. I live in a very rural town, Beaver Falls, NY. I'm 19 years old and plan to write poems for many days to come.

OWENS, CARRIE

[title] "I Promise" [pers.] "I Promise" is an example of our oneness with the Creator. I am humbled by the words that flowed from my spirit. To me, this is evidence of a divine power that is ever present and waiting to come forth from within. We all have a gift. "I Promise" is my commitment, in this life cycle, to develop my "Spiritual Sight," to share, listen, learn, teach, and love more each day. "I Promise" has inspired me to release my gifts to others for their enlightenment, joy, and inner peace. I am thankful for this opportunity.

OWENS, CHET

[a.] Burley, ID [title] "Love at Home" [pers.] This poem," Love at Home," was written as a special gift and message to my wonderful wife, Ann Lee. The words define hers and my closing of a day, retiring, and preparing for the coming days/weeks. I am a retired physician with a love for writing. This poem is one of several I have written, along with a just recently-finished autobiography. The copy of *True Reflections* which I am ordering will be a gift to her, a surprise, as she knows nothing of this order.

OWENS, VERONICA

[title] "A Solution" [pers.] I sit in my ivory tower, often contemplating the famine in the land of humanity and how I might be able to make a difference without judging my fellow beings. The death of my grandmother, who was truly a phenomenal, "turn the other cheek" lady, as well as a mother to me, started me writing to deal with the incredible void her absence left. While her song ended, her melody lingers on and on. Hence, the feelings have been lived through words. To know more, buy the book.

OWENS, VICKIE

[title] "Grandpa" [pers.] Poetry is a way of taking me back to the days I cherished at my grandparents' cabin, nestled deep in the woods, and now seen through their granddaughter's eyes. It has inspired me to put together a unique kind of cookbook, not only of recipes but also of pictures, poetry and short clippings of all that I see as I walk down memory lane. That inspiration will hopefully live on in Grandma's Log Cabin Recipe's. I will always continue to write poetry, as it is my way of expressing what is truly in my heart.

PAISER, HEATHER

[a.] Shawano, WI [title] "The Moment" [pers.] All of my work stems from life experiences and a connection to my spirit. Poetry to me is a collection of innermost untold stories or feelings. I also believe that another person can relate to a poem in their own way, so although this poem has a certain meaning to me, I wish for others to make meanings for themselves. "Poetry is a song without music, and I believe everyone should sing."

PAL, SOPHEAP
[title] "All My Life" [pers.] My poem is about being alone and being in love—it's like holding a red rose that you cannot afford or have, because that rose is beautiful, and she cannot deserve you. Sometimes, that feeling is a wrong feeling. You wanted her, and she wanted you, but you chose to be alone instead of being with that special girl that was just right there. I know I made that mistake, I chose to be a hermit and never commit to anyone, but that feeling gave up on me and wanted to be with her.

PALAZZO, PAUL
[a.] Farrell, PA [pers.] I was born and raised in Sharpsville, PA, and always had a passion for poetry. I believe poetry to be an expression of love—inner feelings put into words. "The Lost Heart" was written during a difficult period of my life that involved a 16 year relationship I thought would last forever. I have always enjoyed gardening and the arts and have a great love for animals. I have two playful and lovable dogs that are a major part of my life. They taught me to take the time to enjoy life to its fullest.

PALMITER, JON
[title] "The Lord Brought Me You"[pers.] I wrote this as a song and sang it to my bride at our wedding. It was my way of expressing my love for her and my appreciation to my God for His gift. I enjoy poems that express love and religious poetry. I often write short poems for my loved ones which I put in e-cards. I live in Michigan where I was born.

PANTON, JOAN
[title] "Requiescat" [pers.] As I grow older, my thoughts often go back to the home of my first childhood memories, a Presbyterian Manse in a small rural district called Ebenezer. My paternal grandparents and the Aunt and Uncle with whom I lived are buried in the churchyard there. Not far from Ebenezer is the village where I was born, and where my maternal grand and great-grandparents are buried. "Requiescat," my only poem thus far, came to me one very early, very beautiful morning, in my quiet time.

PARKER, DUSTIN
[a.] Pittsburgh, TX [title] "Fight the Monster" [pers.] This poem is very important and a way of life for me. This poem is about how everybody has fears, and sooner or later you have to fight them. I hope that for whoever reads this, this poem helps them fight their monster and beat their fears.

PARKER, PATRICIA
[title] "In The Heart" [pers.] I live in Auburn, WA, with my husband, Mike, and our children, Adam and Sarah. My first book of collected poems, *Captured Moments*, will be published soon. Mike did all the illustrations for it. I wrote "In the Heart" for my two dearest girlfriends, Patricia Joyce and Mary Jane Beccaria. I met them in 1966 when we started college together. They're been with me through "thick and thin" and have become for me more than best friends. They are my sisters in the heart. To me, they are precious treasures for life.

PARRIS, DOMINIQUE
[title] "When I Spell before I Think of You" [pers.] I started writing poetry at the age of eight. It was first introduced to me by two of my teachers, Jane McVeigh Schultz and Mary Lynn Ellis as an art form. Poetry soon became much more than a hobby. To me, a poem is the manifestation of emotion. In order for me to write a poem, my entire being must be completely saturated with an emotion. As a teenager, I am constantly being confronted with new and powerful emotions. Often times, poetry is my only outlet. Writing has become my best friend when life throws all the nastiest blows.

PASSER, MELISSA
[title] "My Husband" [pers.] Although I never thought of myself as a poet or writer, I have always loved to write. I don't use fancy words—I just write what is in my heart. This poem was written on my honeymoon. I wrote it for my husband, and it symbolizes my feelings for him. Thank you for giving me the opportunity to share this.

PATEH,
[a.] High Spring, FL [title] "It's Love As Sure As I Am" [pers.] This poem was the result of my dislike of the traditional "Marriage March." I felt a more sensitive song was needed, so these words were received and later turned into a song. I live in a home I built myself, have solar energy, have a successful C.D. out (with my band, Bast), have had three group shows and a one-man-show in Soho, NY. I am known internationally for my art style called "Allism" and am sought out by serious collections. I was born in Cologne, Germany, in 1942, during an air raid, and moved to Canada in 1953, and then to the U.S. in 1973. I live in Florida now, with my three cats and my art and music, performing at concerts, coffee houses, etc. I continue to write poetry, the blood that runs through literature.

PATRICK, MARY
[title] "Mirror Image" [pers.] I am a UCF student studying for his Public Administration and Sociology. I have a thorough interest in writings and poetry. It is a release from daily stress, and I enjoy sharing my writings with others. My inspiration comes from family and the outdoors. People inspire me. I feel that poetry is a form of expression for both men and women. Today's society sets a standard and draws a line that we cannot exceed or hide behind. Men and women are guilty of wearing masks and pretending to be someone else, while at the same time afraid to be themselves. Judgments of the world create a distorted picture of who we really are. Expressing my thoughts in the form of poetry makes my journey to myself and helps others see the image of me. Society has a mirror, and you have a mirror—how you see yourself depends of which mirror you choose to use.

PATTERSON, BETH
[title] "World in My Room" [pers.] Among those things that have inspired me to dream and to appreciate the beauty of life, there are none greater than the two commemorated in this poem. They are first, the love of home and family my grandmother imparted to me, and secondly, the worlds of past and present made real to me by the writers of great poetry and literature. I am grateful for these things above all others.

PAYNE, MARY A.
[a.] Kansas City, KS [title] "Martin Luther King" [pers.] Poetic expression is a gift from God that I cannot remember not having. For me, at times, it has been more like taking dictation. The lines flow through my mind so rapidly that I struggle to write them down. This was the case with the writing of "Martin Luther King." I am a lifelong resident of Kansas City, KS, and a product of the public school system, and the University of Missouri, Kansas City. I have retired after 31 years in the nursing profession. Important in my life are family, friends, and service to God through the Mason Memorial United Methodist Church.

PAYNE, RICHARD
[title] "The Legacy" [pers.] We all know we can't get out of this alive so we want to leave a mark. What we are remembered by becomes the point of our whole life. I want people to know that they are loved, to know that true friendship extends beyond the realm of conventionality. I hope my legacy will be a bridge to the eternal spirit.

PAYNE, TOMMY
[title] "Thief of Mystery" [pers.] This poem was inspired by Elizabeth Barnes, Montel Williams, and all the people going through their own battle with M.S. Montel, thanks for opening of the door on M.S. on August 2000 at our Poetry convention. We can all make it happen, together—Tammy Payne of Princeton, West Virginia. I also want to send a special thank you to my ten-year-old son, Jeffrey Payne, thank you for being so supportive and patient—I love you. To all who inspired most of my poems, thank you all. God Bless. Thanks Mom and Dad and family. Thank you, Lord, for this talent!

PEACE, SUZANNE
[title] "Grandpa [pers.] This poem is special to me because it sums up how I feel about my grandfather, William Gale Senior. It is a poem that I wrote for him to tell him how much he means to me, when I found out he was dying from cancer. God bless you, Grandpa, you'll live on forever in my thoughts and dreams.

PENDLETON, JOY
[title] "I Watch This Child" [pers.] I write poetry at very emotional times in my life. The poem, "I Watch This Child," is no exception. This is my way of sharing this child, my daughter, Heather Lynnette Pendleton, with the world. Heather was born June 24, 1979 and died suddenly May 4, 1997. Heather also wrote poetry. I feel there is no better tribute I can give to her than to tell the world of her in verse.

PENNA, FABIO
[title] "War Helicopters on the Floor" [pers.] "War Helicopters on the Floor" has a special meaning to me, but I'd also like these words to have a special meaning to the whole world. The poem claims people should use, not weapons, but their feelings, so we would live in a better world. Poetry is what our souls tell us and we write in papers, but nothing would be worth it if we don't touch somebody else's conscience, raise someone's smile, or make people love each other. "War Helicopters on the Floor" is also a song I compose, so they can hear it aloud.

PENNER, DARCI
[title] "Captured by Night" [pers.] Poetry has always been an important part of my life. I truly enjoy spinning webs with words and seeing the different effects it will have on each individual. One of the greatest compliments I can receive is that I have a gift at writing poetry. That truly warms my heart to hear, because it is a passion long lived. "As surely as fate will rise up and make himself known, I will always stand tall. I will never give up."

PENNER, DERRICK
[title] "The Process of Becoming" [pers.] Poetry is a fickle thing that can gush forth from writing pens or drip tediously from creative minds. I am very proud to be able to express myself through poetry. This poem came about while watching two people in love sharing their time together over a cup of coffee at my local coffee hang out. I saw a wild look in the man's eyes, a nervousness perhaps. I decided to put myself in his place and imagine what I would be so flustered about. I gave the character in the poem a nonchalant desperation to relate to what I believed the man in the coffee shop might feel.

PEREZ, NICHOLAS
[a.] Cicero, IL [title] "Welcome" [pers.] When I write, I attempt not to plot, so my pieces can be raw and real. My piece, this piece, like many of my others holds a dear spot within me. It has a special significance, which I believe was inspired in me by my deceased mother, Ruth Lebon. This is a form of my vision. It is from my thoughts, my mind, and my soul. It consists of everything that was running through me at

that moment, my joy, my sadness, my love, and tears—because I believe that with every life, there's an untold story.

PERTUZ, CHALYNN
[title] "The Shining Star" [pers.] It had always been hard for me to express my feelings, but poetry seemed to change all that. Through my poems, I am able to put my feelings into words. This particular poem, "The Shining Star," was written for a man named Josh Chasez, the first man I have ever truly been in love with. It shows how he helped me open my heart to love, but all good things must come to an end. Even though he is not with me in person, he is always with me in spirit. I love you, Josh.

PERWAD, NABIL
[title] "Nature" [pers.] I am a thirteen-year-old boy of Indian origin living in Dubai, UAE, with my parents and three younger brothers. I have modest artistic talents which I would like to inculcate in myself and allow my mind to organize my time doing something worthwhile. I was not really inspired by anybody, except nature itself, to make this poem. Leaving the nature and poetry subjects behind, my other hobby is making comic books. I have made a bunch of comic characters of my own. I hope my works will be published and recognized by the world. My greatest ambition is to market my comic character, "Steve Dajee." As a matter of fact, it is quite popular already among my friends and school mates.

PETERS, JENNIFER
[title] "God's Little Angels" [pers.] I wrote this unique poem when I was running a family home child care. We were trying to create a Christmas card to take to the elderly people at Christmas time. I put the poem inside the card, and the children colored a picture on the outside. I tried to create a Christmas greeting for all elderly people from a child's eyes. I dedicate this poem to all the children and elderly people throughout the world, and to my own children: Eric, Katie, Laura, and Jessica.

PETERSON, KASEY
[a.] Delta Junction, AK [title] "Fisherman Boys" [pers.] I began writing songs and poems when I was eight years old. This poem was a school project that I wrote when I was twelve. Writing songs and poems is a creative way for me to express my feelings. I live on a farm in Alaska where I enjoy four wheeler and snow machine riding, snowboarding, skiing, watching wildlife, and hunting with my dad. In school, I enjoy participating in softball, volleyball, and basketball. Someday, I would like to have some of my songs recorded by country music singers.

PETERSON, ROCHELLE
[title] "Little Boston Terror" [pers.] This poem is an excerpt of a larger piece of work, entitled, "Party of Five," describing my family. It includes a section devoted to each one of the three Boston Terriers that were a part of it. The menagerie that lives in this home now include two Boston girls, three rats, two parakeets, goldfish, and tropical fish. This poem is dedicated to my first, beloved, and perfect Boston boy, Oberon. He would be the first to tell you that all Bostons are terrors in their own way. God speed, my friend.

PETTRIE, CELESTINE
[a.] Indianapolis, IN [title] "Spring's Magic Show" [pers.] I am a retired teacher who has tried to encourage creativity in my students. I have never before considered publication of my own compositions. Thank you for this opportunity. I have had a long love affair with dandelions. I believe that they have been maligned as an undesirable weed when they offer enormous possibilities. They are a child's delight. They can serve as food, medicine, nutritional additives, drink, beauty, and a lesson in tenacity. This poem, therefore, says take another look at dandelions.

PHAM, DIEN H.
[a.] Baltimore, MD [title] "Pain" [pers.] This poem is just opening up something that I feel people use frequently without really thinking about it. They take the word "pain" for granted. I wrote this verse to tell people what I think and what I feel. Pain is felt all over: everywhere you go. So then one day it came to me, I had to express it to see if I could change anyone's perceptions. That takes me back to here. Truthfully, I never thought this would have gotten anywhere, the poem that is.

PHAM, NGHIEM
[a.] Tacoma, WA [title] "My Vow to Her" [pers.] A lifetime is too short to be playing with love. When I found mine, I treasured it. Even though it has been so hard for Emmai and me, those theoretical distances only make me love her more. I hope others can find something in their relationship that will keep them together. Truly a lifetime is too short, make the most of it. This poem is the only way I can express what Emmai means to me, yet even this means nothing close to my feelings for her.

PHELPS, DENISE
[title] "Coming Home" [pers.] University of Michigan graduate, majoring in English Education and Advanced Russian studies, married, with two grown children, living in California Low Desert Country.

PHILLIPS, JACKIE
[a.] Council Bluffs, IA [title] "Little Children" [pers.] I have written poems for many people in my life—my husband, Mike, daughter, Jamie, son, John, granddaughter, Hannah, parents, Donna and Roger, grandmother, sister, Jolene, and best friend, Diana. This particular poem is for the homeless people that we feed every day at Mom's place, a homeless feeding site here in my town. God has blessed me with the ability to express myself through poems. In return, I hope that I can bless someone who might be hurting, lost, broken, or discouraged. I enjoy writing my poems and sharing them with the ones I love.

PHILLIPS, TERESA
[title] "Grandma and Tweety" [pers.] This poem is special to me because my grandmother always said that I should write a book or a poem and get it published. She was my inspiration and my friend and she was always there for me. I was blessed to have her as my grandma and my children were likewise blessed to have her as their great-grandma. I am married to a wonderful man named Doug. I have two great-grandchildren, Carie and Brian, and a stepson, Austin, whom I consider my own. I own a medical consultant business called "Oniet Cove Management." I also started a non-profit organization for abused children called "Alone"—all little ones need everyone. My hobbies are gardening, fishing, camping, and hunting. I am waiting my children to give me grandchildren so I can be "Grandma" and give them their nicknames to remember me by.

PISCOPO, STEPHANIE LAURA
[a.] Turnersville, NJ [title] "My Love" [pers.] Poetry, I feel, is a very special gift. It is something I am very thankful to have. People who have this gift should never stop writing. Don't be scared to let people see your work, ask them for their opinions, and think of ways to improve your poems. The poem I wrote was about someone I love deeply. He has always been there for me no matter how much I complained. I pray he will remain at my side as a best friend and a supporter.

PLANGG, HEIDI
[title] "Harbor My Soul" [pers.] Poetry allows me to express my emotions in an artistic fashion. Throughout my life, I have consistently been thrust into situations requiring me to alter my own personal course and follow the course handed me by circumstances beyond my control. I am a single mother of three brilliant children. Struggle has become our motto. However, through perseverance and sheer determination, we prevail. Being a longtime parent has forced me to put "my" needs, wants, and dreams on what seems to began in definite hold pattern. I hold my dreams close to my heart as I hope to find time in life to hold a love as closely as I hold my dreams.

POHLL, DUSTIN
[a.] Freeland, WA [title] "Friendship" [pers.] Mostly poetry is just what you feel inside, your feeling about nature, your surroundings, and your angles on life. What inspired me was a little feeling inside telling me to explain and write about it. Now I can tell people how I feel!

POLLUM, EMMA
[title] "Shadows" [pers.] Writing poetry is the way I like to express myself. In "Shadows," I expressed my thinking about shadows. I have been writing poetry since I was five years old. I write poetry because it is my way of telling people how I feel. And sometimes just because it's fun!

POOR, ANGELA
[a.] Crescent, IA [title] "To My Husband" [pers.] My husband has been such an inspiration to my life. He has taught me how to really love and give myself unconditionally. His love, loyalty, and ongoing commitment to our marriage gives me so much strength and energy. This poem was my gift to him. I hope others can relate to the kind of love that is expressed in this poem as well as feel the incredible emotion I felt while writing it!

POORE, PATRICIA
[title] "Tracey" [pers.] I like writing poetry. At 60, I'm finely putting some of my poems where they can be read. The poem, "Tracey," is about Tracey Falkenstein. She's on the kidney list, but because of her Lupus, she was only put on the list in 2000. If you wish to send her a note of encouragement, you may do so care of The International Library of Poetry.

PORCH, JAMES
[a.] Austin, TX [title] "The Integral Part" [pers.] My poem was written from feelings derived from being one with yourself. If you are married, not only should you love your wife, but also you should really like her. In life, one must truly stop and look around, take a deep breath, and take time to smell the roses. Surround yourself with the basics of life such as sunshine, crystal, blue waters, birds chirping, and stars shining at night, and most importantly, the ones you love. Thus you have the creations that come from within. Take nothing for granted, live life—that is called Poetry!

PORTER, JENNIFER
[a.] Miami, Florida [title] "Reflections" [pers.] My love for flamenco inspired me to write this poem. As a flamenco dancer and performer, I long to know what the future holds. I live for the dance; it is in my heart and in my soul. This poem is a reminder to live each day to its fullest, and let fate take its course. I endlessly thank my family, Greg, Lili, and Kelly Porter for their love and support—without them I would not be where I am today. Jose, Teo, and Rosa: Muchas gracias por darme animo. Arriva con el baile flamenco puro y el duende.

POSCA, MELISSA ANNE
[title] "Brown and Yellow" [pers.] This poem was creatively inspired by our Father, Gene Posca. He has always encouraged us to be creative in whatever we do. Our mother taught us to read and write. We studied hard and learned that isn't soft. For the past year, we have been compiling humorous stories about our family and our childhood. In the future, we plan to write a book about them.

POULER, DAVID

[a.] Grovetown, GA [title] "A Man with Remarkable Blue Eyes" [pers.] Everyone has always told me I never express my true feelings. Just recently, I've discovered that writing is an easy way to do so. Though I don't consider myself a poet, I find that writing just helps me deal with certain things going on in my life. This one is pretty much self-explanatory. I'm 18 and live in Grovetown, GA. I've been a little busy writing a book about overcoming challenges in life after losing my left leg in a train accident at the age of 13. It mainly revolves around my biggest obstacle, high school football.

POWELL, RAY

[title] "Morning Prayers" [pers.] Ray Powell is of Cherokee and Creek Indian descent. It was not that many generations ago that his ancestors survived "Jackson's Trail of Tears" to be relocated in the Oklahoma Territory. Mr. Powell began reacquainting himself with his Native American culture while obtaining his degree in Anthropology at Georgia Southern University. It was during his early college years that he began writing poetry and making Native American artwork. He volunteers time to local schools educating children on American Indian Cultures and Issues. He does consulting work in the deserts of the Southwest, thus, giving him ample ideas on which to dwell upon.

PRATT, LORAINE

[title] "The Look of Joy" [pers.] A few years ago, I became very sick and no longer could do many things I had always enjoyed. I felt like giving up, when this poem came to me, and I know now there is always something to be joyful about.

PRESCOTT, LORY

[title] "Truth Within" [pers.] Thanks, Daddyo, for guidance in my quest for Truth, happiness, and unconditional Love. You're the Cat's Meow! When all people awaken the truth that sleeps within each of us, our animosity towards one another will abate, love will grow, and the future for all will be beautiful. Please begin by having respect for our environment, yourselves, and all living creatures. Never hurt anyone purposely. Give love, receive love. Laugh, play, and have fun, and everyone else will also. Feel free, for you are! Love and peace to all in their quest for truth. Let's begin tomorrow with today!

PRIDDY, CAMILLIA

[title] "Seasons" [pers.] My grandmother, Lillian Forsyth, instilled in me the love of nature, music, and poetry. She and my sister, Shirley, taught me poems before I started school, and I have been writing them since. I spent my early childhood on a little farm surrounded by majestic oaks and many species of birds. My sister, Kathy, and I spent many days playing around the trees and beautiful flowers my grandmother planted and cared for. This, I think, has been the inspiration for me to write. I have no formal training but create from my emotions and what I see and feel.

PROVOST, JOHN

[title] "Personal Highway" [pers.] Poetry is about the moment. It should be spontaneous. It lives in each of us as a passion. If poetry is appreciated and learned as a vehicle for expression, we can all learn to find the poet within us. I do not pretend to be a poet that will be remembered but if I can use poetry to express feelings, emotion, and experience, then poetry will always be a source of joy for me. I thank my parents who have always been a source of inspiration for the visions I hold and the person I am.

PRUE, ROBERT

[a.] South Bend, IN [title] "Now" [pers.] Robert Prue in memoriam. Born in June 1941, he unfortunately past away in early November 2000, after a three year struggle with cancer. His bleak prognosis in May 1997 was six months. After being momentarily deterred, by the news, he spent the ensuing couple years adventuring into several areas and aspects of life, which he had never the mind to accomplish before, including poetry. May "Now" be an inspirational to all of beginning.

PRZYGOCKI, LYNN

[title] "The Ceremony" [pers.] This poem is very special to me. I had dreamed of my graduation day for many years, and when it finally arrived it was one of the most emotional days of my life. All that is written in this poem is true—you never realize how difficult it is to locate your family within hundreds of people until you've experienced a graduation ceremony. Also, I'd like to thank the love of my life. You've given me the strength and the willpower to begin writing poetry. Thank you and I love you.

RAELSON, NOELLE MARIE

[8.4 that runs through my veins. Yet it is also the thorn in my side. Writing poetry forces me to expose the raw innards of myself to the virgin paper. I write because I have to and I write because I love to; simply put, writing is my catharsis and writing is the monkey on my back. Only when I put pen to paper am I truly satiated. Yet when I do not write, the compulsion is ever present, like a nicotine fix to a cigarette addict. Tantalus had his thirst; I have my writing. Yet will I remain forever grateful to my mother, who gave me her precious gift of writing so that I instead may prosper and she may write through me. Her gift will not be wasted.

RAMIREZ, ANA

[title] "My Yesterday" [pers.] This poem, as do all of my other poems, expresses a day, or event, that happened in my life. I sometimes write what I imagine other people feel. Also. I believe that poetry is one of the few ways that feelings and emotions can be expressed. My poetry is about different aspects that I have of life. So therefore I will always have something to write about.

RAMOS, NORMA LINDA

[a.] Runge, TX [title] "Art" [pers.] This poem was written in memory of my beloved brother, Arturo V. Mendoza, Sr. On February 2, 2000, the angels swept down from Heaven and came to escort him "Home." His death inspired me to write this poem, because I wanted everyone to know how special he was, and I also wanted him to always be remembered. He may not have known what it was to be wealthy, or to live in a mansion, but he was a very rich man because he had something that far exceeds that "Faith" and "Love" in his heart for God.

RANSOM, LISA

[title] "A Tragic Loss" [pers.] Lisa Ransom was born April 1, 1980, from Ravenna, MI. "A Tragic Loss" was written in memory of Nanci Kay Mackay Graves. Nanci died three days after her twenty-fifth birthday, in a tragic accident involving her husband. Nancy wasn't only a close friend and cousin, she was someone I looked up to. She taught me a lot about being a mother. Her children were her life; now they have to grow up without her. The lesson here is, don't hold grudges, cherish every day you have with the people you love. I dedicate this to her two children, her family, and everyone who loved her.

RAO, KIRAN

[title] "You Are to Me" [pers.] Sometimes when I have an opportunity to watch my wife as she does the little things in life, and she is not aware that I am observing her, these poems drip from my thought to my fingers. Most of my poems are a reflection of my life with her. I do not believe I am poetic enough to do justice to her personally, but I try!

RAPER, DEBRA

[title] "Mighty Tree" [pers.] I feel that all life is precious and special in God's eyes. Everything is put in space and time to play a part in the creation of life. But because not everyone sees life as precious; their neglect and ignorance can and does cause harm, such as it did to my son, Kenny. He died, August 1990, from a low power line through a "Mighty Tree" that God gives us to sustain our life. I pray my poem touches your heart. If so, my son's death was not in vain, and he will forever be remembered in our hearts.

READ, LINDSIE

[title] "Paramedics" [pers.] I am 14 years old and I was recently diagnosed with panic disorder. It was an unfortunate way to be introduced to paramedics up close and personal, but that's how it all began. I admire what the paramedics did for me. It triggered something inside of me that made me realize I want to go into the medical field and devote my life to helping others. That is exactly what I'm starting to do now. When I turn 16, I plan to become a first responder. I dedicate this poem to paramedics everywhere.

REASKA, HEATHER

[a.] Beloit, WI [title] "Torn between Two Places" [pers.] Poetry has always been my outlet, a way to explore and understand my innermost feelings, to let my emotions untangle and run loose across the page. A poet has no real boundaries, limits, forms, or rules. It can be anything you want it to be. You don't have to be someone "important," to write something beautiful. James Lowell, a favorite of mine, describes the art of poetry best in a verse from "The Fountain," "Full of a Nature, nothing can tame. Changed every moments, but ever the same."

REED, HOWARD

[title] "that Reflection I Never See" [pers.] I am a retired Law Enforcement Officer. The people I came into contact with were the ones who really needed the Lord in their lives. This poem is a reflection of when one realizes that there could be more to live for and a higher level of thought. I have a beautiful family, and we live on lines with the Lord as our anchor.

REPPUCCI, PATRICIA

[title] "On The Mend" [pers.] Born in Cardiff, Wales. Having raised three beautiful children to independence, I sought a new challenge in the United States. I am proud to be a naturalized U.S. Citizen. After fracturing my ankle, I had plenty of time for reflection. "On The Mend" just flowed from within. I believe that from a change of circumstances comes a different perspective to life. Changes are out to embrace. My philosophy towards life—unfurl your wings, show your true colors, and soar as high as you can. Hence my nickname, "Butterfly." I hope to be inspired to write more.

REYNOLDS, JESSE JOSEPH

[title] "All I Worked For" [pers.] I am a proud American Indian, full of passion and respect for the wonderful gift of life. My best expressions are words, and I have written many from my heart. I now am humbled you would take the time to share my feelings by reading my simple works.

RICE, ASHLEIGH

[a.] North East, MD [title] "My Secret Bottle" [pers.] Many people tell me that at age 15, I don't know what stress is. Well, let me tell you, they are wrong. My poem is about the many stresses that come from holding my feelings inside. When I wrote this poem, it was at a point in my life where I had bottled all my feelings inside and felt like there was no way to let them out. This poem helped me express the way I felt in a calm and rational manner.

RICH, ANGELA M.

[a.] Buffalo NY; [title] "Angel's Wings" [pers.] I

hope others find comfort in my words. Poetry is an expression of one's true self. It enables us to release our weaknesses and vulnerabilities. The poem, "Angel's Wings," is dedicated to the memory of Monica Rich and Pearl Phillips. These two women have made a great impact on my life. May they rest in peace. "God" had given me the gift of comforting others in their time of need. I pause to give Him thanks. . . . To my family and friends for your constant love and support, "I thank you." A special thanks to Del Rae Alexander, who encouraged me to believe in myself. Without you, Del, none of this would have been possible. Thank you for your undying love and acceptance.

RIDEOUT, RONNETTA

[title] "The Way I Wished He Looked at Me" [pers.] The poem I have written is very dear to me. It has a sense of the love and passion a girl feels for her boyfriend. This poem expresses love and passion between two people. I love writing meaningful poems to people, it gives them a new sense of love, courage, and hope. Thank you for your support!

RIGOR, TIARA

[title] "Learner" [pers.] Life is a continuous learning process. It is a journey that simply never ends. We all have our share of mistakes and trials, but what matters most is to keep ourselves humble and open to more opportunities to grow and be better. So as they say, we all live and learn. Indeed, everyone should know that because even the greatest thinkers of our time were students once.

RIVERA, LILLIAN

[a.] Fort Worth, TX [title] "A Carnation's Wish" [pers.] A carnation's wish symbolizes my feelings and thoughts personalized in a natural form of a flower. The descriptive words can transport the reader to experience a series of emotions. This poem is dedicated to all the dreamers who are endlessly seeking for the love of their life.

ROBBINS, AMBER

[a.] Higginson, AR [title] "Mixed Feelings" [pers.] I live in Arkansas. I had never really been interested in poetry until I studied it in the eighth grade. My poem, "Mixed Feelings," was written about my ex-boyfriend. I wrote it the night that he broke up with me. I was very upset, and writing helped me get everything out. He hurt me so badly but he helped me discover my talent. He was something very special to me, and losing him made me realize how much I really cared about him. The poem expresses that. If it wasn't for Ian, this wouldn't have happened.

ROBINSON, KEVIN

[title] "True Love" [pers.] This happens to be the first poem I had ever written, some ten years ago. Poetry gave me an outlet for all of the crazy emotions we experience during our teenage years and continues to be an avenue for relaxation in my adult life. I thank you for the opportunity to share it with everyone.

ROBINSON, WILLIAM G.

[a.] Birmingham, West Midlands [title] "The Carbon Copy" [title] Pen name, William; Born September 11, 1939; Sutton Coldfield; Educated at Secondary Modern and C.F.E. and D.I.Y. Studied Electronics, Report Writing, Photography, Astronomy, Bk/kg and Accounting, etc. as General Basics on Varied Subjects; Member of H.M. The Royal Air Force Association; Honors include Poetry to ILP and ISP, received a number of Editor's Choice Awards; As a blood donor had a further award for having helped life via having given 75 blood donations. I have written other poetry that I have managed to put forward to ILP, ISP, and for sharing poetry aquaints of promotion. In literature, poetry appears to me as one ablement I do contribute toward. For the joy of readers, via the light of life, I'm able to put forward.

ROMAN, SHERRY

[a.] Fairfield, OH [title] "A Special Love" [pers.] I believe that my poetry is attributed as a gift from God. That is my true inspiration. This poem was written for my mother. She is a special person who loves her daughters very much. She would be proud of such an honor. I'm thankful for all the people who have contributed to this poem's success and for encouraging me to pursue this God given talent. I hope others will be able to share this poem with someone special in their lives.

RORICK, AMANDA

[title] "Wishes" [pers.] Wishes are what dreams are made of, and dreams help you escape this harsh world of reality. This poem is for all of those people who have given up on wishing for unattainable things. Without these wishes, these dreams, there is no reason to strive to surpass your potential goals. Wishes give you something to look forward to in life, but one realizes most that not all wishes ever come true. Even though they don't always come true, they are still a part of you. Wishes may be unrealistic, but we shouldn't be real all the time.

ROSE, J.

[title] " A Smile on My Heart" [pers.] I feel the world needs to know there are "still" happy marriages, people who care, and that some of us are "still" fond of old fashioned, chivalrous lifestyles. We don't hear many stories of today where the "wonderful, handsome prince rescued the fair lady from the evil villain (acting as the prince), and the two lived happily ever after!" This is no doubt how our lives have come together. People need to hope that marriage is not a waste, and it can work, and is usually found in places we don't even think to look. My poetry is the "me" that's unseen.

ROSS, MICHAEL

[a.] Ipswich, MA [title] "A Poem From Your Angel" [pers.] I did not write " Poem From Your Angel" for myself. I wrote it for anyone who reads it to show them that there is always hope. I also wrote it for the sake of poetry itself. Poetry is the language of passion, so it bothers me when people write angry words, play with fonts, and then call it poetry. Beowulf and Siegfried gave hope in dark times with their legacies. Today, poetry has become a way of mouthing off at society. Another message of hate is not what we need, especially in our literature. What we need is hope.

ROUSE, DOMINIC

[title] "The Harsh Words" [pers.] I wrote this for my soul mate, Courtney. It was from a stupid argument we had. We were both able to forgive each other for the words said. That is what's important, the ability to forgive and to "Never go to bed mad at each other." I love you, CJ.

ROVEGNO, NICOLAS

[title] "When It Will Happen" [pers.] Born in Lima, Peru, Nicolas has been engaged in writing since 1980. Poetry is one of the best ways to express true things. Language is such a powerful tool—poetry is definitely art and craftsmanship.

ROWINSKI, LINDSAY

[title] "Remember" [pers.] My poem is simply about dreams that are accomplished and dreams that are ruined. That was my main idea when writing this poem, but I like to leave room for the reader to interpret poetry to their life. I want to dedicate this poem to my Uncle Mike. He is also a great poet, an actor, and a director. So this one is for you, Uncle Mike! In addition to this, I also want to thank my family members for supporting me in my artistic developments.

RUNESON, ERIK

[title] "My Winter Poem" [pers.] I am a fifteen-year-old student with a great interest in writing. In the past, I have published various poems and short stories in books and papers. At the age of twelve, I won first price in a big essay competition and received the prize from King Carl Gustaf XVI of Sweden. Recently, I got a job at a major Swedish daily newspaper.

RUSSELL, CYNTHIA

[a.] Houston, TX [title] "Thank You" [pers.] I am 29 years old and began writing about a year half ago in hopes of creating songs as an aspiring singer. The particular poem was inspired by the selflessness of family and friends in my life. I wanted to communicate the importance of never forgetting the true significance of saying, "thank you." No amount of money or gifts can replace the humility associated with thanking someone for their kindness.

RUTHERFORD, DEREK

[title] "One Day" [pers.] Poetry is like my first love! It's like my baby, like my only seven-year-old daughter, Khadijah, who I believe is the main reason why I'll be one of the greatest writers one day! . . . I grew up in Washington Heights, New York City, and moved to Harlem. I now live in the Bronx! I work as a security officer in the South Bronx, my bread and butter 'til I become published. My poetry is about love, relationships, women I've fallen in love with, the woman who's in my life now, and other women who I come in contact with. I also write about my pain, my battles with former drug addictions, life, my family, and friends. My writings came from my bleeding heart—it comes through my pen. My passion for poetry will never stop, and hopefully one day I can share that love I have for writing with the world.

RYAN, WILLIAM T.

[a.] Boca Raton, FL [title] "Soul Mate" [pers.] Dr. William T. Ryan holds a Ph.D. from Indiana University in Bloomington, ID. He is a professor of International Business in the College of Business at Florida Atlantic University in Boca Raton, Florida.

SADIQUE, SABRINA

[a.] New Haven, CT [title] "When Harkness Tolls" [pers.] The sound of tolling bells from Harkess Tower in Yale University induces almost a shamanistic sense of communication . . . as though the Gods are looking down and asking passersby to reckon their losses, gains, defeats, and dreams. Freshman, like me, can't help but surrender to it. The poem is thus hardly a predesigned endeavor on my part. It is rather a reflex to the eerie appeal of Harkness with its centripetal quality of directing all passers-by toward its solitude, punctuated by tolling bells. I am just a carrier of a poem that would have inevitably come through—such is the power of Harkness.

SAFFOLD, E. LEE

[title] "Croaking Frogs" [pers.] A native of Alabama, a graduate of Southern Christian University, and an officer in the United States Navy, I live in Atlanta, Georgia and work for AT&T. Man is most like God when speaking with written language to his fellowmen as God speaks in his holy word. Writing with simple metaphor, parables, Psalms, Proverbs, Divine Linguistics, poetry is designed by the creator to convey between hearts insights captured in dreams and visions. By these means, images branded upon the tender surface of the mind can be traced, shaped into a "Branding Corn," heated by strong emotions, and seared into our common conscientious hearts.

SAMAYOA, JUAN MANUEL

[a.] El Paso, TX [title] "Tear of Pain" [pers.] This poem is just words. The meaning of this poem is what you make of it. The uniqueness of my poetry is that everyone could relate to it. This poem is dedicated to a really important person in my life. She made me look at the world in a totally different way. I just want to end this with a couple of words that a wise person once told me, "Live without respect." "God gave me the ability now, and I give Him the glory."

SARGENT, BETTY

[title] "Fun" [pers.] This poem is based on my motto for life. "If I can't have fun, I ain't gonna do it." I have been ill for almost 20 years and have come to realize—life is what we make it. I have chosen to live life to its fullest, enjoying it the best I can. God has blessed me with many talents, poetry being one of them. One of my greatest enjoyments is writing poetry for those I love. In doing so, I share a piece of my heart with them.

SCATCHELL, ANTHONY

[a.] Chicago, IL [title] "Up Or Down" [pers.] I wrote this poem when I was 13 years old in my seventh grade English class when the teacher asked us to write something about Heaven and Hell. If you read this poem carefully, you will see it spells "Heaven" going up and "Hell" going down. I enjoy writing as a hobby and especially giving poems an unusual twist like this one.

SCHARENBROCH, ERIC

[title] "Walk On, Lost Angel" [pers.] I wrote this work in Spain, where I had the privilege to study in a fantastic city called Valladolid. It struck me while I was there, how different everyone's priorities were there as opposed to here; they seemed to enjoy life more. It made me realize what I've always known to be true: Human beings are absolutely incredible, living miracles with endless potential . . . and their worst enemy always ends up being themselves. I guess you know others best from what you know about yourself, right?

SCHERB, DAVID

[title] "Promise" [pers.] This poem was written as a gift to my wife about six months before our wedding. I wanted to let her know how I feel and to show her my commitment to her and our marriage. She liked it so much that it ended up on our wedding program.

SCHERER, MONICA

[title] "I'm Gone" [pers.] My poem sums up my early childhood. Writing poetry about my childhood helps me heal and forgive those ignorant kids (now adults) who have forever changed my life.

SCHMALFELD, CHRISTY

[a.] St. Louis, MO [title] "Whole" [pers.] To love someone completely, with your entire soul, and know they feel it too . . . well, that's everything. That is why we live. Because if you find this, then you are home. You don't have to search anymore, because you've found what most never do, true love. And then you are whole.

SCHOENFELD, AMBER

[title] "Mission Statement" [pers.] This poem serves as a constant reminder of the importance of life. It is a never ending cycle full of turbulence that needs goals to keep everything on track and running on schedule. "Mission Statement" is my everyday criteria for my life.

SCHUMACKER, CHARLES (CHUCK)

[a.] Thorold, ON [title] "Tiger in My House" [pers.] "Tiger" was my first attempt at self-awareness many years ago, and being alone in that house, I was very afraid. It wasn't until I realized who the Tiger was that I became at ease with myself. Now, forty and change years later, I've learned not only how to face the tiger, but how to control him as well. I've written essays, short stories and poetry of one type or another all of my life, and this is the first poem I've ever felt confident enough to share. Thank you, ILP.

SCHUPMAN, JEANNIE

[a.] Lincoln, AR [title] "Remember" [pers.] This poem was written to my husband during a very rocky period in our marriage. I wanted to remind him of all we had shared, and that it hadn't all been bad. He has since passed away, and I would like to dedicate the poem to his memory. In memory of Albert L. Schupman.

SCHWABE, KATIE

[a.] Greenfield, WI [title] "Turmoil to Freedom" [pers.] This poem means a lot to me because it tells the story of how I got my life back. With the help of my mother, Toni, stepfather, Gary, brother, Jeff, and sisters, Kelly and Andrea, I was able to free myself of the binds my father had on me. I finally was able to stand up for myself. So for that, I would like to thank my family and friends that helped me through this ordeal. I could have never done it without you guys. This poem is dedicated to you all. I love you all very much.

SCHWARTZ, JONATHAN

[title] Heaven Sent" [pers.] I believe that all poetry has a certain meaning or inspiration behind it. For me, inspiration comes from my family and close friends. If it weren't for my experience with them, I would have nothing to write about. Thank you, Mom, Dad, Ruchie, Moshe, Eli, Gavriel, Shaya, Sara, Leemor, Taippi, and Cathy. You have all made a huge difference in my life.

SCHWARZ, DAVID

[a.] Clovis, CA [title] "Bitterness" [pers.] For me, poetry is never a chore to do, find time for, and read. It gives me a way to express myself in a truly free and unique way. When I wrote "Bitterness," I was in high school, frustrated with the teachers that tried to teach, tried to motivate, and tried to inspire. Instead, they just discouraged. When it came time to write poetry in my English class, I took the opportunity to express my feelings in a way that best suited me. This poem is the end result.

SELLARD, MERLIN

[a.] Federal Way, MA [title] "Can You Hear the Rainbow?" [pers.] A few years ago, I had a cat that ran to the door only when there was a rainbow or sunset. This made me wonder what a rainbow might sound like, and finally after a few years, the only way I could express this was in a poem. Whether we can actually hear the rainbow or see its refraction of light, an imagination can help bring about new discoveries, like the earth being round. It is a joy to express this and share it in poetry.

SELMER, PHILIP

[title] "Wolf" [pers.] This poem is one of only a few that truly represents my inner self. The wolf is in many ways similar to me. I would like to thank my Mom and Dad for helping me throughout my life, and my favorite English teacher, Ms. Jane Campbell, who helped me release my creative writing talent. I dedicate "wolf" to Ms. Campbell.

SEMENDYAI, OLGA

[a.] Washington, DC [pers.] Pen names: Victoria Clinton, Mary Flahouston; Born September 3, 1955; St. Petersburg, Russia; Divorced with one son; Education: Ph.D. (psychology), University of the District of Columbia; Member of AOPA, AAA, GWU Club, Video Warehouse, Hollywood Video, AMC, Sky Miles, Student Advantage, NAFE; Honors include Letter of Recognition is given by President Clinton for a good job as a volunteer in Tobacco Campaign 1996, 21st Marine Corps Marathon—Finisher, Citation of Merit from the American Air Museum in Britain; Other writings include several unpublished poems in national magazines, articles for the *Washington Post* and the *Washington Times*, an article for *Town and Country*, and a short story for *Reader's Digest*; I believe in the unlimited creative possibilities of the human being. I have been greatly influenced by Longfellow and Frank Sinatra.

SERRANO, RICHARD

[title] "No Reason" [pers.] This poem is special to me, as it was written at a time of great confusion and pain. It helped me to realize that you cannot expect anyone to love you as may love them.

SEVERA, JAIMEE

[title] "Falling Love" [pers.] I am grateful for the gift of poetry. It is the living breath of many writers . . . our fingerprints in time.

SHERWOOD, EDNA

[title] "Unfailing Love" [pers.] I have been writing short articles and readings for several years. Recently I began putting them together in a book but I found myself feeling overwhelmed. I became discouraged, even though I felt God was in it. My devotion time led to me the Psalms, and I read about God's unfailing love for His people. Soon I saw and felt that love for me. A radiator was provided for my car, a hearing loss was restored, and my wardrobe was given a face lift. "Unfailing Love" is the result of reading God's word and these evidences of God's continual care and love for me.

SHORE, MICHAEL

[title] "Hide No Longer" [pers.] Never too young to die, nor too old to live. Life is to the young what living is to the spirit.

SHORES, CHERE

[a.] Long Beach, CA [title] "An Angel Whose Earned His Wings" [pers.] This started as a prayer to my two-and-a-half-year-old, precious, courageous baby boy who was violently taken from this earth. Then I saw it as a voice, the voice of all the innocent, helpless children who are unable to have a voice. I want everyone to hear it. Then maybe someone will hear my plea and join my fight, the fight to pass a law that states, "anyone who takes the life of a child, using malice, should have to plea for theirs." The death penalty should be an option. Please help!

SHORT, SHAWN

[title] "Reflections" [pers.] To: Page, you took your hand from me, showing that love is a form of insanity. I could not breathe and yet could not live, knowing that I have so much more love to give. And now I stay in this awful world, having dreams of my baby girl and that future family that will never be. Things have changed, and I'm not even me . . . anymore. I see things about you that I didn't before. And now that you're gone, I see my life as Shawn a bore.

SIDMAN, DONALD

[title] "Down Deep" [pers.] Poetry is a gift from God. This poem was written on feeling of twenty years ago. It was the pits. Now life is filled with love and joy.

SIEBERT, RYAN

[title] "Riding a Dream" [pers.] This poem is more than just words, it's a part of my life. It's a memory, a lesson, and an inspiration that nothing is impossible. It's a summary of a summer spent on a bicycle with nothing but an open road, love of my family, and my best friend, Stephen Burch. We traveled from the Pacific to the Atlantic Ocean, fulfilling a childhood bet. But the bet was more than just a coast to coast of a dream.

SIMERLY, INGER

[title] "Poems" [pers.] I have always loved poetry, and when I was young, dreamed of becoming a writer. But as my poem says, busy years flew by. Raising a large family and helping to earn a living left little time for writing. Now in my eighties, I finally have time. "Poems" is one of my first attempts.

SIMS, APRIL

[a.] Steelton, PA [title] "Simply You" [pers.] Sunday morning fits her like warm biscuits and syrup, tea with a splash of lemon. When she speaks, her words are full of wisdom and wonder. She can take you somewhere, and you never knew you left. Strong like sisters of old.

No curve in her back, no breaks on her face. My ganny, as I call her, is pure essence! Like rain without acid, air without pollution. She's real love. My mother is her only living child, who inherits her mother's enchanting spirit and fortitude. My grandmother, (ganny) is 94 and still strong. Yes! We've been blessed by simply love.

SIP, ERICA LATOYA
[a.] Baton Rouge, LA [title] "Till the End of Time" [pers.] In a violent explosion of hatred and bottled up feelings, my life was abruptly changed. And during that time of change, I felt very alone, and often spent my time crying in my room. Life was just so unbearable. Then one night, I dried my tears, grabbed a pen and some paper, and began to write down my innermost thoughts and feelings. "Till the End of Time" was what I wrote that night, and it made me feel a little better. Even now, I still use poetry to express myself and ease the strain of my problems, but I'm not alone this time. I now have David and I love him with all my heart and soul.

SLADKOVA, MARTINA
[a.] 150 Mile House, BC [title] "To the Moon" [pers.] Born March 5, 1985, I was inspired by my emotions, all the emotions you have living the teenage years. Being able to write is a gift, but being able to write well is believing. Having English as my second language and living in a small town, Williams Lake, British Columbia, this is a great achievement for me. I would like to thank my family and friends (Jana and Ryan) for believing in me and my dream of wanting to write and be read. I achieved my goals. Thank you for helping me prove that at 16, you can do anything you want with your life. I love you lots.

SMEDLEY, FOSTER
[title] "Lost" [pers.] Poetry is my life, because every time I feel depressed or upset, I write out a verse or two. It helps me get my head on straight without getting too sad or angry. Most of my poems are about ones that have hurt me or the way I feel about life in general. This particular poem is about how lost the human race, as a whole, is. I mean we are all setting ourselves up, but the human race is just too blind to see it. I think we need to realize our ways and clean up the mess we've made on this beautiful planet.

SMITH, AMBER
[title] "Vision of Me" [pers.] I feel honored to be included among the many poets in this publication. Thank you for the opportunity to share my joy of writing with others. "Vision of Me" was written during a time when life had emptied my soul of its joy. I found myself searching for the person I used to be. I began writing a few years ago as a way to work through my circumstances. Writing has become my source of comfort. I'm glad to say that I have found my "springtime" and I am in full bloom once again.

SMITH, BRUCE
[title] "The Wind" [pers.] The wording for the poem is mine. I did have some help with the spelling. The teacher who helped is Mr. Dennis Rolheiser. I love writing poems. To me, poems are a release from things. To any poet having spelling trouble, just don't let it beat you.

SMITH, DIANE
[a.] Bakersfield, CA [title] "One Thousand Dollar Poem" [pers.] First of all, I want to thank you for selecting the "One Thousand Dollar Poem" to be published in *True Reflections*. I believe that poetry is a gift and I enjoy writing poems on many different topics. The "One Thousand Dollar Poem" is very special to me, because it was a pleasure to write this poem for the Montel's "Cure For Multiple Sclerosis" poetry contest announced in the *Bakersfield Californian*, and a delight to use Mr. Williams' name in it. I also enjoy bowling and would like to be a professional bowler.

SMITH, DOUGLAS
[a.] Caddo Mills, TX [pers.] For a 16-year-old, being published is an exhilarating experience. Dreams of college become a little more visible. My poems represent everything that is me and my experiences through life. It prepares me for disaster and for challenges in my near future. I have to once more express how ecstatic I am. The publication of my poetry is a real accomplishment for me.

SMITH, ENDORA
[a.] Enfield, NH [title] "1-800-Heaven" [pers.] All my life, writing poems has become away to express my feelings. My most cherished poem is "1-800-Heaven." It flowed from my heart to a piece of paper when I was missing my father after he passed away. Even today, rereading this poem makes me feel better. I wanted to share this poem with others who have lost a loved one like I have.

SMITH, GARY
[title] "The Day" [pers.] A good ole' boy from the south, born in Georgia and raised in Florida. Been in Data Processing for the last 35 years, same company the last 25. Love to listen to country music (old country). Writes both poetry and country music songs. I am 53 years old and thoroughly enjoy life, especially the simple things, birds singing, flowers blooming, and children playing. I plan to retire as soon as I possibly can, then enjoy spending my time with my lovely wife Debbie and my three wonderful kids, Derek, Adriene and Patrick. Hobbies include, riding motorcycles and growing roses.

SMITH, JENNIFER
[title] "His Turn" [pers.] This poem means a lot to me because it shows how I felt when I lost my uncle and friend from my school. Poetry is a very important part of my life because it lets me express myself in a new way. When I am feeling down, I usually write a quick poem and I just let my feelings flow on a sheet of paper, and it usually lifts my spirits. I would recommend anyone to try writing a poem to either ease their pain or just to express their individuality.

SMITH, JULIE
[title] "Somewhere in Time" [pers.] I am the mother of three children, David, Brittney, and Cody. Like many people in the world, I dreamed of finding the one with whom the Lord had intended for me to share my life. What better way can you express to someone how much in love with them you are, than in a poem of words and feelings that will last forever? My poem, "Somewhere in Time," is my way of saying, Chad, you are the man of my dreams, and I will love you through all eternity.

SMITH, KATIE G.
[a.] Troy, VA [title] "The Misdirection of a Broken Heart" [pers.] Poetry is a talent that I am very proud of. I am in the process of putting my collection of poems and short stories together, in hopes to publish a book someday. I probably wouldn't have written this poem if my English teacher hadn't given me a specific poetry assignment. Aside from poetry, I enjoy drawing, playing the trumpet, and collecting frog paraphernalia, and TV basketball. I also love to spend Sunday nights watching the *X-Files* religiously! I am an honor student, and a member of my High School's Key Club. I hope you enjoy my poem! Ribbit!

SMITH, LINDSEY NICOLE
[title] "Dreams Come True" [pers.] My name is Lindsey Nicole Smith. I'm from Leechburg, Pennsylvania and I'm in the seventh grade. In my leisure time, I like to do gymnastics, swim, and of course, write poetry. My dad encouraged me the most to start writing poetry. He asked me to write a poem, and I did! That is how it all started. After that, I started writing even more. Then I had my poems printed in newspapers, magazines, and now my greatest accomplishment, in a book. I enjoy writing and hope to accomplish more.

SMITH, LISA
[title] "Today" [pers.] Poetry is a powerful tool to express one's innermost feelings. I hope others who find themselves struggling at a crossroads in their life will be comforted by this poem. We are not alone in our feelings of love and joy, or in the dark corners of our hearts.

SMITH, MARK S.
[a.] Drexel Hill, PA [title] "Girl with Overcoat" [pers.] My poem was written for a young woman who was the "first American girl" I noticed after a long trip back from Singapore via a four month tour in the Persian Gulf. I was instantly and absolutely smitten. I couldn't find her the next day, but I did eleven years later. Oh, she did remember me . . . but she slipped away in 2000.

SMITH, MONICA
[a.] New Orleans, LA [title] "Sweet Seduction" [pers.] This poem is dedicated to my loving spouse. For without him, I would not have been inspired to write this beautiful piece. To have someone to share a whirlwind of life changes and still feel that same mesmerizing and loving power that was initially sparked with the very first encounter is amazing and simply phenomenal. I love my spouse and I wanted to express the emotional escapades that are still shared between us even after all of the storm clouds have past.

SMITH PIERRE, CARI
[title] "Broken Soul" [pers.] I see poetry as a gift and an outlet. Whenever I am stressed or in emotional turmoil, I transform my pain into creative energy. In my poem, "Broken Soul," I wrote about how the negative comments and attitudes of a person or group of people can sometimes turn a happy person into a troubled one. The key to staying happy, I believe, is to find a positive outlet for your pain, and to keep in mind that one only gets one life. Therefore, one should live his or her life for him or herself and not to please anyone else.

SMITH-TAYLOR, P. R.
[title] "Life or Death" [pers.] "Creativity is such a personal thing. I believe my best works are those that come easily." I, Pia're, (P.R.) have been involved in artwork and creating since I was a small child. I was encouraged by all my art teachers, all through my schooling, to pursue art. At age 16, my drawing of Former President John F. Kennedy and First Lady Jacqueline Kennedy gained recognition in newspapers while at a state fair. I studied Beauty, Culture, and Design and have been involved in photographic modeling, film, television, and music while always maintaining my artwork, poetry, and writing lyrics. I have lived in California, Hawaii, Texas, and am from Vermont. "My poetry is always connected deeply with my personal emotions and feelings."

SNETSINGER, CHARLES, II
[title] "Chance" [pers.] "Chance" was written for someone that I had met through a close friend. The title pretty much says it all. Thought the relationship may not have worked out, the poem remains very special to me. I think that life's truest rewards are the results from what we experience. "Chance" is my reward.

SNORTEN, MARGARET
[a.] Nashville, TN [title] "Fear Not" [pers.] Poetry can brighten or bring joy to your life. I write to make one feel good. I often write for weddings or special celebrations. My poems are related to the person I write about. They come out a winner. A poem can cheer the lonely and inspire those who are sad. I write to bring cheer, express a good feeling, or tell a story of love.

SNOWDEN, ASHLEY
[title] "Glass Tears" [pers.] My poem was about a

really bad breakup I just went through, but I am surviving. I guess when it comes down to it that's what I am—a survivor.

SOBIERAJ, JEFFREY

[title] "The Little Things Matter the Most" [pers.] You spend your whole life searching for that person of your dreams, that special someone that can make your fairy tale fantasies come true. This poem was written for that person, a very special friend of mine named Emily. Every little thing about her, things that no one else sees, I see. Even though it may never work out as I would like, at least I know that there is someone out there, not only for me but for everybody, as long as they believe and never give up searching with their hearts. True love always finds a way.

SOBIESCZYK, KAREN

[title] "Teacher" [pers.] This poem was originally written to tell a friend the influence he had on my decision to leave a longtime, abusive relationship, but now I believe it serves as a plea from many women and men, who are longing to find a life free from such abuse. If this poem touches you in that way, please know that there is, truly, a better life.

SOILEAU, JESSIE

[a.] Gonzales, LA [title] "Boot Camp" [pers.] Eighteen month after retirement from a major oil company, my wife was diagnosed with lung cancer. Surgery proved unsuccessful. She was prescribed chemotherapy. I would give her a card for encouragement, every time I took her to the doctor, or for a treatment. Having enjoyed writing poems in High School although I had quit writing when I began working, I started writing one every time I gave her a card. I soon realized she would wait for that card, especially enjoying the poems I wrote. What a therapy for her and I! She passed away six months after diagnosed. "Boot Camp" is to my grandsons in military service.

SOLOMON, HOWARD

[title] "The Sea" [pers.]This poem is one of peace. The tranquility of the sea, the freedom of the bee. It's a plea for the dawning of the age of the Messiah when war, famine, and hatred are no more, when man is at peace with man and woman is at peace with woman—a Utopia. A prayer in which the "people's" vote counts, "All" of them, and the electoral college is no more. An age in which "wisdom" returns, and we "see" things as they really are—we see that we need new highways, that we can't have a green light for the man to turn and a green light for people to walk, that we need "smaller" classrooms. . . .

SOULE, RICHARD

[a.] Lincoln, NE [title] "Paper Weight" [pers.] Paper Weight parallels my own relationship to writing. I had an affinity for words at a young age. It wasn't until adulthood that I realized it was something deeper. Poetry has become the validation of my existence—prosody.

STACK, ERIC PHILIP

[a.] Melbourne, FL [title] "Cocaine" [pers.] Born January 8, 1974; Miami, FL; Parents are John and Susan Stack; Educated at Brevard Community College; Honors include Amra Motocross Champion at age eleven for the State of Florida, Most Valuable Player in Football and Little League, lettered in Wrestling in sixth grade; Other writings include several poems that have all been copyrighted. *That Champion* is the name of his book.

STANDIFORD, SHANNON

[a.] Maysville, MO [title] "My Lonely Heart" [pers.] I live in a family where tragedy strikes often. Upon those tragedies, I believe that greatness happens in many ways. I started writing poems when I fell into a multi-year depression over the loss of a loved one. In that time, many of my friends and family say that I published many outstanding works. "My Lonely Heart" is a story about a man who is in love with the woman of his dreams, yet to his dismay, he just can't tell her. I and others an relate to this problem. Personal staff: I go to Maysville R-I in Maysville, Missouri. My parents, and the people that were always behind me are Teresa and James Willtrout, Loretta Crouch, Brother, Matt, Sister, Becky. Aunt Cathi, Ruby, Debbie, and Laura, Uncle Ronnie and my late Uncle Roy. Cousins Malinda, Chad, Heather, Brod, Brit, Bambi, and "J." Everything that I do is because of them and my angels above me, Hope and Gramps, my many friends as well. Thanks to them, poetry is my life's blood and forever will be a past of me.

STANFORD, PETER

[title] "Options" [pers.] The earliest date I can find for "Options" is May '98, but I'm sure it's at least six months older than that. It is one of the first things I wrote that doesn't scare me. I think it is also one of the best things I've ever written. It says exactly what I want it to say, elegantly and concisely, in an interesting way, without just stating it plainly—the essence of poetry, to my mind. I was trying to write something else that didn't scare me, and it wasn't really working, when "Options" just occurred to me. It appears in almost exactly the same form as the original draft. The inspiration for both was the same. I've survived leukemia, alcoholism, drug abuse, depression, self-destructive behavior, suicidal thinking, a stress/anxiety problem, and a seriously dysfunctional family. Almost everything I write comes from these experiences, and it is usually dark. I write what I think about. It's for the relief value. Other people usually don't want to hear it. They've got their own agenda. I write to stay sane. I don't know if it's working.

STANLEY, CATHERINE LORRAINE

[a.] Buckley, WA [title] "Skippy" [pers.] This poem was written when I was fifteen years old. I wrote this poem to commemorate a very special friend in my life: my dog, Skippy. When Skippy died, everyone that knew her was saddened. I made a poem so that she would never be forgotten. Skippy was one of the most faithful creatures alive. She was always there to protect anyone who needed protection and she would never harm a soul. Rest in peace, girl. We all love and miss you.

STAVRIDES, KELLY

[title] "Iris" [pers.] Iris joined my family when I was only eight months old and left when I was twelve years old. Up until the day she died, I'd never known a day without her. I wrote this poem about Iris about a month after she died, during some free time at school. A poem seemed the best way to express myself and tell her how much I loved her, although it was too late for her to "hear" the words.

STEPHENS, DONNA

[a.] Richmond, VA [title] "Charity Shows We Care" [pers.] This poem came to me from a higher power in a dream at 3:00 a.m, so I got out of bed and wrote it down. I was watching TV and saw Montel Williams requesting a poem to help MS; I knew this was a small request for help. My brother-in-law, Earl Bowles, came down with MS last year, and I knew I had to help. Earl has always helped others in life like Montel does, and I feel this is my way to express my love to them. Earl and Montel, "I love you both," and I'm now looking forward to more dreams.

STEPHENSON, LORAINE

[a.] Grayling, MI [pers.] This is dedicated to 18-year-old Vicki, who came up missing one Friday. A week of anxiety, anger, and a frantic state-wide search by family, friends, media, and police passed, before Vicki called, assuring her family she was safe . . . in Virginia! The ensuing tears, threats, questions, and general emotional upheaval prompted me to write these words to strengthen and uplift her as a young woman who is just learning to fly from her nest. I'm happily married, living in Northern Michigan on the Manistee River, and am a 70-year-old grandmother of 17 and great-grandmother of 10. Victoria is my granddaughter.

STERUD, FRANCINE

[a.] Wintersville, Oh, [title] "The Darkness Doesn't Answer" [pers.] I am attending Duquene University. However, I consider myself a lifelong student of knowledge. I sat in darkness of the new early morning with the quiet freshness of a quite peaceful moment. Inspiration overwhelmed me with this feeling that I just had to allow to manifest into words and then become this poem. The words overflowed. This poetic piece of work truly came from a loving heart; my poems have always been written from the joy that comes from my life and my children. I write poetry for the sheer joy of happy expression, not for reward. When I awaken daily, I have a natural sense of peace and love. Life can being goodness from laughter as with sorrow. I live life and thank God for all of life's experiences—great experiences and not so great experiences. Mia Angela has been a huge influence in my depth of soul and spirit. I thank you for the opportunity to share this poem with others.

STEVENS, HAROLD

[a.] Norwalk, CT [title] "Picture of Perfection" [pers.] My inspiration is the only woman on earth whose soul is an exact fit to mine. I am forever thankful to my soul mate and "Picture of Perfection," Peggie.

STIETZ, GEORGE

[a.] Hayes, VA [title] "Mother Sun" [pers.] The Sun—let it enrapture you. Let it love and hold you in times of dark loneliness, with the night on your heels and your heart on the run. A mother with child—let her enrapture you. She is divine. She is perfection. She is the grace and dignity we have been waiting for. Thank you, both.

STILL, EVELYN

[title] "Motherhood" [pers.] Poignant occasions elicit deep emotions, and poetry is my outlet. For me, only words on paper can speak to these lessons in life. To commemorate Mother's 70th birthday, I wanted a simple and heartfelt gift—a thank you for her love and generosity. As a divorced, single parent in a time when this lifestyle was rare, Mother gave her all. Through her, my sisters and I know a great deal more about the meaning of all. A retired legal secretary, I currently enjoy freelance proofreading. This is my first published work! I am inspired to continue poetry and fiction writing.

STOKES, JESSICA

[title] "Mister Reaper, Sir" [pers.] My poem is my plea for peace for my family, which at the time was experiencing loss after loss. Writing is my way of dealing with life's problems. This poem is special to me because it helped me deal with two very unfortunate events in my life.

STONE, SHIRLEY

[a.] Seattle, WA [title] "Heroes" [pers.] My poetry is usually limited to or for special persons or occasions. I begin writing what I called ditties for just my family. Then somehow, it broadened to include friends and sometimes friends of friends. Most of my writings are light and are meant to make the subjects and audiences laugh. Initially they are read aloud by me. Many of my compositions have personal innuendoes, and consequently, would not mean anything to most readers. "Heroes" is different. It was inspired by a good friend who is battling M.S. You see, sometimes I do get serious.

STORK, TAMI L.

[a.] Aurora, CO [title] "My Daddy" [pers.] I wrote this poem while visiting my father for the very last time. He was dying of lung cancer. My father and mother have always been my inspiration to write. After my father died, I had a dream of him and mama remarrying; my dad was in a black tuxedo and mama was in a white wedding gown. We were a family again. They will forever be my inspiration. My father, Donald "Duck" Stork died on December 4, 2000 at 11:58 a.m. I never thought both of my parents would be deceased before I was 40 years old.

STRAIT, AMIE
[title] "Love" [pers.] Sometimes I write poetry to get away, to get my feelings out. It makes me feel better. I am a high school student and proud to have a poem of mine published! I would like to give a special thanks to my parents, Mark and Andrea Strait.

STRANGE, SUSAN
[title] "Michael, My Friend" [pers.] I have enjoyed poetry since I was a child. I wrote my poem to express to Michael that he is a very special person who came into my life when I needed a friend. A poem is my way of thanking him for being there for me. I would like for my poem to be an inspiration to others that find themselves in need of the gift of friendship.

STRATTON, DAVID
[title] "My Dear Phyllis" [pers.] I'm a welder by profession, 52 years. I started writing poems about six years ago. I write about things closest to my heart and family. This poem was written a few days after my beloved wife suddenly passed away. This is my dedication to her for her 47 years of devotion to me. She was always by my side. She left me in the loving care of our six children, 19 grandchildren, 29 great-grandchildren, and our Heavenly Father. I feel the closeness of her always as she watches over us all as our special guardian angel.

STRAWN, JEFFREY
[title] "Campus" [pers.] Poetry, good poetry, is something only few humans possess the talent to produce. It is essential to have a different outlook on life and a deeper understanding of the things around you to write poetry. This poem reflects my views on how people go through each day, blind to the deep beauty behind everything.

STROTHER, NANCY SUSAN
[a.] Golden, CO [title] "The Land of the Forgotten Lovers" [pers.] Writing has always provided me with a convenient outlet to express my deepest thoughts and feelings. I am fortunate enough to have a loving husband who has wholeheartedly supported me and my writing endeavors. My three children have provided me with many reasons to smile, and I thank God for the blessings they have brought to my life. I hope that my poetry provides a clear insight into what events have impacted my life the most.

STUART, TERRANCE
[title] "Quest" [pers.] This poem was written quickly but surely, as I have experienced the void and realize we are more fundamental than our fleeting thoughts—we are beings with eternal qualities to which time neither adds nor subtracts.

SULLIVAN, ANDREA
[a.] Indian Trail, NC [title] "On Raven's First Birthday" [pers.] This poem was written on the way home from a week long family vacation at Myrtle Beach. A three and a half hour drive gave my mind time to wonder. Raven learned to walk really well that week before her birthday at the beach, up and down the beach, all over the beach house. We all had a blast. The words came to me on the way home that afternoon. I replayed them in my mind until we got home. I'm thankful to God for blessing me and my husband, Stephen, with this wonderful addition to our family.

SULLIVAN, KAREN
[title] "Tortured Soul" [pers.] For someone not able to express feelings through her voice, the best way for me to show the world my thoughts has always been to write. Writing has helped me through some of the hardest times of my life.

SUMMERS, NANCY
[title] "Your Eyes" [pers.] Poetry to me is a unique way to express and understand life. Each poem that is written is as diversified as the individuals that make up this world. Yet feelings that are expressed in poetry are not only felt by the artist, but have been experienced by others. Happiness, sadness, surprise, anticipation, and fear can be conveyed in the writing of poems. Feelings and messages we need to know of and express take on a new meaning in poetic form. Something we can pass on from generation to generation, poetry is a gift to both poet and reader alike.

SUPRENAND, JEFF
[a.] Fond Du Lac, WI [title] "All These Tears" [pers.] I have often used poetry to express my feelings and emotions. I often base my poetry on human thoughts and emotions. "All These Tears" is about people's feelings when they have almost lost someone they love and also when there is a tremendous distance between them and the one they love. I believe poetry should come from the heart and touch the heart of many. I would like to thank my mom, dad, brother, and my kids, Kegan, Kimberly, and Braden. I hope people will read my poem and want to share it with someone they love.

SURRATT, JESSICA
[title] "The Price of Freedom" [pers.] I love Jesus Christ with all my heart so I decided to share this love as an essay for my government class. I derived this poem from my essay. I hope that in the future I can tell even more people about Jesus Christ, my Lord and Savior.

SWAIN, CHARLES R.
[a.] Beaver, PA [title] "Tell Me You Love Me" [pers.] This poem was written especially for my wife, Susan. Both of us found love late in life, I being 65, and my wife, 59. This is the poem I wrote to her before our wedding in 1995. I had never written a poem before, but Susan thought I expressed my feelings so well through poetry, she wanted me to continue writing. I have written many other poems, this one having special meaning for both of us. Susan's continuous love and encouragement has brought me happiness, along with a newfound love in a great field of dreams. I have been truly blessed.

SWANSON, KENDA
[title] "A Prayer for Peace" [pers.] When I wrote the poem, "A Prayer for Peace," I was pondering about the war. I would find myself intrigued by the mystery of it all. I spent hours just imagining what it would be like to be one of those poor children—knowing that any minute, my world could be blown to bits. I realize now how fortunate I am to have a caring, loving family and a safe environment to live in. This poem is very special and distinctive to me. It represents how I feel about "peace" as well as my everlasting love towards God.

SWINTON, TWANNA
[title] "My Angels" [pers.] To me, this poem is one of my own personal favorites. Stepping out into the real world, being single, not knowing anyone, special people were placed in my life. Being away from my family, on my own, I had to survive, and I did with my angels. This poem is also a prayer. No one wants to be left alone. Even when you're going through trials in your life, there is always a little ray of sunshine that peeps through the dark clouds. My angels were my sunshine, and they kept happiness flowing all around me—such a great experience, I had to share it with everyone and anyone willing to read. If you have angels in your life, let them know how special they are, and let them know they should never go away.

SYMES, ANDREW
[a.] Perth, West Australia [title] "Pure Conscience" [pers.] For me, poetry is an emotional outlet, so it does not have to be about love or nature. "Pure Conscience" is a dark satire of how man thinks of himself as God, but we cannot deal with the consequences of our actions, and our naive cry for forgiveness. Living in Perth, Western Australia, I see this playing of God every day, with the logging of our old grown forests and the proposed dumping of nuclear waste in our outbrook. I wish to thank my parents, Lan and Peta, my friends, and Hayley for always encouraging me to express myself in life.

SZANY, WILLIAM
[a.] Hammond, IN [title] "The Schedule of the Week" [pers.] I am very grateful for this honor which has been bestowed upon me. However, in my eyes, the true author of all of my poetry is God. Thank you so very much, God, for the wonderful gift of poetry. I would like to dedicate "The Schedule of the Week" to my mother and father for believing in me and for supporting me in my poetic endeavors. Julie Kmak, thank you so much. I might have never written poetry to begin with, if you had not entered my life.

TAJIK, JAMIL
[title] "I Saw a Dead Woman Smiling Today" [pers.] The poem that I wrote has certain meanings to me, but I hope you will find your own meaning in it. I never thought a poem I wrote would be good enough to be published; I stand humbly corrected. I am honored to be among these artists of words. I would like to give thanks to the countless people that have inspired me, most dearly to my family and friends with whom I have spent a life, but truly just a drop in time.

TALAYKA, JOSH JAMES
[a.] Reno, NV [title] "People and Me" [pers.] I currently reside in Reno, NV. I never wrote until I moved here from AZ, at least, never from the heart. Most of my work is my way of crying out—crying out to the people of the world. We must stop hating, for we all are images of ourselves. I feel a great amount of joy, knowing that my work will be read across the world. May my work, and all the work in this book bring joy, hope, and an ultimate wisdom to those who read it.

TARPLEY, JOSIE
[a.] Glencoe, AL [title] "Country Road" [pers.] As I grew up in the country, one of nine children, I developed a great love of nature. At age seven, I began to write poems for family and friends on holidays and special occasions. Today, at age eighty-one, and a cancer survivor, I still love to write poetry. I thank God for this talent and for being able to share it with others. I would like to dedicate this poem, "Country Road," to my brothers and sisters as well as to the memory of my beloved parents.

TATE, FARRAH
[title] "Parting and Departing" [pers.] For me, writing poetry is an absolute pleasure and a passion to treasure always. I am forever grateful to the International Library of Poetry for this unique publication opportunity. My greatest desire is to mature further as a writer and correspondingly to achieve further exposure and publication of my work. My poetry explores common life themes and circumstances, whether they be struggles or joys, thereby reflecting a collective western world experience. I thank those who share my vision and who have supported me in this trek, so far departed from my scientific foundations.

TAYLOR, KELLY
[title] "Angels . . . " [pers.] This poem means a lot to me because it is about people whom I have loved and lost, but they'll always be my angels. I have always loved to write poems and hope to keep doing so. It's a way to get my feelings out, besides singing/dancing. All my life, writing has been a favorite hobby of mine,

and I hope this poem has showed many people that there are other ways to tell someone how much you love and care for them. Thank you. Also I wish to thank my family, friends, and my teachers. Thank you to them.

TAYLOR, ROXANNE

[title] "Broken Flowers" [pers.] Unlike many others, this poem doesn't come from any experiences within my life. Rather, I had been trying to put myself in another person's perspective. I find that most of my better poems are created from trying to imagine another's feelings, which I find is easier than expressing my own through a poem. Poetry is a gift, and I am glad that I have received it and that I am able to pass it on to others for their enjoyment.

TEALER, KAY

[title] "Why Are You Mad at Me?" [pers.] I did this poem when I was fifteen years old. I had a terrible crush on a boy who was nineteen, and we both had hobbies using CB radios. I guess I was too young for him, and he ignored me for the most part, but at I could tell at times he was flattered and not totally resistent. This poem is a result. I am a marvel to a wonderful husband Dennis, I love my 19 year old daughter, Christian, a sheltie named Roddis who is my best friend. I love antiques, reading, and being with my family.

TERRY, AMBER

[a.] Hicksville, Oh, [pers.] My name is Amber Marie Terry, and I'm 12 years old. I live in Hicksville, Ohio with my Dad, Paul, and my younger sister Ashley. I was six when I wrote my first poem. I have loved writing poems ever since then. I'm inspired by mostly anything. Lots of times I will be sitting around just thinking about anything, and a poem will come to me. I really love writing poems and I'm planning on making a career out of it. I would like to thank Howard Ely for getting my dream off the ground. Thank you so much.

TESSIER, TINA

[a.] Shelburne Falls, MA [title] "To Our Sweet, Loveable Damien" [pers.] I have loved poetry ever since I could remember. Poetry is a way for me to express my feelings in words. It is a way to lighten the world.

TESTA, MICHELLE

[a.] Depew, NY [title] "They Are Yours Too" [pers.] Poetry takes me to a place where I can express my fears, and anger towards the neglect our nation's children are suffering every day. My children, William and Laura, are my inspiration. All of my work is in their honor. I cherish them with all of my heart and soul. I write poetry in hopes that I can reach out to the deadbeat parent who remains, all too often, absent in their children's life. Only by choice do they miss out on the beauty of their children's everyday living. Our children's souls are at stake!

THERRIEN, CHRISTINA

[a.] Fairfield, ME [title] "Dreams of a Dancing Soul" [pers.] My poem is based partly on my divorce in 1998 and the gentlemen that I am now dating. It signifies my two year journey of trying to find a person who makes my soul feel alive again. I hope it helps others in their search for happiness.

THOMAS, LEE

[title] "Drowning" [pers.] This poem focuses on the time when I almost lost my youngest brother. He jumped into the ocean of the Gulf of Mexico. My sister ran for help, and my father saved him. I watched the whole event and was in terrible shock. I almost lost my brother and best friend. My little brother and I have grown up together. We were always together when we were young. That day was one of the scariest days of my life, and I will never forget it. Thanks to my big sister, Shannon, and my father, Prentice, my little brother, Charles, is still with me today.

THORNTON, CORICE

[a.] Randallstown, MD [title] "Winter Wonderland" [pers.] I am a college freshman majoring in Interior Design at Philadelphia University. My mother has always believed in me and had the utmost confidence in everything that I have done. Her faith and my trust in God have truly helped me to believe in myself and work hard toward achieving my goals. As I read my poem, "Winter Wonderland," and think about past winters, a smile comes to my face as I think of the wondrous works of God. My hope is that everyone else reading my poem will be touched as well.

THRASH, CLARA

[title] "Nights of Giving" [pers.] I have been a 50-year-old certified Nursing assistance for seven and a half years. This poem was inspired in me two months after I started working at the home for the elderly. I have never felt so complete in my work until I started working with the elderly. I could not express the care and love that I felt in any other way then in my poem and through my true feeling in sharing this poem with others.

TILLEY, JOEL

[title] "It's Morning Over There" [pers.] I have been writing poetry most of my life. I feel impressed from time to time, by what I experience in day to day living, to write this down in poetic form. Most of my inspiration comes from the Bible, the Holy Spirit, and Christian activity. I will continue to write rhyming verse at various times when the spirit of God moves me.

TILTON, DELOISE

[a.] Olympia, WA [title] "An Evening Prayer" [pers.] Deloise Tilton, a northwest native, began writing poetry at age eight and has had a lifelong interest in the study of poems and poets. She became a mystic in her 30's and organized an interracial church in her 40's in the hope that the church would be a place for people to solve their problems. Much of her life has been devoted to helping others, including a variety of stray animals. The mother of three grown sons, she now lives in retirement with her husband, dividing her time between tending a large vegetable garden, writing, reading, and playing a little bridge.

TIMIAN, TRACEY

[title] "Waiting" [pers.] My poetry reflects events that have happened in my life. My mom and I have always written poetry as a way to express our feelings. I enjoy writing poems and am open to criticism. Poetry comes from my heart, and I hope others will enjoy it as much as I do.

TITLBACH, CARSTEN

[a.] Darmstadt, Germany [title] "Next Winter, Maybe"

TONEY, AISHA

[a.] Worcester, MA [title] "A Birthday Wish" [pers.] This poem is a memorial to my late mother, Nadine Toney. My words represent all the love that I will eternally have for her. She was a beautiful person, regardless of all her trials and tribulations. She brought me into this world to follow into her footsteps and to strike for and achieve my goals. This poem commemorates her life, the love her family will always have for her, and the love of a daughter, me. She shall never be forgotten.

TOOTLE, DEBRA

[a.] Reidsville, GA [title] "Trials" [pers.] My parents are Helen and Buddy Hallman. I was raised in Baxley, Georgia. I have two brothers and three sisters. My husband is Cary Tootle. We have six children and five grandchildren. Coedy, our grandchild, died when he was only one month old. He was born premature. Coedy, along with my dad and father-in-law, are what inspired me to write "Trials." I lost my dad and father-in-law to diseases. I wanted to let people know we all have trials, but we have to trust God to help us through.

TORRES, AIDA

[title] "A Question Unanswered" [pers.] My name is Aida Torres, and I'm a 26 year old mother of four and wife of Malachi Torres, my high school sweetheart. I used to write a lot of poems in high school, but after a while I stopped, until I lost my five-year-old nephew, Jose', my little brother's son. I've always loved poetry, but the loss of my nephew brought the beauty out of my writings. Jose' was taken from my family very suddenly one day when he and his father were crossing the street for ice cream along with his little sister, Sheyla. He was struck by a truck and killed. My family will mourn his loss for a very long time, but the publishing of this poem in his memory will make it just a little easier. Thank you, *True Reflections*.

TRANCYNGER, SUSAN D.

[a.] Spearfish, SD [title] "The Wolf's Round" [pers.] Writing poems like "The Wolf's Round" has been healing physically and emotionally for me. I am most inspired when I am at my worst. During the lowest time in my life, writing has helped me get through the most difficult days. This poem is very important to me, because it expresses the pain and difficulty I have experienced every day living with lupus. I can only hope that others can find the strength it has given me and take comfort in it. I would like to thank my friends and family for all the love and support they have given me.

TRAPIER, BRYCE

[a.] Dallas, TX [title] "Down" [pers.] Travelling the globe in the military has allowed me to see many wonderful things and meet some truly spectacular people! We each have our ups and downs, but we all survive with our friends, old or new. I am originally from Layton, Utah, and, as of December 2000, I live in Dallas, Texas. In the upcoming years, I expect to travel to the Middle East and to Europe before returning to Utah. I have a wonderful mother, two sisters, and three brothers. Hi, mom!

TRAVITZ, TYLER

[a.] Millersburg, PA [title] "Commitment of a Lifetime" [pers.] God can change your life and He will, if you let Him. I wrote this poem because, at one time in my life, I was lost. Now I am a child of God, and it is my wish that you find His love as well.

TRICHE, MARTI QUAY

[a.] Mathews, LA [title] "A Father Dearly Missed" [pers.] This poem was written because it was an English assignment from my 11th-grade English III teacher, Mrs. Connie Duet, for which we had to write a poem about something that meant something to us. I want my family and a very good friend of mine to be noted as supporters of this poem. My family members are my mother, Betty B. Triche; my two brothers, Pernell and John Triche; my sister, Angela Lee; my nieces, Ashley and Regina Lee; my grandmother Willis Triche; and, last but not least, my cousin Crystal Triche. I would like to thank all of you and anyone I've left out for your support.

TRIPLETT, TERA

[a.] Tucson, AZ [title] "A Mother's Peace" [pers.] Poetry is an expression of one's inner self. It is a way to release bottled-up feelings about anything going on in one's life. My poem is about my daughter, who was born with trisomy-18. Basically she wasn't given much of a chance at life. I wanted to share with others my experience. Life is precious, my Desiree taught everyone who came in contact with her cute little smile, even though she couldn't speak. People learned to love someone, even if they're going to die. She showed us that people are stronger than they think, my angel.

TROUPE, ELIZABETH

[a.] Fortescue, NJ [title] "The Fears and Hopes for MS" [pers.] Montel Williams was my inspiration for my first try at writing this poem. I watch him every day and see him battle with MS. I am 68 years old, married 50 years to my first love, Jim. We have three children, Theresa (she has five children), Jimmy (three children), and Mary Jane (one child). We live in Fortescue, New Jersey, on an island. It's a fishing port. I love using my computer for e-mailing my friends and family. I like to play bingo. Reading poetry is very calming to me. I dedicate my poem to all with M.S.

TRUEBA, BARBARA

[a.] Miami, FL [title] "Mireya" [pers.] I was 26 when my mother passed away. She was the only constant in my life, and without that I soon had a nervous breakdown. I was diagnosed bipolar manic-depressive, and since that time life has been a roller coaster ride. I find healing and satisfaction in writing. In fact I cannot live without it. It is only now that I have given writing the attention needed. I still need polishing, but I believe that to be able to put thoughts in writing is truly a blessing and a very powerful instrument. Mireya was my mother.

TURNBALL-JACKSON, JASON

[a.] Durban, South Africa [title] "To My Death Be My Truth" [pers.] Everyone seems to be settling for mediocrity and second best. No one thinks anymore. There's no one real out there, all with their everything's-okay-and-life's-having-fun attitude. I lie frustrated in my search for something real and true. This poem is about just that. Our wasted lives spent searching in vain for someone of value, someone worth hanging onto. It's all made in environments with made-up people living off others' dreams, too scared or comfortable to realize their own. Our happiness is transient and fake. The only truth out there is that we're alone.

TYLER, MARY

[a.] Troy, NY [title] "Daughter" [pers.] I wrote this poem in loving memory of our daughter, Heather. My husband, Bob, and I decided that we would like to have another child in addition to our two daughters, Ruth (11) and Lori (nine). We were blessed with a third daughter, Heather. She was with us for six short hours. A year later, we were blessed with a son, David. Since one child can never replace another, we missed her deeply. In memory of Heather, I trust that this poem will touch some other parents' hearts during their time of sorrow, in the loss of their child.

TYNAN, KELLY

[a.] Worth, IL [title] "Rhythm of Raindrops" [pers.] There is distinct beauty in creating and rearranging words on a piece of paper and computer screen. Writing has remained my constant passion in life. I am grateful for the talent. As my life changes with the setting and rising of the sun, I will always be proud of the experience of the publication of my "Rhythm of Raindrops."

UNDERWOOD, NANCY

[a.] Saint Joseph, MO [title] "If I Had a Star" [pers.] This poem was written for my adopted son, Gene. I wanted him to know how important he was to me and how special he was. A friend told me to send it, and I did. I hope my poem will let others know how much I've always loved poems.

UPYR, MARIA

[a.] Toronto, ON [title] "A Babe" [pers.] I love to write poetry, as it fills me with peace and serenity. Poetry gives me an escape from my everyday life and helps me to express the true way of human life and what it has become.

URBAN, CARRIE

[a.] Casa Grande, AZ [title] "When Christmas Comes" [pers.] Christmas is a special season of thanksgiving. When depressed, it reminds us, gently, to be thankful for many blessings. I'm a 31-year-old male-to-female transsexual from Casa Grande, Arizona. I have an MBA in information systems. I enjoy movies and music.

UWAJEH, MONICA

[a.] Orlando, FL [title] "Someone to Love Me" [pers.] I am 19. Due to cerebral palsy, I am forced to use a wheelchair. Poetry allows me to let go of my fears and frustrations.

VALDEZ, FIDELIA

[a.] San Antonio, TX [title] "Mansion on the Hill" [pers.] Several things inspire me to write: love for my son, Rene, to whom I dedicate this poem; faith in God, for he has always been with me—He taught me to see beauty in everything, no matter what; hope, which became reality with my God-sent husband, Jose, who has brought joy to my life. "Mansion on the Hill" describes my vision of our humble abode in the country, which, with nature's beauty, peace, and serenity, provides the perfect setting for me to write my thoughts and visions.

VARNER, LILLIE

[a.] Bluffton, SC [title] "Mixed Emotions" [pers.] Being products of poor but proud parentage, my siblings and I were always exposed to all forms of art, including music, dance, crafts, and, most recently, silk floral arranging. Intertwined with these activities has always been my love for poetry. My family has consistently been a source of encouragement to keep reaching for higher goals. With this in mind, I stepped out on faith and entered the poetry contest, and, thanks be to God, my work is being published. My son, Paul; daughter, Cynthia; granddaughters, Ebony, and L'Oreal; and great-granddaughter, Essence all share the excitement of this wonderful opportunity.

VAUGHS, REBECCA

[a.] Miami, FL [title] "Don't Give In" [pers.] A native of Miami, born on March 25, 1972, under the zodiac sign of Aries, I began writing at age ten. Poetry is my passion. It's that voice expressed through ink. My work is inspired by life, love, spirit, and what happens to me or around me. The essence of poetry is the creativity. To have a particular title of a piece repetitiously but different words is amazing, like three of four singers with the same song title but varying verses. Now, that is artistry. Poetry is conversation between the heart and soul expressed with in-depth emotion.

VAYDA, SYLVIA A.

[a.] Phillips, WI [title] "An Ode to My Loving Husband" [pers.] I believe it is evident from my poems that my inspiration for writing them derives from love of family, nature, and country. These all have much to do with who I am and what and who are important in my life. I love poetry of every kind. With this poem I wanted my husband to know how very important he is in my life and always has been over the years.

VICK, SUE

[a.] Enka, NC [title] "I Will Wait" [pers.] First and foremost, I am a wife and mother. I feel I have always seen things from a different perspective. Besides poetry, pen-and-ink drawings are my passion. As with my poetry, I draw what I feel. On my dark side, I am disabled due to a spinal condition. I have spent many hours in my wheelchair. Yet thanks to my art, I do not feel handicapped. Though chronic pain does, at times, make things difficult, it is in these times that my best work comes forth. God's grace is sufficient.

VINCENT, ELOISE

[a.] Oxnard, CA [title] "Princess Remembered" [pers.] Experience is, at times, an unforgiving teacher who painfully shows us that often we do not appreciate as much as we should what we have when we have it. My four-footed friend was the best companion I have ever had, and I miss her dearly to this day although she has been gone for several years. I truly believe that I will one day again see her and that thought makes her loss easier to bear.

VOLPE, LINDA

[a.] Tyngsborough, MA [title] "My Child" [pers.] I have always written my thoughts and feelings in poetry. The birth of my two sons gave me such joy, I wanted to share it with the world. This poem is for them and every child with which this world has been blessed.

WAGNER, JOSEPH

[a.] Sioux Falls, SD [title] "Life As I Know It" [pers.] My name is Joseph Philip Wagner. I grew up bouncing around from town to town; my father kicked me out at age 14. The words in the poem resemble my life to a T. Every time I get on my feet, I get knocked right back down—but I get right back up.

WAKEFIELD, CATHERINE

[a.] Phildelphia, PA [title] "How I Love Thee" [pers.] In 1997 my granddaughter was born and became very ill. I started to pray for a miracle. I would write sweet things about her. She died in 1998; I thought my faith and poems would, too, but they got stronger. Her brother was born in 1999 with the same disease and died in May 2000. God has a reason for everything. I still write poems and have faith. I know someday we will stand side by side, if we believe, pray, and never give up. I thank Him for everything he gave me, no matter how briefly.

WALTERS, ROBERT

[a.] Overland Park, KS [title] "Morning Star" [pers.] Poems are written, bringing forth the heart of a soul that has a desire to be creative and allowing others to know their innermost thoughts. It is my desire to bless others in some way that allows me to give back to mankind. Writing of the love between two souls gives others hope and confirmation that God is ever present.

WALTON, WHITNEY

[a.] Conroe, TX [title] "Fall" [pers.] This poem was a classroom assignment using metaphors, personification, and similes. I was so much fun! I am a sixth-grade student in junior high in Conroe, Texas.

WARD, JULIET

[a.] Tofino, BC [title] "Colors" [pers.] This poem is about communing with nature, which is my inspiration to write and take many photographs. I live in an area of Canada (Tofino, in the Clayoquot Sound) that has been designated a protected biosphere by UNESCO (United Nations Educational, Scientific, and Cultural Organization). Living in such an environment brings more meaning to life and a feeling of being close to the greatest artist of all—the Creator.

WARNER, JASON

[a.] Boalsburg, PA [title] "A Lifestyle" [pers.] Not wanting to say too much . . . I'll say only this: To see or not to see, that is perception.

WARNER, THOMAS

[a.] Redondo Beach, CA [title] "Each Morning and Evening" [pers.] I've lived a pretty good life. . . . My poem is my testament. Although not my first, it will hopefully be the first of many more inspiring words to my worldwide family of the SGI and others. Los Angeles is my domicile, tax law is my forte, photography is my hobby.

WATERS, LORA

[a.] Memphis, TN [title] "I Love You" [pers.] I like poetry because it helps me tell what I am feeling in my own way. The poem "I Love You" is about my friend who tried to commit suicide. Her mom died when she was seven, and her dad remarried a woman who always beat her. She overdosed on 34 antidepressant pills and was put in the hospital. I am really glad she survived, and I want her to know how much I care about her, no matter what.

WATSON, DI

[a.] Harbinger, NC [title] "Promised Land" [pers.]

Living on the Outer Banks of North Carolina has provided me with a wealth of inspiration. Being so close to some of God's most beautiful creations is a blessing that I cherish.

WEATHERINGTON, RUTH
[a.] Brooklyn, NY

WEIR-SMITH, BECKY
[a.] Houston, TX [title] "The Power of Your Love" [pers.] Writing poetry after the loss of my beloved husband, Barry, helped to heal my heart, feed my soul, and fill my spirit. The words just flowed from the heart and soul. There was such a strong and deep connection with the heavens and Barry. My hope is to always keep my heart and soul alive to express and reveal poetry to others, to also nourish their hearts and souls. I truly treasure the ability bestowed upon me to write words in such a beautiful fashion. I celebrate Barry's life and spirit with this poem.

WEISS, JUDITH
[a.] Durand, WI [title] "For God I Am Challenged" [pers.] Writing poetry comes very easily and naturally to me! I feel I possess a gift and am compelled to verbalize by writing it down. I pick up pen and paper and just start jotting down words with no particular theme in mind. I write poems for my husband, children, and grandchildren, for all occasions. I love the arts, including painting ceramics and plaster (in detail), and I love to draw also. I am at times compelled to write poems and to write in general.

WEMUS, STEVE
[a.] Wyoming, MI [title] "Mourning" [pers.] "Mourning" was written when I was in high school. I was depressed, lonely, and mad at my friends. Writing "Mourning" was very helpful in my attitude toward life in general. I had hope that in the future I would meet someone with whom I could share my life. I am happy now, with a beautiful wife and a group of friends that I would not trade for anything. This is for my only love, Kathy.

WESSNER, GARY L., JR.
[a.] Hyde Park, PA [title] "Start with One" [pers.] For every action there is an equal and opposite reaction. When sitting down with pen in hand, I keep in mind this basic theory in physics (which is interesting as well with others throughout life). What is written on paper and shown to others can have a major impact on them from that moment on. If what I feel through writing can cause a positive reaction, my goal has been reached and life is a little more complete.

WEST, LORI
[a.] Wilmington, NC [title] "A Time to Accept" [pers.] Poetry, for me, has always been a way of expressing experiences in my own life. It has been a way for me to write down my emotions when they have been difficult to verbally express. It is a safe haven and a blessing. God has truly blessed me, and I am truly grateful.

WESTON, LARRY
[a.] McLoud, OK [title] "Internet Friend" [pers.] I write poetry and songs because they express my experiences in life. My escape is in the words I write and the stories they tell. I write in hope of touching the hearts of the world, as the world is my reason for thought. I write to express myself to the ones I love and to the ones who have touched my life. My God-given ability with the piano and my words have allowed me to write songs. May my words and my music touch your heart the way they touch mine.

WESTON, TASHA
[a.] Oklahoma City, OK [title] "Overcoming" [pers.] This poem means a whole lot to me, as I wrote it while living in South Africa for 12 years of my life. My youth and I had gone on an outreach to a coastal town in South Africa, and it was during my quiet time on the beach when I was struck by the awesome beauty of the sun's rays hitting the clouds and the sea itself that God inspired to write this poem.

WEYANDT, NELSON
[a.] Dysart, PA [title] "Ask to Be Heard" [pers.] I have been writing poetry and songs since childhood. I have four brothers and four sisters and dwell in the Pennsylvania mountains. My mother is the bravest person I have ever known. She raised all nine of us. We were poor in riches but rich at heart. She instilled in us to never make jokes of those who were less fortunate than us, and there weren't too many. I faithfully served in the armed forces, just as my father who was a POW of World War II. My brothers have a history of military service, which is a family tradition.

WHITE, BROOKE
[a.] Gray, KY [title] "Angel, I Do, I Do" [pers.] I am only ten but love to write and read poems. It lets me express how I feel. My mother and I have never really had a relationship where we could just talk and express our feelings. When my mother and grandmother read this poem, they were delighted to see a talent so special as writing poems. Not everyone understands poetry, but my poem "Angel, I Do, I Do" is written in a way for people as young as or even younger than myself to understand and lets them know that there really is an angel watching over us.

WHITE, JERI
[a.] Las Vegas, NV [title] "My Journey" [pers.] We all embark on our own journey. Currently I am 18 years into mine and pursuing a degree in psychology. The pathways I have chosen have led me to many wonderful people and helped me gain insight on life's lessons. I owe my inspiration to my Marine, who travels with me along the winding paths. Sometimes life presents its trials and tribulations, and it feels like our path is a never-ending circle. Never forget there is always new ground to be discovered.

WHITE, SHARON
[a.] Middlefield, MA [title] "Some Thoughts for My Child" [pers.] When my cousin had a miscarriage, it brought back many old feelings. I loved my daughter, yet I still missed the children to whom I never gave birth. My sister-in-law suggested writing down my feelings, and the result is this poem. It gave me a sense of closure, of permission to feel this way, and of hope for the future. I dedicate it to Janice and to Mary, who have also lost a child and have shown tremendous strength and courage to "pack up their memories" and go on with their lives.

WHITE, TIMOTHY
[a.] Newark, NJ [title] "Still" [pers.] Poetry, to me, is a gift from God. He gave me the mind and the heart to express myself to others in a very unique way. I know the world can be a cruel place to live in, but God always reminds me that there is beauty in everything and everyone. You just have to search deep within your heart. I grew up in Newark, New Jersey, and I have stayed away from the street life and kept my mind focused on school and God. I thank my family, my mother and father who have been married for 30 years now, for my belief and trust in God. It's so beautiful to express yourself because words can soothe the soul.

WHITFIELD, TANYA
[a.] Denver, CO [title] "Why Is the World Going Crazy?" [pers.] I'm sincerely grateful for your interest and this opportunity. My heart leads my thoughts to write about the trials and tribulations of life. "Why Is the World Going Crazy?" I asked myself, "Where did we go wrong?" as I wrote this poem. We are people of a society; we have to find a way to unite and make a difference. We have to stand up for our rights and the rights of our children. We share the whole world in our hands.

WHITMIRE, SHARON
[a.] McDonough, GA [title] "Open the Door" [pers.] In this poem the door is my heart. The key is the heart of the man I love: my husband. Many times, people are afraid to truly open up to those that they love, in fear of failure or pain. I hope this poem will touch the heart of others and inspire them to open up their own hearts and see what they will find as they make their journeys in life.

WHITNEY, BYRON
[a.] Glendale, AZ [title] "Soul Mate" [pers.] I live in the beautiful Grand Canyon State. I have written poetry as a hobby throughout my life. I feel very fortunate that my poem was selected for publishing and thank God for having blessed me in this way. It has been both uplifting and encouraging. I enjoy writing poetry and sharing it with others. I believe it's a magnificent way to convey your thoughts, desires, dreams, and innermost feelings. This poem is dedicated to D'Aun Douglass, the love of my life. The time we shared was my inspiration for the poem.

WHITTAKER, LARA
[a.] Cincinnati, Oh, [title] "Vampiress" [pers.] I grew up in the inner city in Cincinnati. My mother worked ten and one-half hours at night to support my three brothers and me. We did not have much money, but we had a lot of love. My mother always said to go for our dreams, so I guess that's what I'm doing. Every poem I write comes from the heart, no matter how I'm feeling.

WHITTINGTON, CHRIS
[a.] Adelaide, Australia [title] "Forever Love" [pers.] This poem is one of many I have written and dedicated to a good friend of mine. She has brought meaning to my life and my expressions are shown in my poetry for the friendship she has given me. Good friends like her are hard to find. Sarah, thank you heaps. Thank you for the opportunity for allowing me to express myself through my poetry. It is great for people of all ages to find comfort and joy in either reading or writing poetry. It is a gift we all should have been given.

WICKS, GEMETRA
[a.] Clarksville, TN [title] "Unconditional Love" [pers.] Poetry is my way of expressing how I feel. My poem "Unconditional Love" is about forgiving the unforgivable and still being able to love that person endlessly. It's also about my baby girl, who was born out of that love, my love child, Kayla Nicole.

WIETRZYKOWSKI, VALERIE
[a.] Monongahela, PA [title] "Life" [pers.] At a certain time in my life, questions were appearing to which I had no answers. Now instead of looking for answers, I just take the time to appreciate everything that I've been blessed with, like my beautiful children, Christopher and Darla; my wonderful husband, Chris; and, most of all my mother, Darla, who is and always will be my hero in life. I was born, raised, and live in the city of Monongahela. My hobbies are writing poetry, drawing, and, most of all, spending time with family and friends. It is truly an honor to have my poem published, and I hope to write a book of my own poems and have it published someday. Thank you so much for this wonderful honor.

WILHELM, TIFFANY
[a.] Bethel, Oh, [title] "End of a Beginning" [pers.] Poetry is a way to express myself freely and creatively. This particular poem is about wanting something so bad it seems hopeless. I dedicate this poem to Joshua Brockman, a very important person in my life. My poetry is a reflection of myself and the people closest to me. I consider my poetic abilities to be a gift. Putting thoughts and feelings into words can be very difficult. I feel that everyone is artistic in their own ways. I appreciate anyone who is willing to share their artistic abilities with me, and I am honored to do the same.

WILKINS, MARY
[a.] Downey, CA [title] "Big Sister" [pers.] This poem was written as a tribute to my sister. I was to read it at her funeral but was overcome by emotions and couldn't. To have the poem published means more than words can express. My sister and I had a strained relationship at times, but over the years we put our differences aside and were truly sisters—and best friends. I miss seeing her, but I know she is always with me.

WILLIAMS, ANN
[a.] Flat Rock, MI [title] "My Best Friend" [pers.] I am a free spirit and love all of the arts. I was an only child and very lonesome at times, that lonesomeness led me to an awareness of many things that some never attain in their lifetimes. I wrote "My Best Friend" when I was about 12 years old. I found it tucked in one of my books recently. I am a senior citizen now with great-grandchildren, and I hope it enriches their heritage. I dedicate "My Best Friend" to all my family andespecially to my dear daughter Lynette, who died from cancer in September 1999.

WILLIAMS, ANTHONY
[a.] Bourbonnais, IL [title] "Something about You" [pers.] My home is Gary, where I began to write poetry three years ago. I found my gift through Christ. Poetry is very special to me, because it is a part of me. It is a gift that is me. I believe poetry has no limits; therefore, it can be used for anything. This particular piece, "Something about You," was about a young man who really cared about a special young woman but couldn't tell her. It took the fear of losing her to get him to tell her how he felt. Many people can relate to this poem. I've written enough poems to start my own book, which I plan to do through Poetry.com. I mostly write inspirational poems dealing with God.

WILLIAMS, BRELEA
[a.] Joplin, MO [title] "What You Did to Me" [pers.] I never thought a poem of mine would end up here; it was written about my now ex-husband, whom I loved dearly. I enjoy my days with my daughter, Nicole, and a wonderful man, Paul. Poetry seems to come to me when time is tough or depression is strong. It is a way to deal with life and the hurdles we face daily. I am proud and pleased to have my poem entered in this book. Love and live life to its fullest. Thank you Nicole, Mom, Paul, and family.

WILLIAMS, MICHELLE
[a.] Jacobsburg, Oh, [title] "I Miss You" [pers.] The story behind my poem is the feelings that I wanted to share with several men with whom I had relationships. I wanted to tell them how I really felt about them, but I didn't want to scare them off and away from me forever. Now as I think about it, I wished I told them how I really felt about them, and, maybe, just maybe, they would be with me now and not with someone else.

WILLIAMS, MYNIDA
[a.] Benton Harbor, MI [title] "You Whom I've Never Met" [pers.] Poetry is something I feel God has given me to do, since I have no educational background in writing. I pray that he continues to bless me with the inspirational words that may touch all those who read what he has given me to write. "You Whom I've Never Met" is a poem from my heart to my dad. I'd like to thank my husband and daughters for all their love and encouragement. I would like to give special thanks to my dear friend Jessica McGinnis, for all of her spiritual conversation and that extra push when I needed it. Last and certainly not least, I give honor and praises to Almighty God, who has continuously blessed me, for without him I would be unable to write.

WILLIAMS, SHELBA
[a.] Bowie, TX [title] "My Life with MS" [pers.] My poem is a way of educating the world on the disease of MS (multiple sclerosis). This is my first poem, but it was so easy to express myself. My immediate family knows stress effects a person with MS mentally and physically, but the rest of my family and friends do not understand. It is extremely hard for me to even be socially active with my church, friends, and family. I have put myself in God's hands, hoping the next day will be better.

WINKELMAN, VENETA
[a.] New Lisbon, WI [title] "Hungry?" [pers.] I am a trucker's wife and proud of it. I travel with my husband and have seen a lot of the United States firsthand. My poem "Hungry?" was inspired on one of those many trips. A homeless man in Virginia was the inspiration behind my poem. When I witnessed firsthand how people survive on the streets, it started me to really think. People have choices in life. How they act on their choices determines whether the choice they made was right or wrong.

WONG, ASHLEY
[a.] Aurora, ON [title] "The Hue of You" [pers.] If you have ever been in love, you know that tingle you get in your chest and the way your heart swells at the sight of your lover. I wrote this poem in hopes of putting those feelings into words. I dedicate this poem to my lover, Chris, as a "thank you" for everything he has ever done for me, for the patience, understanding, sensitivity, sympathy, fun, good times, pleasure, and love he has shown me. Chris, every day I love you more than the day before; every time I see you, how handsome you are takes my breath away; every time I hear your voice, I know how important you are to me. I love you now and I always will.

WOOD, NANCY JANE
[a.] Wheeling, WV [title] "It" [pers.] I was born on May 3, 1950, in Wheeling to Davis Wilison Wood and Gue Irene Fry (divorced). I graduated from Wheeling High School in 1969 and attended Wheeling Beauty College and WUNC College where I studied computers. I have two children, Bryan L. and George K. Nagy. I am unemployed due to medical reasons and am a member of St. Matthews Episcopal Church. The only honor I have received was having my poem "It" published. I have written around six other poems, and I'm in the middle of writing a book and hope someday to have it published as well. I would like to say never let your dreams die. I believe if we never dream, then how can we live? Life begins with one little dream.

WOODBURN, DALLAS NICOLE
[a.] Ventura, CA [title] "Who Are You, Teenager?" [pers.] Dallas Woodburn is 13 years old and enjoys writing, reading, playing basketball, and running track. Dallas has been writing for as long as she can remember. In fifth grade, she even wrote and published her own book of short stories and poems, titled, "There's a Huge Pimple on My Nose!" That has sold more than 700 copies nationwide. Dallas is now turning her attention toward her nonprofit organization, Write On!, which encourages children to write through projects such as essay contests. To learn more about Write On! or to purchase Dallas's book, visit her web site.

WOODEN, DONNA
[a.] Lincoln City, OR [title] "My Lake" [pers.] I have written poetry since at least high school days. I usually write about what's around me that moves me. Many times my poems are about nature. Sometimes they are about the love of friends and lovers. Always my poems express my innermost feelings. Rhymes come easily to me. I could almost talk in rhyme. Sometimes my poems are serious and sometimes numerous. Often there is a reflection of my imagination. At this time I live beside my lake and enjoy "poetizing" the wildlife and acts of nature: wind, rain, stillness and ducks, caterpillars, herons and beavers, dogs, deer.

WOODFELL, ROBERTA
[a.] West Palm Beach, FL [title] "Is God in My Life" [pers.] I volunteer at a nearby geriatric center, giving their Sunday lesson once every month. I wrote this poem in the early morning hours, while spiritually inspired, before giving my Sunday lesson to this often forgotten group of senior citizens.

WOODS, T.
[a.] Des Moines, IA [title] "Christ Has Died, Christ Has Risen, Christ Will Come Again" [pers.] There are several reasons and ideas behind this poem. Poetry is one of my greatest gifts and the pride and joys of my life. This poem is dedicated to my late father, who passed away in 1999; my entire family; closest friends; and, especially, my late mom, who inspired and influenced me so much. As I mentioned in *The Radiance of Summer Sun* book, cartoon characters (like "Tweety") and children's shows have influenced me. Several musicians from all genres of the music business also have influenced me, not to mention God. I also use Prairie Woods as a pen name. John 3:16 is another one of my all-time favorite scriptures.

WOOSLEY, MARY
[a.] Waddy, KY [title] "Best Friend" [pers.] Many times I have trouble saying how I feel out loud. Writing helps me to express myself. When I write, I can let my emotions out, but no one else has to know unless I choose to let them in. Perhaps it's a power trip, but I see it as healthy release.

WORTHY, EILEEN
[a.] Bronx, NY [title] "Headtrippin'" [pers.] I started writing poetry at age seven. I had a speech impediment, as I lisped and stuttered terribly. Reciting and writing my poetry became a passion, and my speech got so good that poetry sustained me through a marriage to a composer who turned my words into songs. We sang, which was a sounding board; that marriage fell apart. Writing was also solace from the harsh realities of life I heard for 15 years in N.Y.R.D. as a 911 dispatcher. Now in early retirement due to diagnosis of multiple sclerosis, this poem is self-love and elevation above it all (that I'm sharing).

WOWOR, ANDY
[a.] Magnolia, AR [title] "Love" [pers.] I composed this poem when I wrote an essay about home. Whenever or wherever I feel intimate and safe, I feel home. Sometimes we feel that no one loves us, and I think we all do feel that. We always search for love. What is love, anyway? Love is an abstract matter that is hard to explain in words. For me, love creates the feeling of home. Being accepted or being part of a society gives a sense of love. If we feel love, we are home.

WRIGHT, JOHN HENRY
[a.] State Farm, VA [title] "What a Father Is to Me" [pers.] My grandmother Pearl Kesner was a seed planted long ago. Her words of prayer before she left were to see her grandchildren grow, but these storms in life most do not perceive until they are home with the Father. Then they will truly believe. The seeds of prayers they planted will begin to grow. Unless a seed falls to the ground and dies, it abides alone, you should know. In loving memory of all those who passed away and for those members still alive, we'll see. The blessing of a loving Father for us all is exactly what we need, blessed through our Heavenly Father's seed!

WRIGHT, MARY
[a.] Marshall, MI [title] "For You" [pers.] I feel God gives us all a "Gift" to use—some people can speak words, while others of us write our words. This poem is dedicated to my sister, Teresa, who died from cancer and to my sister, Sarah, for her prayers and love, for Sarah Welsh who lives in Adrain, Michigan is the angel sent to me as a sister. I love you, sis.

WRIGHT, ROLANDA

[a.] Richmond, VA [title] "Too Bad" [pers.] When I sat down to write this poem, I was thinking, "Eh, there is really a lot here I have to say." However, I wanted to make a statement as clear and concrete as possible. I remember talking to my father quite recently about my writing. He called me up and told me about this old notebook of stories I had written a long time ago. I didn't remember it and still find it funny today. Oh, well, Pop, thank you, thank you, and thank you for inspiring me to write.

WYMAN, DANIELLE

[a.] Middletown, CT [title] "Losing You" [pers.] When I write a poem, I base it on my feelings at the time. In this particular poem, I'd just gone through a difficult breakup and was feeling really sad. I wished that I could have him back but knew I couldn't. There are other poems I've written that have to do with happiness. My poems are usually based on heartbreak or love. When I'm feeling sad or lonely, poetry gives me a way to express those feelings to all who'll listen.

XIE, JOAN

[a.] Lansdale, PA [title] "The Sky" [pers.] This is first time anything I have done has ever become published. Writing is my special talent, and I am happy that more people will recognize my work. My poem "The Sky" explains all the wonders of the sky. Planets, constellations, and stars are all included in my poem. I have always wondered about the sky, gazing up and asking questions to myself, endless questions, which I believed would never be answered. I wrote this poem because I wanted children younger than myself to be able to understand the sky through a poetic interpretation.

YANG, JOHN

[a.] Fitchburg, MA [title] "A Piece of Mind" [pers.] After so many mistakes in my life, it seemed as if no one appreciated the fact that I was trying to turn my life around. Asking for help wasn't helping at all. Usually, I was receiving the same line: "You're nothing but a mess-up." No one wanted to help, because no one wanted to be a part of a failure. With all the frustration, I was determined to do something with my life. Then, poetry came into it. . . . The thought of being able to express myself with no boundaries amused me. It's amazing how far poetry has taken me, helping me cope with the past, plans for the future, and bringing me one step closer to the main goal in life, which is to succeed, even through the toughest times.

YARBOUGH, LISA

[a.] Missouri City, TX [title] "My Brother's Keeper" [pers.] Most of my poetry comes from inner expressions that I want to say to others. I have to say that the better choices are conversations that I have with Jesus. I thank God and His Son for my gift. I pray that my poetry becomes a blessing to someone as much as it has to me.

YBANEZ, NICOLE

[a.] Tucson, AZ [title] "A Slave's Day" [pers.] Everyone has something that they are truly proud of. I don't think I had anything to be proud of until I started sharing some of my poetry with a few people. The response I got was surprising. It is so amazing to have others recognize your emotions, views, and thoughts to be of such high quality. All those who encouraged me to keep writing, because they saw what I had not yet seen, I thank you from the bottom of my heart.

YEAGER, ROBERT

[a.] Charlotte, NC [title] "Truth" [pers.] I never really understood poetry until, one day, words were dancing in my head. I didn't know what they were. I finally decided to write them down. When I was done, I looked at the page and my first poem was created. I wrote this poem in the main library in Charlotte, North Carolina, waiting for the copies. The poem is about a friend of mine and what she needed to know. My poetry reflects much of my life and what I've experienced.

YOUNGBERG, BRIAN

[a.] Marietta, GA [title] "Making the Person" [pers.] This is actually my first attempt at poetry in a very long time, almost ten years. This is actually the second poem I have written since beginning to dabble in poetry. I have usually enjoyed writing short stories and novels. This poem is very special to me. It helps me realize that I am the only person that determines what my destiny is and the kind of person I am. For too long in my life I allowed others to rule my life and to shape me. I hope that if nothing else, you can enjoy reading this poem as much as I enjoyed writing it.

ZABINSKI, JEREMY

[a.] Clay, NY [title] "Becoming" [pers.] I wrote this poem as a senior in high school, after going through the problems of growing up and just getting through school.

ZAHM, JULIANNE MARIE

[a.] Newark, CA [title] "The Life of a Butterfly" [pers.] I feel that my poem has many different meanings. To a young child it may be a short story; to an adult it may show the simplicity of life. To me, my poem expresses the unawareness we as people have of one another. I hope that whoever reads my poem will relate to it in the best way for them.

ZAMORA, MELVIN, JR.

[a.] Saucier, MS [title] "Poem for Peace" [pers.] My desire for poetry and music began when I was born and raised in New Orleans, Louisiana. Early musical training under the direction of Professor Taverna became instrumental in obtaining my scholarship for music and education at St. Aldysius College. There and through his guidance I realized the strong link between poetry and music, while learning diversely to be creative, stylish, artistic, unique, and competitive. Hear and feel the rhythm and rhyme working together each and every time. Poetry in music, music in poetry: I hope it works for you as it does for me.

ZEIGLER, DANIEL

[a.] Magnolia, TX [title] "Breathlessness" [pers.] This poem basically describes my life, throughout the whole teenage experience. Some of my problems are more than typical teenage experiences, but some aren't. This poem helped me realize how I really felt about myself and my life.

ZIEMAN, DANETTE

[a.] North Saint Paul, MN [title] "I Love You, Mother" [pers.] I truly enjoy writing poetry. I get the greatest enjoyment writing poems for or about people who have touched my life and people who have influenced all Americans. "I Love You, Mother" will always be my favorite. Previously I have written poems about JonBenet Ramsey, O. J. Simpson, and Princess Diana and recently finished a poem on JFK. I have received a lot of positive feedback from the select few I have shared those with. Poetry is very inspiring. God bless you all.

ZUNIGA, MANDY

[a.] Houston, TX [title] "This Woman" [pers.] This poem, in particular, is a "thank you" to my mother for everything she is and has done. Poetry is my release, my pleasure, my pain, and those elements alone.

Index of Poets

Index

A

B

C

H

I

J

K

L

M

N

O

P

Q

R

S

T

U

V

W

X

Y

Z